Received from the
Leonard Warren tion
7 November 2000

OPERA BIOGRAPHY SERIES, NO. 13

Series Editors
Andrew Farkas
William R. Moran

Studio portrait of Warren, early 1950s. Credit: James Abresch; Vivien Warren Collection.

Leonard Warren

American Baritone

by

Mary Jane Phillips-Matz

Foreword by Tony Randall

Discography and Chronology by Barrett Crawford

AMADEUS PRESS
Portland, Oregon

Copyright © 2000 Leonard Warren Foundation
All rights reserved

ISBN 1-57467-053-0

Printed in Hong Kong

Published in 2000 by
AMADEUS PRESS (an imprint of Timber Press, Inc.)
The Haseltine Building
133 S.W. Second Avenue, Suite 450
Portland, Oregon 97204 U.S.A.

Library of Congress Cataloging-in-Publication Data

Phillips-Matz, Mary Jane.
     Leonard Warren, American baritone / by Mary Jane Phillips-Matz; foreword
by Tony Randall; discography and chronology by Barrett Crawford.
          p.   cm.—(Opera biography series; no. 13)
     Includes bibliographical references and index.
     ISBN 1-57467-053-0
     1. Warren, Leonard, 1911–1960. 2 Baritones (Singers)—United States
Biography. I. Title. II. Series.
     ML420.W188P47   2000
     782.1′092—dc21
      [B]   99-40444
                                                                 CIP

*To the memory
of
Vivien Warren*

*My respected colleague
and cherished friend*

✦

Contents

Photographs follow pages 80, 112, and 224.

✦

Foreword

by Tony Randall

Leonard Warren was the great Verdi baritone of our times. The term requires some explanation. Before the era of Napoleon, opera was a much smaller affair than Grand Opera: the orchestra was much smaller; the chorus, if any, was much smaller; and the house was much smaller. The singers' voices were probably much smaller although more was required of them in the way of acrobatic technique: trills, staccati, and runs, for example. Male singing was dominated by the castrati who were idolized for more than a hundred years for their oddity and extraordinary vocal agility. Power and range were of secondary importance. Tenors took their high notes in falsetto (a misnomer— there is nothing false about it). The other male singers were basses. The voice in between, the baritone, was not recognized as a category, as it still is not in male choruses. But with the rise of the middle class in Paris, a new art developed that satisfied their desire for opulence, and opera became, with the addition of ballet, Grand Opera. Its fathers were Meyerbeer, Verdi, and Wagner, and they required a new kind of singer, one who could be heard in a house seating two or three thousand or more, over an orchestra of seventy-five or more, and a chorus of one hundred. The natural male voice came into its rightful glory as an instrument of ringing power and passion, the tenors began singing their high Cs in full chest voice, and the higher bass, the baritone, found his voice in Verdi. Verdi was extremely partial to this sound, so versatile and human with its full, round, lower half and its top going up to a trumpeted A flat, only a third lower than the tenor's high C. Rigoletto, Nabucco, Macbeth, Simon Boccanegra, and Falstaff are eponymous roles he wrote for this beloved category—obviously he thought it the most expressive—and in most of his other operas the baritone is the equal musically of the leads, or better.

What Verdi expected of his baritone is that he express a Shakespearean range of emotion from blackest rage to pitiful heartbreak, from sardonic cruelty to sublime forgiveness, all in a voice of great beauty and power and effortless high notes. Few have filled the bill.

It is an odd fact that many of the great Verdi baritones of the last seventy years have been American: Lawrence Tibbett, Leonard Warren, Robert Merrill, Cornell MacNeil, and Sherrill Milnes.

There is no question that Pavarotti is a tenor. His is a naturally high voice. But is Domingo? He sings tenor gloriously, but he could also sing baritone. His voice is naturally a little lower. The incomparable Melchior—the only true heldentenor to my ears—began as a baritone and firmly believed that only baritones could become heldentenors. It is a matter of training, and many men and women have changed vocal category. Battistini on records sounds to me more like a tenor than a baritone. Warren could sing up to high C, but the weight of his voice was baritonal.

How to describe his voice? If you know his records you have a pretty good idea, but not completely. His voice in the opera house had a warmth that records never caught. It was huge and filled the house like black smoke. His *piano* and *pianissimo* singing had to be heard to be believed, for it filled the house like his full voice. It was an unusually round, fat voice. He was very musical, and he responded to the beauty of the music as if he were listening to it. He loved his voice. Its color was of a gleaming mahogany. To people like me, susceptible people, opera is about one thing: voice. This cannot be explained. Beautiful voices make me cry, and Warren's was the most beautiful I have heard.

He made a different sound than baritones before him, a sound that has influenced his followers. Baritones before him seemed to favor a resonance that was centered in the mask, the front of the face, the nose. As an extreme example, think of the sound of Nelson Eddy. This kind of placement (the word is anathema to some) makes for a bright, ringing sound. Warren added to this the "back sound," the resonance in the back of the mouth that you hear when you yawn. This gave him his rounder, darker sound. It is not for everyone. Generations of young tenors have ruined themselves trying to sound like Caruso on his records, and if you try to sound like Warren, you'll kill yourself.

We have only one vocal instrument, used for both singing and speaking. A well-trained singer uses his instrument well, but few speakers do because they don't train. The principal difference between the good speaking voice and the good singing voice is the addition of vibrato. Like everything else vocal, including breathing, there is much controversy over the importance, desirability, and production of vibrato. But vibrato is the life of the voice and part of its beauty. Listen to the young Sinatra. As we get older it slows down sometimes. In his prime, Warren's vibrato was a miracle of throbbing sweetness. In his last years, although he was still young, it slowed to a wobble in his lower voice. Why he came to have this problem, almost inevitable in older singers, is a matter of guesswork. His upper voice remained as brilliant as ever.

The voice is made of registers (although of course some deny it). The vocal cords are not cords at all but are gatherings of two muscles each, which make two different sounds: the lower sound, much more pronounced in men although women have it, too, and the upper sound of a man's falsetto. Training the voice consists of strengthening these muscles. (There is enough difference of opinion among teachers and singers on this issue to start a shooting war.) These are often called head and chest voices. To complicate things, there is also head and chest resonance, and each "voice" has both. (Of course some will claim that there is no such thing as resonance.) But what no one can dispute is that as the baritone voice ascends the scale, it wants to crack around E. And this, the *passaggio*, is the bane of the baritone's existence, for the E comes right in the middle of his singing range. Some change must be made in this area to keep from cracking, and most employ a technique known as "covering" (although of course there is a whole school, exemplified by Robert Weede and his pupils, which maintains that you must never cover). Vowels are the names we give to various positions of the mouth and throat. Say *Ee*, *Ah*, and *Oh*, and you will see what I mean. In covering, the vowel is modified toward *Aw* or *Oo* and the voice seems to go over the soft palate instead of straight out of the mouth. Try singing easily an upward scale while yawning and you'll get some of the feeling.

Warren used this technique religiously. His cover was quite far back—which we call "hooking"—and his upper voice from F to A only became bigger and more beautiful. And miraculously, he could achieve a diminuendo on these top notes. The problem is to disguise this change in production so that it doesn't sound like two different voices. Warren solved this problem by singing everything in the covering position. This, some think, cost him a measure of clarity in his middle range and may have contributed to the eventual wobble. Warren's voice sounded deeper than it was because of its weight and dark color, but it was a high baritone, a Verdi baritone. Other great baritones, like Ruffo, have simply thrown away the low notes. Warren insisted on singing them fully, and I think this is what cost him.

Of the glorious nights I spent at Warren's performances, one stands out as perhaps the best night I have had at the opera. It was *Ernani* with Del Monaco, Siepi, and Milanov, Mitropoulos conducting. I have a tape of the broadcast of 29 December 1956, and Warren's role could never have been better sung. His opening arietta is simply overwhelming in its power, beauty, and tenderness. In the second act, his aria "Vieni meco" is heartstopping: the deeply felt pathos, the love, the exquisite musicality spun endlessly. The entire aria is sung *piano*. He did not sing it to the audience; he turned and sang it to Milanov, who was a little upstage of him. I will remember it till I die. The third act is all his. He showed his uncanny dramatic intuition at one moment. The great aria "Oh de' verd' anni miei" is climactic, but Warren found in the words "Gran dio" before the aria the true climax of the scene. And how his voice soared over the chorus on "O sommo Carlo." Lord Byron said of the fabled Shakespearean actor Edmund Kean that seeing him was one of the great consolations, and *that* was Leonard Warren.

✦

Preface

To many of his colleagues and even to his friends, Leonard Warren remains something of an enigma, a man of strange contradictions. As a person who rarely encouraged familiarity, he managed to hide most of his private feelings, even from those close to him. My acquaintance with him reached from the mid-1940s until his death in 1960; I was first his fan and later his colleague, particularly after I began to write about him in *Opera News*. And although Warren proved difficult for me to interview and even more difficult to fathom, it was my job to find the person inside, to discover whether he was outrageous, as he sometimes seemed, or completely closed, or lovable. As I found, he was truly lovable, although he sometimes hid his better nature. Throughout Warren's life, he remained a relentlessly private man. He rarely relaxed his guard with strangers.

Warren sang at the Radio City Music Hall, the Metropolitan Opera, and many other theatres and concert halls from 1934 to 1960 without ever making more than a dozen close friends from the ranks of his colleagues. Unlike many genial, outgoing souls who work in the music business, unlike singers who learned to trust their close associates, Warren often seemed aloof, even to those with whom he worked for years. Many people who worked at the Met still remember him coming to the Opera House, tending to his business, putting on his coat and hat, and going home. Collegiality rarely entered into his professional transactions. Interviewers and publicity agents alike despaired of him. However, many of Warren's early colleagues in opera such as the conductors Wilfrid Pelletier and Fausto Cleva and singers such as Rose Bampton Pelletier, Licia Albanese, Risë Stevens, Robert Merrill, Jan Peerce, and Richard Tucker were unfailingly friendly to me and to other colleagues. Initially Warren was not, but when he began to feel he could trust someone, he gradually revealed himself as surprisingly erudite, the simple, warm, generous, boyish kid from the Bronx.

I first heard Warren sing at the Met in the mid-1940s, as he was struggling through the thickets of his early career in opera. Over the years, I learned more about him. Born Leonard Warenoff, he was the son of two Russian Jewish immigrants, both of whom came from solid middle class families. Expectations for this first son ran high, but Warren was a listless and unresponsive student in the New York City public schools. Nor did he show any particular gift for the stage, for he remained anonymous even in simple school plays. He played no musical instrument and never learned how to read music. After Warren entered City College of New York and the extension program at Columbia University, his parents expected him to go into and eventually take over their traditional fur business, but he was unsuccessful. Fired from his first position as a sorter of raw skins, he ran through a series of demeaning temporary jobs. He tried the garment business, where he made feather boas and trimmings for women's hats. Next he was a grease monkey in gas stations. As Vivien Warren, his younger sister, said, "For years, he was going nowhere."

Reserved and even shy, young Warren kept his frustration to himself. However, even in his youth, his major asset was his big voice. Aunts Bert Warenoff and Mary Kantor kept encouraging him to sing and urged his mother to find a voice teacher for him. Warren sought work, singing for private parties and in a resort in the Catskills. Soon he was able to profit from one aunt's senior position with a New York radio station. Nevertheless, he was a late starter. Not until he was twenty-three did he finally find a place in the Radio City Music Hall Glee Club. He also found his voice. Four years of scattered lessons and coaching gave him some control over an uneven instrument that ranged from tenor highs to baritone lows. At first, his style was coarse and sometimes marred by broken phrasing and his habit of throwing inappropriate high notes into any song. But he was determined to learn and to succeed. He mastered his voice and learned diction, whether in English or foreign languages. He came to the fore in two competitions and finally got a contract with the Metropolitan Opera.

To the Met, Warren brought his raw material and, ultimately, his art, as he progressed from secondary roles to stardom. When he sang, he put forward his inner self as few singers could. Tenor Carlo Bergonzi said of Warren, "He had something inside, something that he had to convey to others; he wanted to *talk* to people when he sang." Yes, the baritone "talked" with his singing voice—getting him to talk with his speaking voice was another matter! As I discovered over the years, interviewing Warren became an exercise in strategy. As our interviews began, he was courteous and almost prim, but would say little of interest. But when we turned the conversation to one or the other of his passions, he blossomed. The warm human being emerged. Then a genial, intelligent Warren spoke freely about his love for history, his tireless research for his roles, or his attempts to master the art of operatic acting. He loved his rose garden, his electric trains, his boat, his fishing expeditions, and the recipes he had perfected as an amateur chef.

This was the man his family knew. I could never have written this biography without the help of Warren's sister, Vivien. Wise, honest, fair, marvelously intelligent, and funny, she proved to be the most valuable colleague any writer could have. Beyond that, she became a beloved friend. From the autumn of 1996 until the end of her life, she devoted most of her time to this book, providing thousands of details that no researcher could have unearthed. She also had a healthy influence on the research and the text itself. As we were going through boxes of clippings in the Leonard Warren Collection in the New York Public Library for the Performing Arts, Vivien would frown when she discovered a bad review of a performance. Then she would show it to me. Slyly, she would smile and whisper to me, "We can't use this." She would put it in an envelope, write "Bad" on the outside, and then say, "Use it!"

This book is hers, much more than it is mine.

◆

Acknowledgments

V ivien Warren worked with me on the book from 1996 until the spring of
1998. Although she was very ill, she contributed to almost every page
before she died, because she introduced me to everyone she knew who might
remember her brother. She and I either talked on the phone (sometimes more
than once a day) or met several times a week to discuss every aspect of
Leonard Warren's life. For hours Vivien would answer my questions as I took
notes. Then I would write up the material and take it over so she could check
it for errors. Back would come my typescript, with Vivien's little Post-it Notes
attached. Because she was so fair-minded, she determined from the outset not
to collaborate in a panegyric about her brother. "No whitewash," she would
say. Straight as an arrow herself, she wanted this to be a straight book.

Before and after Vivien's death in 1998, her daughter, Linda Warren
Tirdel, generously contributed her ideas and knowledge and her own recollections of Uncle Leonard. Linda's son, Edward Warren Haber, and her
daughter-in-law, Siobhan Flaherty Haber, also agreed to carry on Vivien's
work. Siobhan was particularly helpful with research in the Leonard Warren
Collection at the New York Public Library for the Performing Arts.

Particular thanks are owed to Barrett Crawford, president of the Leonard
Warren Foundation, whose unflagging interest in this biography extended
over many years and embraced his own extensive research and correspondence. Barrett's help in reconstructing Warren's career in Puerto Rico, South
America, Mexico City, and San Francisco proved positively invaluable. He
shared books with me and sent dozens of photocopies of relevant material.
Without his chronology of Warren's opera performances and the Met's chronology of Warren's appearances there and on tour, I could never have been
sure of the details of Warren's career. Barrett's masterly discography is worthy of its subject.

I thank my children for their contributions to this book. Margaret Spen-
cer Matz provided guidance at every stage, particularly in matters of content

and design. Clare scouted the Warren sites in the Bronx, took photographs, and did research here and in Italy. Carlino, my son, gave me practical help and moral support. He also took photographs and spent months teaching me how to use the computer, master word processing programs, scan photographs and documents, and plan layouts. In this project, as in all my work, my children are an unfailing source of strength.

No book about Leonard Warren could have been written without the help of Robert Tuggle, director of the Metropolitan Opera Archives, and John Pennino, assistant archivist. Bob searched for documents that I could never have found on my own, while John gave aid and comfort as I hunted down Warren's contemporaries and did research on contracts and other material from the Met files. Raymond Gniewek, concertmaster of the Metropolitan Opera, filled in many details about the last years of Warren's career. John Grande, chief librarian of the Metropolitan Opera, was also helpful.

My colleagues from the Metropolitan Opera Guild and from *Opera News* have helped me with this project, as they have helped with others over the years. I am particularly grateful to Rudolph S. Rauch, managing director of the Metropolitan Opera Guild and editor and publisher of *Opera News*, and to friends on the masthead: Patrick J. Smith, editor-at-large; Brian Kellow, executive editor; Jane L. Poole, senior editor; John W. Freeman, contributing editor, whose detailed review of the manuscript is greatly appreciated; Gregory Downer, art director; and Louise T. Guinther, Jennifer Mellick, Marylis Sevilla-Gonzaga, Elizabeth Diggans, and Lorraine Rosenfeld. Paul Gruber, executive director, program development, for the Guild, deserves particular thanks for helping me to resolve difficult problems I encountered as I researched and wrote about Warren.

At the New York Public Library, I had surefire support from many valued colleagues. Among them are Jean Bowen, director of the Center for the Humanities, the great library at Forty-second Street; Susan Sommer, chief, Music Division, and her staff, including John Shepard, George Boziwick, Frances Barulich, and Linda B. Fairtile, at the New York Public Library for the Performing Arts; and Alice Hudson, chief, and Nancy Kandoian, map cataloguer, Map Division.

For information on Warren's engagement in Milan, I am grateful to M. Contrini, Ph.D., and Andrea Vitalini, Ph.D., of the Museo Teatrale and Archivio Fotografico at the Teatro alla Scala. Giuseppe Pugliese, critic and former director of the press office at the Teatro La Fenice, provided his personal recollections of Warren's performances at La Scala.

Several prelates, priests, and others associated professionally with the Catholic Church directed me as I tried to understand the process that led Leonard Warren to be baptized as a Roman Catholic in 1950. I am indebted to the Very Rev. Edwin Broderick, Bishop of Albany (Ret.), whom I called many times; Patricia Keegan, Church of St. Vincent Ferrer, New York City;

Rev. Charles Kraus, Church of St. Charles Borromeo, Brooklyn; Mrs. Rose Ruffolo Smeriglio, Church of St. Catherine of Siena, Riverside, Connecticut; Barbara Brandon, Equestrian Order of the Knights of the Holy Sepulchre of Jerusalem, Archdiocese of New York; Father Royal Gardner, Warren's close friend, who now has a parish in Pittsfield, Massachusetts; Frank and Barbara Schwarz; and Rev. Father Tarcisio Bolzoni and Rev. Monsignor Stefano Bolzoni of Busseto, Italy.

John F. X. Walsh, manager, contract administration, BMG Classics, found Warren's contracts with RCA Victor and gave me photocopies of them. B. C. Vermeersch, director, Greenwich House Music School, showed me where Warren studied voice and let me examine some of his scores and visit the classroom that is named for him and contains his piano. Robert Morris, director, National Archive, Northeast Region, New York Office, helped me find documents relating to the presence in Manhattan, the Bronx, and Brooklyn of the Warenoff and Kantor families. Also helpful in this matter were Marian Maidenberg, archivist, Evander Childs High School in the Bronx; the librarians of the Mormon Family History Center in New York City; and the secretary of the Mt. Zion Cemetery Office, Queens, New York City. James Slater, M.D., of St. Luke's Roosevelt Hospital, New York City, offered his professional opinion on the circumstances of Warren's death onstage at the Met. Various non-Met moments from Warren's career could be reconstructed because of the help of Ann-Marie Harris, Berkshire Athenaeum, Pittsfield, Massachusetts; Mary Campbell, Associated Press, New York City; Cyrilla Barr, Ph.D., Catholic University of America; and Diane Jaust, archivist, Radio City Music Hall. Special thanks are owed to James B. McPherson, whose expert review of the final text is most appreciated.

Many events recalled in these pages come from my interviews with Warren's Bobrow-Hoffman cousins and with much-loved and dependable colleagues and friends. They are Licia Albanese, Ethel Bobrow Altschuler, Lucine Amara, Charles Anthony, Tina Appleton Bishop, John Appleton, William Appleton, Judith Goldberg Apy, Therman Bailey, Rose Bampton Pelletier, Vera Bardelli Perinati, Cesare Bardelli, Cyrilla Barr, Ph.D., Carlo Bergonzi, Anders Björling, Patricia Brown, Bruce Burroughs, Margaret Carson, Pinuccia Cellini, Vladimir Chernov, Joseph G. Chisholm, Alan Coleridge, Nancy Conrad, Anthony L. Coppola, William Crawford, Mary Curtis-Verna, Peter G. Davis, Constance De Caro, Donna De Laurentis, Norman Dello Joio, John De Merchant, Eileen Di Tullio, Mignon Dunn, Carl Edwards, Andrew Farkas, Martin Feinstein, Richard Fischer, M.D., Eleanor M. Forrer, Reva Freidberg Fox, Vera Giannini, Sonya Haddad, Marilyn Halla, Ward Halla, David Hamilton, Helen Hatton, Ph.D., Floyd Herzog, Ph.D., Lucia Evangelista Hines, Jerome Hines, Daniel Hladik, Joel Honig, Alfred F. Hubay, Merle Hubbard, Paul Jaretzki, Jerry Kagan, Ginger Dreyfus Karren, Henry Kaston, Thomas Kaufman, Alan Kayes, Arge Keller, Herman Krawitz, Bruce Kubert,

Jesús M. López, Mark Lyons, Aldo Mancusi, Ralph Mead, Nathaniel Merrill, Robert Merrill, Anne Midgette, Sherrill Milnes, Richard Mohr, Horacio Molina, Perry Morrison, Patrice Munsel, William Murphy, Danny Newman, Lyric Opera of Chicago; Inna and Howard Ockelmann, Nino Pantano, Roberta Peters, Emil R. Pinta, Marise Angelucci Pokorny, Florence and Ralph Postiglione, Louis Quilico, Roald Reitan, Regina Resnik, Elise Revson, Maria Rich, Martin Rich, Charles Riecker, Wally Cleva Riecker, Delia Rigal, Tony Russo, Joseph V. Siciliano, Giulietta Simionato, Giovanni Simone, Donald Sisler, William R. T. Smith, Louis J. Snyder, Regina Sokol, Armand Stepanian, Risë Stevens, Yolanda Oberding Stivanello, Anthony L. Stivanello, William Mayo Sullivan, Renata Tebaldi, Blanche Thebom, Elaine Troostwyk Toscanini, Walfredo Toscanini, Giorgio Tozzi, Marylin Noble Tracy, Barry Tucker, Jean Seward Uppman, Theodor Uppman, Edgar Vincent, Martha Dreyfus Wagner, Alan Wagner, Sandra Warfield McCracken, William Weaver, John S. White, Seth B. Winner, Richard Woitach, Ellen Wolf, Esther and Michael Wurmfeld, and Dino Yannopoulos. I thank them all.

♦ CHAPTER ONE

From Russia to America

L eonard Warren was born on Friday, 21 April 1911, at eight-thirty in the evening in New York City, in the Bronx, the first of the three children of Solomon Warenoff and Sara Selma Kantor Warenoff, who came from Russia. A descendant of three generations of furriers, Warren turned his back on his family's trade and rose to become one of the greatest singers of this century, with a career that took him from the Radio City Music Hall Glee Club to pinnacles of achievement in celebrated theatres and halls in America and Europe. No other baritone of his time made such a mark in the parts that became his signatures: the title roles in *Rigoletto*, *Macbeth*, *Falstaff*, and *Simon Boccanegra*, Count di Luna in *Il trovatore*, Amonasro in *Aida*, Iago in *Otello*, Barnaba in *La Gioconda*, Tonio in *Pagliacci*, and Scarpia in *Tosca*.

Warren was born in the right environment for a young man who wanted a career in singing. Fortunate in his family, which had preserved much of its European culture and encouraged its young people to love music, he grew up surrounded by parents, grandparents, aunts, uncles, and cousins who nourished in modest ways his own musical aspirations and those of his talented younger brother, a tenor who later worked as a song promoter for a music publisher. An aunt held an important position at the Mutual Network's station WOR and was later the secretary of Robert Wagner, mayor of New York City. Another aunt sang on radio in New York. A cousin on the Warenoff side, Ethel Bobrow, married Richard Altschuler, president of Republic Pictures International and an associate of William Paley of the Columbia Broadcasting System. Francine Kantor, a first cousin, married a partner of Louis Nizer, one of America's most powerful attorneys. Warren was certainly not without resources. Apart from these connections, Warren found professional opportunities in opera because he sought them at a moment when American singers were welcome in the field. His childhood and youth were spent in the very era when, for the first time, American singers without European training or experience could hope for a career.

In the hallowed halls of opera this meant a significant reversal of tradition, which had held that singers had to have experience in Europe before undertaking an American career. In 1912 when Warren was one year old, the Pennsylvania-born tenor Paul Althouse became the first American without European experience to sing major roles at the Metropolitan Opera. When he proved himself, the tide began to turn for Americans. As World War I cut off the supply of European singers, Rosa Ponzillo, born in Connecticut, became Ponselle. The Canadian tenor Edward Johnson sang for years as Edoardo Di Giovanni. Ponselle and Johnson were just two young North Americans added to the Metropolitan Opera roster, but Ponselle alone became an international celebrity without ever having studied or sung abroad. In 1923 Lawrence Tibbett, Warren's greatest American predecessor, began his long career at the Metropolitan, opening a door that Warren stepped through some fifteen years later.

Warren's Russian origins explain some aspects of his profoundly grasped art, and his family's roots are particularly important to any understanding of his early life because his antecedents had so recently arrived in this country, bringing their traditions with them. Their culture was the daily fare of his childhood and youth; his parents and maternal grandparents, David and Brina Kantor, spoke Russian, Yiddish, and English. The Bobrow cousins spoke several languages and traveled and studied in Europe. The family's prayer books were in Hebrew, and it was this culture that helped to shape the man-of-theatre that Warren became. Between his family's beginnings in Russia and his own triumphal return to their native land for his concerts of 1958 lay a distinguished career.

Russia: The Land They Left

The Voronovs, as Warren's family was known in Europe, lived in urban centers in what is now Belarus. They were naturally influenced by a culture where the ideas of western Europe met those of the czars' world. Of all the intellectual and political currents moving in the last half of the nineteenth century, none were more powerful in Russian cities than those of the Romantic movement and nationalism, both of which profoundly influenced the art and music of the time. The ideas they embodied gripped the imaginations of rich and poor alike, and cries for freedom raised hopes in all of Europe. Romanticism fostered a new kind of thinking, one that reached some of the darkest corners of the world. At this same time, the Industrial Revolution was beginning to reach remote places. As early as the 1860s, trains made travel so easy that people could move from Paris or even from Italy to Moscow in relative comfort.

It was Winston Churchill who defined Russia as "a riddle wrapped in a mystery inside an enigma," but some areas of that empire had long been familiar terrain to invading soldiers, well-meaning English Protestant missionaries, tradesmen, theatre folk, architects, and craftsmen. In particular, commercial exchange among the peoples of Belarus, Ukraine, Poland, and Scandinavia flourished without interruption from the Dark Ages into the modern era. For centuries, two heavily traveled trade routes lay between Scandinavia and the Black Sea: in a north-south direction, and between Moscow and Warsaw, from east to west. Several important cities lay on those routes. To the north was Vitebsk (Vicebck), barely inside the present border between Russia and Belarus. Ukraine and its capital, Kiev, lay to the south. One of Warren's grandfathers came from Kiev.

Nathan Hoffman, Warren's great-grandfather, came from Vitebsk. To the southwest lay Minsk, the cultural and political heart of Belarus and a center of Judaism. A Voronov uncle lived in Minsk. Another important city in the region was Orsha (Orsa), a provincial center in Belarus, where Warren's aunt, Sonia Voronov, lived. His father's ancestors came from the town of Sklov, about 60 miles south of Orsha and 125 miles east of Minsk in the district now called the Mahilev, on the main road to Kiev. This northeastern area of Belarus is a hilly, fertile upland with broad fields and dark forests of spruce, oak, maple, and elm. On the Dnieper River, a route that became the grand highway between the Baltic and the Black Sea, Minsk was always important. Orsha and Sklov, the principal seats of the Voronovs, enjoyed an advantage over other small cities because they were on the upper reaches of the Dnieper. Down the rivers came furs and timber; upward streamed the treasures of the Black Sea and the Mediterranean. Orsha also lay on the main road from Moscow to Warsaw and was a strategic bridge between East and West. Now the St. Petersburg–Kiev highway runs through it. Many of these cities had been exposed to Polish Catholic, Lithuanian, Lutheran, German, and French cultures. They knew Western ideas of intellectual awakening.

When Leonard Warren's uncle was living there, Minsk was the capital, while Orsha was an administrative center with a busy river port. Its Jewish communities had for centuries been in somewhat better condition than the ghettos of other larger centers. Intellectual openness brought Russian Jews a knowledge of Pan-Slavic nationalism and the national movement called Zionism. Hans Kohn described them in *Revolutions and Dictatorships*:

> Both [of these] broke the rigid traditionalism of the established social order . . . [just as] the Jewish Enlightenment movement helped to break down the traditional orthodox structure of Russian Jewish society and "open up a window toward Europe." [The way was opened to] secular learning, participation in the general movement of European ideas and to new careers. There was an awakening of individualism [that] prepared the modernization of Judaism.

This is the culture of Warren's ancestors. It was a secular culture. Ethel Bobrow Altschuler, Warren's cousin, described their family as "children of the

Enlightenment" and said the men in the generation of Solomon Voronov and Jacob Bobrow "did not even have bar mitzvah ceremonies because they did not believe in that sort of thing. They were assimilated Jews." Solomon had already Americanized his name to Warenoff in 1900. The family photographs, made in Belarus in 1898 or 1900 and 1919 and 1921, show well-dressed, sophisticated people in the fashionable city photographers' studios. In the earliest of these, Warren's paternal grandparents, the Voronov-Hoffmans, are posed against a backdrop with a formal garden and ornamental architectural details. Leon Warenoff, who later became Warren's uncle, is a child in a handsome full suit. The photograph shows a modern family of the time and could have been made in London, Paris, or New York.

The Voronovs

By the 1890s, when the oldest of the family photographs was made, several branches of the Voronov clan were already comfortably settled in the heart of New York's Lower East Side. The first immigrant in the family came in 1891, when young Isaac Chaitian (later Chaitin), Solomon Voronov's cousin, left Belarus for New York. Several Bobrows followed in 1893. Chaitian was followed in 1898 by his brother, Samuel, who arrived with the boy Solomon Voronov and Nathan Hoffman, Leonard Warren's great-grandfather, the oldest of the group, having been born in 1827. They came to live with Hoffman's daughter and son-in-law, Hannah and Solomon Bobrow. Solomon was just twelve when he and his grandfather came to America. When he arrived at the port of New York in 1898, young Solomon Voronov had his name changed to Warenoff at the customs depot. Solomon's grandfather, Nathan Hoffman, kept his surname. Those earlier immigrants who had reached Forsyth Street were Solomon Bobrow, born in Belarus in 1852, and Chaitian, born in 1871, who became his son-in-law. Together they founded and operated Chaitian and Bobrow, a large international corporation that imported furs. Solomon Bobrow was a distinguished, educated man whose library was so valuable that it was later sought by and donated to the Jewish Seminary in New York. Bobrow brought with him his wife, Hannah (Anna) Hoffman, born in 1858, and their children, Raya (Rosa), Jacob, and Pauline. Raya Bobrow married Isaac Chaitian and had daughters, Augusta, Elizabeth, and Frances, born in New York. The teenage Solomon Warenoff and two of his cousins worked for Chaitian and Bobrow. "Little Leon" Voronov, the attentive younger son in the family's Russian group photograph, later joined his brother and became a fur dyer in New York, changing his name to Leon Warenoff.

Enlightened members of this family saw in the hope of emigration not only a flight from desperation but a move toward a richer future. At that same time several other Jewish families from Orsha also left for America. These were the Cohens, the Hambourgs, the Kalkins, the Kirsons, the Pasenkers, and the Tiemkins. So many people emigrated from Sklov that they eventually formed a society of their own in New York and have descendants scattered from the suburbs of New York and Boston to Idaho and California. Almost three hundred Jewish families, including some of the Hoffmans, emigrated from nearby Vitebsk to America. Like thousands of urban, secularized Jews from Germany, these Russians had understood emigration originally in terms of moving to another large, European city, going first to Warsaw or to Germany or London, where the Thames-side Tower Hamlets of Stepney and Wapping soon began to register large concentrations of Eastern European Jews. But these places were only one step for those who dreamed of America.

When Solomon was fourteen, he described himself to the census taker in the 1900 Federal Census as a furrier, as did Jacob Tanenbaum, one cousin who lived with him in the Bobrows' apartment. The Bobrows, Chaitians, the Schilkits, the elder Hoffman, and young Warenoff were then living in Manhattan on the Lower East Side. Their building at 108 Forsyth, on the northeast corner of Forsyth and Broome, was at the corner of Grand Street. The four households living there were virtually all related. Almost everyone in the building was born in Russia; one Italian family lived around the corner on Broome Street. At 108 Forsyth, almost all of young Warenoff's relatives were in trade or commerce. One family member sold insurance. As we have seen, Isaac Chaitian and two of the Bobrows were furriers and importers, one of the Schilkits was a confectioner, and a daughter of that family made pocketbooks. It was a tightly knit clan. Surprisingly, everyone could speak English. This was clearly a house full of middle-class families. In the early years of this century, Jacob Bobrow frequently traveled to Russia on business; he sent his daughter, Ethel, to school in Switzerland, where she studied at a private girls' academy in Montreux. Vivien Warren said her mother also intended to send her abroad for study though she did not; Leonard was offered a chance to study abroad when he was fifteen, but he declined. Later the Bobrows and Warenoffs remained close. One Bobrow was the obstetrician who delivered Vivien Warren's daughter, and the Altschulers once had "Cousin Leonard" as their guest. Mrs. Altschuler remembered a night in the 1940s when Warren sang in their apartment. "The walls came tumbling down," she said.

Other Bobrows became importers. A close friend of Jacob Bobrow was Armand Hammer, the financier. The Bobrows' business and social contacts reached from England, France, and Switzerland to Belarus and Krasnoyarsk, then into the depths of Siberia, later into Canada and the West Coast of the United States. These families were held together and protected by what Vivien called "associations," which helped them to get to New York and provided for education and financial assistance as needed. It also helped them get established in business. Vivien, like Mrs. Altschuler, remembered her grandparents' participation in the Sklover Benevolent Aid Society, which was named for their native town of Sklov. The Bobrows, like the Warenoffs and David Kantor, also belonged to that protective association; Leonard and Vivien's oldest uncle was an officer of the Sklover Society.

Vivien said her father, Solomon Warenoff, told of sleeping "on the floor of the kitchen of one of the people from the [Sklover] association," soon after he came to this country; this landlord was Solomon Bobrow, for Warenoff went into the Chaitian-Bobrow fur business before he was fourteen. A similar story has been told by the Metropolitan Opera tenor Jan Peerce, who recalled his early life on the Lower East Side in interviews with Alan Levy, the writer who collaborated in his autobiography, *The Bluebird of Happiness*. Born on Orchard Street in 1904 as Jacob Pincus Perelmuth, in a household like the Bobrows' about three blocks from where Solomon Warenoff was living, Peerce remembered his parents' boarders in the apartment they later rented on Madison Street. Peerce and his brother slept on pillows on the kitchen floor, keeping warm at night near the stove, while their paying guests occupied the beds.

Vivien never forgot her family's pride of origin, for, as she said, her grandparents and parents always took pains to point out that they were "Litvaks, not Galitsianas," Jews with historic ties to the ancient Lithuanian Empire, which had once reached to the Black Sea, rather than to Poland. "Galitsianas," she said, were thought of as "foreigners." Yet the immigrants knew they had to learn a new language and a new culture. Solomon Warenoff's relatives probably learned English from members of the Sklover Society or from one of the educational foundations that flourished in the neighborhood. The most famous of these was the Educational Alliance, an institution that stood next to the offices of the *Forward*, the nation's most widely read Jewish newspaper. The Educational Alliance, the Henry Street Settlement, and other such charitable organizations were bulwarks of support for these immigrant families. The Educational Alliance had been founded in 1898 as a Hebrew Institute to help "Americanize" the newcomers. According to Ronald Sanders, writing in *The Lower East Side*, "the focus on Americanization was so strong that none of its many classes, such as those in American history and government, were given in Yiddish." Young Jacob Bobrow, who arrived in America when he was just fourteen, was immediately enrolled in school here. Years later, when Leonard Warren's sister was a child trying to speak Yiddish to her Kantor grandmother, the older woman said, "Vivi, speak English to me." It was a matter of pride, although the Warenoff children had also learned some Yiddish from their cousins.

Just at the corner of Solomon Warenoff's block is the beautiful Forsyth Street Synagogue, at 126 Forsyth. It was the home of the Congregation Anshei Illeya, whose Star of David window is still intact over the main door. Nearby, at the corner of Grand and Allen streets, was Ridley's Department Store, America's largest retail establishment at that time. Commerce was the heart of the Lower East Side, with its push carts, "appetizings," and shops selling religious goods. In many areas street vendors flourished. Many of this country's best loved entertainers, singers, and actors came from the Lower East Side, among them Eddie Cantor, Zero Mostel, and Walter Matthau. Although he was born in Brooklyn in 1913 as Rubin Ticker, the Metropolitan Opera tenor Richard Tucker had ties to the Lower East Side for a long time, from his boyhood to his years as a young adult, chiefly because his parents moved back and forth from there to Brooklyn. The Tickers were affiliated with the Romanian synagogue; Tucker studied to become a cantor in the Tifereth Israel Synagogue on Allen Street, where he also sang in the choir. Jan Peerce, Tucker's future brother-in-law, also studied on the Lower East Side; his family lived near the Etz Chaim Anshei Wolozin Synagogue at 209 Madison Street. Among the most famous synagogues was the Shaarey Shomoyim, on the south side of Rivington Street. Ronald Sanders identifies its Talmud Torah (religious school) as the finest in the neighborhood. This synagogue was home to some of the century's greatest cantors, among them Yossele (Josef) Rosenblatt and Moishe Koussevitzky. Moyshe Oysher performed in movies, radio and television, and on the stage. Both Peerce and Tucker served the best traditions of their culture. So also did Robert Merrill, who was born Moishe Miller. As we shall see, Peerce preceded Warren into the Radio City Music Hall and later went on from there into opera. Merrill followed.

The Kantors

Quite different from this predominantly Jewish quarter was the Italian neighborhood a few blocks to the north and west where David and Brina Kantor settled. The Kantors, Leonard Warren's maternal grandparents, came from Kiev. According to Vivien, they had a troubled history. Although Ukraine was the historic center of one of Europe's largest Jewish communities, Jews of Ukrainian origin were more often driven by fear than emigrants from other regions were. Even before the assassination of Czar Alexander II in 1881, repression there had led to persecution. In 1882 it continued. Terror ran like fire through the Jewish communities, where pogroms brought destruction of property and mass slaughter. The horrors aroused the *Times* of London to denounce the "organized massacres." On 17 March 1882, using an angry editorial tone, the newspaper described the *Pogromen* as "riots against the Jews," which "must be stopped." But they continued, leading the *London Daily News* in June 1905 and the *Westminster Gazette* in 1906 to carry further frightening reports. David Kantor, Leonard Warren's maternal grandfather, evidently carried scars from the memory of the terror in Russia long after he reached New York in 1891. Kantor was born on 8 July 1854. His wife, Brina, was born in August 1862. In Russia their first daughter, Sara Selma, was born in 1881. She later became Leonard Warren's mother. A son,

Solomon, followed in December 1884; then came Fanny, called Flo, who was born in Russia in November 1888. The rest of their children, Miriam (called Mary), Harry, and Samuel, were born in New York City.

Vivien said that no one in the Warenoff clan ever spoke of pogroms, but the Kantors did. The fear learned in Ukraine never left them. She said that even when her grandfather lived in Manhattan, the Bronx, and Brooklyn, even decades after he arrived in New York, he slept with his American passport under his pillow and told his grandchildren tales of murderous Cossacks and their reign of terror. From the 1870s through the 1880s, through the earliest years of that century's Russian emigration to the United States, reports had reached the old country of an America where everyone could work and earn and practice religion freely. Men and women like David and Brina Kantor were encouraged to escape to a new life here. For them, the port of Hamburg was the gateway to a new world, a world without pogroms. From Hamburg, then, the Kantors and their first three children sailed in 1891. They raised their family at 68 Spring Street, in Little Italy, near the corner of Lafayette Street and a few yards from Broadway. The Kantors' neighbors were Italian wine merchants, sailors, stone masons, embroiderers, and caterers. The 1900 census shows the Kantors as the only family living in their home, a private residence. It was a three-story wooden structure with a brick façade and a large back yard that took up about a third of their lot. Shown in *Bromley's 1902 Atlas of New York*, the house seems to be an old Federal style or Greek Revival structure. The Kantors, like the Warenoffs, were furriers. Although Solomon Warenoff originally worked for Chaitian and Bobrow, he went into the business founded by his father-in-law, David Kantor; later he founded his own firm. Vivien said the Kantors also owned a drygoods store in Manhattan's East Eighties, the area known as Yorkville, a center of German culture. The crowded living conditions in Lower Manhattan eventually led many immigrant families to move to other boroughs. The Bobrows moved to fashionable Upper Manhattan, while Solomon Warenoff and the Kantors moved to the Bronx.

CHAPTER TWO

A New York Way of Life

When Leonard Warren was born in 1911, his parents were living in the home of his Kantor grandparents at 1822 Clinton Avenue in the Bronx, just north of Crotona Park. Another son, Martin, was also born there four years later on 26 April 1915. The Warenoffs' third and last child was Vivien Zoe, born on 26 November 1920. Before she arrived, the Warenoffs had moved from the Kantors' house to an apartment of their own at 1360 Ogden Avenue. After each birth, Solomon Warenoff entered his children's birthdays in his copy of *The Form of Daily Prayers*, a beautiful book with ivory and silver inlay on the cover; gold is also overlaid on dark velvet. It is in Hebrew and English, and as its subtitle indicates, it contains the prayers used "in the rituals of German and Polish Jews."

Registering his independence and his new firm, Warenoff filed a certification of his status in the business community on 13 December 1911 when Leonard was not yet a year old. "I, Solomon Warenoff, of the City, County and State of New York do hereby certify that I transact the business of buying and selling furs and skins at Number 162 West Twenty-fourth Street, Boro of Manhattan under the name of Sol Warenoff and Company." With this business he provided well for his family, although their way of life was threatened when World War I broke out. On 13 June 1917, when Leonard was six and had just finished first grade, Sol received a Notice of Enrollment Under Military Law from the State of New York. From then until the end of the war, he was an enrolled soldier in the New York State Militia, able to be called up for service in the National Guard or in the Naval Militia. So far as we know, he was never asked to serve.

The Family Home

The Warenoffs lived in a tastefully furnished upper-middle-class house, which Vivien remembered from her childhood and youth: "It was filled with good furniture and had Oriental rugs on all the floors; an old wind-up Victrola with its black wax platters provided much of the family's entertainment. We had a big green velvet sofa. In the dining room stood a long table, with enough chairs to accommodate large family gatherings; two of the mahogany sideboards had heavy marble tops." She described the living room chairs as "huge." One of them, an imposing Jacobean armchair, was handed down to her, together with the table. "My mother had beautiful and very expensive taste," she says. The Warenoff family always had a live-in maid, often a Jamaican woman hired through a clergyman in the South.

Vivien said that the members of her immediate family were "reformed Jews, not Orthodox Jews." Her father went to temple only on Yom Kippur, but the family, including the aunts, uncles, and cousins, celebrated Passover with the customary rites. Everyone gathered in the Warenoff home for the traditional first-night Seder. "We had gefilte fish, pickled herring, soup, brisket of beef, roast chicken, and wine. The bitter herbs were in a big round dish. The ritual questions were asked by the youngest son, Martin. Every Friday night Mother would light the candles; we had challah and roasted meat, but there were never any blessings with hands being laid on our heads. Brina Kantor, our maternal grandmother, kept a kosher home, and my mother kept a kosher cupboard in our kitchen because if she hadn't, my grandmother would never have come to visit. But we ate ham and eggs, bacon, and pork roast. No one ever thought anything about it." After her grandparents died, the Warenoffs no longer kept kosher. Vivien and her brothers were taught proper behavior and learned to take care of others. Their mother did charity work in children's homes and hospitals.

The family prized records and books. Brina Kantor gave Vivien Warren a prayer book of her own in 1928. Also in the library was *The Jewish Encyclopedia*, on which Solomon Warenoff relied because he was largely self-taught after he left Russia. He made up for his lack of higher education by reading. Vivien said her father always intended to go back to Russia and had saved for the trip, but after World War II broke out, he could not go. Because he had left when he was still a boy, Warenoff was firmly rooted in America, and much of the family lore was about his early life in New York. Nevertheless, he always considered *The Jewish Encyclopedia* his "general textbook," Vivien said. It was handed down to her, and Leonard turned to it decades later when he was studying to sing the title role in Giuseppe Verdi's *Nabucco* at the Metropolitan Opera.

Like other children in the neighborhood, Leonard attended P.S. 11 on Ogden Avenue, near his home. Built in 1859, the school now enjoys national landmark status and is marked with a plaque. There one of his teachers was Marguerite Thoesen, his mother's friend. Occasionally she was invited to the Warenoffs for dinner. Vivien admitted that her brother was an indifferent student. Their mother was often called in by the principal, who asked, "Why does your son just sit there?" In a conversation with Harold C. Schonberg,

Warren described his childhood by saying, "I was very much to myself, the dreamer type." He told other interviewers that he had his first stage "role" at P.S. 11 when he was cast as an Indian guide in a play about Daniel Boone. Apart from that, we know of no other experience he had onstage. After eighth grade, Leonard entered Evander Childs High School in the Bronx. He went out for football but gave it up when he was cleated in the face during a practice session. Famous graduates of Evander Childs included Carl Reiner, the comedian Red Buttons, and the real estate tycoon Harry Helmsley. Martin and Vivien Warenoff had much of their education in Brooklyn, and she later attended the University of Washington in Seattle.

Recalling their early family life, Vivien said she always looked up to her brothers but particularly loved Leonard. "I adored him, and he always loved his 'baby sister.' I was always sketching with pastels on sketch pads, and he would hang my drawings up on the wall." She also studied elocution and dancing with a woman in the neighborhood. The Warenoffs always had a piano in the house, but Vivien appears to have been the only one of the children to have taken formal piano lessons; Martin learned on his own. He was "fun, high-spirited, and amusing." Vivien recalled the boys' early experiments with music. "Martin tried to play the piano and tried the saxophone, which did not work out very well, but he did have a beautiful tenor voice. Leonard never played any instrument, but he always sang. Even when he was a boy, people remarked on how good his voice was."

Vivien said recorded music played a large part in their lives because both her parents and the Kantors had collections of classical platters. "The phonograph was on all the time in our house, and Grandmother Kantor was always playing records." Every Saturday, Leonard, Martin, Vivien, and several cousins would go to their Kantor grandparents' home for lunch. A favorite record was Victor Herbert's *March of the Toys*, which the young cousins and the Warenoff children played for their accompaniment as they marched around the dining room table, keeping time to the music. "When the whole family got together at bigger holiday celebrations, everyone was an entertainer," Vivien recalled. "Samuel Kantor, my uncle, was the comedian of the lot. He did magic tricks. After the meal everyone in the family sang, and we were all proud of the voices of our aunt and uncle, Mary and Harry [Kantor], both of whom sang. Cousin Helen played the piano for us all. Aunt Mary had a lovely voice. She sang 'Indian Love Call' on the radio, on WOR," one of New York City's oldest stations. Not surprisingly, the family's favorite opera singer was Enrico Caruso. When it came time for the young Warenoffs to entertain, they would get together and sing their version of pieces from *Rigoletto*, making up the words as they went along. "Gibberish, and la-de-da," Vivien said. "We learned the melody from the recording, as we learned other classical music from listening to records. We sang opera at these gatherings. The Kantors sang pieces from musicals."

Vivien also spoke of her great fondness for her grandparents and her love for her brothers. When she was a child, they coddled and played with her; when she was older, they used to lift her up to sit on the piano so she could pretend to be Hildegarde. "It was all part of growing up! Leonard and Martin were always singing around the house," she recalled. "I would pipe in. Martin, a good-natured extrovert, had a fine voice, a lovely tenor, but did nothing with it. After he finished high school, he worked for a music publisher as a song promoter, trying to get his firm's music played on New York radio stations."

As the brothers were growing up, Martin took part in school athletics. Both brothers played stickball, New York's official street game. Both joined the Boy Scouts, had girlfriends, and often double-dated. Family vacations, two weeks in the summer, were sometimes spent at the New Jersey shore and sometimes in a hotel at Spring Valley in New York's Catskill Mountains. Martin often took his "baby sister" around with him. As Vivien said, he was trying to get ahead, to be successful. As a family they had an orderly life. The three occasionally argued, as all siblings do, but "Mother would stop us with a look. That was enough. Mother's look. That was the only 'discipline' any of us ever needed." She described her mother as a proud woman who was always perfectly groomed, in the house and when she left it. "She carried herself as though she were six feet tall, although she was only five feet, three inches. She and Leonard both had a presence about them. Head up, chin up." Vivien said everyone teased Leonard by calling him "The Impresario" or "The Imp" because of his desire to control every kind of situation. About manners, she said, "No one in the family swore or used coarse language, and Leonard had a lifelong aversion to crude jokes."

Even when they were young, the three had notably different tastes and different characters, Martin being outgoing, Leonard and Vivien being reserved and even shy. Martin loved parties, but Leonard did not. Vivien said, "Leonard was a loner, although both he and Martin had a lot of friends." Martin, like their mother, was a good cook, while Leonard helped with the housekeeping and liked to vacuum the carpets. Like many other young men of their time, Leonard and Martin were interested in cars. Together they bought a used Essex sedan and fixed it up, but the axle broke, and, Vivien said, "That was the end of their car." Leonard always tinkered with electrical things and built model railroads, a hobby he carried with him into adulthood, just as he continued to repair and build things, to help others and just for his own pleasure. Young and older, he was known as someone who could fix almost any mechanical object. His sister said that even after he was singing at the Metropolitan Opera, he used to stop at the Travel-Tone Radio Shop on Broadway after rehearsals and offer to help the owner fix broken television sets and radios. "Nothing made him happier."

The Warenoff and Kantor families remained very close, with the Kantors respected as the family's elders because none of the older Voronovs came to America. Vivien remembered that Leonard "really loved" their Kantor grandparents. Brina Kantor was looked up to as the "wise old woman" of her generation. Warren also spoke of the counsel offered to him by his grandfather, who said, "A voice is a gift." Warren told an interviewer from *Musical America* in 1956:

> A singer has to have humility, because no matter what kind of a gift you have, sooner or later you're going to have to account for it. I remember my grandfather telling me that, when I was a boy. He was a frail old man, something of a philosopher, and he used to sit me on his knee and feed me raisins and say, "You know, Leonard, we all carry a sample case as we go through life. One of these days you're going to be carrying that sample under your arm and you're going to have to show it. When the time comes, be prepared to deliver." He was right. A gift is a great responsibility.

Earlier, speaking to Rose Heylbut of *Etude*, Warren used his grandfather's phrase: "Auditions mean nothing unless you can deliver, and continue to deliver what you have in your sample box."

Family members evidently began to take notice of Leonard's voice when he was about twelve. In 1938 in an interview for the Boston *Sunday Post*, Warren told writer Hazel Canning that his aunt, undoubtedly Mary Kantor, was the first person to show an interest in his voice. He said:

> My mother took me over one afternoon to call on my aunt, as we often did. I sat down at her piano and went banging away, as I did generally. Then I played more softly and sang to my own music. My aunt listened. She stopped her sentence right in the middle. I was rather young, but I still remember that silence, and then my aunt's comment: "I think you should take that child to a singing teacher. He has an organ voice."

In 1924 when Leonard had his bar mitzvah, he was thirteen. He was prepared for the rite by Morris Goldberg, who was then a rabbinical student and family friend, eight years older than Leonard. In fact, Goldberg and his wife remained close to the Warenoffs for many years. To get the boy ready for the ceremony, Goldberg first had Leonard memorize passages in Hebrew from the Torah, then he taught him to chant with a particular intonation. Leonard learned his lines and appeared to be adequately prepared. Although his sister was too young to remember the event, she told the family's traditional version of how the day went. Leonard had studied his speech in Hebrew and the prayers he was to sing, but when the moment came, he forgot part of his speech. Just then there was a loud clatter as a row of chairs went down. "So God put His hand on the chairs, and they all fell over," Vivien remembered their mother saying as she told the story. The interruption restored Leonard's memory, and he picked up the forgotten lines, successfully finishing his program. Afterward the Warenoffs hosted a large party for their son. Among other guests at Leonard's bar mitzvah were Jacob and Blanche Bobrow and their thirteen-year-old daughter, Ethel, who was born in the same year as Leonard and remembered the event clearly. She also recalled the bar mitzvah of her brother Herbert. By the 1920s, she said, the family had become "more religious" and thus favored having these ceremonies for their sons. After the rite for Herbert, they entertained the guests at a party at the Hotel Roosevelt, where the soloist was Carmela Ponselle, Rosa's sister. The Bobrows also knew the Metropolitan Opera mezzo-soprano Margarete Matzenauer, whose son dated a Bobrow daughter.

Leonard's cousin Blanche Bobrow, his aunt Mary Kantor, and later his aunt Bert Green Warenoff all believed that Leonard had an unusual voice and urged his parents to let him study. Bert made an extra effort and eventually played a substantial role in Leonard's early career. The wife of Leonard's uncle, Leon Warenoff, she was the executive assistant to the founder of the radio station WOR in New York. Leon and Bert lived in an elegant apartment in The Century at 25 Central Park West, one of the city's most expensive buildings. Her insistence that Leonard get voice lessons truly launched the boy's musical education. He was about fourteen at the time and was about to enter Evander Childs High School. Sara Warenoff was urged to enroll her son in the Greenwich House Music School, where his true gifts became apparent. Much later Warren spoke to Harold C. Schonberg about his experience in this neighborhood music school and said his voice had changed when he was sixteen.

The Greenwich House Music School

One of the oldest and most respected settlement houses in New York City, Greenwich House was founded in November 1902, and incorporated by Felix Adler, Jacob Riis, Carl Schurz, and Mary Kingbury Simkhovitch, who was its director. Like its sister institutions, it had a staff that tried to remedy some of the economic and social ills of its time and improve the quality of community life. As the Educational Alliance and the Henry Street Settlement served the Lower East Side, Greenwich House served Greenwich Village and Little Italy, where recently arrived immigrants, chiefly from Sicily and the south of Italy, lived in tenement squalor and misery. Greenwich House was a pioneer in several areas, including social reform, tenants' rights legislation, health education, general education, and child care. As an institution, it still enjoys a reputation for excellence.

In 1905 the Greenwich House Music School was added to the founding institution. Located in several handsome former private townhouses but with its main entrance at 46 Barrow Street, it is dedicated to music education, offering classes and individual instruction. It also has a theatre company and boasts a year round calendar of concert events. Children, young people, and adults are taught in a variety of programs. They play orchestral instruments, and chamber music is featured together with voice. Over the years, the Greenwich House Music School has had support from Mrs. Gertrude Payne Whitney, conductor Julius Rudel, Ossip Gabrilowitch, Edgard Varèse, the actor Kirk Douglas, the painter Jackson Pollock, and, of course, Leonard Warren, its most famous voice student. The school's library has some of Warren's music, and his grand piano stands in the room dedicated to him. The effort made to keep Leonard in the Greenwich House Music School was considerable, given the distance from the Warenoff home to the school, which was just off Seventh Avenue in Greenwich Village. But he persisted, traveling by streetcar, subway, or the el to get there. In later interviews he mentioned the importance of his studies at Greenwich House in the voice classes of Will J. Stone.

In a 1938 Boston *Sunday Post* interview, Warren said that he continued his lessons there for two years. "So I left and got myself a teacher. I was earning money then and going to school, of course. I have to laugh about [my work], and I'm very glad, for the fact is that I've done more odd jobs than any boy outside of a success story. I've run errands, sold papers, worked as a clerk. Well, if I went on, people would say I was exaggerating."

According to family tradition, when Leonard was fifteen and still in high school he attracted the attention of a man who admired his voice. "As he was singing at Greenwich House," Vivien recalled, "a man came to Mother and said that he would take Leonard to Europe and pay all his expenses, if she and my father would agree to send him abroad for a year. There was a family conference, but Leonard decided that he was too young to leave home." Although Vivien did not recall this benefactor's name, it is remarkable that anyone would offer support of that kind to anyone so young and inexperienced. He did attract further attention, though.

Before he was sixteen, it was clear to many people in the family that Leonard had an exceptionally good voice, although no decision was made about how he might best use it. But two people remained uneasy about his ambitions: Leonard's mother and father. Warren told the *Sunday Post* interviewer that his mother wanted him to go to college to become a civil engineer, or to go into the Warenoff fur business. He said she wanted him to "enlarge it, save money, put it in the bank, bring up a family, and become a pillar of society." Vivien recalled the family discussions over her brother's singing. Sol Warenoff believed quite strongly that his son had no future in music. Vivien recalled him saying, "Nobody makes a living as a singer" and asking, "How will you earn a living?" His question was very much to the point because Leonard neither played the piano nor showed any interest in singing in synagogues, although cantors' jobs provided steady work for many young men and offered a springboard to a career performing in hotels or clubs or at weddings, bar mitzvahs, and public events; they could even lead to opera, as singers such as Peerce, Merrill, and Tucker proved. When Leonard Warren was interviewed by Frank Merkling in the autumn of 1956 for *Musical America*, the singer said that his "musical leanings were not encouraged." Solomon Warenoff's skepticism about his son's future may have discouraged Leonard from seeking other engagements at that time, for he neither studied piano nor enrolled in a New York City conservatory, as he might well have done. Neither did he ask for any other formal music instruction or try to get on the stage, which would surely have been easy for him, particularly after Martin became a song-plugger, promoting songs for radio and stage events. Some years later, though, the experience Leonard got at Greenwich House proved invaluable to him; particularly important were the solid vocal training and ideas about music as an art.

Finding a Job

Leonard went into the family's wholesale fur business briefly after high school. In the *Sunday Post* interview, Warren said he worked for his father, going "up north" and "examining furs offered by trappers." He had to "pick out the skins taken in the right season—winter—and reject the damaged ones, then hurry back to New York." Mrs. Altschuler remembered that her father, Jacob Bobrow, gave him the job of sorting raw skins for color and quality in the basement of the Chaitian and Bobrow building. She also said that Leonard often sang as he was working. This was perhaps the setting for an anecdote Warren later told about himself, saying that he had worked in the fur business and had been fired because his singing bothered the other employees.

Warren clearly was not sure what direction he would take. He told Hazel Canning that when he started classes at City College of New York, he was filled with doubt about whether to pursue a singing career. At one point, he said, he became very discouraged because everything was going wrong when one private teacher tried to train him as a tenor. But he went on singing and left college, although he said he "nearly" finished. But he told Canning that although he studied voice for five years after his lessons at Greenwich House, he remained unsure about singing. He said, "I was not altogether sure I wanted to be a singer. I like family life; I am devoted to my father and mother and brother and sister. And I have a very profound respect for money in the bank and the status of pillar of society." He also later confided to Harold C. Schonberg that he had "no definite idea of making a career in music." He must have had some hope, though, for once he stole away to a small radio station and asked for an audition, only to be discouraged by the music director who told him he had no voice at all.

It was at that moment that his Grandfather Kantor gave him further advice. In 1958 Warren told an interviewer for *Parade Magazine* that he had spoken to Grandfather Kantor about his fear and confusion.

> One morning at home [in the Bronx] I was reviewing my dreary saga for my grandfather. Between us there had always been a sympathy and warm affection, so I was startled to hear him say, his voice edged with impatience, "Leonard, a goal never came to a man." I replied, "It's easy to say that." And he said, "It's better to DO." "Do what?" I asked. He gave me a long look over his spectacles. "You KNOW what," he said.

The baritone said this gave him renewed determination; he went on singing. He also completed one year of night classes in business management and marketing at Columbia University. In several interviews, conducted after he was engaged by the Metropolitan Opera, he said almost everyone thought he should go into business. In these classes he may have met a woman, Vin Lindhe, who later played for him at Radio City Music Hall. She, too, was taking business courses in the extension program at that time. Throughout this period, when Warren was in his late teens and early twenties, his life was marked not by great events but by the ordinariness of it. He stayed at home with his parents and siblings, commuting to Manhattan for his business courses and small jobs or looking for work. Although he lived through the stock market crash of 1929, he and his family seem to have been largely unaffected by it. Vivien said that nothing changed in their way of life. Solomon and Leon Warenoff, the Bobrows, and the Kantors continued in the fur business, where Richard Tucker, then still known as Rubin Ticker, was also working. He, too, was struggling to find a niche in the music business but was singing regularly as a cantor, something Leonard never did. The Warenoffs, long settled in the Bronx, eventually moved.

The New Home in Brooklyn

Sometime just after 1931, when Leonard was about twenty, David and Brina Kantor moved to Brooklyn to be near their daughter Mary, who had married Charles Goldberg and was living at 625 Avenue M with her husband and children. Also in Brooklyn were Flo Kantor and her husband, David Cohen, with whom the elder Kantors later lived. The Warenoffs followed, into the middle-class neighborhood of Flatbush, about a block from Flo Kantor Cohen's home. They lived on the second floor of a red brick double house that still stands at 1315 East Eighth Street. It was a comfortable apartment with a large sun parlor, living room, and dining room, all connected by French doors, and three bedrooms, a breakfast room, kitchen, service area, and back porch. "We had a dog," Vivien recalled, "and Mother fed it steak."

When the whole family gathered, Sara Kantor Warenoff would put leaves in her long dining table to extend it through all three rooms. Here the Warenoffs continued the tradition of hosting many of the family's big parties. Apart from those, however, the family lived a quiet life, Vivien said, with Leonard and their father going out to work in the mornings as she and Martin left for school. The whole family was thrown into mourning, though, when David Kantor died in March 1932. He was buried in Mount Zion Cemetery in Queens, under the auspices of the Sklover Independent Benevolent Association.

Warren, just twenty-one, was still trying to find his way. Vivien, who was then preparing to enter Abraham Lincoln High School in Brooklyn, remembered several years when her brother was working at all kinds of unimportant jobs in one little firm after another. He said in interviews that he spent one year "just walking around" and even worked as an accountant and as a "grease monkey in a service station." When his attempt to help the Bobrow cousins or his father did not work out, he turned to other areas of the garment business. Among other things, Vivien said, he worked in the "feather trade," making feather boas and artificial flowers. "But he kept on singing around the house all the time. He said singing was his hobby." Although he did not know exactly how to find a job in the music business, he had not given up hope. Warren was attracting more and more attention from relatives, friends, and colleagues who heard him at clan events.

It was Warren's aunt Bert Green Warenoff who used her influence at WOR to get him his first chance to sing on the radio. This she had also done for his aunt Mary Kantor Goldberg, although no career had resulted from that effort. Through Aunt Bert, Warren, then an adult with a full man's voice, was given a chance to sing on a fifteen-minute weekly radio program in 1933, the first real opportunity he had ever had in the world of professional music. He said he had "two sustaining programs" on WOR. For him this was an enormous step forward, for it was a popular station. It survives still on radio and television as one of the city's most venerable broadcasting systems. In the 1930s, short musical programs were vehicles for pianists and singers in particular. They provided showcases to musicians who later became his first professional colleagues, among them the pianist Vin Lindhe, the soprano Viola Philo, and the tenors Jan Peerce and Richard Tucker. The singers delivered popular ballads and an occasional piece from operetta or an opera aria, but there was one considerable difference between these other artists and Warren: before going on radio, they had had experience in the music business, while he had none.

Speaking of his tenure as a solo artist on WOR, Warren told Rose Heylbut of *Etude* that he felt the fifteen-minute programs were a curse for young singers, not an advantage:

Perhaps the most dazzling obstacle to genuine artistry is the fifteen-minute radio spot. The young singer who captures one of those is likely to be transported with joy. Then he finds that his entire day must be devoted to mastering the kind of song that the fifteen-minute program favors, for in reality you can seldom repeat a song. The result is that he works hard enough for his good salary, but if he has his eyes on a bigger opportunity, and it really comes [to him], he isn't prepared for it. All he knows are some scores of semi-popular numbers.

That is exactly what happened to him. When his "bigger opportunity" came, he was not ready.

It was either just before or just after he had his first opportunity at WOR that Bert Green Warenoff became her nephew's agent. She added him to the list of the WOR Artists' Management Bureau, which then operated under the direction of its president, Samuel O. Jacobson. She also began to introduce Warren to influential figures in New York City such as the popular raconteur and columnist Harry Hirschfield, who had a hand in trying to get work for the young singer. Bert Warenoff also arranged for Warren to meet Louis Nizer, who acted as his representative for several years. It is clear that these people, at least, thought Warren had some kind of career in music ahead.

In the late spring of 1934, the WOR Artists Bureau got Warren a job that appears to be his first as an adult singing live on a stage. The letter contract, dated 18 June 1934, reads:

Dear Mr. Warenoff:

The following is the arrangement between us regarding your employment at the Fairmont Hotel at Tannersville, N.Y. for the season commencing on or about June 28 and terminating after Labor Day, 1934, as an entertainer. You are to receive the sum of $100 for the season, payable weekly, and also room and board and fare both ways. It is also understood that out of the two weeks salary, 10% is to be deducted for commissions to the WOR ARTISTS BUREAU for obtaining this engagement for you. You will also receive part of the proceeds of a performance which will be arranged later on, and whatever percentage is allowed you by us will be satisfactory to you. It is understood that in the event of any disagreement between us whereby we desire to terminate this agreement during the period herein, we will have the privilege of doing so upon payment to you of one week's salary. Kindly acknowledge this agreement by signing the annexed copy.

Yours very truly,
[Samuel O. Jacobson]

The young artist signed "Leonard Warenoff."

This engagement put him squarely in the Catskills, with a modest salary and room, board, and transportation all paid in the mountain vacation paradise where dozens of hotels opened just before the Fourth of July to welcome summer guests from New York City. Although the salary seems small, at about ten dollars a week, it was no worse than the fees paid to many minor Metropolitan Opera singers who earned seventy-five dollars a week and had to cover all their own personal and many professional expenses out of it. Among other singers who promoted their early careers in the Catskills were Peerce, Tucker, and Merrill. They were also engaged in the Catskills as cantors for Jewish holidays, but Warren was not. This first appearance as a concert entertainer at the Fairmont Hotel gave him a live audience for an entire season, something he had never had before.

The Tannersville-Hunter area, where Warren sang, lies west of the Hudson River near Kingston, New York, the earliest of the mountain communities to become popular with Jewish families from the city. A vacation "in the mountains" signified that the guests were "people of the better class," as the hotels advertised. At one point in its early history, this neighborhood was called "the New Jerusalem." Alf Evers, in his book *The Catskills from Wilderness to Woodstock*, notes that in the early 1920s Tannersville had a hundred hotels serving kosher food and keeping seven kosher butchers working full time. Later the Sullivan County area became the more popular resort region, with Grossinger's and other huge hotel complexes, including those at Lake Kiamesha, where the Peerces and the Tuckers stayed. Warren's Bobrow cousins had a farm at Ellenville, where they spent their summers. At the time Warren was engaged to sing in the Catskills, Tannersville was still a respectable resort town, while Sullivan County was just emerging as a refuge for New Yorkers. Traditionally the owners of the summer hotels in the area hired social directors to oversee the organized games and entertainment programs that kept the guests amused. The larger establishments had singers, instrumentalists, lecturers, and even an occasional theatrical troupe on hand. Peerce first appeared in the Catskills as a singing fiddler with his own small band. Boris Thomasshevsky performed in Yiddish plays in Hunter, while Moss Hart became known as "The King of the Borscht Circuit." Here Danny Kaye, Milton Berle, Jerry Lewis, Tony Curtis, and Red Buttons got their start.

In spite of the opportunity offered by the engagement in the Catskills and although Warren now had an important manager in the head of the WOR Artists Bureau, nothing else materialized for him. It seemed then that his father's fears were justified, yet he persisted for several years in his quiet way, with the same humdrum jobs that had kept him going for years.

CHAPTER THREE

Radio City Music Hall and the Rising Musical Star

For New Yorkers like Warren, the new Radio City Music Hall became a veritable theatrical mecca in the 1930s. It had its origins in a failed attempt to build an opera house on a plot of land leased from Columbia University. Nothing came of the original project, but after the stock market crash of 1929, Radio City was built. Samuel "Roxy" Rothafel, an impresario with a reputation of almost mythical proportions, took control of two large performing-arts spaces, Radio City Music Hall and the nearby Center Theatre. The Music Hall opened on 27 December 1932 to a capacity audience of 6200. It soon became one of New York's most popular houses. Its opening show, which played twice a day, had nineteen variety numbers. On this bill were comedians Joe Weber and Lew Fields, soprano Dorothy Fields (Lew's daughter), Jimmy McHugh, Martha Graham and her dance troupe, the soprano Vera Schwarz from the Berlin Staatsoper, the Flying Wallenda acrobatic act, tap dancer Ray Bolger, the actor DeWolf Hopper, the Tuskegee Choir, and well-known singers in several scenes from Georges Bizet's *Carmen*. Original plans for the programs were soon modified, as the variety show was shortened and scheduled for four times a day; it was also supplemented by motion pictures.

In 1957 Warren told Jesús M. López that he saw the opening night and that it had changed his life.

> I was very impressed by the opening of the gigantic Radio City Music Hall in 1932. I went there with several of my classmates, and we sat in the top balcony, the cheapest place, to hear *Carmen*. Titta Ruffo sang the part of Escamillo; and it was impressive to me to see how the voice of that giant truly filled that immense room with a power I have never heard since. This was [one of the reasons] that made me choose a career in singing.

Sara and Solomon Warenoff took Vivien to a stage show soon after the Music Hall opened. The *Carmen* cameo, according to the program in the

Radio City Music Hall Archives, featured the chorus, the company's classical ballet with Patricia Bowman as prima ballerina, the Roxyettes (as the famed precision dancers were first called), "matadors, soldiers, and cigarette girls." Its stage director was Désiré Defrère, who later spent decades at the Metropolitan Opera as a singer, coach, and director and was identified in the program as "formerly of the Chicago Civic Opera." The Carmen was Coe Glade, an American mezzo with a cult following in New York, Chicago, and Cincinnati. "The Theda Bara of opera," she was rumored to have been born in Brooklyn as Gladys Cohen. Among her trademarks were nearly transparent voile gowns, low-cut blouses, artificial eyelashes, dark eye shadow, and sexy poses that left little to the imagination. Glade also had a rich voice that was ideal for Carmen, Amneris, and Dalila. Aroldo Lindi, the Don José, sang for several years with American regional companies. For Ruffo, even at the end of his career, the Music Hall opening was an important event. He was considered by many to be the greatest baritone of his time. Giuseppe De Luca, a legend in his own right, said of him, "He was not a voice, but a miracle." The 1932 *Carmen* excerpts at Radio City were actually Ruffo's last appearance in the United States and almost the last of his entire career. He returned to Italy, where he ran afoul of the fascists, dying there in 1953. That Warren heard him, even at the end of his career, was remarkable.

Jan Peerce sang in Radio City's Center Theatre and in the Music Hall. By 1932 he had undergone several transformations from Perelmuth to Pinky Pearl, the singing violinist, to Jascha Pearl in the Catskills. He was listed in the opening night program at the Music Hall as John Pierce. Warren, in his interview with López, remembered calling Peerce "Pinky" in the Radio City days. It was Rothafel who invented "John Pierce" and "Jan Peerce." With support from that old theatrical fox, Peerce became a soloist, but it took him a long time to earn that title. Under the eye of the music director, conductor Erno Rapee, and Leon Leonidoff, who handled staging, he finally got to sing popular ballads and an occasional aria, sometimes in evening clothes and sometimes in costume. Peerce was also on the Radio City Music Hall of the Air and had his own fifteen-minute program on NBC, and he sang regularly for a Jewish station under yet another name. Later he was on the prestigious Chevrolet Sinfonietta. In 1936 the Music Hall stage program introduced Peerce singing a simple melody that became his hit and trademark song. This was "The Bluebird of Happiness," commissioned by Rapee.

The very popularity of the Radio City Music Hall entertainment and its spinoff radio program encouraged Warren to ask for an audition, although his experience was limited to weddings and parties, his programs on WOR, and his single engagement in the Catskills. Later, in his interview with Harold C. Schonberg of the *New York Times*, he told about asking for a job: "One day I went to Radio City Music Hall and saw a bass onstage. Well, I said to myself, if he can get the job, I certainly can. So I went backstage and asked for an audition. I got it and got the job." This was at the end of 1934. Rapee and Vin Lindhe auditioned him. Lindhe, a woman of Swiss origin, pronounced her name "Landy." She had joined the Music Hall staff as director of the men's chorus just before Warren was hired. Her odd background and peculiar ways led the *Radio City Music Hall Program Magazine* to describe her as "one of the most unusual figures in radio and theatre today." A workaholic and relentless self-promoter, she had worked in Texas for a detective agency, a fountain-pen factory, two radio stations, a modeling agency, and a Dallas newspaper. As a pianist, she used her real first name, Vindhe. Eccentric in the extreme, she talked aloud to herself, even while she was on the air, a habit that soon led her listeners to dub her "Windy Lindy" and "Dizzy Lizzie." This drove her to shorten her given name to Vin. Another big break came when she conducted the Dallas Symphony for two performances. She also organized an "all-girl" dance orchestra before auditioning at the National Broadcasting Company in New York. Rapee had her coaching singers for his variety programs at Radio City.

When Warren went for his audition, Lindhe was directing the all-male Radio City Music Hall Glee Club. Unlike singers who had mastered the classical and operatic repertory, Warren was struggling with semiclassical numbers and popular ballads. His handicap was that despite the great effort made for him to attend classes at Greenwich House Music School, he still could not read music and did not play an instrument. Vivien remarked on how difficult it was for her brother to learn music at that time: "Leonard could not play the piano; music was very, very hard for him." Of course other singers have had this problem as well. In the past, as today, some were trained in conservatories and became instrumentalists and even composers. On the other hand, there were many singers who could not read music but had grown up in theatrical families or simply absorbed the music along the way. Others learned by rote in sessions with coaches and voice teachers. In the twentieth century, for the first time, singers have also been able to learn from listening to recordings, as Warren did.

When Warren's big chance came, he had no serious material ready. Nevertheless, Lindhe was impressed and referred him to Rapee. He was hired at a salary of thirty-five dollars a week, not bad when the country was trying to recover from the market crash of 1929. Said Herman Krawitz, who was later Warren's friend and colleague at the Met, "Any job was a good job then." But Radio City provided more than a job. It was a way of life, demanding complete commitment from its performers. The men in the glee club sang four times a day and rehearsed when they were not singing. What free time they had was supposed to be spent in the rooftop gymnasium and recreation rooms that the management had furnished for all its employees. Vivien said her brother used that recreation space for his own purposes, listening to records he bought at the Liberty Music Shops. Recordings became a significant learning tool for him.

Lindhe and Rapee had a strong preference for men and women with operatic voices, and among the men, they favored Peerce and the American baritone Robert Weede, whom Warren admired. Weede had won the Caruso Memorial Foundation award, which gave him eighteen months of study in Italy. After a single personal audition with Rothafel, he was engaged for "Roxy's Radio Gang." This led to his solo status at Radio City Music Hall. Weede later went on to a career in opera. The favored women soloists were Edwina Eustis and Viola Philo. Eustis was a contralto who had sung with the Philadelphia Opera. Philo came from a solid musical background. Born in New York City in 1905, she had support from an aunt and uncle who had a radio program and from her father, Josef Philo, a violinist, conductor, and composer, and her mother, a lyric soprano. When Philo was nine, she made her stage debut as a child-artist. In Brooklyn, she studied music with her parents and took drama for three years from Luigi Albertieri, a famous coach. She knew five languages and took voice at the New York College of Music from the great Wagnerian Karl Jörn; she later studied with Anna Schoen-René. At fifteen, Philo gave her first public recital in New York. By the time she was sixteen or seventeen, her grandfather got her on the Met roster with the help of Otto H. Kahn, the chairman of the board. Philo was paid one hundred dollars a week in the 1921–1922 Met season and sang the Priestess in all performances of *Aida*. The casts she sang with included Rosa Ponselle, Florence Easton, and Claudia Muzio as Aida; Giovanni Martinelli, Giulio Crimi, Aureliano Pertile, and Manuel Salazar as Radamès; and Margarete Matzenauer, Jeanne Gordon, and Julia Claussen as Amneris. Philo also appeared on the Met's Sunday night concert programs. She was a close friend of Ernestine Schumann-Heink, with whom she sang recitals. In 1924 Philo became a soloist at the Capitol Theatre and on the popular Edison Hour. She was also heard on WEAF, a station known for its interest in opera. Carmela Ponselle was promoting her Opera Cameos programs on WEAF, having sung Amneris in the station's important broadcast of the complete *Aida*. Philo owed her later career to Rothafel, who hired her for the Roxy Theatre in 1928. By 1934 she was the leading soprano at Radio City Music Hall and a soloist on the Radio City Music Hall of the Air. Tall and handsome, with dark hair and large eyes, Philo was stage-wise, and audiences loved her. Her manager, Annie Friedberg, a powerful agent and promoter, claimed she was the "direct descendant of a king, Philo Judeas of Alexandria, Egypt." This claim notwithstanding, the Philo family was of Russian origin and was probably Jewish.

When the Music Hall Symphony Orchestra offered its ambitious, month-long Festival of Wagnerian Music, Philo, Eustis, Peerce, and Weede were the soloists, heard on four consecutive Sundays over WJZ and affiliated stations. Eustis also sang Magdalene in *Die Meistersinger* at the Metropolitan Opera in a gala on 12 April 1935, with Lawrence Tibbett as Hans Sachs and Helen Jepson as Eva. On the Music Hall's regular programs, Jepson and Philo remained the favorites. In 1935 the director of press relations at the Columbia Broadcasting System asked Philo what she would do if someone gave her a million dollars. She said she would set up a foundation to "help establish singers, promising, young musicians; and set aside a sum for the sick and poor." One of the singers she befriended was Warren.

Philo's husband, a physician, Henry A. Schroeder, taught voice, as both her parents did. In their home at 1645 Forty-ninth Street in Brooklyn, Philo and Schroeder gave Warren lessons. In his 1938 interviews, Warren said he started studying voice seriously in 1933 and started with Schroeder a year later. Vivien remembered Schroeder's problems with his unsettled pupil: "Leonard had a peculiar voice, sounding like a tenor above, yet dark in the lower registers. He was singing as a baritone, but at the same time he could sail out on those high B-flats. He loved to show off his high C." The breaks between his registers were marked; Vivien said that he could not sing an even scale, substituting "immoderate blasting" for broad sound. As far as Schroeder could see, this huge voice was out of control. For a while he believed Leonard should be a tenor. Later Schroeder admitted that he had been able to solve only a few of Warren's vocal problems; but in the early years of the baritone's career, Vivien said, Schroeder's lessons proved invaluable. She thought he was also partly responsible for directing her brother to the Metropolitan Opera.

When Warren joined the Radio City Music Hall Glee Club, the men were sometimes costumed in evening clothes with top hats, canes, and black evening capes lined with white satin. In the autumn of 1957, in an interview with W. G. Rogers, arts editor of the Associated Press, Warren laughed as he recalled those costumes. "Imagine me with a tall hat and a cane, doing dance steps." To show how silly he had felt, he "ducked his head" and "went through the motions of the old routine." Vivien remembered her brother coming home with tales of Radio City Music Hall, teaching her his dance steps, and showing her how to flourish his cane. She was convinced he was the "handsomest one of the Glee Club lot." One photograph in her collection, dated the week of 11 July 1936, shows him in a clown costume that may have come from the Music Hall days. On the back someone wrote, "He was great!" Vivien also remembered Warren's "extra" chore at the Music Hall, helping Peerce get onstage and off. Plagued with severe myopia, Peerce in his memoir, *The Bluebird of Happiness*, told of barely being able to make his way to the footlights in the darkened theatre. He was sometimes in place when the curtain went up, but when he was not, the stage manager had to invent a "delivery system," with Warren escorting Peerce out from the wings. When the staging had him drive on in a car, Warren opened the door and led him to his position near the footlights, then shepherded him back again.

Warren Finds a Friend

Three or four months after Warren was hired for the Radio City Music Hall Glee Club, he and twelve other members were called to hear the audition of John De Merchant, an aspiring young baritone who was also a pianist and composer. Lindhe played for De Merchant's tryout in the NBC studio from which the Music Hall program was broadcast every week. De Merchant had studied voice and composition at the University of Washington and in Europe before moving to New York. Once settled on the West Side in the heart of the music business, he found a reliable voice teacher in Douglas Stanley and began looking for work. By Radio City standards, he was quite sophisticated. De Merchant, who in 1998 was a retired pianist of eighty-eight, said, "I heard about an audition at the Radio City Music Hall and went to the stage door. Looking at me, the doorman said, 'I doubt that this is for you.' But he let me in. My first audition number was an Italian popular song. Lindhe was not a very good pianist," he recalled, "and she was very impatient. I was supposed to sing one aria and one song, but she leafed through my music and decided to let me sing only the last eight bars of an Italian number. When I finished those eight bars, Leonard and the other guys all cheered." He got a job.

De Merchant first became aware of Warren when he heard him vocalizing in the bathroom next to their dressing room. "He was practicing an aria, I think from *Trovatore*, with a cadenza that was incredible. I had never heard anything like the sound of that voice, especially with the acoustics of the bathroom. Leonard had a huge, dark, rich sound. He got to like me and joked with me. He laughed and said, 'Next to me, you have the best voice here.'" De Merchant remembered Warren as casually dressed in neat clothes. "He had a big chest, and at the Music Hall he would come in wearing a shirt with a zipper-front cardigan over it. While he was talking to you, he would run the zipper up and down."

About the atmosphere at Radio City, De Merchant said, "It was sheer culture shock. I spoke proper English and was going to the Metropolitan Opera all the time. Many of my colleagues spoke New York English and had never been inside the Met. Viola Philo was very Brooklynese." Anti-Semitism was rampant at Radio City, he said. "Leonard was not treated at all well by many people at the Music Hall," De Merchant recalled.

> He was Jewish, and there was a lot of prejudice against Jews then. He had terrible problems because he was Jewish. I think at that time he was the only Jew in the Glee Club, and I do feel he was discriminated against many times. When he asked for solos, he was always turned down. People really did treat him badly. He hated them. But I remember one man named John Bennis, whom Leonard liked a lot. He also got on well with Chris Pollard. But in general it was a very unpleasant place for him.

De Merchant said no one got along with Lindhe, who felt superior to everyone. "She was very unfriendly. She barely spoke to me. And she really did have it in for Leonard." In his memoirs Peerce also recalled being badly treated at Radio City, where the conductor and stage director kept him out of sight behind the curtain or hidden in the orchestra pit of the Music Hall. But because Peerce was Roxy Rothafel's protégé, he eventually got what he wanted. De Merchant felt Warren suffered a great deal from his inability to read music, which was so important for Glee Club numbers. "He just had to get that into his noodle. He lost a lot from not knowing how to read music. That cost him anguish, and he had arguments with the conductor because he would always want to put in a high note where it did not belong." Later, when Warren got to the Met, his arguments with conductors became fairly commonplace.

As the accompanist for Peerce and Weede in their time off from Radio City, De Merchant gradually built up enough confidence to look for outside work. Michael De Pace, a well-known music manager, hired him to accompany singers on his roster, which then included Peerce and Weede. On one occasion, De Merchant was sent to accompany Peerce for a concert in Detroit. He also played for Weede at Carnegie Hall, where both men earned good reviews. This led Warren to ask De Merchant to play for him. "Weede was annoyed that I spent time playing for Leonard," De Merchant remembered. Over the years, De Merchant became quite close to Warren, although he always found him "shy and quite reserved." The baritone first approached him about diction lessons, not music. "Leonard asked me to help him because when he sang you couldn't understand him as clearly as he would have liked. He had a dark sound that made it very hard for him to sing English in the American style. We had to work on British English." De Merchant taught Warren how to correct his Bronx accent when he sang and roll his Italian *R* perfectly. However, to the end of his life, Warren spoke "Bronx."

De Merchant first made a tentative offer to help Warren, and this led to their later, serious coaching sessions. He remembered Warren struggling with something from a Verdi opera, "where Leonard had difficulty with the recitative and couldn't get the rhythm going right." One problem was that he sounded like a tenor: "He could sing a high B-flat and then had no trouble at all getting up to C. But he did have a problem with his low notes. I remember once we tried Amonasro's music from Act 2, Scene 2, of *Aida*, where he goes down to an A on the words 'Morte invan cercai.' It just wasn't there." In the course of their collaboration, he said, "Warren only talked about voice, nothing else. He was only interested in getting his vocal line well established, in getting the registers working. He knew his upper register and lower register didn't quite match." De Merchant felt that Henry Schroeder and Philo, who had a "cold soprano voice," never provided what Warren needed. "In all those years, Schroeder was not very successful at putting Leonard's vocal line together," he said.

Once Warren invited De Merchant to Brooklyn to meet his family. "I think I was the only man in the Glee Club that he ever invited home." In their breaks from the routine of the Glee Club, the two men also went out for meals. "Dinner cost twenty-five cents and we would leave five cents for the tip. Dinner at the Hotel Algonquin was fifty cents. We hardly ever went there." Eventually Warren found another teacher in Sidney Dietch, and was then able to help his friend by taking him to see Dietch when De Merchant became dissatisfied after studying with Douglas Stanley. De Merchant said:

> That was probably in 1937. I found Dietch more a coach than a teacher; he had played piano around in vocal studios. During the first visit, when Leonard was with me, Dietch said to me, "I can put you in the Metropolitan in three months." Of course, I didn't believe him. Dietch was very diplomatic and highly musical, a nice-looking man. I thought of studying with him, but his lessons cost too much.

De Merchant also said, "Dietch handled Leonard better than anyone else had before. He equalized that freak-of-nature voice and was responsible for putting it together."

Gaining Confidence

Warren's experience at Radio City Music Hall might have been similar to Peerce's and Weede's, with eventual promotion to soloist rank, had Weede not already claimed the leading baritone post. Rose Bampton Pelletier said, "Lindhe's preference for Weede made it impossible for Leonard to succeed. Weede followed Rapee's instructions and got outside engagements that put his name on billboards, printed programs, and marquees, but Leonard was never able to do that." Warren's situation was also compromised by his ongoing conflict with Lindhe. He kept asking for at least a few solo passages. As he often said, he stayed in the Glee Club for three years, hoping for his chance, and Lindhe always promised him his solo, but after he learned the music and rehearsed it, she canceled his assignments. Vivien said, "Leonard was discouraged by everyone at the Music Hall, but he rarely talked about that in front of the family. He was very introverted."

In fact, Lindhe's rejection haunted him, and he later told W. G. Rogers of the Associated Press that he even appealed to "Erno Rapee, the big boss, and asked for some solo parts. He answered bluntly that I would stay in the chorus for keeps unless I picked up some reputation outside his hall. That was a blow." Warren told Hugh Thomson, a critic for the *Toronto Star*, "I was getting nowhere fast." He said that he also begged the stage director, Leon Leonidoff, to give him a better position and solos, but he never got anything. "The baritone was Robert Weede, and the only times [I] got his spot were when Weede got sick. He was disgustingly healthy," Warren said.

In 1948 he told John Reddin, a reporter for the *Milwaukee Journal*, that when he asked for a solo he was "turned down flat. I was told that I was not the type." This was not the first time Warren had been discouraged by important figures in the music business. He told the editor of *Etude* magazine that he "studied privately [with Schroeder] and, after a few years of lessons, sought the advice of a famous teacher, who told me to seek a different profession." We do not know who that teacher was. Quite naturally, he was angry at these rejections.

Warren confided to Rose Heylbut of *Etude* that by 1937 he had become "extremely despondent" over his situation at the Music Hall.

> There I was, stuck in a chorus. In a low frame of mind, I went for a walk between shows. Passing a Fanny Farmer candy store, I chanced to see an advertisement card in the window: "You can HAVE CONFIDENCE in our candy" it said, the word CONFIDENCE printed in large letters. Something inside me clicked. I went into the shop and bought the smallest quantity of their cheapest candy, which was all I could afford. On the counter lay some blotters with the same CONFIDENCE slogan. I picked up a handful of them. Then I cut out the word CONFIDENCE and pasted it on everything I used. One I pasted inside my make-up box, and it is still with me. From that moment on, my thought-pattern changed. Instead of letting myself get low, I strove for confidence in myself, my work, my future.

Speaking to Rogers for the 1957 Associated Press story, Warren admitted that he had been buying peanut chews in his favorite candy store for years, but this was the first time he had noticed the slogan. Much later, during an interview in a city where Warren was presenting a concert, a tattered Fanny Farmer blotter fell out of his wallet, leaving him to explain to the reporter how it got there. Vivien said, "He had them everywhere, even on his bathroom mirror. They were his security blanket!"

Warren also related these events in a partly unscripted broadcast interview with Deems Taylor, a popular composer and critic. Although he had been at the Met for more than a decade when this interview was conducted, he still sounded like a wonder-struck boy, laughing often and laughing at himself. His youthful, high speaking voice rings like a true tenor. He pronounced the words *Taylor* as "Tayluh," *store* as "staw," *blotter* as "blottuh," *counter* as "countuh," *there* as "theah," and *air* as "ayeh," with a solid Bronx accent. Taylor asked him how he "made the Metropolitan" in one jump. Warren replied, "For three years I had been singing in the Radio City Music Hall Glee Club. Then one day I went to Mr. Rapee, the musical director, he was a very nice man, and I asked him for a solo spot. He said, 'You go and find yourself a name, my boy, and I'll give you a solo.'" Rapee's dismissive attitude and Lindhe's spitefulness were very much in the Radio City

Music Hall tradition. Rapee called Warren "my boy," as if this hefty six-footer were a child.

During his Radio City days, Warren also went twice to the Met. He kept a record of the performances he saw in his copy of Irving Kolodin's *The Story of the Metropolitan Opera 1883–1950*. "I saw this one," he wrote beside Kolodin's description of the performance of 3 January 1934. It was *Don Giovanni* with Ponselle, Tito Schipa, and Virgilio Lazzari, with Ezio Pinza as the Don. Pinza, who was having an off night, had to omit "Finch'han dal vino." Warren also wrote, "I saw this" beside the reference to Giulio Gatti-Casazza's farewell gala of 19 March 1935. This marked his retirement after twenty-seven years of service as general manager. The program included Act II, Scene 2, of *Lucia di Lammermoor* with Nina Morgana, Giovanni Martinelli, and Armando Borgioli; Act IV of *Otello* with Lauritz Melchior and Elisabeth Rethberg; the Act III duet from *Norma* with Ponselle and Gladys Swarthout; the Prologue from *Pagliacci*, sung by Lawrence Tibbett; Act IV of *Manon*, with Lucrezia Bori, Richard Crooks, Giuseppe De Luca, and Leon Rothier; and the Act III duet from *Die Walküre* with Kirsten Flagstad and Friedrich Schorr. Warren told Harold C. Schonberg in 1959 that he had also seen one performance of *La traviata*, though not at the Met, and that he cried "like a baby."

Vivien characterized her brother at that time as "very determined. Leonard did not want to be anything but a singer, an opera singer. He studied, took lessons, and was very, very serious about them. He was devoted to his lessons. He grabbed every opportunity offered to him." She also remarked that Radio City was "a stepping stone. He took the job as a stepping stone." One day he told De Merchant he had managed to arrange a preliminary audition for the Metropolitan Opera Auditions of the Air. As De Merchant recalled, "We were working on some Verdi thing at that time. After his first audition, Leonard was sure that he was going to win. I felt he was kidding himself. The next thing we knew, he left the Music Hall, and it was in the papers that he had won. After that, the Music Hall offered him work as a soloist, but he turned it down."

The Rising Musical Star

Warren began to judge his own progress by listening to his voice on privately made recordings and recordings of his early radio programs, some of which survived in Vivien's collection. Restored by Daniel Hladik, they show an emerging artist in halting search of the right road. On 25 September 1936, Warren and an unidentified accompanist made a private recording of the *Pagliacci* Prologue and "Ol' Man River" in the Radio Recording Studio on Broadway. In some early recordings, the singer's considerable potential in the Radio City days was on full display. In the Prologue, his surprisingly clear

Italian diction, complete with perfectly rolled R's, is matched by a bright, forward delivery. What the piece lacks in polished phrasing, it makes up in drama, because Tonio is present, front and center, and in full settle. "Ol' Man River," much less successful, shows Warren's problems with the lower register of his voice. It is also marred by exaggeration that suggests the style of another "showbiz" singer with Russian roots: Al Jolson. However, the echoes of "Mammy" and "Sonny Boy" in Warren's early private recordings completely lack the Jolson magic. Intrusive high notes, shouted phrases, and explosive *parlando* stress on key words were no substitute for singing. A second, undated recording of "Ol' Man River" is more uneven than the 1936 version. If Warren was singing like this in the English-language repertoire at Radio City, Vin Lindhe and Erno Rapee probably had good reason to refuse his requests for solos. At this same time, Weede was in full operatic cry, and Peerce was delivering pure sugar in "The Bluebird of Happiness."

About the time Warren was listening to himself on private recordings, his Aunt Bert also began to seek other opportunities for him on the New York radio stations. On 20 June 1937, he sang a taxing and even risky WQXR Artist Recital. His accompanist, then and for years to come, was Byron Warner. The recording, which survived in Vivien's collection, was made almost nine months after the first private studio test recordings. This one shows Warren clearly at home in Giuseppe Torelli's "Tu lo sai" and in two bolder songs, "L'esperto nocchiero" and "Three for Jack," both of which he continued to include in his recitals for years. However, "The White Dove" from *The Rogue Song* reveals a thin style, while "De Glory Road" comes close to farce. Already opera was his forte, for he delivered "Cortigiani" from *Rigoletto* with great understanding and command of voice. Here the plangent, velvety "heartbreak" quality of Warren's middle register is paired with brilliant top notes. Ruggero Leoncavallo's "Mattinata" is lyrical and sincere.

On 13 July he sang "The Song of the Vagabond" on WOR on a Chevrolet Sinfonietta, an engagement booked by his aunt. That was followed on 30 September by another private session in the studio of Advertisers Recording Service, where Warren made a recording of "Largo al factotum" from *Il barbiere di Siviglia*. As on all these early recordings, the large operatic voice is heard, together with the singer's penchant for blasted high notes. On 25 October 1937, according to a press release from the National Broadcasting Company, Warren was booked to sing on an unidentified network program, perhaps Philo's, perhaps Lindhe's. He offered two numbers: "Largo al factotum" and "Widmung" by Robert Franz, a nineteenth-century composer and arranger. An agent named W. P. Ainsworth also got Warren an engagement to sing on the Magic Key of RCA program on 15 May 1938. Later, in a 1939 letter to Edward Johnson, general manager of the Met, Ainsworth praised Warren's "great natural voice" and said, "I looked after his interests until he sailed for Europe." Like Rapee, he referred to the baritone as "a boy."

Some time while Warren was still a regular in the Radio City Glee Club, he had a great deal of encouragement from another member, Jack Arthur, a baritone who also often sang as a soloist on NBC programs. "Why don't you try a competition?" Arthur asked. He directed Warren to the Sealtest Rising Musical Stars program, then being broadcast weekly on WEAF. Warren told W. G. Rogers that three months after he picked up the Fanny Farmer blotters, "a fellow in the chorus nagged me. 'If you think you're so good, why don't you try for the Metropolitan Opera auditions?'" That also was Arthur. At that point, Warren made a bet that he could at least get a hearing at the Met. He was still coaching with De Merchant, preparing his "five arias."

When Warren finally got around to entering the Sealtest competition, it was well under way. By then he had also been heard for the first time in the preliminaries of the Met Auditions of the Air and was scheduled to sing on one of their programs. One prize winner of the Sealtest Rising Musical Stars competition was Edwina Eustis, the contralto from Radio City, who won five hundred dollars. (Several years later, Eustis and Warren gave joint recitals.) The first contestant of the fourth and last cycle was Warren, who was announced in an NBC press release of 21 December as the featured artist on the Sealtest Rising Musical Stars program at ten in the evening on Sunday, 26 December 1937. He was the first New York man to be heard in the competition, the release said. A mixed chorus of sixty voices and sixty players from the New York Philharmonic backed the artists. Alexander Smallens conducted. With his big voice, Warren made his mark and was called back twice, singing "Pari siamo" from *Rigoletto* on 27 March 1938 and "Il balen del suo sorriso" from *Il trovatore* on a later program. Before the Sealtest finals were scheduled, Warren had every reason to be more interested in the Auditions of the Air. Although he did not win first prize in the Sealtest competition, he was given an award and a chance to appear on a later program as a "returning winner."

Encouraged by professionals, family, and friends, he set out for the Met. To improve his chances in auditions, he had begun early in 1937 to work with Byron Warner, who accompanied his June recital on WQXR. The young coach had had extensive experience in Italy. Vivien described him as "handsome, pleasant, and nice, and absolutely inseparable from Leonard." Much of Warren's day-to-day training in these pre-Met years came from Warner, who was also an important source of moral support.

Warren told Rogers of his final, unpleasant encounter with Lindhe in mid-December 1937. He said, "I asked the woman in charge of the Glee Club for two weeks off to work up some numbers to sing for the [Metropolitan Opera] audition. She told me, 'Sure, take a couple of weeks, and don't come back!' Well! I was ready to quit anyway!" He never forgot how she hurt him. In the early 1950s, in a conversation with the head of public relations for the Sol Hurok organization, Warren said that when he asked Lindhe for "a leave of absence to prepare for the [Metropolitan Opera] audition, she said, 'Don't bother coming back. Your voice isn't virile enough anyway.' So there I was, without a job." His remark later got into print in a Hurok organization press book that survives in the Leonard Warren Collection.

Even twenty-two years after Lindhe dismissed him from the Music Hall, Warren had not forgotten the event. In 1958 he told Fred Danzig, a feature writer for United Press International, "I still don't know how to feel about being fired. It turned out for the best, so I suppose I shouldn't be hurt, but I am." Warren rarely aired his bitterness at home. However, Vivien said he described his battle with Lindhe over "twelve bars here and twelve bars there that he never got to sing. Angry after years of arguing, he sought the best situation for that voice."

CHAPTER FOUR

The Metropolitan Opera in Transition

W arren used his lunch hour from Radio City to go to the Metropolitan Opera House and ask to be heard. He was only one of the several hundred people auditioned in 1937–1938 by the management. Given his small repertory of songs, ill-prepared arias, and the "one presentable aria," as Rose Bampton described it, his chances seemed slim, even though the company had begun to favor young Americans in its recently launched program of national outreach. Nearly thirty years of stability had come to an end at the Met with the Great Depression and the death or withdrawal of men who had guided it. Otto H. Kahn had resigned as chairman of the board of directors but had stayed on the board as president of the company; he died in 1934. Veteran conductor Tullio Serafin, the musical and artistic heart of the Met, left for the Royal Opera in Rome and the new Florence May Festival, the Maggio Fiorentino. And in the spring of 1935, General Manager Giulio Gatti-Casazza, who had ruled the Met with a benevolent father-dictator's hand since 1908, had retired and returned to Italy, leaving behind a corps of bewildered singers. The company was at great risk.

Gatti's successor was Herbert Witherspoon. Just as he took the reins of the company, he died in his office after suffering a heart attack. Understandably, the organization was thrown into chaos. The next general manager, Edward Johnson, a Canadian-born lyric tenor, had a distinguished stage career behind him. Johnson had sung for years, first as Edoardo Di Giovanni and then under his own name. The period of his transition was not easy. Financial problems and the shifting of bureaucratic gears were aggravated by the intervention of critic John Erskine, who had a plan to "save the Met" with an infusion of funds. The company was to add to its roster a number of graduates from the Juilliard School of Music. Soon this policy brought charges that the Metropolitan had become a training camp for immature young Americans. Many other ideas for broadening the financial base were considered by the directors and by Eleanor Robson Belmont (Mrs. August Belmont), whose influence matched or even exceeded Johnson's in some Met matters. She was bent on developing the Metropolitan Opera Guild as a fund-raising and educational arm of the company. *Opera News*, its magazine, grew to win national and international readership. The weekly Saturday afternoon broadcasts became a fixture of national radio programming. In the early years of this period of growth and changed direction, Warren decided to try his luck at the Met.

Wilfrid Pelletier and the Auditions of the Air

Of all the new and well-intentioned programs, the one that most captured listeners' imagination was the Metropolitan Opera Auditions of the Air, an open competition that awarded prizes for further study or, to the top winners, money and a one-year Met contract. The "godfather" of the Auditions of the Air was conductor Wilfrid Pelletier. Born in Canada in 1896, he had joined the Metropolitan staff in 1918 as a coach and conductor. In his autobiography, *Une symphonie inachevée*, he described how he launched the Auditions of the Air, "Talking with Jack Warwick, [in] the public relations firm of Warwick and Legler, I told him about the number of young artists that I had to audition for the Met's recruitment and [spoke about] how qualified they were." Pelletier said a large audience would enjoy hearing them on the radio. Two days later, Warwick told Pelletier that he could push on with the project. To find a sponsor, Pelletier called George A. Martin, president of the Cleveland-based Sherwin-Williams Paint Company, and asked him to launch the program. When Martin wondered whether the Met would have enough young singers for thirteen broadcasts, Pelletier reassured him. "When I went to see him, he agreed in principle, but my plan to have the young singers accompanied by an orchestra scared him because it would cost so much. I explained to him that with good arrangements, an orchestra of thirty-six musicians would be enough and would add a good deal to the quality of the broadcasts. Mr. Martin accepted my proposal." The Metropolitan and Sherwin-Williams agreed to give the winners a one-year contract and a prize of one thousand dollars, which the sponsor would pay. Each week, Pelletier said, he listened to about fifteen singers in Studio 8-H at the National Broadcasting Company, then chose a few to work in his studio in the old Metropolitan Opera House studio building at 1425 Broadway. When they were better prepared, he heard them again in Studio 8-H, to be sure they could sing over an orchestra. Pelletier said, "A great many artists went on to careers after being discovered by the Auditions of the Air."

Emil R. Pinta, a writer and discographer, described the programs in an unpublished essay.

The winners of the individual programs were brought back to New York for the semifinals and finals, broadcast in March or April. . . . The first Auditions broadcast was heard on December 22, 1935, over New York station WEAF, an NBC affiliate. The winners, Anna Kaskas, mezzo-soprano, and Arthur Carron, tenor, were announced on March 29, 1936. Both went on to have successful careers with the Met, each singing for eleven seasons. [The 1937 winners were soprano Maxine Stellman and baritone Thomas L. Thomas.] In 1938 station WJZ began airing the Auditions.

Many "graduates" of the Auditions of the Air went on to careers in film or opera or in concert or on Broadway. Among them were Josephine Antoine, Pierrette Alarie, Jean Dickenson, Robert McFerrin, Robert Merrill, Patrice Munsel, Regina Resnik, Dorothy Sarnoff, Risë Stevens, who was the runner-up to Kaskas and went abroad to further her career, Eleanor Steber, Thomas, and, of course, Warren. Richard Tucker, although he did not win the Auditions of the Air, first came to the Met's attention through them. The auditions provided high-level programming, and because they were part of a competition, they attracted public interest. Beyond that, Pelletier said, "[They gave] these young artists a chance to make a debut with an invisible audience, before they had to face the . . . stage."

When Warren was asking to be heard, he still had his steady job at Radio City Music Hall. He said he was only sure of one aria, "Largo al factotum" from *Il barbiere di Siviglia*. According to Rose Bampton, whom Pelletier had married the previous year, the conductor was astounded that anyone with such an operatic voice had only one aria ready. Pelletier described the day he first heard Warren. "I was in the sound engineer's control room, listening to the contestants. Suddenly I was astonished to hear a voice that was truly exceptional. I turned for a moment toward the auditorium and realized right away that I was in the presence of a particularly gifted young artist." Pelletier thought the technicians were playing a joke on him by putting on a recording of some famous baritone, perhaps Giuseppe De Luca, and pretending it was a young singer.

> Suddenly over the loudspeaker came a rich, ringing baritone. In the control room, I [stood still and listened], peering through the glass panels at the young man who was ostensibly doing the singing. After a moment, I turned angrily to the staff at the control panels. "This is no time to joke! You've put a recording on to fool me. Take it off and let's give this boy a chance. He's doing his best, and the least we can do is to do ours."

The technicians told him he was really listening to Warren.

Bampton said, "Pelly came right home and could talk of nothing but this great voice that he had discovered. He said that at their first meeting he had thought Warren was Italian and had spoken to him in Italian. 'Maestro, I don't understand a word of what you're saying,' Warren responded." She remembered Warren as she first met him, "decently dressed, plainly dressed," when he came to the auditions.

Warren told his family he was among the last singers heard that day. "Pelletier was ready to pack up and go home," Vivien said.

> [Then] he heard an unusually good voice and turned to ask the technicians, "Who is the baritone on the recording we just heard?"
>
> "That's not a recording. It was the young man standing next to the piano."
>
> Pelletier shot back, "Oh, no, stop fooling me. I've had enough for today." After Pelletier was told who the singer was, he turned to a technician, saying, "Leonard Warren. I wonder why I haven't heard that name before."

However, in keeping with Metropolitan practice, the conductor gave the young man no encouragement at the time. He simply thanked Warren and Byron Warner, his accompanist, and left. In 1957 Warren told Jay S. Harrison of the New York *Herald Tribune* that he had competed that day against twenty-seven other singers. In his interview with Deems Taylor, he laughed as he told of the audition with Pelletier. He said if Pelletier had asked him to sing anything else, "I'd have been sunk." He said that at the end of the afternoon, "I left the studio with the feeling I'd flopped." He and Byron Warner went to Radio City and sat through a double feature that included a Nelson Eddy–Jeanette MacDonald singing extravaganza. Warren returned home just before midnight. His mother greeted him at the door. "Where have you been?" she asked. "The Metropolitan has been trying to reach you all evening!"

The caller was Pelletier, and his reason for calling is clear from his own account:

> I met [Leonard] again to try to find out more about him. He told me that he was singing in the chorus at Radio City. I invited [him] to my office the next day, because I wanted to confirm with one further trial the stability of his voice and convince myself that I had just heard a voice that was truly extraordinary. My ears had not deceived me! Once again I was absolutely amazed as I listened to him. I asked this young artist to wait a moment, and I went straight to the General Manager, [Edward] Johnson. I told him that he absolutely had to hear Warren. We made an appointment for the next day. Johnson, Edward Ziegler, the administrative officer [of the Met], Earle Lewis, the treasurer, and I went to the auditorium of the Metropolitan. I was asking myself whether his voice would still have the same magic,

the same beauty that I had heard in the broadcasting studio. I was reassured immediately. As soon as Warren began to sing, I realized that his voice was even more impressive than I had thought, being fuller than it had sounded in the preceding hearings. As we listened to him, we were truly moved, but, as usual, the management was restrained and did not compliment him. Anyway, it was clear that Warren was far better than [everyone else in] the competition and that he would win, getting the prize of a thousand dollars and a contract with the Met.

Warren on the Auditions of the Air

The auditions broadcasts gave the judges ample time to hear the new baritone. For the first program, on 31 October 1937, Warren sang "Largo al factotum" and Robert Franz's "Dedication," then joined the soprano Josephine Chekova and tenor Frank Hornaday in "Drink to Me Only With Thine Eyes." All three pieces later became staples of his recital programs. Returning on 2 January 1938, he offered "The Song of the Open Road" and "Cortigiani" from *Rigoletto*. The other contestants were Florence Kirk, who sang with Warren later, and Hornaday. The trio sang two New Year's songs, "Sing Out, Wild Bells" and "Here We Come A-Wassailing." A third program fell on 13 March, when Warren sang the Prologue from *Pagliacci* (a recording of which survived in Vivien Warren's collection) and "Roses for Remembrance" by Loyal Curtis. Another contestant that day was tenor Felix Knight, who won honorable mention and later joined the Met roster. Bampton remembered Pelletier's coaching Warren "night and day for one week before the March finals and being more and more thrilled with him every day."

These were crowded weeks for the young baritone, who was also scheduled for the Sealtest Rising Musical Stars competition in March. As it happened, the finals of both competitions fell on the same day, 27 March 1938. The finals of the Auditions of the Air were broadcast in the late afternoon from Studio 8-H in the NBC Building at Rockefeller Center. In the audience of 1300 people were many celebrities including Rose Bampton, Mrs. August Belmont, Lucrezia Bori, Lotte Lehmann, Giovanni Martinelli, Ezio Pinza, Lily Pons, Rosa Ponselle, Friedrich Schorr, Gladys Swarthout, John Charles Thomas, and Lawrence Tibbett. Three winners had originally been selected, the first being Kathleen Kersting, a soprano who had sung with Warren on 13 March. She, however, did not appear in the finals. Instead John Carter and Warren were the declared winners. In the final program they were both coached by Pelletier for the duet from *Les pêcheurs de perles*. For his first solo Warren offered a lusty "Largo al factotum," with ringing high notes. When he finished, the announcer said, many in the audience offered him a standing ovation. He also added a short song, "Duna," by Josephine McGill.

The panel of judges included John Erskine, Johnson, Earle Lewis, Lee Patti-
son, Pelletier, and Edward Ziegler. Warren and Carter were introduced as
co-winners. George A. Martin then made a speech and presented a silver
plaque and a check for one thousand dollars to each winner. When Warren
was introduced to the radio audience, he departed from the prepared, printed
script, saying that his father was listening in Seattle and his mother had come
from there for the finals, while his sister and brother were also in the studio
audience. Sometime before March 1938 Warren's parents and sister had
moved to Seattle, leaving Warren and his brother, Martin, in New York. In
Washington their father went into business. Vivien remembered that the official Auditions of the Air winners' party marked the end of the Met's spring
festivities. Warren, his brother, sister, mother, and their friends celebrated
with John Carter and Met luminaries in the famous Rainbow Room in the
RCA Building in Radio City. A huge cake was brought out, to be cut by
mezzo-soprano Swarthout.

   About five hours after he sang in the Met Auditions finals on NBC, Warren sang on the Sealtest Rising Musical Stars competition on WEAF, billed as
"a returning winner." Alexander Smallens conducted the orchestra while he
sang "Il balen del suo sorriso" from *Il trovatore*. The next morning, both
competitions announced him as a winner—although Warren did not win first
prize in the Sealtest competition, he was given an award. The National Broadcasting Company issued a press release headlined, CARTER AND WARREN WIN
MET CONTRACTS. Carter was described as a twenty-six year old who had
already made a name for himself as a soloist of the Chase and Sanborn Hour
on the NBC Red Network. (When Nelson Eddy left that program to do a concert tour, Carter became his successor.) The press release said that both Carter
and Warren would make Metropolitan debuts during the next regular winter
season. Some of the information published about Warren was incorrect:

   Leonard Warren, also 26 years old, sang only as a pastime when he
   worked with his father, buying furs from trappers in the woods.
   When he had saved enough money, he decided on singing as a career
   instead of a hobby. He studied in New York City with private teachers. Warren was born in the Bronx, New York City, of Russian parents. He attended public school in New York City and later enrolled
   in extension courses of Columbia University. He was a member of the
   Radio City Music Hall chorus until last December, when he was "discovered" and turned to a radio career. The day he was announced as
   a new member of the Metropolitan Opera also marked his participation in another competition. He sang in the "Sealtest Rising Musical Stars" program over the NBC Red Network last night to compete
   for the grand award of $1,000 to be made to the best musician to
   appear in the series, held over the last few months.

The final broadcast of the Auditions of the Air was reviewed by Irving Kolodin of the New York *Sun*, one of the city's most important critics. He called Warren's voice "vigorous and finely textured" and said it would "adjust itself with ease to the spaces of the Metropolitan auditorium." Pierre V. R. Key, the respected critic and historian, sent a special dispatch about the auditions to the Dallas *News*. Out of seventy-eight singers in the twenty-six broadcasts, he picked Warren as the most promising. "Of the two first prize winners," he said, "Warren seems to have the equipment for opera. Well advanced in musical knowledge and repertory, he speaks several languages. His voice, as heard via radio, is a full-bodied and virile baritone with facility in the upper reaches. He sings with authority and a degree of finish that speaks well for his future."

In such circumstances the suspicion of partisanship is often voiced. Danton Walker, writing in his "Broadway" column in the *New York Daily News*, showed a great deal of courage when he revealed something about the infighting that had riled the highest ranks of the Metropolitan Opera management as the final decisions about the competition were being made and even after the awards were presented. Reading between the lines, one can see that Earle Lewis's preference for Carter might have led to his being the sole winner; Warren would then not have received any award at all. On 12 December, commenting on the "feuding," Walker said that Lewis was promoting "a big build-up for John Carter" while "Edward Johnson favors giving Leonard Warren the breaks." Lewis's daughter was dating Carter at the time; their association may have robbed Lewis of his objectivity as a judge. Whatever the situation, Warren passed this first big test of his skills as an opera singer.

George A. Martin's Gift

From the start, Pelletier was in charge of Warren. The conductor understood that the award Warren had won would not cover his needs. Pelletier then called George A. Martin of Sherwin-Williams and asked to see him. "I told him about the discovery of this extraordinary voice. Martin asked me what I wanted." Pelletier told him, "We have to help this young man in his career. Right now he is singing in the chorus [at Radio City] and is helping his mother, brother, and sister financially. The Metropolitan is offering him work, but if he goes there with no preparation, he will soon be written off [as inadequate] and we will have lost an extraordinary voice."

"But he will have a thousand dollars, like every other winner," Martin replied. Pelletier said the amount was not enough to send Warren to Milan for study, and that he had to go to Milan. Bampton remembered her husband's telling Warren he needed to learn all the music for five operas before leaving New York for Italy. "Pelly was absolutely determined to send Leonard to Italy, but he had to be prepared," she said. "'He has to go to Milan,' Pelly kept on saying. 'He has to go abroad.'" Martin did not flinch when the conductor asked him to underwrite Warren's continuing study, although, according to Bampton, he argued that Warren did not need a pianist with him. Martin then asked how much the preparation would cost. When Pelletier asked for five thousand dollars for several months of study, the trip to Milan, and Warren's obligations to his family, Martin agreed to cover that amount himself, saying that Sherwin-Williams could not do it. He did, though, make Pelletier promise to monitor Warren's progress, which the conductor did.

Warren clearly had a future, and Johnson's preference for him may have brought the young baritone an offer from Walter Damrosch almost immediately after the Auditions of the Air winners were announced. On 7 April 1938, Warren sent Johnson a telegram saying, "Desirous consulting you concerning Damrosch offer. Please hold decision until your return New York. Respectful regards, Leonard Warren." Damrosch, whose opera *The Man Without a Country* had had its premiere at the Metropolitan Opera on 12 May 1937, may have wanted Warren for a concert. What Johnson did about this matter is not known, but it is significant that such an important figure in the New York music world should have shown interest in the inexperienced artist that Warren surely was in April 1938.

At that same time a troubling matter arose concerning the spring concert that young singers from the Auditions of the Air offered each year in Cleveland under the auspices of the Met. This concert was understood by all to be a gesture of gratitude toward the Sherwin-Williams Company, which sponsored the auditions. The singers' expenses were all paid, although they were not given a fee. Ordinarily these participants welcomed the chance to appear, but when Warren was told to put the concert on his calendar for mid-April at the end of the 1938 Met spring tour performances there, he refused to go unless he got paid. His reaction stunned Pelletier and other Met executives. Bampton recalled her husband's chagrin, for he intended the concert as Warren's first official performance under the Met banner. She said:

> Every year when the Metropolitan went on tour to Cleveland, the auditions winners were asked to give a concert there on a Sunday, without being paid. The hall was always filled—six thousand people. When my husband asked Warren to participate, he asked for a fee of a thousand dollars, saying, "I am now with a manager and have to be paid." My husband said, "But that's impossible. All the winners go to sing free, but they have their expenses paid."

Bampton said Warren's agent, perhaps Bert Green Warenoff, perhaps Louis Nizer or a representative of the WOR Artists Bureau, refused to let him sing the concert. "But everyone else does it for nothing," Pelletier protested to Warren's representative. "He must go, because I have other things in mind for him," referring to the planned trip to Milan. Above all else, the conductor needed Warren there so that Martin and the other Sherwin-Williams executives could hear him in an auditorium. Finally Pelletier prevailed; it was agreed that Warren would receive nothing more than his reimbursed expenses, as the other young singers did. Bampton remembered Pelletier also promoting Warren's cause with George Martin's wife. "After the [Cleveland] concert, Mrs. Martin had a big dinner for the singers. Pelly said to her, 'I think Warren is going to go far, but right now he can't even read music. I think we should send him to Rose's teacher in Italy.' Pelly convinced her. With both Martins behind him, Warren's summer abroad was guaranteed."

On 14 April, Warren was called for his first full, serious audition in the main auditorium of the Metropolitan Opera House. His audition card, preserved in the Met's archives, shows he repeated Figaro's aria and sang something from *Rigoletto*. There is no record of who heard him, other than Pelletier, although it is virtually certain that Johnson was present. Through all this, Pelletier was a pillar of wisdom and strength. First and last, he stood behind his young baritone, loyally nurturing the career that followed.

✦ CHAPTER FIVE

The Italian Experience

Warren had very little time, from mid-April 1938 until the end of October, to learn his assignments for the Met, but at least he was not alone. Strong support came from Byron and Florence Warner, and Pelletier was planning to be in Italy with Warren and also have Rose Bampton watch over him. This would be the Pelletiers' second trip together, for they had spent the summer of 1937 in Como. Bampton had commuted to Milan for her sessions with Giuseppe Pais, a respected coach from the Teatro alla Scala. Near the Pelletiers' hotel on Lake Como was the villa of the Met's chorusmaster, Giulio Setti. He would call for Bampton and Pelletier in his motorboat and take them to an island for picnics. Setti's wife, a good cook, accompanied them on these outings.

Two documents in the Metropolitan Opera Archives outline Pelletier's plans. One, a letter dated 19 April from Warner, describes how Warren would be prepared for his career. The other, a note, summarizes the budget for the Italian trip. Warner's letter stated that he was willing to accompany Warren to Europe and help him prepare for his appearance at the Metropolitan Opera House. Warner wrote, "He intends to go to Italy and travel there in various cities for the purpose of receiving instructions from several Maestros in Italy, as well as perhaps appearing in some small opera companies for the purpose of obtaining actual experience." Warner was to act as "interpreter, guide, companion and teacher" for a period of approximately four and a half months. He would act as translator, accompanying him daily for all coaching sessions, "so he might better understand their instructions, but also for the purpose of hearing the outline of his studies, so that I can properly rehearse them with him when he returns to his quarters." He would spend as many hours a day with Warren as his training required: "five, and perhaps as many as ten or eleven hours a day, and, on special occasions, such as his debut, all the time required, which may on some occasions be twenty hours a day." He would arrange for Warren's "living quarters and expenses" and "the cost of

63

his lessons"; on these Warner promised to economize. He also was to handle "the purchase of his wigs and costumes" and Warren's "entrance into small opera companies." Warren and the Warners planned to leave New York in tourist class on the Italian liner *Conte di Savoia* at the end of May and return on 19 October. The typewritten budget sheet headed "Estimate of Expenses for Leonard Warren's Musical Training and Education in Europe" shows how Martin's five thousand dollar gift was to be spent. The two fares were $290 each. The men would spend $150 on train fares in Italy. "Hotels, living expenses, including food" were estimated at $3.50 a day for Warren. "Miscellaneous expenses" included "laundry, purchase of music, etc." They would total $250. Pais's coaching sessions were estimated at three dollars each, and he would give Warren five lessons a week for three months or more. Riccardo Picozzi's "staging" lessons cost four dollars each, with four lessons a week planned with him. Pelletier apparently vetoed the "costumes and wigs" at five hundred dollars, for he wrote "No" beside the item. Warner's own fees for the trip were estimated at one thousand dollars, "including his professional services to Mr. Warren in coaching, accompanying him and guiding him." Out of Martin's gift, Warner was also paid for "two months intervening before his actual work at the Metropolitan [for the] continuation of studies during this period in New York, in accordance with previous rates, $1,500." Warren's personal situation had also been taken into account, for the budget had an item that covered more than two months of help to his family, a "Contribution to Mr. Warren's mother @ $30.00 a week for a total of $350." This may have made up for the income Warren could no longer provide after he was fired from Radio City. Vivien said that after she moved with her parents to Seattle, she and her mother returned occasionally to New York, even for fairly long periods. She added that her father sent checks to help with the family's expenses. During these visits Vivien, her mother, and her brothers stayed in cramped quarters at the Empire Hotel at Seventy-first Street and Broadway. When Warren's parents decided to separate, Sara Warenoff remained in New York and moved with her three children into a large apartment near Central Park.

With this arrangement for Warren's Italian trip, Warner could be paid in Italy and receive his regular fee in the States. Warner made a very substantial contribution to Warren's training. A note in Pelletier's hand at the bottom of the first page of the document read: "8 weeks at $175." That, apparently, is what they settled on for Warner's fee at the end of summer. When all this was approved and the preliminary study period ended, the little group was ready to leave. Vivien said Leonard trusted the Warners "absolutely. The three were very close, and Leonard may even have been the best man when they married."

Under other circumstances, Bampton and Pelletier might have accompanied Warren in May, but the soprano had a contract with the Cincinnati Sum-

mer Opera to sing Leonora in *Il trovatore* and the title roles in *Norma* and
Aida, all conducted by Fausto Cleva. So it was not until late July that Bampton and Pelletier arrived in Milan, where they stayed in a hotel near the Teatro alla Scala. Bampton, in effect, spent the summer with Warren and the
Warners. A native of Cleveland with English origins, she was three years older
than Warren and was becoming a polished, versatile performer. She had studied in Milan in 1937 with Pais, the man Pelletier chose for Warren. As Bampton was leaving for Cincinnati, Warren was on his way to Italy.

Warren and the Warners sailed on the *Conte di Savoia* on 28 May. Florence Warner's friend Eugenia Buchanan, another singer, may have sailed with
them. Bampton remembered seeing her frequently with the Warners and Warren in Italy. That was quite natural, because it was Buchanan who had introduced Warren to Sidney Dietch. She and he were studying voice with Dietch
in 1938. The trip to Genoa via Naples took more than a week. Although the
Italian Line's *Rex* held the speed record for a time, the company's other ships
made stops and stayed in port, sometimes for a full day. Many people got
off, while the continuing passengers took a short tour of the city and returned
in time to sail again. Warren believed they would have an easy crossing, but
when they encountered rough seas on the first two days out, he was miserable,
though he swore he did not get seasick. News of his distress got back to the
Met in a letter Warner sent to Marino Villa, director of the Met's travel office,
on 6 June from the Grand Hotel in Genoa. Warner said Warren had "suffered
from the vibration of the boat until he was transferred to a very pleasant stateroom," and "the vibration in the dining room was such that he could scarcely
eat." Most tourist class passengers probably had the same complaints, but
after Warren griped, he was given a better accommodation. The day they
landed in Genoa, Warren and Warner, armed with a card of introduction to
the head of the Italian Line, went to his office and asked for more comfortable
staterooms on the return trip, but the only cabins offered were "undesirable,"
Warner said. It took Villa two months to get Warren something on the outside, with a porthole.

In a letter to his family dated 11 June, Warren described his trip. He wrote
on printed stationery brought from home.

LEONARD WARREN

NEW YORK, N.Y.

Dear Mom, Pop, Viv, Mart:

Well, we at last settled ourselves in Milano, and, boy, is it a relief to
get down to business; . . . I have already started with Maestro Pais
and Mrs. Picozzi in Italian lessons. We expect Mr. Picozzi Monday
and I will start with him then. Well, Mom [and all], it certainly is a
great and marvelous thing to go to Europe. You don't realize or even

comprehend the great difference until you come here. Also the amount of water you see in traveling on the boat. We had a fair crossing because [only] two days were very rough, and, by the way, I did not get seasick. Then it was windy till the last two days of the trip. We had a wonderful buggy ride in Napoli and saw Mount Vesuvius. Boy, oh boy! Then we went to Genova, and we had a wonderful stay overnight there. We took a trolley car ride up the side of a mountain and ate dinner there. It overlooked the Bay of Genova and part of the city. Then we railroaded to Milan.

Warren and the Warners also went sightseeing in Genoa with Verdi's *Simon Boccanegra* in mind. The baritone had evidently prepared part of the opera in New York and studied something of its history. To Frances J. Freeman, during an interview in January 1950 in *Opera News*, Warren recalled his first visit to Genoa in 1938, saying, "I wanted to make a study of life in Genoa in the middle of the Fourteenth Century. I [also] went back to it when I prepared the title role [later]. The feeling of the place and time is important, how those people worked and fought, and how most of them had something to do with the sea." With these remarks, Warren described the most basic precept of his learning process. For each opera assigned to him, he researched the history of its period, the lives of the characters or other relevant historical figures, the setting in which they lived, and, finally, any literary analogues or sources of the libretto.

William Appleton, later a professor of English literature at Columbia University, became Warren's close friend in 1939. He analyzed Warren's study methods, saying that his skill at tinkering with machines served him well with his opera scores. "He loved mechanical things, any kind of gadget at all. It was something instinctive. If he didn't know how things worked, he wanted to learn all about them right away. He had a utilitarian mind, something one would not have expected to find in a singer. It carried over into his music. Whenever he studied a role, he looked at it as if it were something to be taken apart and rebuilt. He wanted to know how it worked, what made it the way it was, what made it tick." Thus Warren dragged his friends all over Genoa, looking for the historic Boccanegra.

The little company soon took the train to Milan, where they stepped out of their carriages in the recently opened, monumental Stazione Centrale. With its soaring pilasters, ceilings 120 feet high, and winged marble horses guarding the entrance, it was a model of imperial style. At first they stayed in a hotel, but Warner, who had lived and studied in Italy before, soon found a comfortable lodging in the heart of the city, behind the huge Gothic pile of the Milan cathedral. Their rooms were in the Pensione Agostini at 1 Galleria del Corso. This was a nine-story building that was then considered a wonder of Italian architecture, design, and engineering. It had a street-level gallery of shops and cafes that ran from Piazza Beccaria to one of the city's main streets, the Corso Vittorio Emanuele. A two-minute stroll through the most fashionable part of Milan brought them to the door of the Teatro alla Scala.

Warren wrote of his life in Milan in a June letter to his family:

> We live in the highest building in Milan, nine stories. It has self-service elevators which one must have a key to run, or else it is impossible to go up to our home. We live on the ninth floor. On a clear day we see the Alps. I have a very large room with a piano and a radio; and Byron and his wife have a large room adjacent to mine. As there are only three rooms in our wing of the building, we use [my] room for the studio and rest in his room when we do not work, which is almost never. We have planned to have two days, Sunday and Monday, as rest days. Sunday, no work and Monday mornings, [we] review. It is very hot here, so we may take a day and travel to Como to ride in the boats [operated by the Italian national rail system]. I feel very well, and so [do] Byron and his wife; and they send their regards. [I] received a letter from Mr. Martin, so I have to answer it soon. It was very nice, and he was very anxious to hear from me. . . . By the way, I became very friendly with [Luigi Lucioni], [Giovanni] Martinelli's assistant, who was on the same boat. In fact, [he] was in the same room with me until I was changed to first class. We might come home on the same boat as Martinelli. . . . I took my first trolley ride today and nothing happened. You know, if you don't know where you're going in Italian, you're sunk. But I conquered and made it.
>
> So, arrivederci,
> Leonardo

Bampton remembered Warren's working every day with Pais for an hour or more. The teacher would then devote another generous session to her. Warren brought his assignments home every day so that he could go on studying with Warner. Bampton said Pelletier told Warren, "I'm going to give you five operas to learn. I'm not saying that you are going to sing any one of these right away, but you must prepare them." She said that her husband was

> very severe with Warren because he understood his lack of musicality then. Pelly was doing a lot of coaching in those years. He understood what these young people needed. Leonard and I saw each other every day in Milan. Pelly left me there on my own. I was learning five roles of my own that summer. After our lessons Leonard and I would have coffee together and talk. We also took long walks in Milan and saw all the wonderful things there. He came eager to learn. He was a good student, and having Warner there to play for him [during his lessons and other study sessions] was a very good thing

for him. His lessons [with Pais] always lasted longer than the standard hour, longer than they otherwise might have done.

She also said that Pais coached the opera scores phrase by phrase, giving the singer the exact interpretation of the lines and revealing all the nuances of character. "He was not a voice teacher, but he was a pure coach. You had to know the music before you got there," Bampton recalled, "because he was a terrible stickler musically. No slurs. No extra notes thrown in. You had to know every phrase to perfection. He did not teach voice, but if there was something you did not understand, he would always take time to explain."

Warner interpreted Pais's instructions for Warren. "Leonard was beginning to learn Italian," Bampton went on.

> Pais and his wife lived just out of the center of Milan, in a big apartment with a grand piano. Both Pais and his wife would chat with Leonard, making him speak Italian. "What did you do today?" they would ask, forcing him to answer in Italian. He was open to the experience, normal, and curious. He always took advice from Pelly, and he accepted the words of Pelly, Pais, and Picozzi as the law. Leonard's ties to Pelly led him to a profound study of style, for Pelly was very, very strong on style. And Leonard respected him more than anyone. Pelly made you think about what you were doing. "What is the full meaning of this phrase?" he would ask. He instilled in you the meaning of the words; he forced you to think about them. I remember very well that Leonard would say, "This is the way I learned it; and this is the way it has to be" after Pelly taught him the final definition of his roles.

Bampton recalled Warren's voice at that time as "heartwarming. He was so warm; there was a spiritual sense to him, and that came out when he sang. He had a huge extension, top and bottom. This was one of the greatest voices of the Met."

Licia Albanese came to the Met just after Warren did. She arrived in New York on 1 January 1940, made her Metropolitan Opera debut on 9 January that year, and later sang often with Warren. She described Pais as a careful musician who taught the traditional Italian style of singing. She also remembered Picozzi: "Picozzi was strictly a coach and stage director, more focused on stage acting for men than for women. He was a great actor."

Warren, writing on 27 August 1938 to Edward Ziegler of the Met, gave a detailed account of the trip. His fare had cost $329 for the round trip, as Warner's had, he reported. They spent thirty-five dollars for "incidentals" on shipboard. They stayed in hotels in Genoa and during their first days in Milan. Warren had begun his lessons at once. During his first accounting period, from 4 June to 13 June, he studied six hours with Pais, his "opera coach," three hours "acting" with Picozzi, and five hours with a Miss Borchetta, who was teaching him Italian at that time. Warner, his other "opera coach," was paid for thirty hours of work in that nine-day period, "as per agreement approved by Mr. Martin." Warren also bought five opera scores, *Simon Boccanegra, Falstaff, Pagliacci, Traviata,* and *Cavalleria rusticana.* Later he added *Boris Godunov* to his collection. The scores cost 260 Italian lire or (according to his conversion of currency) $12.20. As one can see from these figures, he kept meticulous weekly accounts and sent reports of his expenses back to the Met and to Louis Nizer, who still represented him. When Warren needed more money, he asked Ziegler to cable it to him in care of American Express in Milan, and in this letter he thanked Ziegler for forwarding funds promptly. Warren's expenses for food, lodging, transportation, and coaching came to $96.50 a week in the city in June and early July, then dropped to $89.50 a week in mid-August when everything in the city is closed.

Warren's fourteen lessons a week, in addition to coaching about five hours a day, six days a week, with Warner, meant working without respite, and Warren fell ill with exhaustion. In June and July he had to spend thirty-eight dollars for doctors and medicine, a very large amount for the time. He also described these problems in his letter of 27 August to Ziegler, saying, "I am afraid the strenuous months I passed through this past spring and the hard study that I did in the first month and a half I was here were a little too much for me." He went on to explain. "For a time I was quite ill and had to stop driving myself so hard." His doctor told him he was in "danger of a nervous breakdown." His illness led Bampton to take him out of the city occasionally, driving a rented car north to Lake Como. There they visited the Settis and took a picnic to their favorite island. The picturesque towns and hills along the shore had been a traditional summer refuge since Roman times.

Riccardo Picozzi, Warren's dramatic coach, also had a villa on the lake. He spent his summers in Varenna on the eastern shore, and he asked Warren to join him and study there. Warren and the Warners left Milan for Varenna on 11 July. To save money, they rented rooms in a modest pensione on a hill, with a row of trees behind it. Outside their rooms was a balcony where they took coffee and relaxed in deck chairs. The lake was nearby. Gradually the Americans became a part of daily life in the town, for Warner, who knew Italy well, felt quite comfortable there. For Warren, who had been so ill, the beauty brought welcome relief from hectic Milan. There were also fewer lessons to prepare. He found time to relax, and his health improved. Warren and the Warners spent a month in that supremely beautiful place, surrounded by the Alps of northern Italy. Varenna stands on the broad promontory where the three branches of Lake Como meet. It is so well situated that the eye can see the spectacular panorama sweeping from one horizon to the other. The gardens were famous for their palms, eucalyptus, citrus trees, magnolias, azaleas, and roses. Warren, always a great lover of nature and particularly of flowers, took long walks, as he always did in New York, and continued his acting studies for four weeks in July and August in Picozzi's villa. Even at the height of summer, they did five sessions a week. A Miss Mahoney became Warren's "pantomine" coach, seeing him three days a week in July and the first week of August; she later also taught him in Milan. Warren again took Italian lessons from Picozzi's wife. More than any other teacher, Picozzi is the one Warren always credited with having taught him the staging of many roles. The Picozzis took Warren into their home, treating him like family. They also arranged for him to meet the widow of Luigi Mancinelli. On a snapshot he sent home, Warren described Mancinelli as "one of the great conductors in the world before Toscanini." As the heirs of this celebrated conductor who had died in 1921, the Picozzis had easy access to his widow. They owned a large collection of Puccini's letters to Mancinelli, covering the whole range of the composer-conductor collaboration. Warren even found a pet of his own in Picozzi's friendly dog, Gandhi. Warren returned to his first teacher for additional sessions over the years; the association between Warren and Picozzi lasted for decades.

Warren's budget in 1938 did not allow many diversions, as his accounts in the Metropolitan Opera Archives show, but he and the Warners clearly enjoyed Varenna. They hiked in the mountains, stopping at saints' shrines to take snapshots. As we know from photographs Warren sent to his mother, brother, and sister, he also went boating on the lake. He signed one such snapshot: "I'm still exercising, Volga Boat Boy." Even then, boats were his passion. In August he and the Warners allowed themselves a two-day vacation, and Warren spent thirty-eight dollars on this getaway. Bampton, who went along with them, remembered renting a Fiat and driving to Verona, where they heard *La favorita* at the famed Verona Arena. She and Warren dressed up for the evening performance. In a snapshot in Vivien Warren's collection, Bampton is wearing a handsome tailored suit with a white jabot at the neck, a hat, and white gloves. This is post-Como: Warren, tanned and robust, wore a well-tailored dark suit and tie.

Finally Picozzi returned to Milan, followed by Warren and the Warners. As before, the Americans stayed at the Pensione Agostini and kept to their June budget. Warren resumed his study of the operas with Pais on 8 August, going back to their old schedule, six sessions a week with him, five Italian lessons with Miss Borchetta, and three acting lessons with Miss Mahoney, who had been coaching him in Varenna. To these Warren added his usual work with Warner. His score of *Pagliacci*, published by Sonzogno in 1893 and bought secondhand in Milan that summer, shows how he labored to master his roles. His longhand stage directions, written with his distinctive *L*, *R*, and *I*, begin with his first note. "Left hand higher, left foot forward, look first L then R." With that he presented himself to the audience. Further notations in the Prologue read, "step up, then step back," "apologetic," "more energetic," "long," "go on," "watch," and "slow," "slower," and "not too slow." The duet with Nedda, punctuated with "hurt" and "grimace, wry face, simper," also shows the problems he faced when he had to sing with others. He ran his English translation above the Italian line. Sometimes he misspelled the English words, writing "here" for *hear*, or "quik" for *quick*. Breaks for breaths, which Dietch considered all-important, are noted, together with Warren's phonetic versions of Italian words. In the line "le vecchie usanze," he wrote VEKIE. The common Italian *e* (for "and") is marked *eh*. Under "Andiam!" he wrote, "Let's go" and "Take it away." As in his later scores, he had to write out the tempo, even in many simple measures, as "1—2—3" or "1—2—3—4." Elemental rhythmic patterns are marked in this way. Later he developed other, more complicated schemes for deciphering tempos. Among these were the vertical lines he drew through both the musical notation and the text, marking the beats and the syllables. Syncopation evidently required extra attention, and ensembles were extremely difficult for him.

In Warren's August letter to Ziegler he said:

[Pelletier] has told me that the Metropolitan Opera was worried about my affairs here because they had not received any letters from me. . . . First of all, I did not know that they wanted to know of my work here, outside of my expenses. But since talking to Maestro Pelletier, I feel that I must apologize for not writing to you to tell you of what I have accomplished and also [to send you] the correct record of my expenses to date.

He said his work was "going beautifully" and that he had learned *Traviata, Trovatore, Simon Boccanegra, Pagliacci, Rigoletto,* "and practically all of Ford in *Falstaff*. The acting is done for *Boccanegra* and *Traviata* and I begin acting lessons [with Picozzi] again next week. This leaves me only Alfio in *Cavalleria* and Ford in *Falstaff*." The five operas he mentioned and the additional role of Ford were the ones Pelletier had assigned to him. In his letter, Warren reassured Ziegler, saying "I have not wasted my time."

At the end of summer Bampton and Pelletier returned to New York, leaving Warren and the Warners in Milan. The lessons with Pais and Picozzi continued as Warren mastered the music and stage action of Ford in *Falstaff* and polished *Pagliacci*. In his August letters, Warren never mentioned the rapidly deteriorating international situation, but by late September war seemed imminent. In March 1938, Hitler had annexed Austria. His drive for more territory led to further appeasement. The fatal date of 29 September marked the signing of the Munich Pact by Hitler, Mussolini, and the French and British prime ministers, Edouard Daladier and Neville Chamberlain. After the conference, Chamberlain announced that there would be "Peace in our time," but not everyone believed him.

On 23 August, a representative of the Italian Line wrote to say that Warren and the Warners had been assigned two cabins in third class on the majestic *Rex*, the celebrated flagship of the line. It stood as a veritable icon and
symbol of the power of Mussolini's state and was featured as such by Federico
Fellini in his film *Amarcord*. In it he showed the people of Rimini going to sea
in small boats to meet the *Rex* in the waters of the Adriatic. Men, women, and
children shed tears as the huge vessel passed, lights blazing in the night. Seeing it, they cried "Viva l'Italia!" from their rowboats as the liner raced on to
Venice. Warren and his friends were to leave Italy on 19 October. Warren was
to pay a "room supplement" for a berth in an outside cabin for four, where
the ship's engines would not bother him. Long before their sailing date, however, the three Americans had become alarmed over the international situation. Tourists and expatriate American residents were fleeing Italy in droves,
fearing they would be stranded. Given the peril, Warren and Warner cabled
to Ziegler for additional funds, which were sent by return cable to American
Express.

On 30 September, one day after the Munich Pact was signed, Warren
wrote to thank Ziegler:

> I received the extra money that I cabled for this morning and am
> writing this note to explain why I asked for it. I am sure that every-
> one in America knows the circumstances that were shaking Europe
> this past week, but here we have been through a greater tension than
> you could imagine without having been through it yourself. Under
> the circumstances, I felt that it was wiser to have several hundred
> dollars surplus, in case of an emergency. We tried desperately to
> change our passage to an earlier boat, but there were no places to be
> had, excepting on German boats, which, of course, were out of the
> question; and we could do nothing but wait for developments. Since
> news of the conference of the Powers was made public this morning,
> we feel much safer and will [sail on] October 11th from Trieste.
> Thank you so much for sending the money immediately. If war does
> not break out, there will be no need to spend the extra money, which
> I hold and will bring back to New York with me.
>
> With kindest personal regards, I am,
> Sincerely,
> Leonard Warren

Shortly before Warren left Italy, George Martin of Sherwin-Williams
wrote to praise him, saying he had been keeping up with him through Pelletier. He must also have heard how exhausted Warren was, for he hoped he
could get some rest on the way home. He congratulated him on having "concluded the work assigned to you by the Metropolitan" and thanked him for

having "applied himself to the limit." Pelletier, Martin said, seemed "tickled as a boy with a new drum at the progress you have made and [at] the information [Pelletier] has gathered from the 'Big Tops' of the [opera] world, such as Maestro [Ettore] Panizza and others." The baritone by then felt comfortable enough about his achievements to report to his patron with one of his rare letters. This correspondence is important in revealing Panizza's early interest in Warren.

In Italy Warren's lessons continued until the second week in October, when he and the Warners left Milan. Their rebooking for 11 October was on the venerable Italian liner *Saturnia*, an old luxury ship of the fleet. Compared to the *Rex* and the *Conte di Savoia*, the *Saturnia* looked like a dignified, elderly lady, but she was broad of hull and reassuringly stable for an autumn trip on the roiling reaches of the Mediterranean and the Atlantic. The three travelers spent the evening of 10 October in Venice and splurged on one last romantic gesture: they hired a gondola and rode down the Grand Canal. Thinking of his family, Warren bought a panoramic watercolor postcard showing an old-fashioned gondola with its black *felze* canopy. The gondolier is rowing on the Grand Canal toward San Marco; in the background are the bell towers of the basilica and the churches of San Giorgio and Santa Maria della Salute. "Dear Mom," Warren wrote on the card, "Can you imagine! I rode in a gondola on the Grand Canal in the moonlight and sang. Boy, oh boy! Wait till I get home to tell you more. My best regards to all. Your Leonardo." The postmark is from the Venice railroad station, 10 October 1938 XVI [Fascist era], between eleven o'clock and midnight. It was Verdi's birthday.

Warren and the Warners had to reach Trieste in time to board the *Saturnia* and sail at five. They surely left Venice by the midnight train, which accounts for the postmark at such a late hour from the railroad station post office. The next day they were safely on board. Warren traveled in stateroom 459 and paid his outside-cabin supplement. The long route of the *Saturnia* often went from Trieste to Patras in Greece, then to Sicily (two stops), Naples, perhaps Gibraltar and Lisbon, and the Azores, where the Italian Line served Flores. From the Azores it took six or seven days to get to Boston and New York. Passengers and freight were taken off and loaded at each stop. After an uneventful crossing, Warren and the Warners landed in New York. When he got home, he told his mother, sister, and brother about his summer and described a young woman he had met in Italy and come to love.

Agatha Leifflen

Sometime after Warren arrived in Milan, he met Agatha and Roy Leifflen, brother and sister, two young Americans who were spending the summer in Italy. By midsummer, although he did not mention them in his letters to Ziegler, he had already become their close friend. Agatha later became Warren's wife. Her brother, Roy, sent by their parents to Italy with her for the summer, gradually became Warren's friend and associate. He was three years older than Warren, having been born in Brooklyn in 1908. Both Leifflens were excellent musicians. Both had studied music, Agatha at the Institute of Musical Art, where her voice teacher was Ella Toedt, and Roy at the Juilliard Graduate School in New York, before Juilliard and IMA merged. Roy managed to become an accomplished amateur pianist. Realizing that he would never have a career, he turned to law, graduating from the law school at Columbia University. Tall, multilingual, elegant, and amusing, he collected records and scores and went regularly to the opera. Agatha, a slender blonde, was a lyric soprano. She had been taking private lessons with Giovanni Zenatello, the celebrated Italian tenor who was then living in New York, and with his wife, mezzo-soprano Maria Gay. In fact, Roy's friend William Appleton said that Agatha had gone to Italy that summer of 1938 to study in Verona with Zenatello who had been born there and had become the originator and engine behind the summer opera seasons in that city's famed Arena. At the time Zenatello met Agatha, he was the artistic director of the Arena opera and was among the more influential teacher-managers in the international music business.

Born in 1876, Zenatello had begun singing as a baritone in 1898 but had moved successfully into the tenor repertory, where his most famous opera was Verdi's *Otello*, which he sang more than three hundred times. He first made his reputation at La Scala, singing Pinkerton in the badly received world premiere of Giacomo Puccini's *Madama Butterfly* on 17 February 1904. A grand career followed. Zenatello and Maria Gay lived in a luxury apartment on Central Park West in New York City in the winters and taught many students. Gay autographed Agatha's score for *Carmen*, which Roy had given her on 8 March 1936: "Maria Gay. The Carmen of a 100 (*sic*) years ago, to my dearest pupul (*sic*), Agatha Leifflen." Beneath the inscription she wrote "Victor Seguidilla 91085" and "Habanera 92059," her recordings. Among the Metropolitan stars in the Zenatello-Gay studio were Lily Pons and Nino Martini. Many of the Zenatellos' New York evenings were spent at the Hotel Ansonia, having dinner and playing cards with Bidù Sayão, Giuseppe Danise, Virgilio Lazzari, and his wife. The singers were close friends; Gay and the three men were teaching voice. While Agatha was taking lessons from Zenatello and his wife, Zenatello was regarded as the doyen of many opera matters, national and international. Later, in the 1940s, he also engaged both Nicola Rossi-Lemeni and Maria Callas for the Verona Arena and launched their careers. Zenatello introduced Callas to her future husband, Giovanni Battista Meneghini, and wielded a great deal of power, whether in Italy or in New York. He could choose the students he wanted, and Agatha was lucky to be working in the studio he ran with his wife.

The Leifflens, a family of Alsatian origin, lived in a handsomely furnished apartment in Brooklyn Heights, a historic neighborhood in New York City. Harry B. Leifflen, the father of Agatha and Roy, was in business. His music-loving wife was called Big Agatha or Agatha, Senior. They were all Brooklyn-born. As Vivien described the family, they were "very religious Catholics. . . . One of Agatha's aunts was a nun, and they always had priests in the house as their guests. The Leifflens were very quiet, middle-class people." An attractive young woman with large hazel eyes, Agatha was in her early twenties when she and Warren met. Then and later, she impressed many people with her prim, ladylike, serious demeanor. Margaret Dempsey, writing of her in the Baltimore *Sun* in 1949, described her "aristocratic nose and very white teeth" and found her "direct and friendly and without pretense." Above all, Agatha possessed determination. She, like Warren, hoped to have a career in opera; she was a serious music student who had gone to Italy to study, as Warren had.

Much later, after she was married, Agatha recalled to an interviewer the first time she heard Warren sing. In the Pensione Agostini she heard a man's voice belting out "Home on the Range" and knew he had to be an American because of his delivery and diction. This Western chestnut, discovered in 1910 by John Lomax during a sweep-search for authentic American music, had been recorded and used by classical and folk singers alike. Gene Autry's recording of it set a national standard, making it a favorite song of the president, Franklin D. Roosevelt. Because Warren later chose to sing "Home on the Range" in radio and recital programs, it is not surprising that Agatha heard it coming from his room in Milan. At that moment she decided she would like to meet the man behind the voice. In the autumn of 1942 she told Mary Ellis Peltz, the editor of *Opera News*: "I fell in love with his voice before I ever saw him at all. . . . I was pleased at the thought that I could find someone to say good morning to in English in a strange city. But I never realized I would marry the young student with the beautiful voice." In this interview, she said he had been singing an opera aria.

Warren described that day in a January 1956 interview with Sidney Fields, a columnist for the New York *Daily Mirror*. "I was bellowing away, practicing; and she walked into this boarding house, asking if any Americans lived there. The owner told her the voice she heard was an American's. We met at the dinner table that night and were married four years later." Although Warren had dated and double-dated with his brother, Martin, he had never been seriously involved with any woman, Vivien said. But it was evident that he felt strongly attracted to Agatha. Bampton saw them together in Milan in July and August, and it is certain that from the moment of their first meeting, they had shared interests that drew them together. For their first date, Warren later said, he took Agatha to a cafe in the Galleria Vittorio Emanuele, where they had a soft drink together and sat, watching the Milanese throng this popular haunt. Because Warren was on such a tight budget, he could not offer her anything more. At the end of the summer, the Pelletiers returned to

New York. Agatha and Roy soon followed, and after Warren returned to the city, he resumed his friendship with them.

More than anything else in Warren's early life, the months in Italy changed him. He expanded his musical and cultural vocabulary and got a basic understanding of the Italian style, which later became his trademark. Beyond that, his coaching sessions with the sophisticated Pelletier in Italy and the United States brought Warren up to the level of polish needed for the kind of career he clearly hoped to have. As Vivien said, "He wanted to be the best there was."

◆ CHAPTER SIX

A Novice at the Met

W arren returned to New York in apparent good health, but the same problems that had brought him to a complete breakdown in June and July again took their toll in the autumn. After settling in at home with his mother, sister, and brother, he had to admit how ill he was. Frightened and unable to sing, he called Pelletier, who realized they might lose everything they had worked for. Warren's Met debut, set for the end of 1938, might have to be postponed. Acting on long experience, Rose Bampton said she and Pelletier worked to save the situation. She had been so close to Warren all summer that she felt he would listen to her. She reassured him, and Pelletier ordered him to rest and stop singing completely until he could recover. Warren obeyed. Vivien, who was eighteen at the time, remembered that he stopped his lessons, stopped vocalizing, and never left their apartment. "He stayed in bed most of the time and only got up to play with his electric trains. They were a hobby he had just begun to cultivate seriously, although, like many American kids, he had always had some around," she said. A natural mechanic, Warren built many pieces of his miniature railroad himself. He took locomotives and cars of the New York Central Line as his models and laid the tracks on ties that Vivien remembered him whittling from matchsticks. Then and later, the model railroad was a resource whenever stress threatened his health. The cure of rest and play worked. In less than a month Warren regained his strength. His voice came back, and he was ready to report to the Met.

Through this and later crises, Warren always had a lot of support from Pelletier and Bampton, his own family, Byron and Florence Warner, and the Leifflens. But he was under great strain because his mother looked to him for help. Martin, a song-promoter for music publishers, was bringing home a tiny salary; Warren was earning nothing. One big expense was Warren's voice lessons, but Sidney Dietch was a reassuring figure. An organist and pianist, he became Warren's most trusted teacher. In 1943 Warren even moved his family to an apartment in the Sherman Square Studios, where Dietch and many other voice teachers lived and worked. Linda Warren Tirdel, Warren's niece, remembered Dietch, who was also Martial Singher's teacher, as tall and broad-chested, bursting with an air of authority. He chatted with her grandmother and mother in the foyer of the building. It was easy for Warren to come for lessons because he visited his family so often. The Detroit-born bass Therman Bailey studied with Dietch for five years, four of them while Warren was the studio's unchallenged star. Bailey remembered his teacher, saying:

> He was definitely and strictly *Mr. Dietch*, with never an air of confidentiality. He always wore shirts and ties; he had white hair; he was robust without being fat. Yes, Mr. Dietch was impressive, vigorous, and sizable! He had a great air of authority and kept a very strict work relationship with his students. This is not to say he was unfriendly, but he never mixed anything with business. He worked strictly on fundamentals of technique.

An accomplished pianist, Dietch was also a "wonderful technician," Bailey said. "The production he taught was very much on the breath. He would say, 'Take a breath, and sing on that breath right away.' He taught us how to turn the breath into sound immediately. Voice back in the throat, then a quick breath, and move the voice to the front. Breathe. Sing. Breathe. Sing." Bailey also studied with Dietch's associate, Vera McIntyre, who later taught Margaret Truman, the president's daughter.

Bailey said Dietch was so modest that he spoke about Warren only once in five years:

> In 1957 Mr. Dietch seemed quite perturbed, which was unusual for him. He told me he was upset with one of his students who had sung on TV. Maybe it was the Firestone Hour or something like that. "It was so sloppy!" Dietch said. When I asked him who the student was, he replied, "Warren"—no further remarks, just "Warren." For him to mention Warren was unusual because he never promoted himself.

Dietch did not tell Bailey that he called Warren all the time to let him know what he had done wrong or right. Throughout his career, Dietch provided counsel in good times and bad. Vivien remembered Dietch getting in touch with her brother after almost every broadcast, telecast, or performance. "He was a monitor," she said. "He kept day-to-day contact with him for all those years." Warren described himself as an artist who never stopped "checking in with Dietch." He told one interviewer he called whenever he thought he had problems, even if they were meeting later that same day. Once, dissatisfied with his own work, he called from South America to ask for advice. Dietch's importance to Warren can hardly be overstated, for they had a professional rapport that lasted to the end of Warren's life. In a rare moment of unguarded frankness, Warren told an interviewer that he had an important psychological boost from Dietch's sessions. It wasn't the voice, he said, it was the sense of security.

Dietch, interviewed in 1959 by Harold C. Schonberg for a *New York Times Magazine* profile on Warren, described his early impressions of the baritone: "When I first heard the voice, it was of very fine basic material, but the quality was not good.—A little rough. I would never have expected him to make the career he has made. But all of a sudden, after two years or so, the voice grew in size, got its characteristic color; and I realized it was a great organ."

Personal Matters

As Warren recovered his strength and voice and waited for Pelletier to call him to the Met, his personal life was being transformed by his growing love for Agatha. Many people in Warren's world, professionals and nonprofessionals alike, believed the shy, wary baritone was probably destined for a great career, but the Leifflens were sure of it. They lived in a large apartment at 128 Willow Street in Brooklyn Heights, a beautiful neighborhood of short, tree-lined streets, dignified apartment buildings, handsome private brownstone residences, and gardens in the shadow of the Brooklyn Bridge. The area had become a refuge for well-to-do New Yorkers before 1900, with the blocks around the Leifflens' home remaining a little enclave of respectability. The Heights also provided housing for writers and artists. Willow Street, where the Leifflens lived, was near the East River, a walker's paradise, with spectacular views of the Manhattan skyline and harbor. Brooklyn Heights and the Leifflens' home provided a comfortable environment for the driven Warren. After he met Agatha's family in the autumn of 1938, he was often invited to Willow Street to join them at dinner and on Sundays. The Leifflens' circle of relatives and friends centered upon Agatha's mother—Big Agatha—whose maiden name was Agatha Schmitt. An affectionate, generous woman, Mrs. Leifflen was widely respected in the parish and loved in her family. Warren also grew closer to Roy. Inevitably Warren absorbed a lot of information about Catholicism just by being around this family. He met the many priests who were their guests and got to know Roy's and Agatha's aunt, who was a nun in the Convent of St. Bernadette in Brooklyn. Gradually he became comfortable with the Leifflens' everyday Catholic practices. Roy and Agatha had attended parochial schools; Agatha and Mrs. Leifflen went to the Nativity Institute. Their whole family lived by the Sacraments, said grace before meals, recited the "Our Father," the Rosary, and other Marian prayers in church, prayed at home, ate fish on Fridays and other fast-days, kept Lent, and went regularly to Confession and Mass. They observed Christmas, Easter, and other holidays with traditional celebrations and hearty meals. Afterward there was music in the parlor, where Agatha sang, and Roy, the amateur pianist, played. The sister-and-brother team used piano-vocal scores that Roy had been buying for years as gifts for Agatha. These included *La sonnambula*, *Carmen*, and *Lohengrin*, and Roy also had a large collection of scores of his own. Even during the first winter of their acquaintance, the elder Leifflens began to act like surrogate parents to Warren.

Soon after, William Appleton, a close friend of Roy's, was introduced to the Leifflen family circle. A descendant of two distinguished families, he was at that time an English instructor at Columbia University. After serving in World War II he resumed his friendship with the family, and Leonard often consulted him on the interpretation of his operatic roles—Rigoletto, Otello, Macbeth, and Falstaff. "We talked about Shakespeare and the concept of tragi-comedy that Victor Hugo expressed in his Preface to *Cromwell* which applied equally well to Hugo's *Le roi s'amuse*, the source of *Rigoletto*. Leonard was quite serious in his research. He really wanted to know." Later the two similarly explored *Macbeth*, *Otello*, and *Falstaff*.

In the Leifflen home, Agatha and Warren got to know each other as they could never have done in Italy. Soon they told their families they wanted to marry. In 1939 Warren also told John White, his coach, about their engagement. The couple did not marry for more than two years after that, a delay probably related to professional and financial concerns. The only objections came from Warren's mother. Vivien said she expressed reservations about the marriage, saying quite frankly that she was sorry her son had not chosen a Jewish girl. However, their grandmother, Brina Kantor, "set her straight." Vivien remembered the afternoon when Agatha came to visit in the Warenoff apartment on Sixty-seventh Street. There she was to meet Mrs. Kantor, who was then an elderly widow living in Brooklyn. Warren and his mother were also there. "Grandmother knew Agatha was a Catholic," Vivien said. "Leonard introduced them in our apartment. Never one to waste words, my grandmother spoke directly to Agatha. 'You love my grandson?' Agatha said she did. Gran turned to Leonard and asked him whether he loved Agatha. He, of course, answered, 'Yes.' Gran said, 'Then get married.' That was the whole story." Vivien also said the Leifflens "were very happy with Leonard, and he truly loved them." William Appleton said Warren simply adored Mrs. Leifflen, whom Appleton found to be "very friendly, a warm, outgoing person." William Mayo Sullivan, who was at one time president of the Metropolitan Opera Club, described Mrs. Leifflen as "a mother to Leonard. I respected Leonard personally just because of his lovely, lovely relationship with her." Margaret Carson, who headed the Metropolitan Opera press office from 1944 to 1954, felt that the younger Agatha's serenity and sense of humor helped to sustain Warren, who in those years was often "playful, but only in the family," as Vivien remembered, and serious and shy with strangers.

The Voronov family, Leonard's paternal grandparents and their children, in Russia, now Belarus. Credit: Vivien Warren Collection.

Above: Sonia Voronov, Leonard's aunt, in Orsha, Belarus, 1919.
Right: Leonard's maternal grandparents, David and Brina Kantor.
Credit: Vivien Warren Collection.

Leonard's father, Solomon
Warenoff, age fifteen, with
his new American name,
photographed in a studio on
Second Avenue in New York
around 1900. He was born 4 July
1885. Credit: Spiess Studio;
Vivien Warren Collection.

Sara Kantor Warenoff,
Leonard's mother. Credit:
Vivien Warren Collection.

The newborn Leonard Warenoff in his mother's arms. Taken on the back steps of the Kantor home, where he was born. On the reverse the inscription reads: "1822 Clinton Avenue, The Bronx, on 10 June 1911." Credit: Vivien Warren Collection.

Leonard as a playful baby. Credit: Vivien Warren Collection.

Leonard Warren's birthplace, the Kantor home at 1822 Clinton Avenue in the Bronx. Credit: Carlino Matz.

The building on Ogden Avenue in the Bronx, where the Warenoffs lived for more than a decade. Credit: Clare Ann Matz.

Leonard, the favored first son, riding a pony, and at right as "Master Leonard Warenoff 1914," according to the inscription. Credit: Vivien Warren Collection.

Leonard boating with his father. Leonard, age four, is rowing. Right: Leonard (top), his brother, Martin, and his sister, Vivien. Credit: Vivien Warren Collection.

Vivien Warenoff, Leonard Warren's sister, in January 1944. She later changed her surname to Warren. Credit: Vivien Warren Collection.

Martin Warenoff, Leonard's brother, relaxing at home. Credit: Vivien Warren Collection.

Leonard, a teenager in sports clothes. Credit: Vivien Warren Collection.

Radio City Music Hall Glee Club in the mid-1930s. Leonard, then using the name "Warren," is third from the left in the second row. The pianist is Vin Lindhe, his nemesis. Credit: Vivien Warren Collection.

Warren costumed as a clown. "During the week of 11 July 1936. He was great!" reads the inscription on the back. Credit: Vivien Warren Collection.

Warren and his friend John Bennis on the roof of Radio City Music Hall in 1937. Credit: Vivien Warren Collection.

Warren at the microphone
at New York station WOR,
1933. Credit: Walter Engel;
Vivien Warren Collection.

Byron and Florence Warner, Warren's best friends, on their wedding day. Warner
was Warren's coach, accompanist, and confidant for many years. Credit: Vivien
Warren Collection.

During and after the Auditions of the Air, Warren's most enthusiastic supporters were conductor Wilfrid Pelletier (left) and his wife Rose Bampton. They congratulate the winners in March 1938: Warren (right) and tenor John Carter. Credit: Vivien Warren Collection.

Warren in Italy, summer 1938, at Varenna on Lake Como. Before sending the snapshot to his family, he wrote on the back, "I'm still exercising, Volga Boat Boy." Credit: Vivien Warren Collection.

At the Verona Arena with Rose Bampton, August 1938. Credit: Vivien Warren Collection.

Warren as Paolo in *Simon Boccanegra*, his first operatic role at the Met, January 1939. Credit: Metropolitan Opera Archives; *Opera News*.

Warren as Valentin
in the Met's *Faust*,
December 1939.
Credit: Metropolitan
Opera Archives.

The Met's *Faust* cast for Boston, March 1942, Warren with Richard Crooks, Licia
Albanese, and Norman Cordon. Credit: Metropolitan Opera Archives.

Warren as Amonasro in *Aida*, his
first professional opera performance
outside the Met; Cincinnati Summer
Opera, 1940. The leopard skin was a
gift from Warren's father. Credit:
Vivien Warren Collection.

Warren as Barnaba in the Met's *Gioconda*,
January 1940. Credit: Vivien Warren
Collection.

The Cincinnati Summer Opera, 1940, rehearsing *Aida* with Bruna
Castagna and Rose Bampton, with Fausto Cleva (extreme right)
conducting. Credit: Reuben Lawson; Vivien Warren Collection.

Left: Agatha Leifflen, whom Warren married in 1941. Credit: Jean Duval Studio; Vivien Warren Collection. Below left: Warren in 1942. Credit: Metropolitan Opera Archives. Below right: Roy Leifflen, Warren's brother-in-law, in uniform during World War II. Credit: Michael Shuter; Vivien Warren Collection.

Leonard and Agatha Warren at their modest dinner table in their first apartment, 305 Lexington Avenue, New York City. Credit: Roy Pinney; Vivien Warren Collection.

Five months after their marriage, Warren and Agatha went to Buenos Aires for his Teatro Colón debut, May 1942. Credit: *Opera News*.

Warren in the kitchen, tasting one of his favorite sauces. Credit: Roy Pinney; Vivien Warren Collection.

Warren as Escamillo
in the Met's *Carmen*,
December 1940.
Credit: Vivien Warren
Collection.

In 1941 Warren sang
the High Priest in the
Met's *Alceste*. Credit:
Metropolitan Opera
Archives.

At the Met, Warren, Astrid Varnay, and Raoul Jobin sang in Gian Carlo Menotti's *Ilo e Zeus*, called *The Island God*, February 1942. Credit: Metropolitan Opera Archives.

Warren's first Renato in *Un ballo in maschera*, Buenos Aires, 21 July 1942, with Frederick Jagel as Riccardo and Ferruccio Calusio conducting. Credit: Vivien Warren Collection.

Warren as the Count di Luna in the Met's *Il trovatore*, which he first sang on 5 February 1943. Credit: Metropolitan Opera Archives.

Agatha had a special relationship with Warren, whom she understood. She learned how to calm him down when he became upset, and later told an interviewer that in these early days she learned how to reassure him, saying, "*Pazienza*, Leonard." Gradually the personal bonds between them were reinforced by a professional cooperation they quickly put to the service of his voice. Agatha gave up any idea of having a career of her own, devoting herself entirely to Warren's well-being. Vivien described their relationship, saying, "All he had to do was sing. She did everything else."

Warren's First Opera Contract

Warren had barely recovered from his 1938 breakdown and gotten his voice back when Pelletier told him to come to the Met to sign a contract. Like all first offers to inexperienced artists, his agreement stipulated many conditions for his employment and provided nothing more than a modest salary, which could not cover even the basic needs for himself, his mother, and his sister. He and Martin were their family's main providers after Solomon and Sara Warenoff legally separated; they would later divorce. Warren's father married a second time. Discussing her brother's plight, Vivien said, "The expenses of launching [Leonard's] career were enormous."

Warren's first contract with the Metropolitan Opera Association is dated "the eighteenth day of November, 1938." So far as one can see, he represented himself, for none of his three previous managers is named. He was engaged for the season of 1938–1939 for a period of sixteen weeks, "from November 21, inclusive, 1938, to March 12, 1939." Had he signed earlier in the year, he would have been required, as all singers were, to report for two weeks or more of rehearsals. Warren's fee was "Seventy-five ($75) per week, during the period of his engagement," payable "at the end of each week or each half-month, at the option of the association." He was paid fortnightly, as his paybook records show. Another young singer, Frank Sinatra, was also earning seventy-five dollars a week at that time, singing with the Harry James band. Like all weekly-fee artists at the Met, Warren could be required to sing as often as three times a week, although the company was not supposed to force anyone to sing in three consecutive performances. Matters concerning the Met spring tour were also covered, as were those applying to performances in Philadelphia and other nearby cities. Warren would be allotted ten dollars a night for hotel expenses, if he had to sing outside of New York with the company. Any train fares would be covered by the Met. He would forfeit "one-fourth (1/4) of his weekly salary" for each performance he canceled "on account of sickness." If he were out "for illness or personal reasons" for more than seven days, the association could deduct "one seventh (1/7)" of his weekly salary for each additional day of "such disability." Each artist was also required "to sing in one or two performances or concerts during each season" without "any compensation whatsoever," at the association's option. In other words, Met artists contributed their services once or twice for benefits or galas and did not get paid for them. Paragraph XVIII of the contract stipulated that the association "shall have the option on the services of the Artist for the season 1939–1940, on the same conditions as those in his original contract" but with a "salary which shall be One Hundred Dollars ($100) per week." The option could also be extended to the season 1940–1941 "at a salary of One Hundred Fifty Dollars ($150) per week," if the company decided to renew the contract. Each year before 31 May he would be notified of the management's decision whether his contract was to be renewed.

Warren had his costumes furnished by the company but had to buy his own "gloves, feathers, jewelry, wigs, tights, boots, shoes and other similar articles." He also had to "place at the disposal" of the Metropolitan any costumes that he had; these would be used if they conformed to "the artistic style of the ensemble for the respective performance." He could not leave his house for more than two hours without leaving word at his residence where he could be found, so the Opera House management could be notified of his whereabouts. He could not leave New York City without written permission from the Met. He had to give official notification of illness and submit it with a doctor's certificate. He was obliged to replace any other artist on orders from the management, so long as he was asked to sing in his own repertoire. Lateness at rehearsals or any other "dereliction of duty" would be fined. The singers were forbidden to appear at rehearsals with "canes, cloaks or hats" as Caruso had done. Smoking and alcoholic drinks were forbidden.

An additional clause, typed in, stipulated that "The Artist agrees immediately to become a member of the American Guild of Musical Artists, Inc., and to remain a member in good standing for the duration of this contract." This referred to AGMA, the musicians' union that had been founded two years before. It was described by Quaintance Eaton in *The Miracle of the Met* as "the single most important idea in the musical world at the time," a union to protect the solo artist against the opera companies' demands. "By its charter in 1937," Eaton wrote, "AGMA got jurisdiction over concert, recital, oratorio and grand opera." It later also absorbed the Opera Choral Alliance, which had been founded earlier.

Warren's contracted repertoire consisted of eight roles in eight operas, all to be sung in Italian: "*Boris Godunoff*, Tchelkaloff (*sic*); *Cavalleria Rusticana*, Alfio; *Falstaff*, Ford; *Pagliacci*, Tonio; *Rigoletto*, Rigoletto; *Simon Boccanegra*, Paolo; *Traviata*, Germont; and *Trovatore*, Count di Luna." The "roles or parts" clause of the contract also stipulated that "the Artist also agrees, at the request of the Association or its representative, to study and sing and perform in new and additional roles or parts." This was a daunting assignment for such an inexperienced opera singer. Clause XII of the contract stipulated that "the Artist" must not "sing or perform or render any professional services either in opera, operetta or public or private concert, on the stage . . . or in vaudeville . . . without the consent of the general manager or assistant general manager of the Association or the Board of Directors." A related "permissions" clause covered the phonograph, radio, broadcasting, television, and "the reproduction of silent or sound motion picture film." The singer had the

> right to sing concerts, for his own account, outside of the period mentioned in paragraphs II and III of this contract. The Artist shall also have the right to sing some concerts, for his own account, during the periods mentioned in paragraphs II and III, but such concerts must not be gratis and the dates and localities of the same must be submitted to the Association for its written approval.

The right to sing concerts and recitals was a matter of great urgency to singers, for many were paid such small fees that they earned much of their living outside the Metropolitan Opera House. The Met claimed that without the prestige of its name, singers could not get outside dates; and quite beyond that, the management believed that the singers' first loyalty belonged to the Met. Disputes over outside concerts were frequent and often bitter. The signatures on the contract read: "Leonard Warren, 40 West 67th Street, NYC" and "Edward Johnson." With the contract signed, Warren was officially a member of the roster of the Metropolitan Opera.

In *The American Opera Singer*, Peter G. Davis described Warren as one of "Johnson's Babies," American singers whom Edward Johnson recruited for the Met and nourished after he got them under contract. Prepared for his debut chiefly by Warner and Pelletier, Warren first appeared onstage at the Opera House just nine days after signing his contract. The event was a concert, not an opera.

In Warren's situation, it would have been easy for a young singer to falter under the twin burdens of overwork and ambition, as he already had nearly done. Margaret Carson is convinced that Warren was spared that fate by his protectors, Pelletier and Frank St. Leger, the conductor who became Johnson's de facto assistant manager. They coddled Warren and literally directed his life because "they knew everything about the care and feeding of singers." She said, "St. Leger played a big part in Warren's career by bringing him along safely and sensibly. He directed his repertory and chose his roles." Described by Carson as "the Number Two man" after Johnson and "the man who knew more about opera than anyone else in the world," St. Leger "could identify a good voice faster than anyone." He had had extensive experience in the music business long before he got to the Metropolitan. "Johnson's most faithful buffer," Quaintance Eaton called him. When Gatti-Casazza's music secretary died in 1940, St. Leger was "the logical one to slip into the tiny cubicle next to Johnson's corner office at Thirty-ninth and Seventh Avenue,"

Eaton remembered. A true cosmopolitan, St. Leger was born in India and had lived in England and Australia. He had been Nellie Melba's accompanist and then had established himself as a coach and conductor. St. Leger became Johnson's assistant in the autumn of 1939, just one year after Warren joined the company. From that moment on, he was a power to be reckoned with at the Met, remaining there until the arrival of Rudolf Bing in 1950.

When Warren joined the company in 1938, the Metropolitan had a contingent of several dependable baritones for the repertory he believed he would eventually be able to sing, but none of them surpassed Lawrence Tibbett in reputation and popularity. Tibbett was the foremost American opera baritone of the time, an international celebrity whose huge, vibrant, looming presence overrode all other singers in the men's wing at the Metropolitan. The California-born singer, fifteen years older than Warren, had joined the Metropolitan Opera in 1923. He soon became a pillar of the roster. Tibbett had also sung abroad, in long, far-flung tours that took him from Stockholm and London to Australia and Hawaii. His radio and film careers had brought him great wealth and made him into an international celebrity. Among the other baritones on the roster were Richard Bonelli, an American, who had joined the company in 1932; Carlo Morelli, who joined in the 1935–1936 season; and Carlo Tagliabue, who came in the 1937–1938 season and sang many Amonasros in *Aida*. By 1939–1940, Tagliabue had returned to Italy, but Morelli stayed on. John Brownlee, born in 1900, had made his early career in his native Australia and gone on to London, where he sang Marcello in Nellie Melba's 1926 farewell performance. He also had sung principal roles at the Royal Opera, the Paris Opéra, and Glyndebourne. At the Met, Brownlee, a graceful, beloved figure, was active across the general repertory. He was also a respected concert artist and was later among the candidates for the post of general manager when Johnson decided to retire.

One American baritone Warren already knew was Robert Weede, his friend and former colleague from Radio City. Although Weede's Met career was limited and even modest at the beginning of his tenure, he gradually gained ground, particularly after Tibbett began to have severe vocal problems. Weede, like Warren, eventually became a dependable "Tibbett-in-reserve," but he never won true star status at the Metropolitan, as Tibbett had. Nonetheless, Weede had a long, serious opera career and was also a favorite in radio concerts and recitals. Jerome Hines, quoted in *Dear Rogue*, Hertzel Weinstat and Bert Wechsler's biography of Lawrence Tibbett, said of Weede, "[He] was a very fine singer, a superlative technician, one of our truly great baritones. But he just did not have the vocal scope that Tibbett had." Weede last sang at the Metropolitan in 1953. He later gained fame on Broadway as the star of *The Most Happy Fella*.

Warren's First Appearances at the Metropolitan

Warren's debut at the Met fell on 27 November 1938 in one of the Sunday concerts that had been a popular feature of the company's programs for years. Fortunately for this nervous tyro, the conductor was Pelletier, on whom he could count for support. His first number was the duet from the second act of Verdi's *La traviata*, performed in costume and fully staged. He sang the elder Germont to the Violetta of Marisa Morel, another young artist. The role of Germont was one that Warren had studied the previous summer with Pais and Picozzi. His second and far more challenging assignment consisted of excerpts from Leoncavallo's *Pagliacci*, also sung in costume. Because he had prepared it in Italy, he used his well-marked score in the rehearsals. Cast as Tonio, he opened the Prologue, introducing himself: "Si può?" This gave him a chance to show off his brilliant top notes. He then sang the duet with Nedda, who was the soprano Hilda Burke, wife of the stage director and former baritone Désiré Defrère. She also sang Nedda's showy soprano aria. There followed another scene with Burke, Martinelli, Warren, and George Cehanovsky, who had joined the Met in 1926.

The next day, Warren's first reviews appeared in the New York papers. The *New York Herald Tribune* headline read: WARREN MAKES VOCAL DEBUT AT METROPOLITAN, while the subhead read: "New York Barytone (*sic*) Who Won Radio Auditions Appears in Costumed Excerpts from Two Operas." The cautious Francis D. Perkins wrote:

Leonard Warren, one of the two young New Yorkers who received Metropolitan Opera contracts for this season as a result of victory in the 1937–1938 radio auditions, faced his first audience in the Metropolitan Opera House last night as one of the soloists in the first weekly opera concert of the season. . . . The first impressions to be derived from his singing were very promising; his voice proved to be of pleasing quality and was produced with commendable style and fluency. In the self-possessed performance of the *Pagliacci* Prologue, his top notes had effective resonance, and his vocal volume in general seemed satisfactory, if not yet fully adjusted to the acoustic conditions of this theatre. The young baritone received warm and extensive applause from a large audience.

A review in the *New York Times* said:

Though a single scene is scarcely enough to reveal fairly a man's ability, it was, in this instance, enough to make one want to hear more of Mr. Warren. His voice is good-sized, round, healthy and altogether one of the most attractive of the company's younger set. It has the appeal of warmth that derives from the very nature of the instrument. To what degree this warmth derived from innate musicianship will be told definitely at future hearings, but the scene augured well for the newcomer. If his acting was somewhat wooden, put that down to the nervous ravages of a Metropolitan debut. He was sincerely encouraged by his listeners.

These favorable reviews showed Warren himself, George Martin, Pelletier, and the opera company management that their large investment in this career had not been wasted. Warren received his first Metropolitan Opera paycheck, for $150, on 30 November. The amount, as per his contract, was for two weeks. One week after his first appearance, Warren sang Act II of Verdi's *Rigoletto* in costume, again in a concert. This was a critical test for the young baritone because Tibbett, for all his fame, had been so successful in the title role of that opera, although Tibbett's first appearance in *Rigoletto* at the Met, about three years earlier, had been greeted by some indifferent reviews. The *New York Times* critic had observed then that "Mr. Tibbett will probably be a more convincing Rigoletto when he has given the opera further study. As yet he has not wormed his way fully beneath the surface of the jester's psychology. Nor has he realized completely the vocal possibilities of the jester's music. At times . . . the voice lost color and volume to a surprising degree." This, like other compromised performances of these years, was perhaps owed in part to overwork and in part to Tibbett's alcoholism. This is not to say Tibbett was a failure as Rigoletto, for it became one of his greatest portrayals. But it is clear that as Tibbett aged and as his personal and vocal problems began to take their toll on his career, the management's need to find a replacement for him in this important opera left a door open to Weede and Warren, among others. In 1938 and 1939, Tibbett still had a long career ahead, but both younger men seized the advantage later, each approaching the role of Rigoletto in his own way.

In this costumed and fully staged second act of *Rigoletto*, the Gilda was Morel. Nicholas Massue sang the Duke, and John Gurney was Sparafucile. The conductor was Fausto Cleva, a native of Trieste who had come to the Met as a chorusmaster and remained there for many years as a principal conductor in Rudolf Bing's regime; he also conducted in Chicago and Cincinnati. Vivien laughed as she remembered that Sunday concert because her brother forgot his words toward the end of the scene, just before he cries "Gilda! Gilda!" but "he made something up, and managed to get through it. Afterwards, he was desperate because he made a mistake." A third concert followed on 18 December, with Warren's solo "Eri tu" from Verdi's *Un ballo in maschera*, which he had sung earlier on radio programs. This day also marked his repeat of the duet from Bizet's *Les pêcheurs de perles* with John Carter, the co-winner of the Auditions of the Air. Again Cleva conducted. Warren was also assigned another long excerpt from *Rigoletto* for the concert on Christmas night, 1938. With Natalia Bodanya, Lucielle Browning, and Massue again as the Duke, he performed the entire last act of the opera in costume with Pietro Cimara conducting.

Warren's first complete, fully staged opera came on 13 January 1939, when he was cast as Paolo Albiani in Verdi's *Simon Boccanegra*. Pais had helped him prepare the score in Italy, and Picozzi had taught him its stage action. In this production, Warren's voice could be weighed for the first time against that of Tibbett, who sang the demanding title role. The cast also included the recently arrived and justly famous Italian soprano Maria Caniglia as Amelia, Martinelli as Gabriele Adorno, and Pinza as Fiesco. Ettore Panizza, an early Warren admirer, conducted. In the *Herald Tribune* Francis Perkins again wrote a supportive review. "[Warren] displayed a voice of good size and generally commendable quality, if leaving room for more emotional color. In acting, the young New Yorker left some of the dramatic significance of the role unrealized, except at the climax of Simon's curse; but some allowance is in order for what was virtually a debut."

One young man who heard Warren's opera debut in 1939 was Martin Feinstein. Brooklyn-born, he had attended City College of New York, as Warren had, and had become an enthusiastic opera fan. Feinstein told me that the first opera he ever heard was a Met dress rehearsal of *Otello* with Martinelli, Tibbett, and Rethberg. He soon found a job at the Met as, he said, "a libretto boy," selling librettos in the lobby of the theatre every night before performances and during intermissions. Feinstein said:

> Most librettos cost thirty cents, the bigger ones cost more. *Der Rosenkavalier*, for example, was sixty cents. We were paid two cents for every one we sold. I didn't earn much, but I heard a lot of opera. We sold librettos until about ten minutes after the curtain went up, then we went inside to watch the opera from the standing room area. I usually picked out three operas a week and heard them all. I'd call my mother to say I'd be home late on those nights.

Recalling Warren's debut, Feinstein spoke of his first impressions:

> He was Paolo, and he was just overwhelming. The voice was splendid, and it had a unique quality, a sound that you would recognize immediately as soon as you heard it. Even that first time, even in those early years, you could tell that a major, major career lay ahead for him. People at the Met realized that Warren's voice was phenomenal, one of the greatest of the century. And keep in mind the fact that these were the days when Tibbett was still king.

Comparing Warren's voice to Tibbett's, Feinstein said, "Warren had a more mellow quality. Tibbett's voice had more bite to it." About the course of Warren's early career, Feinstein said, "Warren was lucky because the Met groomed him very, very, very carefully. Gradually he became a great artist."

Feinstein heard many Warren performances over the years. Warren's first Paolo had Tibbett, Martinelli, and Caniglia in the cast, but soon Feinstein heard him with Rethberg as Amelia/Maria, again with Tibbett and Martinelli. Feinstein then went into the army. After the war, he returned to New York and joined the Sol Hurok concert management firm. Beginning in the early 1950s, when Feinstein was the head of the publicity department in the Hurok organization, he was directly involved with Warren, who had joined the Hurok roster.

Warren's Met broadcast debut was announced in a press release from an unidentified management agency; it was dated 20 January 1939, a week after his debut as Paolo. It began with a phrase about "one of the most promising of the new singers . . . added to the Metropolitan Opera Company last fall" and went on to announce his first radio broadcast for the Met, which was scheduled for 21 January. His role was again Paolo in *Simon Boccanegra*, in which he had made his opera debut. When the radio audience had its first chance to hear Warren, the *Boccanegra* cast was unchanged, save for Elisabeth Rethberg, replacing Maria Caniglia. Because the opera has been released in the Metropolitan Opera Historic Broadcast recording series, one can hear how he handled the complex character of Paolo Albiani, the goldsmith who inspired the people of Genoa to choose Boccanegra as Doge. Musically and dramatically, this is a long, difficult part for any debuting artist. In *Saturday Afternoons at the Old Met*, Paul Jackson said Warren's "superbly resonant instrument more than held its own among the grand sonorities of Tibbett, Pinza and Martinelli. For once, the malicious Paolo was a credible rival for the powerful Doge." An excerpt from this broadcast was played by George Jellinek on 14 January 1989 in a Metropolitan Opera intermission radio profile on Warren and Jussi Björling. In Paolo's monologue, one can hear a forceful young baritone with a fair low range and a remarkable, flexible high register. Although at this point he shows little command of dynamics, his crisp northern Italian diction and forward production make much of the text clear.

Warren again appeared in January in the popular Sunday concerts. He was Count di Luna, first with Arthur Carron as Manrico in *Il trovatore*, then with the Leonora of Croatian soprano Zinka Milanov, with whom Warren often sang. In the second concert Warren sang "Il balen del suo sorriso," also from *Trovatore*; the *Pagliacci* excerpts were repeated, this time with Carron and Muriel Dickson, while Tibbett sang Germont's aria from *Traviata* and excerpts from *Otello*. Warren was away from the Met from 29 January to the end of February, perhaps on a concert tour of his own. Later in the season, he sang in the Metropolitan Opera Guild benefit *Boris Godunov*. He did two roles, Rangoni, the "Gesuita segreto," which he had been assigned after his return to New York, and Shchelkalov, which he also sang that night. In all, he sang seventeen Rangonis from 1939 to 1944. For his first performance on 7 March 1939, Pinza was Boris; Alessio De Paolis, Shuisky; Charles Kullman,

Grigori; Norman Cordon, Pimen; Virgilio Lazzari, Varlaam; and Kerstin Thorborg, Marina. The conductor was again Panizza. Not altogether successful, Warren's Rangoni was sometimes criticized (oddly enough, given his large voice) for a lack of power. When it was repeated in 1939–1940, Olin Downes, writing in the *New York Times*, dismissed Warren's performance with few words: "Where was the craft and the Mephosthelian triumph of Rangoni, the Jesuit, in Mr. Warren's interpretation?"

Warren's handwritten notes in his *Boris* score, as in his other scores, show how hard it was for him to learn his roles. Some notations are in black pencil, some in red. Following Pelletier's suggestion, Warren had bought the score of *Boris* in a Russian-Italian edition in the summer of 1938 in the Sonzogno store in Milan. Because he could not read music and did not understand the time values, Warren learned everything by rote. He often wrote the time values above the notes as "1—2—3—4" and also marked the measures with vertical lines that ran through the vocal part and the text. While it is not unusual for students and coaches to mark scores in this way, it is odd that Warren did it for the simplest tempos. An example from *Boris* follows:

1 — 2 — 3 — 4   1 — 2 — 3 — 4
D'infer | nal | fiam | ma or | luco | no | gli occhi | tuoi.|

The phrase "Oh! Distruggi il settenario spirto!" was marked DARK. Many passages like this provide a guide path through the scenes he found most difficult. Warren's collection of Riccardo Stracciari and Titta Ruffo and complete opera recordings were used as teaching tools. Later he said that he wore records out so quickly that he had copies made of those most valuable to him. A few of his scores even have notes showing how he used complete recorded operas, writing "Side 1" and "Side 2" and "Side 6" over relevant passages.

His first Met season closed with a repeat of *Boris* (Rangoni only) and another concert. In his first year at the Met, Warren sang only twelve performances, two of which were *Boccanegra*, but he gave a very reasonable account of himself. His salary was regularly paid every fortnight, and he could keep it all, save for one payment in February of fifty-five dollars to Earle Lewis, the Metropolitan Opera Association's treasurer. The nature of the payment is not specified, but Louis J. Snyder, a former member of the Met press office, guessed Warren might have repaid a loan.

On 1 March 1939, Warren was given a letter of contractual renewal, signed by Edward Johnson. The letter said, "We beg to notify you hereby that your engagement is renewed for the season 1939–1940 for a period of sixteen weeks, from November 27, inclusive, 1939, to March 17, inclusive, 1940, at a salary of One Hundred Dollars ($100.00) per week. You will place yourself at our disposal for preliminary rehearsals on November 13, 1939." Normally reserved, even among friends, he told his sister how pleased he was. Vivien remembered his pride and awe at being in the Met. At home, he would say to her, "Just imagine! Me up there on that stage, where Caruso sang!"

But his career was not limited to opera. He had sung an aria from *Rigo-letto* on the Magic Key of RCA on 15 May 1938, and now, less than two weeks after the last of his 1939 performances for the Met, Warren returned to radio on Consolidated Edison's Echoes of New York on 21 March 1939. The booking was through an agency called Leading Attractions, Inc., which gave Warren a recording of the broadcast. He sang "Eri tu" from *Un ballo in mas-chera*. For it, he was paid two hundred dollars as his fee and was reimbursed $24.25 for train fare. Leading Attractions, Inc., deducted a commission of twenty percent, forty dollars, and his Social Security tax and a "franchise fee," leaving him with $157.25 for his work. Yet by the time of these broad-casts, his identity as an Italian baritone was becoming evident. Robert Mer-rill remarked, somewhat ruefully, on how valuable the months of studies in Italy had been to Warren. "Leonard was fortunate that the Met sent him to Italy. They sent him to *Italy*! I didn't have that opportunity. I had to go to Brooklyn," Merrill concluded with a laugh.

An important non-Met broadcast that spring came on 9 April, when War-ren was chosen to be one of four soloists with the New York Philharmonic in Carnegie Hall. Gioachino Rossini's *Petite messe solennelle* also featured the soprano Ria Ginster, the mezzo Bruna Castagna, and the tenor Charles Kull-man—all, except for Ginster, Metropolitan Opera artists. The Westminster Choir was directed by the respected John Finley Williamson, while John Bar-birolli conducted the orchestra. The concert, heard on WABC, was reported in the *New York Times* as the first complete American broadcast of this work. Deems Taylor was the commentator for this important event. As he had done before, Warren managed to get a recording of his performance so that he could hear how he sounded.

On 3 May 1939, the baritone reported for work to record part of the Council Chamber Scene from *Boccanegra* for RCA Victor under Pelletier's baton. This was Warren's first official studio recording session. The scene begins with Boccanegra's words "Plebe! Patrizi! Popolo dalla feroce storia!" and gives Tibbett a free rein in Verdi's great oration on factionalism and peace. Thus ended Warren's professional obligations for the season. When summer came, Vivien said, he spent his time in New York, learning new roles. There would be no return to Italy, no vacation in the Catskills. Instead, he set-tled again into the numbing routine of study.

CHAPTER SEVEN

Tending the Career

F or his second season at the Met, Warren had to prepare Valentin in *Faust* with Pelletier and have it ready for December 1939. His first Herald in *Lohengrin* and his first Amonasro in *Aida* were likely to come in January; he also had to brush up the role of Rangoni. His first Barnaba in *La Gioconda* might follow, although that was not certain. Again, Warren's scores reveal how he struggled with his assignments. As he tackled *Faust* with no knowledge of French, he wrote his phonetic version of the words over his usual tempo notations. The French word *de* is rendered with a pure New York DUH, while *et* is marked AY and *sür* has a German umlaut over it. He first sang Valentin, coached and conducted by Pelletier. Warren's score of *Gioconda* also shows how he was struggling. Still shaky in Italian, he again wrote phonetic values over the words, so that *scheletro* has SKAY written over the first syllable. His stage directions to himself are CENTER, in capital letters, when he had to move to center stage; his musical instructions include phrases like "much contrast" or "a little faster." Despite help from Agatha, Dietch, and several coaches, he still could not recognize the time values of the notes and resorted to the system he had used in the past.

A Teacher and Friend

In October 1939 the Austrian conductor Erich Leinsdorf asked Warren to study texts of his roles with John S. White, a recent émigré who helped Warren for years and became close to his family. White, a Jew born in Vienna, had first met Leinsdorf at school, when they went to performances together. Leinsdorf was by two years the younger of the two. Fleeing Austria in 1938, White went first to Paris, then to the United States, "because it was the only country where I was admitted." Almost penniless, he rented a furnished room on West End Avenue in Manhattan. Although he had arrived in New York just as Warren was being introduced to Met audiences, he had not yet heard the singer because, as White said, "I did not have the money for a ticket."

White remembered Leinsdorf's urging Warren to learn German roles, among them the Herald in *Lohengrin* and Biterolf in *Tannhäuser*. Both were on Warren's repertory list at the Met. "He even thought he should sing Alberich in the *Ring*," White said.

> Leinsdorf understood the importance of Leonard's voice, but he really did not know what he should do. Pelletier, on the other hand, knew exactly where Leonard belonged. The one person who was really interested in him at that time was Pelletier. He had a fine ear for potentially great voices; he was really interested in voices. Leonard could have gotten to the top without Pelletier, but it was Pelletier who pushed him.

Warren was restudying Rangoni in *Boris* when he and White first met. White coached him in the Italian text of this and almost every other work he was assigned, then and for years to come. For their first session, White presented himself at the door of the building on West Sixty-seventh Street where Warren, Martin, Vivien, and their mother were then living, having moved in 1938 from the Hotel Embassy where they had settled when Warren's sister and mother returned from Seattle. A few doors from Central Park, their house was next to a riding academy. Because White was evidently in dire financial straits, Mrs. Warenoff arranged for him to come at an hour when she could offer him a meal. "She knew I was destitute, so when I left each day, she filled the pockets of my topcoat so full of apples and knishes and other things that there was no more room for my gloves." He described her as "a lovely woman, very maternal, very interested in her children, and very proud of Leonard. This family led a pleasant, middle-class Jewish life." White added that he was paid at the end of each session, perhaps because Sara Warenoff realized how much he needed cash. He soon learned about his pupil's passion for model trains and found him "very self-confident about the music, although he might sometimes have been a little bit nervous. But the general impression was that he had a lot of self-assurance." Warren was tall and burly, with a thick neck and large chest. In a rare moment of confidentiality, Warren told White he was engaged to Agatha.

At some sessions, with an accompanist present, Warren would ask White to hear him sing. "This [accompanist] was either Byron Warner or, later, William Tarrasch, who was more *pesante*, heavier than Warner, out of the German school. He had come from Chemnitz." Tarrasch, White recalled, was "a highly professional man, a conductor." He created arrangements that Warren began to use in his recitals in the early 1940s. White said, "I would stop Leonard and point out what was not right, and he would stop the pianist and go back and sing it again. He never argued with me about correctness. He had the most trouble with foreign vowels but he also had trouble with the [English way of] pronouncing Italian consonants: 'Puh' and 'Kuh' and 'Tuh.' In

Italian there is no aspiration on the consonants." White pronounced the Italian word "*appellare*," then added, "Leonard had a very, very fine ear. When I showed him what I meant, he was able to pick it up as if he were playing an instrument."

Asked exactly how Warren learned, White said, "When we were alone, we would read the texts through in French or German or Italian—all the parts. He took his pencil and wrote down everything, word for word, in English. He was very meticulous about picking out the accent of the words, the sounds of the vowels, and especially the consonants." Warren also made White go over his roles with him before each performance,

> even if he sang three or four times a week. Several days before the performance, I would come to the house and we would go over everything, from start to finish. Then I would also go to rehearsals. During rehearsals, Leonard insisted on having as many props available as possible. This caused a problem because if you have props, you have to have a stagehand there to pass them to you. This ran up the costs, but he insisted and got his way. He was completely professional.

White, who was allowed to stand in the wings during the performances, said:

> I never saw any sign of nerves. Before he went onstage, he was as cold as a fish. In those days, though, he was always cordial toward his colleagues. He loved Jussi Björling and particularly liked Salvatore Baccaloni, the great comic basso. After performances, Leonard liked to go to a restaurant, where he would sometimes sing. He loved to sing when he was with friends.

Some time after his first meeting with White, Warren briefly rented a studio in the Hotel Buckingham on Fifty-seventh Street and Sixth Avenue, an apartment hotel that, like the Wellington at Fifty-fifth Street, catered to many professional musicians. The Buckingham's most popular long-term tenant was Martinelli, whose assistant had shared a stateroom with Warren on the way to Italy in 1938. It was perhaps shortly after this that Warren began to be friendly with the genial Baccaloni, who joined the Met in the 1940–1941 season and lived nearby. After Warren and Agatha married, White conducted their sessions in their small apartment at 305 Lexington Avenue. White recalled the newlyweds' making room for the electric trains, which they pushed under the bed when guests came. White was also the Warrens' guest after the end of World War II in their country home in Connecticut and visited them after 1951, when they were among the first tenants of Manhattan House on East Sixty-sixth Street. White remembered Warren as a generous, amusing man, sometimes given to practical jokes and vocal stunts. One day after White and Warren began their sessions, Tarrasch was also there. On impulse, White said to Warren, "You know, you could be a tenor." That was not the first time Warren had been told that, for Henry Schroeder had believed all along that Warren had a nimble tenor voice in his throat. In response, Warren boasted that he could sing Rodolfo's aria, "Che gelida manina" from *La bohème*. Tarrasch gave him the correct pitch, and Warren, to show off, "lay on the floor on his belly, with his head up like a fish" and sang the whole aria with Tarrasch accompanying him. According to White, "He held the high C of 'la speranza' for so long I could not believe it. . . . He did it just to show me he could do it." Warren also sang "Di quella pira" in the original key, but only when he was with friends.

Of Warren's most important roles, White found Rigoletto his best characterization. He said:

> It was the emotion [and] his involvement that made it great. Leonard was a man who was not an intellectual. He was not a thinker. He was psychologically involved and certainly not interested in theories. The more he intellectualized a role, the more ineffective he would have been. Spontaneity was the source of his richness. He was fascinated by the music, and completely involved in the character's emotions, the basic, human emotions. He knew how to translate them into sound.

As for Warren's coaching for the physical aspects of his early roles, he was first taught action by the independent Picozzi, then briefed by Désiré Defrère, occasionally by Armando Agnini and other directors. White described Warren's acting as that of someone who

> had the spontaneous and right reactions onstage. His actions were a reaction to what others did, a reaction to their feelings. From them he derived the authenticity of his own actions. He was always very conscious of his partners' actions onstage. He was an instinctive actor— not intellectual at all—but a man who had gut reactions to what was going on onstage. Leonard was born for the stage. Onstage was where he was most comfortable. He was not born for the parlor. He was born for the stage. When he was onstage, he was the *real* Leonard Warren. He was born for the stage and for the emotions of the stage.

Comparing Warren with Tibbett, White said, "Tibbett's voice was not as beautiful as Leonard's, but he had a strong personality that added to that voice. Tibbett was never just a voice *per se*." Of the great Italian baritone Tito Gobbi, White said he was "much more intellectual than Warren, but he never had the voice of Warren." White felt that Enzo Mascherini, who came to the Metropolitan in 1949–1950, was "a peasant, there to sing his aria, and nothing more." Giuseppe Valdengo, an Italian baritone who sang at the Met from 1947 to 1954 and was favored by Arturo Toscanini, had a voice that was "brighter than Mascherini's but not as strong as Warren's." White felt Warren's voice meshed best with those of Renata Tebaldi, Tucker, and Björling, "but Björling was the best match. Warren also interacted well with Mario Del Monaco, but only with the most dramatic part of Del Monaco's voice. Warren's voice was like a beautiful instrument; he was a natural singer. The brilliance of his voice, the beauty of it, were not easily matched."

Old and New Roles: 1939–1940

When the new season opened, it was clear that the Met management was bringing Warren along very slowly. He sang Paolo in the revival of *Simon Boccanegra* on 27 November, with Tibbett, Elisabeth Rethberg, Martinelli, and Pinza. The next day, two important New York critics took note of Warren's performance. One was Olin Downes, who wrote in the *New York Times* about "the excellent singing of Edward (*sic*) Warren" and his "exceptional talent." Oscar Thompson in the *Sun* found him "materially improved over last year" as a "stage personage" and said, "The young American's singing was such as to prophesy important progress in him in time to come." *Boris* was repeated with his rarely successful and occasionally criticized Rangoni. Pelletier helped him learn Valentin in *Faust*. One brief review called him "admirable." The Met continued to cast him in this role for many years, but he had to work hard to master French style.

Warren's first venture in the German repertory came with the Herald in *Lohengrin* on 3 January 1940. Kirsten Flagstad headed the cast as Elsa, while Lauritz Melchior sang the title role. Although, as John White said, Leinsdorf was sure Warren would eventually become a great Wagnerian, nothing further came of those hopes. Many years later Warren told an interviewer how miserable he had been during the rehearsals and first performance. He said he then decided on his own to sing it "in my own way, in the way that made me happy," in an Italian style. When he did that, on impulse and without telling Leinsdorf of changes he intended to make, the conductor was furious. He came up to Warren after the performance and cursed at him for ruining the opera and his reputation as a conductor. Vivien said Leinsdorf shouted at her brother, saying, "You destroyed the opera. If you ever sing like that again, it will be the last time you sing with me. You have to keep to the style we rehearsed." In other interviews Warren said he found the Wagner roles too low for him, although the "lowest two or three notes" were actually in his range. If he persisted in singing Wagner, he said, he felt he would lower his voice, losing the notes at the top. Without them, he would be forced out of the Verdi repertory.

Two solid assignments fell to Warren later that season, when Johnson cast him as Amonasro in his first *Aida*, a student performance, and Barnaba in his first *La Gioconda*. Hearing Warren in these two roles, so suited to his voice, the Met management, the critics, and the audience began to understand that an ambitious young baritone was gradually emerging in the Italian wing. Some New York critics never failed to write about his vocal progress and great natural gifts, but several times his weaknesses showed. Warren was often faulted for excessive volume and forcing; his four-square characterizations also drew the critics' fire. Paul Jackson, in *Saturday Afternoons at the Old Met*, said his Rangoni in the *Boris Godunov* broadcast of 9 December 1939 was "strong-voiced" and "dark-hued." As the Herald in the *Lohengrin* broadcast of 27 January 1940 he had "big, bright tones," although Jackson found some fault with the baritone's effort. A later *Lohengrin*, on 17 January 1942, evidently showed why Warren infuriated Leinsdorf by infusing the Herald's lines with Italian panache, for Jackson compared Warren's "slightly overblown pronouncements" unfavorably with Herbert Janssen's "authentic German style." Reviewing several early broadcasts, Jackson also seemed uneasy with Warren's self-consciousness. In two performances of *Faust*, Warren was hailed for his "sheer vocalism" and "noble" phrasing, his "rich tones mounting with absolute ease to the top Gs" and "splendid subtleties," although Jackson found that his "burly tone robs the line of French elegance." Warren's Escamillo in the 15 March 1941 *Carmen* radiated "star quality splendidly," but a repeat of the role on 24 January 1942 showed him "stolid in inflection but bright in song." His attempts at head voice showed him a "conscientious, if unfinished, artist." These evaluations are not unlike Warren's reviews in the New York papers and others outside the city.

In the spring of 1940, Warren was chosen to sing in the first televised Metropolitan Opera performance in history, a concert on 10 March. Broadcast from the NBC Television Studio in Radio City, it could have been received by just over two thousand television sets in and close to New York. The best-known piece on the program was the quartet from *Rigoletto*, which Warren sang with the Italian coloratura Hilde Reggiani, Bruna Castagna, and the tenor Frederick Jagel. Warren's "Largo al factotum" shared the rest of the program with excerpts from other operas. Two selections from *Carmen* were Micaëla's aria, sung by Albanese, and Castagna's "Habanera." The program was completed by Jagel's "Cielo e mar!" from *Gioconda* and excerpts from Act I of *Pagliacci*, sung by Burke, Armand Tokatyan, Bonelli, Cehanovsky, and De Paolis. Johnson served as master of ceremonies while St. Leger conducted the NBC Orchestra.

Early Recordings: May and June 1940

It was Pelletier who made possible Warren's recordings in 1940. The executives of the New York *Post* asked Pelletier to conduct French and Italian operas for a series of recordings sponsored by some of the nation's newspapers through the Publishers Service Company of New York. No artists' names appeared on the labels of the records.

On the VAI Audio recording (excerpts reissued on CD in 1992), young Warren's voice was impressive in the measured Prologue from *Pagliacci*, where one can hear his mastery in broadening a *pianissimo* note or a whole phrase from a thread to a generous forte. The carefully spun vocalism on "Un nido di memorie" was as fine as the resounding climax that ended the aria. He delivered a rough-and-ready "Toreador Song," sung with chorus. One scene from *La traviata* included the duet "Pura siccome un angelo" from Act II, Scene 1, and ended with "Dite alla giovine." Eleanor Steber, then twenty-six, sang Violetta to Warren's Germont. She was being welcomed to the Metropolitan as the most recent of Pelletier's finds, having won the Auditions of the Air a few weeks earlier. Her scheduled Met debut was planned for December. In spite of the beauty of Warren's and Steber's voices and her careful phrasing in this track, the Violetta-Germont duet remained emotionally thin. The large ensemble with chorus from Flora's party was brought to life by Warren's dignified denunciation; Tokatyan's appropriately contrite Alfredo was lyrical. Here Steber's silvery soprano line, although somewhat confined by Pelletier's rigid tempos, soared above the other voices, clearly foreshadowing her later triumphs as a great American artist.

Much less impressive was the first of the 1940 *Rigoletto* selections on the VAI CD, which included an undistinguished and hard-driven opening scene from Act I, Scene 1, with Warren in the title role and Tokatyan as the Duke. Warren's next track, "Cortigiani, vil razza dannata," made a fine display of his full fury and despair. After a bad start, "Tutte le feste al tempio" became serious and coherent as Warren and Jean Dickenson (Gilda) took fire. The baritone's conviction, command of phrase, and emotional gear-shifting at the words "Piangi, piangi" were worthy of a singer much more mature than Warren was in 1940; at the phrase "Un vindice avrai," he was in full cry. In the quartet from the last act, "Bella figlia dell'amore," Dickenson and Tokatyan, two light voices, were joined by the mezzo-soprano Lucielle Browning, a routine Maddalena, and Warren, who easily dominated the voices and the orchestral fabric. Two excerpts from *Aida* featured a limpid young Bampton in the title role and Warren as a menacing Amonasro. Notwithstanding his inexperience and the somewhat uneven quality of the tracks, many dramatic moments sent signals about his full-throated vocalism and his interpretations.

Leaving New York City

Soon after the New York *Post* recordings were made and the Metropolitan Opera closed its season, Warren set off for his first operatic appearance away from New York. In late June 1940, he left to join one of America's oldest and best-loved companies, the open-air Cincinnati Summer Opera at the Zoo,

where Bampton had sung in 1938. The informal atmosphere proved com-
forting for an inexperienced artist such as Warren. Part of the Cincinnati
Zoo's charm and many of its perennial aggravations came from the proxim-
ity of the stage to the cages of lions, tigers, and squawking exotic birds, adding
their voices to the musical event. Between the 1920s and 1940, the company
had drawn leading singers from New York, the Chicago Opera, and even foreign companies. But just before World War II, the Cincinnati Summer Opera
became known as "the summer Met."

Warren's first performance in Cincinnati was the opening of the season,
an *Aida* on 30 June. Bampton repeated her Aida there. Arthur Carron, the
Auditions of the Air winner who had appeared with Warren in Met Opera
concerts, was Radamès. Bruna Castagna, a Cincinnati Zoo favorite, sang
Amneris; Nicola Moscona, the Greek bass, sang Ramfis; the King was the
Hungarian Lorenzo Alvary. It was an all-Met cast, with Cleva conducting.
John P. Rhodes, reviewing the event for the Cincinnati *Enquirer*, had high
praise for the "brilliant" voices, with Castagna and Bampton heading his column. The newspaper also ran a photo of Warren, standing in his dressing
room door, towering over two men from the ballet, and wearing a real leopard skin. Vivien said it was a gift from their father. "Jungle-cut summer
wear," the writer commented.

Warren returned to the East Coast to sing in another *Aida*, again in an
open-air theatre, the Robin Hood Dell in Philadelphia. There the Aida was a
winning, lissome soprano, Rosa Tentoni, who sang with the Met, Chicago,
and Cincinnati companies. Carron was again the Radamès, and Enid Szánthó
sang Amneris. Alexander Smallens, whom Warren had first met during the
Sealtest competition, conducted. After these spring and summer engagements,
the baritone had about six weeks to begin study for his new roles; he then set
out for his first foreign performances.

Opera Puerto Rico

Warren sang his first engagement outside the continental United States under
the auspices of Giorgio D'Andria, a glib, resourceful impresario who operated
out of a studio in Carnegie Hall. The productions, mounted at the University
Auditorium, were sponsored by the Pro Arte Musical de Puerto Rico for its
1940 festival. The stage director was Defrère, whose wife, Hilda Burke, was
engaged for Nedda. Warren was under contract for three operas and was also
the artist-in-reserve for Francesco Valentino, who sang Rigoletto. Sailing from
New York on the liner *Cherokee* with D'Andria and several members of the
company, Warren arrived in San Juan early in mid-September for rehearsals.
The whole troupe lodged at the Hotel Condado.

Warren made his San Juan debut on 26 September 1940 as Count di Luna
in Verdi's *Il trovatore*. The conductor was Angelo Canarutto, who also

worked at the Chicago Opera and the Met and later became Richard Tucker's coach and accompanist. Again Carron was the tenor. Leonora was Delphina Samoiloff, a prima donna from the Teatro dell'Opera, the royal theatre in Rome, while Azucena was a young Chicago-born mezzo, Eleanor Longone. The dependable bass Nino Ruisi, a pillar of the Chicago Opera, sang Ferrando. Writing in English for the *World Journal*, Dwight W. Hiestand left no doubt about his feelings when he wrote of Warren, "His is unquestionably one of the finest voices of the present time, a voice of tremendous power and range, yet susceptible to fine modulations. His 'Il balen' stopped the show." Jose A. Balseiro, the critic of *El Mundo*, praised Warren's "very energetic realization" of the role. "His voice is powerful, beautiful, very well placed. . . . He really is a great young baritone."

Warren's second role in San Juan was Germont in *La traviata* on 28 September. The conductor was László Halász, who had also been assigned Valentino's *Rigoletto*; later he became the founding music director of New York City Opera and headed the company until 1952. The Met soprano Helen Jepson was Violetta. She and Nino Martini, the dashing tenor, had a high glamour quotient, but neither satisfied Balseiro. He dismissed Martini as a handsome, passable concert singer and mediocre Alfredo who often sang flat. Jepson, he found, could not negotiate Violetta's difficult first-act aria. Once more, Warren was singled out for praise. "Warren is not a singer who forces; he is not out of control. He follows a sober line, with well-contained emotion, which [he uses] to express his state of mind with sincerity, clarity and good taste. And he manages to instill an authentic human warmth in his role." Hiestand found Warren's Germont "excellent," calling him "the phenomenal baritone" who "nearly walked off with the whole show."

Tonio in *Pagliacci* was Warren's last assignment on the island. Hiestand compared him to Tibbett but handed Warren laurels of his own. Writing in the *World Journal*, the critic claimed that he had "stopped the show" with his "marvelous rendition of the Prologue. . . . He was a very fine actor throughout the opera." Balseiro, again in *El Mundo*, compared Warren's Tonio to that of Titta Ruffo, devoting more than two hundred words of his column to him.

Warren's first engagement in San Juan had shown him how quickly he could become a star in a Latin culture, where his big voice was an asset and his youth and stolid stage presence were not liabilities. When Warren arrived back in New York, a recording contract with the RCA Manufacturing Company gave him further validation of his progress. Dated 26 September 1940, it offered Warren a one-year commitment and a minimum of four recordings "or more, if the Company so desires." His royalty would be ten percent of the retail list price; a clause was added covering sales in England and "elsewhere." This began Warren's long affiliation with RCA Victor, which endured until his death. Warren's most remarkable early recording was Ford's monologue,

"È sogno? O realta?" from *Falstaff*. Years later when George Marek, a vice-president of RCA Victor, asked Irving Kolodin to select nine favorite little-known recordings for a *Critic's Choice* album, Kolodin chose Warren's 1941 interpretation of Ford's monologue and wrote, "Such abundance of sound is certainly appropriate to the distracted Ford's monologue, but when does one hear it? The answer: this recording." Some of Warren's other early recordings attracted important critical attention when they were released; and even decades later, they kept their luster. From his first professional work, recorded when he was twenty-eight, to his last releases, Warren proved an invaluable asset to RCA Victor. His contracts were duly renewed, covering him for all the years of his career.

The Three-Year Marker

Warren's next important season as a full-fledged Met artist began with a Sunday night concert on 8 December 1940, which was soon followed by his first Escamillo in *Carmen* on 18 December, a Metropolitan Opera Guild performance for more than three thousand school children. Pelletier conducted while Swarthout sang the title role. Some major critics took little note of Warren, preferring to devote their columns to the students' clothes and their boisterous outburst at the end of the opera. However, Kolodin, writing in the *Sun*, and Robert Bagar in the *World-Telegram*, mentioned him. Grena Bennett of the *Journal-American* praised the "robust-voiced Escamillo," while the critic of the New York *Staats-Zeitung* commented on his style and vocal heft. Edward O'Gorman, in the *Post*, described a "fledgling" who was "moderately successful in his first attempt at the part."

On Christmas Day in 1940, Warren aroused only faint interest with his Valentin in *Faust*, which was plagued by "lagging" and "inertia" and again conducted by Pelletier. In the *Tribune*, Jerome D. Bohm praised Warren's "rich baritone voice" but noted that it "needs a more concentrated projection to make the most of its considerable potentialities. Had his tones been more 'pointed,' his singing would have carried greater conviction." No one was spared by the reviewers, neither the popular Jepson, who lacked the "technical virtuosity" for Marguerite, nor Björling, who cracked on high C, nor Moscona, a "leaden, gray-voiced and unimaginative" bass. Warren sang a total of twenty-two performances of *Faust* at the Met and three with other companies, leaving the role behind in 1951.

His first Alfio in *Cavalleria rusticana* came on 9 January 1941; it was a role he sang only six times in his career. He followed it with his first High Priest of Apollo in Gluck's *Alceste* later that month. This production, a rendering of "Franco-German Greece," as Virgil Thomson dubbed it, featured the Australian soprano Marjorie Lawrence. Her singing was "entirely below par" and off pitch. René Maison showed "good schooling and sense" but otherwise found scant favor. Panizza, who conducted, won high praise. Walter Terry wrote in the *Herald Tribune* that it "would be hard to imagine worse choreography and worse dancing" than the Met offered in *Alceste*. In the *New York Times* of 25 January, Olin Downes declared that Warren, as the High Priest, "sang the part with unctuousness and a voice that carried, but brassily, for he pushed his tone." Even the critic of *Variety* faulted him because "he unnecessarily forced his sufficiently powered voice past the requirements of his part." Thompson, writing for the *Sun*, criticized the ballet's "near-ridiculous goings-on" and said of Warren that he "gave more voice than style." In the *World-Telegram* Pitts Sanborn advised the baritone to revise his *Alceste* makeup and costume and improve his vocal delivery before the next performance. Virgil Thomson, ever the loyal admirer of Warren, said, "Of the singers, only Mr. Warren was really satisfactory. He was quite fine." Out of town, John Haughton of the Baltimore *Morning Sun* thought Warren did "the best singing in the performance." He also had kind words for Lawrence's "sincere effort" but lamented her uneven singing and shrill high notes. He was stunned to see a copy of the Apollo Belvedere from the Vatican used as the statue of the god in the temple scene, "fig-leaf and all. When one realizes that the legend deals with pre-Adamite antiquity and that the statue in question is of the Hellenic period, (with foliage added by a Pope of the sixteenth century), the thing became laughable."

References to Warren's excessive volume were common in those early years. Fairly typical were the words of Noel Straus, who reviewed *Lohengrin* in the *New York Times* in February and accused him of blasting "stentorian sounds, not always too well focused." A different criticism was aimed at him in a March review of that opera. Jerome D. Bohm found that Warren had "sufficient weight to lend the appropriate accents to the Herald's music, but his topmost tones wanted brilliancy." Here was a charge rarely aimed at Warren. Bohm also launched a broad attack upon Rethberg's Elsa, writing regretfully that only "in scattered measures her tones in full voice recalled their former shimmering transparency." He added that she sang with poor focus and was frequently off pitch. Warren was always sensitive to criticism, whether directed at him or colleagues he liked. Vivien said, "He sometimes seemed near tears when people criticized or corrected him. But he was also bent on self-improvement. He swallowed the criticism and strove to do better the next time. Only rarely did he make unkind remarks about critics." She said he took most bad reviews in stride, saying, "Every knock is a boost."

In that same season, Licia Albanese's Micaëla and Warren's Escamillo saved *Carmen*. Thomson criticized Warren's acting but praised his voice. It was "distinguished and beautiful. As Escamillo he neither looked nor even pretended to act the part; but oh, how beautifully he sang! What vigor of musical line! What refreshing variety of *demi-teints*! What constantly accurate resonance, at all times placed in the upper part of the face!" This was his second Escamillo at the Met. Swarthout as Carmen was credited with a "warm and beautiful and friendly voice" but was faulted as "jolly" and "athletic," a Carmen who "grins all the time . . . and has about as much sex-appeal as a Chesterfield cigarette advertisement."

Albanese, the fresh young Italian soprano, got a fine review. Having arrived in the United States on New Year's Day of 1940, she soon became friendly with Warren. "Pais taught him how to create an aria, not just sing it the way it is written," Albanese said. In her first and second seasons, she and Warren sang in Sunday evening concerts. After she married Joseph Gimma and Warren married Agatha, the two couples often met for dinner. Albanese recalled Warren fondly:

> I loved him very much. He was such a sweetheart—so warm and affectionate! When I arrived in this country, I heard him singing "in the style of Gatti-Casazza." He sang the Italian way, from the heart. Later, we visited back and forth. Joe loved electric trains, those Lionel trains, so he and Leonard got on famously. My son also had model trains. I remember when Leonard got a new movie camera, and he took movies of all of us. He was clowning around and fell down on the floor, pretending to be hurt. And there was that great quality of voice; even before he sang, the voice was there. He came on softly, not screeching. Soft! He just opened his mouth, and out came those pianissimos!

That spring, if Johnson and his team in the Met management had had to worry only about reviews mocking Swarthout as a Chesterfield Girl, they might have looked to happier times. It was a tradition in the Italian opera business that "Everyone stinks in March": "In marzo tutti fanno schifo." But things always improved by autumn. Indeed the Met management had another, far more serious concern: Tibbett's alcoholism, which a summer's rest apparently could not cure. The possibility of losing the international celebrity left the Johnson team with a serious dilemma. George Cehanovsky, a reliable source, said Tibbett's "vocal difficulties" began in 1938 in Cincinnati, where he sang *Rigoletto* with Lily Pons in the open-air theatre. "He was never himself again," Cehanovsky declared. According to Tibbett's biographers, he had also given a local manager in Australia cause for concern about his drinking in 1938. The first months of 1940 marked the beginning of his real decline, as he fought dryness in his throat and a choked quality in his voice. His top notes cracked. There were moments when he simply could not sing at all. Tibbett considered canceling all engagements after the spring and summer of 1940. He had a long bout of what Downes called "indisposition" just at the start of the 1940–1941 season. By January and February, he was coping with unsteadiness, vocal blackouts, and pitch problems, wrestling with a heavy schedule of Iago, Tonio, and Rigoletto. In *The American Opera*

Singer, Peter G. Davis called Tibbett's voice "veiled and unwieldy" in an *Otello* broadcast in January. Downes, writing in the *New York Times*, called his "Sì, vendetta" in *Rigoletto* "insufficient." Oscar Straus remarked on tones that were "hollow and lacking in body." Tibbett's biographers heard trouble with the Prologue of *Pagliacci* on 1 February, where he shared the stage with Norina Greco as Nedda and Martinelli as Canio; he was "completely authoritative" in the rest of the opera but "not the Larry of the past." When Tibbett reached New Orleans with the Metropolitan spring tour in *Pagliacci* in April, one critic had the courage to bring the issue out into the open. He lamented Tibbett's vocal ruin, saying that his "glorious voice has rung out in the past" but his Tonio that season was barely acceptable. "It is hoped that this was only an unusually bad night for Mr. Tibbett and that in the future he will do better by us." Unfortunately, he did not always "do better," although he still had many gripping performances in his future. However, in his Cincinnati Summer Opera seasons of 1945 and 1946, Tibbett's voice had a harsh quality, and his alcoholism continued to be a major problem in the free-wheeling environment at the Zoo.

An unmatched opportunity presented itself to young baritones. Among the Americans who might have emerged as Tibbett's successor were Bonelli, a native of New York State; the Colorado-born Francesco Valentino; and the two former Radio City Music Hall performers, Weede and Warren. Bonelli continued in his sometimes brilliant and often stolid way. Valentino proved to be good and reliable. Of them all, Warren showed the most promise, as he gradually became an American original, not just "a second Tibbett," a title he scorned.

In the 1930s Warren had begun to collect photographs of his famous colleagues. Among them was Tibbett, who gave him an autographed portrait with a cordial expression of good wishes. In the 1940s the two men often saw each other backstage at the Met, where Tibbett remained a vital force and was even considered for the post of general manager when Johnson retired. After that, Tibbett and Warren saw very little of each other. They met again on the first night of the new production of *Simon Boccanegra* of March 1960. Warren was then singing the title role. Joseph G. Chisholm, a young fan who had met Warren several years earlier, recalled that evening. He went backstage after the performance and was waiting outside Warren's dressing room. "I heard footsteps on the stairs and saw Tibbett coming up. I had also seen him in the theatre earlier that evening. He knocked on Warren's door and put his head in, saying, 'Hello, Leonard. Remember me?'" Chisholm said the two men were together "no more than two minutes" before Tibbett came out. Tibbett's appearance had changed so drastically in his retirement years that in fact Warren did not recognize him at first. Vivien also remembered Tibbett's brief visit. She said her brother was resting after the performance and that when he opened the door, he "saw a man he did not recognize."

Hertzel Weinstat and Bert Wechsler, Tibbett's biographers, describe his long battle with alcoholism and the toll it took on him. They said that his condition deteriorated significantly after his close friend Betty Fox committed suicide in January 1960. Tibbett died on 15 July that year, four months after this last meeting with Warren.

✦ CHAPTER EIGHT

Solid Ground

Sometime before 1940, Warren changed management, leaving Louis Nizer, Bert Green Warenoff, and the WOR Artists Bureau. He chose Columbia Concerts, Inc., America's largest agency for classical music. First with the division called Haensel and Jones, and later with Mertens, Parmelee, and Brown, another division of Columbia, he began singing recitals and concerts on the North American circuit. Columbia, with its prestige, dominated the field; its nearest competitor was National Concerts and Artists, Inc.; later Sol Hurok became the czar of the arts wars. Columbia and NCAC (as National was called) shaped public taste to a remarkable degree through their tight control of the concert circuit. These well-organized events were the main musical fare of small cities, where opera rarely played. Columbia handled its artists under its Community Concerts umbrella, while NCAC oversaw Civic Music Association events.

The New York management agencies organized some engagements with major orchestras in large halls; others were offered in civic or high school auditoriums, some of which held only three or four hundred people. When an orchestra was involved, the soloist had to allow an extra day for rehearsal in the scheduled city. But even for a solo recital, the local presenter and the management agency wanted the artist to arrive a full day ahead and attend social functions scheduled around the recital, a luncheon, or a late evening supper. The Met also put pressure on its singers to appear where its own tour would later play. These concert tours were exhausting but necessary, unless the singer were rich enough to pick and choose the dates and sites. Singers, supported by accompanists whom they had to pay, tried to do two tours a year, fall and spring, about twenty concerts each, with an average of three events a week. For decades before Warren got to the Met, stars such as Maria Jeritza, Rosa Ponselle, Lucrezia Bori, Lawrence Tibbett, and John Charles Thomas had rarely accepted engagements in small places, although they all sang for important presenters in big cities.

For young artists like Warren, concerts and recitals became a matter of financial necessity if they were to keep their careers going. Never offered a choice of cities and towns, they were given their itineraries by their managers, with their contracts often tied to those of other performers under the same agency. Under these "tie-ins," a manager would sell an important singer or instrumentalist only if the local presenter accepted one or more of the manager's lesser artists as well. In practice this meant that from the beginning of their careers, young singers were caught in a web of managers' relationships that snaked across North America. Just preparing these concert tours added hours of work and expense to the singers' budget. Under some contracts they had to pay for publicity brochures, flyers, press photographs (head shots and candids), and postage, and also had to pay the accompanist's transportation, food, and lodging. Some unscrupulous managers asked for kickbacks, illegal commissions charged under the rubrics of "postage" or "printing."

On the road, the singer and the accompanist always stayed in the same hotel. During Warren's early career, he and his accompanist even shared the same room to save money. Too often the accompanist also served as errand boy and secretary; in 1944, when Warren came down with pneumonia in New Orleans, his accompanist took him to the hospital. With their tightly packed schedule, the singer and the accompanist traveled from one city or town to another, almost always by train. A neophyte on the concert circuit traveled in coach class when possible or booked two berths. Even for a train buff like Warren, this was an uncomfortable way to travel. Trains rocked along over rough lines. They were dirty, pulled by coal-fed steam locomotives that belched smoke and black soot particles into the coaches and sleeping cars. In winter, the passengers were hot; the dining car and club car were filled with smoke; and in summer, open windows provided the only ventilation. Yet for decades singers had to travel in these circumstances. And so it was with Warren, during his concert season and the opera tours, until diesel engines came and air travel became an alternative. Local facilities also presented a challenge. A recital before four hundred people in a high school auditorium could become a real *mano a mano*, where a barely elevated stage put the seated audience right in the singer's face. The piano was often badly tuned, as singers regularly complained to their managers. Technical facilities were so poor that some singers carried their own footlights with them.

Yet Warren emerged as early as 1940 as a serious recitalist. Genial with the audience in spite of his reserved character, he won people over, almost at sight, although Vivien said that recital deportment troubled him at first. Warren thought he seemed stiff and awkward in recitals, where he had no operatic stage business, costumes, wigs, and props to fall back on. Vivien said he never knew what to do with his hands. At home, he practiced a variety of things, holding a piece of paper in his fist, putting his hands in his pockets, clutching his lapels, or leaning against the piano. He finally arrived at his own solution, she said. He stood firm and let his voice and face convey his message. Still, Warren had to work hard to conquer the recital field. During his entire operatic career, he was dependent on cues, always insisting that prompters pass him the words as he sang. In concerts and recitals, in the days when singers always memorized their programs, he was unable to lean on a prompter, and this made him uneasy. It is very much to his credit that he quickly became a favorite of local presenters whose many letters to Columbia Concerts prove his popularity. Soon he was regularly singing around fifty concerts a year; in the war years, when he was singing for the USO, he tallied up even more.

Many of his earliest reviews outside the Met show how good he was on the small stage. Journalists discovered in him a simple American artist utterly without mannerisms and airs. In Ohio in 1940 for a concert with the Cleveland Summer Programs, Warren entertained a local feature writer over breakfast in his hotel. "Been here twelve times," the baritone volunteered to a reporter from the *News* as he recalled his Amonasro and Barnaba from the 1940 Met tour. The writer was surprised to hear Warren say he "had none of the cultural training that is the background of most opera singers." He admitted that he had not attended conservatory and had studied voice for only a short time before the Auditions of the Air. In fact, he was remarkably outspoken about his tribulations. At the height of the Great Depression, he said, "I'd been singing with a glee club in Radio City Music Hall; and since my own business was going wrong, I thought I'd try this singing business." When asked how the two compared, he pointed to his plate of ham and eggs and replied, "Well, look, I'm doing all right." In the course of this interview, Warren also stressed the need for more good works by contemporary composers. "Let the English and American composers give us something good, [and] we'll sing it." He felt that American composers had not "made the grade" in the classical world. "Gershwin, yes, symphonically." He also praised Roy Harris and "some of the younger writers." Warren followed the career of this Oklahoma native who had entered the University of California in Berkeley before moving to Paris to study with Nadia Boulanger. Harris's reputation grew, and in the middle and late years of the 1930s, he had become a famous American symphonist.

Early reviews also give a fair idea of how successful Warren was in concert with a full orchestra. He got headlines in the San Antonio *Express* on 14 November 1940 for his VOICE AND PERSONALITY. The critic wrote of his appearance with the San Antonio Symphony, which was then conducted by Max Reiter, founder of the San Antonio Opera. After the first group of songs on the program, he had five solo curtain calls; later he sang the "Toreador Song" from *Carmen* and "To the Evening Star" from *Tannhäuser*. The San Antonio *Evening News* critic hailed him as "an established favorite with local audiences" and no longer "a Metropolitan Opera newcomer." "Gracious with encores," he came back with "Drink to Me Only With Thine Eyes,"

Leoncavallo's "Mattinata," Valentin's aria from *Faust*, and Bizet's "magnificent Agnus Dei." The critic called his voice "clear and resonant in its softer passages" but said that it "achieves its peak of performance in the great fortissimo tones that ring out as if they were amplified by microphones."

A good example of how well Warren did in a small town came in the winter of 1940–1941, when he sang in New Hampshire in the Keene High School auditorium under the auspices of the Cooperative Concert Association. He was especially lucky that night because a new Steinway concert grand piano had been provided. His accompanist was Miguel Sandoval. The first group on the program began with Handel's "Thanks Be to Thee," Giuseppe Torelli's "Tu lo sai," and Giovanni Bononcini's "L'esperto nocchiero," followed by "Eri tu" from *Ballo*. His second group began with the "To the Evening Star" from *Tannhäuser* and ended with numbers from *Songs of the Sea* by Sir Charles Villiers Stanford, a composer of opera and symphony who was also a master of the narrative ballad. These were "Drake's Drum," "Outward Bound," and "The Old Superb." Warren sang "Drink to Me Only With Thine Eyes" as an encore before intermission. As was customary, the accompanist then offered a few piano pieces. The fourth group included one unusual selection, "Qui donc commande" from Camille Saint-Saëns's *Henry VIII*, followed by "Vision fugitive" from Jules Massenet's *Hérodiade*, both probably suggested by Pelletier. An old Scottish Highland melody, "Turn Ye to Me," was followed by Roger Quilter's "Go, Lovely Rose," Charles Griffes's "An Old Song Resung," and Bizet's "Agnus Dei." Encores included Figaro's aria from *Il barbiere di Siviglia*; "If You Love Me," a popular song; and Warren's old standby, Franz's "Dedication."

The review of this "brilliant" recital, with its twelve column inches of praise for Warren, gives a fair idea of the effect his programs had on the Community Concerts circuit. A large, imposing figure onstage, he was praised for "singing with simplicity and richness of tone and revealing a beautiful technique." Most notable was his mastery of contrast, when he followed "To the Evening Star" with the sea songs. The "tender delicacy and reverence" of the "Agnus Dei" was wholly convincing. Warren proved equally effective in simple pieces such as Albert Hay Malotte's "The Lord's Prayer," which he also included on his recital programs.

One important concert in Newark in June 1941 featured a variety program that had Warren sharing the stage with Jepson, Edwina Eustis, and Jagel. Frieder Weissmann conducted the Essex County Symphony. In *Carmen* excerpts, Eustis took the title role, Jagel was José, and Warren sang Escamillo. Eustis and Jepson sang the "Barcarolle" from *Les contes d'Hoffmann*; and Warren joined them in the trio, adding "some intelligent vocalism of his own." The Spinning Quartet and the Good Night Quartet from *Martha* were followed by selections from Acts I and II of Verdi's *Otello*. Offered at the Newark Schools Stadium, this event attracted eighteen thousand people.

Warren's Radio City Music Hall experience served him well, simply because he knew what the general public liked to hear. He chose accessible pieces, and his diction was pristine, as reviewers often observed. Warren also won people over during backstage encounters because he had an easygoing rapport with autograph seekers and well-intentioned fans. Good reviews soon began to fill the Columbia Concerts files, leading his agent to book him all across America. In an odd way, his highly personalized, unsophisticated approach to concert audiences seemed to win him as many admirers as his opera roles did. His appeal seemed to depend largely on his unwillingness to intellectualize his programs. No one ever accused Warren of belonging to the effete school of song delivery, for his attitude was straightforward, direct, and physical. Unlike many other American singers, who returned from abroad with affected British accents and who flaunted Continental manners and mannerisms, he never put on airs or tried to conceal what he was: a simple man from the Bronx.

Opera and Concerts in Canada

Pelletier chose Warren as his leading baritone for the five-day opera season he had been asked to organize at the Théâtre St-Denis in Montréal in the autumn of 1941. He was also its leading conductor, with an orchestra made up of Montréal Symphony instrumentalists. The first work on the program, scheduled for 26 September, was *Aida*, which had a sold-out house. Thomas Archer, writing in the *Gazette* on 26 September and again on 1 October, praised it as the "best all-round production of its kind we have seen in this city for many years." That Verdi's Egyptian drama was "of a Metropolitan standard" one can easily believe, for Bampton sang the title role, while the Radamès was Martinelli; Norman Cordon sang Ramfis, the High Priest. As Amneris, Anna Kaskas revealed great "personal beauty" and used her voice with "intelligence and grace." Warren ran away with the review. "Vocal honors belonged to Leonard Warren. This is a gorgeous baritone, dramatic in quality, supple and with a great range. [He] manages his voice so that he can sing softly and lightly as well as give his audience the full benefit of a singularly rich organ." *Carmen* was "the greatest of them all" for an audience whose "old-timers" had seen the Bizet work a hundred times. Warren sang Escamillo to the Carmen of Jennie Tourel. Tokatyan, who also sang Des Grieux in *Manon*, was less than successful as Don José. Lillian Raymondi, a "very youthful Metropolitan Auditions Winner," sang Micaëla. As one might expect, Tourel, a stunning artist, won superlative praise, but the critic admitted, "The ovation of the evening went to Leonard Warren for a magnificent, swaggering Escamillo. Here was a Toreador with a gorgeous voice and a real chest measurement [to match]. You really believed [in his] extraordinarily natural performance, unique in its way. And this in spite of the fact that the vocal part lies a little low for Mr.

Warren." In *Une symphonie inachevée*, Pelletier wrote about this important season, the last before the United States entered World War II in 1941.

While Warren was in Canada, Community Concerts also arranged for him to sing a recital for the Société des Concerts in Sherbrooke. Milford Snell, on whom the baritone depended for several years, was his accompanist. Again with Valentin's aria from *Faust* and the Toreador Song, Warren faced the challenge of singing in French in the new and untested auditorium of Christ-Roi church. To his credit, he won unstinting praise from the critic of the French newspaper *La Tribune*; he hailed him as a "remarkable singer, with a rich and supple voice." His *Songs of the Sea* went over particularly well, but the critic said that his greatest success was in the "Italian music" that he "interpreted rigorously and faithfully." The English-language reviewer headlined his column with LEONARD WARREN THRILLED AUDIENCE. He had a "grand and truly magnificent baritone voice." One fine touch was Warren's rendition of Handel's "Thanks Be to Thee," sung on Canada's Thanksgiving Day. Pelletier probably deserves credit for the singer's excellent French, demonstrated in arias from *Carmen* and *Hérodiade* and the stunning "Scintille, diamant" from *Les contes d'Hoffmann*. Warren closed the program with a simple Irish air. These were the first of his many appearances in Canada, where he later drew a large following of dedicated fans in many cities. Among them was his strong supporter Helen Hatton, who was then a teenager. She later became a professor at the University of Toronto. From his very first engagements there, audiences developed a particular loyalty to him.

An Important North American Tour

The autumn schedule in 1941 also included concerts and recitals that took Warren from Canada and the East Coast into the heart of Kansas, Nebraska, and Wyoming, always with Snell at his side. In reviews of these events, Warren won high praise from a variety of critics. In Norfolk, Virginia, his "excellent voice" impressed the audience, especially when he led it in "The Star Spangled Banner" at the end of his program. In Cleveland, he appeared in a "pop" concert under the direction of Rudolph Ringwald. He got twelve column inches of print in October for a Community Concert recital, reviewed in the Battle Creek *Enquirer News*. Its critic wrote of "a considerable triumph for the young singer," although "too much horsing around" marred the "Toreador Song." In Cheyenne, the reviewer for the *State Leader* called his recital "one of the most beautiful and satisfying ever heard here." Warren's *pianissimo* passages were "threads of exquisite beauty. The tones were so soft but clear that the audience scarcely moved, so as not to miss a note." He wisely cut back on power to avoid swamping the acoustics of a junior high school auditorium.

Warren and Snell functioned well as a team, whether on the stage or in joint interviews. Warren again delighted in describing his trains, the "three engines, twenty-one cars, yards of track and all the accessories." He admitted he did not know how to play any instrument. And Snell chimed in, saying, "If he can play an instrument, he has kept it from me." Not the least on the defensive, the baritone swore he would not apologize for his inability to play. He believed it was "better to do one thing well," he said. "I work six days a week from nine in the morning until ten at night. Even after one sings the same thing over a thousand times, one can still improve by studying and practicing." When he and Snell did this interview in Lincoln in November 1941, Warren said he had already memorized twenty-eight operas. He and Snell had arrived in Lincoln on a Saturday at midnight; they did their scheduled recital and were planning to leave on Tuesday at eleven in the morning for Ottawa, Kansas. From there they would go on to Newark, Ohio, to perform their sixteenth and last program. From Ohio they started back to New York, so Warren could begin his scheduled rehearsals at the Met. He also expected to make recordings for RCA in December.

Fitted into the middle of Warren's recital tours were wartime USO camp shows, which he did under a contract with the government that included "travel overseas," to "provide entertainment for the Armed Forces of the United States." He took the required oaths, signed the necessary releases, obtained clearances from the War Department, and set out. His first scheduled appearances were with the soprano Agnes Davis, the cellist Ana Drittelle, and the pianist-accompanist Carolyn Gray. To set the tone, the pianist opened with Gershwin's "Rhapsody in Blue," followed by the soprano's first-act aria from *La bohème*, Schubert's "Ave Maria," and "Thine Alone" by Victor Herbert. Drittelle played three cello solos and provided an obbligato to the Schubert and to "The Lord's Prayer," which Warren sang. His other numbers were "Captain Mac," Figaro's aria from *Il barbiere di Siviglia*, and two soprano-baritone duets with Davis, "Là ci darem la mano" from *Don Giovanni* and "Will You Remember?" from Sigmund Romberg's *Maytime*.

Warren appeared at bond rallies and sang more than thirty wartime concerts in camps and hospitals for the USO on Navy and Coast Guard bases in the United States and in the Caribbean. Among his USO events were concerts in Puerto Rico in 1943, where he sang for soldiers stationed there. Included on this tour were Camp O'Reilly, Ramey Field, Fort Buchanan, and Lossy Field in Ponce. His accompanist was the distinguished Puerto Rican pianist Jesús María Sanromá. Angel Armada, a soldier who later shared his recollections with journalist Jesús M. López, remembered how popular Warren was with the troops. Among his standard USO program numbers were "Largo al factotum," "Danny Boy," "Over the Rainbow," and "Over There." Later he received a citation from the American government for being the first person to sing concerts in tuberculosis hospitals during and after the war. He was the first major artist to visit them, as more patients, most of them former prisoners of war, were brought home with this disease. Warren sang in hospitals on the East Coast and as far afield as Missouri, continuing this activity even after the war ended. He also received a United States Treasury Department citation for "patriotic services to our country, rendered on behalf of national defense" for his participation in a nationwide broadcast of 10 November 1941, "For America We Sing," even before Pearl Harbor. Warren broadcast regularly on Armed Forces Radio and continued singing for the USO from early in 1942 through the end of the war. In January 1944, he appeared with Perry Como and the actress Patsy Kelly in the *Daily News*–WABC War Bond Appeal, staged at the Versailles Restaurant in New York City and broadcast on the ABC network. Columnists Ed Sullivan and Danton Walker and the drama critic John Chapman were the masters of ceremonies. For all-American events such as this, the USO programs, and his radio engagements, Warren reveled in being able to sing popular songs, belting out "While Hearts Are Singing," "Love, Here Is My Heart," "Love Me and the World Is Mine," "Until," and "Romance." When the occasion was right, he added "Invictus" and "Home on the Range." For radio, he later added his sea shanties, arranged for him by Tom Scott, most of which he recorded in 1947. A tape made by Arge Keller, a former Met staff member, from Warren's radio broadcasts includes these romantic and heroic songs and the comic "Captain Mac" and "Three for Jack," both about a sailor's on-shore encounters with women. In fine form and loving every word of the lyrics, Warren seems to burst with pleasure as he tells these stories, turning his voice into an instrument rich with laughter and fun. His "Home on the Range" is serious and limpid. While Warren was serving his country in the USO concerts, Agatha enrolled in the Red Cross and American Woman's Volunteer Corps programs; she contributed time and money before and after she married.

Toscanini's Red Cross Benefit Concert

Warren was also chosen to sing Rigoletto in one of the most stirring of these wartime charity events, Arturo Toscanini's huge American Red Cross concert of 25 May 1944 in Madison Square Garden. As a musical and patriotic celebration, this concert simply had no equal during World War II. According to the critics, it was also the biggest concert in the entire history of New York. The Garden was decorated with huge American flags and Red Cross banners. More than eighteen thousand people attended. The box office registered an intake of $100,000 from ticket sales, the largest amount ever tallied for classical music up to that time, and the sale of souvenir programs brought an additional ten thousand dollars. During the intermission, an additional eleven thousand dollars was contributed by Mrs. James P. Donohue, who outbid everyone else when Mayor Fiorello H. LaGuardia auctioned one of Toscanini's batons for the benefit of the Red Cross.

Warren's first *Falstaff*,
Buenos Aires, summer
1943, with Rogelio
Baldrich, who sang
Bardolfo, and Norman
Cordon, who sang
Pistola. Credit: Sudak,
Teatro Colón; Vivien
Warren Collection.

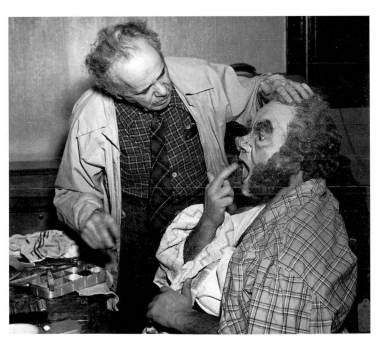

Being made
up by Eddie
Senz for the
Met *Falstaff*,
March 1944.
Credit: Louis
Mélançon,
Metropolitan
Opera
Archives;
Vivien Warren
Collection.

In *Lucia di Lammermoor*, November 1943 at the Metropolitan Opera. Left to right: Thelma Votipka, Warren as Enrico Ashton, Cesare Sodero, Lily Pons, Jan Peerce, and Nicola Moscona. Credit: Vivien Warren Collection.

Warren in *Un ballo in maschera* at the Met, December 1943, with Jan Peerce. Credit: Metropolitan Opera Archives.

Warren's wartime service included many concerts for the USO. He was photographed with Agatha in Trinidad on 28 September 1943. Credit: Signal Corps, U.S. Army; Vivien Warren Collection.

At the U.S. Naval Training School in the Bronx, the musical program included Warren; Carolyn Grey, pianist; Ana Drittelle, cellist; and soprano Agnes Davis, all posing with an unidentified officer. Credit: U.S. Naval Training School, Bronx, New York; Vivien Warren Collection.

The film *Irish Eyes are Smiling* brought Warren to Hollywood in 1944 where he and Agatha became friendly with director Gregory Ratoff and his wife. On the set (left to right) are Blanche Thebom, Warren, and Ratoff (standing, holding a cane). Credit: Vivien Warren Collection.

Warren in a Hollywood portrait shot. Credit: Paul A. Hesse Studios; Vivien Warren Collection.

Warren in an early *Rigoletto* at the Met, 1945. Credit: *Opera News*.

Above: Warren with conductor Wilfrid Pelletier at the RCA Victor studio where he recorded an aria from *Faust* in September 1941. Credit: Metropolitan Opera Archives.

With Ronald Wise and Fred Lynch at the RCA Victor studio on 8 October 1945. Credit: BMG Classics/RCA.

In Connecticut, Warren found true peace. His house in the Willowmere section of Riverside became, as he said, one of his two homes, while the other was the Met. Linda Warren Tirdel, Warren's niece, sits on the pier in 1998. Credit: Linda Warren Tirdel.

Warren fishing in Long Island Sound. Credit: BMG Classics/ RCA.

Roy Leifflen and his parents with Warren and Agatha at the breakwater at the Warrens' Willowmere house in Riverside. Credit: Vivien Warren Collection.

In 1947, baritone Giuseppe De Luca began three years of coaching Warren. He became a major influence in refining Warren's style. The two men in the garden of Warren's house in Riverside in July 1947. Credit: BMG Classics/RCA.

Piloting his beloved *Troubadour* in the waters off Greenwich Cove. Credit: *New York World-Telegram and Sun;* Vivien Warren Collection.

The captain of the *Troubadour.* Credit: Milone Studios; Vivien Warren Collection.

Warren trying out a Delco ship-to-shore telephone at the Boat Show. Credit: Graphic House, New York; Vivien Warren Collection.

With Agatha, relaxing at the Willowmere house in Riverside. Credit: Vivien Warren Collection.

Warren's rose garden was his particular pride. Credit: *Hartford Courant;* Vivien Warren Collection.

Warren spraying for bugs. Credit: Werner Wolff; Vivien Warren Collection.

Jussi Björling and his wife, Anna-Lisa, with Agatha and Warren in Central Park in New York City, 1948. Credit: *Aftonbladet*. Stockholm, Sweden.

Warren cooks spaghetti for student guests in the Memorial Union at the University of Wisconsin in Madison, 3 May 1948. Credit: Gary Schulz; Vivien Warren Collection.

Warren with his father, Solomon Warenoff, after a concert in October 1948 in Seattle. Credit: Solomon Warenoff Collection, Vivien Warren Collection.

Warren's early Iago, for the Met production of *Otello* on 29 November 1948. Credit: Metropolitan Opera Archives.

Warren as Tonio in the Met's *Pagliacci*. Credit: Metropolitan Opera; *Opera News*.

In Rio, Warren's *Rigoletto* of May
1949 at the Teatro Municipal.
Credit: *Vieira, Revista da Semana;*
Vivien Warren Collection.

Un ballo in maschera in
Mexico City, June 1949,
with Warren as Renato
and Zinka Milanov as
Amelia. Credit: Ruffino;
Vivien Warren
Collection.

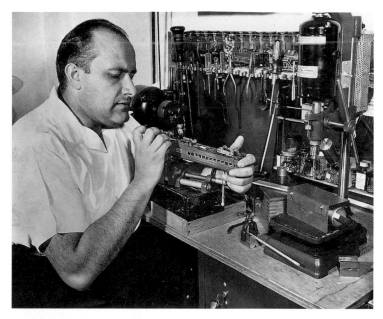

Warren tinkering with a coach from his electric train set in the study of his Lexington Avenue apartment. Credit: Vivien Warren Collection.

Honored for his 1948 RCA *Sea Shanties* album, Warren was greeted by Regimental Commander William Llewellyn at the U.S. Merchant Marine Academy at Kings Point, New York. Credit: Constance Hope Associates; Vivien Warren Collection.

Warren as Santa Claus in December 1949 in New York, as a volunteer for the Women's Aid Society benefit. At the rear is Mrs. Rudolf Gaertner, president of the society, which was celebrating its 110th anniversary. Credit: Vivien Warren Collection.

Warren in the title role of the Metropolitan Opera's *Simon Boccanegra*, November 1949. Credit: Metropolitan Opera; Vivien Warren Collection.

The long musical program at Madison Square Garden included the overture to *Tannhäuser*, the "Daybreak and Rhine Journey" from *Götterdämmerung*, the Prelude and "Liebestod" from *Tristan und Isolde* and the "Ride of the Valkyries." The last act of Verdi's *Rigoletto* and his "Hymn of the Nations" completed the classical portion of the program. John Philip Sousa's march "The Stars and Stripes Forever" provided a rousing finale. Under Toscanini's baton were his own NBC Symphony Orchestra and the instrumentalists of the New York Philharmonic, both seated on a platform ninety feet long. To the professional NBC chorus, used for part of the program, were added six hundred voices from the All-City High School Chorus. Peerce was the tenor soloist in Verdi's "Hymn of the Nations" and in the now legendary performance of the final act of *Rigoletto*. Warren was cast in the title role, Milanov was Gilda, Nan Merriman was Maddalena, and Moscona was Sparafucile. Writing of Milanov's recordings in *Opera Quarterly* in the spring of 1990, William Albright called the event "the vocal equivalent of the 1943 Carnegie Hall broadcast of Tchaikovsky's First Piano Concerto with Toscanini and Vladimir Horowitz." He also said that in the recording of the last act of *Rigoletto*, Milanov, then thirty-eight, was in full command of an "amazingly keen and vibrant voice that seems to leap out of her. Warren's baritone sounds nearly as resonantly cavernous as Moscona's solid bass, yet he can slim it down to the pillowiest *pianissimo*." He compared Merriman's "gypsy quality" with the singing of the brilliant Spanish mezzo Conchita Surpervia, who had died in 1936. In the *World-Telegram*, Robert Bagar singled out Peerce and Warren for the luster of their voices. The only problem was the uneven and "raucous" amplification system, which distorted the quality of the voices in the great hall. None of that, of course, can be heard on the recording of the program. As David Hamilton observed, the audience in the gigantic reaches of Madison Square Garden suffered, while we can hear the true quality that engineers took directly from the microphones. This electrifying recording of *Rigoletto* is superb, from the menacing opening chords to Warren's final tragic cry of "La maledizione!" In the early moments of the act, Warren's exchanges with Gilda and Sparafucile bring into full play his sumptuous voice and meticulous diction, with pristine Italian vowels and consonants audible. In the quartet's heavier texture, his weight binds the piece. The scene closes on Milanov's last, whispered words and Warren's desperate cries. Toscanini's inspired casting carried the day.

The New Season: Autumn 1941–Spring 1942

Warren moved quickly into a demanding program with the Met. On 3 December he sang the High Priest in *Samson et Dalila* for the first time, with Pelletier conducting a cast that included Risë Stevens as Dalila, René Maison as Samson, and Norman Cordon as Abimélech. Stevens, whom Peter G. Davis praises in *The American Opera Singer*, falls into the group called "Johnson Babies." Like Warren, she came from a Bronx background. Unlike Warren and other "Johnson Babies," she had gone abroad to get experience, so she was better prepared for opera than they. In 1998 she said that she and Warren were "good friends as colleagues," although they never had any kind of social association. "We sang great together," the mezzo-soprano recalled.

> It was one of those incredible voices. I think Agatha was a tremendous help to him because she was a singer too, you know. But he was truly magnificent. We did both *Samson* and *Gioconda* together. He was a wonderful colleague, just because of the volume of the sound and the sheer magnificence of the voice. It was such an honor to sing with him. In my time, he was *the* voice of the company.

For all its dignity, *Samson et Dalila* did not satisfy the critics. Then, as now, the work was seen as an oratorio. Louis Biancolli wrote in the *World-Telegram* that Warren did some "pontifical shouting" in the second act but "rounded up some fine tones for the part of the High Priest." Howard Taubman, in the *New York Times*, found the opera "frayed around the edges" but praised Warren, "whose baritone is truly lavish," adding that he "has also developed as an actor." In the *Herald Tribune*, Bohm called his High Priest "impressive" and said he was "ripening rapidly, and he possesses indubitably the best voice of its kind to be heard here at the present time. The richness and unforced fullness of his tones were highly satisfying to hear, and his impersonation has grown more convincing from the histrionic point of view," praising his acting. In the *Post*, Edward O'Gorman also remarked on Warren's vocal and artistic progress. "[He] drew the evening's first and most spontaneous applause for a performance that was more dramatically animated and that carried more conviction and address than most baritones have been able to wrest from this role." When he sang it again in February 1942 with Kerstin Thorborg as Dalila, Robert Lawrence wrote, "This young baritone is gaining in finesse on the stage. All his singing was subordinated to the carrying power of the role; and it was superb."

On 12 December Warren was Amonasro in yet another student performance of *Aida*, sharing the stage with Stella Roman, one of his most frequent partners, and Carron. O'Gorman, writing in the *Post*, said he was "exceptionally fine, which seems to be the rule this season." Virgil Thomson wrote that Warren "gave an example of beautiful singing, as is his habit." Biancolli felt that neither Warren nor Carron "made life along the Nile look very real" and said the ballet "brought guffaws from the kids." This performance marked Paul Breisach's debut as a conductor at the Met.

During this period, the company was in rehearsal for new works and operas with multiple cast changes for repeats. Warren was preparing for *Traviata* and his first Germont, which he sang on 14 January 1942. Not many singers could garner long reviews by appearing in the fourth or sixth performance of any given production in a season. So it was with Warren's first Metropolitan Germont. The New York *Sun* reviewer mistakenly called him Frederick Warren but said he was warmly applauded after singing "Di Provenza il mar" and again at the end of the act. His voice sounded "particularly full and resonant" in the finale of the third act. Perkins, writing in the *Herald Tribune*, also commented on the applause and described him as singing "effectively" although perhaps with too much "vigor," another of the many early references to his excessive volume. Perkins noted, however, that when Warren delivered the aria, he showed a full command of lyricism and expressiveness. In the audience were Warren's sister and brother, who rejoiced when he scored his first big success on the Met stage.

Early the next day, Martin Warenoff sent news of the event to their father, who was living at the New Washington Hotel in Seattle. Leonard "knocked the people in the aisles," Martin wrote.

> When he finished the "Di Provenza" aria, there was such an ovation that you would think the conquering hero had come home. The orchestra got up in unison and applauded, and that is the first time I have ever seen anything like that in the Opera House. Mr. Johnson nearly fell out of his box applauding, and there were so many "bravos" that the house actually resounded for five or six minutes. Pop, let me tell you something. In spite of all the obstacles put in Leonard's way, he is absolutely considered the best baritone in the Metropolitan today, and this tidy bit of information comes from none other than Mr. Edward Ziegler. I just couldn't wait until this morning to tell you how proud you should be of "The Imp." Never have I heard such an ovation; as a matter of fact, when Leonard stepped off the stage, he cried.

(Vivien said her brother often cried; she recalled a time when he cried during a Met rehearsal.)

On 24 January, a *Carmen* that marked the debut of the Belgian mezzo Lily Djanel brought Warren on for his fifth Escamillo. Downes was "not much struck" by Warren's portrayal. His voice was wrong for the music, and his character, though burly enough, was not romantic. A far more damaging review by Thomson described the baritone as "much too fat" and "a little comic" as Escamillo. "I do think Mr. Warren might reduce a bit," he concluded. Biancolli, writing in the *World-Telegram*, also found him "a mite portly for toreador footwork, though tonally fit." O'Gorman characterized his Escamillo as heavily and unsympathetically acted.

Although he had never been overweight as a teenager, Warren had begun to put on weight during the early years of his opera career. In photographs made during the Radio City Music Hall years and in Italy in 1938, he looks sturdy but not unusually heavy. However, he added pounds later. Vivien said that both he and Martin had exemptions from military service for health reasons; they had high blood pressure and were too heavy to qualify for service in World War II. As he aged, Warren added substantial girth but remained a very handsome and imposing man with an almost military bearing, which Vivien said, he learned from their mother. Warren had dark brown hair and expressive eyes; he never lost his broad smile. Almost six feet tall, he dressed impeccably for all public appearances. He remained elegant, even at rehearsals, where he would appear in his zip-front jackets or wool cardigans. His suits were beautifully tailored; after 1950 he began to have most of them made in Italy.

Less than two months after the *Carmen* reviews, Warren exacted a fine revenge on the New York critics. Singing with the Met at the Lyric Theatre in Baltimore, he did so well that the performance came to a full stop after the "Toreador Song." WARREN STOPS SHOW AT LYRIC ran the headline in one paper, while the other said, LEONARD WARREN STOPS SHOW AT PERFORMANCE OF "CARMEN." "Tall and robust, [he] broke through the stage crowd" and sang. "Bedlam broke loose. Calls of 'Encore' and 'Bravo' accompanied his bows." Minutes passed as Thomas Beecham stood quietly, baton in hand, but the noise did not subside. Finally he gave a signal. Warren stepped to the footlights and repeated the aria. This was only the second time in the history of grand opera in Baltimore that a singer had sung an encore.

Among Warren's most important assignments that season was his role in the world premiere of Gian Carlo Menotti's *Ilo e Zeus*, the work billed in Met programs as *The Island God*. Warren was Ilo. Menotti's first commissioned opera at the Met, it attracted attention because his earlier work had been well received. It was first performed at the Met on 20 February 1942, in an English translation by Fleming McLeish. With Warren as the lead, Astrid Varnay as Telca, Raoul Jobin as the Fisherman, and Norman Cordon as the God, it was conducted by Panizza and staged in sets painted by Josef Novak from Richard Rychtarik's designs. Rychtarik also designed the costumes. The opera earned mixed reviews after the first night, although on second hearing one critic praised the composer for his "adroitness," another for his "beguiling melody." Grena Bennett, in the *Journal-American*, praised Warren, saying that he was "generous in revealing his magnificently robust baritone voice." Thomson, writing on 21 February in the *Herald Tribune*, said of Menotti's work, "It sounds like an opera, reads like a short story, [and] actually is a secular cantata." However, he added, "Musically the work is more than a fair job." Downes, reviewing the opera that same day for the *New York Times*, set forth a long musical analysis and said the cast was "able." Oscar Thompson, again writing about "Frederick" Warren, said, "The orchestra gives him plenty of competition. Mr. Warren's voice is undoubtedly one of the most powerful to be heard at the Metropolitan today, but there were times when his hard driven tones were obscured" by Menotti's "lyric expansions" and Panizza's heavy-handed conducting. The audience laughed at one piece of serious stage business. "The performance was competent rather than distinguished," Thompson concluded.

Although the principals worked diligently at it, the audience simply did not accept the opera. Kolodin attributed its failure to heavy symbolism and "limited musical interest." *The Island God* played for only four performances (three in New York and one in Philadelphia) before it was removed from the Met program. At the end of its brief run, the composer withdrew the score from his catalogue. Two interludes from it were played in a symphony concert in 1949, with the composer's permission. The opera has never been performed since the Met produced it.

In that season Warren also sang *Aida*, *Lohengrin*, *Carmen*, and *Faust*. On a weekly salary, he appeared in more than forty Met performances, including the concerts in New York and the Met tour cities of Baltimore, Boston, Cleveland, Bloomington, and Dallas. Forty performances in a season might have suggested that Warren's future at the Met could be defined by routine. For the next Met season, his contract stipulated a list of twenty-nine roles. He would be paid $171.50 per week. His Italian roles were Manfredo in *L'amore dei tre re*, Renato in *Ballo*, his two old parts in *Boris*, Alfio in *Cavalleria rusticana*, Belcore in *L'elisir d'amore*, Ford in *Falstaff*, Don Carlo in *Forza*, Barnaba in *Gioconda*, Enrico in *Lucia*, Iago in *Otello*, Tonio and Silvio in *Pagliacci*, the title role in *Rigoletto*, Paolo in *Boccanegra*, Germont in *Traviata*, and Di Luna in *Trovatore*. His French roles included the High Priests in *Samson* and *Alceste*, Escamillo and Valentin, Dapertutto in *Les contes d'Hoffmann*, and Mercutio in *Roméo et Juliette*. In his German repertory were the Herald in *Lohengrin* and Biterolf in *Tannhäuser*. The English roles were Kruschina in *The Bartered Bride*, Ilo (in case *The Island God* came back), and the title role in *Falstaff*. With assignments like these, Warren's apprenticeship was over. Burdensome for a musical illiterate, this list meant months of study, even though he never sang six of these roles. He did, however, have to memorize them all. As he admitted to a reviewer in Lincoln, Nebraska, he needed "five teachers" to prepare him. Seeing the record of Warren's performance schedule in 1941–1942 and his plans for 1942–1943, few people could have imagined that he could have found time to consider important personal decisions, but the choices he made then changed the entire course of his life.

✦ CHAPTER NINE

Courtship and Marriage

W arren and Agatha spent part of the summer of 1941 on a farm near
Hinsdale, Massachusetts, where both were guests of J. Joseph Noble
and Ruth, his wife. Noble was a senior partner in Roy Leifflen's law firm. In
winter, the Nobles and their children lived in the Dakota, a landmark building on Central Park West and Seventy-second Street. Marylin Noble Tracy,
the daughter of the family, remembered meeting Warren at the Met. "Leonard's career was just taking off," she said. "I remember going to his first *Aida*,
a student performance in 1940. I was taken backstage, and there was this
huge man in a leopard skin with horns on his head. I was obviously impressed
and a bit frightened, so he wanted to calm me down. He tore a piece of metal
off his costume and handed it to me as a gift. That made it all right."

The following summer, the Nobles left New York for their farm. The
eight-year-old Marylin was told that "Aunt Agatha," their houseguest, would
have a friend come up. It was Warren, whom the Nobles lodged in a furnished room near their house. Mrs. Tracy remembered him as "so sweet and
so nice, dressed conservatively in a plain white shirt and brown trousers."
One afternoon "Uncle Leonard" (as Marylin called Warren) sat beside her on
the porch and pointed to the clouds, saying, "See how beautiful they are?
Look at them. That cloud's a lion and that one's a bird." When she said, "I
don't see anything," Warren told her, "You have to watch them. See the legs?
See the tail? That's what they are."

"There was really something childlike about him," Mrs. Tracy said. "He
would pull my sister and me all over the hay field in our wagon. But he was
there for Agatha; he was courting her." That summer marked the beginning
of a long friendship between Warren and the Nobles, who were ardent opera
fans and members of the Metropolitan Opera Club. While he was single, he
often visited them in the Dakota; after marriage, he and Agatha entertained
the Nobles and their children in Manhattan and at their country home in
Connecticut. Warren and Agatha were honored guests when Marylin Noble
married. The friendship reached across two generations.

Sometime during the early autumn of 1941, Warren and Agatha finally decided to marry. After all, they had been dating for more than three years and had been engaged for nearly that long. Neither had shown any interest in anyone else. However, the matter was complicated by the fact that both were marrying out of their faiths. On his side were his Jewish origins, although Vivien always emphasized the Warenoffs' status as nonpracticing, secular Jews. But marriage with a non-Jew had no binding force under Jewish religious law and was not recognized as religiously valid. When Warren married, fewer than five percent of American Jews were choosing partners out of their faith. Of these, most married Episcopalians. Agatha's strict Catholicism also weighed on the scale, for in families of fervent belief, few women would marry a Jew.

All differences of faith notwithstanding, Warren and Agatha defied convention and quietly made their plans. The Leifflens' complete acceptance of Warren made it easier for the couple to wed. Warren's parents both had reservations about their son's choice, but Warren had already turned his back on his family's Jewish traditions. He was clearly thinking of becoming a Catholic by the time of his marriage, for in 1941 he had begun his instructions in the Roman Catholic faith with the priest of Agatha's home parish. Although he stopped some time after they were married, the lessons marked a first step in his nine-year progress toward conversion. Money was another issue, for Warren's income would barely cover his own needs. Agatha was earning nothing; gradually she made his affairs her full-time job. She also helped him with his music, playing for him when he studied at home. Then and later, no one raised doubts about their love for each other and Warren's absolute devotion to her and her family. In his interview with Sidney Fields in 1956 for the New York *Daily Mirror*, Warren made a rare remark about his private life, saying, "Marriage is so much a matter of luck. Agatha is a Juilliard graduate and has great musicianship. But she gave it all up to handle me. She's a great counterbalance to all my impractical ways." In this interview, Warren was not quite correct: Agatha had attended the Institute of Musical Art, before it merged with Juilliard.

Although no one knows what motivated Warren and Agatha to act just when they did, the entry of the United States into World War II may not have been a factor because their plans had been put into motion months before the 7 December 1941 Japanese attack on Pearl Harbor.

Warren and Agatha told her priest they wanted to marry in her parish, the Church of St. Charles Borromeo, which still stands at 21 Sidney Place in Brooklyn Heights, six blocks from the Leifflens' home. Because of Warren's faith, a time-consuming process preceded their wedding. First, their request for a dispensation had to be sent to the Chancery. After it was reviewed, the Bishop of the Diocese of Brooklyn had to give his approval, granting the dispensation. Finally it was sent to the priest, the Rev. Charles W. Gordon. Warren also had to sign the "Three Promises." First, he guaranteed to the Roman Catholic authorities that only one wedding ceremony would take place; second, he promised he would do nothing to interfere with his wife's practice of her religion; third, he agreed that all children of both sexes would be raised as Catholics. Edwin Broderick, a friend of the Warrens and later the Bishop of Albany, was then a Right Reverend Monsignor and the secretary to Francis Cardinal Spellman. He said Father Gordon also had to ask Agatha to pray that they might "breach the chasm" that divided them in their faiths. While she apparently did not urge Warren to become a Catholic, she did have to pray that he would do so.

On 23 December 1941, they went to the New York State civil registry offices of Kings County in Brooklyn to fill out an affidavit of license to marry. Warren stated that he was thirty years old and lived at 40 West Sixty-seventh Street in Manhattan. He gave his occupation as "singer." His father's name is given as "Sol Warren," while his mother is listed as "Sara Kantor." Agatha Margaret Leifflen, born 21 February 1911 in Brooklyn, stated that she lived at 128 Willow Street, her family's home in Brooklyn Heights. She gave her father's name as Harry B. Leifflen, her mother's as Agatha L. Schmitt Leifflen. The license was good for sixty days. Warren and Agatha were married on 27 December 1941, in the rectory of St. Charles Borromeo, adjoining the church. Because of his faith, the ceremony could not take place in the main church building. Warren's "disparity of cult" is noted in their marriage record, where his religion is listed as "Hebrew." Father Gordon read the vows with Roy Leifflen and Margaret Mary Paisley, Agatha's cousin, as witnesses. Marylin Noble Tracy said her father, Joseph Noble, was Warren's best man. Only after the ceremony did Warren tell his mother, sister, and brother that he had married. The Leifflens then sent out a formal announcement:

Mr. and Mrs. Harry Bourgart Leifflen
have the honour to announce
the marriage of their daughter
Agatha Margaret
to
Mr. Leonard Warren
on Saturday, the twenty-seventh of December
one thousand nine hundred and forty-one
at Brooklyn, New York.

Setting Up Housekeeping

The Warrens began their life together in simple circumstances that were appropriate to his position at the Metropolitan. His rehearsal and opera schedule allowed them no time for a honeymoon, as he had to sing just before and just after their marriage. For their first ten years together, they lived at 305 Lexington Avenue, near the corner of Thirty-seventh Street, a short walk across town from the Opera House. They had a four-room flat "the size of a closet," as Agatha later described it to an interviewer. She also called it "a telephone booth" and "a shoe box." With the groom came his model trains, which he mounted on a large board that he first slid under a bed in the guest-room. Soon, though, he brought the tracks out in plain view and began calling the room "my den." His full mechanic's workbench arrived, as did his growing library of scores and phonograph records. One corner of the living room was taken by the spinet piano Pelletier had given him.

From the start, Warren's career came before all else. Agatha ran all practical aspects of their lives. She kept their accounts, wrote checks, mended costumes and sent them to the cleaners, interviewed young composers who wished to write music for her husband, listened to new songs for his recital repertory, answered fan mail, vetted journalists' requests for interviews, maintained contacts with his managers, monitored his calendar, authorized his engagements, accompanied him when he studied at home, attended all his Met rehearsals and performances, and traveled with him whenever possible for opera engagements on the Met tour and with other companies. Edgar Vincent, whose office began to handle Warren's public relations in 1952, called Agatha "a genius at investing" and said she built the fortune they eventually accumulated. As a matter of pure business, Warren and his wife collaborated in what he later called "the organization" and "the corporation" that drove his career.

"My wife is a very important part of this corporation," he told a feature writer in Kitchener, Ontario, in 1947. "She looks after all the social end of things and is the best private secretary in the world. I don't know what I would do without her handling all the telephone calls and some of the problems that come up in the way of a singer." He then laughed as he told the reporter about a young singer who called repeatedly, asking to speak to him. Agatha fended the man off, but he persisted and finally revealed the purpose of his call; he had an audition the next day and "wanted to sing like me," Warren said. "What does Mr. Warren do with his diaphragm when he sings?" the man asked. Warren said, "If I had been there, I would probably still be explaining to him."

Warren and Agatha had a very solid marriage. She devoted her life to him, and there can be little doubt that her training as a pianist and singer helped him. As a husband, he remained unshaken in his devotion to her, and that was unusual in the music business, where extramarital affairs were common. Their marriage was never troubled by infidelity. When he and his accompanist were out of New York for recitals, he telephoned Agatha every day. They kept to themselves, moving in a small circle of family members and close friends. Roy Leifflen, Warren's brother-in-law, became his most trusted male friend, and he became particularly important as the lawyer who could help with legal matters. As an accomplished musician, Roy was helpful in other ways as well. Roy went with Warren to South America in 1946 for his long engagement there, serving as coach, translator, and "right hand." Warren grew close to Roy's friend William Appleton, and Warren and Agatha also kept up friendships with the many priests and nuns. Yet their social life was quite circumscribed by choice and necessity. They rarely socialized with singers. Their closest friends on the Met roster were Albanese and her husband, Wilfrid and Rose Bampton Pelletier, Blanche Thebom, and Fausta Cleva and his family. Some colleagues found them aloof. Roberta Peters, in our interview, spoke of Warren as "distant" and Agatha as "cool" offstage. Risë Stevens also said she never socialized with them. Both women, though, had only the highest praise for him as a stage partner.

In Warren's expressions of love for his wife, seriousness was sometimes matched by pure whimsy. In December 1946 he was in the Hotel Benson in Portland, Oregon, where he was booked for a recital. Wanting to send a loving message to Agatha to mark their fifth wedding anniversary, he took scissors and paste to the Sunday magazine supplement of the local newspaper to make his own card. Words from brightly colored advertisements were pasted on a sheet of hotel stationery. His message, all in inch-high letters cut from the paper, read:

COMING UP!

HAPPY DAYS!

GET READY

THE SECRET'S OUT!

Beneath the last line, he wrote in big capital letters, FIFTH ANNIVERSARY (SOON). The couple's happiness, their sheer trust in each other, continued to impress writers. Late in 1942 Mary Ellis Peltz, editor of *Opera News*, wrote about the Warrens' life in their crowded Lexington Avenue apartment, describing the baritone in her opening lines. "Dark complexion, stern, handsome features, brooding eyes, dignified build, quiet, serious demeanor, Leonard Warren takes his art without levity." Showing Mrs. Peltz his model trains, he relaxed a bit, turned on his "boyish humor," and laughed "like a twelve year old" when an electric switch he had "worked on all afternoon" lit properly "on the drawing room carpet." He described his early life as "a long, slow pull" but soon began to tell her about the hard work that gained him recognition for his voice. She described it as "one of the finest organs in the baritone roster." But only by "constant application and an almost religious devoutness" was he able to advance. "Infinite industry," Mrs. Peltz concluded, "has turned one more young American baritone into a mature artist." Four years later in another interview, she added, "In spite of the villainy or dignity of his stage demeanor, Leonard Warren is very much a child at heart."

✦ CHAPTER TEN

Star Status in South America

W arren may have seemed boyish to Mary Ellis Peltz and other interviewers, but to his mother and younger siblings, he effectively served as head-of-household after his parents separated and finally divorced. So long as Martin was living at home, he shared some of the responsibility. However, after he moved to Buffalo and took a job with Bell Aircraft, Warren had to deal with his family's problems alone. After Warren's own marriage in 1941, he shouldered a double burden, taking care of his mother's home and his own. His mother and sister stayed on Sixty-seventh Street for the first five years of Warren's Met career; then, at his suggestion, they moved in 1943 into the Sherman Square Studios at 160 West Seventy-third Street. There Sidney Dietch, Bruno Landi, Hilde Reggiani, and many other musicians lived or worked. Vivien lived there for more than fifty years. Of her brother's help, she said:

> Whenever we needed help, we called on Leonard. No matter how small the chore, he took care of things. If I said, "The lamp is broken," even during a phone call, Leonard would break in, saying, "I'll be right over." If a family crisis arose, or if he heard our mother or me on the other end of the line, upset or in tears over something, he would say, "I'll come right now. Agatha isn't dressed, but she'll come later." Soon he would be at the door. He was like a father and a brother to me.

Vivien said, "He was so conscientious. His presence was so gentle. When he walked in, he made everything right. That sweet, kind, loving person!—so sweet!"

Warren's mother's troubled emotional state became a major problem in the family in the 1940s. Vivien said her parents' divorce had left her mother "shattered" and feeling rejected by her husband. "She saw herself as a discard in the Jewish community, even in the circle of her sisters, brothers, their families, and friends." As Sara Warenoff grew older, her fury was often directed at those closest to her, and she even hurled invective at Leonard. He, Vivien, and later Vivien's daughter, had to meet the daily challenge of coping with the outbursts of this disturbed, angry woman.

Soon there was a second divorce in the family, when Vivien left her husband, but Warren felt better about that. Vivien said that when she told Warren that she and her husband were separating, his eyes filled with tears. He hugged her and said, "Thank God I have my sister back!" The strong bond between the two was strengthened by Warren's love for Vivien's daughter, Linda. Through the years of Linda's childhood and adolescence, he treated her as if she were his own child. He monitored her education and encouraged her to study piano and violin. When she was older, she announced that she wanted to be a nurse. Vivien became upset, thinking she should choose another profession. And, as Vivien had always done, she turned to her brother for help. He consoled her but asked her to accept Linda's decision. "It's a calling, just like being a priest or a nun," he said. Vivien described her brother as a man who never complained about his family responsibilities. He simply helped. He often seemed difficult to his professional colleagues, even when he was singing in Radio City Music Hall. He began to tell others what to do soon after he got to the Met. Nonetheless, he remained accommodating and even generous with those closest to him. Roy Leifflen, in a letter to a professor in Kentucky, described Warren as a man with "an open, amicable disposition. It was a family joke that we, the nonmusicians, were more temperamental than he was. He was a very easy man to live with."

Buenos Aires and the Teatro Colón

As Warren was struggling to keep his operatic life on course, he persisted with his studies and sought important roles, which the Met management was not yet ready to give him. His main chance came in 1942, when Ettore Panizza decided to cast Warren in major roles and gave him his first contracts for South America. This debut came two years after André Mertens, director of the South American and Mexican division of Columbia Concerts, had tried in vain to place Warren in Buenos Aires; he was turned down because he was not sufficiently experienced to be considered for the Colón. At that time, Erich Engel of the Teatro Colón had exchanged letters with Edward Ziegler of the Met. Ziegler described Warren as "a man who, up to now, has had very limited stage experience . . . but he is ready with quite a number of roles. He has an exceptionally beautiful voice." It was Mertens who in 1942 acted as Warren's agent, using his local counterpart, the Conciertos Daniel in Buenos Aires, as an intermediary. As Warren and Agatha were on their way to Argentina, they stopped in Balboa, Panama, so he could sing under the USO banner for American service men in the Canal Zone. His program was also broadcast on the radio.

Buenos Aires, with its huge Italian presence, was the capital of opera in South America. Its earliest important opera house had opened in 1757, more than two decades before the Teatro alla Scala was inaugurated in Milan in 1778. The Teatro Colón was known as the "South American La Scala," located in the "Paris of South America." It opened in 1908 and quickly became the major opera-producing organization of the continent. By the 1920s, 1930s and 1940s, Panizza had become Argentina's beloved national musical celebrity, known as "Hector" in his native land and "Ettore" in Italy and the United States. Born to Italian parents in Buenos Aires in 1875, Panizza was sent to Milan to complete his studies. He made his debut in 1890 and by 1907 had established himself at London's Covent Garden. He then moved back to Milan, where he became Toscanini's assistant at La Scala. He soon rose to the role of leading conductor, with a tenure that reached from 1921 to 1929, from 1930 to 1932, and from 1946 to 1948. At La Scala, Panizza was assigned that theatre's first production of Puccini's *Trittico* and the Italian premieres of *Khovanshchina* and two works by Ermanno Wolf-Ferrari. In these years he also emerged as a serious opera composer in his own right.

Critical to Warren's early career, Panizza was under contract to the Metropolitan Opera from 1934 to 1942; during that period he had been informed about Warren's studies in Milan. He rehearsed and conducted for Warren's operatic debut on 13 January 1939 as Paolo in *Simon Boccanegra*. He was the only leading conductor Warren worked with in that debut year. In Warren's second season with the company, Panizza conducted the repeats of *Simon Boccanegra* and *Boris Godunov*, with Warren as Rangoni. He was on the podium for Warren's first Amonasro in *Aida* in the fortuitous student performance matinee broadcast of 19 January 1940 and his first Barnaba in *La Gioconda*. He also conducted Warren's first Met tour role in 1940 and his first High Priest in *Alceste*. In 1942 he conducted the first Warren *Traviata* at the Met, the performance that won the baritone the huge ovation that Martin Warenoff described to his father. Panizza also conducted the world premiere of Menotti's *Ilo e Zeus* (*The Island God*). In all this, Panizza had learned to trust Warren; he remained an important influence in many of the major events in his early career. He gave Warren his first chance to sing four of Verdi's most important roles, beginning in Buenos Aires with his first performance of the title role of *Simon Boccanegra* and his first Renato in *Un ballo in maschera*, both offered in Buenos Aires in 1942. His first *Rigoletto* and *Falstaff* came one year later. These ventures into a difficult repertory would have challenged any young artist, but they raised very high hurdles for an unschooled and even uncertain musician, one who was obsessed with perfection. Warren was still a very slow study, sometimes needing six or eight months to master a major role, still learning everything by repetition. Yet he sang so well that Panizza decided to give him his first big chance.

Warren and Agatha were welcomed to the Teatro Colón and introduced to the society of the city, which both loved. Like the cities of Spain and Italy, from which so many of its people came, Buenos Aires was built on European models. With its dignified public buildings, grand hotels, fashionable shopping streets and broad avenues, parks, fine restaurants, comfortable cafes like those in Milan or Paris, and splendid mansions of the rich, the city took second place to none on the South American continent. In the countryside not far away were the huge cattle ranches where the country's fortunes were made. On these estates, gauchos gave colorful riding displays for visiting tourists, the Warrens among them.

Warren's debut opera in Buenos Aires was *Aida* on 29 May 1942. At the Colón, he found a comfortable environment as he rehearsed with Zinka Milanov, Bruna Castagna, and Frederick Jagel. The day after the first performance, he awakened to excellent reviews in the city's papers. His Amonasro was "a triumph in voice and acting," said the critic of the Buenos Aires *Herald*, who added, "He sang with thrilling quality and invested the role with significant power." According to the critic of *The Standard*, "He possesses a voice of enormous volume; it could distinctly be heard above all the chorus and principals in the finale of the second act; it floats easily [and has] an intensely expressive timbre. His acting was undoubtedly the finest of the evening; and his stirring interpretation of Amonasro won him enthusiastic applause." In *El Mundo* Warren was praised for his "gallant figure" and "voice of beautiful timbre, generous volume and excellent range. His diction, technique and musicianship are impeccable, his acting impressive." *La Prensa* found him a "vigorous tragic actor" and "a singer who knows how to place his ample, virile voice at the service of dramatic expression."

A much riskier assignment followed on 12 June when Warren sang the title role in *Simon Boccanegra* for the first time. This was an opera he knew well, but his role in it had been Paolo, not Simon. Between those two roles lies a sea of terror for any baritone, for Simon is perhaps the most difficult of all Verdi roles for that voice. It requires rigorous examination of motive and character development, for Simon is crucial to every act in the opera. The role's subtle moments also need a refinement and delicacy that normally only a mature singer can command. In agreeing to sing the title role in *Boccanegra* at this stage of his development, Warren took a very great risk, having sung Paolo at the Met only four times.

At the Colón, his Amelia/Maria was Milanov in two of the five performances; her alternate was Delia Rigal, an Argentine soprano who later joined the Metropolitan. Jagel sang Gabriele Adorno. When the newspapers came out, Warren made a clean sweep in their columns. His surprising mastery of this supremely difficult characterization dominated their appraisals. *La Prensa* led by praising this "young [artist], gifted in every sense, [whose] creation of the role of the Genoese corsair was expressive and colorful." *La Tribuna di*

Rosario called him an "exceptional singer" whose interpretation "was outstanding, characterized by the emotional and dramatic quality with which he outlined the most important moments of the [opera]. A master of the middle register, he spun tones of such perfection as to cause astonishment [in the audience]." The *Diario Español* praised his "ample voice and sweet timbre" that gave the noble figure of Boccanegra "all the requisite expression and power." A writer for the musical weekly *Cronicas Musicales* called Warren "the hero of the evening" and a "great artist who represented perfectly the multiple emotions and vocal opportunities of this complicated role." And he continued to get excellent reviews throughout the season.

After four Amonasros and five Boccanegras, Warren sent news to Edward Johnson. On 3 July he wrote to say that he had been busy "with a new company and season and a new audience to face." He was happy working with Panizza, he said, "It felt quite like home to be working with him again. I am enjoying the work at the Colón tremendously and, of course, my wife and I are having great fun seeing the sights." Everything was "going smoothly, and everything points to a successful season." Warren sent off an unduly modest report, for he could have said more about his achievement, but he just mentioned his operas.

Warren's *Boccanegra* was followed by his first performance of a much less demanding role, Renato in Verdi's *Un ballo in maschera*, which Ferruccio Calusio conducted. Again Warren was fortunate in these South American "firsts" because Calusio knew him from the Met. Jagel took the leading tenor role in *Ballo*, where he was transformed into a noble Riccardo. Amelia in this production was the American soprano Florence Kirk, a former Auditions of the Air participant. Tall and attractive, with fair skin and long reddish-blonde hair, Kirk had developed a sophistication and confidence that propelled her into a career in radio and opera. When she reached the Met in 1944, *Opera News* described her as someone "with a bit of the mantle of greatness, something of the dignity, high seriousness and smoldering fire of an operatic prima donna in the grand manner." These are the very qualities that best served her for Amelia. Reviews of Warren's Renato show the sumptuous quality of his voice and the sensitivity of his interpretation that made him a fair rival of the other, more experienced singers. In *El Mundo* he was described as "magnificent, ingratiating in the middle register, vibrant in the climaxes and authoritative in [his] acting. He is an artist destined for the heights." The critic of *La Prensa* praised his gifts as an actor and singer and remarked on the fact that he dominated the production with his "vigorous" Renato. The review in *Le Courier de la Plata* called him "the discovery of the season," one who made a "profound impression with his voice and stage presence . . . [and as] an actor, rare today, who brings to mind the memory of the great Feodor Chaliapin." In the Buenos Aires *Herald* he was hailed as "a truly great artist whose rendering of the aria 'Eri tu' brought him one of the longest outbursts of applause that this reviewer has ever witnessed at the Colón." The *Standard* also took note of this ovation:

> The climax of the opera was reached when Leonard Warren brought all the power of his magnificent voice to bear on the famous aria. Not even the habitués who have witnessed many seasons with singers who are worshipped all over the world could have criticized such expressive and beautiful singing, singing that must place this young American artist in the first rank of today's baritones. The deafening applause that followed his rendering of this aria was a tribute from the Argentine public to an artist who has definitely won their heartfelt admiration.

Among other colleagues from the Met who were at the Colón that year was the soprano Irene Jessner. On 12 September she sent Johnson a report on the season, devoting her first paragraph to "the Italian season" and the "outstanding success" Warren had had. "In every one of the roles he sang here, he captured the fancy of the public." In fact, of all the earliest conquests in Warren's career, none matched what he achieved in Buenos Aires. With ample rehearsal time, backed by good conductors and an excellent orchestra, he could perform without fear. It is no wonder that Buenos Aires, São Paulo, and Rio, three great South American cities, would remain Warren's home away from home for years to come. Honored by theatre directors and the authorities, he became comfortable in this Latin American world. For the American Society of the River Plata's Fourth of July celebration in 1942, he was the guest of honor, seated at dinner with Argentina's minister of foreign affairs and the American ambassador, Norman Armour.

A Soprano's Debut in Buenos Aires

Delia Rigal was just launching her career when Warren came to Argentina for the first time. In a personal interview with Horacio Molina in 1998, she said that Warren's engagement for *Boccanegra* was "greeted with joy and happiness" by everyone in the company. It was Panizza, she said, who contracted her to sing in the second cast of the opera. This was her operatic debut. Rigal described herself as "very young and very shy" toward other singers. Toward Warren she felt "much respect . . . because of his personality, his expertise as a singer, [and] his seriousness." She said she was "trying to learn everything related to singing," so she just listened to Warren and "tried to do her best." Rigal recalled the great respect he enjoyed: "Everyone took Leonard as a master, and no one wanted to miss one single bar sung by him during the rehearsals." In the next season, Rigal sang Violetta to Warren's Germont in *Traviata*. They met again in South America in 1946, when she sang Amelia in *Un ballo in maschera* with him, and then again after 1950, when she joined the Met roster during Rudolf Bing's first season as general manager.

The Teatro Municipal in Rio de Janeiro

The singers' move to Brazil was made during the last week in July, when Jagel, Kirk, Warren, and Agatha set off together for Rio. The baritone was armed with a little dictionary and phrase book for conversation in Portuguese, a gift from the War Department of the United States. Although the Municipal was a much less prestigious house than the venerable Colón, it was the foremost theatre of Brazil. For his first appearance, Warren again starred in *Simon Boccanegra*, with Jagel as Gabriele, Kirk as Amelia/Maria, and Calusio as the conductor. The reviewers all agreed on his success. The *Diario* had nothing but praise for "the opulent voice, full of majesty, and the management of that voice, to whose exuberant sound he gives an ingratiating sweetness. His pianissimos and mezza voce were magnificent. As an actor, he maintained a noble, austere line, fulfilling the demands of the role." *Vanguarda* called him

> serene, majestic, rich in pomp, a true Simon Boccanegra. Not for one moment was it a question of an actor who had merely "studied" a role. Never. He gave it life, expression, emotion. A baritone of exceptional resources, his voice is magnificent and powerful, of extensive range and ample volume. In our opinion, he was greatest in his high pianissimos, a veritable marvel of emotion in art. He is a singer who will find few rivals in the world. To cite fine examples of his singing would mean writing about the whole opera.

Meio Dia hailed a voice that was "absolutely marvelous. We had the impression that his vocal cords vibrated like those of a beautiful instrument in the orchestra, played with absolute musicianship." *A Notícia* called his voice "phenomenal, with impeccable pitch, beautiful timbre, magnificent volume and range, and [mastery] of the art of singing. [He made] us remember past evenings of glory with Titta Ruffo and Stracciari."

Again under Calusio's baton, and again with Kirk and Jagel, the company offered *Un ballo in maschera*, with Warren as Renato. Warren's Germont in *La traviata* came on 1 September, again with Calusio as his conductor and with Kullman as Alfredo. The Violetta was Norina Greco, who had joined the roster of the Met in December 1940 and had sung with Warren in a concert in December 1941. The sister of the celebrated flamenco dancer José Greco, she came to the Met and South America via the Bronx, just as Warren did. The Grecos, natives of the Abruzzi region in southern Italy, had emigrated in the 1930s and set up housekeeping on Digby Avenue. Greco studied voice in New York with her cousin, Aldo Di Tullio, who lived with her family. A high-spirited, intelligent woman, she became a fine singing actress with such a good voice that some compared her to the young Ponselle. In Rio, Greco had been the favorite partner of Beniamino Gigli and was very popular in South America.

Faust on 11 September was conducted by Albert Wolff, with Tokatyan in the title role and Warren as Valentin. The next opera was *Aida*, conducted by Edoardo De Guarnieri. Greco did one Aida with Warren and sang Leonora to his Di Luna. Radamès was sung by Jagel. Warren was Amonasro, Julita Fonseca was Amneris, and the dependable Nino Ruisi was Ramfis.

While the company was in Rio, Brazil entered the war. A gasoline shortage led to an edict prohibiting the use of private cars in the nation. Because there were many pro-German factions in the country, riots and civil disorder of all kinds broke out. The baritone heard a pro-Nazi agitator shouting "Heil, Hitler!" in the street during a demonstration. Quickly a mob gathered and almost beat the agitator to death, Warren later said. The opera performances stopped, box office returns fell, and the theatre was closed for several days before it could reopen.

The Teatro Municipal in São Paulo

Several of the singers, Warren among them, moved to the Teatro Municipal in São Paulo at the end of September. *Il trovatore* followed on 3 October, with Greco as Leonora, Warren as Di Luna, Vera Eltzova as Azucena, and Elia Reis e Silva as Manrico. The conductor was Armando Belardi. The last opera of that South American season was a repeat of *La traviata*, this time with the beloved Maria Sá Earp as Violetta and Armando De Assis Pacheco as Alfredo. The city was calm, in spite of wartime shortages. Here, as in Buenos Aires and Rio, critical response showed Warren had established another important beachhead.

News of his success was sent home over the wire services. As early as 18 September, a special dispatch to the Chicago *Daily News* and other North American newspapers described his triumphs in Buenos Aires and Rio. He was "the unexpected sensation of the opera season" in both cities. "Warren has been bringing down the houses," the unnamed writer noted. Warren's excellent 1942 reviews and his popularity brought him a virtual guarantee of success in Latin America. Sylvio Piergili, the impresario at Teatro Municipal in Rio, was so pleased with his first performances that he asked him to sing fifteen performances instead of the eight originally planned. By October, Mertens, working through the Conciertos Daniel agency, could promise a reengagement for the summer of 1943, twenty-five performances in all. Warren loved Latin America, and the South American public loved him. Many in his audience were sure he was Italian, and he delivered the kind of performance they preferred.

At the end of the 1942 season, Warren and Agatha had a difficult trip to

New York in a mail plane, whose pilot learned that another plane just ahead had crashed in the South American jungle. He circled low until the survivors could be seen, waving and signaling. He then radioed their position to a rescue team farther south. As the Warrens were over the Caribbean, they were told that a German U-boat had just torpedoed an American tanker. As required, their plane landed and picked up survivors, some of whom who had reached an island, and then dropped them off in Trinidad. These were among the hazards of wartime travel.

CHAPTER ELEVEN

The Struggle at Home

With his 1942 South American performances behind him, Warren was ready for his next autumn concert tour and the Met. Any singer returning with superlative reviews might have expected better assignments at home. But as Warren soon learned, being a star in South America did not necessarily translate into promotions at home. At the least, he wanted to sing some first performances of the operas he had mastered. The first performance of a given work in each season drew the critics and usually guaranteed reviews in the newspapers.

To be certain of getting reviews, every Met singer fought for four things: opening nights, the first-night casts of repertory operas, new productions, and broadcasts. Warren felt he was entitled to first-night casts as well. To win these, either the singer or the agent had to convince Edward Johnson and his aides to assign them. Managers' careers rose and fell on their ability to secure these showcases for their artists. While Johnson could never guarantee anyone a respectable review, he could help by handing out important roles in the productions that the critics, the wire services, and the major magazines would be certain to cover. Sometimes big assignments were agreed upon in letter contracts between Johnson and the agent; sometimes the agreement was only verbal. The importance of these events, however, can hardly be overstated, especially for Warren, who complained for years that he was "the singer who never got reviewed." To sing in the fifth *Faust* or the eighth *Aida* often meant either getting no review or else, worse, a one-line mention (sometimes with the wrong name) far down the column.

Whatever Warren's expectations were in 1942–1943, he was disappointed. Opening night went to Lily Pons in *La fille du régiment*; the first Escamillo and the first Amonasro went to Alexander Sved. Francesco Valentino got the first Enrico in the new Richard Rychtarik production of *Lucia* and the first Valentin in *Faust*. Not until 11 December did Warren appear, to sing his first Enrico in *Lucia*, as a second-cast baritone following Valentino. *Travi-*

ata with Albanese followed on 26 December, with Warren taking the role Tibbett had sung in the first cast. On 1 January 1943, he again appeared in the second tier, taking the role sung earlier by Sved in *Carmen*. In the broadcast of this opera in March, Paul Jackson heard an "artistic ripening." Warren had one chance to sing in the first cast of a February *Trovatore* with Martinelli, Milanov, and Anna Kaskas as Azucena. The conductor was Cesare Sodero. As Carlo in *La forza del destino* in February, he followed Tibbett. Otherwise Warren's program tended toward Sunday night concerts and repeats of operas. Not until 20 March did he have another chance at a show-case role, and that was Tonio in the broadcast of *Pagliacci*. Again he sang opposite Martinelli, and again Sodero conducted; Marita Farell sang Nedda. Jackson felt that neither Antonio Scotti nor Pasquale Amato could have sung Tonio better than Warren did that day. With "absolute security of tone" he included "a brilliant high A-flat" and had "clarity of focus." It was "one of Warren's finest efforts." The *Trovatore* (5 February) and *Pagliacci* (20 March) were his first at the Met, and the *Forza* (11 February) his first anywhere. Warren was also cast as Germont in the Met's *Traviata* of 25 March at the Civic Opera House in Chicago. That was only his fourth try at the role under the Met banner, and his ineptitude caught the eye of Cecil Smith, who gave him a mixed review.

> Leonard Warren, in his Chicago debut, contributed to the static effect of the performance by substituting conventional gesticulation for communicative acting, and by turning his stalwart young baritone into a strange mush in his attempt to sing with restraint. When he opened up into a superb high A-flat, full voice, at the end of the second act, the effect was electric, and one realized what a good Amonasro or Escamillo he might be.

Helen Jepson and James Melton were the other principals in what Smith called "the dismal charade" that rolled on under Sodero's baton. Another writer said the disastrous *Traviata* might have stirred excitement in Kokomo but was not fit for Chicago. When the company returned to New York, Warren sang a better Germont on another Met broadcast on 24 April, that time with Sayão as Violetta and Kullman as Alfredo.

A Return to South America

Because Panizza wanted Warren in Buenos Aires early in May to rehearse his first *Rigoletto* and first *Falstaff*, he and Agatha left New York soon after the Met closed. Invited back to the Teatro Colón for June, July, and August of 1943, Warren returned as Germont in eight performances of *Traviata*, again with Panizza in charge. He sang the first *Rigoletto* of his career on 11 June and followed it with five repeat performances, four of which Panizza conducted.

Warren's Gilda and the Duke were his family's neighbors in the Sherman Square Studios, Hilde Reggiani and Bruno Landi. As it happened, they were well cast, the secure Reggiani having a crystalline voice, and Landi coming out of the shell of his shyness to portray a nearly ideal Duke. As for Warren, *Rigoletto* was an opera he seemed born to sing. As with his Boccanegra of the previous year, he stunned the audience with the power of his voice and acting. On 12 June the critic of the Buenos Aires *Standard* praised "the enormous success of the evening" and the "majestic voice" and added, "The strength of Warren's performance lay in his electric dramatic climaxes." On the same day, the other papers weighed in. *La Prensa* praised Warren for capturing the "psychology of the unhappy and sinister [jester]." The reviewer of *La Nacion* said, "It is a long time since we have heard on this stage a singer [with] a voice so generous, homogeneous, and virile," but added that because this was Warren's very first Rigoletto, he had not yet fully developed the character. *El Mundo* took a broader view in its review of 13 June, summing up the "resounding triumphs" of his short career. WARREN A MAGNIFICENT RIGOLETTO, the headline read. "The voice has everything, volume, color, and emotion. Warren handles this admirable organ with security, and is equally fine in half-voice and when he uses his tones to their full power. . . . Seldom has the unfortunate buffoon been impersonated with such vocal amplitude and theatrical power."

In the middle of the run of *Rigoletto*, Warren attempted the first *Falstaff* of his career, in a production conducted by Panizza, with Jarmila Novotná as an authoritative Alice and Landi perfectly cast as Fenton. The *Buenos Aires Herald* critic rightly congratulated Warren on 26 June for creating his second huge part in two weeks. "Doubly astonishing is the way this admirable artist steps out of one part and into another. . . . He is an incomparable actor." His Falstaff was "a remarkable feat, [and] admirable." *La Nacion*, reporting on the 23 July performance, said his "magnificent voice and gifts as an actor served him brilliantly." The critic of *La Prensa* congratulated him on such a successful debut in the role and said his originality and faithfulness to Shakespeare's character won the audience. In *El Mundo* he was hailed for his "magnificent voice, extensive range, . . . mastery of details, noble diction, absolute musical sureness." He was "a first class artist, one who consecrates all his gifts to the composer—an unforgettable Falstaff."

Summing up Warren's accomplishments, the critic of the *Standard* hailed his "genius" in singing Rigoletto, the noble and historic Boccanegra, and the comic Falstaff, which he portrayed "with the finesse of any Shakespearean actor. . . . Warren presented his character without a flaw in style and with an understanding and enthusiasm that communicated itself to the audience. Vocally and scenically, Warren's Falstaff is a large masterpiece." The writer said Buenos Aires could boast that "Leonard Warren's genius was first appreciated in this city." At the end of the season, the director of the Colón honored

Warren by giving him the Rigoletto costume he had worn there, together with the jester's bauble. The costume, made in the company's shop, was maroon and beige velvet with gold braid trimming. The jester's hideous "grotesque," a jester doll on a stick, matched Warren's appearance exactly, even to the hat and bells. In 1964, four years after Warren died, Agatha donated the jester's bauble to Gordon M. Eby, who had a collection of memorabilia from Geraldine Farrar, Mary Garden, and the Ponselle sisters.

Warren also returned to the Teatro Municipal in Rio in August 1943, singing a reprise of his Boccanegra and offering his new Rigoletto. Both were successful, but his Germont in September 1943 proved disappointing. Novotná, the Violetta in this *Traviata*, got discouraging mixed reviews, which described her as lacking freshness and sounding thin. Her high tones were forced, and she evidently had some difficulty getting through the first act, but she saved the evening with her acting. She would be judged on her "artistic qualities," not on her voice. Warren fared better with two major critics, but one reviewer wrote unfavorably about him on 15 September, saying that although his voice was as great as ever, "powerful, beautiful, truly phenomenal," his acting was unacceptable.

> Considering the warmth of his voice, we are surprised at the coldness and rigidity of his face. When he sings, everything in him is life and movement, excepting, strangely enough, his face. Even in the emission of the voice, his lips scarcely move. His face is entirely without expression, and [is] immobile. No Buddha has a face that is more inexpressive. This aspect gives the impression that his voice comes not from the mouth but from some other point in space. What this singer seems to practice resembles ventriloquism.

Given Warren's good Italian diction and his spirited manner in the Voice of Firestone videos we have available, these comments seem scarcely credible, but they do represent an established critic's view. At the end of the Rio season, Warren and Agatha traveled on to São Paulo, where he returned to the Teatro Municipal for *Traviata* and *Rigoletto*.

By August, news of the American singers' triumphs had filtered back to New York and appeared in news stories taken from the wire services. On 30 August, a feature story in *Time* described the "Yankee Invasion" of Buenos Aires. It featured four singers. Bampton, the writer said, had been the season's top box office draw, but the "Number one artistic hit" was St. Louis–born Helen Traubel's Isolde. The bass Norman Cordon also drew praise. Warren, whose large portrait photograph ran beside Traubel's, was described as "born in the Bronx" and "stocky [and] swarthy, one of the Met's good stock-in-trade baritones." He made a "much bigger noise in Buenos Aires than any baritone since the great Titta Ruffo." Warren had become a "gran divo." An earlier story in a San Mateo, California, newspaper stated that he had also received an invitation to extend his South American tour and sing six additional performances in Chile. He could not fit them into his schedule because he was to make his debut in San Francisco.

Merola's Regime

The San Francisco Opera often seemed like an American La Scala in the 1940s because it imported so many of its stars. Gaetano Merola, its chief, also drew heavily on the South American theatres, whose seasons ended just as his own were getting under way. The turmoil of World War II forced him and other impresarios further south to change policy, using more Americans in his casts. Particularly, this meant more singers from the Met. Most were grateful to be able to earn good fees with Merola's distinguished company in the months when the Met was "a dark house."

For Warren, San Francisco was a "sandwich date" between South America and his annual concert tour, and he did not reach the city until late in September. His West Coast debut came on 7 October 1943, the season's opening night, with a full house, and the theatre crammed with standees. Warren debuted as the High Priest in *Samson et Dalila*, an ungrateful role in a static opera. His colleagues were Raoul Jobin, hard of voice on top but fully qualified to sing a grand Samson, and Kerstin Thorborg, made ridiculous by a grotesque wig and makeup. Her failure to realize "the Dalila type" (as one critic wrote) led to her being blasted for lack of stage know-how, though she scored with her voice. Nonetheless, respected critics hailed Warren for his performance. In the *San Francisco Chronicle* of 8 October, Alfred Frankenstein alerted his readers to the possibilities of Warren's "immense voice," which was supported by "the endless power, suppleness, and fire of a young man at the height of his capacity." Alexander Fried, writing in the *Examiner* on the same day, called the newcomer "remarkable" and rejoiced in a voice that had "a good old operatic thrill" and was "large" and "expressive," packing "punch and magnetism." His acting also won plaudits. To get good reviews for the High Priest in *Samson* was no small task.

Warren's next opera, more suitable to his gifts, was *La forza del destino*, in which his acting, voice, diction, and conviction were all recognized as exceptional. Frankenstein, writing on 12 October, thanked Verdi for giving the opera its "marvelous roster of first parts" and praised Pinza, Baccaloni, Irra Petina (the Preziosilla), and Milanov, who was later replaced by Dusolina Giannini. Jagel and Warren earned a few words at the end of his column; the phrases dedicated to Warren mentioned the "huge, virile, youthful, and vivid baritone, [who is] a top notch musician and a most intelligent actor." Frankenstein said he looked oddly like Beniamino Gigli, "descended into the bass clef." The first *Forza* was surpassed by the repeat, when Kurt Baum took over from Jagel, but that time Warren won headlines. Fried's column in the *Exam-*

iner on 18 October ran with boldface type that read, OPERA REVEALS SECOND RUFFO. Warren was no less than "an American Titta Ruffo." His "magnificent, free, and charming baritone" won him repeated ovations during the performance and wild curtain calls. When *Forza* was repeated in Los Angeles in November, the baritone's accomplishment was called "a tour de force."

Warren's last opera in San Francisco that season was *Lucia* with Pons and Peerce, formidable competition for any baritone singing Enrico. That was never a good role for him, but Fried, writing on 19 October, found him "superb," although he said Warren sang loud all the time. His voice, a "creamy" baritone, literally covered the audience with sound. Risking a great deal, Fried added, "It is, I think, the most luscious sound that comes from any throat at the Met; and if he doesn't use it with more discretion, that must be because he loves to hear it himself. It is hard to blame him." Pons, a San Francisco favorite, walked away carrying big bouquets and backed by the press. Frankenstein, a day later, said Pons's fans "tore the house down" but added that Warren was the best Enrico he had ever heard, possessing the "depth and weight and darkness" of voice to let him portray "the ultimate villain." Frankenstein faulted Warren for outsinging his colleagues in every scene and outshouting the whole company in the sextet.

With such an initial success, Warren easily got contracts to return to San Francisco in subsequent years of the 1940s, repeating *Forza* and adding *Aida* with Roman and Jagel and *Ballo* with Peerce and Roman in 1944. A single *Faust* followed that year, with Vivian Della Chiesa and Jobin. Warren's grand *Rigoletto* of 1944 with Pons and Peerce was deemed the best opera of the season. In 1947 both *Traviata* and *Gioconda* were added to Warren's San Francisco repertory, the former with Albanese and Peerce, the latter with Roman first and Regina Resnik in the other cast. Baum was the dramatic tenor. Not until 1948 did Warren carry the prime assignment of Iago in *Otello*, with Set Svanholm in the title role and Albanese as a moving Desdemona. Several of Warren's performances on the West Coast in 1947 and 1948 were conducted by the gifted Dick Marzollo. William Steinberg conducted only the *Otello*. Later, Warren had a dispute with Merola, bringing this string of successful autumn engagements to what seemed to be an end; after 1948 he was not invited back until 1954, when Cleva, a strong ally, arranged for his return.

"A Very Big Year"

For the Met administration, struggling with limitations imposed by the war, the idea of calling 1943–1944 the Diamond Jubilee Season was pure promotion. It promised more newspaper coverage than might be garnered in a normal year because the company was celebrating sixty years of life. The opening night was *Boris Godunov*, sung in Italian and produced as a gesture toward Russia, America's ally. Warren's prospects improved somewhat when he was assigned Rangoni in that production, not because he did the role particularly well, but because he sang on opening night. That, at least, assured him a mention by some critics.

In these midcareer seasons, success in concerts carried him forward. Early in 1943–1944, shortly before the Met opening night, Warren sang with the Colorado Springs Symphony and drew a good review from the local critic. In the *Gazette* of 10 November, Elizabeth Hylbon wrote, "One carried away the impression that here was one of the great operatic voices of the day. The timbre is rich and distinctive, and though inclining to darkness of tone, it is nonetheless brilliant and versatile, while the singing itself is robust and virile, shot through with temperament and high spirits, and ornamented with entirely natural and suitable histrionics." The critics mean acting, of course. That autumn many of Warren's other concert reviews fairly matched this one.

This Met season proved crucial to his future. By the end of 1942–1943, he had sung eighteen roles there. Yet in spite of having tried a broadly varied repertory, he felt he had not yet found his place in New York and complained constantly about not getting his big chance. As he saw it, and sometimes said in interviews, he felt the management failed to give him what he deserved, the roles he wanted to sing. Time after time, these were given to Valentino, Sved, or Bonelli, and Warren feared that his Met career might become a repeat of his years at Radio City, years of standing by. Although Warren was bitter, feeling that he had been cheated of the leading parts, he was being protected by two guardians in the Johnson administration. One, of course, was Pelletier, and the other was Frank St. Leger. As Margaret Carson observed, St. Leger helped Warren in subtle ways, mostly by not pushing him. Less aggressive than Pelletier, who had a large vested interest in his protégé, St. Leger cultivated Warren as a pure Italian baritone and nudged him in that direction. Unlike Leinsdorf, St. Leger never pushed Warren into Wagner; he kept him on a narrow path. Warren's progress was slow but steady from 1938 almost until 1950; his first Met assignments in *Trovatore*, *Forza*, and *Pagliacci*, all in 1942–1943, had given him a secure foothold in those works. In 1943–1944 he was assigned another secondary role in the opening-night opera, *Boris Godunov*. Warren's Rangoni was not particularly successful. In the past he had had some good reviews for it, balanced by mixed or bad ones. On opening night this year, inches of space were given over to the Diamond Jubilee and to a horse that the handlers and the tenor, Armand Tokatyan, could not control. In some articles Warren was not even mentioned, and he chalked up one more disappointment. When Warren looked to see what his next rewards might be, he saw himself left out of important productions. Finally, better days came with two new Italian roles. His Enrico in the season's first *Lucia*, which starred Pons and Peerce, was overshadowed somewhat by the coloratura's new costumes. Henry Simon, in the newspaper *P.M.* on 26 November, praised Warren for his "rich, creamy baritone" and "the most luscious sound that comes from any throat at the Met." He sang too loud, Simon wrote, but he sang well.

Much more important was his Renato in the season's first *Ballo in maschera*. This had Milanov as Amelia and Peerce as Riccardo, with Bruno Walter conducting. Downes, writing in the *New York Times*, credited the "uncommonly fine performance" to the conductor, saying he "transformed the opera from an old-fashioned Italian piece to a lusty, full-blooded music drama, which, despite its conventions, strikes home again and again in a manner only possible to Verdi's powerful genius." He also praised all the principals and said Warren's Renato "was robust and sonorously sung. It is a splendid voice, better employed in forte than in piano, but one that was used with marked intelligence and with more than roaring melodrama, if not with the best production in the pronouncement of 'Eri tu.'" Bohm, in the *Herald Tribune*, faulted Warren for poor singing style in the lyric phrases but praised his "huge, rich baritone voice, [which] was so tellingly employed in full-throated passages." Bohm said that Warren "ruined the most touching portions" of "Eri tu" with "breathy, throaty projection." Oscar Thompson finally had Warren's first name right in the review in the *Sun*, but criticized his wooden acting and "burly" singing. However, he praised the control on the "prodigious" crescendo in "Eri tu" and admitted that the applause for Warren was astonishing. Henry Simon, Warren's staunchest supporter and ever loyal, loved the baritone's "glorious" interpretation of "the old war horse."

Warren's First Met *Rigoletto*

On the morning of 18 December 1943, the first of these *Ballo* reviews came out; but before Warren had a chance to read them all, he had an opportunity that turned his Met career around. He was recovering from *Ballo* about ten in the morning when the call came from the Opera House. Tibbett, ill with influenza, had just notified the management that he could not sing that day's matinee broadcast of *Rigoletto*. Warren, who had sung the role the previous summer in South America, was fully prepared to take over. Lucky in having trustworthy colleagues in the cast, he was matched by Kullman, Kaskas, Nicola Moscona as Sparafucile, and Pons, whom he knew well, having sung every one of his *Lucia* performances with her. Sodero, Pons's favorite, a conductor considerate of singers, took the baton.

Both the press and the public love surprise debuts, so Warren was guaranteed a certain measure of success. In the *New York Times*, Noel Straus dedicated most of his column to Warren's performance. He mentioned the singer's youth and attributed the majority of his problems to it, saying that only a "matured artist of long experience" could manage Rigoletto's emotional demands. Although his interpretation was "more conventional than distinguished," Warren deserved compliments for "saving the management" and "making a debut against such odds." He was "thoroughly conversant" with the role, and Straus went on to praise his "seriously considered" portrayal, although Warren became fully convincing only in the "Cortigiani" aria, where he could pour out his "elemental rage." Again the singer's use of full voice entered the equation. His music was "pleasingly and sometimes impressively sung, especially in the moments asking for full volume." The *World-Telegram* also mentioned his primacy in the "Cortigiani" scene. In the short news stories in the *Herald Tribune* and the *Daily Mirror*, Warren's Bronx origins and South American experience were mentioned, but there was no real coverage of the performance itself. Oscar Thompson, however, was present for the matinee and had also heard *Ballo* the night before. His balanced review in the *Sun* praised Warren for being "measurably better" as Rigoletto than as Renato and lauded his "liberal use" of his "secure and expressive" half-voice and the fine effects he achieved when he "employed the full volume of his resonant organ. His highest notes were particularly full and ringing." Warren's characterization was "very acceptable routine," though not distinguished. Grena Bennett, a dedicated Warren fan, wrote a measured review, saying he was "basically intelligent and compelling" and praising his "rich, dark" voice and his "power and artistic control." She also mentioned the hideousness of Warren's portrayal. His insistence on the grotesque in his interpretation set him quite apart, then and later, from baritones who remained their handsome selves in this role. On 27 December, Warren repeated *Rigoletto*, but after Tibbett recovered, he did not do it again for more than a year.

On Christmas Day 1943, Warren also sang an exceptionally fine Tonio in the first cast of *Pagliacci*, joining Albanese and Jobin, with Pelletier on the podium. His reviews were all excellent, with Henry Simon heading his column in *P.M.* by saying, "Warren was the outstanding success" of the double bill. Simon said he earned the most applause of the evening after the Prologue and sang with a "voice that sounded like an impresario's dream." The *Herald Tribune* critic said he was greeted with "cheers" after the Prologue and even overwhelmed the powerful Jobin in later scenes. The *Wall Street Journal* added its voice to the chorus of praise, hailing the "magnificent singing by Leonard Warren. The baritone was at his best, particularly in the [Prologue], and got the biggest ovation of the day. Mr. Warren always had a substantial voice, but it has grown immeasurably with the years, and its sonorous tone . . . is perhaps the best in the company." Pelletier's splendid interpretation carried the opera, the writer said. Paul Jackson, in *Saturday Afternoons at the Old Met*, reviewed the broadcast of 25 March and gave Warren his full due, saying that he provided "the adrenaline of the performance." He was thoroughly convincing in most scenes. Only one or two overly dramatic moments marred the whole. But Jackson concluded that Warren possessed "incipient greatness" and that he was "the new sovereign" of the baritone roles.

All in all, Warren's first Rigoletto at the Met, his Tonio, and the entire season proved to be a great success. The loyal Warren-watcher Henry Simon wrote again about "Warren's magnificent voice," in a long profile in *P.M.* on 19 January 1944. It was headlined GREAT BIG VOICE. Simon stated that Warren had "the finest natural male voice now to be heard at the Met." Although he had been a "musical illiterate" when he won the Auditions of the Air, his hard study had readied him for his Met debut. Warren told Simon that in Italy, "All the sightseeing [I] did was in the hotel room and the teacher's studio." Discussing Warren's reviews, Simon noted that he "chafes under criticism . . . that he sings really well only when he sings loud, and that he sings loud too much of the time." Yet Warren said he had to hold himself back because the Met had so few large voices in the operas he sang. Simon remarked that Warren did not want to sing German operas. Virgil Thomson had just published what Simon called a "Sunday sermon" about how few large voices there were on the opera stage at that time and how radio techniques were killing big voices. Simon commented that if Warren let his voice out full, a "duet with James Melton" would no longer be a duet. In the sextet from *Lucia*, Simon said, Warren's voice rang out over those of the other three principals and the chorus. When Simon asked Warren if he had read Victor Hugo's play *Le roi s'amuse*, Warren replied, "Sure," and then delivered a William Appleton discourse, returning to Simon's favorite subject when he said how much Verdi meant to him. "When Verdi wants a father to tell his daughter to cry, he does it in music and does it so well you can't miss it. I almost have to cry myself when I sing that part. Sure, I've read Hugo, but I didn't have to do that to understand *Rigoletto*." Simon praised Warren's "fierce seriousness" and his modesty. He was only thirty-two at the time and, by his own admission, had a long road ahead, if he were to become as fine an artist as he could become.

Articles on Warren, several of which were beginning to appear in New York and in syndicated newspapers, brought him to the fore across the United States. RCA Victor Red Seal Records also began to run full-page ads featuring sketches of him, portraits, and lists of his recordings, with text about the "bright new luster" he had brought to his art. Whatever satisfaction these things gave him, they certainly did not turn his head. In the middle of the winter in 1944, fighting his way through a sleet storm, he went to Philadelphia to be honored at a city high school assembly. Five thousand Philadelphia students in a citywide poll had voted him "Distinguished Layman" of the year for taking over *Rigoletto* when Tibbett fell ill. The previous honorees were Woodrow Wilson, Albert Einstein, Marian Anderson, and Babe Ruth. During the ceremony, the eighteen-year-old head of the student council presented a large silver loving cup to a smiling, youthful-looking honoree. Warren sang four arias for the students and faculty and thanked them for the honor.

When Warren sang his third Di Luna in *Trovatore* at the Met on 25 February, he stopped the show with "Il balen del suo sorriso." Thomson, in the *Herald Tribune*, reviewed Warren as the "admirable" leading singer of the evening, praising his "beautiful voice [and] dependable manner, and his fine musical style. He is in the process of becoming one of the greatest singers in the world of Italian baritone roles." From the discerningly critical Thomson, this was indeed high praise. By March 1944, Warren was ready with his second title-role opera of the season, *Falstaff*, which he had sung in South America in Italian. In New York, the opera was given in English with an American cast, conducted by Beecham. Because of Tibbett's primacy, Warren was in the second cast, but his earlier successes meant he got long reviews in all the papers. Downes singled him out as "a very competent Falstaff" who "sang the music very well," without "exaggeration or affectation." His discourse on honor was "exceptionally scrupulous and intelligently executed." Bohm, in the *Herald Tribune* of 12 March, found Warren's impersonation "well rounded" both vocally and dramatically, praising his "powerful resonant baritone voice" and his skill in using it. Simon, with his usual frankness, said his acting "was not as good as Lawrence Tibbett's" but "vocally he was little short of superb." Kolodin went farther than other critics, saying the Met would have done better to give the first night to Warren, not Tibbett. Warren's biggest reward came on 20 March, when the weekly *Time* dedicated a two-column profile and a large photograph to him. Under the title "Ample Leonard," he was described as the Falstaff "from the Bronx," the man who had elevated his performance of Sir John above "Tibbett's now rather threadbare version."

At the end of the Met's New York season, Warren returned with the company to Chicago, where he redeemed his reputation and erased memories of his poor performance the previous year. In *Traviata* he had BIG HIT headlines; he also did well in *Un ballo in maschera*. In the *Herald American* he was called "the rightful successor" to Titta Ruffo. When *Rigoletto* reached the stage of the Civic Opera House in November 1944, under the Chicago Opera Company, bold black headlines in the *Sunday Tribune* ran WARREN CLIMBS STARRY ROUTE IN "RIGOLETTO." The review by Claudia Cassidy, who was even then a feared critic, welcomed the "young American baritone [who has] climbed so high so fast that he gives the illusion of flying." She recalled his early efforts with a "big, unwieldy voice, hampered by its own bulk." Now he had "stepped out in the light of his own stardom" as a "stalwart" Rigoletto. His superb acting, even to the tiniest gestures and expressions in his eyes, was matched by a "magnificent voice" that he controlled perfectly. "It is not yet a complete performance—nothing so new could be—but it is a superb working sketch for a masterpiece, to be manipulated and enhanced as a brilliant career develops."

Hollywood and Beyond

With other Metropolitan Opera stars winning added fame in films, Warren accepted a role in *Irish Eyes Are Smiling*, signing a contract with Twentieth Century-Fox. By June he had slimmed down for the film and, with Agatha, found a place to live in California, where he was to make a surefire musical formula picture. It told the story of the romantic and professional battles fought by Ernest R. Ball, a composer of popular songs who had won fame before World War I. Also in the cast were Dick Haymes, June Haver, Monty Woolley, and Blanche Thebom. Like Warren, Thebom had been engaged because of her Met credentials. Gregory Ratoff, the director, came to like Warren as a personal friend, as did Ratoff's wife.

In Hollywood, Warren and Agatha were held in some awe because of their simple ways. Interviewed by John Selby for the Associated Press at the end of his movie-town adventure, Warren talked, as he always did, about his electric trains. "My doctor told me [in 1938] I could either find a hobby or keep on paying doctor bills. I decided to become a railroader and make my own." Bragging about the five locomotives and eight cars he had originally put together, he went on talking about signal equipment. Selby tried to get Warren to talk about his concerts for the Armed Forces and also mentioned his volunteer efforts in army and navy hospitals. Warren refused to discuss these, saying, "Nobody who has sung in a hospital has any right to say anything about it."

After a short stay in New York, Warren and Agatha returned in the summers of 1944 and 1945 to South America, where he sang in August and early September. He was reengaged for São Paulo in 1945, singing *Rigoletto*, *Traviata*, and *Forza*. His career in Buenos Aires effectively ended on 1 August 1946 with a performance of *Ballo*. He later told his sister that Evita Peron fired him. Fittingly, Panizza, Warren's mentor, conducted many of his performances there. At this time, the baritone's career took a different turn, for more and more of his time away from the Met was spent in San Francisco and Chicago. He had also decided he had to rest in the summer. He did not return to South America until 1950, when he returned to Rio and São Paulo.

San Francisco, Autumn 1944

Warren, who had made his San Francisco debut the previous season, was re-engaged for *Aida* with Roman, Jagel, and Margaret Harshaw. He then sang *Forza* and tackled the title role in *Rigoletto* for the first time before this sophisticated audience. With him were the dependable Pons and Peerce. An article by Margery M. Fisher devoted about half the available column space to Warren. Her only reservations concerned his "Pietà, signori," which, she felt, was not sufficiently tragic, but she predicted that he would master this, too, in the future. "He is young and is making steady progress both as singer and actor [and] is destined for a prominent place in the parade of great American baritones, headed by Lawrence Tibbett, Richard Bonelli and John Charles Thomas." Fisher added that Pons sang "the finest Gilda" she had ever done in San Francisco. "Her Gilda was human, even as Warren's jester [was]." Fisher faulted Peerce and the rest of the cast for erratic pitch and unconvincing interpretation but praised the sumptuous staging of the ballet in the first act and the "highly spectacular" storm in the last. Before leaving the city, Warren also sang Valentin in *Faust* and Renato in *Ballo*. Warren then took the train for Chicago, where he repeated *Rigoletto* in two November performances under the baton of Giuseppe Bamboschek. His Gilda was Antoine; Peerce was again the Duke, while the veteran Lazzari sang Sparafucile, and Browning was Maddalena. With all these performances and several concerts behind him, Warren prepared to return to New York and his regular concert and opera routine.

By any standard, this season stands as a milestone in Warren's career, marking his route from second baritone to leading artist. From the autumn of 1944 onward, as Cassidy wisely noted, his upward climb was virtually guaranteed; it would continue if he controlled his voice and improved his acting. Even Kolodin, who had doubted in 1941 that Warren's voice could long survive the heavy use it was getting, had come around. With these critics and Downes, Thomson, Bohm, Simon, Johnson, and other important writers on his side, real progress seemed assured.

Regina Resnik, a Wise Colleague

Warren was still the struggling artist at the end of 1944 when he met Regina Resnik. She recalled her own Met debut, which fell on 6 December of that year. She had won the Auditions of the Air. Her debut was on the schedule, but about a week before it, St. Leger and Johnson called her into the office and asked her whether she knew the score of *Trovatore*. "I know it well, but I've never seen it," she answered. At that, they asked her whether she could make a surprise debut by taking over Leonora the following Wednesday night. "I had never rehearsed even once with the cast because Johnson wanted to spring me on the public. I met the other people in the cast for the first time onstage that night. *After* that performance, we rehearsed together!"

Baum, Warren, and Harshaw were the other leading singers in the performance. Resnik described the event, saying, "All the papers picked it up: nine New York newspapers on a Cinderella story!" She remembered only one bad moment: "I missed a step on a staircase, but I didn't fall. I heard the whole audience gasp." In 1948 performances, she sang Leonora to Warren's Di Luna, Björling's Manrico, and Cloe Elmo's Azucena. "Then I knew I was in the midst of something unforgettable. Björling walked right through the part, singing gorgeously. And Leonard? I found his voice rich and mellow, *pastoso*, as the Italians say. It was a black velvet voice, something much more than just 'a baritone.' When Leonard sang Rigoletto, he sounded more like a bass and Sparafucile sounded like a baritone." Resnik recalled Giuseppe Danise, her teacher, saying of Warren, "It probably could have been the greatest baritone in the world, if we could have removed some of the hot potato from it." Danise, who was then retired but had been a famous baritone in his own right, remained extremely critical of others. Resnik also recalled singing Alice Ford in *Falstaff* with Warren as Falstaff and Fritz Reiner conducting in 1949. About Warren's Scarpia, which she saw at the Met, although she never sang Tosca with him: "I thought he was extremely impressive as Scarpia." Summing up Warren's career, Resnik said that his failure to get basic musical training made things very hard for him. "There wasn't anything he could not do vocally. In the end, it didn't make any difference whether he was trained as a parrot or as a puppet. Leonard was well prepared, a big presence, and not a bad actor at all. He was a very well manufactured package, but that package walked out on the stage and became an artist!"

That artist, seeking growth and struggling with an overloaded schedule, took a critical step in September 1945: Warren asked the Met management to relieve him of several roles he no longer wanted to sing. These included Alfio in *Cavalleria*, Escamillo in *Carmen*, and the Herald in *Lohengrin*. He also asked to be freed of Silvio in *Pagliacci*, Mercutio in *Roméo et Juliette*, and Biterolf in *Tannhäuser*, none of which he ever sang. One odd request concerned *Simon Boccanegra*, for Warren wanted both Paolo and Simon taken off his repertory list. Although he was not freed of all the roles he named, he did get a shorter list, while St. Leger helped him focus on making the Italian operas his special province. By cutting out the roles he felt he had progressed beyond at that time, he laid the foundation for growth in the works he did best.

♦ CHAPTER TWELVE

The Waiting Game

A fter Warren's progress in the early 1940s, some reviewers obviously believed he would soon become as great a star as Tibbett, but for a long time he seemed destined to remain a house baritone. The Met management gave him no new roles. Although he sang on Saturday broadcasts, he felt he was being overlooked. Iago in *Otello* proved to be his only fresh challenge from December 1944 until May 1949. So many of his operas were repeats that the press had little to say about them. He later described the first ten years of his career as sheer frustration, and it began to show. By 1945 Warren was earning a reputation for being difficult with professional colleagues and even unpleasant at times.

Margaret Carson at the Met

At the Met, Warren needed an ally, and he found one in Margaret Carson when she became the new director of the Met's all-important press office in 1944. She replaced Alan Kayes who had been called into service; after the war, he worked for RCA Victor. Carson ruled her world with a strong hand for the next ten years. Her first impression of Warren was of "a gorgeous voice," which she heard in the Opera House, not in a rehearsal room. "It was a voice with an identity, a voice with a face to it. You could hear Warren and Milanov, for example, and the moment you heard those voices you could see their faces in your mind." Carson discovered over the years that Warren had what she called "intellectual curiosity," and she found it astonishing that he "would go up to Columbia University to study his Shakespeare roles, Iago, Macbeth, and Falstaff, with the most respected Shakespeare scholar of the time." That was William Appleton. Carson saw in Warren "a man who had no ambition to be a 'second Tibbett' or a 'second Ruffo.'" Instead, she said, "He was striving to be the very best there ever was." After 1951, Warren and Agatha invited Carson into their home in Manhattan House, where she also lived. As neighbors, they visited back and forth for nearly sixteen years, sometimes at dinner, sometimes at small parties. Carson and Agatha remained close friends for about thirty years. "She was a lot of fun," Carson remarked.

She remembered Warren on the Met spring tours. "Some social events were obligatory. These were the parties given by the local sponsors for the leading singers when they came to a city for their annual visit. Few singers could decline these invitations. They couldn't be avoided, not even by someone who disliked them as much as Warren seemingly did." At some of these affairs, Carson, a handsome woman, younger than Warren, "loved dancing with him" and found him "a wonderful dancer." During her tenure, the baritone gradually turned around his publicity and received fairly steady support from the press office. "I never heard him complain," she said, "nor did Agatha complain to me. Even when he did not get rave reviews, he never said anything." He most certainly did complain to others in the press office, although while Carson was there, he had fair coverage, something remarkable for a man who believed he was mired in routine.

Warren was also getting professional help from a distinguished vocal coach who became his accompanist. Willard Sektberg, a pianist and organist, maintained a studio on Seventy-second Street from 1939 until 1979, just around the corner from Vivien. Born in New Jersey, Sektberg, a child prodigy, had become a church organist when he was twelve. He studied in New York and Paris. When he and Warren first met, Sektberg was accompanying the Met tenor Richard Crooks, whom Warren admired. From 1945 until 1960, Warren and Sektberg traveled the baritone's recital circuit as an effective team.

At the same time, Warren was becoming more aggressive around the Opera House and even snapped brusquely at the supernumeraries. On 23 March 1945, the Met offered *Aida* as the student performance matinee. Alan Coleridge, who was then in high school, already stood well over six feet tall and had become a regular super. "I was paid a dollar for each performance," Coleridge said.

> In *Aida*, one other super and I had to carry a golden calf in the Triumphal Scene; it was very, very heavy. Backstage, we were waiting for instructions. We had set it down and were standing with other supers, talking. Warren, just in front of us, was waiting to go on. Suddenly he wheeled on us, and, in a loud voice, barked, "Shut up!" We obeyed, and he marched onstage.

A Trusted Colleague

He was not always so brusque. To others, Warren would show both the lion and the kitten. The Met tour of 1945 marked the beginning of a rare personal friendship between the Warrens and a fellow singer. Blanche Thebom, a leading mezzo-soprano with the company, was, like Warren, an American who had never sung professionally abroad. Her antecedents were Scandinavian. A native of Pennsylvania, she was raised in Canton, Ohio, and had worked with private teachers, making a career in concerts and radio before joining the Metropolitan roster in the autumn of 1944. Trim, attractive, and proper, she was respected for her musical correctness and artistry. She was also remarkable because of her dark brown hair, which was five feet long; it reached her ankles when it was unpinned. Thebom combed it into braids that were wound into a splendid crown. Anyone who came to know her well discovered a no-nonsense "working woman," as she called herself, an expert at time management and a person of enormous dignity and self-respect. Like many novices who tried to learn as much as possible by listening to colleagues, Thebom often sat in on rehearsals and performances. Thus she heard Warren onstage before they began to sing together.

The rehearsals of *Gioconda* in Thebom's first season gave her the chance to work with Warren, and on her first Met tour, she became friendly with Warren and his wife. "Leonard and Agatha and I got to know each other socially because of the tour," Thebom said.

> We were always on trains. It took a long time to get from one place to another on the tour in those days. Agatha always went along with Leonard. I was so impressed with his artistry, and I let him know it. I got to know him perhaps better than most of his colleagues did because I was so overwhelmed by him as a performer. Leonard and Agatha were comfortable with me, and I with them. He thought the sun rose and set with Agatha. He absolutely adored her. She was "the other half of Leonard," and he was "the other half of her." His devotion to her was absolutely on a par with his total devotion to his profession. He was completely involved with her. They had the world's most perfect marriage. He was just incomplete without her, and she lived for him. He talked about nothing except his career and Agatha. We were very close friends. Leonard was really a kitten, so approachable and so lovable. I felt very comfortable with him on a social level because of his sense of service as an artist and friend.

In Cleveland on the 1945 tour, Thebom sang with Warren for the first time. The opera was *Gioconda* on 21 April. She was Laura, the role that had often been assigned to Bruna Castagna in that and earlier seasons; Roman was Gioconda; and Warren was Barnaba, while Jagel sang Enzo. Thebom and Warren often appeared together in *Gioconda* over the next ten years. After 1946 she also sang Amneris to his Amonasro in New York, Philadelphia, Cleveland, Chicago, Atlanta, Denver, Boston, Washington, Birmingham, and Des Moines. Frequently standing in the wings when she was not onstage,

Thebom heard these works at close reach. She also attended many rehearsals, even when she was not singing.

Of Warren's work Thebom said:

> As a total artist he had integrity, a degree of integrity that no one else had. Everything he could possibly know about something, he *knew*. He had that total immersion into character. When you saw Leonard onstage, you forgot it was Leonard. He had a way of becoming the character. His interpretations were always matched with his large, rich vocal sound. He could be so stunning because he was always so in character. It was artistry wholly put to the service of the character. I was completely in awe of his Amonasro. I have to confess that I cannot imagine anyone else doing that part. I was always in the wings listening to him. When I did Amneris, I am onstage when he comes on. He was awesome, so total and so powerful, a real entity, just as he was offstage. When he turned from side to side onstage, you could physically feel his power. His entire energy and projection and emotional life burst out. He was like a flame-thrower.

Thebom admitted that she also saw Warren display his temper.

> Yes, he was "hell on wheels" sometimes because he felt he had to have things his way. When anyone tried to get him to do something he did not feel was right, it was like butting up against a stone wall. I remember once he climbed all over Herbert Graf during a dress rehearsal. I don't even remember what opera it was; I was in the auditorium, and he just blew up.

Thebom described frequent evenings as the Warrens' dinner guest in Manhattan House. "They never had another guest when I was there, just me. It was not a formal thing, just getting together. We talked about singers and plans for our careers and said, 'Wouldn't it be great if . . . ?' That was his whole life: Agatha and his career as a singer. Period."

Although Warren sometimes felt discouraged at the Met, he had years of successes in concerts and opera out of town. He also returned to his beachhead at the San Francisco Opera, where he won over the audience and found a comfortable niche. In 1946 he appeared with the Chicago Opera Company in *Rigoletto* and *Aida*. John S. White, his coach, said Warren prepared for each of these repeats, never losing sight of two main areas of study, the history and the text. The complex tempos and his cues in duets, trios, and ensembles were a challenge throughout his career. Vivien said he "loved the solo work but was scared of getting lost when he sang with others."

He also focused on acting, and, as he had always done, he looked outside opera for models. After he was invited to sing at Glyndebourne, Warren spent many free hours in preparation by watching the Old Vic Theatre Company, which came to New York with Laurence Olivier and Ralph Richardson as its stars. Warren was already a fan of Olivier's, having seen several showings of the film *Henry V*, which was sponsored in New York by the Theatre Guild. He loved its flat sets, which offered no perspective and, he said, seemed ideal for opera on film. "They could then be melted into a life-like and existing filmed scene," he said. He aired all this with an interviewer for the Buenos Aires *Standard* that summer, calling the Old Vic performances "super-stupendous." He also said how happy he was when the company scheduled an extra performance of *Henry IV, Part II*. As it happened, he could not use his new ideas abroad because the Glyndebourne engagement could not be arranged.

Warren's New Gilda

Before that summer 1946 trip to South America, Warren sang his tenth *Rigoletto* at the Met with a very young partner, Patrice Munsel, who was his Gilda on the Met's spring tour. Billed as the company's youngest coloratura soprano, she had seen her name appear on the roster in 1942–1943, after she won the Auditions of the Air. Munsel was introduced to the Met audience in a Sunday night concert, just as Warren himself had been in 1938, and soon was thrust into leading roles. She was the youngest person to sing a leading role at the Metropolitan Opera House in the entire history of the company and the youngest ever to be signed to a contract. Facing well-meant criticism, she worked until she became an invaluable member of the company. Munsel's Gildas in 1946 were the first of a long series of collaborations with Warren in *Rigoletto* that lasted until 1952. She had also played Lucia to Warren's Enrico in *Lucia* in December 1944, but, as Munsel said, "I didn't know him that well before *Rigoletto*. You really don't have a lot to do with Enrico, the brother, you know." Before 1946, Warren had played Rigoletto opposite Pons, Antoine, Mimi Benzell, and Sayão, but he was still relatively new to the part himself. Munsel said she had been singing Gilda with Tibbett,

> the most delicious man to work with, so charming and so talented. So I was a bit worried when I learned I was going to start singing with Leonard. I must say that I was more than impressed with him; I was thrilled with his interpretation of Rigoletto. Thrilled and moved. When I've heard people do it recently, I keep wondering why they have not carried on some of the great tradition he represented. He had a whole different feeling for the role, where the drama was so important. He moved me every night.

Munsel, who had worked toward her goal of being an opera star since she was twelve, said, "The drama of the opera appealed to me as much as the music.

That's why I was so moved by Leonard. He lived it every single time. Was he too melodramatic? Never! After all, *Rigoletto* is melodrama from the very beginning, and Gilda and her behavior are melodramatic, and so is her death. Leonard made Gilda's death believable to me as an actress. I found that very gratifying."

When she was asked about Warren's development in the role, she said, "Of course, he kept polishing it, but musically it was so right from the beginning. I think his whole performance was right. In 1952 I did my last performance with Leonard and was sorry when I realized it would be the last. I was always excited by the prospect of doing Gilda with him. He had such personality, such a wonderful characterization in that role." Munsel added that although Warren never openly criticized her, as he did many other singers, she learned by chance that he had told other company members he was unhappy about her. "I heard through the grapevine that some things I was doing distressed him. I was upset to hear that." Although she doesn't remember what bothered him, Munsel suspected that Warren was a bit wary of her.

> I had a reputation for not taking any nonsense. In 1946, on tour in Rochester, I was singing Rosina in the *Barber* with Baccaloni and Nino Martini. In the Lesson Scene, they were horsing around a lot. Martini was pretending to play the piano, and Baccaloni walked over and sat down beside him, and the two of them kept pounding on it until it started moving up and down on the stage. They made so much noise I couldn't hear the orchestra, so I just stopped singing and went downstage and spoke to the conductor [Pietro Cimara] and said "When all this stops, I'll start over again." Martini and Baccaloni marched off the stage at the end of the act, and I could hear them backstage, shouting in Italian, saying "We'll never work with this woman again." Maybe that's why Warren never said anything directly to me about the problems he had with my Gilda.

Asked whether she had ever had the chance to become friendly with Warren, she said:

> No, not really. Although he was a magnificent artist, I never "found a person" in him, as I did with Pinza and Peerce. With them, I knew the person inside and loved them dearly. But I found Warren remote, whether in New York or out of it. On tour, he stayed to himself, mostly with Agatha and Earle Lewis and his family. So I really only knew him very casually. But nothing can detract from him as an artist.

Willowmere

During these early middle years of Warren's career, he was driving himself almost to exhaustion, as he had done in Milan and New York in 1938. With his passion for tinkering with cars, radios, television sets, and gadgets of all kinds, he surely must have felt confined by the four walls of his New York home. Agatha, after all, described their Lexington Avenue apartment as "a telephone booth" when Margaret Dempsey interviewed her in Baltimore. They decided they had to find a place in the country, a refuge for them both. Needing space and time to relax, the couple had begun searching at the beginning of 1946 for a place close to New York and the Met. They scouted New Jersey and Connecticut in their new Mercury sedan, which Agatha drove. So far as is known, Warren never drove after he married. The Mercury was their first luxury purchase after the sacrifices of wartime. Their choice for a small country place finally fell on Connecticut, where they found "a dream home" in the Willowmere section of Riverside, near Greenwich. In choosing Connecticut, Agatha and Leonard Warren acted as other colleagues did; also there were the Tibbetts, Wilfrid Pelletier and Rose Bampton, Geraldine Farrar, and, later, Licia Albanese and her husband, Joseph Gimma. The house the Warrens bought in 1946 stood on a narrow peninsula that reached into Greenwich Cove. A picturesque site on the north shore, it had a full view of Long Island Sound backed by distant hills. With a backyard reaching into a grove of trees and a waterfront and sandy shore, the house offered the best of the country and the beach to its new owners.

The house itself, with its quaint pitched front gable, had a curious history. It was an exact copy of the dressing room cottage that Mary Pickford had had built on her studio lot in Hollywood. Just two shallow steps up from the lawn, the ground floor had a large living room with a gabled ceiling with heavy oak beams. Its walls were painted a smoky blue. Large windows provided a view of Long Island Sound on three sides. A dining room took up much of the main living area; the kitchen, out-of-date and plain in 1946, was the first room the Warrens remodeled and expanded, adding a dishwasher and other amenities. Two light-flooded, airy bedrooms, each with private bath, completed the ground floor. Upstairs was a third bath and bedroom; it had an entire wall of windows. Warren called it "The Admiral's Bridge." Surrounded by a lawn that ran down to the beaches on three sides of the peninsula, the house had a garden bursting with hollyhocks, Canterbury bells, and asters, which the Warrens had started in a cardboard carton on the bathroom windowsill in New York. A large mulberry bush behind the house sheltered a nest of Baltimore orioles. The pride of the garden, though, was the rose bed, which Warren loved to describe in interviews. He learned about drainage and sunlight, and he and Roy gradually learned to fertilize the roses with fish heads and mulch, but spraying for bugs was Warren's job. In a later remodeling, two other bedrooms and baths were added on the second floor. The Warrens began moving to Connecticut late in the spring and officially became residents of Riverside at the beginning of July. Agatha bore the burden of the main move from mid-June until the first of August, while Warren, accompanied by Roy, was keeping engagements in South America. Warren called his wife almost every day while he was away. Interviewed that summer by Carol Jackson of the newspaper *Greenwich Time*, Agatha described their new house as a "little English cottage" and "a storybook house, just like the gingerbread cottage in *Hansel and Gretel*."

One neighbor and close friend of Leonard and Agatha in Connecticut was Tina Appleton Bishop, the sister of William and John Appleton. She said the Warrens bought the house for "about $25,000, maybe $27,000. They got it for a song." Three regular visitors were Roy Leifflen, who left the Navy with the rank of Lieutenant Commander and was practicing law in New York and Washington, and Agatha's parents. Mrs. Bishop recalled the Warren household:

> Mrs. Leifflen loved fishing, and so did Leonard. But these were not born country folk! Mrs. Leifflen wore her pearl earrings when they went fishing! She was very rigid and very prim. She dressed in Riverside exactly the way she dressed in Brooklyn. And she brought her "parish values" with her. I remember that there were several children with their nursemaids on the beach in front of Leonard's house. When they came out of the water and changed out of their swimming suits, Mrs. Leifflen was horrified. I had the impression that all the Leifflens were very cut-and-dried, very strict Catholics. Leonard converted to Catholicism, of course, and so did their maid, Lottie, and that is unusual. They had very rigid ideas. I remember Agatha being critical of Jussi Björling because of his drinking. "He ruined himself with alcohol," she would say. And Pinza was "that animal" because of his womanizing.

Speaking of Agatha's conservatism and her dread of looking sloppy, Vivien remembered her own attempt to get her sister-in-law to wear tailored slacks and a blouse. "I went to Bloomingdale's and picked out four pairs of slacks and four tops, but Agatha just stared at them. She was totally a city person. She and her mother simply could not be casual." Agatha also tried to keep her husband in fairly dressy clothes, even in the country. Father Royal Gardner, a priest from the Church of St. Vincent Ferrer whom the Warrens entertained in Riverside, said that Warren was "very relaxed there, never sloppy, but very comfortable in the country with his captain's hat and his baggy shorts. He kept his shirt outside his shorts or trousers, and Agatha hated that." Father Gardner remembered their country house as "so homey and lived-in."

Mrs. Bishop recalled the Warrens' Riverside life as

very simple. They loved the outdoors, the terrace, the garden and the roses. Roy was the indoor cook; when he came up from Washington, he always brought with him a freezer full of food. Leonard took over the outdoor meals, preparing chicken or steak on the grill with fresh corn on the cob. He had a fancy barbecue and flourished the tools around like a pro. Leonard and Agatha, with Roy or her parents, when they visited, used to ride all over the countryside looking for the best vegetable stands. They shopped in Old Greenwich and then went to Mass together at the Church of St. Catherine of Siena in Riverside every Sunday. Leonard moved some of his electric trains into the house, where he could play with them, leaving the rest in New York. He also loved his boats.

When I interviewed Warren in his Manhattan House apartment in the early 1950s for *Opera News*, he talked mostly about his "paradise" in the Willowmere section of Riverside. As the interview began, he seemed as buttoned-up as the vest and jacket of his three-piece suit, but gradually he relaxed. Because I already knew him from previous interviews and from sitting in on many room rehearsals as the guest of Mario Del Monaco or Cleva, he seemed quite comfortable as we talked. About his boats at Willowmere, he said, "The water was right there, and we just had to put something into it." First, he said, he bought a flat-bottomed rowboat, which he fitted with an outboard motor. It served for brief trips off the pier and short jaunts up and down the shore. Then came an eighteen-foot craft with an outboard motor. It was followed by a twenty-four-foot inboard, a Sea Beaver with one hundred horsepower, "equipped with every gadget manufactured for boats," as he described it. Agatha laughed, saying she was sure it would sink under the weight of all the accessories he had bought. Even then his pride and joy was his ship-to-ship and ship-to-shore phone. He said he used it to call friends and his manager, play practical jokes on people, and call Agatha to tell her what fish he had caught. It would be their dinner. He told me he took up fishing "primarily because I got tired of just reading and doing crossword puzzles while I was out." His eyes lit up when he told of piloting his boats up and down Long Island Sound. He said that Agatha, his in-laws, and their friends came with him on fishing trips; sometimes they would pack a lunch and swim from the boat, about a mile offshore. Occasionally they would take friends to Norwalk or other shore towns, tie up, and have lunch on shore. Agatha said they had never had any serious accidents, although they had picked up a couple of children who had fallen from other boats. Warren was like a boy, popping with pride when he told me about his rose garden. Again, the catalogues came out. The idea of this rough-hewn man cultivating roses boggled the imagination, but he was deadly serious when he talked about them. In the end, he said only the sea offered him "great tranquillity," something he said he could not find on land. "I always do my best thinking on water," he said, "and that's where I love to be."

He named his first important boat *Troubadour*. It was followed by *Troubadour II*, nearly thirty feet long, built in St. Simons Island, Georgia, and bought in 1957. He spoke triumphantly about ordering it by phone while he was in a hotel on Capri. *Troubadour II* had a planked mahogany hull, twin Nordberg engines, more than one hundred horsepower each, a separate twelve-volt generator system for emergencies, a galley, and two bunks. When I interviewed him in the early 1950s, he said he had taught himself everything about boats. As he had taught himself to sing, he learned water safety by reading books and magazines because he never had time to take the Power Squadron courses. All things considered, Warren became quite an expert boatman, although years passed before he could call himself that.

Tina Appleton Bishop recalled a funny incident on the water from Warren's early days at Willowmere.

> Once he came in from fishing and ran aground. This was in the days when he knew almost nothing about the tides. He got his boat stuck in the mud because he was not yet experienced enough to handle it. So he had to anchor it off the dock and wade in. Here came this enormous man, out of the sea, covered with muck up to his knees! The children were terrified. But he smiled broadly and picked up one of them and began to sing Figaro's aria to the children in a soft voice. "Figaro here, Figaro there!" That broke the ice, and everyone laughed.

In the evenings, Mrs. Bishop said, "Agatha and Roy played a lot of backgammon with us, but Leonard was not a 'game person.'" Nonetheless, he, Vivien, and Agatha played a card game called "Spite and Malice," for which Agatha kept score on legal pad sheets. Mrs. Bishop said Agatha also loved to paint, but Warren was her main concern.

> She babied him, and he babied himself. She took wonderful care of him. Leonard was a very simple, direct, almost childlike person with absolutely no airs. He was about as simple and straightforward as you could ever imagine anyone being. And helpful! If you brought him your broken TV set, he would thank you for it and then go straight to fixing it. He was always repairing something for someone.

Mrs. Bishop remembered how kind Warren was to her children, who were six and four when they first met him.

Warren became a regular at the annual New York City Boat Show, setting aside days in his calendar for it. When he found out its dates, he ordered his manager to set aside three days without concerts so he could spend all his time there. He showed me his catalogues of equipment, most of them picked up at the recent Boat Show, where he said he had spent most of a week. He had been unable to find his favorite fishing reel, a Pflueger, which had formerly been made by Enterprise Manufacturing Company in Akron. During the war, Enterprise stopped making tackle, and gradually the Pflueger reels became collectors' items. Warren told many people about his search for this reel. "You can't find one anywhere," he complained. Finally John S. Pflueger, the president and treasurer of Enterprise, heard of Warren's search and asked his employees to look for the reel he wanted. In a salesman's old sample line, one was found. Pflueger gave it to him. "And that was the beginning of a beautiful friendship," the baritone said. The reel became the pride of his tackle box.

A Companion for Fishing

Warren's most dependable fisherman friend was Henry Kaston, a violinist from the Met orchestra, who recalled, "I drove over to Willowmere from Scarsdale to visit on Sundays. Leonard was a very dear friend." Born in Poland and educated in Paris, Kaston joined the Met orchestra in 1943 after auditioning with Pelletier, George Szell, and Emil Cooper. He met Warren, he said, when he went backstage to congratulate him after a performance. Because Kaston had a flat in the old Met Studio Building, he was around the Opera House all the time. He said:

> Leonard and I became very close friends. He invited me to their apartment on Lexington Avenue all the time. I would have dinner with him and Agatha, then he and I would play with his electric trains. He had the whole thing set up on a big table. When I went to Paris in the summer, I always had to bring him back some new model railroad cars for it. To some extent, he was like a child, and a little naïve; and the trains were his toys.

After the Warrens bought the Willowmere house, Kaston became a regular visitor there, especially on summer weekends. "We fished, we talked about singers and music. We always went out in the boat together, half a day at a time, and came in for dinner." Kaston, who also made fine gold jewelry for many of the singers, made jewelry for Agatha. Kaston found her "very kind, but she was always bossing Leonard around. He did everything she wanted because he loved her so much."

Recalling Warren's artistry, Kaston said he watched Warren develop over almost two decades.

> His acting and singing became perfect. He had a voice like a tenor, very clean. I honestly never heard him make a mistake. He never missed a note. He was just so perfect all the time. The Met was everything to him, just as singing was everything to him. I've never known

anyone so devoted to music and acting. He was very convinced about what he did. He wanted to have everything his way, and he rarely looked at a conductor. He did watch the prompter, though.

Kaston said Warren, when he was downstage, often looked into the pit to make eye contact with him. "I was at the third stand in the first violin section, and it was easy for us to see each other." Warren trusted him, and the two men remained friends for years.

A Kindred Spirit: Marylin Noble Tracy

Another frequent and welcome guest in the Warrens' country house in Riverside was young Marylin Noble, the daughter of Roy Leifflen's law partner. As we have seen, she first heard and met Warren at the Metropolitan Opera in 1940. After Warren and Agatha visited the Nobles' farm in 1941, Marylin followed the baritone's development for almost two decades. As she grew up, she became the Warrens' close friend, seeing them at the Met and visiting first their small Lexington Avenue flat and after 1951 their Manhattan House apartment. She recalled an afternoon in the 1940s in the "not very attractive" Lexington Avenue apartment. While she was there, Warren told her how hard it was for him to achieve the career status he aspired to. "He said he was having a terrible time getting started and talked about singing and how hard it was. He was working on his acting all the time. I remember he spoke about his concentration on *Rigoletto*. He was a perfectionist, and acting was very difficult for him." She added:

> Agatha thought his voice was the greatest on earth. She was very protective of him. All he wanted to do was sing. She was his real business manager, a very strong-minded woman. She could be very sharp with people when she got upset or excited. Leonard didn't care anything about money or contracts. Agatha did all of that. She also discussed Leonard's contracts with my father [Roy's law partner]. Roy did a lot for Leonard, making arrangements for travel and investments, things like that. He was a very good pianist. When I first knew them, Agatha would occasionally sing when Roy played, but she was very reticent about singing after Leonard became a famous artist.

The Riverside trips had a routine to them, Marylin Noble Tracy recounted.

> [Leonard] would have a Saturday matinee or evening performance; and they would leave New York the minute it finished. Mr. and Mrs. Leifflen also went up all the time. Leonard loved that house, but more than the house, he loved his boat. He was like a boy when he got on that boat. He also had a ham radio in the house, in one of the upstairs

bedrooms. It was a big black box that he tinkered with all the time. He just loved to go up there and talk to people on his radio. Leonard loved gadgets. After they moved to Manhattan House, one of his pleasures was walking down to Hammacher-Schlemmer on Fifty-seventh Street and looking at all the gadgets and toys. He loved to walk. Oh, such a sweet, natural person! He never changed. He was just Leonard, always talking about some mundane thing.

Whatever else Warren did for pleasure in Connecticut, he never studied opera scores, except during the summer when he had Giuseppe De Luca as his guest and mentor. The house had no piano. As Warren told everyone, he went there to sail, fish, cook, and cultivate his roses. John S. White, a frequent guest, said:

> When you saw Leonard there with his boat, he was nothing spectacular. As you were sitting in the house with him beside you, you would never have guessed that he was the greatest baritone and singing actor in the world. You would never have suspected that this man was a world-shaker in his profession. He never struck poses. He liked simple things like the beach, the water, his boat; he liked people around him.

White recalled a visit when he and Warren, exhausted after a day of boating and gardening, were napping in the late afternoon on the sofa in the living room. "Agatha came in and saw us asleep and was very angry because we weren't working at something! But Leonard never worked on music in Connecticut. He went to rest."

From the summer of 1946 on, Warren and his wife spent their free time in their comfortable private refuge on the water. Vivien said her brother loved the Willowmere property so much that when he got there, at the end of the car trip from New York, he sometimes kissed his fingertips and touched them to the front door, saying, "Oh, my little housie."

◆ CHAPTER THIRTEEN

Art As a Work in Progress

In 1946 Warren and others on the Met roster went through the summer without new contracts because the company was threatened by a labor dispute with AGMA, the American Guild of Musical Artists. At issue was Edward Johnson's attempt to fire sixteen chorus members who had been with the company for twenty years or more. He was not wholly successful, for one of them, a woman, survived to chalk up fifty years in the ranks. When no resolution was reached in early discussions, Johnson threatened to close the Met. A final agreement was not signed until 24 September. Then and only then could formal negotiations with singers officially begin, although wise managers had already agreed with Johnson about their clients' schedules. During the litigation, Warren, who was singing in Chicago, told André Mertens, his manager, that he understood the Met's problems and was "willing to cooperate to the utmost" and show his loyalty to Johnson and to the company. Mertens passed his words on to Johnson, in a letter now in the Met Archives, then set forth Warren's terms. His spring tour dates were at issue because they overlapped with other engagements, but in general the outlines of the season were clearly drawn. He was still on a weekly salary of $500 at the Met, $550 per week on tour. The most important improvement in his position was this: two title-role operas, *Falstaff* and *Simon Boccanegra*, were added to his repertoire list. He was not guaranteed either that season and did not sing them, but as he knew, when they came, his career would take a leap forward. Because of the dispute with AGMA, he did not sign his contract until late October.

In the spring of 1946, just a few weeks after buying the property in Riverside, Warren embarked on another recital tour, from one end of this country to another, and into Vancouver, Canada. The 1946–1947 Met season opened with Pons in *Lakmé*; Warren's first *Otello* of the season reached the stage on 16 November. Like his first Iago, it was a broadcast matinee. Again he had Roman as Desdemona, with Torsten Ralf as Otello, but in December the Chilean tenor Ramón Vinay, a former baritone, moved into the title role,

159

which he was to claim as his own for many years, singing it on three continents. Perhaps the most significant performance for Vinay was Toscanini's NBC Symphony *Otello* broadcast, released on RCA Victor. Fritz Busch conducted at the Met from 1946 to 1949; *Otello* was a favorite with him, and he gave his singers full rein. It was also a great success with the public, but Warren, who had sung Iago only five times, did not fare well with the New York critics. Biancolli, like his colleagues, criticized Warren's interpretation. In the *World-Telegram* he said it was "hardly adequate for so malicious a character."

Perhaps stung by the reviews, Warren decided to consult William Appleton about *Otello*. Appleton had returned from army service in 1945 and, by his own account, was seeing a great deal of the Warrens and Leifflens. He remembered Warren's work on Iago as focusing chiefly on motivation. Appleton said:

> At the end of the play, when Otello asks Iago why he had acted as he did, Iago refuses to say. In the opera, too, Otello says, "Discolpati!" In his desperation he demands that Iago explain his evil deeds. Iago cries "No!" I told Leonard this represented what Samuel Taylor Coleridge called "motiveless malignity." Evil exists for its own sake, and it doesn't need motivation. There are some people who are evil by nature.

He urged Warren not to suggest that Iago loved Desdemona, was burning with jealousy over Cassio's promotion, or believed that Otello had "played hanky-panky" with Iago's wife,

> nor should he play to the homosexual idea that Iago was in love with Otello. All these ideas had been aired by critics. I told Leonard they were all wrong. In fact, I think the "Credo" in Verdi's *Otello* is one of the great strengths of the opera because it does establish in some way the idea that evil is innate, that it exists for its own sake. Leonard became a very persuasive Iago, simply because he didn't buy any of these limited views of the text. He was pure evil. Rangoni in *Boris Godunov*, which Leonard had sung for years at the Met, is different; he is working for the church; there is his motive. But Iago is something else. His whole being is put to the service of evil.

Clearly Warren took Appleton's counsel to heart, for as he developed Iago, he gradually expunged all melodrama from his characterization, developing a silken character who was refined and frightening. Appleton particularly admired Warren's new subtlety. "Because his voice was so large, and because he became more confident of himself, he finally reached a goal he had had for years: to sing certain scenes with Otello with his back to the audience, letting the full horror of what he was saying be seen on Otello's face, not his own." This piece of stage action had to be reserved for artists, not hacks; and if it was hard for singers who were good musicians, it was almost impossible for some-one who always depended heavily on the prompter, as Warren did. None-theless, he finally developed enough confidence in himself to be able to turn away from the footlights and let his voice, back, and hands tell the story. In the course of his career, Warren was lucky in having two superb Otellos to play against. Vinay was Warren's passionate, dark victim from December 1946 to March 1952. He was followed by Mario Del Monaco, who made the Moor his signature role.

Warren and Agatha celebrated Christmas in 1946 by inviting the Björ-lings and their children to their apartment on Lexington Avenue. Anders Björ-ling, who was ten at the time, told me he visited the Warrens twice during that holiday. "Leonard had a whole room devoted to his model railroad. He would turn out the lights in the room and let the lights from the trains blaze in the darkness. He loved things like that." Anders also remembered seeing television for the first time in the Warrens' apartment. "The set had a little rounded screen, and the image rolled up and down all the time. It didn't quite work, but it was very exciting. Leonard impressed me so much because he was almost childlike in his enthusiasm."

As the 1946–1947 season progressed, Warren went back to roles he knew well. When he sang his next Amonasro, the attention of the audience was focused more on the Duke and Duchess of Windsor than on the singers. *Aida* made "a very welcome return," Downes wrote in the *New York Times*, but he had little good to say about the Radamès of Vinay, who, the critic felt, should have remained in his original baritone range. Thebom, "now officiating as a contralto," was "almost certainly a soprano." Downes said the "two great voices of the performance were those of Zinka Milanov and Leonard War-ren." But, oh! Milanov's appearance! "Where, by all the snakes, in the name of all that is incredible, did Mme. Milanov get her costumes? They were masterpieces of ridiculousness, incongruity with period, and style." Downes praised Warren's "sonorous voice" and said that he sang "with breadth, dig-nity and fire" in the role of Amonasro, in which he "is heard to the best advan-tage." Bagar in the *World-Telegram* said, "Two richer, more exciting voices" than Milanov's and Warren's would be "hard to imagine," but he, too, found Vinay's voice short on top. Another plus for Warren was tallied when Thomas B. Sherman reviewed RCA's recently released *A Treasury of Grand Opera* album: "Mr. Warren's baritone has the agility of a lyric tenor and a masculine power and frontal resonance that make it a supple instrument for all dra-matic and musical purposes."

This was also a season of good reviews for *Rigoletto*. Warren's fifteenth performance of it followed in February 1947; the opera stayed in the repertory until spring. Kolodin, brittle as he sometimes was, did listen to singers. On 8 February in the *Sun*, he called Warren "the dominating figure of the evening," with "imposing vocal strength and much more subtlety than in the past. The superb flow and richness of Warren's voice are notable, and he has worked hard to augment an acting ability that is by no means innate." Twelve days later Kolodin added:

> Warren has verged on becoming a great Rigoletto for some while; and the line of separation is narrowing all the time. He has all the vocal resources one could wish, and he has mastered enough plausible dramatic action to make a reasonable show as an actor. But he is so enamored of the sound and weight of his voice that he forgets too often that color is as much a part of tonal effect as emphasis. There were some exquisite details of modulated tone, but a little more [care] in "Cortigiani" would have underscored the meaning that Verdi wrote into this great scene.

In March, Kolodin reviewed Warren's newly released recording of "Pari siamo" and "Cortigiani" from *Rigoletto* and congratulated him on having been "superbly recorded." It was "a first-rate accomplishment." In the *New York Times* Downes wrote, "Warren is growing constantly as an actor and dramatic interpreter. His fine voice is constantly under better control for purposes of color and diction as well as those of mere sonority. He was given a special demonstration by the audience after the curtain of the third act." Biancolli said Warren's voice was "getting bigger by the week"; he would "never forget Rigoletto's scream after the kidnap scene." In a later review he called his jester "a truly tragic figure." Warren marked up another important "first-cast" evening with *Gioconda* on 12 February, singing with Milanov, Tucker, and Stevens, with Emil Cooper conducting.

Giuseppe De Luca

On balance, one could say that Warren was gradually turning the corner in his career. He was solidly seated at the Met, though not where he wished to be, and was winning major-artist status in North America, as he had in Argentina and Brazil. His recitals and concerts were also showing new polish and refinement. Part of this growth derived from his own persistent and blind determination to improve himself. But another factor, Warren's decision to take coaching lessons and serious advice from the veteran baritone Giuseppe De Luca, brought about a remarkable refinement of his stage persona and his singing. Roy Leifflen, interviewed by Joseph G. Chisholm, said Agatha had decided that De Luca would help Warren. "She called him and said, 'Come by and say hello.'" Discerning critics soon sensed that something was happening to Warren and began asking who caused the turn-around. They learned it was De Luca.

Like Ruffo and Stracciari, De Luca had become a baritone standard-bearer in his career. Born in Rome in 1876, he had made his debut before the turn of the century; he quickly gained both reputation and experience, so that he was offered a contract for La Scala in Milan. The season 1903–1904 found him there, just in time to create the role of Sharpless, the American consul, in the disastrous world premiere of Puccini's *Madama Butterfly*. De Luca was engaged by Covent Garden and by the Metropolitan Opera, where he sang from 1915 to 1935 and from 1939 to 1940. As a major artist he sang more than eight hundred performances of more than one hundred operas. Again he appeared in a Puccini world premiere, *Gianni Schicchi*, produced at the Met in 1918. Although De Luca had frequently traveled between Italy and the United States over the course of his career, he made his home in New York City before and after the end of World War II. Young singers often sought his advice. In the 1930s, the young baritone Samuel Barber asked De Luca to give him an audition; Gian Carlo Menotti was Barber's accompanist that day. By the 1940s, De Luca had returned to Italy, but after the war he came back to teach voice at the Juilliard School of Music and celebrate his golden jubilee with a concert in 1947. Defying age and time, De Luca sang a stunning Sharpless to Licia Albanese's Butterfly during the late 1940s in Newark. He died in New York in 1950.

It was in 1947, near the end of this master's life, then, that De Luca agreed to accept Warren as his pupil. For a major artist this step meant the start of a new search for a more polished dramatic style and vocal refinement. The seasons of 1946–1947 and 1947–1948, when Warren was with De Luca, were among the most productive of his career. When they had been working for about a year, Warren told Mary Ellis Peltz, the editor of *Opera News*, about his debt to "that incomparable Rigoletto, Giuseppe De Luca." The coaching gave him a new direction, he said, and he was "striving for a more perfect balance in the part" so he could have a "maximum impact" on the audience in the heightened dramatic moments of the opera. "It is necessary to exercise considerable restraint. The passages with Gilda must be kept within a purely lyrical frame. Verdi's music provides a marvelous opportunity to create a character that must always arouse sympathy, whether as the cynical court jester or as the tragic and tender father." Warren stressed the "new possibilities" and the "subtlety and nuance" he was finding, as he went on hoping "to perfect this extraordinary character."

All the "new insight" from De Luca also made an impression on Alfred Hubay, whom De Luca knew. Hubay had begun working as an usher at the Met in 1943 and later rose to become the house manager. He acquired an extraordinary appreciation of voices. Speaking of Warren's debt to De Luca, Hubay said the older man taught him "to be a little more nuanced than he had been before. Above all, he taught him more about how to use bel canto singing in his middle voice." In 1947 Warren invited De Luca to spend the summer with him in Connecticut. They fished in the morning, usually catching small fish that Warren could grill for dinner, but once De Luca landed a sand shark, which he insisted on bringing in, "so it wouldn't bother anybody else," Warren told a reporter. He and De Luca studied the roles, then lounged in deck chairs on the patio. At night, they cooked on the barbecue. Sometimes they ate "Leonardo's" special Milanese risotto or pasta. This study period with De Luca was the only occasion when Warren brought opera into the sanctuary of his "little housie."

The middle and late 1940s were among Warren's busiest seasons. In Indiana in May 1948, he told Clarence Newman, a writer for the Fort Wayne *News-Sentinel*, that he traveled 165 days a year "to fill concert and radio engagements," regularly singing three times a week on his recital tours. On tour, major artists fought to keep away from small cities and, worse, towns. Pons, Tibbett, and Björling always demanded bookings within easy reach of New York. Warren, though, continued to accept less important concert and recital sites throughout his career. Even on the road with the Met, he tossed in an occasional radio or concert engagement. Warren told Newman that he sang either a rehearsal or performance every day at the Met and studied operatic roles five hours every day. "I haven't any time for my personal life," Warren claimed. About the great singers of the past, he said, "Most of them I've never heard in person, so my desire is not to copy anyone but merely to sing and stay happy and healthy." Nevertheless, he admitted to leaning heavily on De Luca. When Newman asked about his success in recitals and concerts, Warren changed the subject, saying opera was "my favorite, it's my career, and it's still the most gratifying thing. Each [opera] is a different adventure, but they demand great research in different periods, how characters in history behaved and the mannerisms of their times." He also analyzed his study of *Rigoletto*, describing all the "period details." Warren believed that the stage and movies were "a constant reminder to operatic performers to be on their mettle as far as their dramatic work goes. People demand polished performances in addition to fine music." As he often did, he mentioned contemporary composers, saying he was "an ardent admirer of *The Telephone* and *The Medium* by [Gian] Carlo Menotti." The failure of *The Island God* did not come up. At the end of the interview, Warren repeated his creed, saying, "A voice is a thing God gives you. What you do with it and how long it lasts depends on how hard you work and how well you take care of it."

The End of a Decade

Warren's next Metropolitan season began with the new production of *Un ballo in maschera*, with Giuseppe Antonicelli conducting, Graf directing, and Daniza Ilitsch as Amelia. Peerce was Riccardo, and Harshaw sang Ulrica. One particularly difficult critic, John Rosenfield of the *Dallas Morning News*, came to hear *Ballo* on an evening in January 1948 when Warren was singing it with Roman, Björling, and Harshaw, with Fritz Busch conducting. A significant comparison between Warren and De Luca appeared in the column, which carried the headline LEONARD WARREN SINGS SENSATIONAL RENATO. Almost six column inches were devoted to him. "We sent our hats sailing up into the Family Circle [of the opera house]," Rosenfield wrote. "Warren [in this performance] was a new and phenomenal baritone, and the only thing old about him is his name." The astute critic asked a member of the Met administration about Warren's progress and particularly about his study with Giuseppe De Luca. He added, "The sort of vocalism Warren now represents is his own. He has more voice than De Luca had, and his high fortissimos, while covered, are more stentorian, more dramatic and better supported [than De Luca's]." Rosenfield went to say that this performance surpassed in large measure his "other operatic appearances and his rather tasteless Civic Music recital . . . or [his] generally well-sung Rigoletto of the Met's 1946 Dallas season." He concluded by saying the baritone had not yet reached the level of artistry of Pinza or the Golden Age's Scotti or Chaliapin, but he was surely well on his way to the highest reaches of his profession. By the middle of the 1947–1948 season, then, Warren's studies with De Luca were paying huge dividends in terms of reviews on the road and in New York. Louis J. Snyder, by then a stalwart of the Met press office, recalled De Luca's return to New York and spoke of Warren's development at that time. He said, "I remember that Warren sort of burst forth as an artist as he was studying with De Luca. I always thought it was amazing that he was able to absorb what he did, absorb the information he got from people about language and acting, and then make it his own in such a forceful way."

It is to Warren's credit that he won these victories in spite of never having paid the men hired to applaud in the Met claque, not even when Ferruccio Tagliavini, Giuseppe Di Stefano, and other colleagues were paying the claqueurs for every performance. By never being bludgeoned into paying, Warren put himself at substantial risk, for the claque was a force to be feared. At the old Met, the claque was headed by Max Bennett and John De Luca. John De Luca was known among the Italians as "Lingua d'oro" (Golden Tongue) for his vicious attacks on those who would not pay. He sneeringly referred to singers who paid as "our clients." Once he guaranteed Tagliavini a ten-minute ovation for "Una furtiva lagrima," and he was perfectly capable of holding up a performance for that long if a singer was willing to pay for enough claqueurs to create that "storm." On another occasion when one singer refused to pay for a claque, Bennett and John De Luca organized a gang and went to boo and whistle, teaching him a lesson. The humiliating spectacle, staged in an audience that included Björling and Giuseppe De Luca, showed the claque's ugly power. Even Björling (or perhaps his wife) was said to have put money in the claqueurs' hands after they began orchestrating huge demonstrations for Di Stefano. The bass Giorgio Tozzi said that claqueurs let each singer know how much they wanted, saying, "Well, I like white liquor, vodka, and it's expensive," or "Steaks are good, aren't they?" Tozzi said he gave the claqueurs ten dollars once in a while, just to keep them quiet. Notwithstanding the Met's efforts and those of the stars that resisted them, Bennett, John De Luca, and the claque survived. Alfred Hubay said one of his specific jobs was patrolling the dress circle to keep the claque under control.

As the New York 1947–1948 term ended, Downes wrote a "Retrospect of the Season" article in the *New York Times*, weighing in with all his prestige: "Highest praise must go to the fine baritone, Leonard Warren, and his constant advance in his art. He seems to take his Metropolitan engagement with a seriousness and sense of obligation to his employers, his public, and his art." One month earlier John Ball had put it succinctly when he reviewed *Rigoletto* in the *Brooklyn Eagle*. The headline read: GIUSEPPE DI STEFANO DEBUTS AT THE MET; LEONARD WARREN STEALS THE SHOW. The critic said, "He opened up his gifted throat and proceeded to sing and act with such quality that the show was his, lock, stock, and libretto. Mr. Warren took this opera home in his already well-filled back pocket."

Warren often reflected on his own voice and methods of study. Once in 1946, in the Hotel Vancouver, he was obviously comfortable during an interview, when he curled up in the depths of a big chair, "boyishly, hugging his knees." He told a reporter for the *Daily Province* that he believed his voice was

> a gift from God. I can only use it with humility. The voice is a responsibility, a bridge. I ask myself, "Why did my brother not get it? Why not my sister?" The only way I can deserve it is to study. The voice is only a conveyor of great emotions, but how can I feel them unless I understand not just the music, words, voice, production, conductor, orchestra [and] action, but also the life of the man [I am playing] and the life of his times. What is the conflict inside him?

He spoke of recent work on *Rigoletto* and *Simon Boccanegra* in particular and said of Verdi, "He was a great master of emotional music. There is something in Verdi to wring even the most hardbitten heart." Another Canadian writer spoke to Warren about his studies when they sat in his hotel suite in Kitchener in 1947. Warren said, "A singer is like a doctor, he is never through with learning." Experimentation, he said, was the road to understanding.

> Sure, God gave you a voice, but a lot of people have a voice and don't know what to do with it. A singing teacher can tell you when your voice is right, but you have got to experiment and experiment, and keep on trying yourself until you get it right. You have to learn how to make it right with your own particular equipment. You will always be learning something new as long as you live.

In January and February 1948, the "new" Warren covered the eastern half of the United States from Maine to Georgia in six weeks in concerts, winning star treatment everywhere. He and Sektberg, his accompanist, were "greeted with a veritable storm of applause" in Portland, where the critic said, "His magnificent voice and vibrant personality" enriched all his music, from "Ombra mai fu" to "Eri tu." Warren created the impression that he was having great fun. In a 1948 review from an unidentified newspaper, the writer said the audience created such an uproar when Sektberg struck up the "Toreador Song" that he and Warren broke up laughing and had to stop. More "tumultuous applause" followed. Only then could they begin again. In Troy, New York, the music ranged from Handel through Figaro's aria to "A Little Bit of Heaven," and the audience was "wildly enthusiastic." Warren closed with "The Lord's Prayer," which was so moving that there was a moment of "stark silence" before a storm of applause rocked the hall. The local critic found him "a jolly, big man who loves to sing." In Macon, Warren was rewarded with "one of the greatest receptions" anyone could recall. The critic said:

> Warren is more than just a great singer. It is the brain behind that voice that, having brought its training to a degree near perfection, plays with it and upon it like a great pipe organ. In "Sebben crudele" by Antonio Caldara, Warren's control of breath and phrasing suggested the perfection of [the] bowing of Fritz Kreisler and Pablo Casals. Though the medium is different, the perfect art is of the same flawless character. It is rare indeed to hear from a vocal organ of such capacity a mezza-voce as beautiful as that of Leonard Warren. He is first, last and always a great artist.

Offstage, Warren's simplicity proved to be an asset almost as great as his voice. Sektberg, who was handsome and even taller and more imposing than Warren, made a handy stand-up comic for him in their encounters with the public. The two men made friends with fans before or after their programs. And if Warren managed to get someone to listen to him talk about his model railroad and his skill in building trains and track, he would bubble with pride. The best of his boyish nature came out in these encounters. In May 1948, when Warren was to sing at the University of Wisconsin, he bragged about his skill as an amateur chef and proved his merit by cooking a spaghetti dinner for fifteen people in a university kitchen. "Complete with salad and meat balls," Warren boasted.

Mexico City

Warren's earlier successes in South America suggested he would also do well in Mexico, where the Ópera Nacional first welcomed him in 1948. His debut role there came in May as Di Luna in *Il trovatore*, with a cast that included Baum, Varnay, and the American mezzo Winifred Heidt. Guido Picco conducted. A description of the outcome survives in the memoir of the noted Mexican stage director Carlos Díaz Du-Pond. He described Varnay as "the authentic dramatic soprano" and Baum as an egomaniac who hung on to his high C in "Di quella pira" even after an angry conductor stopped the orchestra and laid down his baton, and even after the stage manager brought the curtain down. Warren stole the show. "What a beautiful timbre he had!" After "Il balen del suo sorriso," the audience "went mad." Heidt, Varnay, and Baum then sang with Warren's Barnaba in *Gioconda*, which marked the farewell performance of the great mezzo Fanny Anitúa, who sang La Cieca. Warren, Baum, and Varnay were "magnificent." Vinay joined Warren and Varnay in *Otello*, with Warren's friend Renato Cellini conducting. "Warren was already an idol," Díaz Du-Pond wrote, "and I think that took away applause from Vinay, who was maturing from day to day in the role of the Moor but who kept his baritone timbre." It was clear by summer of 1948 that Warren's artistic growth, unsteady in the past, had finally become a constant.

CHAPTER FOURTEEN

Leading-Artist Rank

A mong the symbols of power sought by ambitious singers on the Metropolitan Opera roster, few carried more weight than a contract securing a per-performance fee. In the company's ranks, two classes of soloists worked side by side. In steerage were the singers on weekly salaries, and in first class were the leading artists, paid by the performance. In theory, this was a fair system, but some per-week singers sang better and even had better reviews than their better-paid colleagues. Under Johnson, the younger Americans sometimes felt their promotions were delayed by Europhile attitudes because so many Europeans came to the Met as leading artists. Even after the Americans moved into leading roles in new productions and opening nights, some were still being handed their weekly salary and kept firmly in their places. In annual negotiations, the Met generally had the upper hand because it ran a virtual monopoly. Anyone who did not like it could leave, but there was nowhere else to go.

Warren, whose importance to the company grew steadily, pressed for years to be paid on a per-performance basis. He believed he deserved that, but not even André Mertens of Columbia could convince the Met management of his merit. Eventually, though, the company could no longer pretend that he was not a star. Yes, he occasionally got a mixed review in New York, but he rarely got a bad one; most critics wrote glowingly about him. The Met management knew full well how important Warren was to the company, with Tibbett's gradual withdrawal from the stage and the failure of any other baritone to take his place. Johnson was always ready to hand Warren a compliment, but sometimes that was not enough. The baritone also wanted to be treated as the serious artist he knew he was.

An overview of Warren's Met contracts shows how hard it was for him to gain the recognition he thought he deserved. In 1942–1943, he was earning $171.50 a week. This was raised to $250 a week in 1943–1944. A big leap brought him to $400 a week in 1944–1945. In 1945–1946, he was engaged for $450 a week for seventeen weeks. A slightly more compromised contract was offered in 1946–1947, when the Met gave Warren $500 a week but cut his time down to fourteen weeks. All this fell in a financially tight year, when he and Agatha were carrying substantial new burdens incurred in Connecticut. One year later, a further increase to $550 a week came for 1947–1948, but this, too, proved inadequate to his needs because his contract period was cut to thirteen weeks. The Met usually had the option of adding extra performances or requiring the artist to sing on the tour, but those options did not always work to the singer's advantage. Managers complained, saying contracts with other opera companies or extended concert tours could not be planned until the Met performances were in place. Sometimes singers even had to wait until late in the season for their tour assignments. Concerts, both in and out of New York, always had to be approved by the Met management if they overlapped in any way with the artist's Met schedule. Especially vexing to the Met were singers' outside concerts in the middle of the tour. These were attempts to earn extra income, but the Met might well ask for the event to be postponed.

Although he was doing opera, radio, recordings, recitals, and concerts, Warren felt he was still badly paid and was overlooked for the big Met productions. At that time, he and Agatha traded their Mercury for a used black Rolls-Royce sedan, which she and Roy drove. Vivien said, "A luxury car was not inappropriate for the Warenoffs because Uncle Leon owned a Silver Cloud Rolls, but that secondhand Rolls was the only showy thing Leonard owned." He and Agatha also lived modestly in another important way, for they never pushed socially at the Met. Unlike many singers, they rarely dined with members of the Met's board of directors or prominent subscribers. This made them seem distant and probably contributed to Warren's slow progress because the management favored popular singers who appeared at Metropolitan Opera Guild events and worked for fund-raising drives.

Not until 17 September 1948 did Johnson offer Warren a contract with the status of per-performance artist. He was covered for 1948–1949 and was given a minimum of twelve "individual" performances at five hundred dollars each. Any additional performances were to be paid at the same fee. He was to begin rehearsals in mid-November and sing until 8 January. He got a favor: a break for his concert tour. Then it was back to the Met on 14 February for the rest of the season. His tour dates would fall between 21 March and 25 May 1949, and he would be paid six hundred dollars for each of them. All the usual penalties for noncompliance were written in. How this Metropolitan Opera contract translated into reality can be seen from the record of Warren's engagements. He still had a long list of contracted roles and was required to prepare the works of many composers. The Met casting system then required singers to prepare many operas so they could cover for one another in emergencies and sing in the second- or third-tier casts. This meant dozens of hours of coaching sessions for works that singers might never perform.

Warren's first season as a per-performance artist brought several visible tokens of stardom: the opening night *Otello*, which was also a telecast, and three Saturday broadcasts. Two of those were his title roles, Falstaff and Rigoletto. He also did Germont. With the new contract, he earned first-cast assignments in *Rigoletto*, and *Falstaff* in Italian, a new Met role for him. No longer did he have to follow Tibbett, his prestige grew, and his self-image improved. Singing only Verdi operas that season, he was completely focused, further proving his right to the grand Verdi characters. De Luca continued coaching him on his scores, while William Appleton, for whom Warren had developed a particular affection, worked with him on Verdi's Shakespearean operas. Appleton recalled their sessions that season, saying that they developed the idea of Falstaff as a

> decayed gentleman. Leonard never forgot that he was, after all, *Sir John Falstaff*. We talked about this character first as Shakespeare portrayed him in the history plays, [which Warren had seen performed by the Old Vic]. We saw Falstaff as this antiquated, elegant figure, and that is how Leonard played him. He was never vulgar, never gross. I will never forget how he came down the stairs of the Garter Inn, dressed in his finery for the visit to Alice Ford. His clothes were old-fashioned, but they had clearly been fine clothes. He had a beautiful pair of gloves, and as he came down, he was pulling them on in the most elegant way. That was a good example of how he utilized the details of character that we worked out. Yes, Leonard's Falstaff had disreputable friends, but he never lost his essential nobility. Leonard acted him as a figure of great dignity.

It was his studies with Appleton that led Warren to make notes in his *Falstaff* score on specific acts and scenes from Shakespeare's *The Merry Wives of Windsor*.

Falstaff was in rehearsal at the Met from December on, with early sessions that were a concession to Warren's midseason concert tour. The interrupted preparation resumed upon his return in mid-February 1949. Regina Resnik, who sang Alice Ford, recalled:

> We rehearsed it for six weeks, with Reiner at the piano. He only gave up the piano when he actually had to conduct! For a week, he started every rehearsal with the fugue from the last scene. Of course, it is the most difficult thing in the opera. Every day, Leonard would say to Reiner, "I don't know why we can't start the rehearsal at the beginning. Why do we have to start at the end?" He wanted to start at the beginning because that was the way he had learned the opera, and it was hard for him to break away from the way he learned things. Leonard was excellent as Falstaff. I liked working with him, and I

liked watching him as Falstaff. He enjoyed himself so much with it. You know, everybody thought he was humorless, but Leonard was very funny. I played the bad little girl with him and even piqued him a bit during rehearsals. Then his big, wide smile came out; he would say something to me in that high tenor speaking voice of his, and he would laugh. As the Fat Knight, he was enormously impressive vocally, as you can hear in the *Falstaff* CDs in the Art of Fritz Reiner series.

The matinee, a broadcast on 26 February, brought out the critics in full cry. VIRTUOSO STYLE, INTENSE MUSICAL REFINEMENT, and TRIUMPHANT blared from the headlines, with Reiner getting full credit for his extraordinarily polished rendering of the score. "Mr. Warren's Falstaff was a worthy center of [the excellent cast]," wrote Downes in the *New York Times* the next day.

His voice gains constantly in quality, richness of color, and technical control. He gains in authority and nuance with each season. . . . Mr. Warren gave the Knight a trace of dignity and contemptuous superiority to his comrades of the dung heap in the first scene and a suggestion of the courtly in his reception of Dame Quickly and later of the disguised Ford. And he made Falstaff a human and appealing character throughout. Above all, he was able to bring changes in the character in terms of masterly song.

Other critics were equally glowing, with Thomson calling Warren "vocally grand and dramatically satisfactory," giving a "thoroughly distinguished performance." In the *Sun*, Kolodin greeted Warren's Falstaff as "magnificently vocalized," a characterization that "stands beside his Rigoletto as the most mature things he has done as an actor." Along with Warren and Resnik, Elmo and Valdengo bustled with energy as Dame Quickly and Ford, and Albanese sang Nannetta, with Di Stefano as Fenton.

Kolodin, reviewing the last *Falstaff* of the season, counted more than two hundred standees at the back of a full house and voiced the hope that the opera would return in the next season. It did not. The Falstaff of 7 March 1949 was Warren's last at the Met. Although Warren begged for years to sing it again, not until 1956 did Renato Cellini arrange another *Falstaff* for him. This New Orleans Opera Association production of 5 May featured Vivian Della Chiesa and Richard Torigi. What Warren could not get at the Met, he later also achieved that year in San Francisco and Los Angeles, singing *Falstaff* in September and October, four months after New Orleans. The last Sir John of his career came on 23 October 1956 in San Francisco, with Elisabeth Schwarzkopf, Oralia Dominguez, and Frank Guarrera, with William Steinberg conducting.

Warren's last performance at the Met for 1948–1949 was *Otello*. He and

Agatha then left with the company on the long spring tour, traveling to Baltimore, Boston, Cleveland, Atlanta, Dallas, Los Angeles, and Minneapolis. It was during these coast-to-coast sweeps that Jerome Hines, the young American Metropolitan Opera bass, really got to know Warren, although they had been acquainted for some time before they appeared together in the same production. Hines sang his first Sparafucile to Leonard Warren's title role in *Rigoletto* on the 1950 tour in St. Louis on 22 April and in Atlanta on 26 April. For years, the two were often cast together in that opera. They also worked together in the 1959 *Macbeth*. Asked about his recollections of Warren and other colleagues, Hines said:

> Warren was very well settled at the Metropolitan when I came there in 1946. He was generally regarded even then as having the potential to be one of the two or three greatest baritones in history. He had a world-class sound, he had the top, and he had the sound that fills the hall. I'll never forget those pianissimos on his high notes. His middle voice was not as colossal as Bob's [Robert Merrill's], but to each his own, one might say.

He described Warren's register and remembered him as "throaty in the high voice," while Ettore Bastianini sang with an "all-chest voice; it had a narrow sound. He became the leading baritone in Italy, of course." Merrill sang with a voice in "the dome of his head," Hines said, while Robert Weede "sang with a high voice; he sang 'behind the eyeballs,' in my opinion. I think Weede studied Tibbett's records. Warren didn't. He was an original. George London had a throaty sound like Warren's, a good high voice and a gorgeous sound." Hines and Warren established a "good colleague" relationship that lasted until the end of Warren's life. Warren extended his "Good Samaritan" hand to Hines on more than one occasion. As we shall see, Hines even convinced Warren to go with him to sing in mission houses for alcoholics and the homeless on the Bowery. It was a close bond. Both men believed in the Almighty, Hines said. "Neither of us was embarrassed by using the word *God*. For us, God was a real presence and source of strength."

Back to Mexico City

When Warren returned to the Ópera Nacional in 1949, he was greeted as a hero and reassured by the presence of his friend Renato Cellini, who conducted two of his three operas. In his memoirs, Carlos Díaz Du-Pond described Warren's 1949 Rigoletto as "fabulous." The critic of *El Redondel*, writing on 29 May, called Warren the successor of Riccardo Stracciari, Titta Ruffo, Giuseppe Danise, and Carlo Galeffi. Another review mentioned his "monumental voice." *Un ballo in maschera* followed with Warren and Gianni Poggi. The review of this opera in *Excelsior* hailed the baritone in "another great dramatic role" and tagged him "a colossal interpreter of Verdi." A feature article in the same newspaper declared that Warren was "absolutely the top baritone of the era." Going even further, the writer said that Warren could match or even outdo Ruffo and Stracciari, whose performances many in the audience remembered. He was "today's idol." Warren's last opera was *Traviata*, in which Poggi was a "cold" Alfredo and Onelia Fineschi of La Scala fell short, lacking the top notes and failing as an actress. Again Warren's artistry won the day, while Cellini's conducting was called "magisterial" in *Ultimas Noticias* on 9 June.

Before Warren left, the city's dignitaries honored him with a large cocktail party and reception, complete with orchestra, at the University Club. Among the guests were writers, diplomats, artists, and journalists. The British and American ambassadors and the American consul all attended with their wives. Directors of the Anglo-American Cultural Institute and the National Archive of Mexico were also among the guests. Reporters described Warren as "young, very distinguished, and jovial," and "portly." With Agatha at his side, Warren heard speakers call him "the principal singer of the season" and "the darling of the public." At the end of the affair, the city and the opera society presented him with a large round silver platter that bore an inscription commemorating his appearances. During the evening, Warren was interviewed by Virginia Snow, who wrote for the *Mexico City Herald*. To her he confided that he had had problems with the altitude, which was "a challenge to my breathing capacity." He also said that he had changed his schedule to accommodate Mexican custom, having his main meal after noon and taking just a glass of pineapple juice before a performance. He ate supper afterward, he said. The program of the day, including all the speeches, was recorded and broadcast later on a local station, and the prestigious event sent the Warrens back to the States in grand style.

CHAPTER FIFTEEN

Ends and Beginnings:
1949–1950

With Johnson's retirement imminent, the Metropolitan Opera Board of Directors set out to find someone to replace him. Among the candidates for his job were the baritones Tibbett, Brownlee, and Bonelli, the tenor Lauritz Melchior, and Frank St. Leger, but the final choice fell on a man who had no direct ties to the company. This was Rudolf Bing, an Austrian-born theatrical administrator and former artists' representative. To ease his entry into the company, Bing was asked to move to New York in May 1949 and spend the next season as a paid observer. His contract as general manager would take effect on 1 June 1950. Johnson continued to produce the planned works of his final season, while Bing, assigned an office in the old Met Opera Studio building, began to assemble his own staff. In theory his team was to do nothing but plan for 1950–1951, but as Quaintance Eaton observed in *The Miracle of the Met*, Bing soon began to wield power and a chaotic year followed, a year "of schizophrenia" marred by partisan and factional struggles, jealousy, fear, and conflict. Bing often fell afoul of Johnson and his staff, while singers were pitted against each other as they fought for contracts.

As it happened, Bing's arrival in May coincided with a difficult moment for Warren. He had changed managers, was ill with influenza, and had been sued for a contract violation. Having left Mertens and his other handlers at Columbia Concerts, he signed with a new agent. This was James A. Davidson, an independent, who ran his management firm from an office in the Steinway Building on Fifty-seventh Street. He functioned as a concert manager and personal consultant, managing the careers of musicians on his own roster and those of other singers as well. While Warren never needed Davidson as a consultant, he did believe he could profit from having a manager with a small list. Because he was ill that spring, he had canceled three concerts in Illinois and Iowa. Thus he became caught in a legal tangle involving himself, Columbia, and Harry Zelzer, a Chicago concert presenter. Zelzer lost money on Warren's cancellations. When he learned that Warren had sung in Michigan on 9 May after calling in sick for the Chicago-area recitals, he tried to hold him liable for the losses and demanded reimbursement for all box office refunds. At that point, Warren had to hire Albert Gins, a respected partner in the law firm of Gins and Massler, to represent him. Influential in the American Guild of Musical Artists, Gins had a solid reputation for handling theatrical matters. He later turned impresario, producing summer opera seasons in the University Theatre in Puerto Rico and engaging Warren as his leading baritone.

Just after Gins resolved the dispute with Zelzer, Davidson published an expensive twelve-page brochure featuring "the greatest" singers on his 1949–1950 list. Jeanette MacDonald headed it, and was followed by Melchior, Steber, Warren, Traubel, Morton Gould and his String Symphony, and Robert Shaw with his Chorale. Large portraits of Davidson's artists showed he was happy to promote them, but with so small a roster, he wielded limited power. Soon Davidson found himself negotiating with Bing for the reengagement of four of his singers: Melchior, Traubel, Steber, and Warren. At that moment, Bing's first priority was to organize a company of "stars, not comets," as he said when he described his plans for reining in Met singers who seemed out of control. He hoped to be able to cajole or force them to commit large blocks of time to the opera season, attend all rehearsals, and give up some of their lucrative concert engagements. Some artists rebelled at once, and openly. Others stood by in fear.

The last opening night of Johnson's tenure was *Der Rosenkavalier* on 21 November 1949. One week later *Simon Boccanegra* followed, with Warren in the title role, Varnay as Amelia/Maria, and Valdengo as Paolo, the role of Warren's Metropolitan Opera debut. Antoine Oberding designed the principals' new costumes, and Fritz Stiedry conducted. Warren had waited a long time to sing this opera in New York, having learned it with Panizza and sung it in South America.

Sitting in the living room of his apartment at 305 Lexington, Warren talked with Frances J. Freeman in an interview for *Opera News* about his approach to *Simon Boccanegra* and his love for it. He spoke of his trip to Italy in 1938, saying that when he prepared Paolo, he made "a study of life in Genoa in the middle of the Fourteenth Century. I went back to it when I prepared the title role. The feeling of the time and place is important; how those people worked and fought, and how most of them had something to do with the sea." He then began to speak of his love for his favorite composer. "Verdi! I always say to myself, 'There's nobody who was so kind to the voice.' He wrote for it. He really loved the voice! How grateful that makes the singer, how he wants with his whole heart to do his best!" Warren then proudly showed Freeman an aquatint of Verdi and a tattered copy of Francis Toye's biography of the composer. It bore a dedication from the great Verdi scholar on its first page: "To Leonard Warren, in gratitude for a dream of my past life

—and two splendid performances of Simon and Rigoletto. September, 1943."
Warren explained that he had met Toye in Brazil, where the musicologist had
been appointed cultural attaché at the British embassy. "We had a long talk,"
the baritone recalled. "He explained many of the subtler phases of the music."
Verdi was always willing to have "the artist study how he could best portray
a role. Verdi didn't believe in iron-bound stage directions," he added.

Warren said he had originally studied the figure of Boccanegra from
Paolo's point of view; as the opera began, he saw both as young pirates. Simon
was "first a rough, forceful fellow who changes into a man of simple, great
dignity, but who never loses that fierce fire within him." Warren said he had
studied Verdi's original 1857 version as well as his later revisions of the opera.
Declaring that *Boccanegra* has "some of the finest [music] Verdi ever wrote,"
Warren then explained his development of this character from young lover to
the great Doge of Genoa. Before Freeman left him that day, Warren had also
expounded on the life of the historical Boccanegra. He then went on to the
libretto. After years of seeking pardon from Maria's father, "[Boccanegra]
began to see his mistake, perhaps even to feel the first desire for peace surging
within his heart." Warren also stressed the man's compassion. He then
described the makeup techniques he used to transform the young pirate into
the old Doge and the psychology of the character, which turned on Boccanegra's awareness of the wrong he had done. "What would you feel if you were
lonely and old, and knew that you had done wrong? Then you meet [Amelia/
Maria] and wonder, 'Could she be my daughter?' You'd muse to yourself,
think how wonderful it would be if you could give her everything you, the
wealthy Doge, possessed. The music is deep and vivid, yet gentle." At that
point, Warren sang a few lines of the recognition scene for Freeman and spoke
again of the text and insight into the main character.

Talking about the Council Chamber Scene, he focused on Boccanegra's
"warning tones." He found the ruler's power to be psychological as well as
worldly. Speaking about Boccanegra's death, Warren told Freeman he had
even discovered the name of the drug Paolo used to poison the Doge. "It
means slow death. Simon's strength must leave him gradually." At that point,
Warren illustrated Boccanegra's weariness and waning power. "He loses
more strength, and yet a little more." At the end of the interview, he spoke
modestly about how he worked. "When I'm the Doge, and Verdi's music is
there to guide me, I just act as he feels. If I sang the scene now, I could show
you. But tell you? How could I tell you?"

His performance spoke for him. In the *Herald Tribune*, Thomson wrote
almost ecstatically about the evening, saying, "Beauty, grandeur, distinction,
and infinite variety were clearly its qualities. Never before has Leonard Warren, always a handsome vocalist, seemed to your reporter so completely the
servant of his role. . . . [His] glorious singing and commanding stage presence lifted the title role to a level of musico-dramatic expression rarely to be

encountered these days." Harriet Johnson, a great lover of refinement, wrote in the *Post*, saying Warren displayed "his beautiful voice" and demonstrated "an immense artistic growth. He produced a real characterization." Robert Bagar, the critic of the *World Telegram*, said, "It is always an absorbing thing to witness an artist's progress right under one's eyes and ears; and it was definitely absorbing for me to gaze upon the polished embodiment of Simon given by Leonard Warren." The high level of execution and the great reviews wholly validated Warren's new leading artist status.

Regrettably, RCA Victor never recorded the complete opera with him as Boccanegra. In *Saturday Afternoons at the Old Met*, Paul Jackson called the broadcast of 28 January 1950 "one of the finest Verdi performances of the decade." According to Margaret Carson, Warren begged the directors at RCA Victor to record it. She said George Marek, an officer of the company, refused, believing that it would not be profitable. Only a single duet survives on an authorized recording. This was made on 4 February 1950 and released by RCA Victor in November of that year. One moment from this important production is captured, the father-daughter recognition scene, in which Warren is paired with Varnay. Beginning with the phrase "Dinne, perchè in quest'eremo," it gives Warren full rein, revealing the depth and brilliance of his characterization in every subtly modeled phrase. The whole of Warren's mighty Boccanegra also rings out on unauthorized recordings taken from the Met broadcast. There we hear Warren's remarkable range of color and feeling matched against Valdengo's clever villainy.

Carl Edwards, a stalwart employee of the Met Gift Shop and long-time fan, recalled Warren's first Simon Boccanegra, saying, "The thing that sticks in my mind is the rapport between Warren and Varnay in the [recognition] scene in the garden. There was a great deal of tenderness and understanding. There was the great freedom Warren had; he seemed so at ease on the stage. No one else had that tremendous ease. And there was the music! He followed the markings in the score beautifully; all the gradations were right there."

By December 1949, Bing's regime, though still unofficial, had laid a solid base in the Opera House. Thus it was effectively the new general manager who sat in the auditorium as Warren rehearsed and performed. Because Warren had never sung in Europe, this was Bing's first chance to judge him. He heard his *Boccanegra* and performances and a broadcast of *Rigoletto*, and *Faust*, which Warren had continued singing. Pleased, he decided to keep him under contract. Negotiations with Davidson continued. They should have been simple, given Warren's long term at the Met, but Davidson evidently soon ran afoul of Bing and Max Rudolf, his closest associate. In September 1949, Davidson wrote to give the Met the dates of some of Warren's concerts and non-Met broadcasts in the next season, all scheduled for November, January, March, April, and May. This approach started the Warren-Met negotiations off badly. Davidson's letter, addressed to St. Leger, was handed off to Rudolf, who was by then managing many artist relations. Then Bing and Davidson had a long talk about Warren in mid-December and evidently also disagreed about his Met assignments, his pre- and midseason concert tours, and the Met spring tour. They could not agree on a calendar for his appearances. On 16 December, Bing wrote to Davidson, opening his letter with the words "I thought a good deal about our conversation the other day, and I don't wish to appear unreasonable. What would you, therefore, think of the following compromise?" Bing proposed that Warren be available for rehearsals from 15 October 1950 and sing straight through until 3 February 1951. The contract would thus include the first thirteen weeks of the season. He then offered to let Warren take time off for his usual midseason concert tour, seven weeks in February and March, although this huge concession violated the very rules he was determined to impose on the company. He also offered Warren the leading baritone roles in proposed new productions of *Faust* and Verdi's *Don Carlos*. Bing planned to present it in Italian as *Don Carlo* for the first opening night of his term. He also wanted Warren for other works, "*Traviata*, perhaps *Trovatore*, etc." But Bing sounded a note of warning with his next paragraph, when he asked Davidson to advise him at once about "whether I have now met your and Mr. Warren's points sufficiently, because frankly, with the best will in the world, I don't see how I can meet you further." He asked Davidson for a quick reply.

Davidson waited more than ten days to answer. On 28 December he said that although he had "every desire in the world to cooperate," he felt it was "impossible" for him to accept the outline of Warren's season, as Bing proposed it. He asked for more time and a second meeting, so they could work out a "mutually satisfactory arrangement." After they met again, Bing wrote to Davidson, reconfirming Warren's terms: he would be available from 19 October for rehearsals and would sing a thirteen-week season, beginning on 6 November. This meant that Warren would indeed sing in the opening night *Don Carlo*. He would have one day free every week for his radio engagements. Bing would also give him advance notice of his schedule, so that no operas would clash with the radio programs. If there were a clash between rehearsals and broadcasts, Warren could be released from the rehearsals "on the actual days of such broadcasts." Warren would sing twenty performances at a fee of $650 each. These arrangements, Bing wrote, depended on Warren's signing "a formal agreement on an AGMA form" and on the Met's "reaching agreement with the labor unions concerning holding a season in 1950–1951." Bing also made a concession about the tour. Again he asked for a quick answer.

Davidson's letter of 5 January raised aggravating issues which he said required "a great deal of thought." The first was the problem Bing had raised by mentioning AGMA and the company's future agreements with the unions.

Davidson wrote, "This in effect means you are asking a definite commitment regarding Mr. Warren's services for the season 1950–1951 when you are in no position to made definite and binding commitments on your end." Warren could not pledge twenty-two weeks to the Met and lose possible income from "other and more lucrative activities." While this is true, it is also true that every singer was being asked to make the same pledge, and many were accepting Bing's terms. In that letter, the wary Davidson also told Bing he would make Warren available only for December, January, and February, but not for the rehearsals and performances of Bing's cherished *Don Carlo*. He also refused to make a definite commitment for the spring tour and advised Bing that he would "hold the foregoing months in reserve for you until 15 April 1950." Bing hated to be given a deadline, but that was a lesson some singers and their agents had not yet learned. When he read Davidson's reply, he was furious. Edgar Vincent, whose firm later handled Warren's public relations for nearly ten years, said, "Bing held talks with all the artists who wanted to go on singing at the Met; and he divided them in his mind into 'likes, dislikes, and so-so.' He was especially against singers who thought they were stars. Somehow Warren was in the 'dislikes' category." From the moment Davidson crossed swords with Bing, Warren's career was in peril, and he almost lost the world he knew.

Late January came, and neither Warren nor Traubel nor Melchior had been reengaged—all three on Davidson's list—although singers represented by accommodating managers were being hired. Rumors about Kirsten Flagstad's imminent return led Traubel to announce on 28 January 1950 that she would not be singing with the Met the following season. Melchior, who laid down a quasi-ultimatum for Bing to respond, was never given a contract. He was dropped from the Met roster. Others from the old guard, including Pelletier and Bampton, Earle Lewis, and St. Leger were dismissed. Then came 1 February, and with it the front-page headlines in two newspapers. The *Post* ran bold type across the top of the page: "FLAGSTAD WILL BE BACK NEXT YEAR; SAY BING FIRES TRAUBEL, PONS, MELCHIOR, WARREN." Alvin Davis's by-line story carried a report on Bing's plans and the "stormiest Metropolitan Opera Board meeting in years." It covered the seventeen-to-one vote to approve Flagstad's return. "At the same time there was an unconfirmed report that Bing would announce today that four of the Met's star performers would be dropped from the roster." They were "Lauritz Melchior, tenor, Lily Pons and Helen Traubel, sopranos, and Leonard Warren, baritone." Head-shots of all four ran across the page. On the cover of the New York *Daily News*, the headlines ran in bold black Roman capital letters that took a quarter of the page: "MELCHIOR, TRAUBEL AND WARREN FIRED." That night Warren had to sing *Rigoletto*, having no idea of what his future with the company might be.

In *5000 Nights at the Opera*, Bing's account of this period stresses his accomplishment in getting Flagstad back. But he also admitted that his delaying tactics with "some of the singers" provoked a "difficult incident" with Melchior and Traubel. He did not renew Melchior's contract, effectively dismissing him. Pons remained. Later, Bing was reconciled with Traubel, although she left the Met later. He failed to mention Warren in the context of these disputes, but what happened between the incoming general manager and Warren can be read in part from correspondence and news reports. The fact that Davidson managed Melchior, Traubel, and Warren, three of the "fired" singers, may reflect Bing's dislike of the disputatious agent. But Bing was also personally angry with Warren for demanding free weeks in midseason to keep his concert career on course. Warren argued that this favor had been extended to Tibbett, Pons, Björling, and other leading singers. Why should it not be offered to him?

Alfred Hubay explained Bing's reaction.

> Here is the reason Warren was fired. Bing was an autocrat. He wanted his own way. In the first months of his year of observation, he studied all the singers' contracts and schedules so he could plan his own debut season. Eventually he came upon Warren's file. When he looked at it, there were things he did not understand. Then he got an explanation; he learned Warren had always had an "unwritten agreement" with Johnson that allowed him to leave New York almost every year in the middle of the season and take four or five weeks off for his concert tours. Johnson scheduled Warren's appearances around those tours. Warren would be away for about four weeks, earn a lot of money from high fees, and then come back to finish the season. That was unacceptable to Bing. During a conversation, he absolutely forbade Warren to go on like that. That is how the dispute began. Warren refused, so Bing gave out the word that he was fired. Bing was right to fire him.

Still, from the start of his Met career, Warren had enjoyed his midseason concert-tour privilege quite regularly. These releases were a favor Johnson granted to him, but they proved troublesome. The rehearsal department could never be sure of where the singers were, whether they were in New York or a continent away; sometimes performances were missed after a singer "called in sick" from a thousand miles away. By the end of 1949, Bing hoped to end these concessions, but singers were determined not to give them up.

After the shock of seeing himself on the "fired" list, Warren passed several days in limbo. However, Hubay said, "Bing soon had a change of heart and decided not to get rid of him. He looked at the roster and saw what trouble he would be in without him. At that point, he, Davidson, and Warren reopened negotiations." After Bing's press conference of 1 February, Max Rudolf took over all Warren negotiations, and not until 10 February did Davidson reach even a tentative compromise with the Met management. Warren got a general letter of agreement about the coming year. At that moment, the apparent animosity between Bing and Davidson, with Warren an informed third party, created a breach between the baritone and the new general director, the last thing Warren could afford, knowing that Robert Merrill and other fine baritones were available to replace him. In the end, Bing said Warren could do concerts in the autumn, but he had to remain at the Met from 18 December until the first week in May. Months passed before Warren's new Metropolitan contract was secure, for he did not sign for 1950–1951 until 4 August. Artistically, Warren lost a very big opportunity when he was left out of *Don Carlo*. Vivien said, "It was the greatest disappointment of his career."

Becoming a Catholic

Warren came to his Roman Catholic faith slowly, having first taken instructions in 1941 from Agatha's priest in the Church of St. Charles Borromeo in Brooklyn. As Vivien said, he then let nine years pass before making a decision about his religion. In the end, his was a total, serious commitment and a deeply felt choice. Recalling the process that led to his conversion, he spoke in a 1957 interview with Jesús M. López in Puerto Rico. Warren said his first serious experience with Catholicism had come when Francis Cardinal Spellman invited him "and other friends" to sing in St. Patrick's Cathedral for the Christmas Eve rite. Warren said, "I remember I sang Malotte's 'The Lord's Prayer' and Bizet's 'Agnus Dei.'" He then began to reflect on the meaning of the words in those pieces and said he was also influenced by a "famous Mexican actor and singer named José Mojica," who had given up his profession to become a Franciscan friar. The historic figures of the Catholic faith also meant a great deal to him. He loved statuettes of the saints and was impressed by the huge Christ of the Andes statue in Buenos Aires. When he was interviewed for *Musical America* in 1956, he described seeing Julie Harris as Joan of Arc in *The Lark*, saying that he experienced "one of the two greatest thrills" of his life. The other unforgettable experience, he said, was playing Carlo to Martinelli's Don Alvaro in *La forza del destino* and seeing the grand, old tenor lie flat and immobile as they sang their battle scene duet. Martinelli's feeling and intensity remained in Warren's mind even years later. Returning to the subject of religion, Warren also told Jesús M. López that he was attracted to Roman Catholic belief because, as he said, "Catholicism has everything well defined."

Early in 1950, nearly a decade after he had had his first instructions, Warren spoke to Father Joseph A. Ganley, the priest of the Church of St. Catherine of Siena in Riverside, where he had been attending regularly. Asking Father Ganley to tutor him, he began his instructions again. Vivien said Warren did not even tell Agatha of his plans; he took her into his confidence when he was ready to be baptized. Warren chose Agatha's parents, "Big Agatha" Schmitt Leifflen and Harry Leifflen, as his sponsors. Father Ganley baptized Warren on 10 June 1950 at the main altar of St. Catherine's. The document in the parish register reads:

Certificate of Baptism
This is to Certify
That Leonard Warren
Child of Sol Warren (*sic*)
and Sara Kantor
Born in New York City
on the 21 day of April, 1911
Was baptized
on the 10 day of June 1950
According to the Rite of the Roman Catholic Church
by the Rev. Joseph A. Ganley
The Sponsors being Harry Leifflen
and Mrs. Harry Leifflen.

Warren did not tell his own family about his plan to be baptized. Vivien said, "I learned Leonard had become a Catholic more than three months later, and then only because gossip about him began circulating at the Met. I had to ask him about it, then he told me." However, Warren never told his sister that he had been baptized in Riverside, for she believed he had become a Catholic in South America.

In February 1977 Louis R. Thomas, a professor from Northern Kentucky State College, wrote to ask Roy about Warren's conversion. Roy answered on 8 February, writing, "I know of no profoundly moving experience that moved [Warren] to convert to Roman Catholicism, and I doubt whether he did it to please my sister." He added after 1946 Warren "often came to Mass with my mother, father, sister, and me in Riverside. None of us tried to influence him in the slightest way, as missionary zeal does not run in the family." Yet in making his critical personal decision to become a Roman Catholic, Warren was certainly motivated by love for his wife and respect for the Leifflens and their faith. Both were constant and absolute factors in his life, from the late 1930s until the day of his death. More particularly, his love for his mother-in-law influenced him. Agatha's "nun-aunt" and many of the Leifflens' friends were priests; Warren and Agatha had been inviting them to dinner or to the opera for years. They also knew several important prelates personally and were very close to Licia Albanese and her husband, Joseph Gimma, and to other devout Catholics of their circle.

Wally Cleva Riecker on Warren's Conversion

The younger daughter of conductor Fausto Cleva, Wally grew up in the opera environment as she, her sister Maria, her mother, and sometimes even her grandmother, followed Cleva across the country, from New York to Chicago, Cincinnati, and San Francisco on his many Met and non-Met engagements. I first met the Cleva family when I was in junior high school in Ohio; naturally I turned to Wally for an interview about Warren because Maestro Cleva was Jewish. Fausto Cleva had been born into the Israelite community in Trieste and is buried there.

When she was a child, Wally said, Agatha and Warren were very close to her parents. The Warrens visited the Clevas in their grand apartment in the landmark Hotel Ansonia; they would then respond by inviting all the Clevas for dinner in Manhattan House. Wally remembered that Warren "went to Mass and took Communion every Sunday, never ate meat on Fridays, and always gave up something for Lent." She said that after he became a Catholic he placed religious objects such as prayer cards or pictures of Jesus, the Virgin Mary, and the saints, or religious statuettes near his dressing table mirror. On the Met spring tours and in Puerto Rico, Mexico, and Argentina, colleagues saw Warren taking Communion at Mass on Sunday. "He never kept his religion a secret," Wally said. Roy Leifflen once even joked with her about Warren's fervor, saying, "He's a better Catholic than I am."

Wally also recalled the problems Warren's conversion raised with some Jews at the Met. She said that people began to realize Warren had become a Catholic in the autumn of 1950, when they first saw his prayer cards and statuettes in his dressing room. She described Jan Peerce as very angry about Warren's choice, and other Jews supported Peerce. "Peerce was totally Orthodox. He was so devout that he would not even drink a glass of water in my family's apartment because my mother did not keep a kosher kitchen." Wally also recalled Richard Tucker's first reaction to Warren's new faith. When she was a child, the Tuckers were very close to her family; after she grew up, they became her friends. Wally said Richard and Sara invited her father to their seders, and Cleva always attended, wearing a yarmulke. Wally remembered Tucker talking about Warren's conversion: "He seemed not to mind it. Richard said, 'Well, everybody does things their own way.'" Tucker liked Warren, whom he fondly called "Lenny," while Warren always responded warmly to "Ruby."

Warren's Catholicism raised serious issues of prejudice for him at the Met. Nancy Conrad, whose family also had Russian Jewish origins, said she understood why Warren was badly treated by some Jews at the Met. "Jews never like to see anyone abandon their religion. With his display of religious objects, Warren shoved it in peoples' faces; and it became an insult." Arge Keller also recalled Peerce being foremost among the Jews outraged by Warren's choice;

but, he said, great animosity was also directed toward another singer, Igor Gorin. "Gorin pushed the Russian side instead of the Jewish side, and everyone hated him for it. Certain people at the Met were just as upset about Warren."

Robert Merrill, another Jew at the Met, took Warren's Catholicism casually. He said, "Only a devout Orthodox Jew like Peerce would have made an issue of Warren's choice. No one else would care." Peter G. Davis wrote about this matter in *The American Opera Singer*, saying "Unlike his tenor colleagues [Peerce and Tucker], Warren never felt drawn to or defined by his Jewish identity; and he converted to his wife's faith."

Warren spoke briefly about his colleagues' anger in a 1957 interview with Jesús M. López, who made his remarks available for this book. Warren said, "My conversion did not set well with all my Jewish colleagues. Tucker understood it, but Peerce has never forgiven me. He's a fanatical Jew."

Warren's Relationship with His Father

Around the Met, gossip also circulated later about Warren's break with his father. It was rumored to have been caused by his decision to become a Catholic. In spite of his parents' divorce, Warren remained on good terms with his father, at least until 1948. Solomon Warenoff collected clippings about his son from American newspapers from coast to coast and even managed to get a translation of the reviews of the 1942 Buenos Aires performances. In the summer of 1946, he clipped Walter Winchell's syndicated column of 4 June, in which Winchell said Warren had been offered a million dollars to star in a streamlined version of *Pagliacci* on Broadway.

Warenoff had provided the leopard skin and other accessories for Warren's Amonasro costume, and he traveled from Seattle to hear his son in cities where he toured. He told one reporter that he went to New York at least once a year to hear Warren at the Met. In September 1946, Warenoff honored his son by entertaining Albanese, Thelma Votipka, Maria Sá Earp, Peerce, Pinza, and Baccaloni at the American-Italian Athletic Club in San Francisco. The event was reported in the Seattle *Times* two days later. In September 1947, he returned to San Francisco to hear his son again. Warren's father also went to Portland on 2 October 1948 to hear him sing a recital, accompanied by Ralph Linsley. Unusual in its Hugo Wolf group, the concert ended with works by Charles Griffes, Malotte, and Victor Hely-Hutchinson. The next day the father and son were together in Seattle, where they did a joint interview for the *Times-Intelligencer* and were photographed at the New Washington Hotel, where Warenoff lived. The writer described Warenoff as "a fur broker" who was "proud of his son" and had gone to New York every year for the previous ten years to hear Warren sing and could hardly believe that "the man on the stage" was his son. In this interview, Warren talked about his relationship with the audience in his Columbia Concert tours: "Sometimes in the smaller towns, the pianos are not too good, but two-thirds of the town is there in front of the footlights, and when one knows that, one sings." The atmosphere was relaxed, and Warren was jovial. The next night, Warren sang and got good reviews.

However, some time after that, perhaps in 1950 or 1951 after Warren became a Catholic, several Met colleagues heard that Solomon Warenoff had demonstrated his anger with his son by sitting shiva, the Jewish ritual of mourning, as though Warren had died. Sitting shiva, traditional especially among the more observant immigrant families, usually involved covering all mirrors in the house with cloth. Friends and family sat on boxes and on low chairs reciting prayers for the dead. Opera director Alan Coleridge commented that this rite of mourning "was not unusual in that period. That was a time when there was a lot of sitting shiva in immigrant Jewish families. With Jews from Russia and Eastern Europe, it was sometimes more a tradition than a strictly religious thing." Herman Krawitz, who became Bing's right hand at the Met in the mid-1950s, said that he had heard of a Jewish family at the time sitting shiva when their son married a non-Jewish girl. We do not know whether Sol Warenoff sat shiva or not, but in his collection of clippings about his son, almost no clippings are dated between 1950 and 1959. There are many clippings about Warren's death in 1960.

In *The Bluebird of Happiness*, Peerce admitted he was furious when Larry, his son, married a Gentile. "I was ready to die," Peerce said. "It was the tragedy of my life. I wanted to sit shiva for seven days, in mourning for Larry. But Alice [Peerce's wife] would not let me." Peerce disowned his son and refused to speak to him; much later the two men reconciled. Warren and his father apparently did not.

Leslie Chabay, the Met tenor, told stage director Dino Yannopoulos that after a concert in Seattle, a man approached him in the Green Room and introduced himself as "Sol Warenoff, Leonard Warren's father." He congratulated Chabay on his performance and asked him to give Warren his regards when he got back to New York. Chabay, knowing nothing of the rupture between father and son, saw Warren in the Met a few days later. He told him of his encounter, only to have Warren turn on him and bark, "I have no father!" Later the chagrined tenor learned the reason for the outburst. Robert Merrill recalled being in Seattle for a concert and having a call from Warren's father. "How is my son?" Warenoff asked. "I hear him on the radio all the time but don't hear very much from him."

Practicing the Faith

Warren made a total, serious commitment to his religion. Long before 1950 he had become familiar with the rites of Catholicism, going to Mass in New York and wherever he and Agatha traveled together. In a rare, unguarded moment on 15 April 1949, one year before he converted, he spoke to Paul Jones, a reporter for the *Atlanta Constitution*, about religion. He said he and Agatha had arrived in Atlanta on Good Friday, three days before the first Met tour performance, just to attend Mass in the Sacred Heart Church. Marylin Noble Tracy, who had known the Warrens and Leifflens since 1941, said, "They were all very devout Catholics; and after Leonard converted, he was also very devout. He didn't just go to Mass on Sunday. I used to meet him in church on weekdays in New York when he would stop to say a prayer at the Church of St. Vincent Ferrer. These were his little visits. I also heard him sing several times at midnight Mass there, once with orchestra, up on the altar, with that voice rolling out."

As Wally Cleva Riecker said, Warren became very proud of his new religion and rather flaunted his faith in ways that were odd for such a reserved person as he was. However, he was utterly convinced of the rightness of what he was doing. Among the few jokes Warren was ever heard to tell centered on Roman Catholicism. After signing autographs backstage in Toronto in the mid-1950s, he suddenly turned to James McPherson and other young fans. He had known some of them for years. Without preliminaries, Warren said, "Do any of you know how to make Holy Water?" They shook their heads. "Well, you put a pot of water on the stove and boil the hell out of it." This single moment of humor about Catholic practice almost constituted a breach of confidentiality for him because in his faith, as in many other matters, Warren was a very private person. He rarely talked about religion to anyone. Apart from telling journalists that his voice was a gift from God, he usually said little about his inner life. He always dismissed questions about his or his parents' religion and origins, saying simply that they were "Americans." Nevertheless, some singers who watched him backstage came to learn how deeply religious he was. Jerome Hines noticed that he always stepped away by himself to seek some quiet spot in the wings so he could pray before performances. "He always made the Sign of the Cross, then he went onstage." Warren told López that Hines wanted to convert him to "the Protestant faith." But Warren said, "His arguments don't convince me." Warren added that he and Hines were "more than good friends; we are brothers, and we appreciate each other a lot."

Charles Anthony and Blanche Thebom Remember

Metropolitan opera tenor Charles Anthony shed further light on Warren's faith. Anthony said that from the time of his own debut in 1954 as the Simpleton in *Boris Godunov*, he often heard Warren in rehearsals and performances. Their first professional contact came during the rehearsals of *Pagliacci*, which Anthony first sang with Warren on 24 March. Warren was Tonio, and Anthony was Beppe. They later worked together in many other productions. Anthony characterized Warren as "a baritone who had a lot of competition, including Robert Merrill and Ettore Bastianini, among others. But to me he was the greatest, because of his voice and his character. I was pretty close to him, although we were never good friends; but he was very complimentary and helpful to me. When I decided to sing major roles like Almaviva and Ottavio and Rodolfo, he encouraged me."

Anthony recalled his first 1954 performance of *Pagliacci* with Warren.

> I was obviously nervous, pacing up and down backstage; and he came up to me and said, "Relax, relax!" I answered him back. I said to him, "It's easy for you to say that, with that big chest of yours." I put my hand on his chest and felt a big lump there. Without thinking, I said, "What's that lump?" He never hesitated. He said, "It's religious things." He had a rosary and maybe even a prayer book and other religious articles under his costume. I said to him, "No wonder you can sing like that! It's not just you singing. You have help from the Almighty." He laughed.

Anthony said he found Warren "very prayerful. He always prayed before he went onstage. Becoming a Catholic was a big thing for him to do, I'm sure. He offered everything up in prayer. He dedicated his voice and his life and his talent to his Maker." Anthony added that he also found Warren quite shy. "I understand that at the beginning of his career he was very sensitive and was almost brought to tears by criticism of assistant conductors, conductors and coaches. He would go off by himself and cry. But as he got more experience, it became easier for him. Once he said his little prayers and got onstage, he was completely relaxed." Remembering Warren's technique, Anthony said:

> He was so loose that even when he was singing the most difficult passages, his face was so free that the flesh would shake if he moved his head. His voice never sounded constricted. Never. The notes came out like thunder. It was a free, remarkable brilliant voice. And think how hard it was for him to make that career, even with that voice! Occasionally he would vocalize in his dressing room before a performance and, rarely, even sing something high like "Che gelida manina."

Speaking of Warren's greatest roles, Anthony said, "Rigoletto was dynamite, and he was a great Gérard in *Andrea Chénier*. He did almost everything better than anybody else, but for me his best role was Tonio. He was spectacular. He takes an A-flat and you don't even realize that it's that high! Then the G! All those notes were in his pocket." Anthony recalled the *Otello* performances of 1958 and 1959, in which Warren was Iago and Del Monaco sang the title role. Anthony was Roderigo. He said:

I remember standing backstage and just listening to the volume created by their two voices in the vengeance duet at the end of second act. It was so overwhelming and so vibrant that you could actually feel the wood on the stage floor vibrate when you were in the wings, and it was so acoustically right that it felt as if the opera house and the stage floor were some kind of instrument. They sounded as if they were singing inside a violin.

Anthony added, "I found Warren a devout, serious man and a sympathetic colleague."

After his baptism, Warren also trusted Blanche Thebom enough to speak to her one day about his decision to become a Catholic. She and the baritone were alone, Thebom recalled. "Agatha was not there. He told me how totally he loved and respected and admired her, then he added that because she had found everything in Catholicism, he wanted to share that with her. He said that if that religion had made it possible for there to be an Agatha, he wanted that religion for himself." The religion Warren wanted was tightly structured, requiring regular attendance at Confession and Mass; a presence at the Communion Rail; the recital of many prayers, including the Lord's Prayer, the Marian Prayers, and the Rosary; the observance of dietary and other restrictions during Lent and on Fridays and other religious holidays; and the practice of all tenets of the church. For him, for a man who had never before practiced a faith, Catholicism filled a need. As a parishioner at the Church of St. Vincent Ferrer, he also found a new place to sing, for he replaced Martinelli as a soloist with the choir in holiday seasons. He was also a faithful communicant at St. Catherine of Siena in Riverside.

Again the Ópera Nacional

Four days after his baptism in Riverside, Warren and Agatha left for Mexico, where Warren was engaged for the summer, his third year there. Arriving on 15 June 1950, they found the season already under way, having opened with *Norma*, featuring Maria Callas, Giulietta Simionato, Kurt Baum, and Nicola Moscona. To honor Callas, the impresario of the company had placed a huge electric sign over the central door of the Palacio de Bellas Artes. One full story high, it ran across about half of the building and blazed day and night with dozens upon dozens of lightbulbs:

ÓPERA NACIONAL CON
MARIA MENEGHINI CALLAS
LA SOPRANO ABSOLUTA DEL SIGLO.

In spite of the publicity, Callas, "the greatest soprano of the century" got a rather cool reception at first, but soon she and Simionato became the darlings of the season. Baum joined the two women and Weede in *Aida*, when Mexico City heard Callas's E-flat at the end of the Triumphal Scene. "The note turned the Palacio de Bellas Artes into a madhouse," recalled Carlos Díaz Du-Pond. Warren and Agatha heard the second *Aida* of the season, again with Callas, Simionato, and Weede, with Mario Filippeschi replacing Baum. Again, the opera was a huge success, but Díaz Du-Pond said Warren was "astonished" that evening by the ovations given to the "divas." Still he remained convinced, as Díaz Du-Pond said, that he was still the "Number One idol of the Mexican audience." He was shocked when it became evident that he had been pushed out of the limelight by two women.

On the calendar were two performances of *Il trovatore*, with Callas's first Leonora, Simionato, Baum, Moscona, and Warren. Trouble started even before the first performance, perhaps because of the uproar over Callas. "Warren's success diminished noticeably that season," said Díaz Du-Pond.

> It was not the same to sing with inferior singers as it was to [sing] next to Callas and Simionato. The reviews also must have come as a shock. One critic raved about "that marvelous woman" and "the truly incomparable Callas," while another wrote about the "incomparable, unparalleled Simionato." Only superlatives would do. In the second performance, the audience was more demanding and applauded Warren less, because he had had a slight slip during "Il balen del suo sorriso."

At one point, the audience shouted for Simionato to come out alone for a curtain call, after the scene in Di Luna's camp. This made Warren furious. In fact, Warren had quite a record of resenting other colleagues' curtain calls and good reviews, and stories circulated at different times at the Met about his fury over the bows taken by Milanov, Tucker, Tebaldi, and Rysanek. He also loved to take his own bows. When he stayed before the curtain too long, Milanov would call out "Enough!" from backstage, "Basta, Leonard. Basta!" In Mexico, Díaz Du-Pond went on, "He refused to sing the fourth-act duet [with Callas], arguing that he had lost his voice." At that point, the director called in three physicians. They examined Warren in his dressing room and determined there was nothing wrong. At that, he became "furious" and "threw down the score." Agatha then appealed to the director personally. Warren should not sing, she said, because both *Simon Boccanegra* and *Falstaff* were on his program for the following week. The director said he gave in, then telephoned to Ivan Petroff in New York, asking him to come to replace Warren for the other performances of *Trovatore*. This account suggests that Warren did not finish the performance.

Simionato's Recollections

However, Giulietta Simionato, when we spoke in Milan, stated unequivocally that Warren finished the Mexico City *Trovatore*, even though he was probably ill. "I would have remembered if he had stopped before the last act. I have a good memory, and I certainly would have remembered something like that." She also said:

> I found him a very polite person, a man who behaved very properly, but truly properly. He was The Voice for the world of classical music, for opera is classical music; he was The Voice exactly as you Americans said Frank Sinatra was The Voice for popular music. As to his voice, he knew how to modulate it perfectly. It was very large, but he knew exactly how to manage it, and that is a great gift. He was very, very expressive and intelligent.

Simionato remembered her performances with Warren in Mexico and those at the Met, where they sang together in the splendid Metropolitan Opera *Trovatore* in the autumn of 1959, with Carlo Bergonzi and Antonietta Stella.

Warren's "illness" in Mexico City evidently became public knowledge, for local journalists referred to it in their columns and wished him well for his next appearances. One might almost suspect that Warren had faked his loss of voice, had he not been a man of great integrity. But he was clearly having problems. Only a few weeks later, he lost his voice altogether and had to stop singing in *Rigoletto* in Rio, so he may very well have felt ill during the Mexico City *Trovatore*.

Closing the Season in Triumph

Fortunately, Warren's *Boccanegra* went well, although the audience found the opera too long. Parts of the performance of 4 July 1950 can be heard on an unauthorized recording, where a bright Filippeschi and a shrill Celia García are paired with Warren's rich Simon, while the rugged, dark voice of Roberto Silva, a local favorite, conveys Fiesco's rage, grief, and joy. The veteran Carlo Morelli is Paolo. Next came *Falstaff*, rehearsals for which, Díaz Du-Pond said, drove him "crazy" because he was caught between Warren, the perfectionist, Defrère, and Cellini, the conductor, whom Warren loved. The Mexican singers lacked both experience and polish; but Simionato sang a lively Quickly, and Petroff sang Ford, while the Met's brilliant comprimario Alessio De Paolis flew in to sing Bardolfo. "*Falstaff* was a success, and Warren had a great triumph," Díaz Du-Pond concluded.

Brazil

When his Mexico City obligations ended, Warren and Agatha left for Rio and the Teatro Municipal, where he was to sing with the great Tullio Serafin as his conductor. The tenor in *Un ballo in maschera* was Gianni Poggi, while the Amelia was Elisabetta Barbato, who had come from La Scala for the production. On 11 August, praise for Warren's Renato headed the column in the *Gazeta de Noticias*, but by that evening, he was in trouble. *Rigoletto* was a gala with Poggi as the Duke and Sá Earp as Gilda. All reviewers agreed that Warren sang very well in the first act and his first scene with Américo Bàsso, his protégé, who was Sparafucile. Signs of trouble appeared during "Pari siamo." In its final bars, said the critic of *Jornal do Brasil*, even the audience noticed something was wrong. He went "off pitch" and "his voice disappeared." The reviewer for *Correio da Manhá* said it "faded out" during the aria. He and Sá Earp started the father-daughter duet, but Warren made only a "strangled sound" and stopped. Confused and angry, he turned to Serafin and the audience and said, "Não posso," in perfect Portuguese, "I cannot." He raised his arm and gestured to the crew to bring the curtain down. A huge ovation swelled behind him as he walked off. Doctors were called. The impresario announced that a substitute had been found in the audience: Enzo Mascherini got into costume and finished the opera. Within a week, Warren had regained his voice.

Preparing for *Il trovatore*, Warren met Mario and Rina Del Monaco for the first time, laying the foundation for a long friendship. During rehearsal the cast faced a replacement conductor because Serafin had "disappeared," as *O Globo* reported. *Correio da Manhá* praised Juan Emilio Martini, who took over. In Warren and Del Monaco, the production had two large, bright voices that meshed perfectly; they got excellent reviews. Said the critic of *A Noite*, "Warren dominated with his fascinating timbre and the finesse of his interpretation," while Del Monaco was a real Manrico, young, handsome, "exuberant," and generous with top notes. *O Jornal* led with an excellent review of Elena Nicolai's Azucena and said that Warren possessed versatility, immense expertise, and imagination. Del Monaco ruled the stage with his "absolute confidence." *Otello*, with Warren, Del Monaco, and Barbato, showed off the tenor's "heroic vigor," said the reviewer of the *Jornal de Commercio*, while Warren had a "full success" as Iago. Antonino Votto conducted. When Warren returned to the States after this engagement, he set up a scholarship for Américo Bàsso, with whom he had often sung, and brought him to the Curtis Institute of Music in Philadelphia.

From Rio, Warren and Agatha and Mario and Rina Del Monaco, traveled with Barbato and Poggi to São Paulo. *Rigoletto* followed, with Poggi as the Duke and Agnes Ayres as Gilda. *Otello* again had Del Monaco, Warren, and Barbato. La Scala's scholarly Votto conducted both operas. His interpretation won almost six inches of column space from the critic of *Diario* on 2 September. Del Monaco's elegant Moor was "on the same artistic level as Leonard Warren," who was "magisterial." His Iago won special praise for the second act.

Warren and Agatha spent most of September 1950 in Connecticut, but he went back to work at the end of the month to record *Songs for Everyone* for RCA Victor, with the popular Frank Black as his conductor. These were issued by RCA on a 45 rpm mini-album in July 1951. They included "America the Beautiful," "Love's Old Sweet Song," "Mother Machree," "A Little Bit of Heaven," "Home on the Range," "On the Road to Mandalay," "Ol' Man River," and "Battle Hymn of the Republic." With this season's recording obligations fulfilled, Warren left New York on the concert tour that kept him out of New York and out of the cast of Bing's first-night *Don Carlo*.

CHAPTER SIXTEEN

Living With Bing

In December 1950, when Warren returned to the Met after his autumn concert tour, Bing's taste had already made itself felt everywhere. The new general manager's sharp tongue and strong will had cast fear into the hearts of many staff members, and Bing had replaced so many of the old Johnson crew that new administrators and functionaries were scattered everywhere throughout the Opera House. Warren felt like a stranger when he went into some offices.

Arge Keller

Soon the baritone found a new fan in a young staff member who worked with him over the years. Arge Keller, who shared many memories of him, said he first heard Warren long before Keller joined the Met staff.

> I was in the audience, shouting bravo for his Rigoletto and his Di Luna in *Trovatore*. I believe I also heard him at the Temple Emanu-El one Friday night in the mid-1930s. Then came the 1940s, and he was singing at the Met. I first met him backstage after a performance of *Rigoletto* or *Trovatore*. He had just come back from Washington and said it had been snowing there and he wanted to tell me what he had seen. "The snow just hung on the trees in great globs," he said. "It was so beautiful." Agatha was there, and Emily Coleman helped me get my first Warren autograph. Then my parents bought me a disk recorder so I could record the Voice of Firestone and other programs. I began recording Warren very early and have everything on disks.

Keller joined the company in September 1950, when Emily Coleman, the distinguished music critic at *Newsweek*, told him about a job opening at the Met press office. "I took it, and my salary went from one hundred dollars a week to thirty-five dollars week. I went to work putting clippings in scrap-books. Later Frank Paola asked me if I wanted to fill an opening in the rehearsal department, where I could earn more money." In his new position, Keller got to know Bing as few staff members did. "I admired Bing enormously and also liked him. He loved a good fight. And he was generous. Bing would take your contract and, without your even asking, he would give you a raise of a thousand dollars a year." In the course of his work, Keller was sent on the Met spring tours. He particularly remembered the glories of Atlanta and the "magnificent" acoustics of the Fox Theatre there.

> Many of the singers and administration people stayed at the Georgian Terrace Hotel, across the street from the theatre. I would see Warren, Tucker, and Mitropoulos, sitting in rocking chairs under the portico, watching the people go by. Warren took home movies of everyone. Cellini was there, and he was very charming and funny, a very decent fellow. I remember once Cellini had a heart attack, and Warren went around to everyone and took up a collection for him to pay his hospital bill. He and Warren were very good friends.
>
> Once Warren talked to me about Cellini, saying they were making a recording together, a set of Italian art songs, Tosti and other composers from Warren's recital repertory. They were recording these for an album. Then neither man heard any more about it. Later both learned that the people at Victor had decided it would not be commercial enough. The whole thing was just dead. No one at Victor ever wrote Warren anything about it. It just died.

Keller said that many years later, he spoke about the recording to Francis Robinson, the head of the Met's press office. He had never heard of it.

> Francis sent a letter to RCA Victor on 21 August 1978, asking whether any tapes or pressings existed and, if so, whether he could copy them. Nothing happened. Many months later, Francis threw a box on my desk, saying, "Have I got a Christmas gift for you!" On the tape Robinson gave me, there were what Francis believed to be some of Warren's "lost" songs. I got "L'ultima canzone," "Ideale," "Occhi di fata," "Canto di primavera" and "Nel giardino." Five pieces, all perfect.

Keller generously provided these to me, together with Warren's splendid "O Holy Night." Talking about that song, he said:

> One year just around Christmas, Warren told me he was going to appear on the radio broadcast of the Catholic Hour, singing "O Holy Night." I recorded it on my disk recorder, and it came out magnifi-

cently. He did the first two verses without the high note. Then there is a repeat of part of the first verse, and then he hits that top note. It was the most beautiful singing you could ever hear. The next morning, Warren came to my office, so I mentioned it to him. "It was magnificent; I hope you're going to record it." He shook his head. "Victor won't let me record it because they don't want two of the same thing, and they already have Mario Lanza doing it."

Warren often came into Keller's office, which was next to his dressing room, but Keller never heard the baritone vocalizing. "I heard him talking and laughing, but never a single vocalise." Transportation for the tours was in the hand of Frank Paola, who began organizing it with pads and maps. Keller remembered a day when William Gengenbach of the New York Central Railroad and John Whelan of the New York, New Haven, and Hartford line were in the office, discussing which lines to use for the tour. Warren came in. He had just come from a rehearsal and had a problem he needed to discuss. "He was in a business suit," Keller said. "He just stood for ten minutes, lecturing the two men on how they should run their railroad. For ten minutes! He told them what was wrong with the dining cars and what night noises he heard when the railroad workers would hook up the cars. He was very nice about it. But he told them what he thought. And they listened."

A Troubled *Pagliacci*

Warren's first season in the Bing regime proved to be fairly undistinguished, although it certainly demonstrated how reliable he was. He was back to New York in time for *Traviata* on 18 December and sang twenty-one performances in 1950–1951, although only two broadcasts. However, he was awarded the role of Tonio in the new *Pagliacci*. Several performances of *Trovatore* followed; then came the repeats of *Pagliacci*, more Germonts, and two performances of *Faust*, one with Björling and Steber, the other with Tucker and a most unlikely Marguerite, Delia Rigal, who had first sung with Warren in South America in 1942.

Of these productions, only *Pagliacci* caused a stir. Warren had reacted unfavorably when he saw the scenery. One colleague said, "It was the first day the sets were onstage. He took one look, turned around, walked out of the auditorium and out of the building, hailed a cab, and went home." Warren later told Vivien that he hated the set and felt as he did "because he hated anything that sullied the Met." Rigal, cast as Nedda in that production, recalled the troubled *Pagliacci* rehearsals. In her interview with Horacio Molina, she said that Max Leavitt, the director, "changed the traditional [setting] and prepared a very modern one, at least according to the standards of those times. This led to many quarrels between Leonard and Leavitt. Leonard did not agree with the way the director mounted the scenes. They argued about this all the time during the rehearsals." Rigal said she sat silently and waited until their quarrels ended, so the rehearsals could go on.

In one extraordinary *Pagliacci* rehearsal, she said, "All the tenors appointed to do the role of Canio were not present in the theatre. Leonard just took the score and sang the complete role of Canio, from the very beginning to the end, and including all the high notes. The artists who were present in the theatre, and the conductor, too, were all delighted." Rigal remembered this as "one of the most striking performances I ever heard." She added, "We finally got to the performances, and after Leonard sang the Prologue, everything was good, and the rest of the singing would be perfect." After the first night, Kolodin wrote that Horace Armistead's setting was "as barren as a bombed-out village," populated by a "fluttery-voiced" Rigal and a "throaty" Vinay. Warren, he said, was the only singer worth hearing. But a series of Tonios was not enough to enhance Warren's standing in Bing's new Met. For a brighter future, he needed title roles.

Negotiations Resumed

Given James Davidson's problems with Bing and Max Rudolf, the agent was probably the wrong person to ask about getting Warren more visibility. In December 1950, Mildred Shagal, an assistant of Davidson, wrote to Max Rudolf about the spring tour performances Warren had agreed to sing, but said she had to "regretfully advise" the Met that Warren would not be available for much of the spring tour that year. "Between April 5 and 30, 1951" he had contracts for concerts. Inexplicably, the manager also offered Warren to the Met for tour dates when the Met was not even on tour. Because Warren had agreed upon his dates in February 1950, he was technically in violation of his contract. "You and Mr. Warren know perfectly well that we are not on tour [on the dates you offer]," an exasperated Rudolf wrote. Davidson also offered to have Warren sing six performances in a period of eleven days, an utter impossibility. Rudolf shot back, accusing Davidson of bad faith, of making an offer that was "entirely unsatisfactory and equally unfair. We have, therefore, to take note that Mr. Warren is disinterested in appearing with us on tour and will advise cities concerned accordingly." In answer to another real threat to Warren, Davidson sent back a sharp letter, accusing Rudolf of being "intemperate." It was peppered with peculiar remarks about the meaning of the words "mutually agreeable." Rhetorical questions—"May I remind you?" and "Do you consider it fair?"—led to more angry exchanges. Rudolf knew how wrong Davidson was. But Davidson kept on writing that Rudolf was "unfair as well as incorrect" and saying, "This is strictly your responsibility, not ours." Finally they settled the matter by agreeing on three tour dates for Warren, with one other performance on option. Warren sailed through his spring concerts in 1951 and brought home large fees for him and commissions for Davidson. He was "tops" in Boston, "ranked with Caruso" in Toronto, and "gorgeous" in Winnipeg. But on 10 May, the Davidson management office informed Rudolf that Warren was ill with "a cold that settled in his throat" and could not sing the tour performance in Chicago—doctor's certificate available!

Once again, Warren's relations with Bing and the management had gone sour. According to Edgar Vincent, whose office began to handle Warren in 1952, Warren and Agatha saved the singer's career. These two reserved people, who did not frequent the Met's party circuit, managed in 1950 to reach George Sloan, the chairman of the board. They begged him to help Warren get the role of Rigoletto in the most important new production Bing was planning. If he did not get it, Robert Merrill would surely be cast as the jester, and Warren would be stuck in routine operas for another season. The direct appeal to Sloan accomplished what all earlier negotiations had not been able to do, for he went straight to Bing. The happy outcome was that Warren was given the new *Rigoletto*, scheduled for November 1951, and the highest honors of that season fell to him when he sang it. Designed by Eugene Berman and graced with a Renaissance setting, the opera set the Met standard for years to come and was described by Kolodin as "the keenest expression to that date" of Bing's sense of style, even surpassing *Don Carlo*. The first night also marked Warren's fortieth performance of the jester at the Met. His first Gilda was Hilde Gueden, who had never sung with Warren before but proved to be a dependable asset. Tucker sang his polished, familiar Duke, and Jean Madeira sang Maddalena. Alberto Erede, by then a veteran of experiences with Warren, conducted. Kolodin praised Warren for his progress, from "manly to mature to magnificent" in the role, and after that first night, no doubt was left about his status. Its success confirmed him as an unchallenged star in Bing's firmament. "After Leonard did that *Rigoletto*, he became Bing's darling," Vincent said. "From then on, Bing actually planned things for him. Leonard's future was assured." *Rigoletto* paved the way for a decade of star turns for Warren. Among other copious coverage, he appeared in *Life* on 3 March 1952 in a full-color spread singing "Cortigiani" in *Rigoletto*, in an article entitled "Bing Shifts into High."

A Brilliant New Gilda

Thirteen days after the production opened, the young American coloratura Roberta Peters sang Gilda, the first of nineteen performances of this role with Warren. Born in 1930, Peters was yet another child of the Bronx to become a star at the Met. In a 1998 interview, Peters recalled her early impressions of Warren. These were formed in the many rehearsals for this near-perfect production. "Warren was like a father figure to me," Peters said, adding that the relationship was also, of course, built into the opera itself. "He loved that role so much and wanted everyone in the cast to be just as good as he was. That is where his so called 'perfectionism' came from. He was absolutely magical in that part. He tried so hard to make every phrase count; he took each phrase and polished it until it was perfect. I remember the legato phrases, above all." Asked about his characterization, she said, "He babied the role. Yes, that's it. He *babied* it. Just as he worked on the score, he also worked on the stage business. I remember how he rehearsed everything to do with the hump on his back: he wanted the audience to know it was there. It had to be perfect, too. It isn't that he wanted to stick out from the rest of us, but he really wanted the opera to be perfect." Warren's emphasis on the jester's deformity contrasted markedly with the ideas of Tibbett, who had minimized the character's awkwardness.

Peters remembered how *Rigoletto* became "Warren's opera" rather than "Erede's" for about four years, beginning in 1951, until the day in early November 1955 when Cleva took over. By then, Warren truly felt that he owned *Rigoletto*, the opera, and not just the title role. Detesting sloppiness and the routine that often marred repeats of even the best productions, he had become accustomed to giving orders to other singers and directors. He also had believed for years that Erede, the Met's regular conductor for this opera, was securely under his control. Erede, who had come to the Met with Bing, had never had the reputation of being a hard taskmaster. With his gentle ways and soft-spoken, almost tentative way with English, he was certainly no match for the strong-willed baritone. Like Sodero, Erede sometimes seemed to look to the singers for cues, a great mistake for a conductor dealing with a man as set in his convictions as Warren then was. By 1951 Warren had tried to tame a half-generation of conductors, among them Sodero, who had the reputation of being Lily Pons's pet poodle, and Cimara, another compliant musician.

Cleva, Peters said, was another matter. He had conducted for Warren's first Amonasro at the Cincinnati Summer Opera in 1940 and for many of his early Met appearances. He had come to regard the baritone as a fine performer but always had a healthy skepticism about singers. A strict disciplinarian, he drove his casts and orchestras. He admitted few exceptions to what he read in the score. For him the composer was sacred, as he often said during rehearsals and private conversations. His tempos and his contempt for the singers' egos led to inevitable conflict between him and Warren when the *Rigoletto* rehearsals began. Peters said:

> Cleva had his own idea of what tempos he wanted, and Warren had other ideas. I remember our rehearsals with Cleva. He didn't want Warren to hold his high notes too long. But Warren loved his high notes! He had glorious high notes. There was quite a bit of sparring

between the two of them about this. One particular point of discussion was the "Sì, vendetta" duet. At the end of it, Warren went up to A-flat, as I recall, and I had a high D or maybe something even higher. During the rehearsal, Cleva made it clear that he wanted us to hold this for only four bars and stop. But Warren was having none of that. He and I worked it out in our own way. Just before the end of the duet, he took a really deep breath. I was watching him, so I took a deep breath, then he glanced at me. We attacked that phrase and hung on and on. We did that every time; we were always hanging on to the end, eight bars or so, in spite of what Cleva wanted.

Hines and Milnes Remember Warren

Metropolitan Opera bass Jerome Hines, a very different kind of singer, had no problems with Cleva, although he was the Sparafucile for many of Warren's Rigolettos. He recalled a particular act of kindness on Warren's part in the season of 1951–1952. Hines had been lying ill with intestinal flu in his compartment on the Met train before the tour reached Minneapolis. It was mid-May when the company arrived. "I was the last one off the train when we got there and was in great pain," Hines said. "When I got to the Hotel Nicolet, there were about a hundred Met tour people lined up at the desk to check in. I got in line. A couple of minutes later, the manager of the hotel came up to me and pulled me aside. He handed me a room key. 'Mr. Warren says you are sick, so he already checked in for you. Just go on upstairs.' As I told you, Warren was such a nice guy."

Sherrill Milnes, who joined the Met roster in the mid-1960s and in a sense was Warren's heir, became interested in Warren's voice while he was in Des Moines studying voice with Andrew White at Drake University.

> White had studied with Sidney Dietch, Warren's teacher. Because of that I knew Warren as a giant, a world name. He was a kind of hero to me. I felt akin to him, as if he were a kind of voice-teacher uncle. White's sound was somewhat similar to Warren's, and there was also a similarity in his teaching of vocal technique. It is an open-throat sound, with that back space and frontal point, a frontal ring. That was Dietch's stuff.

Milnes said he was won over by Warren's timbre. "He was such a vocal presence, with a sound that was warm and round rather than full of *squillo*. He was mellow, even though he had those brilliant high notes. Warren also had the most technical control of any baritone ever. He could do those crescendos and then spin out his pianissimos on any note, every note, if he wanted to." Milnes also volunteered his thoughts on Warren's diction: "Most people would agree that you did not have to know what the words meant when Warren sang. His sound always told you what they meant, that's how expressive he was. His sound, above all, was sincere. That's why you always felt the emotion of the moment."

Speaking of Warren's jester, Milnes said, "His *Rigoletto* is the most perfectly sung recording I have ever heard. He was a father pouring out his heart. I can't imagine anyone ever singing it as well as Warren did. He sounds like a father. And his top register! He could *live* up there, between B-flat and F. That high tessitura was where he lived." Milnes also said he thought Warren's Prologue to *Pagliacci* was "one of the great recorded pieces" and that in *Ballo* he wove "sheer magic with those long spun lines of 'Eri tu.'" His "Oh de' verd' anni miei" in *Ernani* was also perfect. Milnes commented on that aria's orchestration, "a chamber music accompaniment for a long while, and then came Warren's top notes!" Milnes believed that Warren's mellow sound did not make him as good a Scarpia because he could not convey true evil with the voice he had.

He particularly admired Warren because "he studied very hard, and locked in the character and locked in where the voice wanted to be. Maybe that was why so many people found it difficult to make him change. He studied for months or even a year or longer on every role. Then he didn't allow anything to change or take a different direction. Once he locked the role in, he was like a bulldog."

Margaret Truman and Roy Leifflen

The new Berman production of *Rigoletto* came two days after the season's opening night, 13 November 1951, which was distinguished by Margaret Webster's new production of *Aida*, with Milanov, Del Monaco, Elena Nikolaidi, and the Canadian baritone George London, who made his Met debut that night. Cleva conducted. Because opening night at the Met was a social occasion, photographers were out in full force. One elegant couple they caught entering the Opera House was Margaret Truman, the president's daughter, "resplendent in pink chiffon," on the arm of Roy Leifflen, Warren's brother-in-law, whom Miss Truman had begun to date earlier that year. The couple had been photographed at a baseball game in Washington in May. In April 1952 he took her to hear *Aida* with Warren, Milanov, Thebom, and Del Monaco at the Capitol Theatre in Washington; a month later they were photographed together at the races at Pimlico. From then on, they made "the Washington scene" regularly. By 12 October, one newspaper reported that "Roy Leifflen has the inside track to marrying her." In November that year, he took her to the Met's opening night *Forza*, which again had Warren and Milanov, with Tucker as Alvaro and Stiedry conducting. Danton Walker reported on Roy's relationship with Miss Truman in his column in the *Daily*

News, saying, "If Margaret Truman does marry that young Washington attorney, Roy Leifflen, she'll quit her show-business career." Nonetheless, she continued her voice lessons, studying in the same building where Sidney Dietch taught, with an associate of his, and on the same floor where Sara Kantor Warenoff, Vivien, and Linda lived. Linda remembered Secret Service agents standing in the hall outside the studio door while Miss Truman took her lessons. For the Met opening of 1954, Miss Truman, Agatha, and Roy arrived in the foyer together. That event was a gala concert that was televised. It included acts from three operas, including *Aida* with Warren. Roy dated Miss Truman over several years and even accompanied her abroad, where they were photographed together in a gondola in Venice. Their imminent engagement was widely reported in the newspapers, where Roy was dubbed "the most likely candidate" for her hand. Later, of course, Margaret Truman married someone else, but only after a great deal of coverage had been devoted to her dates with Roy.

Aida and More

Warren was not cast in the opening night *Aida* because he had the new production of *Rigoletto* that same week. His rehearsals for it, his concert tour, and rehearsals for *Pagliacci* had kept him from attending or even watching the new production as Margaret Webster staged it. After the first night, stage manager David Pardoll had the job of coaching any late arrivals to the cast. Warren, who was about to sing his fortieth Amonasro at the Met, said he was sure of himself and did not need additional preparation. On the night of 29 December 1951, he went onstage, believing that his old stage business would carry him through. He was wrong. In the production, Webster intended for two young supers to stand first near Milanov, the Aida, then move across the stage to seize Warren, as if to arrest him, after his announcement that Aida was his daughter. One of the supers, Armand Stepanian, recalled the incident. Intimidated at seeing the imposing Warren firm on his feet and a whole stage away, the supers hesitated, and at that Milanov turned to them and gave orders under her breath, "Arrest him! Arrest him!" When they did not obey, she cursed at them and gave them a push. With that, they crossed the stage to Warren and tried to "arrest" him. But Warren, set in his ideas, refused to budge. They finally had to wedge him between two shields and force him to move forward. Afterward, of course, he was furious.

With the exception of performances of *Pagliacci*, this was another all-Verdi season for Warren at the Metropolitan Opera. He sang *Rigoletto*, *Aida*, *Otello*, *Trovatore*, and *Traviata*. Del Monaco sang *Otello* once with Warren at the Met in February 1952; he later played the Moor to Warren's Iago many times. Their meeting in 1950 in South America had marked the beginning of a long association between them; they respected each other as colleagues and loved each other as friends. Del Monaco called Warren "Lenny," joked with him, and treated him with genuine affection.

A New Manhattan Home and New Management

In 1951, after ten cramped years in their first apartment, Warren and Agatha found an elegant place to live in New York. They celebrated by moving on 1 May to a large, handsome suite in Manhattan House, a luxury building that had just opened. Roy had first suggested this move and used one of the rooms when he came up from Washington. On Sixty-sixth Street between Third and Second avenues, Manhattan House took up a whole block. With long lobbies and well-designed, beautifully tended courtyards, it had every imaginable service and even housed a fine restaurant. For the Warrens, it was an ideal city place.

Warren also changed management in the spring of 1952, leaving Davidson and turning to Sol Hurok, with his first full Hurok season starting that autumn. Then his concert tours, with his portrait appearing on full-sized Hurok posters, took him from Indianapolis and South Bend to Toronto and New Orleans in October, to Boston in January, and then Memphis and Sacramento in the spring. Hurok, a giant among impresarios, had a highly professional press office. With so many stars on his roster, he also had more leverage with the local concert and recital presenters. Vivien remembered her brother saying that the day Hurok agreed to manage him was "one of the happiest days of his life." She said, "As proud as he had been when he joined the Met, Leonard was just as proud of being with Hurok. It meant he had arrived. He could say, 'I'm a Hurok artist now,' and he kept one of those big 'S. Hurok Presents Leonard Warren' posters on the wall in his house." Eventually Hurok's power made possible Warren's important engagements in Italy and Russia and kept his career in the United States on a straight course.

When Warren joined the Hurok roster, Martin Feinstein, the former "libretto boy" from the Met, was the director of Hurok's publicity department. Feinstein, as we have seen, had heard the baritone's opera debut in 1939 and had followed his career until the war, and then again throughout the rest of the 1940s. Thus he saw the development of the artist from Warren's debut as Paolo through his early and middle career and then saw the performances at the end of his life. Feinstein felt that Warren's two greatest roles were Simon Boccanegra and Rigoletto. "There was so much growth, and those two roles were very fine," he said.

"When Warren first came to the Hurok office, I was a little overwhelmed by him, and I found it difficult to talk to him. He was terribly serious, and it was hard to get a response out of him. But he was a very great artist." Because Warren felt he never got enough attention from the media, Feinstein made a great effort to get good publicity for him. Nevertheless, his contacts with

Warren were strictly professional. He said, "Mr. Hurok had direct contact with Warren, as he did with all his artists. I really had little contact with him beyond our work. I didn't socialize with him and Agatha, but I did hear dozens of Warren's performances. I was a great admirer of his."

The season of 1952–1953 set a new standard for Warren at the Metropolitan. A sign of his elevated status came when he was cast in the handsome new production of *La forza del destino* for the opening night, 10 November. He was Carlo; Milanov was Leonora; Tucker, Alvaro; and Cesare Siepi, the Padre Guardiano; Fritz Stiedry conducted. The opera was directed by Herbert Graf; like the successful *Rigoletto*, it was designed by Berman. *Forza* was in rehearsal for three full weeks before the opening, which meant the rehearsal department summoned Warren and other cast members to the Opera House for long sessions. With time to spare between *Forza* rehearsals, singers often dropped in on preparations for other productions. But Warren was also being called that autumn to rehearse and perform in the second cast of *Rigoletto* because the first night had gone to Robert Merrill. Roberta Peters was Gilda, Giacinto Prandelli sang the Duke, and Hines sang Sparafucile, with Erede conducting. Warren's nineteenth Barnaba in *Gioconda* reached the stage on 16 December with Milanov, Del Monaco, Fedora Barbieri, and Siepi. Again, Cleva's demanding rehearsals, held in the old Metropolitan Opera Guild Room and on the top-of-the-house rehearsal stage, filled weeks before the first performance. In the Guild Room, the artists sat on old gilt chairs or gathered around the piano. Milanov and Barbieri wore conservative dresses with "princess waistlines" and double-breasted bodices. Del Monaco and Warren usually came in hand-tailored Italian suits, but sometimes Warren turned up in a jacket or cardigan. He always tucked his old beret into his pocket, then twisted and fingered it as the hours dragged on. Cleva, a tiny figure beside Warren's considerable bulk, drilled everyone; he and the singers often quarreled over repeats. The four—Milanov, Barbieri, Del Monaco, and Warren— often sang in full voice, the women's voices as large as the men's, with all generating enormous power. Warren rang out with "Enzo Grimaldo, Principe di Santafior," then Del Monaco whispered, "Scoperto son!" They sailed furiously into the long scene that ended with Warren snarling "Buona fortuna!" and Del Monaco spitting out, "E tu sia maledetto." This was Italian melodrama with huge voices, and at its best.

With such a heavy schedule, Warren spent most of his time at the Met that autumn and winter. So it was that he started to cross the big stage about ten o'clock one morning. The curtain was up, but because the scenery for the rehearsal opera was not yet in place, the playing area was bare. The company's next new production, *La bohème*, was to go into rehearsal later that day. Warren was not in its cast and had never seen its director, the Hollywood celebrity Joseph L. Mankiewicz, who had directed the film *All About Eve* but was new to the Met. "It was early," said Arge Keller, who witnessed the encounter between the two men. "A stage rehearsal had been scheduled but nothing had been set up. Mankiewicz was standing on the stage, looking around, and he had his hat on. Warren came in by chance, on business of his own that had nothing to do with *Bohème*. Of course, he did not know Mankiewicz, and Mankiewicz certainly did not know him. Warren saw that hat and just blew up," Keller said. "He absolutely ordered Mankiewicz to remove his hat and began to hector him about respect for the Met. Mankiewicz just stared. He listened for a while, then he stepped away and took off his hat. He walked off, without a word. I think he must have been in a state of shock all the rest of the day. Warren acted out of love for that stage."

It is easy to see why Warren was so offended by Mankiewicz. By the early 1950s, Warren's awe and respect for the Metropolitan Opera had matured to become a passion. He loved the building and everything it stood for. And he had manners, having been raised by a strict mother who taught her children etiquette and paid a woman to give them lessons in elocution and proper behavior. He believed that a man addressed people in a certain way, tipped or removed his hat, and dressed according to good form. Warren's code was violated when he saw something that offended him profoundly, a man standing in dead center, *wearing a hat*. Mankiewicz lost, and Warren won. Yet his code of etiquette met its match in his temper.

The Abilene Incident

Others who got a taste of Warren's ire that year were seated in the audience during a recital. In 1953 he toured from the first week in February to the first week in March, fighting winter weather all the way. He returned to the Met for a single performance, *Rigoletto* on 7 March, then went on the road again, cramming concerts and recitals into the weeks before the Met tour. At the beginning of April, he and Sektberg reached Abilene, where he was to sing for the Civic Music Association in the Radford Memorial Student Life Center of McMurry College. This was exactly the kind of hall and city that Tibbett, Pons, and other stars fought to exclude from their concert tours. Winter tours were particularly exhausting. Small cities were hard to reach, airports often had to close, trains ran late, snow and ice covered the roads, hotels were inadequate, the food was bad, and audiences were small and sometimes not receptive to recital programs. But Warren, new to the Hurok organization roster that season, may not have felt free to refuse this engagement. As the local critic described the evening, Warren seemed tense "during the first half of the concert," probably because several children were fidgeting in the front row. Nevertheless, the program began smoothly. By 1953 Warren had complete control over his famous pianissimos, which he used generously in his song repertory; in fact, he was used to getting praise for them. But that evening Warren was spinning out the subtleties of the "Credo" from *Otello* when a man, perhaps drunk, broke into the music, shouting, "Louder! Louder!" Warren stopped singing and came to the footlights, then responded inappropriately. Instead of attacking the offender, he pointed down and said, "I won't go on until those children are removed from the front row." His next furious words were directed at the heckler. "I've never been so insulted in my life," he shouted. "And as for you, get your hearing aid rigged up right!" The reporter added, "There were a few more spatting words back and forth between Warren and two or three persons in the crowd." With difficulty, Warren regained his composure. He spoke "abjectly" to the audience, saying he was sorry he had "been so rude." The offending children got up and moved to the rear. Warren then explained that they made it difficult for him to get in the mood for the song he had been singing. "His apology brought the house down in tumultuous applause." Instead of starting the "Credo" again, Warren agreed with Sektberg to do the Toreador Song from *Carmen*, a standard encore. After the intermission, the program went smoothly, but as Warren began the final group of songs, he again "stepped to the footlights and apologized to the audience and told them how nice they all were. He said it was the first time in his life he had lost his poise. He was loudly applauded." He got about nine curtain calls at the end and sang three encores. In the local paper, the headline read, FAMED BARITONE FLAYS ABILENE AUDIENCE THEN APOLOGIZES. The incident was also reported in the New York *Post* and wire-service papers. Whatever else Warren's breach of etiquette shows, it demonstrates what singers had to endure during these concert and recital tours. Most said they had to tour because the Met paid them so badly they needed the extra income. For the manager, the high commissions earned from concerts lent an added incentive to this kind of booking, but the harm to the exhausted singer could not easily be undone.

CHAPTER SEVENTEEN

Honors in Italy and at Home

B ing made Warren happy in 1953, first, by letting him do a long autumn concert season then by giving him a release to sing at the Teatro alla Scala in Milan at the height of the season. As a result, Warren did not appear at the Met at all from May 1953 until mid-January 1954. The idea of sending Warren abroad had been in the air for years, but as soon as Hurok took over Warren's management, serious planning started. Bing's decision came at a moment when he felt he owed La Scala something, for he had been involved in an acrimonious dispute with Antonio Ghiringhelli, the head of La Scala. In the autumn of 1952, as Bing tells the story in his memoir, *5000 Nights at the Opera*, he wrote to the tenor Giuseppe Di Stefano about plans for the 1953–1954 season, which he intended to open with a new production of *Faust*, with Di Stefano in the title role. He asked the tenor to be in New York by mid-October for early rehearsals, but Di Stefano wanted to stay at La Scala, where he could earn better money. This led to an exchange of telegrams between Bing and Ghiringhelli. When the moment came, Di Stefano did not arrive as scheduled. Instead, he notified Bing that "sudden illness" kept him in Italy. But, as Bing discovered from Roberto Bauer, the Met's agent in Milan, "Di Stefano was never ill at all." Bing then charged the tenor with a contract violation and fired him. According to Bing's own view of the matter, "Some good seems to have come of it. La Scala engaged Leonard Warren for what was for us an awkward part of the [1953–1954] Metropolitan season." The "awkward part" included holiday weeks when tickets were hard to sell.

Warren's Milan repertory and dates were *Rigoletto* and *Otello*, at the end of December and the beginning of January. For him, this first Italian engagement was risky and laden with emotional baggage. He would be singing these Verdi operas in La Scala, where Verdi launched his own career in 1839 with *Oberto, Conte di San Bonifacio* and ended it just before the turn of the century with *Falstaff*. Warren would be singing in Italian in the city where he had first learned to speak that language, singing before the very coaches who had taught him in 1938. Apart from his significant "firsts" at the Met, these operas at La Scala were the most important performances of his career up to that time.

Knowing what he did about Italian audiences, Warren was nervous and unsure of his reception. Vivien remembered him as being "hopeful, but not confident" about the engagement. Inside La Scala, trouble was brewing, leading the critic Oreste Noto to describe a season when Italian theatres had failed to hire Italian singers. At the same time, it was rumored that "the foreigners are coming." The headline read, THE THEATRE WITHOUT PEACE on the front page of the *Corriere degli Artisti* of 15 to 30 December. In Italy, "unhappiness" was matched by "cruel joblessness." At La Scala, the claque, headed by Ettore Parmeggiani, had been disrupting performances with whistles and hisses from the top balcony, where it always held forth. The Italian opera business was in turmoil. Outside La Scala, political considerations sometimes also figured in the discourse. For nearly a decade after the end of the war, sentiment against the Allied bombings boiled up regularly in Milan, where La Scala had been restored but dozens of other buildings still lay in ruins. The English were the most despised of the former enemies because people believed they had bombed the city after the signing of the armistice. Many Italians were still wary of foreigners.

Giorgio Tozzi, an Italian-American from Chicago, had been studying in Europe and had settled in Milan before the Warrens arrived. Interviewed for this book, he recalled signing his first contract to sing at La Scala and living with a family in a fourth-floor walk-up apartment, "living very simply," as most of Italy did. "A lot of people were still smarting about losing the war," Tozzi said. "Some people were toying with Communism. Americans were not terribly popular." He also spoke of "the poisoned air" and the "politics of Italy" invading La Scala, the epicenter of the "terribly competitive" opera business. Tozzi felt Warren had risked a great deal by singing *Rigoletto*, "which every Italian considers his personal property."

The Warrens in Milan

This, then, was the atmosphere when Warren and Agatha landed in Italy. The first friends to greet them in their hotel were Mario and Rina Del Monaco; the tenor had just finished singing *La Wally* at La Scala with Tebaldi and Giangiacomo Guelfi, Giulini conducting. The Del Monacos invited the Warrens to their apartment, a showcase for their collection of antiques, chessboards, Old Master paintings, and expensive Oriental carpets. Next came Warren's former coaches, Giuseppe Pais and Riccardo Picozzi, followed by conductor Ettore Panizza. For these three men, Warren's international reputation fully justified every effort they had made for him. This small circle of friends kept company with the Warrens at every turn. The weather was bad.

Warren complained that the fog was so thick he could not even see the top of the spire of Milan cathedral. "And when you can see it, watch out! That means snow," he said.

His *Rigoletto* performances were scheduled between 16 December and 3 January. *Otello* would follow, with a first night on 8 January. Both had to be rehearsed. The *Rigoletto* cast included Di Stefano as the Duke; the lyric soprano Rosanna Carteri as Gilda; Nicola Zaccaria, a young Greek bass, as Sparafucile; and Luisa Ribacchi as Maddalena. Clara Betner sang Giovanna, and Antonio Zerbini, Paolo Pedani, Lucia Mardelli, and other comprimarios completed the cast. Nino Sanzogno conducted. On the first night, Warren made small talk backstage with the wardrobe men and stage director. Then came his cue. The La Scala audience was "edgy," one journalist said, but its displeasure was directed not at Warren, but at Di Stefano. The tenor was clearly in bad voice, starting the first act with off-pitch singing and sloppy phrasing, coming to grief at the end of the opera. One critic faulted him for missing crucial top notes and "slithering through" others. In the *Corriere d'Informazione*, the reviewer wrote, "Poor Mantua! How low have you fallen, with Di Stefano as your Duke. . . . Two thousand people in the audience knew this role by heart, and they were all sitting there, sure they could sing it perfectly," so there was no room for mistakes. When Carteri, whom almost everyone judged wrong for Gilda, began to sing "Caro nome," real disaster threatened. Orazio Vergani, the critic of the *Corriere della Sera*, said, "It is not easy to stop a crisis from developing after a performance begins to wobble." *Rigoletto* at La Scala began "to wobble" early that night, and things did not improve. Incredibly, not a single handclap followed the celebrated quartet, mainly because Di Stefano cracked on the final high note. After the last act, when the audience realized the tenor would not come out for a curtain call, whistles and shrieks of derision mingled with whatever applause there was. It was clear from the reviews that only Warren could tally up a success.

Critics praised him in many local and national newspapers. Giulio Confalonieri, the dean of Milanese reviewers, wrote almost thirty column inches in *La Patria*, characterizing the event as one of the "Great First Nights at La Scala." Critical of Di Stefano and Carteri, who pushed their voices, he found Warren in excellent form. Big expectations had been raised, he said, over the American baritone's appearance. "We got a very favorable impression of him," he wrote.

> Warren has a voice that is equal [from top to bottom], beautiful in timbre, made of noble stuff, and he uses it with great elegance, without showing it off. He prefers dark coloration and a tone that is subtle rather than crudely aggressive. For all these reasons, the audience appreciated him, and we admire him, even though his recitatives were

not always sufficiently incisive; still, he had perfect pronunciation, aside from an occasional [incorrect] double consonant.

In his paternal affection for Gilda, he was "extremely moving"; his private feelings and his suffering were "intense and sincere."

Vergani, in the *Corriere della Sera*, emphasized Warren's style and his studies with Giuseppe De Luca, then praised him for his understanding of the character's psychology and realization of it through the music. "His excellent Italian diction, his use of his profound intelligence, his command of the pathetic elements [in the story], the warm and emotion-laden voice, all let him get to the heart of the character with an intelligence that the audience could feel. Among all the singers, he was the one who was most appreciated and got the most spontaneous applause." Headlines in *La Notte* praised Warren. HE WON HIS BATTLE, in spite of demonstrations coming from an unruly horde of "gangsters." Parmeggiani and the claque got a slap from this reviewer, but "the protesters could not take issue with Warren. He sings like God, and learned from Titta Ruffo, De Luca, and Pasquale Amato." Luigi Gianoli, in *L'Italia*, wrote a mixed review. He found Warren somewhat cold and faulted him for not singing loud enough. However, he said that Warren shaped phrases well, had "great self-assurance" and was "especially dignified and wise." His final judgment was that Warren was "grandissimo" in the second and fourth acts. "He made of this dark, repellent character a truly compassionate and tragic human being," particularly unforgettable and "lacerating." Both critics from the political parties of the left praised Warren. The article in the socialist paper *Avanti* deplored the rudeness of the audience during the "turbulent evening" and criticized "unhappy" Di Stefano for attacking phrases improperly and cracking wide open on a top note in the last act. Warren, though, had a "beautifully trained and excellently placed voice, [and] he knew how to act this role, keeping his humanity central [to it]." *L'Unità*, the voice of the Italian Communist Party, praised Warren's "magnificent technique and dramatic power" and said that he resembled all the great interpreters of Rigoletto in that generation. "Note for note, and word for word, he created the role, and none of its subtlety escaped him. He evidently has studied this part for a long time, profoundly, meticulously—something that is extremely rare today and must be appreciated." The critic of *Candido* hailed Warren's "masterly line" and subtle way with the text. His mezza voce was "extremely beautiful [and] perfectly modulated, his phrasing fine; his legato allowed him to color the particularly tragic moments. A more perfect father could not be imagined." His only fault, the reviewer said, was in making Rigoletto too aristocratic, too much like a diplomat. He lacked the bitterness and fury that should boil in Rigoletto. "But what an admirable Germont, what a splendid father in *Luisa Miller* this excellent baritone would be!"

Oreste Noto, the knowledgeable, cranky editor of the *Corriere degli*

Artisti, felt most of this *Rigoletto* performance was "gray," with the orchestra playing "without soul and without spirit." However, at the beginning of his review Noto praised Warren warmly, offering him congratulations for being the only artist who remembered that "*La Scala is La Scala.*" He was

> entirely worthy of the great reputation that preceded him here. Without betraying the musical line even once, he created a human Rigoletto . . . that stood out magnificently from others. Alone, and so badly assisted [by the rest of the cast], the American baritone often created the right atmosphere. He fully deserved the two ovations he got during the acts of the opera, in the course of the action.

Noto added that these demonstrations favorable to Warren were the only ones of the evening that were not marred by ugly protests. Noto dispatched Di Stefano and Carteri by reviewing them far down the page, after his remarks on the comprimarios! Di Stefano sang "very, very badly, perhaps because he was irritated by the loud whistling that punctuated his truly wretched performance. At the end of the fourth act, he refused to come out for a curtain call; and that was his last off-key note that evening." Carteri, a promising young artist who had only recently made her La Scala debut, lacked the voice for Gilda and committed many "vocal sins."

Warren's next opera at La Scala was *Otello*. The conductor was Antonino Votto, substituting for an ailing Victor De Sabata. Tozzi, who was cast as Lodovico, described Votto as "clear-minded, a scholarly type of conductor. He loved to impart his knowledge in an almost academic way." This production brought Del Monaco's Otello to La Scala for the first time, although he had sung it in other cities, among them Rome, Mexico City, Buenos Aires, and New York. One month after the run at La Scala, he repeated the role at the Paris Opéra. The tenor and the baritone were more than comfortable with each other, having sung *Otello* together in 1950 in Rio and in 1952 at the Met. Renata Tebaldi sang Desdemona in the La Scala production. Giuseppe Zampieri was Cassio, while Anna Maria Canali played Emilia. The comprimarios were Mario Carlin, Paolo Pedani, and Emilio Campi. As in *Rigoletto*, the chorus master was Vittorio Veneziani. Mario Frigerio directed; and the scenes and costumes were by the master hand of Nicola Benois. Of the principals, Warren was by far the most familiar with the opera. Del Monaco called him "the equal of Titta Ruffo" and looked to him for support. For his part, Warren hoped the opera might have a better reception than the "turbulent" *Rigoletto*. On the day after the first night of *Otello*, when the papers came out, it was reviewed in the *Corriere della Sera* by Franco Abbiati, a respected author and critic who was already well into writing his four-volume biography of Verdi.

Comparing this *Otello* to previous productions at La Scala, he found it fell short, although it was generally "satisfying" and had some moments "worthy of high praise." Del Monaco's "splendid voice" and acting matched Tebaldi's "limpid" singing. Both singers satisfied an audience that had just heard them in *La Wally*. Warren "imposed his noble attitude and the contained energy of his [singing] on the evil figure of Iago." Applause for the three leading singers broke out during the opera, and at the end they were called before the curtain "many times."

Confalonieri, who had written favorably of Warren's *Rigoletto*, covered *Otello* for *La Patria*. As Iago, the American baritone was "always correct, always noble in his sung lines." He said, "This worthy artist" was badly costumed in black, "looking like the minister of a Protestant sect." His voice sometimes got "bogged down" between his chest and his throat and seemed strangely "far away" and "abstract," which it had never been before. Although the "Credo" was well sung, Confalonieri criticized Warren's stage business at the end of it. He was too casual as he sang the line "E poi? E poi?" And while the orchestra plays the phrases that follow, Iago should not stroll around the stage, but should stand motionless, staring into the face of Death.

In the newspaper *La Notte*, Alceo Toni, the author of another book on Verdi, described the audience for *Otello* as "restless" but not "up in arms," as it had been in the controversial *Rigoletto*. Nothing went amiss, however, and the stars saved the "beautiful evening." Del Monaco was "the best Otello of the last thirty years" and "stupendous" in the death scene, which left the audience mute and shocked. Toni found Tebaldi "a miraculous singer" with "marvelous" line and perfect bel canto style. Warren, "a polished artist at the height of his power," fell "perfectly into the line of our best traditions of singing" and offered an Iago that was "a masterpiece of psychological understanding."

Claudio Sartori, a distinguished critic and colleague of Confalonieri and Abbiati, wrote in *La Notte* that Tebaldi's Desdemona was "peerless, with a magic sweetness." She possessed a perfect technique and "resplendent timbre." Del Monaco's Otello, Sartori said, was "like a bolt of lightning." His voice and interpretation combined with his "fearlessness" to make a near-perfect protagonist. Writing about Warren, he offered a mixed review of Iago that reflects an anti-American stance. His hostility evidently took root in the first act, for he said that Del Monaco's electrifying entrance with "Esultate!" had "liberated" the scene from the "American element." Warren's reappearance did not "convince us that we need this input from across the sea." Sartori added that Warren was "a noble artist whose musical interpretation of the Verdi character is polished and tight, solid, and secure," although he was not dramatic enough and did not convey the villain's "diabolic nature." To be fair, he concluded by saying, "All in all, Warren as Iago stood in dignity beside Del Monaco and Tebaldi, sharing the extraordinary success of the evening with them." Agatha, who dated most of the Milanese reviews and wrote remarks on some of them, translated Sartori's most favorable words and noted them in pencil at the top of his article. Another listener who remarked on the presence of an American at La Scala that season was Marise Angelucci Pokorny, who attended *Rigoletto* as the guest of a Milanese employee of Decca Records. Marise remembered Warren as being "very, very good" and said she asked her friend how an American baritone happened to be singing in such a bastion of Italian pride. About the demonstrations that are a part of La Scala life, she said, "Well, the Milanese are so terrible." Later Marise became a close friend of Warren, Agatha, Roy, Vivien, and many members of their circle.

Another Critic's View

Giuseppe Pugliese, one of Italy's foremost critics, attended both *Rigoletto* and *Otello*. Based in Venice, where he directed the Press Office of the Teatro La Fenice for many years, he is now the president of the Wagner Society and is in charge of the restoration of the apartment on the Grand Canal where Wagner died in 1883. Interviewed in Venice, Pugliese said:

> When Warren got to Milan and began to rehearse and perform, his voice seemed somewhat tired; and I'm sure all the critics noticed that because we all went to rehearsals, officially and otherwise. But Warren he was a great artist, truly great. He should never be mentioned in the same sentence as Tibbett. Never! Never! Tibbett was a Hollywood singer, a film singer. He could never have risen to Warren's level. Warren had a voice of gorgeous color. It reminded me of the classical line of the great Carlo Tagliabue. Yes! Warren's beautiful phrasing sounded like Tagliabue.

When I asked Pugliese about the noisy demonstrations that interrupted the La Scala performance of *Rigoletto*, Pugliese swore they were nothing compared to the ugliest events in that theatre. Quite beyond the episodes of people throwing things across the auditorium and even coming to blows in arguments over singers, he mentioned the Callas-Del Monaco *Norma*, of sad memory. "She had a moment of uncertainty, and the audience immediately began to shout "Ooooooooo." Then Del Monaco was pushing too much toward a baritone color, and he went flat, and the theatre exploded. What happened with *Rigoletto* and Di Stefano's Duke was nothing like that." Pugliese also felt that *Otello* with Warren, Tebaldi, and Del Monaco was very fine, and that Warren's second Iago at La Scala went better than the first. Tozzi described Warren's two portrayals as "excellent" and said, "I was in awe of his vocal splendor."

After the compromised *Rigoletto*, *Otello* brought relief. Warren had a contract to sing other repeats of *Otello*, but while he was preparing them, a telephone call from New York brought Agatha the news that her mother was dying. This was the second family tragedy she had faced in less than three years because Harry Leifflen had died in 1951, leaving his widow to spend much of her time at Manhattan House with her daughter and son-in-law. The Warrens and Mrs. Leifflen had been living a quiet, intimate family life. Warren was particularly affected, for he had been very close to her from the earliest years of their acquaintance. "She always treated him exactly as if he were her son," Vivien said. When the Warrens first heard the news, Agatha decided to fly back to New York alone, leaving Warren to finish his engagement; but he refused to let her go. Learning from a later telephone call that Mrs. Leifflen could not survive, he canceled the rest of his performances and left for New York with his wife. They arrived too late, for Mrs. Leifflen died on 11 January 1954. Warren mourned her for years. William Mayo Sullivan said the only times he ever heard Warren sing badly were during the Met performances after the death of this woman, who had truly been a second mother to him.

Coverage of Warren's success at La Scala had been widely distributed over the Associated Press wire service while he was still in Milan, although no one mentioned how troubled he had been by the rambunctious audience for *Rigoletto*. After he got home, Kolodin wrote a long feature article about him and Leonard Bernstein. They had made their debuts at La Scala only a few days apart, with Bernstein conducting Cherubini's *Medea*. Warren was the first American baritone ever to sing Rigoletto at La Scala and the first non-Italian to sing it there in years. Quoting the best of Warren's reviews, the critic urged the Met to bring Bernstein and Warren together in one production in the Opera House. "Has the Met Heard?" Kolodin's headline asked. Bernstein and Warren were never paired at the Met.

Herman Krawitz as Bing's Trusted Associate

One man who appreciated Warren more than many young Turks at the Met was Herman Krawitz, who also came to be the baritone's trusted friend. At the beginning of the 1953–1954 season, Krawitz joined the Met administrative staff as a consultant on labor relations. Soon he was offered a permanent post. He said Bing had hired him to "make things work within the budget." His first year at the Met was a time of learning and breaking in, and his first big production was *Andrea Chénier*, which went onstage in November 1954. In the first months of Krawitz's tenure, he got to know many of the singers, Warren among them. Both men were natives of the Bronx, where they both had attended public schools. Krawitz had graduated from DeWitt Clinton High School and gone on to get practical experience on stages on Cape Cod, among them the Provincetown Theatre. The Broadway producer Richard Aldrich recommended Krawitz to the Met at a time when, as Bing said, he needed an expert in backstage organization.

From the moment he entered the Met, Krawitz was impressed with Warren, and he said that Warren "was and still remains my favorite baritone, without question the greatest baritone of our time. He was the most instinctive performer I ever saw at the Met. I could never see where the intellectual side of him was, but he had that too. He was childlike, a sweet, lovely guy. I knew him very well, better than any other artist at the Met. Our friendship started in the House. Even when I was new there, I would be standing around after a performance, and Leonard would give me a ride home. Later I was frequently invited to his apartment for dinner." Onstage and off, Krawitz and Warren got on famously. Krawitz supported Warren the artist, while Warren found a young friend.

To Krawitz's surprise, he, a Jew, was criticized by certain Jews on the roster for associating with Warren. Soon after he got to the Met, he said, he became aware of their prejudice against Warren. It was still in force, three and more years after Warren's baptism. Krawitz said:

Some Jewish performers at the Met disliked Leonard a lot because of his conversion. In fact, very early on several singers mentioned Leonard's religion to me. The Jews were annoyed at him. One of the first things I remember was the feeling that he had done something terribly wrong. We would be standing in the wings while he was onstage during a curtain call, and someone would say, "Look at that guy! Can you believe it? He converted!" Or one Jewish singer or the other would say to me, "Did you know that he converted?" Or they would say, "Why do you get along so well with him? Don't you know what he did?" Once I was even warned not to speak to him. Some of the Met's Jews believed Leonard had done the unthinkable, the one thing that should never be done. They had found out somehow about his Catholicism. Maybe it was Peerce who figured it out first. He could not accept what he saw as Warren's betrayal of his people. The Catholic part of it wasn't important. It was not just that Leonard became a *Catholic*; it was that he became a *Christian*.

Krawitz went on:

Leonard made no secret of his affiliation. He showed up with priests all the time; priests were with him pretty often, in rehearsals and after performances. He really even seemed a lot more Catholic than Licia [Albanese] and [her husband] Joe Gimma. As far as his conversion being possible because the Warenoffs were not very observant Jews, that didn't mean much because among a lot of secular Jews, nonobservance of Jewish tradition is very common. But even among secular Jews, there are a lot of hard feelings over intermarriage. When a secular Jew I knew married a Gentile girl, his family sat shiva for him; they had the mourning services for the dead. Not everyone did that, of course. But even if some Jews forgave intermarriage, it was quite another step to convert, and very few people could ever forgive that. Those Jews at the Met who felt worst about this sort of shunned Leonard.

Asked about Bing's personal feelings about his star baritone, Krawitz said the general manager never showed any prejudice about Warren's Catholicism.

Bing very much wanted Leonard in the company and didn't want him to be unhappy. In fact, he wanted to keep Leonard happy by letting him sing whatever roles he wanted. The only conflict I can remember came because of *Falstaff*. Bing loved *Falstaff*, and so did Leonard, who had sung it at the Met in 1944 and always kept after Bing to let him sing it again. But Bing didn't think Leonard should do it; he thought he would not be good in a comic role. So as long as Leonard was there, Bing couldn't produce *Falstaff* because he didn't want to hurt Leonard. But we gave him everything else. We did everything to keep him happy.

The Lamentation of Saul

In 1954 Warren spent part of his spring and summer in the studio with Willard Sektberg, learning a new work that was unlike anything he had done before. This was *The Lamentation of Saul* by Norman Dello Joio, which was written for Warren. Born in New York City in 1913, Dello Joio was a distinguished composer and pianist, an educator who had taught at Sarah Lawrence College until 1950. He had also gone often to the celebrated music festival at Tanglewood in the Berkshires and had even attended as a student in the first year it opened. By the time the Elizabeth Sprague Coolidge Foundation commissioned Dello Joio to write a new piece to celebrate the birthday of Mrs. Coolidge, he had already achieved a substantial reputation with a repertory of successful operas, ballets and orchestral and chamber compositions to his credit. Verdi was then and still remains Dello Joio's favorite composer. More than a hundred years earlier, young Verdi had also chosen to compose a cantata with Saul as his protagonist, taking Vittorio Alfieri's drama as his source.

Dello Joio, interviewed for this book, said that he took his text for *The Lamentation of Saul* from *David*, a play by D. H. Lawrence.

Actually the play was given to me by Lawrence's widow, Frieda. She had come to Tanglewood, where we heard a concert together. We became friends. She gave me the play, hoping that I would make an opera out of it. I toyed with the idea; but it presented too many problems. The drama itself was basically about David, but I was more interested in Saul. I was intrigued with the role that Lawrence gave him in the play, and even while I composed *The Lamentation of Saul*, I had the opera in mind.

Fascinated by the Biblical character, Dello Joio composed a chamber piece for baritone, flute, oboe, clarinet, viola, cello and piano. He recalled his first meeting with Warren and the circumstances that led the baritone to agree to sing the world premiere of an original, commissioned composition. "I had heard Leonard at the Met," Dello Joio said.

I liked the quality of his voice. That's what drew me to him, especially when he sang *Rigoletto*. I also liked him in *Otello*. I admired his singing very much because the voice was so full and so masculine and so true in terms of intonation. I also understood his lyrics when he sang. At the time I was also a good friend of Roy Leifflen, Leonard's brother-in-law. Then there came a period when I was doing the Metropolitan Opera Saturday afternoon intermission features, and on one of those broadcasts I met Leonard and interviewed him. From then on we became close friends. We visited back and forth outside the Opera House, Leonard, his wife, Roy and I.

Dello Joio said when Warren first saw the score of *The Lamentation of Saul*, he was fascinated with the idea of singing it.

I handed it to him. Then he had the score for some time and was obviously very delighted with the work. I knew he couldn't read music, but that made no difference at all. Many singers I knew could not read music. Leonard studied and rehearsed it alone and with Willard Sektberg. When he had it under his belt, we did the first sit-down together. At that first rehearsal, he was so excited about listening to my accompaniment that at the end of his entrance he sang a B-flat, a tone so high it sometimes even posed problems for tenors. He got so excited that instead of singing a high E-flat he sang a high B-flat. I was stunned. The fact that Leonard could sing that note was astonishing. It was just thrilling, but I told him that I didn't know any other baritone who could sing it. He agreed, and he sang it as an E-flat in the world premiere. He conveyed all the drama in that chamber piece. It was my first experience with Leonard; and working on it with me tended to help him. I just let him go in terms of what he thought he should do and told him where he got out of hand. He took directions from me very well because it was all so new to him. When it came to the problem of controlling such a large voice, I would simply say, "Doesn't that need to be softer? That's too long. Don't make it unnecessarily long. A more subtle approach might be better." He did take directions.

On 21 August, Warren was the soloist in the world premiere of Dello Joio's cantata, *The Lamentation of Saul*, presented under the auspices of the Elizabeth Sprague Coolidge Memorial Festival at the South Mountain Temple of Music in South Mountain, Pittsfield, Massachusetts. The festival's music director, Mrs. Willem Willeke, planned the program with Dello Joio. Both composer and soloist were fortunate because the setting, in the heart of the Berkshires, enhanced the beauty of the evening. The work was also offered in Washington on 30 October, Mrs. Coolidge's birthday, for the Founder's Day concert of the Library of Congress. A review from an unidentified newspaper of 31 October in the Leonard Warren Collection calls the Washington event "the peak of the year's chamber music activity." The writer said it was the most "memorable musical happening of any sort that has taken place in Washington during the past several years." The work itself was "thrilling." Its "exciting, full-bodied, lithe music" and "astringent harmonies and nervous rhythms" heightened the effect of the piece. "Mr. Warren's singing was superb. The great baritone was in magnificent voice and sang the Dello Joio music with obvious affection and deep understanding." Years passed before Warren would sing it again.

✦ CHAPTER EIGHTEEN

A Better Image

The Muriel Francis office had begun to handle Warren's publicity in 1952, and two years later, Agatha asked Muriel to assign Warren's account to Edgar Vincent, a polished European gentleman with roots in The Netherlands and Venice. He had reached the top of his profession. In our interview he said that over the many years of their association, he found Warren a complex person who hid his real character behind the façade of boyish simplicity. "Inside there was a volcano," he said, "a real male prima donna. I wanted him to let people see that." As Warren, Agatha, and Vincent worked on a public relations plan, Warren asked what he could do to improve his image. "I told him, 'Look, you are putting on this face of being very cooperative and dull with the press. Have opinions. Be yourself.' The press really did not know him, although they knew the voice. I believe he was the world's greatest baritone; he had an absolutely unique voice. When he sang, he produced a huge dome of sound. And then he had those pianissimos!" Eventually the two men became good friends. Warren sometimes accepted Vincent's suggestions. They also had common interests outside the music business. Vincent was born a Catholic, and an uncle was a prelate in the great basilica of St. Francis in Assisi. They also shared a love for rose gardens. "I had mine in Rockland County; his was in Connecticut," Vincent said. "I remember he was distraught once because he cultivated a lot of magnificent white roses and then lost them. It pained him more than you could imagine. I asked him, 'Was heaving the problem?' He said, 'No. And we did a wonderful job of mounding them. I don't know what happened.' It was as if he had lost something very, very dear to him."

From 1954 until 1960, Vincent placed stories about Warren in most major American newspapers and magazines and, far more important, saw that he was covered in almost every performance. He remained Warren's press agent until the end. It was a good relationship. Vincent said, "The more successful he became, the more relaxed Agatha became. Leonard, too. Along the way, I realized how much research he did on his operas, and I was very impressed by that." Vincent even coached Warren in some roles and designed one of his most effective costumes, the Iago costume Warren used in the late 1950s. "I bought the material," Vincent remembered, "Pompeiian red taffeta, and I laid black lace over it to minimize his size. He looked better when he was not in a single color." When a press representative took on that kind of responsibility, it meant he and his clients, Warren and Agatha, believed in each other.

Learning from Yannopoulos

The first big event of Warren's 1954–1955 Met season was Umberto Giordano's *Andrea Chénier*, a new production that gave him the richly satisfying role of Gérard. He learned the action in sessions with director Dino Yannopoulos.

This *Andrea Chénier* was not Yannopoulos's first experience with Warren. As the Greek director recalled, the two men had initially worked on Warren's *Rigoletto* in 1946–1947. Yannopoulos did not begin rehearsing for that season until January 1947, about a month before Warren was to sing it. "We didn't get along too well," he said.

> In fact, we didn't get along at all. We immediately disagreed about everything. He was unpleasant and very, very difficult. It's not that I thought he was stupid. Later he reminded me of Callas. Everything had to be his way or nothing at all. Warren had come back from Italy in 1938 with what he had learned. Once he did something in a given way, that was it; it was like something engraved in stone. And it was very difficult to get him to change.

Yannopoulos said he felt Warren "really hammed it up when he shouted 'Gilda! Gilda! Ah, la maledizione!' After the chorus men walked off, they made fun of him backstage for yelling the way he did." Yannopoulos considered their association a failure. Their next encounters came at the end of 1950, for *Pagliacci*.

> By then we got along a little better. There was something there; it just took time to get it out. The Met had hired a stage director from a little opera company; and this guy wanted Warren, the Tonio, to sit on a kind of diver's bell, holding a green canary. Warren took one look and left. He walked out because it was really bad. It made no sense. He was right to protest, and he refused to sing until he got things his way. Then I started working with him. It took years to win his trust, but it was worthwhile.

After these sessions came the Bing era and the new 1953–1954 *Andrea Chénier*, which Yannopoulos was assigned. "Warren had never sung it before, so no one had taught it to him. By then we knew each other quite well. Once he knew you and liked you, he was really quite wonderful." Yannopoulos said Warren could not bear to have anyone correct him in the presence of other people. "He was very sensitive about that, and in that way he was different from other singers, who are used to having the director tell them what to do. Directors are there to teach." But according to Yannopoulos, Warren had "a terrible inferiority complex because of his lack of musical education." In the early rehearsals, the director tried to get Gérard's character across to Warren so that he could find the right expression for the role. "But he rebelled against my advice. I couldn't get through to him until I started talking to him about the French Revolution. History! He loved that. I found that marvelous painting by David and showed him how Gérard should be. It was at that point that Warren invited me to come to his apartment and work privately with him there."

Yannopoulos recalled his first visit to the Warrens' home in Manhattan House.

> Warren was alone with his wife. The one impression I got was of religion. There were crucifixes everywhere. I understood they were all very devout Catholics. Mrs. Warren's aunt, who was a nun, used to come to the opera with her. Seeing Warren there, I began to understand him better. This man was really a boy, and he needed his wife. He was completely hers. We didn't talk much about opera on that first visit because we played with his electric trains. From then on, I started going to their apartment in the evenings, sometimes two or three times a week. I was there only for work. I never had a meal with Warren and his wife, not even a cup of coffee. But he worked very hard, so I thought to myself, "Well, for art's sake, I'll do this." It was worth it.
>
> I believe I really got something out of him for that *Chénier*, but it was a long struggle. I remember how we worked on the third act. Gérard is at his desk. Maddalena comes in. When Gérard suddenly recognizes her, there is a big chord in the orchestra. Warren's instinct was to leap out of the chair, but I told him to let the music do it and just act with his voice. "Just look at her," I said. "Just look at her for some time before the chord. Then the chord tells the story." After that Warren trusted me more.

Quite beyond offering Warren a new role, *Andrea Chénier* gave him a part that was more complicated than his usual opera villains were. The baritone underwent profound character transformations in the course of the action. In his aria "Nemico della patria" he dominated a stunning dramatic moment of self-examination. It was exactly the kind of humanizing role Warren finally learned to master. In the fine cast with him were Milanov and Del Monaco, with Cleva conducting.

Later that season, Yannopoulos also directed Warren in the revised production of *Otello*, which reached the stage on 31 January 1955 with Del Monaco and Tebaldi, conducted by Fritz Stiedry. Its dress rehearsal was the finest performance I ever saw at the Met. It gave the invited audience its first chance to hear Tebaldi's luminous Desdemona matched by the two men who had sung *Otello* with her at La Scala. As the rehearsal ended with her whispered lines, Iago's furious exit, and Del Monaco's last cry, absolute silence hung in the auditorium. People in the invited audience were too stunned to applaud. Finally a roar of approval broke out. The first night of *Otello* came close to matching this unusual event.

Yannopoulos explained how he happened to coach his Iago, saying, "I had seen Warren in the *Otello* directed by Herbert Graf in the 1940s, and I thought he was awful, using all the cliches of the stage villain. He was hammy, leering, and staggering around." But Yannopoulos kept his criticism to himself, and, to his surprise, Warren approached him in November 1954, soon after the premiere of *Andrea Chénier*. "I'd like to get some new ideas about Iago," Warren confided to the director. "You know, I'm not really the old fogey you think I am." The startled Yannopoulos hesitated for a moment, then began to tell the baritone what he hoped to accomplish. Warren, trusting, said, "O.K., I'll work with you," and again invited the director to Manhattan House. "I went to his apartment as I had done before. This time, three times a week. And we got very positive results." This production held the stage until the end of the 1950s, usually with the original cast and, after Tebaldi returned to Italy, with Lucine Amara, Victoria de Los Angeles, or Zinka Milanov as Desdemona. In 1958 it again had Tebaldi, Del Monaco, and Warren, under the baton of Cleva, who had taken over from Stiedry. Warren's last *Otello* at the Met came in January 1959.

Renata Tebaldi as Warren's Partner

The legendary soprano Renata Tebaldi began our interview by describing the "great esteem" she had for Warren, a "very respected colleague." She also had kind words for Agatha, whom she remembered as "very sweet," "molto carina." Tebaldi gently edged into his first name, "Lay-o-nard." She said, "Rather than being just a great singer, Leonard was truly a great artist. Above all, he was a great interpreter, but he was blessed with a voice of velvet; it was a very, very soft, velvety voice. I believe he was just born with that voice." She remembered sharing the stage with him in many Met performances of *Aida*, *Otello*, *Andrea Chénier*, and *Tosca*. They also sang six performances of *Traviata* together at the Met in the new production of February 1957. Outside the Met, their initial encounter at La Scala in rehearsals and performances of *Otello* over the 1954–1955 Christmas and New Year's holidays was followed by their appearances in San Francisco in 1955 in *Aida* and *Andrea Chénier* and in 1956 in *Tosca* and a sublime *Simon Boccanegra*. Recalling Warren's Scarpia, Tebaldi suggested it was not easy for him. Still, she said, "He succeeded in doing it well. In fact, he could accomplish a great deal because he was so intelligent." Asked about his Boccanegra, she blossomed, saying, "He was truly stupendous. It was something marvelous. *He had to sing.* That is what his life was: he had to sing."

Other Productions, Other Colleagues

A historic *Ballo in maschera* reached the Met's stage on 7 January 1955. In it came Marian Anderson's Metropolitan Opera debut as Ulrica. She thus became the first African-American singer on the Met roster. As it happened, Warren had not sung Renato there since 1948, and in the course of those years his voice had developed considerable power and polish. Tucker sang Riccardo, while Milanov was cast as Amelia. Roberta Peters portrayed Oscar, and James McCracken, still a comprimario and not yet reborn as a dramatic tenor, sang the Judge. This production had gone into rehearsal in early December. In the course of preparations, Warren, obviously in fine fettle, took a certain delight in showing the power and beauty of his voice. Arge Keller, still in the rehearsal department, took advantage of his position to listen to the sessions. He recalled a *Ballo* rehearsal on the old roof stage on the Seventh Avenue side of the building. He said, "The singers were sitting in a semicircle near the piano. Most were singing at least part of the rehearsal in half-voice to spare themselves as they ran through the score, and Tucker protected his assets by dropping his voice one octave when he came to the high notes. Warren, though, sang out in full voice, as he generally did." Keller remembered him sitting on a folding chair, completely relaxed, with his legs crossed. When Warren came to his great aria "Eri tu," he stayed where he was and belted it out, sailing through its high emotional seas and hanging onto his top notes. As he finished, Tucker turned to Keller and whispered, "Listen to that! The S.O.B. is a tenor!"

One colleague who got to know Warren in the autumn of 1954 was the American mezzo Sandra Warfield. *Andrea Chénier* had been on the stage only two weeks when she was thrust into the role of Madelon. Having made her company debut in the autumn of 1953, she sang with Warren in three seasons in the Opera House and on tour. "I was so young then, and I really looked up to him." Warfield said, "I didn't even know the operas. You know, the Met had these maestros who taught me, and then suddenly I was on the stage." Warfield recalled her first impressions of Warren's voice. "It was like thunder in your ear. A magnificent sound, a broad, rich sound. It shook the rafters.

No, there was something more. It shook the whole Met." She also sang Maddalena to Warren's Rigoletto and spoke of her experiences with him in *La Gioconda* in 1955. There she was cast as the Blind Woman. "I remember that I had to be led offstage by him, and he was so gentle and considerate. I was afraid I would fall because I couldn't see a thing when they threw that shawl over my head. He took such pains when he guided me. He said, 'Don't worry' and other things like that. I thought of him as a very nice man, always very kind to me."

Also in that *Gioconda* production was Giorgio Tozzi, who had first met Warren in Milan the previous year. "I was a great fan of his, having heard many of his broadcasts. Then I got to see his *Falstaff*, and it far surpassed what I had heard on the air," Tozzi said. "*Gioconda* was my Met debut. Leonard and Zinka were wonderful colleagues, but Leonard was particularly good to me. He took me under his wing. In 1955 we were in *Aida* in San Francisco together; he was Amonasro, and I was Ramfis. Leonard and Agatha had invited some of their best friends there to a picnic at the Bohemian Club, and they asked me to go along. You couldn't imagine any two people more friendly and affable. They treated me as if we had been friends for years." After the *Aida*, Alfred Frankenstein praised Warren as "the cast's most exciting singer" and hailed "the tremendous vocalism, the evenness of his production, the strength and subtlety of the delivery." Tozzi, he wrote, was "next to Warren" in importance, but Tebaldi "was rather disappointing," with "choppy phrasing and other erratic dealings with the music."

The Bowery Mission and Other Good Deeds

For some years the Metropolitan Opera bass Jerome Hines had been contributing his services to the Salvation Army Mission in the building at 370 Bowery on the Lower East Side. At his side was his wife, the soprano Lucia Evangelista. Hines recalled these evenings. "They would have two or three hundred men there, some ill, some alcoholics, all pretty much down on their luck. Lucia and I would sing a couple of gospel hymns and then we would give testimony about our lives. After that, some of the men even spoke up and testified."

Hines continued, "I began to think of expanding these programs to a half-hour of music. Then I would ask other singers to join us. Among the ones who came were [the baritones] Walter Cassel and Leonard, [the tenor] James McCracken, and Sandra Warfield, his wife, a mezzo. Another mezzo who came down was Jean Madeira. Usually we sang opera arias, but once we did a whole program of lieder. After that concert, I said to one of the men that I thought the program had been a mistake because the music was not popular enough. He set me straight. 'Mr. Hines,' he said, 'We didn't come from the Bowery. We just ended up here.'"

The Warrens in the living room of their new Manhattan House apartment, 1951.
Credit: Vivien Warren Collection.

Warren as Germont after the 17 April 1951 performance of *La traviata* on the Met tour in Cleveland. Left to right: Eugene Conley, Dorothy Kirsten, Rudolf Bing, and Warren. Credit: Dorothy Kirsten Collection.

At the RCA recording studio for the complete *Il trovatore* in 1952, Milanov, Björling, and Warren confer with Warren's good friend, conductor Renato Cellini. Credit: RCA Victor; Metropolitan Opera Archives.

The Met's stars rehearse *Rigoletto* for the new Eugene Berman production of 1952. Left to right: Warren, Hilde Gueden, Alois Pernersdorfer, and Richard Tucker. Credit: Sedge LeBlang, Metropolitan Opera; *Opera News*.

Warren onstage in *Rigoletto*. Credit: Metropolitan Opera Archives.

Warren as Don Carlo in *La forza del destino*, the new 1952 production under Rudolf Bing's management. Credit: Metropolitan Opera; *Opera News*.

In Milan, Warren and
Rosanna Carteri rehearse
Rigoletto at La Scala. Credit: E.
Piccagliani, Teatro alla Scala.

Warren and Agatha taking
a nighttime gondola ride in
Venice. Credit: Vivien Warren
Collection.

Warren in 1953, photographed with his coaches Riccardo Picozzi (left) and Giuseppe Pais (right), both of whom had taught him in 1938. His early supporter, the Argentinian conductor Ettore Panizza (center), joined them at the Teatro alla Scala after Warren's *Rigoletto*. Credit: E. Piccagliani, Teatro alla Scala; *Opera News*.

Warren and conductor Nino Sanzogno, after *Rigoletto* at La Scala. Credit: E. Piccagliani, Teatro alla Scala.

Warren and Mario Del
Monaco in *Otello* at La Scala.
Credit: E. Piccagliani, Teatro
alla Scala; *Opera News*.

La Scala performance of
Otello on 8 or 10 January
1954. Left to right: Renata
Tebaldi (sitting), Warren,
Mario Del Monaco,
conductor Antonio Votto,
and Anna Maria Canali.
Credit: E. Piccagliani,
Teatro alla Scala.

A candid shot of Warren rehearsing for American composer Norman Dello Joio's *Lamentation of Saul*, August 1954. Credit: Clemens Kalischer; Vivien Warren Collection.

Dello Joio was Warren's guest in Riverside. Credit: Vivien Warren Collection.

Margaret Truman
arriving for the 1954
Met opening night with
Roy Leifflen. Credit:
Wide World Photos;
Vivien Warren
Collection.

Warren as Gérard in the
Met's *Andrea Chénier* of
1954–1955. Credit: Sedge
LeBlang, Metropolitan
Opera; Vivien Warren
Collection.

Warren with Oralia Dominguez as Dame Quickly, in a San Francisco Opera *Falstaff*, September 1956. Credit: San Francisco Opera.

Backstage after a San Francisco Opera *Tosca* of 15 September 1956, Warren, a genial Scarpia, greets Stephen P. Kennedy, the New York City Police Commissioner. Credit: Robert Lackenbach for the San Francisco Opera.

Verdi's *Ernani*, November 1956,
offered Warren the great role of the
king of Spain who becomes the
emperor, Charles V. Credit: Frank
Lerner, Metropolitan Opera; *Opera
News*. Right: In costume for *Ernani*,
Warren relaxed on a Met balcony
overlooking Seventh Avenue. Credit:
United Press International; Vivien
Warren Collection.

Warren with posters announcing his 1958 appearances in Russia. In a recital there in May 1958, his accompanist was Willard Sektberg. Credit: BMG Classics/RCA.

Warren arrives with Agatha at Rome Airport on 2 July 1957 to record RCA's complete *Tosca*. Credit: Vivien Warren Collection.

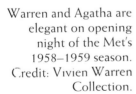

Warren and Agatha are elegant on opening night of the Met's 1958–1959 season. Credit: Vivien Warren Collection.

Warren in the title role of *Macbeth* at the Metropolitan in 1959. Credit: Metropolitan Opera; *Opera News*.

Warren was a dramatic Tonio in the Met's new production of *Pagliacci*, directed by José Quintero in the 1958–1959 season. Credit: Sedge LeBlang, Metropolitan Opera; *Opera News*.

Warren as Count di Luna in the 1959 production of *Il trovatore*. The red plumes on his hat inspired Zinka Milanov to tell him, with a smile, "Leonard, you look just like a rooster." Credit: Louis Mélançon, Metropolitan Opera Archives.

The groundbreaking ceremony for Lincoln Center, 14 May 1959, with Leonard Bernstein, Risë Stevens, and Warren. Credit: Bob Serating; Vivien Warren Collection.

Warren as Simon and Mary Curtis-Verna, the Amelia/Maria, are a father and daughter, reunited in the new 1960 production of *Simon Boccanegra* in Warren's last season at the Met. Credit: Metropolitan Opera Archives.

Warren at a dress rehearsal with Ezio Flagello on 18 February 1960 for the upcoming premiere of *Simon Boccanegra* at the Met. Credit: Eugene Cook.

As Lucia, Hines, and Warren were leaving the Bowery Mission one night, Hines turned to the baritone and said, "Leonard, how can I ever thank you for doing this?" Warren pointed up to the sky and replied, "Don't thank me. We both know we are doing this for Him." Hines felt Warren was profoundly religious. He also recalled something his own accompanist, Alexander Alexay, had told him many years earlier. Born in Canada, Alexay also served Richard Tucker and other Metropolitan artists. Finally came the moment when he was asked to accompany Warren, which he did on several occasions. Alexay, a Jew, noticed that before each recital, Warren, who had by then become a Catholic, would walk away by himself and make the Sign of the Cross. Later, when Alexay himself also became a convert to Catholicism, he came to understand Warren better.

Hines also spoke of Warren's generosity on other occasions. He said that in 1949 when the conductor Renato Cellini first came to the Metropolitan from Italy, he got his working papers and wanted to go back to Europe and bring his wife and family to America. "Of course he did not have the money to do this because he was not earning that much. Leonard lent him three thousand dollars so he could go back. Who knows how many other people he helped like that?" Cellini's widow confirmed in a 1998 interview that Warren had indeed helped her husband in this way. Warren became the godfather of the Cellinis' daughter, who was born in America and baptized in Sacred Heart Church in Bayside, Long Island, in 1954. Warren also helped with the medical bills when Cellini fell ill with heart disease.

Summer 1955

After the Met season ended and Warren finished his concerts, an important interview with him ran on the Associated Press wire service lines. He was introduced as "Six feet, 200 pounds, 52" chest"; his voice was "a power unto itself." To the writer, Hal Boyle, Warren spoke with rare frankness about his life and his career. He recalled the days when he had worked in a filling station and added remarks about the fur business. Of the Met, he said, "This is where I was born, this is where I live. Even to step on the boards of the Metropolitan Opera stage is [an honor]; it is a tradition, a feeling." About his lifestyle, he said, "I have to live very simply. I do nothing to excess. Not in food or liquor. I don't smoke. Some do, I don't. An artist cannot afford excess. I don't take physical exercise, although I do like to walk. I go to bed early." Asked if he sang every day, he said, "No, I don't practice singing [daily], but about once a week, I go to my old singing teacher for an hour whenever I can. It is a kind of psychological checkup." He spoke of the difficulty of defining theatrical character, saying, "You assume the music, but to know the role, to feel it is you, or you are it, well, that is the problem. After singing it a hundred times, you begin to understand the role and feel it fits you, and you fit it."

His views on money included a slap at the government. "The greatest enemies of an opera singer are the common cold and the income tax. I first sang for $35 a week [and kept it all]. Now, if I earn $1,000, I keep for myself about $1.98. And if someone with a cold breathes in my face, I worry about catching cold. Deductions? I can't even deduct the cost of my singing lessons." He also added a few words about discipline. "Discipline is the whole thing in the music business. What am I afraid of? Only that I won't be worthy of this gift I have been given. It carries a tremendous responsibility. The most important thing in the world is to be tranquil with yourself and God."

Warren and Agatha returned to Rome that summer to make a complete recording of *Aida* with Milanov in the title role, Fedora Barbieri as Amneris, Björling as Radamès, and Boris Christoff as Ramfis, with Jonel Perlea conducting. While there, the baritone also recorded two singles, Iago's "Credo" from *Otello* and Ford's monologue from *Falstaff*. For these, Vincenzo Bellezza conducted. In his *Opera Quarterly* review of Milanov's recordings, William Albright described the *Aida* as one of the two "crowning achievements" of her career, the other being her *Trovatore* with Warren. He also had kind words for Björling, but felt Barbieri was "stentorian" without being "subtle." He concluded, though, that her Amneris was perhaps the best on records for its "authenticity of expression and emotional impact." Warren, he found, showed a hint of a vocal problem in this *Aida*. A "shuddery quaver sometimes mars Warren's mellifluous Amonasro," he said. Otherwise the baritone seemed to be in excellent health.

In Rome, Warren renewed his friendship with young Anders Björling, the tenor's son, who recalled spending two weeks in Rome during the *Aida* sessions. He was then eighteen. Anders said, "We stayed at the Grand Hotel, and I spent a lot of time with him. He really was a lot of fun. I had my dad's movie camera, and Leonard had his, and we went around Rome filming. We took pictures of the Spanish Steps, the Castel Sant'Angelo, the Vittorio Emanuele Monument, and the Colosseum." Warren also took Anders with him while he searched for saints' relics for his collection. Anders said:

> Leonard had a little wooden cabinet for his relics. It was about eighteen inches high and eighteen inches across, and six inches deep. It had little drawers with tiny compartments for the relics. Each was mounted on a card about the size of a slide. He explained the different classes of relics. He said a third class relic was a piece of something the saint had touched. Second class was a fragment of the saint's clothing. First class was the best: a piece of the saint's bone. He had at least one of those, a tiny little speck on a small card. Some were in plastic. I remember he took me to this monastery in Rome where he went to buy a new relic. Only six or eight monks were left there, and they were completely cloistered. Leonard had heard they

had relics, and he got very excited about getting one. I think he paid dearly for it.

Warren should not have had to pay for the relic, but he could have made an offering of money for it before putting it in his prized reliquary. Anders also recalled a visit to St. Peter's with his mother and Agatha. "It was very hot, and they were both wearing low-cut sun dresses. When we got to the door of the basilica, the usher said they could not come in unless their shoulders were covered, so we went around the corner and found a niche where they could take off their half-slips. They put those over their shoulders, and we got in." One Sunday, all the cast went to Ostia to go to the beach. "Zinka and her brother, my parents, my sister and I, Leonard, and Agatha. Everyone wore swimsuits, and it was quite a sight because some of them were quite large."

Anders remembered Agatha being difficult during a playback session of *Aida*. "We were all sitting around listening to the tape. Leonard was always O.K. But I remember Agatha was very aggressive in looking out for him. 'Oh, I can't hear Leonard!' she often complained." Anders also recalled Warren being very kind to his sister. When the strap of her sandal broke, he asked the hotel housekeeper for a needle and thread, sat down on the girl's bed, and sewed the strap back together. "Warren was kind, very sweet, childlike in the very best sense," Anders said. A mature and famous singer by 1955, Warren remained a caring person.

Preparing and Singing *Tosca*

Warren had other work to think about because the Met management had guaranteed him a new role, Scarpia in *Tosca*, the evil force that propels the opera from its first note to its last. Although he had been studying Scarpia in New York, his first move in Italy was to contact Riccardo Picozzi, his old maestro, and make an appointment to coach with him again. By the time Warren finished his session in the recording studio, Picozzi was ill, so their coaching sessions took place in the hospital. In 1957, in an interview with Jay S. Harrison of the New York *Herald Tribune*, Warren said:

> I had in my mind what Scarpia should be like. So I went to Italy to coach the part with Riccardo Picozzi. When I got there, I learned that he was in the hospital. I nearly died! But Picozzi had anticipated my concern and had had himself put into a large room. There, day after day, he simply made me walk like Scarpia by tapping out the rhythm of the walk with a pencil. From the tread that Picozzi demanded and from the facial [expressions and] gestures, I began to see the full hateful and sinister quality of the man; and after that, all details quickly fell into place. I then went on to build the character bit by bit, a little at a time. You see, you must give to a character, really give. In fact,

it's what you give of yourself to the lyric art that counts, not what you take out. Fame, glamour—that's all on the surface. Opera wouldn't be what it is if it didn't go deeper than that.

Warren told Harrison how he worked up the role, which he sang in San Francisco in September 1955, weeks before attempting Scarpia at the Met. He said:

I still study to this day. I study voice with Sidney Dietch, and acting and languages and history. Why history? Because if you know history, you learn an enormous amount about the background of the character you're portraying. By reading up on the character carefully, I discovered that he was a Sicilian, that he came from a fine family and that he was once the lover of the Queen of Naples. Immediately you see what kind of person he must have been. And while it is true that studying the psychology and background of a character may not tell you how to portray him, it certainly will tell you how *not* to. Scarpia, in other words, though he may be a wretch, is certainly not an upstart.

Warren told W. G. Rogers, arts editor of the Associated Press, about Picozzi and the pencil. In the course of another 1957 interview, he said:

[Picozzi] told me that the secret of Scarpia, the ruthless police chief, was the right kind of walk. He tapped out the rhythm with a pencil on an ashtray, while for hours I walked up and down beside his bed. Finally the body and the mind were so closely knit in their understanding of this tyrant that without my singing or saying a word, an audience could tell what kind of man I interpreted.

While Warren and his wife were in Rome, he worked out the details of his Scarpia costume, to which he had dedicated a lot of research. He decided he wanted silk stockings with a scarlet clock running up the side of them. Searching in one men's shop after another and finding nothing, he asked someone to make them for him. Vivien remembered how proud he was of them, saying, "Even though no one behind the fourth or fifth row in the auditorium could see them, he knew they were there. That was enough. They contributed to his sense of self on the stage in that opera." Edgar Vincent provided further detail about the stockings. As it happened, even after Warren had "the right ones," he was not satisfied. More research, then new stockings!

Once he came up to me after a *Tosca*, and with the greatest glee he asked me, "Did you notice anything different tonight?" I had to admit that I didn't. Well, he told me he had done more research on Scarpia's background and had discovered that the real baron was a Sicilian nobleman whose family crest had a serpent on it. Leonard pointed to his new white stockings. Running down the outside of each was a serpent. He had had them made to order, and was sure that three thousand people in the audience could see that serpent!

After the sessions in Rome, Warren and Agatha returned to the United States in time to relax in Riverside before his concerts. Then came the 1955–1956 Met season and the *Tosca* rehearsals. Again he would have Tebaldi as his soprano. Yannopoulos faced the task of coaching him. As he had done with Gérard in *Andrea Chénier* and Iago in *Otello*, the director was to come to Manhattan House in the evenings so Warren would not be embarrassed at being corrected in public. Yannopoulos recalled working "months, absolutely months" on Scarpia. "Warren had never read the Sardou play, although he had investigated all the original sites in Rome. So first we went through the English translation of the libretto. We had a lot of work there because he was very slow, but once he had it, you couldn't budge him. It came out nicely because we were getting along very well by that time. Agatha also helped." Yannopoulos particularly remembered teaching Warren his entrance in the first act. "I said to him, 'Come in fast and stand still. Don't move. Everybody else moves, but you don't. The altar boys are running around, everyone is scrambling, but not you.' When he strode onstage, he was like a bomb. From then on, he was immobile. It took time to get it into him, but it worked perfectly. I think his Scarpia was magnificent."

About Warren's *Tosca*, Thebom said:

I loved certain scenes in his Scarpia: so suave—so subtle. He was such a perfectionist in his passion for the details. He went into great studies about his second act black satin costume for Scarpia. He was quite wonderful in the special way he handled his legs onstage. He had remarkably slender legs under his huge barrel chest. His legs and the embroidered red silk "clocks" on the black silk stockings were representative of the vanity of Scarpia and he used them with great dramatic effect. There really was no detail too small for him. When he played Scarpia, he enriched the vocal/musical structure of the composer's opera with similar details—and he got them all from his penetrating background research.

Almost as an afterthought she asked:

How does a kitten become Scarpia? By study. To learn just the music is like ice skating over the deepest water in the world. If you learn just the music, then everything in the explanatory detail remains peripheral. Leonard never did that. He was fully developed as an artist, and he remained at a level that only he ever achieved. But no one else ever reached that level. Leonard was total.

The first *Tosca*, 8 December 1955, was a benefit sponsored by the Metropolitan Opera Guild for the company's production funds. It was conducted by Dimitri Mitropoulos with Tebaldi, Tucker, and Warren, with Baccaloni as the Sacristan.

Reviewing the first night, Kolodin wrote, "Warren brought with him, in addition to a solid command of the vocal line, a well-planned dramatic action. It tended to be a little crude, lacking in finesse, but these flaws were in the characterization rather than in his execution of it." However, he said, he preferred the Scarpia of Tito Gobbi, "a masterly actor who also sang"; Gobbi joined the cast when it changed in January 1956. Vivien Warren thought Scarpia was her brother's greatest achievement. Cesare Bardelli, a former Metropolitan Opera artist who sang several hundred sinister Scarpias in his career, recalled Warren.

> He was a distinguished and exceptionally warm, profoundly human man, for as long as I knew him. Leonard had a marvelous, colorful baritone voice, one that let him do extraordinary things in the upper, middle, and lower registers. He combined a remarkable extension with the greatest facility of production and a pure simplicity in his sound. Here was a rich, mellow, soft, velvety sound; here was a voice that was even through all its range. It was a dream! He had perfect technique, married to an exceptional vocal organ. But Leonard seemed modest and had the conscience of a professional. I found his acting as Scarpia very contained; his every movement, his every gesture was intelligently connected to what he was singing. In art and in life, he was one of the greatest!

In Warren's schedule, the Met *Tosca* was followed by repeats of his standard operas. He also appeared in nine cities on the tour and managed non-Met engagements in Kansas City with Eva Likova and Peerce, and in New Orleans, where Cellini conducted *Falstaff* with Vivian Della Chiesa as Sir John's foil. I interviewed Warren for *Opera News* in March 1956 as he was preparing that *Falstaff*. In his Manhattan House apartment, he offered me a cup of tea from an elegant silver service, then talked about how he had learned to act with his voice, saying, "Acting in the lyric theatre is totally unlike the acting required for any other theatrical medium. Maurice Evans in *Man and Superman* expounded exactly the method that operatic actors must rely on. In opera, there is all too rarely acting as we see it in the modern theatre. Forms are stylized in opera. Most of the standard repertory was written before the Stanislavsky method had been devised." From there he went on about his literal translations of librettos, his study of the music, and his acting style. "Opera, being a living art, must change with the times. Only if a singer knows the libretto from A to Z can he transmit his operatic personality across the footlights." He described *Trovatore* as an opera where he had little acting to do, other than taking out his sword and moving "from one position to another, utilizing a few facial expressions along the way." Warren laughed heartily as he showed what he meant. He then turned sober and talked about *Traviata*, where, he said, "the voice must speak, emote, gesture, and move." He spoke of his love for Verdi but said that *Falstaff* and *Simon Boccanegra* were "the most difficult" for him.

In September and October, the San Francisco Opera honored Warren by giving him both *Falstaff* and the *Simon Boccanegra* that so impressed Tebaldi. He also sang *Tosca* with her. During his season on the West Coast, John De Merchant, Warren's longtime friend from Radio City Music Hall, met him after a performance. Remembering the evening, De Merchant said:

> Chris Pollard, a former Music Hall artist who had been an understudy to John Charles Thomas, had kept up with Leonard and decided to host a little dinner for him, just a handful of us. We talked a bit about his colleagues. Leonard said just one singer in the world made him nervous, and that was Renata Tebaldi, who was singing with him there that season. He told us she was too sure of herself and was always telling others what they should be doing. "That makes me nervous," Leonard said.

De Merchant and Warren never met again. At the end of my interview with him, De Merchant said, "Leonard had one of the greatest voices of all time."

New Productions: *Ernani* and Beyond

Warren began his 1956–1957 season at the Met in very good spirits, showing every sign of his star status and holding a contract for two new productions. As Jay Harrison said, by then he was a "giant" in his profession. After their interview, Harrison remarked on his modesty: "He acts as though he has done nothing more arduous than hum through a verse of 'Sweet Adeline.'" Nothing ever got in the way of the learning process, on which Warren dwelt through every phase of his career. Almost dismissing his vocal prowess, he remained stubbornly proud of how he worked. Remarkably, he was never vain about his person, although he always dressed well and once even did endorsements in ads for men's hats. Offstage he never tried to hide the fact that he was becoming bald, although several male colleagues at the Met were hiding their baldness under full toupees or "comb over" hairpieces.

When Sidney Fields interviewed him for the New York *Daily Mirror* in early January 1956, Warren was photographed at his desk, dressed in a dark suit, white shirt, and rakish bow tie. The bald crown of his head was framed by a neatly trimmed dark fringe over the ears. Pen in hand, he had laid a score open in front of him. On one side of the desk stood his homemade model stage, a three-sided box about a foot wide. Nor was this setup an empty gesture for the photographer. Warren was assiduous about settings, costumes, props, and every position and gesture in his stage action. Fields described him as a man of "44, a six-footer, over 200 pounds, with a disarming directness." Warren said he was "Leonard Warenoff, better known as Leonard Warren. My father was a fur broker." From that familiar starting point Warren recalled his struggles to find himself and to be noticed, noting the same touchstones as he had in those days, including "the best piece of advice I ever got" when his grandfather Kantor told him, "A goal never comes to a man." He reminisced about his early career and went on to credit his emergence as a serious artist to the events of the week when he sang Renato in *Un ballo in maschera* one night and followed it fourteen hours later with *Rigoletto*, with no advance notice and not even a rehearsal, when he was called to replace the ailing Tibbett. In less than twenty-four hours, "His star began to rise," but he had walked a hard road. Fields was particularly impressed by Warren's comment that although he had sung the title role in *Rigoletto* at La Scala in Milan, he still felt he was "just beginning to get it."

In a rare moment of confidence, Warren told Fields about his family, his marriage, his house in Connecticut, his hobbies, and his passion for jazz and Italian popular songs. He recalled meeting Agatha in Milan; he said that after they married, she directed their lives "with simplicity and sense." He described his life in Connecticut as "play at boats and fishing. There are no opera scores, nor is there a piano in the cottage. The only music is from a super-duper radio, TV, hi-fi and tape recorder combination. It does everything but cook our meals. And it can be taken apart into separate units and carried upstairs in case of floods. We've been flooded five times so far."

Warren also spoke of his own Leonard Warren Scholarship Fund for young singers, but he said not a word about the people whose voice lessons he had paid for. Nor did he mention financing Américo Bàsso's studies at the Curtis Institute in Philadelphia. Fields found Warren "an exceedingly devout man" who refused to talk of his own goals except in terms of his belief. Speaking of faith, Warren said, "I know that nothing belongs to us, not even what we call our own. Any gift can be taken away at any time. But as long as I have it, all I want is to be worthy of the gift given to me by God."

New to the Metropolitan Opera staff that season was director Nathaniel Merrill, who had previously worked at the 1954 Glyndebourne Festival with director Carl Ebert. Merrill's early acquaintance with Warren became friendship over the course of five years. Merrill described their association, saying, "I knew him quite well. We had something in common: model railroads." Here was one of the few subjects that could draw Warren into an enthusiastic conversation. "When I went to their apartment, he wanted to talk about his trains. He had his in Connecticut. Socially he was wonderful. He was so nice, though he was not the kind you could make jokes with. It was a time for baritones, but none of them could match Warren. He was Number One." Perhaps Warren's experiences with Yannopoulos had brought him to the point of accepting direction from Nat Merrill that he rarely accepted from others. Asked about how Warren took his direction, Merrill said, "I was transmitting directions from Carl Ebert. Anyway, I was usually able to get Warren to do everything, one way or another. Most of the time." Asked about Warren's manner toward conductors, he said:

> Conductors? I don't know. He was difficult with all of them. He was sensitive about being wrong. Warren was very difficult backstage. He had a fear of the stage, a tension about performing. I found him very nervous, though he was pretty nice during most rehearsals. But he was always tense and wanted things his way. In the Opera House he was a terror during performances. There everyone stayed out of his way. In his relations with other colleagues, he got along fine with singers of his class, Tucker and Milanov, especially. He never had much to do with the second-ranking singers.

With several important principals and much of the rest of the company in rehearsal in mid-October of 1956, the Met management was looking forward to a solid season. Before it opened, most press coverage was focused on the opening night, 29 October, the evening of Maria Callas's Met debut in *Norma* with Del Monaco, Barbieri, and Siepi. As the season began, Warren had just finished his regular autumn recital tour and was facing an overloaded rehearsal schedule. He sang *Il trovatore* on 5 November and *Rigoletto* four nights later. It was not an easy year, as he made clear in a byline article in *Variety*, where he wrote about how male opera stars combat the avalanche of publicity about prima donnas. Published at the height of Callas mania, it is a very funny piece, loaded with Warrenisms such as "young fellow," "I can tell you," "champed at the bit," "paid off," and "Do you know?" All were typical of his everyday speech. Although he never mentioned Tebaldi or Callas, who was about to finish her stormy Met engagement, he slipped in sly references to both. The substance of the piece is: "When there are divas around, a man's lot is not a happy one." A bad review of Callas's *Lucia* appeared on the same page of *Variety*.

The new production of Verdi's *Ernani* was on the Met calendar for 23 November 1956. Warren's leading role was that of the king of Spain who becomes the Holy Roman Emperor. A difficult work unfamiliar to most singers, *Ernani* makes demands on the voice. Composed in the early 1840s, it was the first opera Verdi wrote for Venice, where it had its wildly successful world premiere at the Teatro La Fenice, then swept into the repertory at once. As Verdi's third big success, coming on the heels of *Nabucco* and *I Lombardi alla Prima Crociata*, it became a standard work of its time. Produced at the Met in 1903, it had also been revived in 1921 with Ponselle, Martinelli, Giuseppe Danise, and José Mardones. For its 1956 revival, *Ernani* got a new production with sets and costumes by Esteban Frances. Warren sang Carlo, a character like Boccanegra, who plays against rich historical backgrounds; his role was full of dramatic potential. It was perfectly suited to Warren's ability at that time. Del Monaco took the title role, Milanov sang Elvira, and Cesare Siepi sang Don Ruy Gómez de Silva. Yannopoulos directed. Mitropoulos, the conductor, was a frail, ascetic man of devout Greek Orthodox faith. His uncle, a priest in the monastery of Mount Athos, had almost led him into the clergy. A quiet man and a pacifist, Mitropoulos was passionately devoted to St. Francis of Assisi. During one interview with me, his face was almost transfigured with emotion when he said, "St. Francis offers me the most perfect expression of Christ's intentions." On the shelves of his apartment was his collection of books about St. Francis; on the walls he had hung images of the Umbrian saint, while small statuettes of him stood on a chest and side tables.

At the Met, problems arose during the early *Ernani* rehearsals with orchestra, and as the work progressed, Warren took issue with Mitropoulos over his tempos. Three of Warren's colleagues, Yannopoulos, Vincent, and Krawitz, all recalled the friction between the conductor and the baritone. Realizing that Mitropoulos was not stepping up the pace, Warren became very angry and began to rage at Mitropoulos. Yannopoulos described him as "frightening" and "going on a rampage." Edgar Vincent said this outburst came during the second intermission of the first night of *Ernani*. "Warren had his big aria coming up," Vincent remembered. "He went right down to Mitropoulos's dressing room and literally took him by the collar. He said, 'If you don't conduct this as we rehearsed it, I'll walk right off the stage and you can sing the opera yourself.'" As Krawitz noted when we discussed Warren's outburst, Warren was definitely out of line, but, Krawitz said, in the opera business, personal conflicts such as these become fodder for gossips because they occur in public, while in an office setting they usually happen in private.

In *Ernani*, Warren also had trouble with his costumes, although no one noticed them in time to spare him some embarrassing moments. Krawitz, who was in charge of that production as he had been of *Andrea Chénier*, remembered a large audience, perhaps from the Metropolitan Opera Guild, sitting in the auditorium for the dress rehearsal.

> Leonard's costume was covered with yellowish gold squares. When he first stepped onstage in it, the audience roared with laughter. We didn't know what hit us! In all those early rehearsals, we hadn't seen anything wrong! And I still don't know what went wrong; maybe it was the way he walked in that costume. But Leonard was mortified. We were terribly embarrassed, and that was the only time I saw Leonard humiliated onstage. After the rehearsal, we sprayed the cos-

tume down with dark paint, so it wouldn't look so garish on opening night. To this day, I don't know what was wrong.

Yannopoulos said, "*Ernani* was the reason I left the Met. Bing had insisted on this Spanish designer [Esteban Frances], who geared Warren up in gold-studded armor. He looked like a Christmas tree! When he came out onstage, everyone laughed. I was sorry that I had contributed in any way to that. Warren was absolutely fantastic in the Tomb of Charlemagne scene."

Ernani opened on 23 November 1956. Bing's hopes for it were quickly crushed by the first-night reviews and the audience response. Writing for the *New York Times*, Howard Taubman said the work had merit, but the audience "had outgrown" the early Verdi operas. He did congratulate the company on the handsome production, its "four leading singers, and Mitropoulos, who brought excitement to the score. He found Warren "did the most consistently distinguished work. His singing was in the bel canto tradition." Paul Henry Lang of the *Herald Tribune* said Warren brought Carlo to life "with truly imperial splendor" and "glorious vocalism." Then he added, "Those who listened attentively when he sang his quiet cavatina in the second act must have realized the full measure of this great artist's capabilities." All the critics skewered Milanov, who got off to a poor start with bad pitch and edginess in her showcase aria "Ernani, involami." The writer from *Time* also remarked on her "dizziness" and "staggering." And she also kept twisting one curl of her wig. In sum, nothing looked right. Later, Del Monaco told me that he and Milanov had been frightened by a backstage bat that kept swooping over their heads during the first scene. They both kept staring upward. The critics found Milanov in better form in the acts that followed, but even Siepi was faulted for erratic pitch, although he was sufficiently dignified. In *Saturday Review of Literature* on 8 December, Kolodin devoted two and a half columns to *Ernani*, criticizing the Met for "tinkering" with the score and saying he hated Yannopoulos's "presumed stage direction." Although he faulted much of the singing, he said that Warren's "magnificent 'O sommo Carlo' encouraged silent gratitude" for its pianissimos and "soaring A-flats." In *The Metropolitan Opera 1883–1966*, Kolodin criticized the downward transposition of Milanov's great aria, dismissed the first act setting as "a California-Spanish patio," hated the "exterior" substituted for Verdi's "magnificent hall," and called Yannopoulos's direction "posteresque."

Time called Warren "the star of the evening" and said he "came through, as always, with sane, reliable singing and a beautiful voice." Most reviewers remarked on how uncomfortable he looked when he first appeared in his grotesque costume. It was "toadstool-shaped black armor," said *Time*. Lang objected to the "light-reflecting sequins hung on every square inch of Mr. Warren's imperial costume, fore and aft, and even on his puttees. [It] was quite midway-ish. They would suffice for all the road signs from here to

Charlemagne's tomb." Taubman said his costumes were "so bedecked with
gold and jewels that one wonders how the poor man can stand under their
weight." The audience "snickered" and "guffawed" on the first night, even
after the costume had been spray-painted.

Nothing could match the majesty of Warren's acting throughout the
opera and his delivery of "Oh de' verd'anni miei." This is the very heart of
Ernani, one of Verdi's noblest baritone showpieces. At Charlemagne's tomb,
Carlo, the king, waits to learn whether he will become emperor. *Time* wrote,
"Bronx-born baritone Warren spent a year and a half learning his part,"
something his piano-vocal score clearly shows. First he wrote out the entire
Italian text for his role on sheets from a legal pad, occasionally even marking
his breaks for breaths. Then came the translation. All his usual markings and
penciled vertical lines mark the tempos. He also wrote instructions to himself,
such as "Kind of slowly with a long legato," at the first words of "Oh de'
verd'anni miei," and "Watch carefully. Breathe once in a while" at the words
"bugiarde larve." He marked some notes *pppp* even when Verdi did not, and
added his own nimble, difficult cadenza at the end, closing it in the strato-
sphere. The act ends fittingly with an ensemble, "A Carlo Quinto, sia gloria
ed onor." Warren got the honor. With this interpretation, he celebrated Verdi
and conferred veritable grandeur on the Met. Unfortunately, he sang *Ernani*,
one of his finest roles, only four times, although it marked another step on his
way to becoming *the* Verdi baritone. Reviewing an unauthorized recording of
the Met broadcast of *Ernani* in December 1956 in the *Bolletino* of the Istituto
Nazionale di Studi Verdiani in Parma, Maurizio Modugno said Warren
"offers a really outstanding performance, with a Don Carlo quite different
from anyone else's." He praised Warren's "exceptional high register" and
called his reading something "of the utmost importance" that revealed "the
unbroken threads that link Verdi's baritone figures."

After *Ernani*, Warren returned to his standard operas. Of these, the new
production of *Traviata* on 21 February 1957 was by far the most important
of his professional obligations. Tebaldi was the Violetta, Giuseppe Campora
the Alfredo, and Cleva the conductor. The first night, though, came while
Warren was in mourning. His mother, Sara Kantor Warenoff, had died on 4
February; she was buried in Mount Hebron Cemetery in Queens, New York.
After her death, Warren committed more time than ever to Vivien and his
niece, who also stayed on in the family's apartment in the Sherman Square
Studios. Because Warren still came to Dietch's studio in that building at least
once a week, he found it easy to slip in. But as Vivien said, he also came when-
ever she needed him.

After his marvelous Tonio in *Pagliacci* in March, a feature piece ran in
Time with a review of both *Cavalleria* and *Pagliacci*. These operas brought the
triumph of Warren and Tucker, "Two Home-Town Boys," as the headline
ran. Their early experience in the fur trade made good copy, as did Warren's

Tonio costume, "a disreputable red wig, striped T-shirt and ill-fitting green jacket." Warren played Tonio as a simpleton and "shot the role full of self-pity which honed rather than blunted its edge of evil." The "mahogany hued voice soared with a passion and authority that no other baritone today can top." Not even Mario Ortica, the Canio, got a bigger hand. Soon after this piece came out, Warren did the Met spring tour. He ended it by making a special effort to visit a dear friend, Helen Hatton.

Warren's Friendship with Dr. Helen Hatton

Warren's concern for others was never limited to his family, as many former colleagues have confirmed. During the 1957 tour engagement in Toronto, where Warren was to sing *Trovatore*, he sacrificed time and energy for Helen Hatton, a young woman who may have been his most dedicated fan. In several interviews Hatton spoke of their nine-year friendship. Early on, she said, she began to see him in the dressing room. After they became friends, she named her dog Leonard and joked with the baritone about it. In 1956 when she became pregnant, she decided that if her first child were a boy, she would name him Warren. The baby, born in May, was indeed given that name. Hatton intended to see Warren when he came for the tour but was confined in the hospital and at home for nearly a month after her son's birth and could not get to his performance.

Both James B. McPherson and Helen Hatton told of Warren's visit to her home. After Warren arrived, she had asked a friend to leave a letter for him at the Royal York Hotel. Warren then called McPherson, a journalist, at his office and asked how to get to the Hattons' house in Clarkson, some fifteen miles away. He called her to say he was determined to see her and the baby. "My husband went to get him," Helen Hatton said. "He spent a half-day with us and didn't go back until late afternoon, about four-thirty, I believe. He came with two dozen red and white carnations, his favorite flower. He told me those were the colors of life. Warren met his tiny namesake, my son. Then we talked about opera and his life."

Months after Warren sang in *Ernani*, he told Helen Hatton about his problems with Mitropoulos during the rehearsals. She said that Warren gave this account in her living room in May 1957: He said matters of tempo and interpretation had been agreed upon during the pre–stage rehearsals. However, when rehearsals went to the main stage with the orchestra in the pit, Mitropoulos slowed the tempos, leaving the singers short of breath. "He was so erratic and so slow that we ran out of breath," Warren said. Even though he complained, Mitropoulos continued expanding the phrases. Finally Warren blew up. He said, "I went up to Mitropoulos backstage and exploded. I lifted him up and said to him face to face, 'If you don't conduct this the way we rehearsed it, we'll walk off.'"

Hatton said, "I also remember something he said about an early recording I played for him. It was Giuseppe Kaschmann, singing 'Oh de' verd'anni miei' from *Ernani* with that cadenza at the end. Suddenly Warren's face lit up, and he said, 'I sing that better!' And he stood up, beaming, and sang it." He also talked about Mattia Battistini's recording of "Vieni meco, sol di rose," another aria from *Ernani* that Hatton played for him. "He then sang as Battistini did and said, 'I have to know that I can do it [that way], but in the performance I cannot be outside the style of the others.'" Warren also discussed his Catholicism, which he took seriously but never preached about. Hatton worried about his getting back to the city on time but he reassured her and stayed on. Remembering Warren, she exclaimed, "Oh, what a dear, generous, and trusted friend."

CHAPTER NINETEEN

The Singing Artist

A s the Met season of 1957–1958 got under way, Warren was again work-ing on his public relations and discussing strategies with Edgar Vincent. The big feature profile pieces Vincent arranged pleased him, but he still felt cheated in his day-to-day reviews. To attack that problem on a new front, he turned to his manager, Walter Prude of the Hurok organization, who had managed Warren since the early 1950s when Warren left Davidson. Prude, husband of the dancer and choreographer Agnes De Mille, knew Bing well and was able to go straight to him, but he had little encouragement. In a let-ter of 9 December 1957, Bing explained that Warren had been with the com-pany for many years and probably could not expect more visibility in the press because new artists usually attracted the critics' attention. He had no suggestions. Louis Snyder of the Met press office remembered how angry Warren became when he was disappointed by his reviews. Snyder said, "He would storm in when he got coverage he did not like, and he would always blame it on the press office. When he did complain, it was usually because someone wrote something derogatory about him. It was hard to understand because when he sang, he was always reviewed; he was never left out, and he got dozens of good reviews." That was true, but Warren, as a baritone, often found himself in brief notices well below the soprano and tenor, a big concern in 1957–1958 when he was not contracted for anything new at the Met. His twelfth *Tosca* or fifty-fourth *Aida* there would not get him what he so des-perately wanted, he thought.

One early product of his campaign for better coverage came through Vin-cent; it was a long feature article by W. G. Rogers, mentioned in earlier chap-ters of this book. It began to run on the wire service on 30 November 1957. Rogers, the arts editor of the Associated Press, was a distinguished dean of writers who was fifteen years older than Warren. Slight and elegant, he cut a fine figure with his refined ways; he could chat easily about books and paint-ings and always appreciated good operatic acting. Rogers's interview with

Warren took place in a good restaurant, where the two men struck up a con-genial relationship. Rogers described his guest as "a tall, sturdy man who holds himself straight as a soldier. [He] has a swarthy complexion, a high forehead, hair that is graying a bit and receding a bit more." Over lunch the two men talked of the Warenoff family, which was "of better than average means," and of Warren's futile attempt to join his father's business. As usual, Warren spent an inordinate amount of time talking about his career at Radio City Music Hall. He was "as dramatic offstage as on," Rogers said. "He rolls his eyes, he smiles, scowls, looks at you with affection and glares with ha-tred." Warren illustrated one of his roles for Rogers. "This is Iago," he said, clenching his fingers, baring his teeth, and "freezing you with dread." Even the waiters were impressed by his improvised performance, Rogers said.

During the interview, the two men spoke of Verdi, Warren's favorite composer, who had "provided [him] with perhaps his best parts." Rogers particularly liked Warren's Rigoletto and his moving interpretation of Ger-mont in *Traviata*. He remembered performances where the public had expected to be thrilled by the "featured lead, a soprano or tenor," but found itself more impressed by Warren's "voice and artistry." As the afternoon wore on, Warren discussed his beloved home in Connecticut and described his new cruiser, twenty-six feet long and equipped with all kinds of technical mar-vels, including an intercom, a ship-to-shore telephone, and a full galley. He also spoke of his love of photography and the joy he got from fishing. Before the luncheon ended, Warren was telling Rogers how to make "Chicken Supreme" and using the edge of the restaurant table to roll up imaginary chicken breasts and dip them in batter. Warren was clearly in good spirits.

Outside New York, of course, Warren had no difficulty getting column inches in papers. In January 1958, Arthur Darrack wrote a funny article in the *Cincinnati Enquirer* about an adventure he had had with Warren in San Fran-cisco in 1956. A friend of Warren's appeared at the Fairmont Hotel to take him out for lunch, but the friend had to apologize because his car was not working very well. Perhaps they should eat in the hotel, the friend said. War-ren shook his head. For him, a car engine was a welcome challenge. "Let's take a ride and see what's the matter," he suggested. The two men tooled around the city while Warren listened to the choked machine. He then ordered his friend back to the Fairmont. "It's the carburetor," the baritone said, "but don't worry." Warren jumped out, borrowed the hotel handyman's toolbox, and within about thirty minutes had the engine running right. The two men got back in the car and drove off.

Darrack, who had interviewed Warren, remarked that the singer also knew how to "take a role apart" and put it together again. The particular role they discussed was Scarpia, for the simple reason that the baritone loved to talk about it. Warren repeated his standard story about studying with Picozzi in the hospital. He also talked about stage business and remarked on how absurd it was for him to throw Tebaldi onto a couch in the second act of *Tosca*. "After all, she could throw *me* onto the couch, couldn't she?" Darrack continued, "Warren and Picozzi worked it out a different way. [Warren] would pin her arms behind her back and kiss her on the nape of the neck," an action far more effective than a brutal physical attack.

Long feature articles such as these certainly pleased Warren, but he wanted more. Soon an engagement came his way that put him in all the media. Through the good offices of Sol Hurok, Warren was booked for recitals and operas in four Russian cities. This major effort was not the first for a pioneer of East-West cultural exchange, for Hurok was a man determined to place his artists on programs abroad. Arrangements were made through the State Department and authorities in the Soviet Union. The violinist Isaac Stern, whom Hurok revered, had been the first to go; both he and Peerce performed in Russia in 1956. Peerce sang four concerts in Moscow, one in Leningrad, and one in Kiev. He also did Riccardo in *Ballo* in Kiev and the Duke in *Rigoletto* in Leningrad. At the Bolshoi in Moscow, he sang Alfredo in *Traviata*. Thebom, another Hurok artist, preceded Warren into Russia in 1957; she went to Moscow, Leningrad, and Kiev. The first American woman to perform with the Bolshoi Opera, she remained in Russia five weeks, winning ovations and suffering from the piercing cold. Hurok's 1958 Russian booking for Warren was arranged in a milder season.

An Alan Wagner Interview

As Warren was planning his trip, he let Alan Wagner do a live, unscripted interview for the Living Opera program in New York. Among other things, Warren revealed he was already far along in his study of *Macbeth*, which was still a year in the future. On a tape from a preliminary test, we can hear the two men laughing together before the formal interview began. Not surprisingly, Warren was telling someone how to manage the recording apparatus. "Set it up," Warren ordered in his bright, tenorish voice. The old Bronx accent is still in full flower, with *court* and *courtiers* becoming "cawht" and "cawhtiers"; *part* comes out as "paht," and *short* as "shawt." "And here I am, speaking to you for Living Opera," he joked while the test was being run.

In the interview, Warren mentioned his Russian roles, "Well, I'm doing *Rigoletto* in Moscow and Kiev," which he pronounced as "Keef." Then Wagner led him into a conversation about the character of Rigoletto.

Well, I feel that Rigoletto is a man, a hunchback. He hates the courtiers because he thinks they should have hunch[backs]; he hates the Duke because he is the Duke; the only thing he likes and cherishes is his love for his daughter; and of course, if you've seen me in the role, you see that it is a great fatherly love. Of course, it is so complicated,

I mean, I couldn't possibly do it in such a short time, give you a complete résumé, but he is quite a nasty man when he is in court and a loving father when he is with his child.

The remark about Rigoletto wishing that all the courtiers were hunchbacked comes from Hugo's Preface to *Le roi s'amuse* and is pure William Appleton lecture material.

Wagner next asked about *Macbeth*, Warren's new opera at the Met, and noted that the baritone would complete a cycle by singing all three of Verdi's Shakespearean operas, *Otello*, *Falstaff*, and *Macbeth*. The baritone said:

I don't think anybody becomes complete in any kind of profession, but I feel as though there is a great challenge for me in this part, because it *is* Macbeth. He is a character of great complications, and a man who is one thing one way, and then all of a sudden you find that he is not so bad in another way. So you have a very difficult role to portray.

Asked about the relationship between Macbeth and Lady Macbeth, Warren said:

Now, of course he is a warrior, and at the beginning, in the first act you know his strength, that he is a great warrior and a great man who won battles, and all that, of course. But as the play progresses, you find out his weaknesses, and then all of a sudden he begins to believe how strong he is, from the tremendous power of this woman, who wants things. Of course he wants it too, but you find that she becomes weaker and weaker, and at the end he even says what a stupid woman she is.

Discussing his approach to Iago, Falstaff, and Macbeth, Warren said:

First I read the story. Sometimes I can even do the play; for *Macbeth* I am studying the play now. I have already broken the back of the music, so that the play and the music become one. And of course people say, "Oh, that's wonderful to be a baritone and be able to do Shakespeare's *Macbeth*!"—But let's figure this out. Shakespeare, well, it's bad enough to be able to *do* Shakespeare. I mean you have to have enough knowledge even to be a Shakespearean actor, but then to add the music to it, and especially Verdi's music, well, you have to be a little bit more informed, as I would call it.

When Wagner asked Warren about other aspects of his next year at the Met, Warren laughed.

Well, they're keeping me out of mischief down there. Everything seems to be going very well. *Rigoletto* is coming back, *Ballo in mas-*

chera is coming back, and of course *Macbeth*. That'll happen at the latter part of the season, *Macbeth* will. And I'm thankful for that. And, oh, yes, *Pagliacci* is going to come back with a new face-lifting. And of course we are going to have a wonderful stage director, Quintero, who is on Broadway doing these famous plays.

When Wagner asked Warren what effect the stage director had on his interpretation, he responded, "I think that when the preliminary talks are had at the Opera House, usually we see eye-to-eye, even before the performance or even the rehearsals start. And as far as I am concerned, I'm always looking for something new, and if there is something new, I'm always happy to do it."

At that point, Wagner complimented Warren on his extraordinary growth as an artist. Warren again emphasized his continuing study of his roles, saying, "Well, all professionals, even a doctor, if he didn't go back for a postgraduate course to some hospital or college, he wouldn't even know about penicillin." Asked about American artists and whether they were slighted or whether, on the contrary, foreign artists were being slighted, Warren said:

> Well, I believe that for the first time we're beginning to see that there are great artists in America. [But] maybe we're too hasty in passing judgment on young singers. I think we are too quick in passing judgment and saying, "Well, he's all right." Just, "He's all right." And of course, in all professions—I hate to say this—but in all professions I feel that there is something very, very serious going on, as far as the quality is concerned. That is recording, that is music, that is all the professions, and that is the snake of mediocrity. And every time something happens, people just listen, and the next day, they will say, "Well, it's all right." Instead of saying, "No! It was no good!" or "It was just passable," they'll say, "Well, he's all right. They'll pass." Unprepared artists come and just pass through, and they think that the world owes them a living. And of course, believe me, I am not trying to sell anybody down the river; I'm not trying to be a prude about this thing. It's a God-given gift. You must deserve such a gift. And you must work hard to be able to give this gift, and give this gift an even chance to become a great gift.

Warren in the Soviet Union

It was this "great gift" that Warren was able to take to his parents' native land. In May 1958, he, Agatha, and Sektberg flew first to Stockholm, then on to Moscow. Vivien said they had been told not to overdress, so Agatha took simple clothes, although she packed her fur jacket, knowing that it would be cold; Warren often went about with an unbuttoned shirt collar, plain trousers, sweater, topcoat, and his trademark dark beret. He was to sing three operas and eight recitals. Irving R. Levine, the Moscow correspondent for the National Broadcasting Company, wrote in his program notes for the RCA Victor recording of the tour recitals that there was little or no advance billing for Warren's appearances; few newspaper advertisements and even fewer posters appeared. But word-of-mouth had preceded the American baritone; the halls and theatres were sold out well in advance so "he could have played to packed houses for months."

Russian audiences had difficulty pronouncing the westernized version of Voronov, so they shouted "Oo-or-en!" over and over again at the end of the performance in the Great Tchaikovsky Hall of the Moscow Conservatory, Leningrad's Philharmonic Orchestra Hall, and in the opera houses of Moscow, Kiev, and Riga. Everywhere, Irving Levine wrote, people greeted the baritone with demands for encores and with "insistent, rhythmic applause." He said that a lot of Russians liked Americans, despite anti-American propaganda on Radio Moscow and in *Pravda*. In the audiences were famous figures from the Russian ballet, drama, and folk dance, all professionals who "recognized in Warren an operatic voice and talent greater than any in Russia today." They particularly loved his flair for drama, Levine said.

Warren sang his first recital in Moscow. In a byline article for the *New York Herald Tribune* Warren praised the "courteous and enthusiastic" audience. He was surprised that the house lights remained on during recitals. When he asked for an explanation, he was told that Russians thought a lighted hall created a warm human exchange between the performer and the public. Another novelty was the Russian announcer, who came forward, as Warren wrote in the *Herald Tribune*, "to explain the meaning of the song or aria." There was only one intermission; he had no break between his groups, but he was told he could walk offstage whenever he wanted to take a sip of water. In Moscow and in Leningrad, members of the audience called for many encores; one that quickly became a sensation was "Colorado Trail." Warren was astonished in Moscow to see people walking up to the stage with handwritten notes, asking him to repeat something he had already sung or add some particular work to his program. Some begged for "The Way to Kolorado," which was so popular that one morning a Russian baritone whom Warren had met came to the hotel with a camera and photographed the sheet music to "Colorado Trail." One note delivered to Warren onstage specifically requested American songs. Others, "unsigned, expressed gratitude for the opportunity to hear an American singer after so many years of Stalinist isolation," Irving R. Levine wrote. Warren repeated his Moscow recital in other cities. In the hall of the Leningrad Philharmonic, he generated such enthusiasm that when the concert was over, a shout drowned out the announcer and Warren was called back. After encores, a bell rang and the lights went out.

A far more serious test of Warren's art came when the Soviet critics reviewed him. After his debut recital, the first review appeared in the *Evening Moscow* over the byline of E. Katulskaya. The headline read, simply, RE-MARKABLE SINGER. He showed "great vocal mastery." The critic called particular attention to a Caldara song and "Ombra mai fu" from Handel's *Serse*, saying that Warren's free and easy voice had a beautiful timbre. His technique was used with subtlety and tact. "He succeeded with real professional brilliance, with striking music and dramatic expressiveness." His artistic execution in Ravel's "Chanson à boire" won particular praise; the overall impression was of "mastery and artistic polish," but people loved his simplicity and heartiness. "High musical culture and vocal technique, expressive gesture, excellent [acting skills] and the charm of a true theatrical actor" contributed to his success. Equally favorable was Alexei Ivanov, writing in *Soviet Culture* on 20 May. Here the gratifying headline read: A SINGER OF GREAT CUL-TURE. Warren, the "possessor of a big voice of pleasant timbre," showed his mastery of "vocal coloration to reveal one artistic image or another." He captured the essence of the French composers. Far more demanding were arias from *Acis and Galatea* and two Verdi operas, *Falstaff* and *Otello*. In them, the writer found "dramatic qualities, great force and expression." The baritone's hallmarks were "splendid cantilena, brilliant passagework [and] subtle shading of sound."

No matter how compelling Warren was as a recitalist, he was known everywhere as an opera singer. Thus his opera performances proved to be a more serious test of his strength than concerts. The most important came on 16 May at the Bolshoi Opera, where Warren sang his first *Rigoletto* in Russia. The headline TOAST OF MOSCOW ran in the *New York Times* on 17 May. Howard Taubman, writing for the *Times*, said that during the rehearsals, Warren sang half-voice to spare himself. Finally, though, he was asked to sing "Cortigiani" in full voice for the benefit of several Russian singers who were attending the rehearsal because they could not get tickets for the evening performance. "He did so gladly," Taubman reported, "and they gave him an ovation." He sang in Italian, and the rest of the cast and chorus sang in Russian. With his sumptuous and carefully crafted costume, he appears in official photographs as the commanding figure he undoubtedly was, towering artistically over the other singers on that big stage. In *Soviet Culture*, Alexei Ivanov reviewed him very favorably on 20 May. His representation of the tragic Rigoletto was "unquestionably one of the best creations of this great artist." His "Cortigiani, vil razza dannata" was brilliant, revealing the "desperation and anger he turns on the [courtiers]; at the same time, with what real warmth and softness [he infuses] the scenes with the only joy of his life, Gilda." Ivanov describes Warren as a lyric-tragic singer who "adheres to the musical idea of the curse," which Verdi sounds through all of *Rigoletto*. At the end of the opera, the audience stood and cheered. From a basket of flowers brought from backstage, the baritone plucked a gift for his Gilda, V. M. Firsova, whom Taubman identified as the best of the Russian cast. He embraced the other singers and ended by "applauding the audience in Russian style."

On 21 May, Warren repeated *Rigoletto* at the Ukrainian Opera in Kiev, the home of his Kantor grandparents. There the director was Nikita Khrushchev's son-in-law. Warren said they discussed the schedules of singers and chorus: "He was amazed to learn that the Met had a roster of principals which is larger than the chorus." Then the baritone explained how American houses differ from European repertory theatres. From Kiev he brought back a souvenir book of postcard photos, one of which shows the opera house.

Warren's last engagement in the Soviet Union was at the Academic Theatre of Opera and Ballet in Riga, where he sang Iago to the Otello of A. Frinberg and the Desdemona of Germena Heine-Wagner. The Americans stayed at the Hotel Riga, where Warren had "the best caviar" of his trip and ate "delicious rye bread." He said he drank Coca-Cola and never touched vodka. He arrived and rehearsed one day and sang the next. But the Warrens had time to tour the city and were taken to the seashore by members of the cast. Irving R. Levine noted that he was

> the first American to appear on the Latvian capital's stage in several decades. The ovation was deafening. There were none more enthusiastic than the members of the Riga Opera troupe. At the final curtain they hoisted Warren, a large man, to their shoulders and began parading him triumphantly off the stage. It was only at the last instant that Warren noticed that his bearers were headed straight for a low beam. Warren ducked just in time to save his head!

Afterward, Warren earned a lot of good will at the Ministry of Culture when he declined to accept an additional fee for television and radio rights to his performance. "I thought all Americans were money-hungry," the office manager said. "Not this one," Warren replied. In spite of his warm reception in Riga, Warren complained to William Appleton about the director there. Appleton said, "Leonard clashed with the director of the Latvian Opera in Riga about *Otello*. The director wanted everything according the their tradition, not only the stage action but also the costumes. Leonard was troubled by what was said about his costume. The director was using the kind of control that he very much resented, and the direction was ironclad. Leonard was furious."

In the Soviet Union, Warren let journalists photograph him looking like a tourist in his soft beret, open-necked shirt, and raincoat. Accompanied by an entourage of escorts, bodyguards, and an interpreter, he found time to get out among the people and see some of the tourist sites in cities he visited. He found people curious about the huge success that the Moiseyev Dance Company had had in America. But he was also told in confidence that the Soviet authorities were "not too happy" with the success of American cultural ambassadors like himself in the Soviet Union. He need not have worried about his own reception. Before he left Russia, the directors of the Bolshoi Opera invited him to return in the 1959–1960 season and sing on the opening night. "Any opera of my choice," Warren said, with obvious satisfaction. His artistry was beyond dispute.

Warren, Agatha, and Sektberg stopped over a few days in Stockholm on their way back to New York. While there, they visited the Met tenor Set Svanholm. Björling, a dear colleague, was away. Interviewed there by a writer for the *Svenska Dagbladet*, Warren said he felt flattered by the reception the Russian opera public gave him. "From every audience I received an unusually warm reception.—Yes, so warm it was and so heated that I can think of it only one way. Among the Soviet people, there lies a latent, warm friendship for us Americans." He remarked on the "fine Russian opera traditions" and the extent to which they had been preserved. "I could see only a few little changes in the modern staging," Warren said. He said that he hoped his visit might help "open the Iron Curtain."

In New York, Warren did an unusually long, frank interview with a writer from the Latvian-American newspaper *Laiks*. The Soviet Union was a "backward" place," he said. "The singers cannot go anywhere, they cannot see anything new; they are unable to grow and mature. Moscow is chilly and unpleasant, and there are no trees," he added, comparing it to Riga, "a Western city." He showed the interviewer the gifts he had received, a leather-bound photo album of Riga from his Desdemona and a beer mug from a fan. He said he would use the mug in *Falstaff*.

Warren also gave a long account of his travels in his *New York Herald Tribune* article which ran on 24 August. He said that if he had sung all the encores and extra numbers requested by the audience, the "concert would have been twice its normal length." He had nothing but praise for the Bolshoi's makeup man, the wig-dresser, and the prompter, who was a woman. Warren, who always depended on prompters' cues no matter where he was singing, was astonished that she could cue him in Italian and seconds later cue the rest of the company in Russian. He called the Russians in the cast "of world caliber," but he found it surprising that the highest paid among them earned only the equivalent of six hundred dollars a month. The average salary, Warren reported, was three hundred dollars a month. He also said he had been uncomfortable when he was asked why no leading Russian singer of that era had been invited to sing at the Metropolitan. Warren found the Bolshoi and the theatre in Riga far more organized and disciplined than La Scala. "The physical productions are excellent in Moscow," he said, "often bordering on the stupendous." His passion for the mechanics of special effects led him to criticize the Met and La Scala, neither of which, he said, could offer a "realistic thunderstorm" in *Rigoletto* to match that of the Bolshoi.

Yet in the end, the Russian appearances cost him money. Among the papers in the Leonard Warren Collection is Agatha's memo on the Russian tour; she added a note about the loss he incurred. Headed "Russia, May, 1958," the memo shows that his fee for the tour was $6000. His expenses were $900 for his manager's commission, $1886.10 for transportation, $315.95 for overweight baggage, $775 for Sektberg, and $440 for extra expenses. His profit was $1683. By contrast, his Metropolitan Opera Spring Tour fees would have come to $7200 for eight performances; the commission would have been $360. "$5157 lost for Russian Tour," she noted.

When Warren got home, he told his sister about the problems they had had. "He said the Russian trip was very difficult for them," Vivien recalled. "They believed that their hotel room was bugged, so they had all private conversations in the bathroom with the water running in the sink. Agatha and Leonard wanted to be able to go to church, but when Agatha asked, she was always told that the churches were 'under construction.' Undaunted, she found a way for them to get in some church just the same." Agatha also told Vivien how uncomfortable she was about her clothes; she regretted having brought a fur jacket along. "People stared at them everywhere," Vivien said. "They had bodyguards and interpreters with them constantly, and Leonard was sad that they had not been able to walk around on their own. He said he was also surprised to find that audiences in the Soviet Union did not know more concert music, simply because it was rarely performed there and the sheet music was not available. The American numbers were a great novelty."

Warren also told William Appleton that he was delighted to have been so well received. He explained how he knew their room was bugged. In their Moscow hotel, they had trouble with the plumbing because hot water came of out of the tap marked *cold*, and cold water came out of the other tap, and not much came out. They complained to each other about it in their room but said nothing to the manager. One day when they got back from the theatre they were shocked to see that the taps had been switched, and they realized that the room really was bugged. "This bothered Agatha particularly," Appleton said. Asked about the Warrens' attempt to attend Roman Catholic services in Russia, he talked about his own trip there and added, "I don't think any Catholic churches were open. The Russian Orthodox churches were open, sort of as a token. I think Agatha and Leonard went to a chapel in the Italian and French embassies."

The Russian tour was a milestone in Warren's career. It went more smoothly than his Italian engagement and generated great publicity. Soon the American public could hear what Warren had accomplished in the Soviet Union. Selections from two of his Russian recital programs in Leningrad and Kiev, accompanied by Sektberg, were recorded and later released by RCA Victor in both LP and CD. Warren's recital in Moscow was recorded by Melodiya which issued ten selections on an LP. Among the reviews, one in the

Saturday Review of Literature on 29 November called Warren's voice "audible velvet."

Paris, Spoleto, and Rome

The Warrens soon traveled abroad again, marking the summer of 1958 with a vacation in Europe. They met Appleton in Paris at the Hotel Continental where they all stayed. He remembered their visit:

> We went to the opera a couple of times while we were there. At the Comique they were giving *Tosca*, and Leonard wanted to go. We also saw Poulenc's *Les mamelles de Tirésias*. I was very surprised that Warren wanted to see it. It is an *opéra bouffe* that had been premiered at the Comique in 1947. In it there was a long baritone solo, about ten minutes. When we left the theatre, Leonard said "You know, I'd like to sing that sometime," but he never did because it was not appropriate for American recital audiences.

Warren, Agatha, and Appleton also visited Versailles. Appleton said, "I remember Leonard got onto the subject of French food that day. He had decided that he really liked Italian food better. It had more substance and body, he said. French food was too refined for his taste. He was longing to get to Italy and 'real food.'"

The Warrens went ahead to Italy, agreeing to meet Appleton in Rome. He remembered how comfortable Warren was there. "Socially, Leonard was very outgoing, but he was particularly easy in that Italian setting. When I flew down from Paris, he met me at the airport. As I came off the plane and went to the terminal entrance, Leonard came forward to greet me. He hesitated for a moment, then threw his arms around me and kissed me on both cheeks, Italian style. This was his 'Italian mode.'" In Rome they ran into a lot of singers Warren knew. They were all scheduled to record there. Appleton particularly recalled Agatha's reverence for Milanov. "She thought a divine constellation was Leonard, Milanov, and Björling. That was her dream trio. We dined out many times together in Rome. Leonard talked about food, about music and family things, and about getting a new boat."

While the trio was in Rome, they went to Spoleto, where Gian Carlo Menotti's Festival of Two Worlds was in its first season. Appleton said:

> We went up by car and stayed three nights in a very nice hotel. Leonard was there to see *Macbeth*, which he was to sing at the Met the next year. We also went to see Jerome Robbins and his Ballets U.S.A. Gian Carlo invited us to his palazzo. Tommy Schippers [the conductor of *Macbeth*] was there. Up to that point, Leonard and I had not talked much about motivation in *Macbeth*. I still remember

how impressed we were by the soprano, Shakeh Vartenissian, the Lady Macbeth. [Under Luchino Visconti's direction], she walked forward toward the footlights for her Drinking Song and kicked her train aside before she began to sing. It was just right for that opera in that setting. Very melodramatic, with a lot of reds and blacks. It was given in the Teatro Nuovo, an authentic nineteenth-century house. It was just great for that opera.

Among the friends the Warrens saw in Spoleto and Rome was Marise Angelucci Pokorny, who had first met Roy Leifflen in Washington and whom they had met in 1956. They entertained her for dinner at Manhattan House, and sometimes she and Roy would cook "huge feasts" on Saturday in the Warrens' kitchen, so they could all enjoy a pleasant, low-key evening together. On other occasions, Marise was also invited to the Warrens' house in Connecticut. However, she was Roman; her mother knew Menotti and Schippers well and spent her summers in Spoleto. So it was on Marise's home turf that she was best able to entertain Warren, his wife, and their friends. Later Marise also became Vivien's close friend. She said of the Warrens' trip:

> We went to Spoleto and Orvieto together, anything to get them out of their hotel. One year they were staying at the Majestic on the Via Veneto, another time at the Ambasciatori. When Leonard was recording with RCA, I used to pick them up, and we would go to very simple restaurants for dinner. Sometimes Milanov was with us. I remember one night in a Trastevere restaurant with an outdoor garden. Someone asked Leonard to sing, and he did. This was very unusual because he would not do that often. I think he would have done it more because he was such a warm, nice person, but he didn't want to overtax himself. As Leonard was singing, a waiter whispered to me, "Oh, what a beautiful voice!" Of course, no one knew who these singers really were. They all went around Rome just like ordinary people.

After their stay in Spoleto, they settled in Rome so that Warren could record *Forza* with Milanov, Di Stefano, and Tozzi, with Fernando Previtali conducting. Tozzi, who by then knew the Warrens quite well, said they were all at the Hotel Ambasciatori and often dined together after the recording sessions. In the course of their discussions about singing, Tozzi said, Warren started to talk about his early years with Sidney Dietch. "You have to raise your soft palate when you sing," Warren said, adding, "It's easy for me." Tozzi said he looked in Warren's mouth and was astonished at what he saw. "It looked like the Grand Canyon. His body was a perfect resonating machine, just built to create beautiful sound. But he said he had to work very, very hard to get his voice forward onto his teeth and his lips. It was an open, high palatal sound." Warren told Tozzi, "I've studied the role of Rigoletto so much, and I've coached it so much that today I think if you want to cut open my wrists, little Rigolettos would come out." Tozzi added, "He swore that he had devoted all his energies to that role." Edgar Vincent said Warren wore himself out trying to perfect his Rigoletto. "I think Rigoletto almost defeated Leonard," Vincent remarked. "He insisted on singing the whole role hunched over, which made it very difficult for him to produce his voice. But he was determined to sing it that way. The physical figure of the jester had to be deformed." Wally Cleva Riecker said that in all the performances she saw, Warren never stood up straight.

Warren's 1958–1959 term at the Met began in Eugene Berman's hardy sets of *Rigoletto* on the third night of the season. On 7 November came the new production of *Pagliacci*, directed by José Quintero, with Rolf Gérard's settings. Mitropoulos was conducting. Del Monaco was Canio, and Lucine Amara sang Nedda. As Warren told his sister, Quintero was brought in "to lend a touch of Broadway to the stodgy old Met." And although Warren had assured Alan Wagner that he got on famously with new directors and saw "eye to eye" with them, the truth was he often argued with them when they asked him to change the action that worked best for him. For this new production, he was an unforgettable Tonio. Robert Merrill, who had been assigned one performance of Silvio and was also scheduled to sing Tonio later, was in the rehearsal room with Quintero, Warren, Del Monaco, Amara, and Mario Sereni. Merrill recalled that day:

> We were having our first rehearsal up in the old hall on the roof of the Opera House. We were all sitting around when Quintero began to describe his new concept of the opera. He announced that he had decided to change the [traditional] staging of the opening of *Pagliacci*. He wanted to have the curtain go up at the beginning, with the whole cast onstage. Tonio would sing his Prologue up there, surrounded by people, instead of having the whole stage to himself, standing in front of the curtain, as the composer intended. As he was talking, I saw Leonard's face. He was furious. I said to myself, "Leonard, stop this!" Leonard got up, six feet of him and probably around 250 pounds. Quintero, a slight little guy, weighed about 150. Leonard went right over to him and almost picked him up off the floor. "Listen," he said, "You're not ruining my Prologue!" Quintero gave in right away. After the rehearsal, I went over and said, "Thank you, Leonard!" We never heard about Quintero's "new idea" about the Prologue again.

Lucine Amara described Warren. "He was fine as a colleague, but he could be temperamental. If someone rubbed him the wrong way, he responded." She remembered trying to get him to change some of the action between Nedda and Tonio. "I said to him, 'The director didn't change this, so why don't we do something about it?' But if he didn't like what I wanted to do, he just would not do it." All the same, she said, "His Tonio was fantastic. He *was* Tonio. And he had a phenomenal voice. He could easily have been a heldentenor."

Merle Hubbard, a young man who had joined the rehearsal department staff in October 1958, found Warren "very difficult" to deal with. He called him "a louse, a stinker, but a very great singer, one of the greatest baritones." Hubbard also said that in the last two years of Warren's career "He was as much a faker as a glorious singer; a lot of the time, he just faked it." His *Macbeth*, however, was "a pretty stunning achievement." Hubbard called Warren a man "who loved to wear costumes," and said, "He was always the first to come to rehearsals in costume." Vivien confirmed this, adding, "Leonard always wanted to have all his costumes and props available for early rehearsals, even if that cost the Met money. It did cost money because the company had to pay stagehands just to put things in place for Leonard." Hubbard and Warren often argued over rehearsals, which the baritone protested he did not need. Hubbard said, "He saw no reason to come in just because everyone else needed to do so. I called him for *Otello* in 1958–1959, and he said, 'Why? Why should I come in? I've done them all, and I'm not supposed to come down to teach Uzunov his part.' He was often like that, as if it were a tremendous burden to do things for other people."

Macbeth

As Warren had told Alan Wagner, his study of *Macbeth* was underway more than a year before he was actually scheduled to sing it. He had bought the Ricordi score in Italy, then paid Roy Leifflen five hundred dollars to translate it for him and write the English words over the Italian text in the score. New sessions with Dietch and Appleton began in 1957 or 1958. On some pages of his score, Warren was still marking the time with vertical lines between the notes, just as he had had to do in 1938. Occasionally he also had to write in his phonetic version of the Italian text. "In sua vece" has VECHE over it; and "Di voi chi ciò fece?" is written as KI CHO FECHE. Over the word "ciocche," Warren wrote CHUCKE. In the great aria "Pietà, rispetto, amore," the florid passages are circled in red pencil, and over "Nè sul tuo regio sasso sperar soavi accenti" he wrote DOLCISSSSISSSIMO.

As he began work on the music, he also studied the character. In Warren's score, many pages contain specific act and scene references to Shakespeare's drama. Recalling their sessions, Appleton said:

> In the summer and fall of 1958, Leonard asked me a lot of questions about what kind of character Macbeth was. It is a strange role

because no actor had ever really given a satisfactory performance of it; no actor was "a famous Macbeth." Why was this? I explained to Leonard that Macbeth is a complex character. At the beginning he is a visionary, a decent man; in the course of the play, he is completely transformed and capable of evil. I also talked to him about another overly complex character in Shakespeare, Cleopatra, who is really so many different women, a woman of "infinite variety," if you will. You can't pin down Macbeth to one kind of character because he changes so radically in the course of both the play and the opera. I said to Leonard, "Just sing it." He developed the character, burgeoning and blossoming with it. He had that true "infinite variety," so his Macbeth changed completely in the course of the opera.

Friendship with Bergonzi

In these years, a new and strong bond developed between Warren and the young Italian tenor Carlo Bergonzi. They first became acquainted during the preparations for *Tosca* and *Aida* in 1957–1958, but *Macbeth* put both on their mettle and truly brought them together. Of course, Bergonzi's authentic Verdi credentials were guaranteed to catch Warren's attention. Born in Vidalenzo, the country village where Verdi's parents had lived, Bergonzi also had lifelong ties with Busseto, Verdi's town, and Sant'Agata, where Verdi had his farm and villa. He had come to New York with an expressed commitment to Verdi's style and a clear sense of the art of singing his music.

Warren stood out strongly in a broad, competitive field in the mid-1950s. As Bergonzi remarked:

> There were a lot of baritones around then, but Leonard was always different because he was such a great artist. He sang so artistically. He was serious, though, and rather closed. He rarely opened up to people, but luckily he liked me and even began to joke with me during rehearsals and performances. When we did *Macbeth* together, we really got to know each other, and after that he often invited my wife and me to visit him and Agatha in Manhattan House.

Bergonzi's observations about Warren's art emphasized his seriousness.

> He was a man who wanted to be able to convey every single phrase of the score. A scholar, a true scholar, Leonard was always trying to understand things better. That was his temperament: he was so serious. He often would say to me, "I can't understand this." Or he would ask me, "Carlo, just what does this phrase mean?" In *Macbeth* he was very worried about getting across the mystery of the scenes with the witches.

With Bergonzi, Warren also played games, something he rarely did with other artists. Bergonzi remembered:

> He was determined to do every performance better than the one before, and we had a kind of competition about that. After an aria or a scene, he would say to me, "Carlo, tonight was better than the other night. We were good!" I liked singing with him, and I loved the little contests we carried on, the competition between the two of us. And to think that he could not read music—couldn't even recognize a half-note! But he learned how to commit everything to memory. He accomplished what he did because of his intelligence. He was so wise about his voice that even when he was ill, he knew just how to position it, so he could sing without letting the audience know he wasn't in top form. I loved him because he was so sincere. Leonard always had something inside him that he wanted to give the audience. And of course he had music inside him. *Aveva una musica dentro*. He wanted to talk to the audience with his music.

A Truly Great Role

Bing and Warren both knew *Macbeth* would be important. In one sense, it completed a cycle. Verdi wrote the leading baritone roles of *Macbeth*, *Rigoletto*, and *Traviata* for the high, flexible voice of Felice Varesi, a great Verdi interpreter of the nineteenth century. These "Varesi" operas were also ideally suited to Warren's voice. *Macbeth* was also right for his age and level of artistry. The planned cast included Callas, Hines, and Bergonzi, with Mitropoulos conducting. The designer was Caspar Neher and the director Carl Ebert. Warren probably devoted more effort to *Macbeth* than to any other opera except *Rigoletto*, even going to the New York City Opera, where William Chapman sang the title role. No matter how often Warren sang these parts and no matter whether they were in his immediate future, he wanted to learn. In addition to studying *Macbeth* with Appleton and Ebert, in 1959 he would work with Nathaniel Merrill.

Edgar Vincent remembered Warren being "very worried" about having to appear in *Macbeth* with Callas as his Lady. "What am I going to do to counteract Callas's star shenanigans?" Warren asked. Assiduous publicity was the only answer. As it happened, he was spared by Bing's dispute with Callas and her subsequent firing. Vincent said, "I think Leonard was delighted when Callas got fired. His life was easier then." Callas's replacement was Leonie Rysanek. At the end of January, the whole production was again thrown into turmoil when Mitropoulos was hospitalized with a heart attack. Leinsdorf then took over. Because so few singers had ever sung this opera, extra rehearsals were scheduled in the weeks before the opening night, 5 February 1959. Warren felt that even these were not enough and kept hounding Appleton and others for hints about Macbeth's character.

Jerome Hines in *Macbeth*

Hines recalled in our interview that a worried Warren asked Hines and his wife, Lucia Evangelista, to come to his apartment in Manhattan House for extra rehearsals. "I want to talk to you about the first act," Warren said to Hines after a rehearsal. "Do you mind coming to my apartment to go over this again?" Hines and Evangelista went and were warmly received by Warren and Agatha, as if the visit were social, but in fact it was purely professional. The two men began to go through the act together without an accompanist. "We mustn't sing too loud because this scene should be intimate," Warren declared. Hines listened. They polished the phrasing and then rehearsed as best they could to perfect the musical line of their moments together onstage. After Hines and Evangelista had left the Warrens' building, Evangelista turned to Hines and began to discuss the session. Both knew Warren's ways of upstaging his colleagues during performances. "So!" she said, "he is up there blasting away and you're singing *pianissimo*, so no one will hear you. Forget about it!" Hines, who was by then as stage-wise as Warren, kept the older man's suggestions in mind, but in the actual performances he carefully balanced his own volume against Warren's so as not to be outshone by his Macbeth.

Hines sang seven Banquos with Warren at the Met that season and repeated the role in 1959–1960 when the opera returned to the repertory in January. Hines also recalled Warren's absolute commitment to his work and how great he was in *Macbeth*. "Leonard was not by nature a great actor, but when he had a new role, he would call his teacher or someone like [Armando] Agnini [from San Francisco] and work on that one until he had it right, sometimes one opera for as long as a year."

Lady Macbeth at Risk

Leonie Rysanek was of Czech and Austrian background. At the time she undertook Lady Macbeth at the Met she was thirty-three and feared making a debut as a replacement for such a celebrity, even though she had strong, supportive colleagues around her. Among the stalwarts were young Bergonzi and the mature Warren, who was perfectly prepared. In a 1996 *New York Times* interview Rysanek said, "I was hesitant to debut in a production made for Callas. I already had a major success in Europe. But in New York the attitude was 'Who are you? Who knows you? How dare you?'" When Rysanek came onstage as Lady Macbeth for the first time, someone in the audience shouted "Brava Callas!" But Rysanek did not flinch. She decided at that moment to "show him my high Cs. So I sat on that high C, which is incorrect." (Bing, in his book *5000 Nights at the Opera*, admitted that he had hired a claqueur to shout "Brava Callas!" in the hope of getting the audience to see Rysanek as an underdog and favor her.") Rysanek's debut was a notable success. She sang with Warren in all but one of his performances of *Macbeth*.

The Reviews

Incredible as it may seem to those who heard this *Macbeth*, the reviews were mixed. One day after the opening night, the *New York Times* ran a long profile on Warren, headlined "Methodical Musician," describing his "slow study" of his roles. Paul Jackson, in *Sign-off for the Old Met*, wrote that in *Macbeth* Warren added "yet another strong portrayal" to his list of Verdi characters and praised him as "straightforward" in interpretation, but felt the last high A-flat of the broadcast betrayed "strain" even though he was "at the peak of his form."

When the *Macbeth* recording came out, it was widely hailed as a landmark performance. Among the glowing reviews, a particularly fine one appeared in the New Orleans *Times-Picayune* on 8 November 1959. Written by Sim Meyers, it is headlined METROPOLITAN "MACBETH" A TRIUMPH FOR WARREN. He said, "This is more a triumph for baritone Leonard Warren than any other recorded operatic role has ever been for any other star, man or woman. . . . In Warren, one finds a singer so perfectly suited to the role of Macbeth, and a performance of such glowing vigor that excitement wells forth each time he takes to the stage to sing." Giuseppe Pugliese called the baritone's performance on the recording with Leinsdorf "formidable, something that absolutely no one could surpass." Those who followed opera generally believed that Warren had never before reached the level of greatness he did in this role. Having wanted to sing it for years, he invested his whole being into doing it perfectly.

Breaking Ground for Lincoln Center

Warren was honored by being included on the program for the new Met's groundbreaking at Lincoln Center on 14 May 1959. Plans for a new opera house had been on the table for decades, reaching back to 1908. At that time, Gatti-Casazza, who had just arrived to become the new general manager, complained to Otto Kahn about the inadequate facilities of the old theatre on Broadway. Promises and hopes were raised and dashed in the years that followed, and not until the first year of Bing's tenure did serious discussions commence. A site for a new Met was found at Columbus Circle, where the New York Coliseum now stands. It was abandoned. At that point, several improvements were made to the old Opera House, most under Krawitz's direction. Later, Bing said he bore the burden of the planning and execution of the new Met, saying, "Krawitz and Krawitz alone really understood."

Not until the mid-1950s did a committee begin to explore a site at Lincoln Square, where a slum-clearance project was under way. The new Met would stand beside a hall for the New York Philharmonic and a theatre for the New York City Opera, which was then playing in the old City Center on Fifty-fifth Street. Lincoln Center was incorporated in June 1956. On the day of the groundbreaking ceremony nearly three years later, a limousine called for the Warrens in the morning and took them to the construction site, where they joined the parties of President Eisenhower and other dignitaries. The driver parked behind the orchestra platform to give Warren a place to rest between the early rehearsal and the program. For the event, he sat on the platform with Risë Stevens and the New York Philharmonic, which Bernstein conducted. Warren sang the Prologue from *Pagliacci*. The Juilliard School of Music chorus also sang. Among the speakers were the president, who turned the first spade of earth, the governor, the mayor, and many members of the Met and Lincoln Center administration and the boards of directors. Afterward, Eisenhower told John D. Rockefeller III how much he enjoyed the music. He added, "It would have been worth coming just for the music alone." The first complete performance at the new Met would not take place until the spring of 1966.

Summer 1959

By the summer of 1959, Warren was back in Rome. Margaret Carson, who first met him in 1944, reminisced about his passion for work. She said:

> In 1959 he spent much of the summer recording in Rome. He finished one complete opera, *Trovatore*, with Leontyne Price, Tucker, Rosalind Elias, and Tozzi, with Arturo Basile conducting. Everyone was ready to go back to the States. They were about to leave when Leonard took Agatha aside. He said to her, "I think I'm going to stay a few days longer and work with Picozzi [his coach]. In *Rigoletto* there's one certain phrase that isn't quite right. It should tear your heart out, but it just doesn't. I haven't got it right." Imagine! The phrase he wanted to polish came in the scene where Rigoletto discovers that the body in the sack is Gilda's. What a testimony to the seriousness and commitment of that man! Imagine staying on in Italy to go over one phrase! Imagine that, when he was the greatest Rigoletto in the world!

Carson also felt that one of the greatest disappointments of Warren's entire career came after those recording sessions in Rome. "He very much wanted to record the complete *Simon Boccanegra*," she said, "and that was a time when there was no other baritone who could have done it." Warren asked George Marek of RCA Victor to authorize the recording, but Marek replied, "You don't want to do that." Warren insisted. "I'm willing to give up a full ten days of work to record it," he told Marek. But Marek refused, saying, "It'll never sell." Carson remembered that "Warren was very, very unhappy about that. It broke his heart."

An Honor from the Pope

On 10 September 1959, Warren was honored by Pope John XXIII in a private audience in the Vatican, where he and Agatha were received. He was inducted into the Equestrian Order of the Knights of the Holy Sepulchre in Jerusalem, his knighthood having come through the effort of Francis Cardinal Spellman, the Archbishop of New York. With this, Warren became a Knight Commander. Investiture included a rite that was followed by the robing. The white, gold-embroidered robe was placed on his shoulders; the headpiece fit like a bishop's mitre; and on the gold chain around his neck hung the medallion of the order. The only decorations on the robe were the emblems of the Equestrian Knights, two large red crosses that had four small crosses placed in the corners where their arms come together. The emblems, called cosmic crosses, symbolize the Cross of Christ saving the four corners of the earth. It has been a mark of the Order since the 1300s. Because Warren's favorite colors were red and white, the robe had special importance for him, apart from the honor. Father Royal Gardner, a priest from the Church of St. Vincent Ferrer and Warren's close and trusted friend, said, "He loved the cape and headpiece. He was very proud of it." This investiture gave Warren a kind of second home in Italy, at the seat of the Order on Via Santo Spirito in Sassia in Rome. After he received the regalia, he told Helen Hatton how proud he was to have been honored with this investiture; Vivien said her brother told Agatha that if he were to die, he wanted to be buried in it.

CHAPTER TWENTY

The Career Ends: 1959–1960

W hatever concern Warren had had about his future in 1957, he was fully satisfied with his new Met assignments for 1959–1960. Two were Verdi's grand title-role operas, *Macbeth* and *Simon Boccanegra*, and he would sing the opening night *Trovatore*, two new productions, and the usual Saturday broadcasts. Another leading role lay ahead, for Bing personally promised him Verdi's *Nabucco* for the opening night of the 1960–1961 season. This respect, which underscored his rank above other baritones on the roster, was particularly remarkable in a culture founded on celebrity sopranos and tenors. With such recognition came onerous duties and burdens. Warren's tight schedule of concerts, recitals, and operas added to the draining round of other work: the days and nights of study, voice and coaching sessions, costume and wig fittings, rehearsals, and performances.

Warren won further prestige and had a big success on 20 October 1959, when he sang the New York premiere of Dello Joio's *Lamentation of Saul* in Town Hall. It had been just over five years since Warren had sung the world premiere of this dramatic cantata. The Little Orchestra Society played under Thomas Scherman. Dello Joio said he was "overjoyed" when he was asked to score the work for full orchestra. As he had done before, Warren brought forth all the complexity of the D. H. Lawrence text and showed off his sterling diction. He supported the composer with dignity and grace. A HIT, ran one headline, while Harriet Johnson, writing in the New York *Post*, began her column with the words "The splendor of Leonard Warren's baritone gave epic stature to the supplications of Saul." Francis D. Perkins in the *Herald Tribune* found him in his best voice, "with a wide, finely graded range of hue and volume and a thorough, expressive understanding combined with complete distinctness of enunciation." The *New York Times* said he "sang with compelling force."

When the Met rehearsals began, Warren had just finished a concert and recital tour. Broadcasts and other outside events were also scheduled on free days during his opera season. Warren should probably have cut back on his commitments: he had suffered through a long bout of Asian flu the year before, and his physician was treating him for high blood pressure, a condition he never discussed with friends, colleagues, or the Met management. John S. White, though, suspected Warren was not well. He recalled several occasions that winter when he noticed that the baritone's hands were "cold and covered with perspiration." This, he said, he had never noticed before.

To most people, Warren seemed fine and in high good spirits. Rehearsals for his first four operas were under way; next on the schedule was the new *Trovatore*, the season's opener, which fell on 26 October. One day during the first costume fittings, he met Milanov just inside the Thirty-ninth Street stage door of the Met. Irene Barry and Winifred Short ruled the switchboard and mailboxes and controlled the corridors that led to the offices of Bing and his assistants. They also buzzed people through the door to the backstage and the auditorium. Between the switchboard area and the backstage door, a bench accommodated singers and people waiting for appointments with members of the administration. Arge Keller remembered Warren coming out from backstage in costume to pick up his mail.

> Milanov was sitting on the wooden bench, waiting for someone. Then Warren popped out. He was dressed as Di Luna for the new *Trovatore* in 1959. It was a weird costume, with a fantastic hat with red plumes on it. He stood there for a moment, looking at his mail. He then turned to Milanov and asked, "Zinka, how do I look?" And she, with a smile, said, "Leonard, you look just like a rooster." He laughed. She laughed.

In *Trovatore* Warren was featured with Carlo Bergonzi as Manrico and Antonietta Stella as Leonora, with Graf directing and Cleva conducting. On 2 November *Newsweek* ran a large photograph of Warren that took up nearly a third of a page, with a long feature article on him. He was "the baritone king of the Met," with a voice that had been called "the most gorgeously expressive in the Italian repertory today." The article covered his passion for detail. "Thoroughness is next to godliness" in his world. He moved through fittings for costumes, boots, and wigs, with meticulous attention to everything. Graf said he had "the most consistent career of any American singer." But as the writer added, he was stubborn and could drive "directors, designers and conductors" to distraction. In their interview he fell back on his grandfather's phrase about a salesman with his merchandise in a sample box. This was vintage Warren.

Three days later the Met scheduled Warren's twenty-fourth Scarpia, the first of the season, with Milanov as a riveting Tosca and Italian tenor Eugenio Fernandi as Cavaradossi. By then, Nathaniel Merrill had taken over rehearsing and directing the original Yannopoulos staging of the Puccini work. Merrill was also directing *Macbeth*, his second Warren opera that season because Ebert, the original director, had gone back to Europe. Leinsdorf was the conductor. Merrill, who had become quite friendly with Warren by 1960, recalled the problems that arose with *Macbeth*. Merrill said, "By the time it became my production, Warren had taken over all the direction of it. From the first rehearsal, he began by making us all understand that he wanted everything done his way. Our final dress rehearsal was 30 December." In the first act of the final rehearsal, after he and Lady Macbeth decided to kill King Duncan, Warren launched into the scene that begins "Is this a dagger?" Merrill recalled that he was on a balcony with all the lights on him.

> I was sitting out in the house with Bing and the rest of the management. It looked as if everything was going smoothly, when suddenly in the middle of the aria, Leonard stopped singing. "Stop! Stop!" he shouted to Leinsdorf. The orchestra ground to a halt. "Merrill, come down here," he ordered. I walked slowly down the aisle and stood behind the conductor. Before I could get a word out, Warren said, "Nat! Nat! How do I look? How do I look?" I didn't dare smile, but I said in a clear voice, "Leonard, *you—look—beautiful!*" The rehearsal audience went into a howl. As the orchestra picked up the line again, I passed Bing on my way back to my seat. "Bravo! Bravo!" he said, leaning out toward me.

Macbeth, which brought Warren's eighth performance of the long, taxing, exposed role, fell on 2 January 1960, with Rysanek again a stunning Lady Macbeth. Hines sang Banquo on the broadcast and alternated the role with Tozzi. Edgar Vincent remembered the Warrens' elegant after-performance dinner for the conductor and all the principals.

The next day, Warren began a mini-tour of recitals and concerts. Defying common sense and snowstorms in Ontario and the Midwest, he and Sektberg went first to Orillia, a city at the end of Lake Couchiching, about ninety miles due north of Toronto. Warren's Canadian acquaintance James B. McPherson said, "You can't even imagine how he got there. Train? Car? Maybe even a bus!" His recital of 4 January was covered the next day by the reviewer for the *Daily Packet and Times*, who said Warren "held his audience spellbound" and "proved himself a great artist with a warm personality. At the end of the program, he sang a parody of "Old Mother Hubbard," which brought a storm of applause from the seven hundred listeners. The Orillia date was followed two days later by another in Kitchener, seventy miles west of Toronto. This was a familiar stop on Warren's itineraries. On the eighth he sang in Montclair, New Jersey, and on the twelfth in Fayetteville, Arkansas. Next came a recital in the University Auditorium in Stillwater, Oklahoma, where he appeared on 13 January. James C. Stratton, the reviewer for the Stillwater *News-Press*, thanked Warren for a "memorable evening" and reported that he was in "fine fettle" and displayed "every facet of his range and control, shading and nuance." Particularly beautiful were "three chansons from Ravel's *Don Quichotte à Dulcinée*," where the baritone delivered "a bouquet, avoiding romantic bombast and the over-elaboration of slender materials." Warren ended with his standard contemporary works in English and peppered the program and encore series with arias. The sum: "A prime example of today's golden age of voice" bolstered by "high fun and polished artistry." At the end of the article, Stratton complimented him for being "about as easy as they come and a delicious fellow for whom conversation is a joy and a delight." Warren discussed his trip to Russia with the journalist before leaving Stillwater with Sektberg on 14 January. His goal was to get back to New York in time to spend three days at the Motorboat Show, which he had penciled into his schedule.

Warren sang his next *Macbeth* at the Met on the eighteenth, but even before the repeats of that opera, he had five symphony dates in five different cities, all requiring full rehearsals. He arrived in San Antonio on 22 January, rehearsed, and sang with the symphony there the next day. Next came a rehearsal in Tulsa on 25 January, followed by the concert on the twenty-sixth. Two days later, he rehearsed in Orlando and sang there on 28 January. His next stop on that tour was Daytona Beach, on 29 January. The next morning, Warren flew back to Canada, where he sang with Pelletier and the Orchestre Symphonique du Québec in Québec City on 1 February. Warren's notation on his calendar reads "Pelly sym." His part of the program for this all-operatic concert included Ford's monologue from *Falstaff*, the Prologue to *Pagliacci*, "Ombra mai fu" from Handel's *Serse*, Iago's "Credo," and Valentin's aria from *Faust*. The orchestra played the overture to *La forza del destino* and the Prelude to *Meistersinger*. The next day, the critic of *Le Soleil* declared that Warren's voice had "lost nothing of its richness and vitality." He was much heavier and balder than he had been in his earlier Canadian appearances, but he sang as he had through "triumph after triumph," having lost nothing of his "very sure technique," "incredible mastery," the "richness of voice," and "all his marvelous vitality."

Leaving Québec City on 2 February, Warren was in New York in time to sing *Macbeth* on the fourth. Rehearsals for the new production of *Simon Boccanegra* began the day after he arrived and were fitted around *Macbeth* performances. He had not sung the role of Boccanegra at the Met since the 1949–1950 season, but he restudied it in 1956 for San Francisco, then again for the new Met production. He had even returned to Genoa in the summer of 1959 to revisit the historic sites shown in the opera and verify details of the life of the Doge. *Simon Boccanegra* was, after all, his most important assignment that season. Bing gave it as a showcase for him; the first night was an important benefit, sponsored by the Metropolitan Opera Guild for the Metropolitan Opera production funds. Boccanegra, like Rigoletto, offered high dramatic moments in a rich setting of historical images, and it was an ideal part for the subtle artist Warren then was.

Mary Curtis-Verna as Amelia

During the early rehearsals with a coach-pianist, no problems arose with *Boccanegra*. Although Warren often resisted taking new direction, he even accepted most of Margaret Webster's plan of action. The orchestra rehearsals on the old roof stage went smoothly. Mary Curtis-Verna, the Amelia/Maria, had been asked to sing in the place of Tebaldi, whose arrival in New York had been delayed. Curtis-Verna and Warren had sung together before, in one stress-filled week in 1958, when they had performed *La forza del destino* and *Aida* on consecutive evenings at the Met. Then and in other encounters, Curtis-Verna said, Warren had always been courteous and respectful. "Really, he was the sort of quiet person who wanted to be left alone, such a studious man, and so sincere as an artist." She had also learned of Warren's interest in young singers. "[Giorgio] Tozzi told me that when he first came to the Met, Warren gave him a tour of the stage, showing him where to find the spots with the best acoustics and resonance. George said he was great with beginners."

The preliminary rehearsals of *Simon Boccanegra* began about 1 February. Curtis-Verna remembered their early sessions in rooms and on the roof stage as uneventful, apart from Warren's prodigious vocal displays. "He would take a straight chair and turn it around, sit backwards on it, fill those lungs and just let go. He never, never spared himself and sang full voice all the time." As rehearsals progressed, she said, no friction marred Warren's working relationship with Mitropoulos, who was "so marvelous, just like a monk or a friar, completely dedicated to the music." At that point, she, Warren and the other cast members believed the action and the tempos were set.

The singers' problems began just as the problems with *Ernani* had, during the early orchestra rehearsals when the production reached the main stage. Curtis-Verna said Mitropoulos "changed his ways. When we got to the early rehearsals of *Simon* in the theatre, he got involved with the sheer sound and wanted to draw it out as long as possible, very legato; you could hear him romanticizing the music. Of course, he was best known as a symphonic conductor, so this came naturally to him, but it was very hard on the singers." The slow tempo particularly challenged Warren. Unfortunately, it also reminded him of his previous, ugly exchange with Mitropoulos about the tempos during *Ernani* rehearsals. Curtis-Verna felt that the conductor seemed to care nothing for his singers. By 1960 Warren had a record of more than twenty years of performing works as he had studied and rehearsed them for given productions, and he simply could not tolerate last-minute changes. "He was very particular," Curtis-Verna said. "When Mitropoulos slowed the tempo in the Council Chamber Scene, Warren just couldn't sustain the phrases. They couldn't fall into the pattern he had learned. Changes threw him off because he studied each scene in a certain way, and you just could not go out of that pattern. As he wrestled with the slower tempo, he became over-wrought; his nerves got the better of him. I don't think it was anything personal against Mitropoulos, but the unexpected changes really upset him, and at one point he just stopped singing. He walked down to the footlights and spoke very brusquely to Mitropoulos, saying that the tempo was just too slow. Then he added some other words, which I could not hear. Mitropoulos was speechless."

Two Directors' Views

Yannopoulos remembered Mitropoulos as thin and ill that year, still recovering from a heart attack suffered in 1959. "Warren was this huge man, gigantic, and frightening as hell. He insulted Mitropoulos." Margaret Webster, writing in *Don't Put Your Daughter on the Stage*, offered a slightly different account of what happened. She called Warren affectionately "the old dinosaur" and said she loved him. Before rehearsals began, she had heard "by the grapevine" that he often had fights with people and was "impossible" to work with. As things got under way, she said, she learned he was a perfectionist, "one who cared passionately that everything should be just so." But "unfortunately this led him to think that he knew more about everybody else's business than they did; and he never hesitated to tell them what they ought to do about it." Nevertheless, she and Warren got on "famously" and trusted each other. Webster said all went well until the dress rehearsal during which Warren insulted Mitropoulos and the orchestra.

Webster particularly appreciated Warren's knowledge of the drama and of the Met stage. When she tried to put him in a certain place, he told her he could not sing from there because it was a dead spot. He wanted to sing from a position "not more than a foot away." On the day Warren exploded, he had objected to having a second-cast singer do the rehearsal. Webster said, in her diary of the rehearsal period, "He wanted to sing the rehearsal himself because he feels he needs it" and got "heated and pompous." He said "some silly thing like, 'Well, after all, Maestro, *we* are the singers, and *we* have to give the performance.'" At that a roar of "hostile and derisive laughter" came from the pit. "Warren swings on them and says, 'Well, *you* didn't play so good either!' Uproar!" She said the orchestra men "hurled" many four-letter words at Warren. He, in his fury, looked down into the pit.

Tucker and Raymond Gniewek

At that moment, Richard Tucker, who was singing Gabriele, tried to intervene. Barry Tucker, the tenor's son, was also there. Barry, who was in his twenties, had known Warren almost all his life and considered him a good friend. He said that by the time they got to *Simon Boccanegra*, Tucker "revered Mitropoulos as a father figure," while the conductor considered the tenor "his little boy." When Warren exploded at Mitropoulos during the rehearsal, Tucker stepped out of his role as Gabriele, went over to him, and tried to calm him down. "Lenny, you can't talk to people like that," Tucker said. "We've got to work this out." He tried to be the peacemaker, Barry said. But the situation was out of control, and Tucker had to step back.

Raymond Gniewek, then a young violinist at the Met, was a veteran of the Eastman School of Music and the Rochester Philharmonic. He had joined the Met orchestra in 1957 and became its concertmaster. He also remembered that troubled February day.

It was about ten days before the opening night, a costume rehearsal with scenery and orchestra. A lot of tensions had arisen during the preparation because of the new staging, which some people did not understand, and the fact that some things from [the scenery and costumes] were delayed. Warren got quite uptight, and finally he walked to the footlights, complained to Mitropoulos about the slow tempos, and ended his gripe by giving him an order: "You just follow me."

Mitropoulos didn't take offense, but the players did. They just adored Mitropoulos. So when Warren said that to him, one of the men shouted, "Who do you think you are?" Others chimed in, insulting Warren. Furious by then, he looked down into the pit and said, "You guys don't sound too good this morning either." At that, the whole orchestra just erupted. There were yells and hoots and cursing and raspberries, Bronx cheers. I don't think anyone had ever heard anything like that at the Met, and everyone was stunned. Warren turned and walked away.

Mitropoulos then told us to take a break. We all laid down our instruments and went down into the orchestra room. We sent for the union delegate. After a while, someone came to call us back into the pit, but the whole orchestra, almost with one voice, said "No! No!" We just stayed where we were. We all knew Warren and knew he could get a little nasty at times, but this was over the top.

Finally Bing came downstairs. "I am here to apologize for Mr. Warren," he said. But the orchestra players weren't buying that. A couple of them answered Bing: "Warren insulted the orchestra, and he will have to apologize himself." Bing offered to see what he could do and went back upstairs. About forty-five minutes passed before we were told to go back to the pit. Finally Bing walked Warren through the gold curtain and down to the footlights. Then he spoke to us, but he never did truly apologize. What he said was "It's been a difficult production, really tough. But you know what I think of you guys." We accepted that, and the rehearsal went on.

About a week later, Gniewek said, Tucker was onstage during another rehearsal, without Warren. He was having a conversation with the conductor. "Suddenly he smiled, looked down at the orchestra and said, 'You guys sound great this morning.' Everyone in the auditorium just burst out laughing."

On 2 April, *Opera News* carried a sanitized report of the troubled rehearsal. Warren's name was kept out of the account, as was the fact that Bing ran down the aisle of the Opera House shouting, "Time is money! Time is money!" while the orchestra was out. The *Opera News* account said that when one scene ended, an unnamed singer (Warren) said, "Let's do it again, the tempo is too slow." Mitropoulos protested. Then the singer retorted "All right! I'll get an oxygen tank!" Coverage of the uproar that followed never found its way into the magazine. The writer merely added that "at this point" the singers were "tired."

Warren's Account to His Sister

Vivien was not at that rehearsal, but because she had so many friends among Met employees and subscribers, she heard about the *Boccanegra* rehearsal incident right after it happened. She asked her brother about it. She said, "Leonard admitted he had been disruptive, but he told me he didn't like the way the orchestra was playing and couldn't follow the tempos. Yes, he admitted to me that he told Mitropoulos how to play. He said he insulted the orchestra men, and they walked out and wouldn't return until he stood at the front of the stage and apologized." But Vivien explained his actions, saying, "Leonard was taught a certain way and stood by that. He drove everybody crazy, telling directors how to direct and singers how to sing. That's how he was; he lived by what he was taught, and because he idolized all his teachers, he wanted to do it their way. Whatever they said was right." David Pardoll, the head of production at the Met, had his own view of Warren. Many years later, James McPherson asked him, "Of all the singers with whom you've had to deal, who was the most difficult?" Pardoll answered, "Warren, because he was a perfectionist."

The Production Goes Forward

After the unsettling incident with the orchestra, the preparations for *Simon Boccanegra* continued. After a stage rehearsal, Edgar Vincent mustered the courage to make a suggestion to Warren about his singing in the last part of the opera.

He was singing everything after the Council Chamber Scene *piano* and *pianissimo*. I thought he should sing out, with that glorious voice he had. He said to me, "You're wrong." I persisted. "Why am I wrong?" I asked him. "Because Simon is dying of belladonna poisoning, and it makes you weaker and weaker. I couldn't sing it *forte*. It would not be right." He told me what he had found out about the death of the real Simon Boccanegra, who was poisoned at a banquet. To think that Leonard had even discovered what the poison was and how it worked!

In fact, this was old lore for Warren; he had done his homework on that subject years earlier.

The night of the first performance of *Simon Boccanegra* was Tuesday, 1 March. Barry Tucker remembered the Warrens had planned a big party after the first performance and invited Sara and Richard Tucker and their family to join them. "They were good colleagues. Leonard taught my father a lot," Barry said, "and particularly in *Forza*, where he taught him how to sing the battle scene duet as he is lying on the stretcher." Nevertheless, the Tuckers declined Warren's invitation because Warren's after-theatre supper fell on Barry's birthday. The Tuckers were giving their son a party of his own at a restaurant a block north of the Opera House. Barry said Warren understood. When the opera ended and everyone was out of costume and dressed, the Warrens went off to receive their guests while the Tuckers left for their dinner. Webster went to the "splendid party" at the Warrens' house.

The success of the first *Simon Boccanegra* was beyond dispute because Warren gave the finest performance he had ever sung in the Met. Howard Taubman's review in the *New York Times* began with sublime praise: "If there were nothing more to *Simon Boccanegra* than the Council Chamber Scene, it would repay going miles to hear and see." It was performed with "tense, chilling impact," he added. Margaret Webster's staging was marked with "simplicity and grandeur"; Frederick Fox's sets and Motley's costumes caught "the spirit of early Renaissance splendor." As for Warren, Tucker, and Tozzi, the Met had "led from matchless strength" and had other substantial assets in Ezio Flagello and Norman Scott. Warren was praised for bringing "increased nuance and power" to the title role. The "fullness and lyricism" of Tucker's Gabriele Adorno could not be matched by many tenors. Tozzi, in the role of Fiesco, was praised for the size of his voice and the humanity he invested in "Il lacerato spirito." At the end of the review, Taubman compared the "proud" *Simon Boccanegra* to the glories of Bing's landmark 1950 production of *Don Carlo*.

In the *Herald Tribune* Paul Henry Lang opened with remarks about the "million dollar cast" and Verdi's genius in revising this 1857 opera and sealing it with the hand that would soon write *Aida*, the *Messa da Requiem*, and *Otello*. As for Boccanegra and Warren, he said:

One can search high and low before finding such an overwhelming musical portrait as the principal figure in this opera. It is one of the great baritone roles, and last night it was entrusted to a great baritone, Leonard Warren. [He] made Boccanegra altogether his own, a vibrant, tragic, mesmerizing portrayal, sung with a voice that obeyed [his] every command. . . . *Boccanegra* is one of the season's most exciting artistic triumphs. Don't miss it!

Theodor Uppman's Memories

One Met artist who particularly appreciated that *Simon Boccanegra* was the young American baritone Theodor Uppman, a keen judge of voices. Uppman had first become a Warren fan as he listened to the Met broadcasts; he then met Warren in 1948 and again in the early 1950s in San Francisco. Joining the Met roster in November 1953, Uppman remained on it for twenty-five-years. Evaluating Warren's voice and career, Uppman said:

> I knew Warren, although not well, and I often heard him. What a gorgeous voice! He had a one-in-a-million voice. I loved it and was amazed by what tremendous breadth it had. In fact, he had a voice that could have gone either way, toward Italian opera or the German repertory. Although I didn't think he was all that great a musician, he certainly took his place in opera and kept it. He provided us with one of the finest baritone careers we have ever had.

Warren encouraged young Uppman, who was launching his own career. Uppman remembered an occasion when Warren gave him a pep talk:

> Once in 1953 or 1954, AGMA asked me to sing two or three arias in an open-air concert in Washington Square down in Greenwich Village. I was scheduled to do "Eri tu" from *Un ballo in maschera*, "Cortigiani" from *Rigoletto*, and "It Ain't Necessarily So" from *Porgy and Bess*. When I came out on the stage, I looked down and was stunned to see Warren, Larry Tibbett, and John Brownlee in the front row. Three of the Met's greatest baritones! Tibbett, who was the "father of AGMA," had obviously asked the other two to come. Well, I got through it, and afterward, all three came backstage. When I told Tibbett how frightened and ridiculous I had felt, he helped me by giving me very good advice. But Warren was the first person who stopped to see me. I spoke to him about my nerves; and he reassured me, then said, "Listen, kid, you're going to make it!"

✦ CHAPTER TWENTY-ONE

La forza del destino

As rehearsals for *La forza del destino* began, nothing seemed amiss with Warren, although some in the company understood that he had had a grueling year. He seemed in grand voice, but like other cast members, he was nervous. Sonya Haddad, Thomas Schippers's assistant, remembered hearing superstitious talk backstage during the rehearsals: "Everyone was uneasy and a bit apprehensive because someone circulated a story about an old curse on *Forza*, saying two singers and a conductor had died while performing it. Matters were further complicated because Tommy [Schippers] had an engagement to conduct the Montréal Symphony that week," Haddad said. "He was squeezing it in between Met rehearsals with singers and the orchestra. He was due back at the Met for the pre–dress rehearsal, but between one blizzard in Montréal and another in New York, with about fifteen inches of snow, he couldn't fly out of Montréal. There was a lot of tension."

Warren and Tucker had been called for rehearsal with Schippers at four on the afternoon of 4 March, the day of the performance. But Merle Hubbard recalled that when they got there, they were told that Schippers had just called to say he was still stuck in the blizzard.

> Expecting them both to blow up, I went down and met them at Winnie Short's desk by the stage door, and I said, "Excuse me, but we have bad news. Maestro Schippers is not back." To my surprise, Warren said, "Oh! I'm so sorry! Will he get here in time?" Then he turned to Tucker. "Ruby, what shall we do?" Tucker said, "Let's come early and run through the duets with Tommy then."

Schippers barely got there in time for the pre-curtain rehearsal.

Haddad said, "Tommy called the principals into his dressing room about an hour before the show to review several last-minute details, things he wanted to be sure about." She sat there during the brush-up session with the uneasy singers.

They were in varying states of stress, some in costume and some not yet dressed. Tebaldi seemed very nervous: it was the night of her return to the Met, and there was that horrible snow outside. She was still in mourning for her mother, and people felt she was very fragile. At that moment, Warren looked fine, but he was in bad humor, really grumpy, and his earlier outburst against the orchestra had not helped. Tucker seemed kind of quietly uncomfortable. No one was at ease. They didn't really argue with Tommy about anything, but you could feel that everyone was on edge. Tommy was aware of the delicate atmosphere, but he seemed pretty much together. The session ended with some of the tensions dispelled, and Tommy went down into the pit.

Barry Tucker remembered speaking to Warren just before the performance of *La forza del destino*:

I was backstage with my father before the opera. Leonard came over and started teasing me, saying I had wrecked his dinner party. He laughed and boomed out, "What right did you have to be born on my big day? You ruined my party!" Of course he was kidding. We joked together for a moment, then I said to him, "Go out there and give them a great show."

Hubbard said Warren "dressed on the third floor and came down early, saying hello to everyone."

Hines remembered the night vividly. He said:

I was in my dressing room during the first act of *Forza*. The opera began as scheduled, and I could hear it on the intercom. This occasion was Renata's return to the Met, and all her fans were there. When she first appeared onstage in Act I, the audience broke out in an unusually long and noisy ovation that lasted about four minutes. It brought the opera to a complete halt. After the tumult subsided, she and Tucker continued the first act without incident.

During this scene, Hines, who did not have to be onstage then because he was singing the Padre Guardiano of the monastery, was sitting at his mirror, putting the final touches on his makeup. "Suddenly the dressing room door opened, and Warren walked in, without even knocking. He was clearly upset about the ovation for Tebaldi. 'What are we doing here?' Warren asked. 'Why don't we just go home? There's no place for Americans here.'" He and Hines continued talking because neither was in the first scene. Later, Tucker came up from the stage and, seeing Hines's door open, came in. He, too, was upset about Tebaldi. "Hey, guys, why are we here?" he asked. Both Hines and Warren burst out laughing. They all joked together for a while, then went about their business. Hines said Warren seemed absolutely normal to him.

Nathaniel Merrill, who had taken over Ebert's *Macbeth* production, was also assigned *La forza del destino*. He was upstairs in the men's dressing room area during the performance on 4 March, he said.

> Angelo Casamassa, who was with the wardrobe department, always sat on that straight chair at the top of the stairs that led to the men's dressing rooms. That night when I made my usual rounds, Leonard was sitting on that chair, waiting to go onstage for the battle scene. He made a couple of jokes, then said, "Well, I guess they're not going to get around to me tonight." He seemed perfectly well. Then he went down to the stage, and his act began.

Felix Eyle, the manager of the orchestra, was the concertmaster that night, substituting for Raymond Gniewek. Eyle had long admired Warren for his "profound and unique artistry and the strength of his conviction in musical matters," and spoke with him just before both men went to work. In a letter to Agatha, written after Warren died, Eyle said they had discussed the baton box that Warren was about to buy as a gift for Pelletier. Then Eyle went to the pit as Warren prepared to sing. Martin Rich, a Met conductor, sent him onstage. Rich remembered that Warren had been away and had just come back. He said, "It was the first night of *Forza*. We were together in the wings. I said to Warren, 'Pay attention now,' as the moment for his entrance approached. Warren then stepped onstage." He and Tucker sang the duet; the onstage battle ensued; Don Alvaro, the character Tucker was playing, was wounded and then carried offstage. According to the libretto, the Surgeon was to attend to his wounds. Alone, Warren sang the recitative, "Morir! Tremenda cosa!" and the aria, "Urna fatale."

The closest witness to the onstage events that evening was Roald Reitan, the young singer cast for his first time as Chirurgo. Having just joined the Met roster, he had gotten to know Warren around the Opera House during rehearsals and productions because Reitan, the novice, had sung the Jailer in *Tosca* and the Gypsy in *Trovatore*. He said, "Warren and I had a nodding acquaintance, and we said hello to each other." Reitan was surprised that Warren was "not in good voice" at the dress rehearsal. On the night of the performance, though, he sang splendidly. As Reitan was getting ready to go onstage for his scene with Warren, he stood behind a piece of scenery, center stage, waiting for his cue. "I remember being backstage with Mignon Dunn. Warren sang 'Urna fatale' perfectly. In fact, I don't think he ever sang anything better. When the aria ended, I said to Mignon, 'He still has a lot to teach us!' She nodded." Then Reitan's cue came; he entered through what he called "some sort of portico or doorway" and stepped onstage.

He saw nothing wrong. Reitan recalled:

I walked right toward Warren and sang my line: "Lieta novella! È salvo!" [Good news! He is saved!] I got the whole line out. At that point Warren should have turned back to the conductor and sung his next line, but he didn't. He was still standing just to the left of center stage, facing me and staring at me. He had a very strange look on his face and was immobile. When he missed his cue, I thought he had forgotten his words. I didn't hear the prompter, so I was going to cue Warren or even sing the line for him, but his face was a blank; there was just no one there. He looked as if he had been struck by lightning. He took a couple of steps toward me and fell forward, straight down. He didn't crumple or try to save himself.

When he fell, I went downstage and knelt beside him. He mumbled something, maybe he said, "Help me!" Just a couple of sounds, maybe not even words. I didn't see any blood and had no idea what was wrong. I looked up, toward Schippers, and shouted "Curtain! Curtain!" Someone in the audience also yelled, "Bring down the curtain!" But it seemed like forever before the curtain came down. Osie Hawkins was the first one who ran out from the wings.

Several people remember Warren singing the words "È salvo! Oh, gioia!" just before he died. Among these were several critics and Sonya Haddad. Ralph Mead, who now lives in California, was also in the audience that night. His letter to the editor, published in the *New York Times* Arts and Leisure section on Sunday, 9 May 1999, confirmed that those were Warren's last words.

Just after Warren fell, the violinist Raymond Gniewek reached the stage by chance. He had not been called to play that performance, but he had come in because he had a date with a ballerina.

I came through the Fortieth Street stage door about the time I thought she should finish for the night, and I knew something was wrong because I couldn't hear any music. I walked right onto the stage. The curtain was down. Then I saw Warren lying there, with only a couple of people near him. I thought he had fainted. But within a few seconds, people were shouting and running in from all sides. It was shocking, so I stepped back into the wings.

William Crawford, who was then the general manager of the Festival of Two Worlds in Spoleto, was seated in the audience and had his opera glasses fixed on Warren during "Urna fatale" and kept them there as he waited for him to start the cabaletta. "I wanted to see how he tackled it, what his mouth looked like as he attacked the first phrase," he said. "Reitan was upstage. The orchestra played the ascending phrase leading to the beginning of the cabaletta, but Warren never opened his mouth. He fell, just as a pillar would. He gave no sign, made no gesture of any kind."

When Warren went down, Lucia Evangelista, Hines's wife, was in a box near the stage. With her was their physician, Arthur D'Alessandro. After Warren fell, D'Alessandro turned to her and, just from seeing Warren's fall, said, "He's dead." With Evangelista beside him, the physician rushed to Warren. They met Hines as he rushed down the stairs from his dressing room. He had heard the orchestra stop. Evangelista told him Warren had collapsed. Hines remembered the scene when they walked onto the stage: "He was lying where he had fallen. By that time, people were milling around. D'Alessandro and two or three doctors huddled over Warren. Tucker turned to me and muttered, 'There's a curse on this opera.' A few minutes later, Dr. D'Alessandro stepped over to us and said, 'He's gone.'"

Edgar Vincent had not intended to go to the Met that night even though Doris Pinza had urged him to do so several days earlier. "I hear there's an Italian cabal that is out to boo Americans," Doris had said. As it happened, she and Vincent met again on the morning of the *Forza*. He was going to work, and she had parked and was unloading packages from her car. Snow was knee-deep on the sidewalks, and many streets were blocked. As Vincent stopped beside her car, she repeated her warning, saying that a claque might cause a disturbance during Warren's scenes. "You must go and watch out for him." With that, he decided to do his duty. So it was that even in 1960, on the night Warren died, a claque threatened him. Alfred Hubay said the claqueur John De Luca had a pass to the Opera House for the *Forza*; he had hired his goons and also managed to get a seat at one of the score desks, which were reserved for students. "That night I had to keep an eye on De Luca, to see whether he was going to create a rumpus," Hubay said.

When Vincent left Warren backstage and went out into the audience to listen to the performance, he stood at the back of the House, feeling very pleased with Warren's singing. "When Warren got to 'Urna fatale,' he sang it very well," Vincent said. Then Warren fell. "At first I thought he had tripped, and I thought to myself how awkward he was. Then I saw Tucker come out from the wings, take one look, and retreat. When I saw Richard's face, I ran. It was chaos backstage."

Barry Tucker, who had sent Warren off with good wishes just as the opera was about to start, was sitting in an aisle seat next to his mother when Warren fell. He recalled:

The minute he went down, my mother said, "Something's wrong!" You could hear my father, who was in the wings, shouting, "Lenny! Lenny!" I jumped up, and just as the curtain was coming down, I saw Dad running over to Warren; then I ran backstage. Dad was white as a ghost and was trying to hold Leonard in his arms. Mother came a few minutes later. I never saw so many priests in my life.

In a 1965 interview for *Newsweek*, Richard Tucker said he had run out from
the wings, shouting, "My God! Lenny! Lenny! What is it?" Martinelli soon
joined the Tuckers. They all stepped back toward the wings.

   One priest who reached Warren's side almost immediately was the Right
Reverend Monsignor Edwin Broderick, now the retired Bishop of Albany.
He was then the secretary and master of ceremonies to Francis Cardinal Spell-
man. Bishop Broderick was also a close friend of the Warrens and a member
of the prestigious Metropolitan Opera Club. Broderick had met Leonard and
Agatha originally at a musical-social evening in the Park Avenue apartment of
Albanese and her husband, Joseph Gimma. Warren, Sayão, Albanese, and
Victoria de Los Angeles were rehearsing for a benefit concert. De Los Ange-
les had brought her guitar and entertained everyone by singing and playing.
On later occasions, Broderick was the Warrens' guest for lunch or dinner at
their home in Manhattan House. He also remembered Warren singing as
soloist at St. Vincent Ferrer Church for special concerts at Easter and Christmas. For that evening's *Forza*, he was sitting in the second row in a seat Maria
Jeritza had given him. Other priests from the Jeritzas' circle were in the Opera
Club box; among them were two other priests from St. Patrick's Cathedral,
Monsignor Terence Cooke, later a Cardinal, and Monsignor Patrick Ahern,
later a retired bishop. All were regulars at the Met, and they were the center
of the group of priests whom Barry Tucker saw backstage that night.

   Bishop Broderick said:

> Before Leonard fell, he took a couple of steps, and when he went
> down, my first thought was that he had sprained his ankle. Then the
> curtain came down. There was dead silence because the orchestra
> had stopped playing. I knew something had happened, so I left my
> seat and rushed through the backstage door.
>
>   I was one of the first people to reach the stage. When I walked on,
> several company members were standing around; some were bending
> over Leonard. Osie Hawkins and Tucker and Mignon Dunn were
> there, but Tebaldi was still in her dressing room. Agatha had not yet
> come down from her box. Bing rushed in and got down on one knee
> next to Leonard, then he looked at me and waved me off. "Step
> back," he said, but I did not; I bent down. Bing then spoke softly to
> me: "I think he's dead." At first I thought he had had a stroke, but at
> that moment he certainly seemed dead. I saw no sign of life at all. I
> gave Leonard conditional last rites, absolution, and a last blessing. I
> could not give him Extreme Unction, as the rite was called then
> because I did not have any chrism, any consecrated oil, with me. I
> went backstage then and telephoned to the Church of St. Francis of
> Assisi, asking one of the priests there to bring the oil. When he came,
> we completed the rite.

A member of the house staff went to get Roy to help Agatha. She had Warren's physician, William Goldring, an elderly man, as her guest in her box. They rushed downstairs together, although it took them several minutes to reach the stage. They joined the circle kneeling beside Warren. Later Agatha stepped back from where he was lying and let Evangelista put her arms around her. She clearly did not know that her husband was dead. One of the doctors then drew Agatha aside to tell her Warren was gone. Hines said she was "beyond consolation."

Nathaniel Merrill was watching from backstage when Warren died.

Leonard sang that long recitative that began "Morir! Tremenda cosa!" [To die! What a dire thing!] Then he went back to the table to sing the aria, "Urna fatale." At the end of it, he looked up for a moment, just when he discovered the miniature portrait of his dearest Leonora among Alvaro's possessions. He walked a few steps with it in his hand. Then he sang, "Heaven! Leonora! Don Alvaro is wounded! Now he is alive, and by my hand he shall die!" At that moment Reitan was coming in upstage to tell Carlo that Alvaro would recover from his wounds. Warren turned and moved upstage toward him and in a hoarse whisper pleaded, "Help me! Help me!" Reitan was shocked, but went on as rehearsed, announcing, "Good news! He is saved!" Warren turned and moved downstage toward Tommy Schippers and sang, "È salvo! È salvo! Oh, gioia!" The portrait fell from his hand and he pitched forward onto the floor about fifteen feet from the prompter's box. I felt he was dead as he hit the floor. From backstage and out front, there was a gasp. Tommy stopped the orchestra. Osie Hawkins rang down the curtain as he and I ran onstage. There was just no sign of life in Leonard. Osie and a couple of other staffers started mouth-to-mouth resuscitation while I ran to call for a doctor. Then I came back to help Osie. It was chaos. Bing ran in, and by that time, a priest and the doctors were beside him. Agatha, who still was unaware that Leonard was gone, sat with Bing and two other people on a bench and pieces of scenery upstage. Members of the chorus had come down from upstairs. A lot of them were Italians and Italian-Americans, and they were kneeling on the stage floor and praying, but Bing ordered me to send them away. "Get these people out of here," he said, although a couple of them were trying to console Agatha. It took about twenty minutes for the ambulance to get there; they came from St. Clare's Hospital, as I recall. But it was too late. Leonard was gone. I went to Bing and quietly suggested he take Agatha into the privacy of his office, while I went around asking the choristers and others to leave the stage so that Bing might go out before the curtain to announce that Leonard had passed away.

Sonya Haddad had taken her seat in the audience after seeing Schippers go to the pit and after chatting for a moment with the Tuckers, whom she knew. Speaking of the *Forza* performance, she said, "They came to the fatal scene. Warren was down from center stage. Reitan entered from upstage." Her recollection, like that of the critics who were in the theatre that night, differs from Reitan's account.

> After Reitan made his little announcement, Warren sang "È salvo! È salvo! Oh, gioia!" and fell forward. Reitan hesitated for a second, not knowing what to do; he then went over to Warren and knelt down and looked out toward the audience. He may have been looking at Tommy, and he had a very questioning look on his face and looked shocked. Several people in the audience gasped. Tommy was just standing there in the pit. The orchestra had already stopped playing. The curtain came down. Tommy said something to the concertmaster. I was sitting on the farthest left side of the orchestra, so I ran backstage, expecting to meet Tommy. Onstage, there may have been three people close to Warren and others standing nearby. I got to him just as they were opening his costume. Two men were kneeling over him. I was standing where the wings began at the edge of the stage. One man, a doctor, was pounding on Warren's chest with both fists, as hard as he could. I heard someone say, "They've called for oxygen," but by the time the oxygen arrived it was too late. No one moved Warren from that spot. The stage looked strange: the curtain was down and all the stage lights were on. The Tuckers were standing over toward the right of the stage, toward the back. Tucker was the color of chalk. Sara was with him, just standing, waiting. I noticed Tucker shaking his head back and forth.
>
> Mrs. Warren was standing left onstage, near me. Some people were with her. After the doctor pulled her aside and told her that Warren was dead, she was alone, and for a moment or two she seemed disoriented. She later stepped over to me, although I did not know her. She put her hand on my arm and said, with an incredulous tone, "Leonard isn't dead, is he?" I didn't know. He was still lying there. So I said to her, "Mrs. Warren, I know everyone is doing everything they can for your husband." She then said, "He can't be dead." Suddenly someone said, "Where's Schippers? Has anyone called him?" Tommy was still waiting for someone to tell him what had happened.

Adrian Zorgniotti, a Met house doctor, was in his usual seat on the orchestra level that night. He described the horror to Vera Giannini many years later, saying that Warren toppled over, "just like a falling tree." Dr. Zorgniotti ran backstage and "had to push aside Richard Tucker and everybody crowding around. Warren had already stopped breathing, and his heart was no longer beating." He said he injected adrenaline directly into the heart, but to no avail. At first it was widely reported in the press that Warren had died of a massive cerebral hemorrhage, but when Dr. Zorgniotti spoke to Giannini, he said the cause of death was "myocardial infarction." He found out later that Warren had high blood pressure and had been under enormous "emotional strain." Warren fell so hard that his nose bled.

After Warren fell, Bing went before the curtain to announce that the performance would continue after a substitute, Mario Sereni, arrived. Later, when physicians confirmed that Warren had died, Bing addressed the public again. Some in the audience gasped after his first sentence. "This is one of the saddest nights in the history of the Metropolitan Opera. May I ask you all to rise in memory of one of our greatest performers, who died in the middle of one of his greatest performances? I am sure you will agree with me that it would not be possible to continue with the performance." People filed out quietly. Sonya Haddad remembered the moment. "From backstage, with the curtain down, you couldn't hear much sound at all. At that point, Tommy ran onstage. Everyone was standing around. No one knew what to say. When the audience left, people didn't talk." After Warren's body was removed to a nearby dressing room, she and Schippers went back to the conductor's room. "We didn't know what to do. We just sat there quietly talking for a while; then we left the Opera House and went back to Tommy's apartment. Tommy was just shocked. He was terribly moved by the death, although he did not know Warren very well."

House Manager Reginald Tonry left his account of the evening in the stage manager's log, under the date "Friday, March 4, '60." His report reads:

Evening Show: "Forza del Destino."
About 9:55 PM Walter Price came into House Mgr. Office to say that Leonard Warren had collapsed on stage and doctor was on his way back there. I told Bob Gorman to bring doctor bag from 1st aid room and went to stage. I was notified that Doctor Zorgniotti wanted an ambulance urgently. Called Police Dpt. Asked for same. Then called Scully-Walton for private ambulance—none available. Then called Keefe and Keefe [Ambulance] who said in about 20 minutes. Went on stage to scene—found artificial mouth-to-mouth respiration (*sic*) being performed by Osie Hawkins—summoned Wm. McGowan to assist—went to phone J. Petrich for our oxygen set and mouth-to-mouth resuscitation. Then called police for oxygen. Returned to scene—Petrich responded—Dr. Zorgniotti said Mr. Warren was dead—Petrich responded (*sic*) & set up oxygen for a final try—Capt. Dreiss, who was passing, came in. Set up men to guard the stage & stage door—notified Mr. Hubay what all ushers should tell audience. No police oxygen yet. Called Fire Dpt. Dispatcher for nearest oxygen

but too far away to respond for 10 minutes. Police oxygen then came & went to work—also ambulance arrived. Warren pronounced dead about 10:20 P[M]. Body moved to Star room #15. Coroner [was] called—also brother-in-law of Mr. Warren called Abbey mortician. Coroner arrived. Released body. Police released possessions. Body removed about 11:30 PM. Mr. Warren's private physician Dr. Wm. Goldring, 1088 Park AT-9-1383. Police Emergency Squad #1 P[atrolman] Dowling, P[atrolman] White.
St. Clare's Hospital Amb[ulance]. Special assist from my force: A. Hubay, R. Gorman, Wm. McGowan, J. Petrich.
[signed] Reginald Tonry, 3/5/60.

After the coroner examined Warren's body in a dressing room, he released it. Representatives of the Abbey Funeral Home left with it through the Fortieth Street stage door and went to a waiting hearse. By that time, a large crowd of opera fans and other onlookers had gathered on the sidewalk. As the funeral home crew was making their final arrangements before pulling away, the hearse door was open. Warren's covered body was clearly visible. At that moment, a fan moved toward the vehicle, leaned through the door, and made a silent gesture of farewell. He tipped his hat.

Ceremonies for the Dead

The next day, Schippers, who had gone to bed at five in the morning, had to conduct the Saturday matinee broadcast. Sonya Haddad said that the weight of Warren's death had cast a pall over the entire Opera House. Before the opera began, Bing came before the curtain and spoke a few words in memory of Warren. He then asked everyone to rise. Haddad said, "People were so silent that no one listening to the broadcast would have known that the audience had risen to its feet. Then Tommy lifted his baton, and the orchestra played the prelude to the last act of *La traviata*."

The funeral services were arranged with the Warrens' parish, the Church of St. Vincent Ferrer, and Father Royal Gardner, a former priest whom Warren had known there, was summoned from Providence. Warren's body was taken to the Abbey Funeral Home, where he was dressed for burial in the regalia of his knighthood in the Equestrian Order of the Knights of the Holy Sepulchre, as he had told Agatha he wished to be. He lay wrapped in its symbols of everlasting life, and in his favorite colors of red and white. Seeing his regalia, some singers and Met staff thought it was part of an opera costume. Only later were they told that the cape represented his knighthood.

Over the weekend from Friday, when Warren died, until Monday, the day of his funeral, more than three thousand people passed through the Abbey Funeral Home for the viewing. Several hundred signed the register; most were professional colleagues from the United States and acquaintances from Italy. Among them was Bricktop, who had welcomed Warren and many of the world's celebrities to her cabaret in Rome. "Bricktop's" on the Via Veneto attracted tourists, film stars, writers, artists from the field of classical music, and jet-set celebrities. The proprietor was an African American singer, Ada Smith Du Conge, who had light skin, freckles, and red hair, hence her nickname. A native of West Virginia, she had worked in Black vaudeville before opening her first "Bricktop's" in Paris. William Weaver, remembering visits to her cabaret in Rome, felt she had met Warren when he was recording in Italy.

The first of Warren's Metropolitan Opera colleagues to sign was the tenor Eugene Conley. Among scores of other mourners who followed were Rudolf Bing, Schuyler Chapin, John Gutman, Nicholas Massue, Giuseppe Bamboschek, Licia Albanese and Joseph Gimma, Lorenzo Alvary, Dolores Wilson, Mario Sereni, Cesare Sodero Jr., William Tarrasch, Milford Snell, Giorgio Tozzi, Rose Bampton Pelletier, Charles Kullman, Giovanni Martinelli, Ettore Panizza, Richard and Sara Tucker, and Thelma Votipka. Many members of the Metropolitan Opera chorus also signed, as did stage directors, stagehands, and makeup artists. The directors and officers of the Metropolitan Opera Guild also came to the Abbey. Dozens of priests and nuns added their names; among them were Jesuits from Fordham University, the Dominicans Warren knew from St. Vincent Ferrer, and members of other orders and priests from other parishes in the city. Several nuns of Agatha's aunt's teaching order from the Convent of St. Bernadette on Eighty-third Street in Brooklyn paid respects, as did all the members of the choir of St. Vincent Ferrer. The singers from the choir had come to say goodbye to a colleague, the man who had stood up with them for Midnight Mass on Christmas Eve and sung with them, not as a star but as a member of the congregation. The New York *Journal-American* sent a reporter to check on the line waiting to get into the Abbey. It stretched for more than a half-block, in deep snow, with the temperature below freezing.

Several hundred telegrams also came. Although Agatha had announced in the newspapers that flowers should not be sent, floral arrangements were delivered from the Tuckers, Margaret Truman Daniel, Leinsdorf, the Sol Hurok organization, the administrators of Lincoln Center for the Performing Arts, and several officers of the Metropolitan Opera and the Metropolitan Opera Guild. At her request, Masses were offered for her husband, and a Leonard Warren Fund was established in his memory at the Guild; contributions to it poured in from all over the country. Many came from colleagues in New York, dozens from opera-lovers who had seen him only in concert, and others from those who knew his voice only through the Saturday afternoon broadcasts. The largest single donation was from Doris Pinza, Ezio Pinza's widow; among many other contributors were Jan and Alice Peerce, Robert Merrill, Willard Sektberg, Alice Tully, George Cehanovsky, Lucrezia Bori, Metropolitan Opera board members, and the directors of AGMA, the singers' union. From Seattle, Solomon Warenoff sent his contribution to the fund with a note that read, "In memory of my son, Leonard, who lived and died for opera." By that time, the estrangement between Warren and his father had endured for many years. Nonetheless, Solomon Warenoff was among the first to send his contribution.

In the many expressions of condolence and notes enclosing contributions from members of the opera and concert audience across the country, there were truly moving letters in which people described their impressions of Warren as an artist and a man. The power of his character when he sang in concerts and recitals had left many listeners feeling that they knew him personally, and several remarked in their letters on how accessible and friendly he was during and after these events. Evidently, Warren without "false hair and costumes," as one writer said, deeply affected those who saw him in these settings. Among the dozens of Mass cards, most were destined for St. Vincent Ferrer, but other services were said for his soul at the Jesuit Seminary in Boston and Franciscan monasteries in Chicago and Wichita Falls. The chaplain of the Italian Line ship *Cristoforo Colombo* said Mass for Warren on shipboard. In Rome, a Mass was offered at the church of Sant'Onofrio on the Janiculum Hill and was attended by the knights and ladies who made up the Roman contingent of the Knights of the Equestrian Order of the Holy Sepulchre in Jerusalem.

The Funeral Mass

Warren's funeral service was held at the Church of St. Vincent Ferrer at ten in the morning on 7 March. The Low Mass was said by Warren's close friend and confessor, Father Royal Gardner, the baritone's much loved "Father Roy." He described the morning.

> I was called to their apartment just after Leonard died. Agatha was in shock. Roy was afraid she would not be able to cope with the funeral. He asked whether she could enter the church to the side of the nave and walk down the side aisle to her seat. We asked the curate and got permission. But she did not want to do that. She said, "I'm not going to sneak into church." And she got her way. She followed Leonard's coffin right down the center aisle. The church was packed full, absolutely full.

Father Gardner added, "Agatha didn't want either flowers or music. And I didn't deliver any sermon or homily. It was a very simple service."

More than a thousand people came for the ceremony, and the first of them was Bing; he was followed by Robert Herman and others from the Met management team; Eleanor Robson Belmont, the founder of the Metropolitan Opera Guild; Milanov, Albanese, Thebom, Robert Merrill, Richard and Sara Tucker, the Peerces, the Clevas, Martinelli, Jerome Hines and Lucia,

Munsel, Steber, Swarthout, Brownlee, Osie Hawkins, Mario Sereni, dozens of other leading singers, members of the chorus, orchestra, and stage staff, and a contingent from RCA Victor, headed by Marek. Agatha, sitting in the first row, sobbed uncontrollably throughout the ceremony. Across the aisle was Robert Merrill. He recalled the funeral, adding a light touch. "I was sitting with Jan Peerce, there we were, two Jews, right up front. Here came this priest spraying Holy Water all over us! Peerce caught my eye and said, 'Look at that!' I looked down the row and saw Martin Warenoff, Leonard's brother, who was also a Jew. He was also looking very uneasy." Father Gardner laughed in our interview when I told him what Merrill had said. "It's true I tend to sprinkle a lot of Holy Water. They probably thought, 'He's trying to get us!'" After the rite, Warren was buried beside his in-laws in the Leifflen family plot in St. Mary's Cemetery in Greenwich, Connecticut.

Soon after Warren died, Richard Tucker turned on reporters who came to interview him and told them how bad he felt about the short shrift they had given his colleague. During one interview he railed, "[You] wanted me to say something about Lenny. What do you want to write about him now? Did any of you ever take him out for coffee when he was living? Did any of you give him the honor he deserved? He was the greatest baritone in America, and you took him for granted!'"

After her husband's death, Agatha remained for a while in their large apartment in Manhattan House, while her brother continued to keep his room there. She also kept the house in Connecticut. Later she moved to smaller quarters in Manhattan House, with Roy still a regular visitor. In seclusion for months, she was comforted by him, Vivien, and the priests who had been closest to her and her husband. Blanche Thebom, a close friend who called soon after Warren died, wanted Agatha to go to Japan with her, but Agatha, still in shock, declined. Years passed before she would allow anyone to play Warren's records in her hearing, Vivien said, and if anyone spoke while his records were playing, Agatha reprimanded them sharply. She lived with her grief, but Thebom, whose friendship with Agatha dated back about sixteen years, had the courage to say what many people were feeling: "God was really kind to take Leonard the way He did. If He was going to take him, how good it was that he died at that moment. Leonard had a perfect life, and that was the perfect way to die." As Rudolf Bing observed, "He left this world at the peak of his career in the middle of one of his triumphant performances, without a moment of fear or suffering."

In every real sense, Warren died at home because he died in the Metropolitan Opera House. Once, in an interview, he had said of the Met, "This is my home. This is where I live." Gradually it became a kind of mantra for him, so he died right, in the place where he lived his life and walked his professional road. In that house, the Metropolitan Opera House, his house, Warren's life, career, and even his death became a true celebration of the artist's very being.

Notes

The research material used for this book is primarily in three major collections. The first two, the Vivien Warren Collection and the Solomon Warenoff Collection, now belong to Edward Warren Haber, Vivien's grandson. During her lifetime Vivien Warren kept her private collection in her apartment in New York City. It included the Warenoff and Kantor family photographs and documents; the Warenoffs' Jewish prayer books; the Leifflens' Catholic missals; Leonard Warenoff's (Warren's) earliest contract for a season in the Catskills; scores belonging to Warren and to Roy Leifflen and Agatha Leifflen Warren; books; photographs, snapshots, undeveloped film negatives; programs; typed correspondence and a few handwritten notes; memorabilia; Warren's calendar pages from 1959 and 1960; Agatha's list of his opera performances; a record of Warren's recordings; many private and commercial recordings on disks and tape and videocassettes; and several hundred clippings. The second collection, which consisted of about a hundred items, belonged to Solomon Warenoff, the father of Leonard, Martin, and Vivien. After he died in Seattle in November 1965, this collection was sent to Vivien in its plastic folder. She said she had never opened it before she and I examined its contents in 1997.

The third source is the large Leonard Warren Collection in the Special Collections of the Music Division of the New York Public Library for the Performing Arts. As of this writing, it has not been catalogued. It includes thousands of clippings from North and South America, Mexico, and Europe; scrapbooks; photographs and snapshots; correspondence; programs, press releases, and publicity flyers from Warren's management agencies and RCA Victor; the register from the Abbey Funeral Home; telegrams and letters sent to Agatha Warren after her husband died; records of contributions to the memorial fund established in Leonard Warren's name and administered by the Metropolitan Opera Guild; and much personal memorabilia. In addition to material in this collection, I used the Clipping Files in the Music Division of the New York Public Library for the Performing Arts.

In all these collections, many clippings are badly damaged. A few are in shreds. Some lack the publication's name, some the date. In the worst cases, all identifying information is lacking. Then I used the text of the clipping to try to identify the source. In every case, I have given whatever information can be obtained from the headings, the text itself, or notes written on it.

This biography also draws extensively on interviews. A list of the most important published interviews with Warren appears in the bibliography, which also lists author interviews. Unless described otherwise, quotations in the text are from interviews I conducted for this book.

Chapter One

Much information on the Chaitians, Bobrows, Voronovs/Warenoffs, and Kantors came from my interviews with Vivien Warren and Ethel Bobrow Altschuler and from prayer books, documents, and photographs in Vivien's collection. Most New York vital records (births, marriages, and deaths) are found in family prayer books and in the New York City Municipal Archives on Chambers Street. I used immigration records, ship passenger lists, city directories, and the Federal Census of 1900, 1910, and 1920 in the National Archives Northeastern Division on Varick Street in New York City. The New York Public Library Map Division has *Bromley's 1902 Atlas of New York City* and many real estate records, including those with the description of the Kantor house on Spring Street and the house where the Chaitians and Sol Warenoff lived on the Lower East Side. The general collection of the New York Public Library also has city directories of Manhattan, the Bronx, and Brooklyn that could not be found in the National Archives. Its map collection includes the German and Russian gazetteers.

The *Social Security Death Index* and the *Jewish Family History Information Exchange* volumes in the Mormon Family History Center in New York City contain references to families that emigrated to the United States from the Warenoffs' and Kantors' places of origin. Other information on Russia came from *The Russian Encyclopedia* and other reference books that include the history of Sklov, Mohilew (Mahilev/Mogiljov), Vitebsk, Orsha (Orsa), Ukraine, and Kiev. I also used a modern guide to these regions, *Russia, With Chapters on Ukraine and Belarus*, edited by Anna Benn, from the Insight Guide series. Hans Kohn's *Revolutions and Dictatorships* (p. 301) and his chapters on the Russian Revolution and Zionism (pp. 85 ff. and 299 ff.) were a source for my general remarks on the intellectual history of Russia and the condition of Russian Jews in the nineteenth century.

Ronald Sanders's book *The Lower East Side* (pp. 30–39 and 45–49) was the source of specific information on the sites and institutions in that area. Vivien Warren and I visited the house where her father lived in 1900, the Forsyth Street Synagogue, and other buildings in the neighborhood on one of our day trips to the Lower East Side. Jan Peerce's remarks on the Lower East Side are in *The Bluebird of Happiness* (pp. 13–32). Robert Merrill also spoke of his early life in an interview for this book.

Chapter Two

The birth certificates of the Warenoff children and the death certificates of David Kantor and Brina Kantor are on microfilm in the New York City Department of Records and Information Services, Municipal Archives, Chambers Street, and in the Mount

Zion Cemetery archives. Vivien Warren also had Leonard Warren's birth certificate. Solomon Warenoff's "Doing Business As" declaration was provided to the Leonard Warren Foundation by Joel Honig. Solomon Warenoff's New York State Militia enrollment notice is in Vivien Warren's collection. In interviews Warren often spoke of the early years of his life, particularly between his high school years and his first engagement at Radio City Music Hall. One of the most detailed of these was given to Hazel Canning of the Boston *Sunday Post* and published on 8 May 1938. It seems to be the earliest of all Warren's interviews. The *Etude* magazine profile by Rose Heylbut appeared in March 1949. Warren's interview for *Parade Magazine* of 15 June 1958 (the interviewer is not identified) is in the Leonard Warren Collection at the Library for the Performing Arts. Harold C. Schonberg's profile appeared on 25 October 1959 in the *New York Times* and in *Facing the Music* (pp. 268–275).

Chapter Three

Diane Joust, archivist of Radio City Music Hall, made available the profile of Vin Lindhe in *Radio City Music Hall Program Magazine*, the program book for *The Good Fairy*, January 1935 (pp. 4, 20); profiles of Viola Philo in undated drafts of articles for the *Radio City Music Hall Program Magazine*; an unpublished file of biographical notes on Viola Philo from the Columbia Broadcasting System, Inc., and the Columbia Artists Bureau, Inc., 1935 biography file; the complete record of the opening-night production, including the *Carmen* excerpts and Titta Ruffo's role of Escamillo; and information on Rapee and Leon Leonidoff. The record of Philo's and Eustis's engagements at the Metropolitan Opera are found in the *Annals of the Metropolitan Opera*. Philo's appearances there are also mentioned in her Radio City and Columbia Artists Bureau files, which are also in the Music Hall Archives. I interviewed John De Merchant, several times by telephone to Seattle, about his and Warren's experiences in the Music Hall Glee Club.

According to the entry for Philo Judaeus in *Encyclopedia Britannica*, Philo was not a king but "a Greek-speaking Jewish philosopher and theologian." As James B. McPherson notes, at the time of Philo's birth, c. 10–20 B.C., Egypt had no king; it became a Roman province after Cleopatra's death in 30 B.C.

Warren's copy of Irving Kolodin's *The Story of the Metropolitan Opera 1883–1950* and the WOR Artists Bureau contract for Warren's engagement in the Catskills are in Vivien Warren's collection. Alf Evers's *The Catskills from Wilderness to Woodstock* (passim) was the source of historical material on that region. Again, Jan Peerce's *The Bluebird of Happiness* includes information about his own early work in the Catskills (pp. 54–56) and his career at Radio City Music Hall (pp. 52 ff.).

In the Clipping Files of the Music Division of the New York Public Library for the Performing Arts at Lincoln Center are the National Broadcasting Company's press release about Warren's first broadcast with that network; the announcement of the Sealtest Rising Musical Stars competition; and the Columbia Concerts public relations director's interview. Vivien Warren kept her brother's earliest private studio recordings and recordings of his first broadcasts. Daniel Hladik made these available to me on cassette. Arge Keller sent me a cassette that included Deems Taylor's (undated) interview with Warren and several songs. William P. Ainsworth's letter of 29 January 1939 about placing Warren on the Magic Key program is in the Metropolitan Opera Archives. In the Leonard Warren Collection in the New York Public Library for the Performing Arts are W. G. Rogers's Associated Press interview, which appeared in many newspapers in 1957; Warren's interview for UPI's Fred Danzig, which was published in an undated UPI article from autumn 1958. Rose Heylbut's interview with Warren (mentioned above) was conducted in 1947 or 1948 and published in *Etude* in March 1949, together with the magazine editor's own short article about Warren's career.

Chapter Four

Many personal recollections in this chapter were drawn from interviews I did in 1997 and 1998 in person and by telephone. Wilfrid Pelletier's recollections of this period are found in *Une symphonie inachevée* (pp. 118–121 and 173–175). My copy is a gift from Rose Bampton Pelletier, whom I first met backstage at the Cincinnati Summer Opera when I was in high school. She filled in many gaps in my knowledge of this period. Gatti-Casazza described his method of conducting auditions in *Memories of the Opera* (pp. 101–103). Mary Ellis Peltz's first interview with the Warrens took place less than a year after they married. It was published in *Opera News* on 23 November 1942. Warren's most consistent account of his first audition for Pelletier appeared in Jay S. Harrison's New York *Herald Tribune* interview on 31 March 1957. Again, I also used Warren's taped interview with Deems Taylor. Pierre V. R. Key's special dispatch about the Auditions of the Air was printed in the Dallas *News*; the clipping, lacking a date, is in the Leonard Warren Collection in the New York Public Library for the Performing Arts, together with other documents relating to the Auditions of the Air. A mixed review of Warren appeared in the New York *Evening Post* on 28 March 1938, in Aaron Stein's review of the Auditions of the Air winners. Warren was faulted for overacting and "stressing comedy at the cost of the music, producing two moments that marred an otherwise notable performance." The NBC press release about the Auditions of the Air and Danton Walker's column from the New York *Daily News* are in Vivien's collection. Emil R. Pinta sent his unpublished essay on the Auditions of the Air to Barrett Crawford, president of the Leonard Warren Foundation. Mr. Pinta gave permission for its use in this book. Robert Tuggle, director of the Metropolitan Opera Archives, discovered much original correspondence, the original programs of the 1937–1938 Auditions of the Air, a draft of the script for the program of 27 March, and an angry letter from a listener in California who protested Carter's award.

Chapter Five

Warren's letter to his family, his postcard from Venice, and George A. Martin's letter to him, written on the Sherwin-Williams Company letterhead, are in Vivien Warren's collection. Other George Martin correspondence, including the letter of 5 October 1938 to Warren, is in the Metropolitan Opera Archives. Byron Warner's budget for the stay in Italy (of nearly five months) is also there, inserted into the Warren page of the Metropolitan Opera Paybook for 1938. Warren's recollections of his first visit to Genoa are from Frances J. Freeman's interview with him, "Boccanegra from Pirate to Prince," in *Opera News*, 23 January 1950. Florence and Ralph Postiglione assisted with much of the research about Lake Como, with the help of Count Pietro Giusti and the staff of the Pro Loco in the city of Como.

Leonard Warren's letters of 1938 to Edward Ziegler are also in the Met's archives. Byron Warner's letter to Marino Villa and a carbon copy of the Italian Line's letter of 23 August 1938 to Warren belong to Arge Keller. He also has Warren's *Saturnia* ticket for stateroom 459 and his receipt for a "high season" supplemental payment for the voyage. Other data on the Metropolitan Opera in the 1930s are found in

Quaintance Eaton's *The Miracle of the Met* (pp. 240–311) and in *The Annals of the Metropolitan Opera* (by year). The casts of Rose Bampton's 1938 engagements in Cincinnati are found in Eldred A. Thierstein's *Cincinnati Opera* (by year).

The description of the Milan Warren knew is found in *Milano*, an architectural history of the city by A. Calderini and R. Paribeni, in the chapter "Milano nello stato italiano" (pp. 215 ff). In the same authors' *Milano, notizie utili al turista*, the Pensione Agostini at l Galleria del Corso is also listed. The building in Galleria del Corso was a landmark before World War II; with its nine stories it was one of Milan's tallest modern buildings in the era before the Pirelli Company skyscraper was built. Several other important modern buildings in the center of the city had either just been built or were in construction when Warren arrived in Milan in 1938. Other information comes from Warren's letters.

Margaret Dempsey's interview with Agatha Leifflen Warren was published in the Baltimore *Sun* on 22 March 1949. Warren's interview with Sidney Fields was published in his column, "Only Human," in the New York *Daily Mirror* on 20 January 1956. This was in Warren's father's collection, together with dozens of other items from San Francisco, New York, Boston, and far-flung places. Licia Albanese contributed information on Picozzi and her studies with other teachers in Milan. Professor William Appleton kindly contributed his recollections of the Leifflen household in Brooklyn for this book. His teacher-to-student relationship with Warren, when the baritone was studying Verdi's Shakespearean operas and Victor Hugo's *Le roi s'amuse*, is described in greater detail in later chapters.

Chapter Six

Much information in this chapter comes from interviews with William Appleton, Therman Bailey, Rose Bampton, Margaret Carson, Louis J. Snyder, William Mayo Sullivan, and Vivien Warren. Nino Pantano assisted with research on the Leifflens' residence and parish church in Brooklyn Heights and the Convent of St. Bernadette.

Leonard Warren's Metropolitan Opera Association contracts and paybook entries are in the Metropolitan Opera Archives, together with other artists' salary and tenure data that appear in this chapter. Quaintance Eaton's *The Miracle of the Met* (pp. 256–257) is the source for the summarized history of the founding of AGMA, the American Guild of Musical Artists, and for some of the biographical information on Frank St. Leger (pp. 277 ff.) and his position at the Metropolitan. Peter G. Davis's book *The American Opera Singer* describes "Johnson's Babies: I" in chapter 19. It includes specific information on Warren (pp. 318–321). Jerome Hines's remarks about Weede are in Weinstat and Wechsler's *Dear Rogue* (p. 184); see also pp. 166–179. The reviews are quoted in that book.

Francis D. Perkins's reviews appeared in the New York *Herald Tribune* on 28 November 1938, in an undated clipping, and on 14 January 1939, identified by a handwritten note "F.D.P." on a review of *Simon Boccanegra*. Paul Jackson's *Saturday Afternoons at the Old Met* mentions Warren's Paolo in the Saturday afternoon *Simon Boccanegra* (pp. 197–198). Olin Downes's review of *Boris Godunov* appeared in the *New York Times* on 8 March 1939.

Information on the *Petite messe solennelle* is found in reviews, Barrett Crawford's discography for this book, and documents from the archives of the New York Philharmonic. Deems Taylor's piece on the Rossini work appeared in the *New York Times* on 10 April 1939.

Chapter Seven

I interviewed John S. White in 1997 and Licia Albanese in 1998. I interviewed Rose Bampton Pelletier many times in person and by telephone. Olin Downes's review of "Edward" Warren in *Boccanegra* appeared in the *New York Times* on 28 November 1939. Also of that date is the review in the *Sun*. John Rhodes's review of *Aida* appeared in the Cincinnati *Enquirer* of 2 July 1940. The reviews from Puerto Rico by José A. Balseiro ran in *El Mundo* (30 September and 3 October 1940). A feature article and photograph ran on 26 September. Dwight W. Hiestand's reviews appeared in the *World Journal* (27 and 30 September and 2 October). All are in the Leonard Warren Collection.

Paul Jackson's *Saturday Afternoons at the Old Met* has reviews of the broadcasts of *Simon Boccanegra* and *Boris* (pp. 197–198), *Lohengrin* (pp. 161 and 268–269), *Faust* (p.198) *Carmen* (pp. 252–253 and 281–282). The student performance *Carmen* reviews appeared on 19 December 1940. The *Faust* reviews appeared on 26 and 27 December 1940. *Cavalleria rusticana* was reviewed on 10 January 1941. Reviews of *Alceste* followed on 25 January in all papers. Walter Terry's piece was published in the *Herald Tribune* on 30 January. *Lohengrin* was reviewed on 4 January, again after the performance of 13 January, and, with Flagstad as Elsa, on 24 February. Warren's recollections of the *Lohengrin* rehearsals are from an unidentified clipping in the Clipping Files of the New York Public Library for the Performing Arts. Again, material on Tibbett's problems comes from *Dear Rogue* (pp. 159–179). Barrett Crawford sent me a photocopy of the cover and Irving Kolodin's notes to the Treasury of Immortal Performances recording entitled *Critic's Choice*.

For further information on the World's Greatest Operas series, see the introduction to Barrett Crawford's discography for this book.

Chapter Eight

The Cleveland *News* interview has neither the date nor the reporter's name, but it comes from the summer of 1940. The San Antonio *Express* piece is dated 14 November 1940. The San Antonio *Evening News* article says "November" and has no date, although it was filed with 1940 material; the writer was Mary Louise Walliser. The Keene, New Hampshire, piece, "Start of Winter Series," has neither the name of the paper nor the date. In May 1941 Warren sang in New Jersey, in the very modest Montclair High School Student Singer Auditions and Glee Club concert. The Newark, New Jersey, concert review was written by Louis Biancolli and the New York *World-Telegram* of 18 June 1941. Warren also sang on the "Ford Summer Hour" on 6 July 1941, with soprano Joan Edwards, Percy Faith conducting. Wilfrid Pelletier's *Une symphonie inachevée* and Rose Bampton's accounts in personal and telephone interviews are among my sources for the Montréal opera season. The Canadian reviews, some undated and one without the newspaper's name, are identifiable from Pelletier's remarks about that series. The Montréal *Gazette* reviewed *Carmen* on 1 October 1941.

Warren's spring concert tour in 1941 took him to Chillicothe and Akron, Ohio. His autumn concert tour that year took him to Sherbrooke, Québec, where he was reviewed in the *Daily Record* on 14 October 1941; Norfolk, Virginia, with a review on 23 October in the *Ledger*; and Battle Creek, Michigan, with a review in the *Enquirer News* on 28 October. In Cheyenne, Wyoming, he got reviews in the *State Leader* and the *Eagle* on 1 November; the Lincoln, Nebraska, *Journal* is dated 3 November; the Ottawa, Kansas, paper has neither date nor name. Documents relating to Warren's USO concerts, broadcasts, citations, and other wartime activities are in Vivien's collection. Angel Armada's recollections of Warren's USO tours in Puerto Rico were sent to Barrett Crawford by Jesús M. López. I used Walfredo Toscanini's original house program of the American Red Cross Concert. William Albright's essay "Milanov on Disc" appeared in Volume 7, Number 1, of *The Opera Quarterly* (pp. 148–149). Articles in the Leonard Warren Collection about the Toscanini concert are dated 13 and 26 May 1944.

Peter G. Davis's remarks on Risë Stevens are in *The American Opera Singer* (pp. 383–388). The first *Samson* reviews appeared on 4 December 1941; Robert Lawrence's review, dated 8 February 1942, is from an unidentified clipping in the Leonard Warren Collection in the New York Library for the Performing Arts. The reviews of the student performance *Aida* are from the *Herald Tribune*, the *World-Telegram*, and the New York *Post*, all of 13 December 1941. Martin Warenoff's letter to his father about Warren's first Met Germont in *Traviata* is in the Solomon Warenoff papers in Vivien Warren's collection. The "fourth *Traviata* of the season" was reviewed on 15 January 1942. The *Carmen* reviews are from 26 January. The excellent review of *Carmen* in the Baltimore *Sun* appeared on 18 March 1942. Reviews of *The Island God* appeared in the New York papers on 3 March 1942. Licia Albanese, another artist whom I first met in Cincinnati in the 1940s, was interviewed in 1997 for this book. Margaret Carson, whom I first met in 1947, provided information on Warren's early career and on Frank St. Leger's role in launching him.

Chapter Nine

All documents from the archives of the Church of St. Charles Borromeo were provided by the Rev. Charles Kraus, parish priest at the Church. The civil affidavit, marriage license, and certificate are in Vivien Warren's collection. Nino Pantano, the Brooklyn historian and writer, provided information about the church itself and the Leifflens' home on Willow Street. Vivien Warren, Marylin Noble Tracy, and William Appleton also contributed their recollections of many meetings with Warren and the Leifflens. My interviews with Roberta Peters, Robert Merrill, Risë Stevens, and Jerome Hines took place in 1998. The Canadian interview with Warren was published in the *Kitchener Record* on 10 January 1947. Warren returned to Kitchener often. His last concert there was in the year of his death. Mary Ellis Peltz's interview was published in *Opera News* on 24 November 1942 and later in *Spotlights on the Stars*. Her next interview with him was published in *Opera News* on 8 April 1946.

Chapter Ten

Vivien Warren's remarks about her brother's help to his family are from one of my interviews with her. Roy Leifflen's description of Warren's character appears in the letter to Professor Louis R. Thomas mentioned in chapter nine. The records of Warren's South American career include Erich Engel's letter to Edward Ziegler, dated 11 November 1940, and Ziegler's answer, dated 18 November 1940, both in the Metropolitan Opera Archives. Warren's first-person account of his and Agatha's first flight to Buenos Aires is in *New Horizons*, January–March 1945, a clipping that is found only in Solomon Warenoff's collection. Warren's 3 July 1942 letter and Irene Jessner's letter of 12 September, both sent from Buenos Aires to Edward Johnson, are in the Metropolitan Opera Archives. All South American reviews quoted in this chapter are in the Leonard Warren Collection in the New York Public Library for the Performing Arts. They include those from Buenos Aires newspapers: *Aida* reviews of 30 May 1942;

Boccanegra of 13 June and 26 June; and *Ballo* of 22 July. Translations were sent regularly from Conciertos Daniel to André Mertens of Columbia Concerts, Inc., during Warren's season there. Delia Rigal's interview with Horacio Molina, an attorney in Buenos Aires, contributed further information about this season. The reviews from Rio are only of *Boccanegra*, reviewed on 15, 16, and 18 August. On 10 September 1942 the Toledo, Ohio, *Blade* carried a long feature story by Allen Haden on Warren's success in South America. A special report went to the Chicago *Daily News* and was printed on 18 September. Columbia Concerts sent out a long press release on 9 October 1942.

Chapter Eleven

Paul Jackson's remarks are from *Saturday Afternoons at the Old Met* (pp. 283, *Carmen*; pp. 361–362, *Pagliacci*). The newspaper that carried Cecil Smith's review of the Chicago *Traviata* is not identified, but it is perhaps the *Herald-American*. The South American reviews were published on 12 and 13 June (*Rigoletto*) and 23 and 26 June (*Falstaff*) 1943. The feature story about Agatha Warren donating her husband's *Rigoletto* bauble to Gordon Eby appeared in the Lancaster, Pennsylvania, *Intelligencer Journal* of 2 March 1964. It is in Vivien Warren's collection. The bad reviews of *Traviata* appeared in Rio on 11 and 14 September 1943. *Time*'s "Yankee Invasion," featuring photographs of Traubel and Warren, appeared on 30 August 1943. The San Francisco *Samson* reviews are dated 8 and 12 October. *Forza* was reviewed four days later and again on 18 October; *Lucia* was reviewed on 19 October 1943. The Colorado Springs concert was reviewed on 10 November.

The Met season reviews began with those by Henry Simon in the much-lamented *P.M.* on 26 November and 26 December 1943 and 19 January 1944. The *Ballo* and *Rigoletto* reviews are dated 18 and 19 December 1943. *Pagliacci* was reviewed on 26 December. Jackson's report on *Pagliacci* appears in *Saturday Afternoons at the Old Met* (pp. 361–362). *The Wall Street Journal* article on Warren appeared on 28 December 1943. *Trovatore* was reviewed on 26 February 1944 and *Falstaff* on 12 March. The *Time* profile entitled "Ample Leonard" was published on 20 March.

Claudia Cassidy's important article appeared in the Chicago *Sunday Tribune* on 12 November. Warren's Associated Press interview with John Selby is dated 8 July. *Film Daily* published a piece about Warren on 6 October 1944. Margery Fisher's undated article about Warren in San Francisco does not name the newspaper. The 27 September 1945 letter from André Mertens to Frank St. Leger about Warren's choice of roles is in the Metropolitan Opera Archives.

Chapter Twelve

The interview with Agatha Warren in the newspaper *Greenwich Time* appeared on 19 July 1946, while Warren was in South America. My interviews with Margaret Carson, Blanche Thebom, Patrice Munsel, Tina Appleton Bishop, Henry Kaston, Marylin Noble Tracy, Alan Coleridge, and Vivien Warren were done in 1996, 1997, and 1998. My first interview with Warren was published in *Opera News* and then reprinted in *Stars in the Sun* (pp. 298–301).

Chapter Thirteen

The letter from André Mertens to Edward Johnson setting forth Warren's terms for the 1946–1947 season is dated 17 October 1946; it is in the Met's archives. Louis Biancolli reviewed Warren's Iago in the *World-Telegram* on 17 November 1946. This chapter includes excerpts from my interview with Anders Björling and interviews Warren gave to Mary Ellis Peltz for the *Opera News* of 22 March 1948 and to Clarence Newman. Newman's profile, "Operatic Singing is a Rugged Career," appeared in the Fort Wayne, Indiana, *News-Sentinel* of 6 May 1948. Also included are remarks from my interviews with Louis Snyder, Giorgio Tozzi, Margaret Carson, Alfred Hubay, and Anthony and Yolanda Stivanello about the old Met and the claque. Branches of the Met claque also functioned in many American regional companies, large and small, under the direction of Max Bennett and John De Luca and their henchmen, who organized the applause and often sold librettos.

The reviews of *Aida* appeared on 19 November 1946. William Appleton discussed his sessions with Warren on *Otello. Rigoletto* was reviewed by Irving Kolodin and other critics on 8 February 1947. The information about Samuel Barber's audition for De Luca is from my personal interview with Gian Carlo Menotti in the Hotel Carlyle in New York City in November 1993. Alfred Hubay recalled Warren's sessions with Giuseppe De Luca. The anecdote about De Luca catching the sand shark appeared in the *Twin City Sentinel* in Winston-Salem, North Carolina, on 1 October 1953.

John Rosenfield's article in the *Dallas Morning News* appeared on 10 January 1948, covering the "sensational" 8 January performance of *Ballo*. The New York critics originally reviewed the opera on 11 November. Olin Downes's "Retrospect of the Season" appeared in the *New York Times* on 31 March 1948. John Ball's review of *Rigoletto* was printed in the *Brooklyn Eagle* on 25 February 1948. Warren's interview in the Vancouver *Daily Province* was published on 22 October 1946. He was interviewed for the *Kitchener Record* of 10 January 1947. In Maine the Lewiston *Daily Sun* carried its review on 20 January 1948, while the Portland *Press Herald* review ran on 22 January. Joseph Maerz's article ran in the *Macon Telegraph* of 2 February. Don Haskins wrote of Warren's Troy recital in the *Times Record*. Although the date of the newspaper is missing from the Leonard Warren Collection, the clipping is in the January–February 1948 files.

Excerpts from Carlos Díaz Du-Pond's *Cincuenta años de ópera en México* were translated by Maribel Moheno and made available by Barrett Crawford.

Chapter Fourteen

Robert Tuggle and John Pennino of the Metropolitan Opera Archives provided Warren's contracts and discussed them with me. Jerome Hines, William Appleton, and Regina Resnik contributed important interviews for this chapter. The *Falstaff* CDs in the Art of Fritz Reiner series are unauthorized Met broadcast recordings of 26 February 1949 by Arlecchino. *Falstaff* was reviewed in the *New York Times* and other papers on 27 February 1949. The New Orleans Opera *Falstaff* of 5 May 1956 has been issued on CD by VAI.

The Mexico City review excerpts cited include my translations from *El Redondel* and *Excelsior* (29 May 1949) and *Excelsior* and *Ultimas Noticias* (9 June); the Mexico City *Herald* piece was published on 12 June. Some reviews and articles from the Mexico City newspapers are in the Leonard Warren Collection in the New York Public Library for the Performing Arts. Other information from Mexico was provided by Barrett Crawford, who also gathered clippings and interviews from South America.

Chapter Fifteen

The James Davidson correspondence with the Met management is in the Metropolitan Opera Archives. The Harry Zelzer–Albert Gins correspondence is in Vivien Warren's collection. Frances J. Freeman's long interview with Warren about preparing

Boccanegra appeared in *Opera News* on 23 January 1950. The New York reviews of *Simon Boccanegra* appeared on 29 November 1949. Paul Jackson's remarks about the broadcast of 28 January 1950 are in *Saturday Afternoons at the Old Met* (pp. 472–476). I interviewed Carl Edwards in 1999.

Alvin Davis's article ran in the New York *Post* on 1 February 1950. It and other articles on the crisis are in Vivien Warren's collection. Bing's account of this period is in *5000 Nights at the Opera* (pp. 147 ff.).

Personal recollections of this period and of Warren's conversion to Roman Catholicism come from interviews with Vivien Warren, Edgar Vincent, Alfred Hubay, Reva Freidberg Fox, Paul Jaretzki, Herman Krawitz, Bishop Edwin Broderick, Father Royal Gardner, Marylin Noble Tracy, Wally Cleva Riecker, William Mayo Sullivan, Robert Merrill, Jerome Hines, Charles Anthony, Andrew Farkas, Anders Björling, Blanche Thebom, Yolanda Oberding Stivanello, and Nancy Conrad, among many others. See also Peter G. Davis's *The American Opera Singer* (p. 433).

Warren's Certificate of Baptism as a Roman Catholic was provided by Mrs. Rose Ruffolo Smeriglio, archivist of the Church of St. Catherine of Siena, 4 Riverside Avenue, Riverside, Connecticut. A note in the margin of the original states that he was "converted." Apart from the baptismal certificate, I used Jesús M. López's interview with Warren, which was conducted in the Hotel Condado in San Juan, Puerto Rico, on 13 June 1957 and published in the October 1990 edition of *Correo Musical Argentina*. The article was translated by Maribel Moheno. Roy Leifflen's letter about Warren's conversion to Catholicism is dated 8 February 1977 and is addressed to Professor Louis R. Thomas, a teacher at Northern Kentucky State College. It is in Vivien's collection.

Alan Coleridge, who was a super at the Met while Warren was there, offered his understanding of Jewish religious practice and culture among immigrant families. Floyd Herzog also helped me to understand the Warenoffs' practice of their faith. Jan Peerce's account of his estrangement from his son is in *The Bluebird of Happiness* (pp. 220 ff.). Many years ago Leslie Chabay told Dino Yannopoulos of his encounters with Solomon Warenoff in Seattle and Warren at the Met. Yannopoulos, interviewed for this book, confirmed it.

Solomon Warenoff's collection of clippings about his son is in Vivien Warren's collection. The Seattle *Times* covered the dinner on 18 September 1946; the *Post-Intelligencer* published the photograph and interview with Warren and his father on 4 October 1948. A review of Warren's 4 October concert in Seattle was published in the *Times* on 5 October.

I interviewed Giulietta Simionato about the Mexico City performances in 1998. The account of the 1950 season in Mexico City appears in Carlos Díaz Du-Pond's *Cincuenta años de ópera en México* (pp. 142–151). The translation is by Mirabel Moheno. A large photograph of the electric sign welcoming Callas to the Palacio de Bellas Artes is in *Callas by Callas*, a book by Renzo and Roberto Allegri, p. 59. Patricia Brown helped me to find cassettes of portions of the Mexico City *Simon Boccanegra* and the Met broadcast of that opera on 28 January 1950. Helen Hatton also contributed a cassette of that performance. These are for private use and are not commercial.

Newspaper reviews of performances in Rio de Janeiro are dated from 11 through 26 August. The translations are mine. The single review from the *Diario* of São Paulo is dated 2 September 1950. The biography *Mario Del Monaco ou un ténor de légende* by André Segond and Daniel Sébille refers to Warren's performances with the tenor on pp. 66–69, 75, 81, and 88.

Chapter Sixteen

The letters exchanged in December 1950 and May 1951 between Max Rudolf and James Davidson and a member of Davidson's staff are in the Metropolitan Opera Archives. Arge Keller's recollections of Warren are taken from several interviews he gave for this book. I am particularly grateful to him for sending me the tape of "O Holy Night," recorded from the Catholic Hour; the unreleased Italian songs, recorded for RCA Victor; and Warren's *Sea Shanties*. He also helped me reconstruct Warren's 1938 schedule.

Delia Rigal's interview with Horacio Molina filled out the details of the *Pagliacci* rehearsals. Davidson's further correspondence is in the Metropolitan Opera Archives. Edgar Vincent provided the invaluable information about Warren and George Sloan. Roberta Peters, Sherrill Milnes, Jerome Hines, and Arman Stepanian helped with their recollections of Warren in interviews for this book. Marylin Noble Tracy did the necessary research about Manhattan House. Arge Keller witnessed the encounter between Warren and Mankiewicz.

Reports of the incident in Abilene appeared in the *Reporter* on 3 April 1953, the New York *Post* on 30 April, and other papers during the month. Leonard Lyons featured the story in his column "The Lyons Den."

Chapter Seventeen

Rudolf Bing's account of his disputes with Ghiringhelli and Di Stefano is in *5000 Nights at the Opera* (pp. 190–198). The information on Del Monaco comes from my interviews and conversations with him in the 1950s. The Milanese newspapers of December and January, all identified within the text, and Kolodin's 1954 article on Bernstein and Warren (undated; the publication is unidentified but is probably *Saturday Review of Literature*) are in the Leonard Warren Collection in the New York Public Library for the Performing Arts. I interviewed Giuseppe Pugliese in Venice in 1998.

Norman Dello Joio provided many details about *The Lamentation of Saul* in telephone interviews and one personal interview. A feature article in the *Berkshire Eagle* of 20 August 1954 had further information. It was sent by Ann-Marie Harris of the Local History Department of the Berkshire Athenaeum in Pittsfield to Barrett Crawford. The review of the Library of Congress concert is dated 31 October 1954 but does not identify the Washington newspaper in which it was printed. Like most other clippings used in this book, it is in the Leonard Warren Collection at the New York Public Library for the Performing Arts.

Chapter Eighteen

I interviewed Edgar Vincent, Dino Yannopoulos, Renata Tebaldi, Arge Keller, Sandra Warfield, Giorgio Tozzi, Anders Björling, Blanche Thebom, Jerome Hines, Cesare Bardelli, John De Merchant, Nathaniel Merrill, and Herman Krawitz. My interview with Warren on operatic acting was published in *Opera News* on 9 April 1956.

Hal Boyle's interview for the Associated Press appeared on 3 and 4 August 1955. Neither clipping identifies the newspaper. The Boyle interview that appeared in the Seattle *Times* of 5 August 1955 and his 15 September 1955 story about Frankenstein's review (from an unnamed Seattle paper, but probably from the *Times*) were in Warren's father's collection. Frankenstein's review in the San Francisco *Chronicle* was also reproduced on Associated Press wires. It was returned to Vivien Warren after Solomon Warenoff died. *Aida* is covered in William Albright's essay "Milanov on Disc" in *The Opera Quarterly* Volume 7, Number 1 (1990), pp. 148–149. Jay Harrison's interview about Warren's study of Scarpia is in the New York *Herald Tribune* of 31 March 1957. Jesús M. López also published a long interview about Warren's Scarpia in *El Mundo* on 13 June 1957. It was translated by Maribel Moheno. Kolodin's remarks about Scarpia are in *The Metropolitan Opera 1883–1966* (p. 568). Sidney Fields's interview with Warren was published on 20 January 1956 in Fields's "Only Human" column in the New York *Daily Mirror*. Warren's byline article about fighting the Callas-Tebaldi mania, "How Do Male Opera Stars [Fight] Against the Glittering Prima Donna?," appeared in *Variety* in December 1956. The exact date is not given.

The reviews of *Ernani* appeared on 24 November 1956. Irving Kolodin's remarks about *Ernani* are in *The Metropolitan Opera 1883–1966* (pp. 579–589). The review in *Time* (3 December 1956) is headlined "Travesty at the Met." *Variety* also ran a review on 28 November 1956, saying that Warren was "alone" among the principals in "exquisite artistic coordination" and "up in the part and the score." The reviewer noted that standees and other "characters in the Opera House" wore "Viva Zinka" buttons during the performance. The *Bolletino* Number 10 of the Istituto Nazionale di Studi Verdiani has the title "*Ernani*, Yesterday and Today." It was published in Parma in 1989. My interview with Mitropoulos was published in *Stars in the Sun* in 1955. The *Time* article, "Two Home-Town Boys," appeared on 8 April 1957.

Helen Hatton's account of her friendship with Warren and her recollection of Warren's story about *Ernani* came from several telephone interviews and the essay she sent me for this book. She was also particularly generous in sending cassettes of operas that I did not have.

The record of Sara Kantor Warenoff's death, 4 February 1957, was in Vivien Warren's prayer book, *The Festival Prayers According to the Ritual of the German and Polish Jew*. The book was a gift from her grandmother, Brina Kantor. Vivien also noted the deaths of her brother Leonard in 1960, her brother Martin on 1 January 1963, and her father, Solomon Warenoff, on 8 November 1965. Leon Warenoff, Vivien's uncle, lived to celebrate his hundredth birthday.

Chapter Nineteen

Rudolf Bing's letter to Walter Prude is in the Metropolitan Opera Archives. The long Associated Press profile by W. G. Rogers appeared in the evening papers on 30 November 1957. A galley of it, in the Leonard Warren Collection, notes that other newspapers can use the syndicated piece beginning with the morning papers on 1 December. Arthur Darrack's interview appeared in the *Cincinnati Enquirer* on 17 January 1958. The reviews of *Otello*, which appeared on 28 February 1958, were excellent. I owe particular thanks to Alan Wagner and Martha Dreyfus Wagner for help with this book and for sending me the cassette of Alan's 1958 interview with Warren. Alan also interviewed Warren just a few days before his death. That tape was broadcast on WNYC in March 1960, two days after Warren died. Alan said that after Warren finished his taping, Warren demonstrated his legendary high C, first saying, "I can do it; I can do it." Alan also wrote "The Life and Death of Leonard Warren," published in *High Fidelity* in June 1960.

The chief journalist covering Warren in Russia was Irving R. Levine, whose RCA Victor album cover notes for *Leonard Warren on Tour in Russia* were published in 1958. At that time, Levine was the Moscow correspondent for the National Broadcasting Company. He saw at least two of Warren's recitals and performances and was especially impressed by *Rigoletto* in Moscow at the Bolshoi Opera Company and

Otello in Riga. Howard Taubman's coverage for the *New York Times*, under the headline "The Toast of Moscow," ran on 17 May 1958. His article headlined "Kiev Opens Its Gates" appeared on 1 June. Articles by Russian critics are dated 16 and 20 May. The official government permission to broadcast and telecast *Otello* from Riga has Agatha's handwritten note with the date 29 May 1958. Other articles are the undated piece in the Stockholm *Svenska Dagbladet*, and the Warren byline piece in the *New York Herald Tribune* of 24 August 1958. These are all in the Leonard Warren Collection. Warren had an astonishing amount of coverage in Russia by local and American journalists. In addition to the signed articles, unsigned dispatches on his progress went out regularly. The interview by Janis Klavsons, published in the Latvian-American newspaper *Laiks* on 25 June 1958, is in Vivien Warren's collection. Inna Ockelmann correctly identified this newspaper. Dorothy Kilgallen wrote a long piece that included "the male stars of opera" and Warren. It was syndicated. The clipping of it in the Leonard Warren Collection is dated 29 April 1958, from the Norfolk, Nebraska, *News*. In the piece, Eleanor Steber called Warren "a great prima donna" and said he became angry with her for clearing her throat while he was singing and smearing his makeup with her hat brim during the first act of *Tosca*.

Vivien's recollection of her brother's account of the trip and William Appleton's description of Warren's feelings about his experiences in the Soviet Union are transcribed from my interviews. Jan Peerce's account of his trip to Russia appears in *The Bluebird of Happiness* (pp. 235 ff.). Blanche Thebom spoke of her Russian tour under Hurok's auspices in my 1998 interview with her.

William Appleton and Giorgio Tozzi provided details of the Warrens' summer. I also interviewed Lucine Amara, Nathaniel Merrill, Margaret Carson, and Merle Hubbard about this period. Reviews of *Macbeth* appeared on 6 February 1959, as did the *New York Times* profile on Warren. Although it is unsigned, it may have been written by Howard Taubman. It is in Solomon Warenoff's collection. Leonie Rysanek's remarks about Lady Macbeth were quoted in the *New York Times* obituary of her, 9 March 1998. Rudolf Bing's comment on hiring a claqueur appears on p. 245 of *5000 Nights at the Opera*. The New Orleans *Times-Picayune* article of 8 November 1959 is in the Leonard Warren Collection. Giuseppe Pugliese's comment about Warren's recording of *Macbeth* comes from our interview. Letters about the Lincoln Center groundbreaking ceremony are in Vivien Warren's collection. Carlo Bergonzi, whom I have often interviewed, contributed his recollections of Warren during a 1998 visit. I thank Jerry Hines for his funny story about the session in Warren's house. Rysanek's remarks were quoted in the *New York Times* of 6 February 1959.

Chapter Twenty

The reviews of Dello Joio's *Lamentation of Saul* appeared on 21 October 1959. Howard Taubman wrote about the Little Orchestra Society concert in the *New York Times* of 22 October 1958. I interviewed the composer about this event. Harold C. Schonberg's long feature article on Warren was in the *New York Times Magazine* on 25 October 1959. Arge Keller recounted Milanov's remark about Warren's costume. A *Newsweek* profile of Warren appeared on 2 November 1959, in connection with opening night. Nathaniel Merrill also contributed his recollections of that and other productions. Warren's day-to-day calendar for 1959–1960 is in Vivien Warren's collection, as is James A. Stratton's review for the *News-Press* of Warren's Stillwater, Oklahoma, recital. Dated 14 January 1960, the article has a handwritten note at the top that reads "Warren's last recital."

Joseph V. Siciliano, a Warren fan in Salt Lake City, sent the *Opera News* account of the *Simon Boccanegra* rehearsal to the president of the Leonard Warren Foundation. John Freeman sent me a slightly different version of the rehearsal from David Berkowitz's *Behind the Gold Curtain* (pp. 133–134). Berkowitz recalled that Warren "had a super-ego and was a very argumentative man." He said after Warren complained to Mitropoulos, a violinist "let out a Bronx cheer" and stuck out his tongue at the baritone. This set off the uproar. The rehearsal was held up for more than an hour, Berkowitz said. He also said Agatha "blamed Warren's death on that incident in the pit and never forgave the orchestra." Remarks by Mary Curtis-Verna, Raymond Gniewek, Nathaniel Merrill, John S. White, and Edgar Vincent are from my interviews for this book. In *Opera News* of 4 March 1995, Patrick J. Smith wrote of Warren's Boccanegra, saying, "Anyone familiar with his voice knew that the role was ideal for it, and it for him." He felt that Warren was "past his vocal peak" but "sang strongly." Smith called the opening night "a triumph for Warren." He also said, "What I most remember is not the way Warren's voice dominated the Council Chamber Scene but his single, floated high-F 'Figlia!' as he watches his beloved daughter leave." Theodor Uppman also recalled Warren's Simon.

James B. McPherson contributed recollections of his meetings with Warren, checked information from Canadian newspapers about the baritone's last appearances in Ontario and Québec City, and sent me clippings so that I could check Warren's itineraries. The review in *Le Soleil*, published on 2 February 1960, was also researched by McPherson. It covered Warren's last concert.

Chapter Twenty-one

I gathered many personal accounts of the last week of Warren's life during interviews for this book. Father Royal Gardner answered many questions about the last years of Warren's life and about his death and funeral. Regina Resnik said she was in the audience but did not go backstage. The recollections of Edgar Vincent and others, including Roald Reitan and Mignon Dunn, are from my 1998 interviews. Robert Tuggle found Reginald Tonry's account in the stage manager's log in the Metropolitan Opera Archives. John Pennino found the official house program, which Michael Manuel, the executive stage manager, was responsible for filing. At the bottom of the title page, he wrote, "Performance terminated during Act II when Leonard Warren collapsed and died."

Vera Giannini's interview with Dr. Zorgniotti appeared in *Opera News* in September 1985. Regina Sokol also gave me information about the house physician, her uncle. Andrew Farkas interviewed Dr. Zorgniotti on 17 March 1992 in New York City. The physician said to him, "The moment I saw Warren fall, I wasn't sure whether it was a massive stroke that killed him or a heart attack, but later on I was more inclined to think that it was a heart attack, not a stroke. And I have been haunted by the thought ever since that had I performed a [thoracotomy] and given him a heart massage right then and there, I could have revived and saved him. I had the instruments in my bag, a scalpel to cut the chest open; I could have done it. I probably should have tried it regardless, as there was nothing to lose."

The reviews of *Simon Boccanegra* appeared in the New York papers on 2 March. Richard Tucker's remarks about Warren's death are in *Newsweek*, 11 January 1965. Tucker admitted to the interviewer that after Warren died, he cut back his own schedule, out of fear. Phyllis Battelle's interview with Tucker appeared in the New York *Journal American* of 26 January 1964. Newspapers and obituaries cited are all from the New York papers of 5, 6, and 7 March. The *Journal-American* (4–7 March) was particularly good on covering visitors to the Abbey Funeral Home and those who attended the Mass at St. Vincent Ferrer.

Felix Eyle's letter to Agatha is in the Leonard Warren Collection in the New York Public Library for the Performing Arts. With it are the funeral home registers. For this chapter I also used many articles from the Leonard Warren Collection. A few were only in Vivien's and Agatha's files and the clipping file Solomon Warenoff kept; these are all now in Vivien's collection.

Since Warren's death, a dispute has arisen about the last words he sang onstage. One document from that period is a page from the concertmaster's orchestra part. It is in the Met's orchestra library and was discovered by John Grande, the Met's chief librarian. After Warren died, Schippers, the concertmaster, and the orchestra stayed in the pit because they did not know what had happened. Finally Schippers left the pit; then the orchestra was also free to leave. In this orchestra part, someone made a little arrow on the page of his score, just after the words "Poi muoia!" Below the arrow is a note that says, "Warren dropped dead here!"

This account, however, is at odds with the recollections of many who witnessed Warren's death. It is widely believed that Warren died after singing the line "Oh, *gioia*!" and not "Poi *muoia*!" Sonya Haddad remembered that people even made remarks about the irony of Warren's dying after singing "Oh, *gioia*!" These are the "last words" reported in some newspapers. Roald Reitan, in my 1998 interviews with him, said Warren could not have sung the phrase that ends with "Oh, gioia!" Had Warren been singing those words, Reitan would have been walking away from Warren or would perhaps already have been offstage. But when Warren fell, Reitan said, he was still a few feet away from the baritone, facing him and waiting for him to pick up his cue and sing.

Agatha, the Warrens' doctor, and several priests who were the Warrens' friends were in the theatre that night. Vivien was in her apartment at 160 West Seventy-third Street when her brother died. A friend heard about the death on the radio and called her.

◆

Selected Bibliography

Vital Records, Baptismal Records, Census, City Directories, Immigration Records

Federal and Municipal Records

National Archives Northeastern Division, New York City. Bronx, Brooklyn, Manhattan city directories; Federal Census of New York for 1900, 1910, 1920; immigration and citizenship records, passenger lists.

New York City Municipal Archives. Birth, death, marriage certificates; business and corporation records.

Church and Cemetery Records

Church of St. Catherine of Siena, Riverside, Connecticut. Register of Baptisms.

Church of St. Charles Borromeo, Brooklyn, New York City. Register of Marriages.

Mormon Family History Center, New York City. Social Security Death Index.

Mount Hebron and Mount Zion Cemeteries, Queens, New York City; St. Mary's Cemetery, Greenwich, Connecticut. Cemetery Records.

Correspondence, Clippings, Memorabilia, Unpublished Memoranda, Photographs

Leonard Warren Collection, Music Division, Special Collections, The New York Public Library for the Performing Arts at Lincoln Center.

Leonard Warren Foundation Archive, Leonard Warren Foundation, Alamo, California.

The Metropolitan Opera Archives, Metropolitan Opera Association, Lincoln Center.

Radio City Music Hall Archives, Radio City Music Hall, New York.
Roy Leifflen, private collection, now in collection of Edward Warren Haber
Vivien Warren Collection, including the Solomon Warenoff Collection, now
  in the collection of Edward Warren Haber.

Books, Manuscripts, Periodicals, Program Magazines

Allegri, Renzo, and Roberto Allegri. *Callas by Callas: The Secret Writings of
  "la Maria."* New York, 1998. Originally published by Arnoldo Monda-
  dori, Milan, 1997.
Barr, Cyrilla. *Elizabeth Sprague Coolidge, American Patron of Music.* New
  York, 1998.
Benn, Anna, ed. *Russia, With Chapters on Ukraine and Belarus.* An Insight
  Guide. New York, 1996.
Bing, Rudolf. *5000 Nights at the Opera.* New York, 1972.
Björling, Anna-Lisa, and Andrew Farkas. *Jussi.* Portland, Oregon, 1996.
Bromley's 1902 Atlas of New York. New York, 1902.
Celli, Teodoro, and Giuseppe Pugliese. *Tullio Serafin, Il patriarca del melo-
  dramma.* Venice, 1985.
Columbia Broadcasting System, Inc., and Columbia Artists Bureau, Inc., in
  the Radio City Music Hall Archives. Biographical questionnaire and
  notes about Viola Philo, 1935.
Davis, Peter G. *The American Opera Singer.* New York, 1997.
Díaz Du-Pond, Carlos. *Cincuenta años de ópera en México.* Mexico City,
  1978.
Donin, Rabbi Hayim Halevy. *To Be a Jew.* New York, 1972.
Drake, James A. *Richard Tucker: A Biography.* New York, 1984.
Eaton, Quaintance. *The Miracle of the Met.* New York, 1968.
Edwards, Geoffrey, and Ryan Edwards. *The Verdi Baritone.* Bloomington,
  Indiana, 1994.
Evers, Alf. *The Catskills.* Woodstock, New York, 1982.
Ferrario, Carlo, and Sandro Chierichetti. *Lago di Como.* Como, 1985.
Fitzgerald, Gerald, Jean Seward Uppman, and Geoff Peterson. *The Annals
  of the Metropolitan Opera.* Boston and New York, 1989.
Gatti-Casazza, Giulio. *Memories of the Opera.* New York, 1933.
Jackson, Paul. *Saturday Afternoons at the Old Met.* Portland, Oregon, 1992.
———. *Sign-off for the Old Met.* Portland, Oregon, 1997.
Jewish Genealogical Society, Inc. *The Jewish Genealogical Family Finder.*
  New York, 1994.
Kohn, Hans. *Revolutions and Dictatorships.* New York, 1941.
Kolodin, Irving. *The Metropolitan Opera, 1883–1966.* New York, 1966.
Levy, Alan. *The Bluebird of Happiness: The Memoirs of Jan Peerce.* New
  York, 1976.

London Daily News. [5?] June 1905. Report on pogroms.
London Times. 17 March 1882. Report on pogroms.
Pelletier, Wilfrid. *Une symphonie inachevée*. Ottawa, 1972.
Phillips-Matz, Mary Jane. *The Many Lives of Otto Kahn*. New York, 1963, 1983.
Pinta, Emil R. "Remembering the Met Auditions of the Air." Unpublished essay. Leonard Warren Foundation Archive.
Radio City Music Hall Program Magazine. Profile of Vin Lindhe. January 1935.
————. Program biography of Viola Philo. n.d.
Ruffo, Titta. *Ruffo: My Parabola, the Autobiography of Titta Ruffo*. Translated by Connie Mandracchia DeCaro. Edited by Andrew Farkas. Dallas, 1995.
Sanders, Roland. *The Lower East Side*. New York, 1979.
Schonberg, Harold C. *Facing the Music*. New York, 1981.
Segond, André, and Daniel Sébille. *Mario Del Monaco ou un ténor de légende*. Lyons, 1981.
Webster, Margaret. *Don't Put Your Daughter on the Stage*. New York, 1972.
Weinstat, Hertzel, and Bert Wechsler. *Dear Rogue*. Portland, Oregon, 1996.

Important Print Interviews and Feature Articles

Unsigned Articles in Chronological Order

"Keene Concert Association Presents Famous Soloist." Unidentified newspaper. [Keene, New Hampshire, autumn 1940.]
"Yankee Invasion." *Time*, 30 August 1943.
"Singer Finds Relaxation in Model Railroads." *Popular Hobbies*, 1944.
"Northeast High Hails Operatic Baritone." *The Philadelphia Inquirer*, [January 1944].
"Ample Leonard." *Time*, 20 March 1944.
"O Baritono Leonard Warren Homenageado no Municipal." *La Gazeta* (São Paulo), 19 September 1945.
"Met Baritone First Timer." *The Oregonian*, 6 October 1946.
"Singer's Voice 'Gift from God.'" *Vancouver Daily Province*, 22 October 1946.
"Noted Singer Phones Wife Daily, Even When in Brazil." *The Kitchener Record*, 10 January 1947.
"Leonard Warren Sees Pictures as Opera Boom." *New York Journal-American*, 30 November 1947.
"Leonard Warren Discusses Operatic Films." *Opera News*, 16 February 1948.
"Big Baritone." *Newsweek*, 13 December 1948.

"Meet Mr. Falstaff." *The Youngstown (Ohio) Vindicator*, 20 March 1949.

"Warren Fishing Enthusiast." *Twin Cities (Winston-Salem) Sentinel*, 1 October 1953.

"Leonard Warren in Milan." *Opera News*, 15 February 1954.

"Disguised Baritone." *The Philadelphia Inquirer* (Magazine), 22 January 1956.

"Two Home-Town Boys." *Time*, 8 April 1957.

"Met Singer Turned Bounce into Boost." Associated Press. *P.M.*, 30 November 1957.

"Baritone from USA Acclaimed in Russia." *Svenska Dagbladet* (Stockholm), [May 1958]. Original and translation in the Leonard Warren Collection.

"It's Better to DO." *Parade*, 15 June 1958.

"The Met's Big Men." *Time*, 3 November 1958.

"Methodical Musician." *The New York Times*, 6 February 1959.

"The Jester Reflects." *Opera News*, 23 March 1959.

Signed Articles

B. B. "A carreira de um grande artista." *La Vitrina* (São Paulo), November 1942.

Battelle, Phyllis. "Cultivate Home-Grown Talent." *New York Journal-American*, 26 January 1964.

Boyle, Hal. "Top Operatic Baritone Boasts 52-Inch Chest." Associated Press. *The Seattle Times*, 3 August 1955.

Canning, Hazel. "Fierce Love of Music in His Heart." *Boston Sunday Post*, 8 May 1938.

Coleman, Emily. "Big Baritone." *Newsweek*, 13 December 1948.

———. "Cue for the Met's 75th." *Newsweek*, 2 November 1959.

Danzig, Fred. "A Warren Interview." UPI. Unidentified newspaper, 1959.

Davis, Peter G. "The Met Needs Vision, Not Just Stars." *The New York Times*, 23 February 1968.

Dempsey, Margaret. "Leonard Warren's Wife, a Force in His Career." *The (Baltimore) Sun*, [April 1945].

Fields, Sidney. "Only Human." *New York Daily Mirror*, 20 January 1956.

Fitzgerald, Gerald. "Warren in Search of Scarpia." *Opera News*, 18 March 1957.

Freeman, Frances J. "Boccanegra from Pirate to Prince." *Opera News*, 23 January 1950.

Giannini, Vera. "Caruso Enthusiast Adrian Zorgniotti." *Opera News*, September 1985.

Gutman, John. "Leonard Warren, April 21, 1911–March 4, 1960." *Opera News*, 2 April 1960.

Harrison, Jay S. "Warren a Hard-Working Baritone." *The New York Herald Tribune*, 31 March 1957.

Hatton, Helen. "A Tribute to Leonard Warren." [Toronto] *Record News*, [1960].

Heylbut, Rose. "Profile of Leonard Warren." *Etude*, March 1949.

Jackson, Carol. "Metropolitan Opera Baritone and Wife Settle Down in Greenwich." *Greenwich Time*, [10?] July 1946.

Kilgallen, Dorothy. "Temper and Temperament." *Norfolk (Nebraska) News*, 29 April 1958.

Klavsons, Janis. "Leonard Warren Tells About Riga." *Laiks*, 25 June 1958. Original and translation in the Leonard Warren Collection.

Kolodin, Irving. "Music to My Ears." *Saturday Review of Literature*, 19 March 1960.

López, Jesús M. "Baritono Leonard Warren Explica su Interpretacion [Scarpia]." *El Mundo* (San Juan), 13 April 1957.

———. "Leonard Warren: Barítono de Barítones." Interview with Leonard Warren, conducted 13 June 1957 in the Hotel Condado, San Juan, Puerto Rico. Typescript in the Leonard Warren Foundation Archives. Published in *Correo Musical Argentino*, October 1990.

Matz. See Phillips-Matz.

Merkling, Frank. "Leonard Warren's Credo, Humility and Hard Work." *Musical America*, 1 December 1956.

Miller, Philip L. "Leonard Warren, 1911–1960." *Opera*, June 1960.

Milnes, Sherrill. "The Warren Legacy." *Opera News*, 22 March 1975.

Newman, Clarence. "Operatic Singing is a Rugged Career." *Fort Wayne News-Sentinel*, 6 May 1948.

Owen, Dick. "The Lon Chaney of the Opera." *New York Sunday News* (Magazine), 1 December 1957.

———. "The Ham and Eggs of Opera." *New York Sunday News*, 1 February 1959.

Peltz, Mary Ellis. "Leonard Warren." In *Spotlights on the Stars*. New York, 1943.

———. "Personality of the Week." *Opera News*, 23 November 1942.

Phillips-Matz, Mary Jane. "Dimitri Mitropoulos" and "Leonard Warren." In *Stars in the Sun*. New York, 1955.

———. "Our Little Table." *Opera News*, 7 March 1955.

———. "Warren: Acting With the Voice." *Opera News*, 9 April 1956.

Robb, Inez. "Baritones Are Born Villains." *New York World-Telegram and Sun*, 13 March 1957.

Rogers, W. G. "Singer Leonard Warren Operates Machine Shop." Associated Press. Unidentified newspaper, July 1948.

Rosenberg, George. "'Nyets to You,' Sang Our Top Baritone." *New York Mirror* (Magazine), Sunday, 14 December 1958.

Schonberg, Harold C. "Big Voice, Big Temperament," *The New York Times*, Section 6 (Magazine), 25 October 1959.

Selby, John. "Baritone Leonard Warren Had No Phony Rungs in His Ladder to Met Top." Associated Press. *Springfield (Massachusetts) News-Sun*, 9 July 1944.

Simon, Henry. "Themes and Variations." *P.M.*, 19 January 1944.

Taubman, Howard. "Music: The Toast of Moscow." *The New York Times*, 17 May 1958.

Wagner, Alan. "Living Opera Program." Interview with Warren in 1958. Audio cassette in the Alan Wagner Collection.

———. "The Life and Death of Leonard Warren." *High Fidelity*, June 1960.

Walker, Earle. "Famed Baritone Flays Abilene Audience Then Apologizes." *Abilene News*, 3 April 1953.

Warren, Leonard. "Were Vocalists of the Past Tradition-Bound?" *Musical Courier*, August 1944.

———. "Traveler's Report." (Pan American World Airways) *New Horizons*, January–March 1945.

———. "You Need Steak to Sing Baritone." *New York Post*, [February 1945].

———. "Managers Make Music Too!!" *Music News*, April 1945.

———. "The Molding of an Artist Begins in Childhood." Translation of article in *La Gazeta* (São Paulo, Brazil) 17 September 1945. Based on an interview done earlier on the *Gazeta* Radio Station.

———. "How Do Male Opera Stars [Fight] Against the Glittering Prima Donna?" *Variety*, [early December] 1956.

———. "Hi-Fi in the Home." *Audio*, March 1957.

———. "'The Goal Won't Come to You.'" Unidentified publication, [15 June 1957].

———. "Warren Reports on Russian Tour." *The New York Herald Tribune*, 24 August 1958.

Yumet, Miguel Angel. "Sociales." *El Imparcial* (San Juan), 9 September 1949.

Interviews by the Author

Leonard Warren, 1950s; Linda Warren Tirdel, 1997, 1998; Vivien Warren, 1996, 1997, 1998.

Licia Albanese, 1998; Lucine Amara, 1998; Charles Anthony, 1998; John Appleton, 1998; Tina Appleton Bishop, 1997, 1998; William Appleton, 1997, 1998; Therman Bailey, 1998; Rose Bampton Pelletier, 1997, 1998; Cesare Bardelli, 1998; Vera Bardelli-Perinati, 1998; Carlo Bergonzi, 1998; Anders Björling, 1998; Ethel Bobrow Altschuler, 1997, 1998; The Very Rev. Edwin Broderick, Bishop of Albany, (Ret.), 1998; Patricia Brown, 1997, 1998; Bruce Burroughs, 1998; Margaret Carson, 1997, 1998; Pinuccia Cellini, 1998; Joseph G. Chisholm, 1999; Alan Coleridge, 1997; Nancy Conrad, 1998; William Crawford, 1997, 1998; Mary

Curtis-Verna, 1998; Peter G. Davis, 1998; Norman Dello Joio, 1998; John De Merchant, 1997; Eileen Di Tullio, 1997; Mignon Dunn, 1998; Carl Edwards, 1999; Martin Feinstein, 1999; Reva Freidberg Fox, 1998; Father Royal Gardner, 1998; Vera Giannini, 1997, 1998; Raymond Gniewek, 1998; Sonia Haddad, 1997; David Hamilton, 1997, 1998; Helen Hatton, Ph.D., 1998; Floyd Herzog, Ph.D., 1997, 1998; Jerome Hines, 1997, 1998; Alfred F. Hubay, 1998; Merle Hubbard, 1998; Paul Jaretzki, 1998; Diane Jaust, 1997; Jerry Kagan, 1998; Henry Kaston, 1998; Alan Kayes, 1998; Arge Keller, 1998; Rev. Charles Kraus, 1998; Herman Krawitz, 1998; James B. McPherson, 1998; Nathaniel Merrill, 1998; Robert Merrill, 1998; Sherrill Milnes, 1998; Richard Mohr, 1998; Perry Morrison, 1999; Patrice Munsel, 1998; William Murphy, 1998; Danny Newman, 1997; John Pennino, 1997, 1998; Roberta Peters, 1998; Marise Angelucci Pokorny, 1997, 1998; Giuseppe Pugliese, 1998; Louis Quilico, 1998; Roald Reitan, 1998; Regina Resnik, 1998; Elise Revson, 1998; Maria Rich, 1998; Martin Rich, 1998; Charles Riecker, 1998; Wally Cleva Riecker, 1998; Tony Russo, 1997, 1998; Barbara Schwarz, 1998; Giulietta Simionato, 1998; Donald Sisler, 1997; Louis J. Snyder, 1996, 1997, 1998; Regina Sokol, 1998; Risë Stevens, 1998; Anthony Stivanello, 1980s–1990s; Yolanda Oberding Stivanello, 1997, 1998; William Mayo Sullivan, 1998; Renata Tebaldi, 1998; Blanche Thebom, 1998; Walfredo Toscanini, 1997, 1998; Giorgio Tozzi, 1998; Marylin Noble Tracy, 1998; Barry Tucker, 1998; Robert Tuggle, 1997, 1998; Jean Seward Uppman, 1998; Theodor Uppman, 1998; Edgar Vincent, 1998; Alan Wagner, 1997, 1998; Martha Dreyfus Wagner, 1997, 1998; Sandra Warfield McCracken, 1998; John S. White, 1997; Richard Woitach, 1998; Dino Yannopoulos, 1998.

♦

Discography

by Barrett Crawford

From 1939 through 1959, Leonard Warren participated in more than one hundred recording sessions. From individual songs or arias to complete operas, Warren always recorded well, usually requiring only one take for each selection.

As the world's leading interpreter during the 1950s of Giuseppe Verdi's baritone roles, Warren recorded six complete Verdi operas and a second version of *Il trovatore*, as well as selections from three others. His performances in three Verdi operas are included in the Metropolitan Opera's Historic Broadcast recording series. Although he performed on stage in *Ernani*, no authorized recordings of Warren were made from that opera. Regrettably, the baritone neither performed nor was recorded in *Don Carlo* or *Nabucco*.

This discography comprises seven sections:

		Discography Numbers
I.	Audio Recording Sessions and Selected Public Performances by Date	1001 to 1114
II.	Opera Audio Recordings by Opera	2001 to 2077
III.	Nonopera Audio Recordings by Song	3001 to 3069
IV.	Unauthorized Audio Recordings by Opera	4001 to 4147
V.	Opera Roles Recorded by Opera	5001 to 5020
VI.	Video Excerpts from the Voice of Firestone Telecasts	6001 to 6015
VII.	Metropolitan Opera Radio Broadcast Performances by Opera	7001 to 7024

Section I lists in chronological order Leonard Warren's studio recording sessions and public performances that are sources of his authorized recordings. Sections II and III include all Warren's published and unpublished commercial recordings and those opera, recital, and radio performances that have been authorized for distribution by the appropriate copyright owners. In the interest of scholarship and completeness, unauthorized recordings of Warren's performances are included separately in Section IV. Their inclusion does not represent approval of their sale, which may infringe on the rights of the copyright owners and the artists who took part in the performances. Additional topics include private recordings, radio broadcasts, television, motion pictures, the World's Greatest Operas and Heart of the Opera series, and the Leonard Warren Commemorative compact discs.

Section I. Audio Recording Sessions and Selected Public Performances by Date

Except for two complete operas recorded for RCA by Decca (*La Gioconda* and *La forza del destino*), all Warren's studio recordings were made with RCA Victor. If available, RCA (U.S.) matrix and related take numbers are listed. Warren recorded in various studio locations. The 1940 recording sessions for the World's Greatest Operas series took place in Town Hall in New York City, although RCA files place some sessions at the Academy of Music in Philadelphia. RCA's Italian recording sessions were held at the Rome Opera House. Decca's two recordings were made in Rome at L'Accademia di Santa Cecilia. All other recording sessions were held in New York City at RCA's studios at the Lotos Club (5 East Sixty-sixth Street), Manhattan Center (311 West Thirty-fourth Street), and Webster Hall (125 East Eleventh Street).

The discography includes RCA matrix-take numbers for most recording sessions. The term *matrix* refers to the assigned number of the studio recording session (or sessions) in which an ensemble, a duet, or a solo was recorded. Two or more versions or takes of the same selection, sometimes months apart, might be made. The RCA take number is the single-digit suffix to the matrix number. For example, on 2 January 1947, Warren recorded the aria "Il balen del suo sorriso" from *Il trovatore*. There were two takes. The master recording chosen for release was assigned matrix-take number D7-RC-7101-2 in which D is the decade 1940 through 1949; 7 indicates the seventh year of the decade (1947); R is the label, Classical Red Seal; C is the record size and speed (12" and 78 rpm); 7101 is the matrix number, and 2 is the take number.

Section II. Opera Audio Recordings by Opera

Section II includes selections from twenty operas. Opera highlights and individual selections follow the recording of the complete opera or highlights from which they were taken. Individual arias, duets, and ensembles appear in the order in which they take place in the opera. Beginning with complete operas, the recordings are listed by opera, with the recording session or public performance date; the RCA matrix-take number(s), if any; the producer's catalog number (the related album set number, if any, is also shown); the type of recording; the issue date of the recording; and the album description, if any. If the album comprises more than one record or disc, the number appears in brackets in the "Type" column. The cast is listed for recordings of complete operas and opera highlights. Included are 78 rpm, 45 rpm, LP (33⅓ rpm), compact disc (CD), cassette (CAS), prerecorded tape (open reel, designated as OR), and eight-track stereo cartridge (8T) opera recordings released by RCA Victor (U.S.) and its successor, BMG Classics; opera selections from RCA recording sessions released by the Metropolitan Opera Guild; public performance recordings of complete operas and opera excerpts produced by the Metropolitan Opera Association as Historic Broadcast recordings; opera selections from RCA recording sessions released by VAI Audio (VAIA); a CD of sixteen opera arias on the Leonard Warren Commemorative label; public performances of *Falstaff* and *Rigoletto* released on CD by VAI Audio and the New Orleans Opera Association; three recordings of arias released by RCA affiliates in Germany and Italy featuring Warren only; three complete operas released in both LP and CD versions by two record companies in collaboration with RCA (Decca's *La forza del destino* and *La Gioconda,* and EMI's *Pagliacci*); and operatic selections from an LP recording of Warren's public recital in Moscow issued by Melodiya.

RCA Victor (U.S.) sent masters of several complete operas in which Warren appeared to its affiliates in England, France, Germany, Italy, Spain, and several other countries. The affiliates, in turn, issued recordings of those operas locally under their own labels. Since they replicate the RCA Victor (U.S.) recordings already listed, such affiliate pressings are not also included in the discography. Here is a compilation, provided by Harald Henrysson (*A Jussi Björling Phonography*, 2d edition), of RCA's foreign affiliate pressings of the highly acclaimed 1952 recording of the complete *Il trovatore* (with Milanov, Björling, Warren, Barbieri, and Moscona; see Discography Number 2071). The first RCA (U.S.) issues are catalog numbers WDM 6008 (45 rpm) and LM 6008 (LP). The affiliate LP recordings are:

Argentina	LM 6008
Australia	LB 16012 and AVM 2-0699
England	HMV-ALP 1112/13 and ALP 1832/33
France	A 630.361/362
Germany	LM 6008/1-2 and VIC 6008/1-2 [26.35003]
Italy	B12R 0023/24, KV 6008, MCV 536, VL 43536 and VLS 00699
Japan	RGC 1106/07
South Africa	JALP 1112/13
Spain	LM 6008

Section III. Nonopera Audio Recordings by Song

Section III lists by song title Warren's commercial recordings taken from studio sessions and authorized recordings of public recitals. It includes 78, 45, LP, CD, and cassette recordings of songs released by RCA Victor (U.S.) and its successor, BMG Classics; songs from RCA recording sessions released by the Metropolitan Opera Guild; a CD of twenty-four concert songs on the Leonard Warren Commemorative label; and songs from an LP recording of Warren's public recital in Moscow issued by Melodiya.

The composer is named first, followed by the lyricist. The fifty-seven songs are sung in English, French, Italian, or Latin. Three Italian songs recorded by RCA in 1954 but not made available commercially appear on the Leonard Warren Commemorative CD entitled *Concert Songs*. Eleven songs recorded in 1941, 1944, and 1954, including the three Italian songs, were never released by RCA.

Section IV. Unauthorized Audio Recordings by Opera

At last count, approximately fifty European and American record companies had issued unauthorized (also referred to as "pirate" and "bootleg") recordings of performances in which Warren appeared. They have issued at least 147 unauthorized commercial and private-label recordings.

Many unauthorized recordings were taken from Warren's Metropolitan Opera radio broadcasts as well as from other opera and radio broadcast performances. Regrettably, some were simply copied from RCA commercial recordings. Section IV lists by date within opera sequence the unauthorized recordings of which I was aware in early 1999, as well as eleven additional unauthorized recordings, including Warren's participation in a Carnegie Hall performance of Rossini's *Petite messe solennelle* on 9 April 1939.

For obvious reasons, the information disclosed on many pirate record labels and album covers is not reliable. To clarify the information shown on private labels issued by Edward J. Smith, a prolific producer of unauthorized opera recordings, the Greenwood Press (Westport, Connecticut) published *EJS: Discography of the Edward J. Smith Recordings* in 1994. This monumental work by William Shaman, William J. Collins, and Calvin M. Goodwin catalogs Smith's GAO (The Golden Age of Opera) label from 1956 to 1971. Section IV includes fifteen GAO label selections in which Leonard Warren appears as well as eleven selections from Smith's UORC (Unique Opera Record Company) label and one selection from his ANNA label (*More EJS: Discography of the Edward J. Smith Recordings*, 1999).

I believe that Section IV correctly describes the unauthorized recordings, regardless of what is stated on the record labels or album covers. *There is no assurance, however, that Section IV includes all of Warren's unauthorized recordings.*

Section V. Opera Roles Recorded by Opera

Section V lists, by opera and date, the twenty two roles in twenty operas that Leonard Warren recorded (complete operas, highlights, and individual selections), as well as his roles in authorized recordings made from public opera and recital performances. Warren recorded selections from five operas in roles that he never performed on stage: *Il barbiere di Siviglia* (Figaro), *La bohème* (Marcello), *Les contes d'Hoffmann* (Dapertutto), *Falstaff* (Ford), and *Tannhäuser* (Wolfram).

Conversely, Leonard Warren performed in eight operas from which he made no authorized recordings: *Alceste* (High Priest), *Boris Godunov* (Rangoni and Shchelkalov), *Cavalleria rusticana* (Alfio), *Ernani* (Carlo), *The Island God* (Ilo), *Lohengrin* (Herald), *Lucia di Lammermoor* (Enrico), and *Samson et Dalila* (High Priest). Except for *The Island God*, unauthorized recordings from various public performances of these operas are listed in Section IV.

Section VI. Video Excerpts from the Voice of Firestone Telecasts

Section VI lists video reproductions of kinescope masters of Leonard Warren's performances on the Voice of Firestone telecasts that were simulcast on radio. The videos include excerpts from Warren's four telecasts produced in 1949, 1952, and 1953. The original kinescope masters are preserved in the archives of the Idabelle Firestone Music Library at the New England Conservatory in Boston. They were reproduced on video and distributed by VAI Video. This section lists the date of each telecast, the selection performed, the composer and lyricist, the conductor, and the related VAI Video catalog number.

Warren also appeared in two other Voice of Firestone telecasts for which kinescopes are not present in the Idabelle Firestone Music Library. On 23 January 1950 Warren sang "One Alone," "Drink to Me Only with Thine Eyes," "While Hearts Are Singing," and "Si può?" (*Pagliacci*). On 27 March 1950 he sang "March of the Musketeers," "Romance," "Without a Song," and "Eri tu?" (*Un ballo in maschera*).

Section VII. Metropolitan Opera Radio Broadcast Performances by Opera

Leonard Warren performed in eighty-three Metropolitan Opera radio broadcast performances. Beginning with a January 1939 broadcast performance of *Simon Boccanegra* and ending with his final broadcast performance of *Macbeth* in January 1960, Warren appeared in twenty-four roles in twenty-three operas. Section VII lists, by opera, the date of each Met radio broadcast and the role Warren performed. The only authorized recordings of these performances are the Historic Broadcast series issued by the Metropolitan Opera Association. Warren is heard in the following recordings:

Broadcast Date	Opera	Catalog Number	Issue Date	Discography Numbers
21 Jan. 1939	*Simon Boccanegra* (Paolo)	Met 13	May 1986	1001 [2061]
16 Mar. 1946	*La Gioconda*	Met 17	Apr. 1991	1040 [2035]
29 Nov. 1952	*La forza del destino* (excerpts from Act II)	Met 100	Mar. 1985	1086 [2026]
4 Dec. 1954	*Andrea Chénier*	Met 15	July 1988	1094 [2004]
7 Jan. 1956	*Tosca*	Met 10	July 1983	1104 [2065]
8 Mar. 1958	*Otello*	Met 20	Mar. 1996	1109 [2040]

Private Recordings

Prior to winning the Metropolitan Opera Auditions of the Air in 1938, Warren made several private studio recordings with piano accompaniment: "Si può?" (*Pagliacci*) and "Ol' Man River" on 25 September 1936, and "Largo al factotum" (*Il barbiere di Siviglia*) on 30 September 1937.

Radio Broadcasts

Leonard Warren and tenor John Carter were co-winners of the Metropolitan Opera Auditions of the Air broadcast of 27 March 1938. Warren sang "Largo al factotum" and "Duna." Warren and Carter sang the duet "Au fond du temple saint" from *Les pêcheurs de perles*. Warren also appeared on prior Auditions of the Air broadcasts of 31 October 1937, 2 January 1938, and 13 March 1938.

In addition, Warren appeared on many other radio broadcasts, including the WQXR Artist Recital (20 June 1937), Chevrolet's Sinfonietta (13 and 20 July 1937); Sealtest's Rising Musical Stars (26 December 1937 and 27 March 1938); the Magic Key of RCA (15 May 1938); Consolidated Edison's Echoes of New York (21 March 1939, 3 and 31 October 1939, 2 January and 30 April 1940); Westinghouse's Musical Americana (9 and 30 May 1940, 6 June 1940); The Songs of Your Life (4 September 1940); Ford Summer Hour (6 July 1941); For America We Sing (10 November 1941); Celebration for Edward R. Murrow (2 December 1941); Treasure Hour of Song (8 May 1942); Coca-Cola's The Pause That Refreshes on the Air (19 December 1943, 2 April 1944); What's New? (6 November 1943; 15, 22, and 29 January 1944; 5, 12, and 19 February 1944); Music America Loves Best (1 July and 17 December 1944); The Metropolitan Opera Presents: Sherwin-Williams Hour (25 February 1945); The World of Song (16 April and 2 July 1944); The Ford Sunday Evening Hour (4 January 1942, 11 November 1945, 3 March and 9 June 1946); The Standard Hour (5 November 1944, 19 and 26 October 1947, and 17 October 1954); and The Bell Telephone Hour (25 July 1955; 13 February and 2 July 1956; 4 February, 10 June, and 25 November 1957; and 9 June 1958). This information derives from William Shaman, a log prepared by Agatha Warren, and the Vivien Warren Collection.

As shown below, Warren also appeared on several V-Discs. These were a unique series of 78 rpm phonograph records produced during and soon after World War II by a small service group in New York. Two V-Disc selections of Warren derived from RCA Victor commercial recordings made in 1941. Coca-Cola's The Pause That Refreshes on the Air, the CBS broadcast of 19 December 1943, was with André Kostelanetz and his orchestra in Liederkranz Hall in New York City. On 2 April 1944, another Coca-Cola broadcast with Warren and Kostelanetz took place at Carnegie Hall. This broadcast was pressed on V-Discs, but apparently they were not issued.

Sears Number	Broadcast or Recording Date RCA Catalog Number	V-Disc Number	Selection
KOS-12	19 Dec. 1943 (Navy 68-A)	288A	"Silent Night" (incorrectly identified as "It Came Upon the Midnight Clear")
WAR-8	3 Sep. 1941 18293-A (78 rpm)	130-A	"È sogno? O realtà?" (Ford's monologue, *Falstaff*)
WAR-9	4 Sep. 1941 18420-A (78 rpm)	130-B	"Avant de quitter ces lieux" (*Faust)*

Source: Richard S. Sears, *V-Discs: A History and Discography* (Westport. Connecticut: Greenwood Press, 1980) and *First Supplement* (1986).

On 30 October 1954, Leonard Warren performed at the Library of Congress in Washington, D.C., in the premiere radio broadcast of Norman Dello Joio's *The Lamentation of Saul*. Warren was accompanied by a chamber ensemble with the composer at the piano. This work was commissioned by the Elizabeth Sprague Coolidge Foundation. The world premiere had been performed by Warren and Dello Joio on 21 August 1954 at South Mountain Temple of Music in the Berkshires at South Mountain, Pittsfield, Massachusetts.

Television

In addition to the Voice of Firestone telecasts, Leonard Warren appeared in three pioneering Metropolitan Opera telecasts in 1940, 1948, and 1954. He also performed three times on the Ed Sullivan Show and in a 1956 telecast, Producers' Showcase.

The first televised performance by the Metropolitan Opera, a gala event with nine artists, was held at the Manhattan NBC Television Studio on 10 March 1940. The master of ceremonies was the Met's general manager, Edward Johnson. Warren sang "Largo al factotum" from *Il barbiere di Siviglia* and participated in the Quartet from *Rigoletto*, "Bella figlia del-l'amore." As described in the Metropolitan Opera Guild's *Annals of the Metropolitan Opera* (1989), "This was the first televised performance of the Metropolitan Opera. The audience was limited to viewers on the approximately two thousand sets able to receive the National Broadcasting Company's ten hours of weekly transmissions."

The second Met telecast, a performance of *Otello* on 29 November 1948, was the first telecast of a complete opera from the stage of the Metropolitan Opera House in collaboration with the American Broadcasting Company. The conductor was Fritz Busch and the cast included Ramón Vinay (Otello), Licia Albanese (Desdemona), Leonard Warren (Iago), Martha Lipton (Emilia), and John Garris (Cassio). Regrettably, the kinescopes of these two historic Met telecasts cannot be located.

The third Met telecast was on 8 November 1954. This gala performance from the stage of the Metropolitan Opera House was relayed via closed circuit to theaters throughout the United States. Warren sang "Si può?" from *Pagliacci* and also performed as Amonasro in Act II of *Aida* with Zinka Milanov, Mario Del Monaco, Blanche Thebom, and Jerome Hines. The conductor was Alberto Erede.

On the Ed Sullivan Show of 26 November 1950 Warren sang "Cortigiani, vil razza dannata" in costume from *Rigoletto* and "March of the Musketeers" from Rudolf Friml's *The Three Musketeers*. For the latter selection he was accompanied on the piano by the composer. On 11 April 1954 Warren sang "Si può?" from *Pagliacci*. His third appearance was on 8 October 1950, although what he sang is not known.

On 30 January 1956, Warren sang "Si può?" from *Pagliacci* on an NBC color telecast of Producer's Showcase entitled "Festival of Music" narrated by Charles Laughton. Other singers included Marian Anderson, Jussi Björling, Zinka Milanov, Mildred Miller, Jan Peerce, Roberta Peters, Risë Stevens, Renata Tebaldi, and Blanche Thebom.

Motion Pictures

Warren appeared in only one motion picture, *Irish Eyes Are Smiling*, a 20th Century–Fox production released in 1944. The Technicolor movie features sentimental Irish songs composed by Ernest R. Ball, who was portrayed by Dick Haymes. In the movie, Warren portrayed himself and sang "A Little Bit of Heaven" and a portion of "Love Me and the World Is Mine." Mezzo-soprano Blanche Thebom also appeared in the movie.

The World's Greatest Operas and the Heart of the Opera Series

Leonard Warren's first published recordings appeared in two series: the World's Greatest Operas and the Heart of the Opera. William R. Moran, in his article "World's Greatest Operas Series" (*The Record Collector,* November 1988), described these recordings as

> a project conceived for promotional and educational purposes by Publishers Service Co. of New York, and . . . produced, recorded and pressed by RCA Victor. The records were sold through newspapers in the United States at prices considerably below commercial 78 rpm records of the time. Initially they were labeled in two ways: the edition sold without albums had blue labels with gold lettering, and were titled "World's Greatest Operas." They bore no artists' names, but the statement "Recorded by World Famous Artists and Conductors." There was no manufacturer's name. A more expensive edition, provided with albums and bound-in introductory leaflets authored by Samuel Chotzinoff which usually ran to eight pages, included a brief biography of the composer, the story of the opera, and an English libretto keyed to the recorded material. The labels of this "de Luxe" series bore cream, gold, red and brown labels, and were called "Philharmonic Transcriptions." The recordings of the two editions were identical. At a slightly later date, the Philharmonic Transcriptions were provided in slide-automatic sequence, these with a white, silver and blue label. Still later, sets appeared with a "Music Appreciation" label. In all 78 rpm editions and formats, each side carried a catalogue number beginning with the letters "SR." Opera records were numbered from SR-45 through SR-84. Six sides were used for most operas; *Aida* had 8, and *Tristan* 12. Other SR catalog numbers were used for instrumental material. In 1954, RCA transferred the opera records to LP, and they were issued in seven parts on the Camden (CAL) label, as "The Heart of the Opera." These were cut from the catalogues in 1956, 1957 and 1958. The sets were also at one time available on the Parade label, but I have not examined examples.

As the opera records were published without artist identification, there was much speculation as to the identity of the singers and conductors involved. Charles O'Connell, who had been in charge of the project for Victor, told its history without disclosing full details in his book *The Other Side of the Record* (1947, pp. 329–330). The late Frank Garcia Montes of Havana managed to piece together the casts for the recordings from information obtained from some of his friends who took part in the sessions, and these have proved remarkably accurate in light of the discography by Michael H. Gray (in the ARSC *Journal,* Vol. VII, No. 1/2, 1975), and that of Frederick P.

Fellers (*The Metropolitan Opera Company Orchestra and Chorus,* 1984).

Moran received confirmation from Rose Bampton that all the opera sessions took place in Town Hall, New York City (RCA files indicate that some sessions were at the Academy of Music in Philadelphia). Moran noted, "The orchestra and chorus were drawn from those of the Metropolitan Opera Co. The recordings are technically excellent."

Published sources and a review of the recordings themselves indicate that Warren appeared in five of the twelve recorded opera highlights. The 78 rpm recordings were issued in 1940. Individual LP Camden (CAL) recordings were issued in 1954, and the LP set CFL-101 was issued in 1955. All of the Leonard Warren excerpts from these series were included by VAI on an authorized CD called *Leonard Warren: His First Recordings (1940)*. It was released in 1992 (VAIA 1017). The series also included *Faust, Madama Butterfly, La bohème, Tannhäuser, Lohengrin, Tristan und Isolde,* and *Le nozze di Figaro.*

Recordings with Leonard Warren in the World's Greatest Operas and the Heart of the Opera Series

Opera Highlights	The World's Greatest Operas (78 rpm)	Camden		Discography Number
		The Heart of the Opera LP (33⅓ rpm) CFL-101 (set)	Volume	
Carmen	SR 45, 46, 47	CAL-221	1	2014
Aida	SR 51, 52, 53, 54	CAL-225	5	2002, 2003
Rigoletto	SR 58, 59, 60	CAL-226	6	2052, 2055, 2058, 2060
La traviata	SR 67, 68, 69	CAL-227	7	2068, 2070
Pagliacci	SR 70, 71, 72	CAL-226	6	2047

Source: Frederick P. Fellers, *The Metropolitan Opera on Record.* Westport, Connecticut: Greenwood Press, 1984.

Leonard Warren Commemorative Compact Discs

Under a licensing agreement with BMG Classics, the Leonard Warren Foundation plans to release in March 2000, coincident with the publication of this book, a two-CD set entitled *Opera Arias and Concert Songs* on the Leonard Warren Commemorative label, to be distributed by VAI Distribution, Inc.

Opera Arias (LWC-1) contains sixteen arias from fifteen operas, of which eight were composed by Verdi. The CD includes "O du mein holder Abendstern" from *Tannhäuser,* recorded by Melodiya at Warren's public recital in Moscow on 13 May 1958. Except for unauthorized recordings of Warren's 27 January 1940 performance as the Herald in the Met's *Lohengrin,* this is Warren's only recorded Wagnerian aria and is its first release outside Russia. The May 1958 "O sainte médaille . . . Avant de quitter ces lieux" also comes from Warren's public recitals in Russia, recorded by RCA.

Concert Songs (LWC-2) contains twenty-four concert songs sung in English, Italian, and Latin. It includes three Italian songs recorded by RCA in 1954 that apparently were produced in extremely limited quantities but not made available commercially. It also includes "Agnus Dei" from Warren's public recitals of May 1958 in Russia, recorded by RCA, as well as the first release of Warren's RCA recordings of "Occhi di fata," "Nel giardino," and "Canto di primavera." I have examined a private collector's one-sided 10″ LP with an RCA Red Seal label that contains three 33⅓ rpm bands with three selections. The label's left side has the number M70L0162, which also appears stamped on the inner rim with the take number 1. The right side of the label reads: "Santoliquido: Nel Giardino (In the Garden) E4RC-0256; Cimara-Salvatori: Canto di Primavera (Song of Spring) E4RC-0255; Denza-Tremacoldo: Occhi di Fata (Lovely Eyes) E4RC-0253."

Leonard Warren Commemorative CDs: *Opera Arias and Concert Songs*

Recording Session/ Performance Date	Selection
Opera Arias (LWC-1)	
7 Mar. 1946	Prologo: Si può? (*Pagliacci*)
26 Mar. 1945	Largo al factotum (*Il barbiere di Sivilgia*)
4 Feb. 1950	Di Provenza il mar (*La traviata*)
3 Sep. 1941	È sogno? O realtà? (Ford's monologue, *Falstaff*)
3 Mar. 1955	Nemico della patria (*Andrea Chénier*)
4 Sep. 1941	Allez! Pour te livrer . . . Scintille, diamant! (Dapertutto's aria, *Les contes d'Hoffmann*)
14 Dec. 1945	Eri tu? (*Un ballo in maschera*)
26 Mar. 1945	Chanson du toreador: Votre toast! (*Carmen*)
May 1958	O sainte médaille . . . Avant de quitter ces lieux (*Faust*)
14 Dec. 1945	Cortigiani, vil razza dannata (*Rigoletto*)
13 May 1958	O du mein holder Abendstern (*Tannhäuser*)
7 Mar. 1946	Vanne: la tua meta già vedo . . . Credo in un Dio crudel (*Otello*)
3 Mar. 1955	Era la notte (*Otello*)
2 Jan. 1947	Il balen del suo sorriso (*Il trovatore*)

| 12 Feb. 1959 | Perfidi! All'anglo . . . Pietà, rispetto, amore (*Macbeth*) |
| 16 Feb. 1950 | Morir! Tremenda cosa . . . Urna fatale del mio destino . . . È s'altra prova rinvenir potessi? . . . Ah! Egli è salvo! (*La forza del destino*) |

Concert Songs (LWC-2)

9 July 1947	Shenandoah
9 July 1947	Low Lands
8 July 1947	A Rovin'
9 July 1947	Haul-A-Way, Joe
5 Oct. 1951	Rolling Down to Rio
2 Oct. 1951	Boots
28 Sep. 1950	On the Road to Mandalay
5 Oct. 1951	Danny Deever
5 Oct. 1951	Smugglers' Song
28 Sep. 1950	America the Beautiful
26 Sep. 1950	Home on the Range
28 Sep. 1950	Battle Hymn of the Republic
9 June 1954	Ideale
9 June 1954	Occhi di fata
8 June 1954	Nel giardino
9 June 1954	Canto di primavera
3 Sep. 1947	Danny Boy
26 Sep. 1950	Mother Machree
26 Sep. 1950	A Little Bit of Heaven
26 Sep. 1950	Love's Old Sweet Song
3 Sep. 1947	None But the Lonely Heart
3 Sep. 1947	Because
29 Nov. 1947	The Lord's Prayer
May 1958	Agnus Dei

Acknowledgments

In compiling this discography, I received invaluable help from many people to whom I am deeply grateful. Five people have been particularly unsparing of their time: George Shelby Weaver, Louisiana record collector and discographer; Jack Belsom, archivist, New Orleans Opera; Claudia J. Depkin, manager, Worldwide Archives, BMG Entertainment; Edward F. Durbeck III, founder of the Durbeck Archive and opera LP collector *extraordinaire*; and William Shaman, author of the two-volume *EJS: Discography of the Edward J. Smith Recordings*.

I also acknowledge with gratitude the assistance of Harvey Becker, SOFA Entertainment; Bruce Burroughs, editor emeritus of *Opera Quarterly*; George

Dansker, librarian and producer of the New Orleans Opera Association archival CD series; Eugene Gaudette, BMG Classics; Paul Gruber, executive director, program development, Metropolitan Opera Guild; Daniel Guss, senior director, product development, BMG Classics; David Hamilton, music critic, author, and editor of *The Metropolitan Opera Encyclopedia*; Ann-Marie Harris, senior assistant, local history department, Berkshire Athenaeum; Harald Henrysson, author of *A Jussi Björling Phonography*, 2d edition; Richard Koprowski, assistant archivist, the Stanford Archive of Recorded Sound; Elwood A. McKee, collector and researcher; James B. McPherson, opera historian; William R. Moran, author, discographer, and cofounder and honorary curator of the Stanford Archive of Recorded Sound; John Parry, second exploitation manager, Decca Record Company Limited; Tom Peel, researcher and discographer; the late John Pfeiffer, executive producer, RCA Red Seal Artists and Repertoire; Emil R. Pinta, author of *A Chronological Jan Peerce Discography, 1931–1982*; and C.M. Rodier, director, contracts and business affairs, EMI Classics.

My special thanks to Wanda I. Carney, who typed countless drafts of both the discography and chronology. Her word processing wizardry transmuted my research into readable form. I would also like to express my sincere appreciation for the encouragement of the late Vivien Warren, Leonard Warren's sister, who cofounded with me in 1986 the Leonard Warren Foundation. Finally I would like to thank Eve Goodman, editorial director of Amadeus Press, for her admirable patience in editing the daunting format and endless detail of my discography and chronology.

Notes to the Discography

1. In collaboration with RCA, Decca (London Records, Inc.) recorded the complete *La Gioconda* in July–August 1957 and the complete *La forza del destino* in July–August 1958. Both recording sessions were held in Rome at L'Accademia di Santa Cecilia. Unfortunately, Decca's documentation of these sessions is unavailable so that we do not know the exact recording session dates and related matrix numbers for individual selections.

2. The highlights of *Un ballo in maschera* were recorded in January 1955 and issued in RCA Victor album LM-1911 (LP) in March 1955. Although the entire recording session consisted of matrix numbers F2-RP-0603 through F2-RP-0613, the available RCA recording documents do not reveal the exact recording session dates and related matrix numbers for individual selections.

3. In July 1955, Warren recorded Ford's monologue "È sogno? O realtà?"from *Falstaff* at the Rome Opera House with Vincenzo Bellezza conducting. In the absence of RCA documents for this recording session, we do not know the exact date or the related matrix number. However, on 4 July 1955 Warren recorded "Credo in un Dio crudel" from *Otello* at the Rome Opera House, also with Vincenzo Bellezza conducting. Neither are there RCA documents or matrix numbers for this recording session, but both the *Otello* and *Falstaff* arias appear in RCA Victor album LM-1932 (LP), so it is highly likely that both arias were recorded in Rome on the same day.

4. The complete *Macbeth* was recorded by RCA Victor in February 1959. Although the entire recording session consisted of matrix numbers K2-RB-1106 through K2-RB-1126, the available RCA recording documents do not reveal the exact recording session dates and related matrix numbers for individual selections.

5. In several instances, the description of Warren's opera recordings appearing on RCA album covers is incorrect. Where discovered, the errors have been corrected in this discography. Errors probably occurred because Warren recorded the same aria more than once. For example, the album cover on RCA's German pressing PVM1-9082 Vol. 2 [26.41410] states that the recitative and aria "Alzati! là tuo figlio . . . Eri tu?" from *Un ballo in maschera* were recorded on 14 December 1945 with Dimitri Mitropoulos conducting. The correct date is 9 January 1955 (see Discography Number 2008c). The "Eri tu?" aria recorded on 14 December 1945 was conducted by Frieder Weissmann and did not include the recitative "Alzati! là tuo figlio" (see Discography Number 2009). Similarly, on RCA 447-0802, a 45 rpm recording issued in September 1957 on RCA's Gold Standard Series, the record label on side 2 indicates that "Di Provenza il mar" from *La traviata* was recorded on 2 June 1956 in Italy with Renato Cellini conducting the RCA Victor Orchestra. In fact, Warren recorded "Di Provenza il mar" at the Rome Opera House on 2 June 1956 with Pierre Monteux conducting a complete performance of *La traviata*. However, the "Di Provenza il mar" on RCA's 447-0802 (45 rpm) was actually the same take used in LM-1932 (LP) that was recorded on 4 February 1950 in New York City with Cellini conducting the RCA Victor Orchestra (see Discography Number 2069).

6. According to Frederick P. Fellers in *The Metropolitan Opera on Record* (Discographies, Number 9), Leonard Warren wrote RCA Victor and requested that his name be removed from the *Simon Boccanegra* record labels on the 1939 recording of "Plebe! Patrizi . . . Piango su voi" issued on RCA catalog number 15642. Fellers noted that beginning in 1946, the RCA 78 rpm labels no longer listed Warren's name.

7. In the 1952 recording of the complete *Il trovatore*, the duet "Udiste? Come albeggi" was actually recorded by Leonard Warren and Zinka Milanov on 9 May 1951 (see Discography Number 2077).

8. From the Vivien Warren Collection, I have examined three one-sided 10" RCA Victor test pressings that contain a 78 rpm band with one selection each. Leonard Warren's name and the song descriptions are handwritten in blue ink on a plain white label. The matrix numbers are written in pencil with the designation "RS." "RCA Victor" is engraved in the black plastic on the backs of the records. Never released commercially by RCA, these selections are "L'esperto nocchiero" (Giovanni Bononcini) 065695-1 RS, "Tu lo sai" (Giuseppe Torelli) 060706-2 RS, and "Turn Ye to Me" (arr. by Miguel Sandoval) 065696-3 RS.

Section I. Audio Recording Sessions and Selected Public Performances by Date

Discog. No.	Date	Opera	Selection	Conductor or Pianist*	RCA Victor Matrix-Take No.	Comments
1001 [2061]	21 Jan. 39	Simon Boccanegra	Complete opera (with Tibbett as Simon, Warren as Paolo, Rethberg, Martinelli, Pinza)	E. Panizza	—	Met Historic Broadcast.
1002 [2062]	3 May 39	Simon Boccanegra	Plebe! Patrizi! . . . Piango su voi (with Tibbett as Simon, Warren as Paolo, Bampton, Martinelli, Nicholson)	W. Pelletier	CS-036850-1, 1A	Warren's first studio recording session.
1003 [2002]	28 May 40	Aida	Che veggo! Egli? Mio padre! (with Bampton)	W. Pelletier	CS-050341-1, 1A, 1R, 1AR	
1004 [2014]	31 May 40	Carmen	Chanson du toreador: Votre toast!	W. Pelletier	CS-050352-1, 1A, 1R	
1005 [2070]	31 May 40	La traviata	Di sprezzo degno sè stesso rende (with Steber, Tokatyan)	W. Pelletier	CS-050356-1, 1A	
1006 [2052]	31 May 40	Rigoletto	Ah, più di Ceprano importuno non v'è! (with Tokatyan)	W. Pelletier	CS-050357-1A	
1007 [2047]	17 June 40	Pagliacci	Prologo: Si può?	W. Pelletier	CS-051102-1, 1A, 2, 2A	
1008 [2003]	17 June 40	Aida	Rivedrai le foreste inbalsamate (with Bampton)	W. Pelletier	CS-051110-1, 1A	
1009 [2068]	25 June 40	La traviata	Pura siccome un angelo . . . Così alla misera . . . Morrò! la mia memoria (with Steber)	W. Pelletier	CS-051113-1, 1A, 2, 2A; CS-051114-1, 1A	

Discog. No.	Date	Opera	Selection	Conductor or Pianist*	RCA Victor Matrix-Take No.	Comments
1010 [2055]	25 June 40	Rigoletto	Cortigiani, vil razza dannata	W. Pelletier	CS-051117-1, 1A	
1011 [2060]	25 June 40	Rigoletto	Bella figlia dell'amore (with Tokatyan, Dickenson, Browning)	W. Pelletier	CS-051118-1, 2, 2A	
1012 [2058]	25 June 40	Rigoletto	Tutte le feste . . . Piangi, fanciulla, piangi . . . Compiuto pur quanto (with Dickenson, Alvary)	W. Pelletier	CS-051119-1, 1A / CS-051120-1, 1A	
1013 [3019]	4 Feb. 41	—	Drake's Drum	M. Sandoval*	BS-060703-1, 2	Unpublished.
1014 [3053]	4 Feb. 41	—	Outward Bound	M. Sandoval*	BS-060704-1, 1A, 2, 2A, 3	Unpublished.
1015 [3049]	4 Feb. 41	—	The Old Superb	M. Sandoval*	BS-060705-1, 2, 2A	Unpublished.
1016 [3062]	4 Feb. 41 / 10 June 41	—	Tu lo sai	M. Sandoval*	BS-060706-1, 2, 2A, 3, 3A, 4, 4A	Unpublished.
1017 [3023]	10 June 41	—	L'esperto nocchiero	M. Sandoval*	BS-065695-1	Unpublished.
1018 [3063]	10 June 41	—	Turn Ye to Me	M. Sandoval*	BS-065696-1, 2, 3, 3A	Unpublished.
1019 [2020]	3 Sep. 41	Falstaff	È sogno? O realtà?	W. Pelletier	CS-066748-1, 1A, 2, 2A	Ford's monologue.
1020 [2037]	3 Sep. 41	La Gioconda	O monumento!	W. Pelletier	CS-066749-1, 1A, 2, 2A	

No.	Date	Opera	Title	Conductor	Matrix	Notes
1021 [2018]	3–4 Sep. 41	Les contes d'Hoffmann	Allez! pour te livrer . . . Scintille, diamant!	W. Pelletier	CS-066750-1, 2, 2A, 3, 3A	Dapertutto's aria.
1022 [2056]	4 Sep. 41	Rigoletto	Cortigiani, vil razza dannata	W. Pelletier	CS-066751-1, 2, 2A	Unpublished (remade 14 Dec. 45).
1023 [2053]	4 Sep. 41	Rigoletto	Pari siamo!	W. Pelletier	CS-066752-1, 1A, 2, 2A	Unpublished (remade 14 Dec. 45).
1024 [2023]	4 Sep. 41	Faust	O sainte médaille . . . Avant de quitter ces lieux	W. Pelletier	CS-066753-1, 1A	
1025 [2073]	11 Sep. 41	Il trovatore	Il balen del suo sorriso	W. Pelletier	CS-066766-1, 1A	Unpublished (remade 2 Jan. 47).
1026 [2059]	25 May 44	Rigoletto	Act IV only (with Milanov, Merriman, Peerce, Moscona)	A. Toscanini	—	Red Cross concert, Madison Square Garden.
1027 [2074]	18 Dec. 44	Il trovatore	Il balen del suo sorriso	M. Pilzer	D4-RC-682-1, 1A, 2, 2A	Unpublished (remade 2 Jan. 47).
1028 [3030]	18 Dec. 44	—	A Little Bit of Heaven	M. Pilzer	D4-RB-717-1, 1A	Unpublished (remade 26 Sep. 50).
1029 [3068]	18 Dec. 44	—	When Irish Eyes Are Smiling	M. Pilzer	D4-RB-718-1, 1A, 2, 2A	Unpublished.
1030 [2048]	27 Dec. 44	Pagliacci	Prologo: Si può?	F. Weissmann	D4-RC-695-1, 1A, 2, 2A	Unpublished (remade 7 Mar. 46).

Discog. No.	Date	Opera	Selection	Conductor or Pianist*	RCA Victor Matrix-Take No.	Comments
1031 [2015]	27 Dec. 44	*Carmen*	Chanson du toreador: Votre toast!	F. Weissmann	D4-RC-696-1, 1A	Unpublished (remade 26 Mar. 45).
1032 [2010]	27 Dec. 44	*Il barbiere di Siviglia*	Largo al factotum	F. Weissmann	D4-RC-697-1, 1A	Unpublished (remade 26 Mar. 45).
1033 [2016]	26 Mar. 45	*Carmen*	Chanson du toreador: Votre toast!	W. Tarrasch	D4-RC-696-2A, 2B	
1034 [2011]	26 Mar. 45	*Il barbiere di Siviglia*	Largo al factotum	W. Tarrasch	D4-RC-697-2A, 2B	
1035 [2054]	14 Dec. 45	*Rigoletto*	Pari siamo!	F. Weissmann	D5-RC-1800-1, 1A, 2, 2A	
1036 [2057]	14 Dec. 45	*Rigoletto*	Cortigiani, vil razza dannata	F. Weissmann	D5-RC-1801-1, 1A	
1037 [2009]	14 Dec. 45	*Un ballo in maschera*	Eri tu?	F. Weissmann	D5-RC-1802-1, 1A	
1038 [2049]	7 Mar. 46	*Pagliacci*	Prologo: Si può?	F. Weissmann	D6-RC-5178-1, 1A, 2, 2A	
1039 [2042]	7 Mar. 46	*Otello*	Vanne: la tua meta già vedo . . . Credo in un Dio crudel	F. Weissmann	D6-RC-5179-1, 1A, 2, 2A	
1040 [2035]	16 Mar. 46	*La Gioconda*	Complete opera (with Milanov, Tucker, Stevens, Vaghi, Harshaw)	E. Cooper	—	Met Historic Broadcast.

1041 [2031]	13 June 46	*La forza del destino*	Invano, Alvaro . . . Ah! Una suora mi lasciasti (with Peerce)	E. Leinsdorf	D6-RC-5973-1, 1A D6-RC-5974-1, 1A	Unpublished (remade 27 Dec. 46).
1042 [2028]	13 June 46	*La forza del destino*	Solenne in quest'ora (with Peerce)	E. Leinsdorf	D6-RC-5975-1, 1A	
1043 [2032]	27 Dec. 46	*La forza del destino*	Invano, Alvaro . . . Ah! Una suora mi lasciasti (with Peerce)	J. P. Morel	D6-RC-6653-1, 1A, 2, 2A D6-RC-6654-1, 1A	
1044 [2013]	27 Dec. 46	*La bohème*	In un coupé? . . . O Mimì, tu più non torni (with Peerce)	J. P. Morel	D6-RC-6655-1, 1A, 2, 2A	
1045 [2038]	2 Jan. 47	*La Gioconda*	Barcarola: Ah! Pescator, affonda l'esca	J. P. Morel	D7-RC-7100-1, 1A, 2, 2A	
1046 [2075]	2 Jan. 47	*Il trovatore*	Il balen del suo scrriso	J. P. Morel	D7-RC-7101-1, 1A, 2, 2A	
1047 [2076]	2 Jan. 47	*Il trovatore*	Qual suono! . . . Per me ora fatale . . . Ah! se l'error t'ingombra	J. P. Morel	D7-RC-7102-1, 1A, 2, 2A	Takes 2B and 2C made by electrical transfer 26 Mar. 47.
1048 [3001]	8 July 47	—	A Rovin' (arr. by Tom Scott)	M. Levine	D7-RB-1261-1, 1A, 1B, 1C	
1049 [3008]	8 July 47	—	Blow the Man Down (arr. by Tom Scott)	M. Levine	D7-RB-1262-1, 1A, 1B, 1C	
1050 [3020]	8 July 47	—	The Drummer and the Cook (arr. by Tom Scott)	M. Levine	D7-RB-1263-1, 1A, 1B, 1C	
1051 [3021]	8 July 47	—	The Drunken Sailor (arr. by Tom Scott)	M. Levine	D7-RB-1264-1, 1A, 1B, 1C	
1052 [3026]	9 July 47	—	Haul-A-Way, Joe (arr. by Tom Scott)	M. Levine	D7-RB-1265-1, 1A, 1B, 1C, 2, 2A, 2B, 2C	

Discog. No.	Date	Opera	Selection	Conductor or Pianist*	RCA Victor Matrix-Take No.	Comments
1053 [3055]	9 July 47	—	Rio Grande (arr. by Tom Scott)	M. Levine	D7-RB-1266-1, 1A, 1B, 1C	
1054 [3034]	9 July 47	—	Low Lands (arr. by Tom Scott)	M. Levine	D7-RB-1267-1, 1A, 1B, 1C	
1055 [3057]	9 July 47	—	Shenandoah (arr. by Tom Scott)	M. Levine	D7-RB-1268-1, 1A, 1B, 1C, 2, 2A, 2B, 2C	
1056 [3006]	3 Sep. 47	—	Because	W. Sektberg*	D7-RB-1604-1, 1A, 2, 2A	
1057 [3041]	3 Sep. 47	—	None But the Lonely Heart	W. Sektberg*	D7-RB-1605-1, 1A, 2, 2A	
1058 [3017]	3 Sep. 47	—	Danny Boy (arr. by Fred Weatherly)	W. Sektberg*	D7-RB-1606-1, 1A	
1059 [3067]	29 Nov. 47	—	Until	W. Sektberg*	D7-RB-2544-1, 1A	
1060 [3032]	29 Nov. 47	—	The Lord's Prayer	W. Sektberg*	D7-RB-2546-1, 1A, 2, 2A	Takes 2B and 2C made by electrical transfer 31 Mar. 48.
1061 [3051]	29 Nov. 47	—	On the Road to Mandalay	W. Sektberg*	D7-RB-2545-1, 1A	
1062 [2063]	4 Feb. 50	*Simon Boccanegra*	Dinne, perchè in quest'eremo . . . Dinne, alcun là non vedesti? . . . Figlia! a tal nome palpito (with Varnay)	R. Cellini	EO-RC-108-1, 1A, 2, 2A EO-RC-109-1, 1A, 2, 2A	

No.	Date	Opera	Title	Conductor	Matrix	Notes
1063 [2069]	4 Feb. 50	La traviata	Di Provenza il Mar	R. Cellini	EO-RC-110-1, 1A, 1B, 2, 2A	Take 1C made by electrical transfer 18 Mar. 50.
1064 [2030] [2027]	16 Feb. 50	La forza del destino	Morir! tremenda cosa . . . Urna fatale del mio destino . . . È s'altra prova rinvenir potessi? . . . Ah! Egli è salvo! (with Keast)	R. Cellini	EO-RC-147-1, 1A, 2, 2A EO-RC-148-1, 1A, 2, 2A	Takes 1B and 1C made by electrical transfer 18 Mar. 50.
1065 [2041]	16 Feb. 50	Otello	Brindisi: Inaffia l'ugola! (with Sprinzena, Matto)	R. Cellini	EO-RC-149-1, 1A	
1066 [2050]	8 Mar.–25 May 50	Rigoletto	Complete opera (with Berger, Peerce, Merriman, Tajo, Wentworth)	R. Cellini	EO-RC-154 through EO-RC-181	First complete opera recorded by RCA Victor.
1067 [3027]	26 Sep. 50	—	Home on the Range	F. Black	EO-RB-5668-1, 1A	
1068 [3037]	26 Sep. 50	—	Mother Machree	F. Black	EO-RB-5669-1, 1A	
1069 [3033]	26 Sep. 50	—	Love's Old Sweet Song	F. Black	EO-RB-5670-1, 1A	
1070 [3031]	26 Sep. 50	—	A Little Bit of Heaven	F. Black	EO-RB-5671-1, 1A, 2, 2A	
1071 [3050]	28 Sep. 50	—	Ol' Man River	F. Black	EO-RB-5672-1, 1A	
1072 [3004]	28 Sep. 50	—	America the Beautiful	F. Black	EO-RB-5673-1, 1A	
1073 [3005]	28 Sep. 50	—	Battle Hymn of the Republic	F. Black	EO-RB-5674-1, 1A	
1074 [3052]	28 Sep. 50	—	On the Road to Mandalay	F. Black	EO-RB-5675-1, 1A	

Discog. No.	Date	Opera	Selection	Conductor or Pianist*	RCA Victor Matrix-Take No.	Comments
1075 [2012]	23-24 Mar. 51	La bohème	Highlights (with Albanese, Di Stefano, Munsel, Cehanovsky, Moscona)	R. Cellini	E1-RC-3179 through E1-RC-3185	
1076 [2077]	9 May 51	Il trovatore	Udiste? Come albeggi (with Milanov)	R. Cellini	E1-RC-3421-1, 1A, 1R, 1AR (from 3421-1 and 3422-1)	(Note 7).
1077 [3054]	2 Oct. 51	—	Recessional	F. Black	E1-RB-3731-1, 1A	
1078 [3010]	2 Oct. 51	—	Boots	F. Black	E1-RB-3736-1, 1A	
1079 [3025]	2 Oct. 51	—	Gunga Din	F. Black	E1-RB-3737-1, 1A	
1080 [3059]	5 Oct. 51	—	Smugglers' Song	F. Black	E1-RB-3732-1, 1A	
1081 [3056]	5 Oct. 51	—	Rolling Down to Rio	F. Black	E1-RB-3733-1, 1A	
1082 [3038]	5 Oct. 51	—	Mother o' Mine	F. Black	E1-RB-3734-1, 1A, 1R, 2, 2A	
1083 [3018]	5 Oct. 51	—	Danny Deever	F. Black	E1-RB-3735-1, 1A	
1084 [2071]	21 Feb.–16 Mar. 52	Il trovatore	Complete opera (with Björling, Milanov, Barbieri, Moscona)	R. Cellini	E2-RC-0170 through E2-RC-0191 (no. 0172, 0178, 0181 or 0185)	(Note 7).

No.	Date	Work	Details	Conductor	Matrix	Notes
1085 [2051]	3 or 5 Apr. 52	Rigoletto	Complete opera (with Gueden, Conley, Muhs, Wildermann, Treigle)	W. Herbert	—	New Orleans Opera performance. VAI release.
1086 [2026]	29 Nov. 52	La forza del destino	Act II excerpts (with Tucker, Brazis)	F. Stiedry	—	Met Historic Broadcast.
1087 [2046]	6–29 Jan. 53	Pagliacci	Complete opera (with De Los Angeles, Björling, Merrill, Franke)	R. Cellini	E3-RC-2119 through E3-RC-2130	
1088 [3064]	9 June 54	—	L'ultima canzone	W. Sektberg*	E4-RC-0251-1	
1089 [3028]	9 June 54	—	Ideale	W. Sektberg*	E4-RC-0252-1	
1090 [3047]	9 June 54	—	Occhi di fata	W. Sektberg*	E4-RC-0253-1	
1091 [3060]	9 June 54	—	Stornello	W. Sektberg*	E4-RC-0254-1	Unpublished.
1092 [3011]	9 June 54	—	Canto di primavera	W. Sektberg*	E4-RC-0255-1	
1093 [3039]	9 June 54	—	Nel giardino	W. Sektberg*	E4-RC-0256-1	
1094 [2004]	4 Dec. 54	Andrea Chénier	Complete opera (with Del Monaco, Milanov, Elias, Baccaloni)	F. Cleva	—	Met Historic Broadcast.
1095 [2008]	9 Jan. 55 21 Jan. 55	Un ballo in maschera	Highlights (with Milanov, Peerce, Anderson, Peters)	D. Mitropoulos	F2-RP-0603 through F2-RP-0613	(Note 2).
1096 [2005]	3 Mar. 55	Andrea Chénier	Nemico della patria	J. Perlea	F2-RH-1770-1	

Discog. No.	Date	Opera	Selection	Conductor or Pianist*	RCA Victor Matrix-Take No.	Comments
1097 [2045]	3 Mar. 55	Otello	Era la notte	J. Perlea	F2-RH-1771-1	
1098 [2029]	7 Apr. 55	La forza del destino	Solenne in quest'ora (with Peerce)	R. Cellini	F2-RH-1695	
1099 [2033]	7 Apr. 55	La forza del destino	Invano, Alvaro . . . Ah! Una suora mi lasciasti (with Peerce)	R. Cellini	F2-RH-1696	
1100 [2034]	7 Apr. 55	La forza del destino	Io muoio! . . . Non imprecare (with Milanov, Peerce, Moscona)	R. Cellini	F2-RH-3123	
1101 [2001]	2–18 July 55	Aida	Complete opera (with Milanov, Bjÿrling, Barbieri, Christoff, Clabassi)	J. Perlea	2-F2-RH-4135 through 2-F2-RH-4155 (no 4150 or 4152)	Recorded in Rome.
1102 [2043]	4 July 55	Otello	Credo in un Dio crudel	V. Bellezza	(Note 3)	Recorded in Rome.
1103 [2021]	July 55	Falstaff	È sogno? O realtà?	V. Bellezza	(Note 3)	Recorded in Rome.
1104 [2065]	7 Jan. 56	Tosca	Complete opera (with Tebaldi, Tucker, Corena, De Paolis, Harvuot, Cehanovsky)	D. Mitropoulos	—	Met Historic Broadcast.
1105 [2019]	5 May 56	Falstaff	Complete opera (with Della Chiesa, Torigi, Pritchett, Schuh, Turp, Sachs, Treigle, Velluci, Assandri)	R. Cellini	—	New Orleans Opera performance. VAI release.

1106 [2067]	1–11 June 56	La traviata	Complete opera (with Carteri, Valletti, Marimpietri, Scarlini, La Porta)	P. Monteux	2-G-2-RB-4203 through 2-G-2-RB-4227 (no 4205, 4206,) 4213 or 4226	Recorded in Rome.
1107 [2066]	2–18 July 57	Tosca	Complete opera (with Milanov, Björling, Corena, Carlin, Monreale, Catalani, Preziosa)	E. Leinsdorf	2-H2-RB-2539-1 through 2-H2-RB-2552-1 (no 2540)	Recorded in Rome.
1108 [2036]	July–Aug. 57	La Gioconda	Complete opera (with Milanov, Di Stefano, Elias, Clabassi, Amparan)	F. Previtali	4-H2-RP-37 through 4-H2-RP-42	(Note 1).
1109 [2040]	8 Mar. 58	Otello	Complete opera (with Del Monaco, De Los Angeles, Elias, Franke, Moscona, Harvuot, Anthony, Marsh)	F. Cleva	—	Met Historic Broadcast.

Discog. No.	Date	Opera	Selection	Conductor or Pianist*	RCA Victor Matrix-Take No.	Comments
1110	13 May 58		On Melodiya LP:	W. Sektberg*	—	Tchaikovsky Concert Hall performance, Moscow.
[2044]		Otello	(1) Credo in un Dio crudel			
[2064]		Tannhäuser	(2) O du mein holder Abendstern			The only Wagnerian aria recorded by Warren.
[2007]		Andrea Chénier	(3) Nemico della patria			
[2017]		Carmen	(4) Chanson du toreador: Votre toast!			
[3015]			(5) Chanson à boire			
[3043]			(6) O del mio amato Ben			
[3066]			(7) L'ultima canzone			
[3046]			(8) O That It Were So			
[3069]			(9) When Lights Go Rolling Round the Sky			
[3058]			(10) Shenandoah			
[3022]			(11) The Drunken Sailor			
1111	May 58		Leonard Warren on Tour in Russia, RCA Victor 1958 LP, includes 14 selections**; 1988 CD includes all 22 selections:	W. Sektberg*	—	Public performances, Leningrad and Kiev.
[3002]			(1) Agnus Dei**			
[3003]			(2) Amarilli**			
[3048]			(3) An Old Song Resung**			
[3009]			(4) Blow the Man Down			

ID	Date	Work	Selection	Conductor	Matrix	Notes
[3012]			(5) Canto di primavera			See Section III.
[3013]			(6) Canto popolare			
[3014]			(7) Chanson à boire**			
[3016]			(8) Colorado Trail**			
[3024]			(9) Good Fellows Be Merry**			
[3029]			(10) In questa tomba oscura**			
[3007]			(11) Les berceaux**			
[3035]			(12) Madrigal**			
[3036]			(13) Mattinata**			
[3040]			(14) Nel giardino			
[3042]			(15) O del mio amato Ben			
[3045]			(16) O That It Were So**			
[3061]			(17) Tell Me, O Blue, Blue Sky**			
[3065]			(18) L'ultima canzone**			
[3044]		*Acis and Galatea*	(19) O Ruddier Than the Cherry			
[2006]		*Andrea Chénier*	(20) Nemico della patria			
[2022]		*Falstaff*	(21) È sogno? O realtà?**			
[2024]		*Faust*	(22) Avant de quitter ces lieux			
1112 [2025]	July–Aug. 58	*La forza del destino*	Complete opera (with Milanov, Di Stefano, Tozzi)	F. Previtali	J2-RP-7938 through J2-RP-7953	(Note 1).
1113 [2039]	12–16 Feb. 59 / 1 Mar. 59 / 4 Mar. 59	*Macbeth*	Complete opera (with Rysanek, Hines, Bergonzi, Olvis)	E. Leinsdorf	K2-RB-1106 through K2-RB-1126	(Note 4).
1114 [2072]	15–25 July 59	*Il trovatore*	Complete opera (with Tucker, Price, Elias, Tozzi)	A. Basile	2-K2-RB-3338 through 2-K2-RB-3358 (no 3350)	Recorded in Rome. Warren's last studio recording session.

Section II. Opera Audio Recordings by Opera

Aida (Giuseppe Verdi)

Complete Opera. Jonel Perlea, Rome Opera House Orchestra and Chorus (Aida: Milanov; Radamès: Björling; Amneris: Barbieri; Amonasro: Warren; Ramfis: Christoff; King: Clabassi; Messenger: Carlin; High Priestess: Rizzoli)

Discog. No.	Recording/Performance Date	RCA Victor Matrix-Take No.	Catalog Number RCA/BMG	Other Label	Type	Record Issue Date	Album Description and Notes
2001 [1101]	2–18 July 55	2-F2-RH-4135 through 2-F2-RH-4155 (no 4150 or 4152)	LM-6122		LP [3]	Oct. 55	
			VIC-6119		LP [3]	Sep. 69	
			6652-2-RG		CD [2]	Mar. 88	
			ALK3-5380P		CAS [3]	Feb. 85	
			FC-41		OR	Mar. 57	Acts I, II.
			EC-42		OR	Mar. 57	Acts III, IV.
2001a	Highlights/Excerpts 2–18 July 55		549-5271 through 549-5273	(SEP-19)	45 [3]	Nov. 56	
			549-5274 through 549-5276	(ERC-2046)	45 [3]	Jan. 57	
			LM-2046	(SLP-19)	LP	Jan. 57	
			LM-6069		LP [2]	Aug. 59	Abridged.
			60201-2-RG		CD	Oct. 89	
			60201-4-RG		CAS	Oct. 89	
2001b	Ciel! Mio padre! (with Milanov) 4 July 55	2-F2-RH-4148-1	ERC-2046		45 [3]	Jan. 57	Highlights.
			LM-2046	(SLP-19)	LP	Jan. 57	Highlights.
			LM-6069		LP [2]	Aug. 59	Abridged.

	Catalog	Format	Date	Description
	60201-2-RG	CD	Oct. 89	Highlights.
	Met 503	CD [2]	Nov. 88	Great Operas at the Met: *Aida*.

Rivedrai le foreste imbalsamate . . . In armi ora si desta il popol nostro . . . Padre! A costoro schiava non sono (with Milanov)

2001c   4 July 55   2-F2-RH-4148-1

	Catalog	Format	Date	Description
	ERC-2046	45 [3]	Jan. 57	Highlights.
	LM-2046 (SLP-19)	LP	Jan. 57	Highlights.
	LM-6069	LP [2]	Aug. 59	Abridged.
	60201-2-RG	CD	Oct. 89	Highlights.

Tu! Amonasro! . . . Io son disonorato! (with Björling and Milanov)

2001d   8 July 55   2-F2-RH-4149

	Catalog	Format	Date	Description
	LM-2736	LP	Apr. 64	Jussi Björling: Opera Duets and Opera Scenes.
	AGM1-4889	LP	Jan. 84	Jussi Björling: Opera Duets and Opera Scenes.
	GL 84889	LP	1983	German pressing.

Che veggo! Egli? Mio padre! Wilfrid Pelletier, symphony orchestra (with Bampton, Summers, Carron, Alvary, and Cordon)

2002 [1003]   28 May 40   CS-050341-1R

	Catalog	Format	Date	Description
	SR-52	78 [3]	Aug. 40	The World's Greatest Operas. *Aida*.
	CAL-225 (CFL-101)	LP [6]	1954 (55)	Camden. The Heart of the Opera, Vol. 5. *Aida*.
	VAIA-1017	CD	Nov. 92	Leonard Warren: His First Recordings (1940).

Rivedrai le foreste imbalsamate. Wilfrid Pelletier, symphony orchestra (with Bampton)

2003 [1008]   17 June 40   CS-051110-1A

	Catalog	Format	Date	Description
	SR-53	78 [3]	Aug. 40	The World's Greatest Operas. *Aida*.
	CAL-225 (CFL-101)	LP [6]	1954 (55)	Camden. The Heart of the Opera, Vol. 5. *Aida*.
	VAIA-1017	CD	Nov. 92	Leonard Warren: His First Recordings (1940).
	VAIA-1084	CD	Jan. 95	Rose Bampton Sings Verdi and Wagner.

Andrea Chénier (Umberto Giordano)

Complete Opera. Fausto Cleva, Metropolitan Opera Orchestra and Chorus (Chénier: Del Monaco; Maddalena: Milanov; Gérard: Warren; Bersi: Elias; Mathieu: Baccaloni; Countess di Coigny: Glaz; Abbé: Carelli; Fléville: Cehanovsky; Incroyable: De Paolis; Roucher: Valentino; Madelon: Warfield; Dumas: Hawkins; Fouquier-Tinville: Scott; Schmidt: Davidson; Major-Domo: Sgarro)

Discog. No.	Recording/ Performance Date	RCA Victor Matrix-Take No.	Catalog Number RCA/BMG	Other Label	Type	Record Issue Date	Album Description and Notes
2004 [1094]	4 Dec. 54			Met 15	LP [3]	July 88	Met Historic Broadcast.
				Met 15	CD [2]	July 88	Met Historic Broadcast.

Nemico della patria. Jonel Perlea, members of NBC Symphony Orchestra

2005 [1096]	3 Mar. 55	F2-RH-1770-1	LM-2453		LP	Mar. 60	Leonard Warren: An Appreciation.
			PVM1-9048 Vol. 1 [26.41372]		LP	1976	German pressing. Leonard Warren: Arien und Szenen.
			VL-42432		LP	1978	Italian pressing. Leonard Warren: L'età d'oro del belcanto.
				LWC-1	CD [2]	Mar. 00	Leonard Warren Commemorative. Opera Arias and Concert Songs.

Nemico della patria. Willard Sektberg, piano

2006 [1111]	May 58		7807-2-RG		CD	Jan. 89	Leonard Warren on Tour in Russia.

Nemico della patria. Willard Sektberg, piano

2007 [1110]	13 May 58			MIO 49519-007	LP	1958 (?)	Public recital. Melodiya.

Leonard Warren, Baritone: Arias from Operas, Songs, Romances.

Un ballo in maschera (Giuseppe Verdi)

Highlights. Dimitri Mitropoulos, Metropolitan Opera Orchestra and Chorus (Amelia: Milanov; Riccardo: Peerce; Renato: Warren; Ulrica: Anderson; Oscar: Peters) (Note 2)

2008 [1095]

9 Jan. 55	F2-RP-0603	LM-1911	LP	Mar. 55	Verdi's *A Masked Ball*.
21 Jan. 55	through	LM-1911 RE	LP	June 59	*A Masked Ball* (Abridged).
	F2-RP-0613	DC-33	OR	Feb. 57	*A Masked Ball*.

Alla vita che t'arride

2008a

9 Jan. 55	F2-RP-0603-1	LM-1911	LP	Mar. 55	Highlights.
		LM-1932	LP	Dec. 55	Leonard Warren: Verdi Baritone Arias.
		PVM1-9082 Vol. 2 [26.41410]	LP	1976	German pressing, Leonard Warren: Arien und Szenen.
		Met 525	CD [2]	Feb. 95	Great Operas at the Met. *Un ballo in maschera.*

Ahimè! S'appressa alcun (with Milanov and Peerce)

2008b

9 Jan. 55	F2-RP-0613 (R)	LM-1911	LP	Mar. 55	Highlights.
		LM-1911 RE	LP	June 59	Highlights.
		Met 525	CD [2]	Feb. 95	Great Operas at the Met. *Un ballo in maschera.*

Alzati! là tuo figlio . . . Eri tu?

2008c

9 Jan. 55	F2-RP-1610-1	LM-1911	LP	Mar. 55	Highlights.
		LM-1991 RE	LP	June 59	Highlights.
		LM-1932	LP	Dec. 55	Leonard Warren: Verdi Baritone Arias.
		LM-6061	LP [2]	Oct. 58	Great Moments in Opera: Verdi–Puccini.
		PVM1-9082 Vol. 2 [26.41410]	LP	1976	German pressing, Leonard Warren: Arien und Szenen (Note 5).
		Met 215	CD	Sep. 92	Leonard Warren: Portraits in Memory.

Discog. No.	Recording/ Performance Date	RCA Victor Matrix-Take No.	Catalog Number RCA/BMG	Other Label	Type	Record Issue Date	Album Description and Notes
2009 [1037]	Eri tu? Frieder Weissmann, RCA Victor Orchestra (Note 5)						
	14 Dec. 45	D5-RC-1802-1A	11-9292-A		78	Nov. 46	
			12-0461-B (MO-1245)		78 [3]	Oct. 48	Leonard Warren in Dramatic Scenes from Verdi Operas.
			12-3067-A (DM-1474)		78 [5]	Jan. 51	Verdi Commemorative Album.
			49-0647-B (WDM/WMO-1245)		45 [3]	Oct. 49	Leonard Warren in Dramatic Scenes from Verdi Operas.
			49-3067-A (WDM-1474)		45 [5]	Jan. 51	Verdi Commemorative Album.
			LM-1168		LP	Oct. 51	Leonard Warren: Operatic Arias and Sea Shanties.
			VIC-1595		LP	May 71	Leonard Warren: The Great Hits of a Great Baritone.
			VL-42432		LP	1978	Italian pressing. Leonard Warren: L'età d'oro del belcanto.
				LWC-1	CD [2]	Mar. 00	Leonard Warren Commemorative. Opera Arias and Concert Songs.

Il barbiere di Siviglia (Gioachino Rossini)

Discog. No.	Recording/ Performance Date	RCA Victor Matrix-Take No.	Catalog Number RCA/BMG	Other Label	Type	Record Issue Date	Album Description and Notes
2010 [1032]	Largo al factotum. Frieder Weissmann, RCA Victor Orchestra						
	27 Dec. 44	D4-RC-697-1, 1A	—		—		Unpublished (remade 26 Mar. 45).
2011 [1034]	Largo al factotum. William Tarrasch, orchestra						
	26 Mar. 45	4-RC-697-2A	11-8744-B		78	Nov. 45	
			49-0302-B (WDM-1460)		45 [3]	Mar. 49	A Leonard Warren Collection.

LM-1168	LP	Oct. 51	Leonard Warren: Operatic Arias and Sea Shanties.
VIC-1595	LP	May 71	Leonard Warren: The Great Hits of a Great Baritone.
PVM1-9082 Vol. 2 [26.41410]	LP	1976	German pressing. Leonard Warren: Arien und Szenen.
VL-42432	LP	1978	Italian pressing. Leonard Warren: L'età d'oro del belcanto.
LWC-1	CD [2]	Mar. 00	Leonard Warren Commemorative. Opera Arias and Concert Songs.

La bohème (Giacomo Puccini)

Highlights. Renato Cellini and Victor Trucco, RCA Victor Orchestra (Mimì: Albanese; Rodolfo: Di Stefano; Marcello: Warren; Musetta: Munsel; Schaunard: Cehanovsky; Colline: Moscona)

2012 [1075]	23–24 Mar. 51	E1-RC-3179 through E1-RC-3185	49-3841 (WDM-1709) through 49-3844	45 [4]	Oct. 52	The 1951 recording with Warren conducted by Cellini.
	18 May 49	D9-RC-1040-1C				The 1949 recording of "Sì. Mi chiamano Mimì" conducted by Trucco.
	21 Dec. 50	E0-RC-1970-1				The 1950 recording of "O soave fanciulla" conducted by Cellini.

Dunque è proprio finita! (with Albanese, Di Stefano, and Munsel)

2012a	23 Mar. 51	E1-RC-3180-1	49-3844 (WDM-1709)	45 [4]	Oct. 52	Highlights.
			LM-1709	LP	Oct. 52	Highlights.
			ERA/WEPR-18	45	Sep. 52	Selections from La bohème.
			LM-1709	LP	Oct. 52	Highlights.

Discog. No.	Recording/ Performance Date	RCA Victor Matrix-Take No.	Catalog Number RCA/BMG	Other Label	Type	Record Issue Date	Album Description and Notes
	In un coupé? . . . O Mimì, tu più non torni (with Di Stefano)						
2012b	24 Mar. 51	E1-RC-3182-<u>1</u>	49-3843 (WDM-1709)		45 [4]	Oct. 52	Highlights.
			ERA/WEPR-18		45	Sep. 52	Selections from *La bohème*.
			LM-1709		LP	Oct. 52	Highlights.
			VICS-1672(e)		LP	July 72	Puccini's Biggest Hits (without "In un coupé?").
				Met 215	CD	Sep. 92	Leonard Warren: Portraits in Memory.
	Riposa . . . Sono andati? . . . Dorme? (with Albanese, Di Stefano, Munsel, Cehanovsky, and Moscona)						
2012c	23 Mar. 51	E1-RC-3183	49-3842 (WDM-1709)		45 [4]	Oct. 52	Highlights.
		E1-RC-3185	49-3841 (WDM-1709)		45 [4]	Oct. 52	Highlights.
			LM-1709		LP	Oct. 52	Highlights.
				Met 501	CD [2]	May 88	Great Operas at the Met. *La bohème*.
	In un coupé? . . . O Mimì, tu più non torni. Jean Paul Morel, RCA Victor Orchestra (with Peerce)						
2013 [1044]	27 Dec. 46	D6-RC-6655-<u>2</u>	11-9767-A (M-1156)		78 [2]	Nov. 47	Italian Opera Duets.
			11-9769-A (DM-1156)		78 [2]	Nov. 47	Italian Opera Duets.
			49-0630-A (WDM-1156)		45 [2]	Oct. 49	Italian Opera Duets.

Carmen (Georges Bizet)

Discog. No.	Recording/ Performance Date	RCA Victor Matrix-Take No.	Catalog Number RCA/BMG	Other Label	Type	Record Issue Date	Album Description and Notes
	Chanson du toreador: Votre toast! Wilfrid Pelletier, symphony orchestra						
2014 [1004]	31 May 40	CS-050352-<u>1</u>	SR-46		78 [3]	Sep. 40	The World's Greatest Operas. *Carmen*.

2015 [1031] Chanson du toreador: Votre toast! Frieder Weissmann, RCA Victor Orchestra

27 Dec. 44   D4-RC-696-1, 1A

Issue	Format	Released	Notes
CAL-221 (CFL-101)	LP [6]	1954 (55)	Camden. The Heart of the Opera, Vol. 1. *Carmen.*
VAIA-1017	CD	Nov. 92	Leonard Warren: His First Recordings (1940).
—	—	—	Unpublished (remade 26 Mar. 45).

2016 [1033] Chanson du toreador: Votre toast! William Tarrasch, Victor Orchestra

26 Mar. 45   D4-RC-696-2A

Issue	Format	Released	Notes
11-8744-A	78	Nov. 45	A Leonard Warren Collection.
49-0302-A (WDM-1460)	45 [3]	Mar. 49	Leonard Warren: Four Opera Arias.
ERA-114	45	Nov. 53	
LM-6088	LP	Oct. 60	60 Years of Music America Loves Best, Vol. 2.
VIC-1595	LP	May 71	Leonard Warren: The Great Hits of a Great Baritone.
PVM1-9082 Vol. 2 [26.41410]	LP	1976	German pressing. Leonard Warren: Arien und Szenen.
VL-42432	LP	1978	Italian pressing, Leonard Warren: L'età d'oro del belcanto.
LWC-1	CD [2]	Mar. 00	Leonard Warren Commemorative. Opera Arias and Concert Songs.

2017 [1110] Chanson du toreador: Votre toast! Willard Sektberg, piano

13 May 58

Issue	Format	Released	Notes
MIO 49519-007	LP	1958 (?)	Public recital. Melodiya. Leonard Warren, Baritone: Arias from Operas, Songs, Romances.

Les contes d'Hoffmann (Jacques Offenbach)

Dapertutto's aria: Allez! Pour te livrer ... Scintille, diamant! Wilfrid Pelletier, Victor Symphony Ochestra

Discog. No.	Recording/ Performance Date	RCA Victor Matrix-Take No.	Catalog Number RCA/BMG	Other Label	Type	Record Issue Date	Album Description and Notes
2018 [1021]	4 Sep. 41	S-066750-3	18420-B		78	Feb. 42	
			VIC-1595		LP	May 71	Leonard Warren: The Great Hits of a Great Baritone.
			LCT-6701-5 Vol. 5		LP [5]	May 55	50 Years of Great Opera Singing (Limited Edition).
			PVM1-9082 Vol. 2 [26.41410]		LP	1976	German pressing. Leonard Warren: Arien und Szenen.
			VL-42432		LP	1978	Italian pressing, Leonard Warren: L'età d'oro del belcanto.
				Met 215	CD	Sep. 92	Leonard Warren: Portraits in Memory.
				LWC-1	CD [2]	Mar. 00	Leonard Warren Commemorative. Opera Arias and Concert Songs.

Falstaff (Giuseppe Verdi)

Complete Opera. Renato Cellini, New Orleans Opera Orchestra and Chorus (Falstaff: Warren; Alice: Della Chiesa; Ford: Torigi; Quickly: Pritchett; Nannetta: Schuh; Fenton: Turp; Meg: Sachs; Pistola: Treigle; Bardolfo: Vellucci; Caius: Assandri)

Discog. No.	Recording/ Performance Date	RCA Victor Matrix-Take No.	Catalog Number RCA/BMG	Other Label	Type	Record Issue Date	Album Description and Notes
2019 [1105]	5 May 56			VAIA-1056-2	CD [2]	Oct. 94	Public performance. New Orleans Opera Archives, Vol. 4.

Ford's monologue: È sogno? O realtà? Wilfrid Pelletier, Victor Symphony Orchestra

2020 [1019]	3 Sep. 41	CS-066748-2		
		18293-A	78	Dec. 41
		WCT-1115	45 [4]	Feb. 53	Critic's Choice. Chosen by Irving Kolodin.
		LCT-1115	LP	Feb. 53	Critic's Choice. Chosen by Irving Kolodin.
		F20L-6919	LP	1953 (?)	Critic's Choice. Chosen by Irving Kolodin (Special Saturday Review Edition 10").
		PVM1-9082 Vol. 2 [26.41410]	LP	1976	German pressing. Leonard Warren: Arien und Szenen.
		Met 215	CD	Sep. 92	Leonard Warren: Portraits in Memory.
		LWC-1	CD [2]	Mar. 00	Leonard Warren Commemorative. Opera Arias and Concert Songs.

Ford's monologue: È sogno? O realtà? Vincenzo Bellezza, Rome Opera House Orchestra

2021 [1103]	July 55 (Note 3)			
		LM-1932	LP	Dec. 55	Leonard Warren: Verdi Baritone Arias.
		LM-6061	LP [2]	Oct. 58	Great Moments in Opera: Verdi-Puccini.

Ford's monologue: È sogno? O realtà? Willard Sektberg, piano

2022 [1111]	May 58			
		LM-2266	LP	Oct. 58	Leonard Warren on Tour in Russia.
		7807-2-RG	CD	Jan. 89	Leonard Warren on Tour in Russia.

Faust (Charles Gounod)

O sainte médaille . . . Avant de quitter ces lieux. Wilfrid Pelletier, Victor Symphony Orchestra

Discog. No.	Recording/ Performance Date	RCA Victor Matrix-Take No.	Catalog Number RCA/BMG	Catalog Number Other Label	Type	Record Issue Date	Album Description and Notes
2023 [1024]	4 Sep. 41	CS-066753-1	18420-A		78	Feb. 42	Leonard Warren: The Great Hits of a Great Baritone.
			VIC-1595		LP	May 71	
			PVM1-9082 Vol. 2 [26.41410]		LP	1976	German pressing. Leonard Warren: Arien und Szenen.
			CRM8-5177		LP [8]	Oct. 84	RCA Met: 100 Singers/100 Years (record 5).
			09026-61580-2		CD [6]	Sep. 93	RCA Met: 100 Singers/100 Years.

O sainte médaille . . . Avant de quitter ces lieux. Willard Sektberg, piano

Discog. No.	Recording/ Performance Date	RCA Victor Matrix-Take No.	Catalog Number RCA/BMG	Catalog Number Other Label	Type	Record Issue Date	Album Description and Notes
2024 [1111]	May 58		7807-2-RG		CD	Jan. 89	Leonard Warren on Tour in Russia.
				LWC-1	CD [2]	Mar. 00	Leonard Warren Commemorative. Opera Arias and Concert Songs.

La forza del destino (Giuseppe Verdi)

Complete Opera. Fernando Previtali, Orchestra and Chorus of L'Accademia di Santa Cecilia, Rome (Leonora: Milanov; Alvaro: Di Stefano; Carlo: Warren; Padre Guardiano: Tozzi; Preziosilla: Elias; Melitone: Mantovani; Marquis: Washington; Curra: Gioia; Alcade: Carbonari; Trabucco: Mercuriali; Surgeon: Liviabella)

Discog. No.	Recording/ Performance Date	RCA Victor Matrix-Take No.	Catalog Number RCA/BMG	Catalog Number Other Label	Type	Record Issue Date	Album Description and Notes
2025 [1112]	July–Aug. 58	J2-RP-7938 through J2-RP-7953	LM/LSC-6406		LP [4]	July 59	London Records, Inc. (Decca). The Decca Record Company Ltd.
				OSA 13122	LP [3]	1977	
				443 678-2	CD [3]	Apr. 96	

	Scene / Recording date	Catalog No.	Format	Date	Notes
2025a	Abridged July–Aug. 58	LM-6083	LP [2]	June 60	
2025b	Solenne in quest'ora (with Di Stefano) July 58	LM-6083	LP [2]	June 60	Abridged.
		LM-2391	LP	Jan. 60	Opera for People Who Hate Opera.
		LM/LSC-2709	LP	Feb. 64	Giuseppe Di Stefano: Scenes from La Gioconda and La forza del destino.
2025c	Morir! tremenda cosa . . . Urna fatale del mio destino . . . È s'altra prova rinvenir potessi? (with Liviabella) July 58	LM-6083	LP [2]	Jan. 60	Abridged.
		LM-2453	LP	Mar. 60	Leonard Warren: An Appreciation.
		PVM1-9048 Vol. 1 [26.41372]	LP	1976	German pressing. Leonard Warren: Arien und Szenen.
2025d	Invano, Alvaro . . . Ah? Una suora mi lasciasti (with Di Stefano) July 58	LM-6083	LP [2]	Jan. 60	Abridged.
2025e	Le minaccie, i fieri accenti (with Di Stefano) July 58	LM/LSC-2709	LP	Feb. 64	Giuseppe Di Stefano: Scenes from La Gioconda and La forza del destino.
2025f	Io muoio! . . . Non imprecare (with Milanov, Di Stefano, and Tozzi) July 58	LM-6083	LP [2]	Jan. 60	Abridged.

Discog. No.	Recording/ Performance Date	RCA Victor Matrix-Take No.	Catalog Number RCA/BMG	Catalog Number Other Label	Type	Record Issue Date	Album Description and Notes
2026 [1086]	Act II Excerpts. Fritz Stiedry, Metropolitan Opera Orchestra and Chorus (with Tucker and Brazis)						
	29 Nov. 52		Met 100		LP [2]	Mar. 85	Metropolitan Opera Historic Broadcast Centennial Collection 1935–1959. Side 3/Band 2: Act II, Scene 1 (through "Solenne in quest'ora"). Side 4/Band 1: Act II, Scene 1 (conclusion). Side 4/Band 2: Act II, Scene 2 (through "Sleale! Il segreto fu dunque violato?").
2027 [1064]	Highlights. Renato Cellini and Jonel Perlea, RCA Victor Orchestra (with Milanov, Peerce, Keast, and Moscona)						
	16 Feb. 50	EO-RC-147-2A	LM-1916		LP	Nov. 55	Selections recorded on six dates from 16 Feb. 50 to 7 Apr. 55. Warren's selections from recording sessions of 16 Feb. 50 and 7 Apr. 55, conducted by Renato Cellini.
[1097]		EO-RC-148-2	DC-32		OR	Feb. 57	
[1098]	7 Apr. 55	F2-RH-1695					
[1099]	7 Apr. 55	F2-RH-1696					
	7 Apr. 55	F2-RH-3123					
2028 [1042]	Solenne in quest'ora. Erich Leinsdorf, RCA Victor Orchestra (with Peerce)						
	13 June 46	D6-RC-5975-1	11-9767-B (M-1156)		78 [2]	Nov. 47	Italian Opera Duets.
			11-9770-A (DM-1156)		78 [2]	Nov. 47	Italian Opera Duets.
			12-3064-A (DM-1474)		78 [5]	Jan. 51	Verdi Commemorative Album.
			49-0631-A (WDM-1156)		45 [2]	Oct. 49	Italian Opera Duets.
			49-3064-A (WDM-1474)		45 [5]	Jan. 51	Verdi Commemorative Album.
			Met 215		CD	Sep. 92	Leonard Warren: Portraits in Memory.

2029 [1098]	Solenne in quest'ora. Renato Cellini, RCA Victor Orchestra (with Peerce)					
	7 Apr. 55	F2-RH-1695	LM-1916	LP	Nov. 55	Highlights.
			LM-6061	LP [2]	Oct. 58	Great Moments in Opera: Verdi–Puccini.
2030 [1064]	Morir! Tremenda cosa . . . Urna fatale del mio destino . . . È s'altra prova rinvenir potessi? . . . Ah! Egli è salvo! Renato Cellini, RCA Victor Orchestra (with Raymond Keast).					
	16 Feb. 50	EO-RC-147-2A	12-1336-B (DM-1426)	78 [3]	Nov. 50	Leonard Warren in Great Operatic Scenes (Morir!).
		EO-RC-148-2	12-1335-B (DM-1426)	78 [3]	Nov. 50	Leonard Warren in Great Operatic Scenes (È s'altra).
			49-1390-B (WDM 1426)	45 [3]	Nov. 50	Leonard Warren in Great Operatic Scenes (Morir!).
			49-1391-B (WDM-1426)	45 [3]	Nov. 50	Leonard Warren in Great Operatic Scenes (È s'altra).
			ERA-65	45	Mar. 53	Leonard Warren: Great Baritone Arias.
			LM-1916	LP	Nov. 53	Highlights.
			LM-1932	LP	Dec. 55	Leonard Warren: Verdi Baritone Arias.
			Met 522	CD [2]	June 94	Great Operas at the Met. La forza del destino.
			LWC-1	CD [2]	Mar. 00	Leonard Warren Commemorative. Opera Arias and Songs.
2031 [1041]	Invano, Alvaro . . . Ah! Una suora mi lasciasti. Erich Leinsdorf, RCA Victor Orchestra (with Peerce)					
	13 June 46	D6-RC-5973-1, 1A	–		–	Unpublished (remade 27 Dec. 46).
		D6-RC-5974-1, 1A				

Discog. No.	Recording/ Performance Date	RCA Victor Matrix-Take No.	Catalog Number RCA/BMG	Other Label	Type	Record Issue Date	Album Description and Notes
	Invano, Alvaro . . . Ah! Una suora mi lasciasti. Jean Paul Morel, RCA Victor Orchestra (with Peerce)						
2032 [1043]	27 Dec. 46	D6-RC-6654-1A	11-9768-A (M-1156)		78 [2]	Nov. 47	Italian Opera Duets (Invano, Alvaro).
			11-9770-B (DM-1156)		78 [2]	Nov. 47	Italian Opera Duets (Invano, Alvaro).
			49-0631-B (WDM-1156)		45 [2]	Oct. 49	Italian Opera Duets (Invano, Alvaro).
		D6-RC-6653-2	11-9768-B (M-1156)		78 [2]	Nov. 47	Italian Opera Duets (Ah! Una suora).
			11-9769-B (DM-1156)		78 [2]	Nov. 47	Italian Opera Duets (Ah! Una suora).
			49-0630-B (WDM-1156)		45 [2]	Oct. 49	Italian Opera Duets (Ah! Una suora).
	Invano, Alvaro . . . Ah! Una suora mi lasciasti. Renato Cellini, RCA Victor Orchestra (with Peerce)						
2033 [1099]	7 Apr. 55	F2-RH-1696	LM-1916		LP	Nov. 55	Highlights.
	Io muoio! . . . Non imprecare. Renato Cellini, RCA Victor Orchestra (with Milanov, Peerce, and Moscona)						
2034 [1100]	7 Apr. 55	F2-RH-3123	LM-1916		LP	Nov. 55	Highlights.
			VIC-1336/VICS-1336(e)		LP	May 68	The Art of Zinka Milanov.
			60074-2-RG		CD	Apr. 90	The RCA Victor Vocal Series. Zinka Milanov.
				Met 522	CD [2]	June 94	Great Operas at the Met. La forza del destino.

La Gioconda (Amilcare Ponchielli)

2035 [1040] Complete Opera. Emil Cooper, Metropolitan Opera Orchestra and Chorus (Gioconda: Milanov; Enzo: Tucker; Laura: Stevens; Barnaba: Warren; Alvise: Vaghi; La Cieca: Harshaw; Zuàne: Hawkins; Isèpo: Oliviero; Monk: Hargrave; Steersman: Baker; Singers: Ezekiel and Manning)

Date	Matrix	Catalog	Format	Release	Notes
16 Mar. 46		Met 17	CD [3]	Apr. 91	Met Historic Broadcast.

2036 [1108] Complete Opera. Fernando Previtali, Orchestra and Chorus of L'Accademia di Santa Cecilia, Rome (Gioconda: Milanov; Enzo: Di Stefano; Laura: Elias; Barnaba: Warren; Alvise: Clabassi; La Cieca: Amparan; Zuàne: Valentini; Isèpo: Cottiro; Steersman: Valenti; Singer: Carbonari) (Note 1)

Date	Matrix	Catalog	Format	Release	Notes
7 July–10 Aug. 57	4-H2-RP-37 through 4-H2-RP-42 (Decca Masters)	LM-6139	LP [3]	Sep. 58	Selected by the Metropolitan Opera.
		LSC-6139	LP [4]	Mar. 59	
		VIC-6101	LP [3]	Jan. 65	
		VICS-6101	LP [3]	Jan. 66	
		OSA 13123	LP [3]	1977	London Records, Inc. (Decca). The Decca Record Company Ltd.
		444 598-2	CD [3]	Apr. 96	

2036a Abridged

Date	Catalog	Format	Release
July–Aug. 57	LM-2249	LP	Nov. 58
	LSC-2249	LP	Mar. 59

2036b Voce di donna o d'angelo ... Che fai? vaneggi? (with Milanov, Elias, Di Stefano, Clabassi, Cottino, and Valentini)

Date	Matrix	Catalog	Format	Release	Notes
July 57	4-H2-RP-38	Met 524	CD [2]	Oct. 94	Great Operas at the Met. La Gioconda.

2036c Enzo Grimaldo, Principe di Santafior (with Di Stefano)

Date	Matrix	Catalog	Format	Release	Notes
July 57	4-H2-RP-38	LM-2249	LP	Nov. 58	Abridged.
		LSC-2249	LP	Mar. 59	Abridged.
		LM/LSC 2709	LP	Feb. 64	Giuseppe Di Stefano: Scenes from La Gioconda and La forza del destino.

Discog. No.	Recording/ Performance Date	RCA Victor Matrix-Take No.	Catalog Number RCA/BMG	Other Label	Type	Record Issue Date	Album Description and Notes
2036d	O monumento!						
	July 57	4-H2-RP-38	LM-2249		LP	Nov. 58	Abridged.
			LSC-2249		LP	Mar. 59	Abridged.
			LM-2453		LP	Mar. 60	Leonard Warren: An Appreciation.
			LM/LSC-6138		LP [3]	Aug. 58	Included in a three-record album of Samuel Barber's Vanessa.
			PVM1-9048 Vol. 1 [26.41372]		LP	1976	German pressing. Leonard Warren: Arien und Szenen.
	Barcarola: Ah! Pescator, affonda l'esca						
2036e	July 57	4-H2-RP-38	LM-2249		LP	Nov. 58	Abridged.
			LSC-2249		LP	Mar. 59	Abridged.
	Ora posso morir . . . Così mantiene il patto? (with Milanov)						
2036f	July 57	4-H2-RP-42	LM-2249		LP	Nov. 58	Abridged.
			LSC-2249		LP	Mar. 59	Abridged.
				Met 524	CD [2]	Oct. 94	Great Operas at the Met. La Gioconda.
	O monumento! Wilfrid Pelletier, Victor Symphony Orchestra						
2037 [1020]	3 Sep. 41	CS-066749-2	18293-B		78	Dec. 41	
				Met 524	CD [2]	Oct. 94	Great Operas at the Met. La Gioconda.

Barcarola: Ah! Pescator, affonda l'esca. Jean Paul Morel, RCA Victor Chorale and Orchestra

2038 [1045]	2 Jan. 47	11-9790-A	78	Nov. 47	
		49-0701-A	45	Nov. 47	
		D7-RC-7100-2			
		LM-1168	LP	Oct. 51	Leonard Warren: Operatic Arias and Sea Shanties.
		Met 215	CD	Sep. 92	Leonard Warren: Portraits in Memory.

Macbeth (Giuseppe Verdi)

Complete Opera. Erich Leinsdorf, Metropolitan Opera Orchestra and Chorus (Macbeth: Warren; Lady Macbeth: Rysanek; Banquo: Hines; Macduff: Bergonzi; Malcolm: Olvis; Lady-in-Attendance: Ordassy; Physician: Pechner; Murderer: Hawkins; Warrior: Marsh; Bloody Child: Cundari; Crowned Child: Allen; Manservant: Sternberg) (Note 4)

2039 [1113]	12–16 Feb. 59	K2-RB-1106	LM/LSC-6147	LP [3]	Oct. 59	
	1 Mar. 59	through	VICS-6121	LP [3]	Oct. 69	
	4 Mar. 59	K2-RB-1126	AGL3-4516	LP [3]	Oct. 82	
			4516-2-RG	CD [2]	Sep. 87	
			AGK2-4516	CAS [2]	Oct. 82	

Abridged

2039a	12–16 Feb. 59	LM/LSC-6076	LP [2]	Jan. 60	
	1 Mar. 59				
	4 Mar. 59				

Due vaticini compiuti or sono (with Hines)

| 2039b | Feb. 59 | LM/LSC-6076 | LP [2] | Jan. 60 | Abridged. |

Sappia la sposa mia . . . Fatal mia donna! (with Rysanek)

| 2039c | Feb. 59 | LM/LSC-6076 | LP [2] | Jan. 60 | Abridged. |

Fatal mia donna! (with Rysanek)

| 2039d | Feb. 59 | Met 405 | LP [2] | Feb. 85 | The Bing Years. |

Va' spirto d'abisso! (with Rysanek and Bergonzi)

| 2039e | Feb. 59 | LM/LSC-6076 | LP [2] | Jan. 60 | Abridged. |

Discog. No.	Recording/ Performance Date	RCA Victor Matrix-Take No.	Catalog Number RCA/BMG	Other Label	Type	Record Issue Date	Album Description and Notes
2039f	Feb. 59	Sangue a me (with Rysanek, Bergonzi, and Ordassy)	Met 50		LP [3]	Nov. 85	50 Years of Guild Performances at the Met.
2039g	12 Feb. 59	Perfidi! All'anglo . . . Pietà, rispetto, amore K2-RB-1108	LM-2453		LP	Mar. 60	Leonard Warren: An Appreciation. Abridged.
			LM/LSC-6076		LP [2]	Jan. 60	
			PVM1-9048 Vol. 1 [26.41372]		LP	1976	German pressing. Leonard Warren: Arien und Szenen.
			VL-42432		LP	1978	Italian pressing. Leonard Warren: L'età d'oro del belcanto.
			09026-62689-2		CD	Aug. 95	The Voices of Living Stereo, Vol. 1.
				LWC-1	CD	Mar. 00	Leonard Warren Commemorative. Opera Arias and Concert Songs.
			09026-62689-4		CAS	Aug. 95	The Voices of Living Stereo, Vol. 1.

Otello (Giuseppe Verdi)

Complete Opera. Fausto Cleva, Metropolitan Opera Orchestra and Chorus (Otello: Del Monaco; Desdemona: De Los Angeles; Iago: Warren; Emilia: Elias; Cassio: Franke; Lodovico: Moscona; Montàno: Harvuot; Roderigo: Anthony; Herald: Marsh)

Discog. No.	Recording/ Performance Date	RCA Victor Matrix-Take No.	Catalog Number RCA/BMG	Other Label	Type	Record Issue Date	Album Description and Notes
2040 [1109]	8 Mar. 58		Met 20		CD [2]	Mar. 96	Met Historic Broadcast.

2041 [1065]

Brindisi: Inaffia l'ugola! Renato Cellini, RCA Victor Orchestra and Chorus (with Sprinzena and Matto)

16 Feb. 50   E0-RC-149-1A

Catalog	Format	Date	Release
12-1337-B (DM-1426)	78 [3]	Nov. 50	Leonard Warren in Great Operatic Scenes.
49-1392-B (WDM-1426)	45 [3]	Nov. 50	Leonard Warren in Great Operatic Scenes.
49-3371-A (WDM-1542)	45 [4]	Oct. 51	Treasury of Grand Opera.
ERA-65	45	Mar. 53	Leonard Warren: Great Baritone Arias.
LM-1148	LP	Oct. 51	Treasury of Grand Opera, Vol. 2.
LM-1932	LP	Dec. 55	Leonard Warren: Verdi Baritone Arias.
Met 514	CD [2]	Jan. 92	Great Operas at the Met *Otello*.

2042 [1039]

Vanne: la tua meta già vedo . . . Credo in un Dio crudel. Frieder Weissmann, RCA Victor Orchestra

7 Mar. 46   D6-RC-5179-2

Catalog	Format	Date	Release
11-9292-B	78	Nov. 46	Leonard Warren in Dramatic Scenes from Verdi Operas.
12-0461-A (MO-1245)	78 [3]	Oct. 48	Leonard Warren in Dramatic Scenes from Verdi Operas.
49-0647-A (WDM/WMO-1245)	45 [3]	Oct. 49	Leonard Warren in Dramatic Scenes from Verdi Operas.
Met 215	CD	Sep. 92	Leonard Warren: Portraits in Memory.
LWC-1	CD [2]	Mar. 00	Leonard Warren Commemorative. Opera Arias and Concert Songs.

Discog. No.	Recording/ Performance Date	RCA Victor Matrix-Take No.	Catalog Number RCA/BMG	Other Label	Type	Record Issue Date	Album Description and Notes
2043 [1102]	Credo in un Dio crudel. Vincenzo Bellezza, Rome Opera House Orchestra						
	4 July 55	(Note 3)	447-0802		45	Sep. 57	Gold Standard Series (Note 5).
			LM-1932		LP	Dec. 55	Leonard Warren: Verdi Baritone Arias.
			VIC-1595		LP	May 71	Leonard Warren: The Great Hits of a Great Baritone.
			PVM1-9082 Vol. 2 [26.41410]		LP	1976	German pressing. Leonard Warren: Arien und Szenen.
			VL-42432		LP	1978	Italian pressing. Leonard Warren: L'età d'oro del belcanto.
2044 [1110]	Credo in un Dio crudel. Willard Sektberg, piano						
	13 May 58			MIO 49519-007	LP	1958 (?)	Public recital. Melodiya. Leonard Warren, Baritone: Arias from Operas, Songs, Romances.
2045 [1097]	Era la notte. Jonel Perlea, RCA Victor Orchestra						
	3 Mar. 55	F2-RH-1771-1	LM-1932		LP	Dec. 55	Leonard Warren: Verdi Baritone Arias.
			PVM1-9082 Vol. 2 [26.41410]		LP	1976	German pressing. Leonard Warren: Arien und Szenen.
				Met 514	CD [2]	Jan. 92	Great Operas at the Met. Otello.
				LWC-1	CD [2]	Mar. 00	Leonard Warren Commemorative. Opera Arias and Concert Songs.

Pagliacci (Ruggero Leoncavallo)

Complete Opera. Renato Cellini, RCA Victor Orchestra, Robert Shaw Chorale, Columbus Boy Choir (Nedda: De Los Angeles; Canio: Björling; Tonio: Warren; Silvio: Merrill; Beppe: Franke; Peasant I: Cehanovsky; Peasant II: Wright)

ID	Date					Notes
2046 [1087]	6–29 Jan. 53	E3-RC-2119 through E3-RC-2130	49-4180 (WDM-6106) through 49-4191	45 [12]	Sep. 53	
			LM-6045	LP [2]	Oct. 56	
			LM-6084	LP [2]	May 60	
			LM-6106	LP [3]	Sep. 53	Includes complete *Cavalleria rusticana.*
			IB-6058	LP [2]	Apr. 70	Seraphim. Angel Records. Includes arias by Jussi Björling.
			CDC-749503-2	CD	June 89	EMI Records, Ltd.
			7243 5 66782 1	CD	Apr. 98	EMI Classics.
2046a	Highlights					
	10 Jan. 53	E3-RC-2119-1				
	11 Jan. 53	E3-RC-2129-1	ERB-38	45 [2]	Jan. 55	Highlights from *I Pagliacci* and *Cavalleria rusticana.*
	19 Jan. 53	E3-RC-2130-1	LM-1828	LP	Jan. 55	Highlights from *I Pagliacci* and *Cavalleria rusticana.*

Discog. No.	Recording/ Performance Date	RCA Victor Matrix-Take No.	Catalog Number RCA/BMG	Other Label	Type	Record Issue Date	Album Description and Notes
2046b	Prologo: Si può?						
	10 Jan 53	E3-RC-2119-1 (For ERA-207A and LM-1801, the matrix number is E4-RW-1017. It was made on 3 Feb. 54 from E3-RC-3351-1 recorded on 11 Dec. 53 with Dennis King and from E3-RC2119-1 recorded on 10 Jan. 53.)	ERA-207-A		LP	May 54	Arias Sung and Acted. Acted by Dennis King.
			LM-1801		LP	June 54	Arias Sung and Acted. Acted by Dennis King.
			LM-1828		LP	Jan. 55	Highlights from I Pagliacci and Cavalleria rusticana.
			LM-1847		LP	Jan. 55	Treasury of Grand Opera in High Fidelity.
			LM-2453		LP	Mar. 60	Leonard Warren: An Appreciation.
				PMV1-9048 Vol. 1 [26.41372]	LP	1976	German pressing. Leonard Warren: Arien und Szenen (Note 5).
				VL-42432	LP	1978	Italian pressing. Leonard Warren: L'età d'oro del belcanto.

Commedia: Attenti! Pagliaccio è là, tutto stravolto . . . to end of opera (with De Los Angeles, Franke, Björling, Merrill, and the Robert Shaw Chorale)

Discog. No.	Recording/ Performance Date	RCA Victor Matrix-Take No.	Catalog Number RCA/BMG	Other Label	Type	Record Issue Date	Album Description and Notes
2046c	11 Jan. 53	E3-RC-2129-1	ERB-38		45 [2]	Jan. 55	Highlights from I Pagliacci and Cavalleria rusticana.
	19 Jan. 53	E3-RC-2130-1	LM-1828		LP	Jan. 55	Highlights from I Pagliacci and Cavalleria rusticana.

No.	Date / Take	Matrix	Catalog	Format	Date	Description
2047 [1007]	*Prologo: Si può?* Wilfrid Pelletier, symphony orchestra					
	17 June 40	CS-051102-2	SR-70	78 [2]	Sep. 40	The World's Greatest Operas. *Pagliacci.*
			CAL-226 (CFL-101)	LP [6]	1954 (55)	Camden. The Heart of the Opera, Vol. 6. *Pagliacci.*
			Met 512	CD [2]	May 91	Great Operas at the Met. *Cavalleria / Pagliacci.*
			VAIA-1017	CD	Nov. 92	Leonard Warren: His First Recordings (1940).
2048 [1030]	*Prologo: Si può?* Frieder Weissmann, RCA Victor Orchestra					
	27 Dec. 44	D4-RC-695-1, 1A, 2, 2A	—	—	—	Unpublished (remade 7 Mar. 46).
2049 [1038]	*Prologo: Si può?* Frieder Weissmann, RCA Victor Orchestra					
	7 Mar. 46	D6-RC-5178-2A	11-9288-A (M-1074)	78 [4]	Nov. 46	Treasury of Grand Opera.
			11-9790-B	78	Nov. 47	
			49-0701-B	45	Nov. 47	
			49-3409-B (WDM-1565)	45 [5]	Oct. 51	Highlights from *Cavalleria rusticana* and *I Pagliacci.*
			LM-1160	LP	Oct. 51	Highlights from *Cavalleria rusticana* and *I Pagliacci.*
			LM-1168	LP	Oct. 51	Leonard Warren: Operatic Arias and Sea Shanties.
			VIC-1595	LP	May 71	Leonard Warren: The Great Hits of a Great Baritone.
			Met 404	LP [2]	Apr. 84	The Johnson Years.
			LWC-1	CD [2]	Mar. 00	Leonard Warren Commemorative. Opera Arias and Concert Songs.

Rigoletto (Giuseppe Verdi)

Complete Opera. Renato Cellini, RCA Victor Orchestra, Robert Shaw Chorale (Rigoletto: Warren; Gilda: Berger; Duke: Peerce; Maddalena: Merriman; Sparafucile: Tajo; Monterone: Wentworth; Marullo: Newman; Borsa: Sprinzena; Count Ceprano: Ukena; Countess Ceprano: White; Giovanna: Kreste; Page: White; Herald: Newman)

Discog. No.	Recording/ Performance Date	RCA Victor Matrix-Take No.	Catalog Number RCA/BMG	Catalog Number Other Label	Type	Record Issue Date	Album Description and Notes
2050 [1066]	8 Mar. 50 through 25 May 50	EO-RC-154 through EO-RC-181	12-1262 (DM-1400 Vol. 1) through 12-1268		78 [7]	Oct. 50	First complete opera recorded by RCA Victor.
			12-1269 (DM-1401 Vol. 2) through 12-1275		78 [7]	Oct. 50	
			49-1305 (WDM-1400 Vol. 1) through 49-1311		45 [7]	Oct. 50	
			49-1312 (WDM-1401 Vol. 2) through 49-1318		45 [7]	Oct. 50	
			LM-6021		LP [2]	Nov. 54	
			LM-6101/LM(X)-6101		LP [3]	Oct. 50	
			AVM2-0698		LP [2]	Oct. 74	
			CLK2-5378P		CAS [2]	Feb. 85	
2050a	Highlights/Excerpts 8 Mar. 50 through 25 May 50 (Electrically transferred on 9 June 50 for four selections)		12-1290 (DM-1414) through 12-1295		78 [6]	Oct. 50	
			49-1342 (WDM-1414)		45 [6]	Oct. 50	

Label	Title / Session (recording date)	EO-RC matrix	Catalog	Format	Release	Description
	(continued)		through 49-1347	45	June 53	Gems from *Rigoletto*.
			ERA-84	45 [2]	Sep. 53	Gems from *Rigoletto* (10").
			ERB-7000	LP	Oct. 50	
			LM-1104	LP	Sep. 53	
			LRM-7000	LP	Sep. 53	
			CC-36	OR	Feb. 57	
2050b	In testa che avete, Signor di Ceprano? . . . Ch' io gli parli (with Sprinzena, Newman, Ukena, Wentworth, and Peerce) 4 Apr. 50	EO-RC-156-1A EO-RC-157-2	ERB-7000-2	45 [2]	Sep. 53	Gems from *Rigoletto*.
			LRM-7000	LP	Sep. 53	Gems from *Rigoletto* (10").
2050c	Pari siamo! 25 May 50	EO-RC-159-2	12-1267 (DM-1400)	78 [7]	Oct. 50	Complete Opera, Vol. 1.
			12-1291-A (DM-1414)	78 [6]	Oct. 50	Highlights.
			49-1310-A (WDM-1400)	45 [7]	Oct. 50	Complete Opera, Vol. 1.
			49-1343-A (WDM-1414)	45 [6]	Oct. 50	Highlights.
			ERB-7000-3	45 [2]	Sep. 53	Gems from *Rigoletto*.
			LM-1104	LP	Oct. 50	Highlights.
			LM-1932	LP	Dec. 55	Leonard Warren: Verdi Baritone Arias.
			LRM-7000	LP	Sep. 53	Gems from *Rigoletto* (10").
			VIC-1595	LP	May 71	Leonard Warren: The Great Hits of a Great Baritone.
			PVM1-9082 Vol. 2 [26.41410]	LP	1976	German pressing. Leonard Warren: Arien und Szenen.
2050d	Se non volete (with Berger, Kreste, and Peerce) 8 Mar. 50	EO-RC-160-1	12-1268-A (DM-1400)	78 [7]	Oct. 50	Complete Opera, Vol. 1.
			49-1311-A (WDM-1400)	45 [7]	Oct. 50	Complete Opera, Vol. 1.
			ERB-7000-3	45 [2]	Sep. 53	Gems from *Rigoletto*.
			LRM-7000	LP	Sep. 53	Gems from *Rigoletto* (10").
2050e	A che nomarmi? È inutile! . . . Già da tre lune son qui venuta (with Berger) 8 Mar. 50 9 Mar. 50	EO-RC-160-1 EO-RC-161-1	ERB-7000-4	45 [2]	Sep. 53	Gems from *Rigoletto*.
			LRM-7000	LP	Sep. 53	Gems from *Rigoletto* (10").

Discog. No.	Recording/ Performance Date	RCA Victor Matrix-Take No.	Catalog Number RCA/BMG	Catalog Number Other Label	Type	Record Issue Date	Album Description and Notes
2050f	Povero Rigoletto (with Newman, Sprinzena, Ukena, and White)						
	25 May 50	EO-RC-169-1	12-1295-A (DM-1414)		78 [6]	Oct. 50	Highlights.
			49-1313-A (WDM-1400)		45 [7]	Oct. 50	Complete Opera, Vol. 1.
			49-1347-A (WDM-1414)		45 [6]	Oct. 50	Highlights.
2050g	Cortigiani, vil razza dannata						
	6 Apr. 50	E0-RC-170-1A	12-1271-A (DM-1401)		78 [7]	Oct. 50	Complete Opera, Vol. 2.
			12-1295-B (DM-1414)		78 [6]	Oct. 50	Highlights.
			49-1314-A (WDM-1401)		45 [7]	Oct. 50	Complete Opera, Vol. 2.
			49-1347-B (WDM-1414)		45 [6]	Oct. 50	Highlights.
			ERA-114		45	Nov. 53	Leonard Warren: Four Opera Arias.
		(For ERA-207-B and LM-1801, the matrix number is E4-RW-1018. It was made on 3 Feb. 53 from E3-RC-3352-1 recorded on 11 Dec. 53 with Dennis King and EO-RC-170-1A recorded on 6 Apr. 50.)	ERA-207-B		45	May 54	Arias Sung and Acted. Acted by Dennis King.
			LM-1104		LP	Oct. 50	Highlights.
			LM-1801		LP	June 54	Arias Sung and Acted. Acted by Dennis King.
			LM-1932		LP	Dec. 55	Leonard Warren: Verdi Baritone Arias.
			LM-2453		LP	Mar. 60	Leonard Warren: An Appreciation.
			PVM1-9048 Vol. 1 [26.41372]		LP	1976	German pressing, Leonard Warren: Arien und Szenen.
			09026-68921-2		CD	Nov. 97	The American Opera Singer.
2050h	Tutte le feste al tempio (with Berger)						
	9 Mar. 50	EO-RC-1088-1 (Electrically transferred on 9 June 50)	12-1294-B (DM-1414)		78 [6]	Oct. 50	Highlights.
			49-1346-B (WDM-1414)		45 [6]	Oct. 50	Highlights.

2050i Ah! Solo per me l'infamia . . . Ah! Piangi, fanciulla . . . No, vecchio, t'inganni! . . . Si, vendetta, tremenda vendetta (with Berger, Wentworth, and Newman)

11 Mar. 50   EO-RC-172-1A

Catalog	Format	Date	Notes
12-1293-B (DM-1414)	78 [6]	Oct. 50	Highlights.
49-1345-A (WDM-1414)	45 [6]	Oct. 50	Highlights.
Met 518	CD [2]	Jan. 93	Great Operas at the Met. *Rigoletto.*

2050j E là il vostr'uomo (with Tajo, Peerce, Berger, and Merriman)

10 Mar. 50   E0-RC-175-1B (Electrically transferred to E0-RC-175-1B and 1C on 23 Mar. 50)

Catalog	Format	Date	Notes
12-1275-B (DM-1401)	78 [7]	Oct. 50	Complete Opera, Vol. 2.
49-1318-B (WDM-1401)	45 [7]	Oct. 50	Complete Opera, Vol. 2.

2050k Bella figlia dell'amore (with Berger, Peerce, and Merriman)

10 Mar. 50   EO-RC-1089-1 (Electrically transferred on 9 June 50)

Catalog	Format	Date	Notes
12-1274-B (DM-1401)	78 [7]	Oct. 50	Complete Opera, Vol. 2.
12-1291-B (DM-1414)	78 [6]	Oct. 50	Highlights.
12-3066-A (DM-1474)	78 [5]	Jan. 51	Verdi Commemorative Album.
49-1317 (WDM-1401)	45 [7]	Oct. 50	Complete Opera, Vol. 2.
49-1343-B (WDM-1414)	45 [6]	Oct. 50	Highlights.
49-3066-B (WDM-1474)	45 [5]	Oct. 50	Verdi Commemorative Album.
49-3367-B	45	Oct. 51	
ERA-84	45	June 53	*Rigoletto* Highlights.
LM-1104	LP	Oct. 50	Highlights.

2050l V'ho 'ingannato (with Berger)

11 Mar. 50   EO-RC-1090-1 (Electrically transferred on 9 June 50)

Catalog	Format	Date	Notes
12-1290-B (DM-1414)	78 [6]	Oct. 50	Highlights.
49-1342-B (WDM-1414)	45 [6]	Oct. 50	Highlights.
LM-1104	LP	Oct. 50	Highlights.

Discog. No.	Recording/ Performance Date	RCA Victor Matrix-Take No.	Catalog Number RCA/BMG	Other Label	Type	Record Issue Date	Album Description and Notes
2051 [1085]	Complete Opera. Walter Herbert, New Orleans Opera Orchestra and Chorus (Rigoletto: Warren; Gilda: Gueden; Duke: Conley; Maddalena: Muhs; Sparafucile: Wildermann; Monterone: Treigle)						
	3 or 5 Apr. 52			VAIA 1174-2	CD [2]	Mar. 99	Public performance. New Orleans Opera Archives, Vol. 5.
2052	Ah, più di Ceprano importuno non v'è! Wilfrid Pelletier, symphony orchestra (with Tokatyan)						
	31 May 40	CS-050357-1A	SR-58		78 [3]	Sep. 40	The World's Greatest Operas.
[1006]				CAL-226 (CFL-101)	LP [6]	Rigoletto. 1954 (55)	Camden, The Heart of the Opera, Vol. 6. Rigoletto.
				VAIA-1017	CD	Nov. 92	Leonard Warren: His First Recordings (1940).
2053 [1023]	Pari siamo! Wilfrid Pelletier, Victor Symphony Orchestra						
	4 Sep. 41	CS-066752-1, 2, 2A	—		—	—	Unpublished (remade 14 Dec. 45).
2054 [1035]	Pari siamo! Frieder Weissmann, RCA Victor Orchestra						
	14 Dec. 45	D5-RC-1800-1A	11-9413-A		78	Mar. 47	
			12-0462-A (MO-1245)		78 [3]	Oct. 48	Leonard Warren in Dramatic Scenes from Verdi Operas.
			49-0648-A (WDM/WMO-1245)		45 [3]	Oct. 49	Leonard Warren in Dramatic Scenes from Verdi Operas.
			ERA-65		45	Mar. 53	Leonard Warren: Great Baritone Arias.
2055 [1010]	Cortigiani, vil razza dannata. Wilfrid Pelletier, symphony orchestra						
	25 June 40	CS-051117-1A	SR-59		78 [3]	Sep. 40	The World's Greatest Operas. Rigoletto.

Cortigiani, vil razza dannata. Wilfrid Pelletier, Victor Symphony Orchestra

No.	Date	Matrix	Catalog	Format	Issued	Notes
2056 [1022]	4 Sep. 41	CS-066751-1, 2, 2A —	CAL-226 (CFL-101)	LP [6]	1954 (55)	Camden. The Heart of the Opera, Vol. 6. *Rigoletto*.
			VAIA-1017	CD	Nov. 92	Leonard Warren: His First Recordings (1940).
				—	—	Unpublished (remade 14 Dec. 45).

Cortigiani, vil razza dannata. Frieder Weissmann, RCA Victor Orchestra

No.	Date	Matrix	Catalog	Format	Issued	Notes
2057 [1036]	14 Dec. 45	D5-RC-1801-1	11-9413-B	78	Mar. 47	Leonard Warren in Dramatic Scenes from Verdi Operas.
			12-0462-B (MO-1245)	78 [3]	Oct. 48	Leonard Warren in Dramatic Scenes from Verdi Operas.
			49-0648-B (WMO-1245)	45 [3]	Oct. 49	Leonard Warren: The Great Hits of a Great Baritone.
			VIC-1595	LP	May 71	Italian pressing, Leonard Warren: L'età d'oro del belcanto.
			VL-42432	LP	1978	Leonard Warren: Portraits in Memory.
			Met 215	CD	Sep. 92	
			LWC-1	CD [2]	Mar. 00	Leonard Warren Commemorative. Opera Arias and Concert Songs.

Tutte le feste . . . Piangi, fanciulla, piangi . . . Compiuto pur quanto. Wilfrid Pelletier, symphony orchestra (with Dickenson and Alvary)

No.	Date	Matrix	Catalog	Format	Issued	Notes
2058 [1012]	25 June 40	CS-051119-1	SR-59	78 [3]	Sep. 40	The World's Greatest Operas.
		CS-051120-1	CAL-226 (CFL-101)	LP [6]	1954 (55)	Camden. The Heart of the Opera, Vol. 6. *Rigoletto*.
			VAIA-1017	CD	Nov. 92	Leonard Warren: His First Recordings (1940).

Act IV. E l'ami? to end of opera. Arturo Toscanini, NBC Symphony Orchestra and Chorus (with Milanov, Merriman, Peerce, and Moscona)

Discog. No.	Recording/ Performance Date	RCA Victor Matrix-Take No.	RCA/BMG	Other Label	Type	Record Issue Date	Album Description and Notes
2059 [1026]	25 May 44	—	LM-6041		LP [2]	Jan. 57	Public performance. Verdi & Toscanini.
			VIC-1314/VICS-1314(e)		LP	Jan. 68	Toscanini: Verdi.
			60276-2-RG		CD	Oct. 90	Toscanini, Vol. 62.
			60276-4-RG		CAS	Oct. 90	Toscanini, Vol. 62.

Venti scudi, hai tu detto? (with Merriman, Peerce, and Moscona)

Discog. No.	Recording/ Performance Date	RCA Victor Matrix-Take No.	RCA/BMG	Other Label	Type	Record Issue Date	Album Description and Notes
2059a	25 May 44	—		Met 518	CD [2]	Jan. 93	Great Operas at the Met. Rigoletto.

Bella figlia dell'amore. Wilfrid Pelletier, symphony orchestra (with Tokatyan, Dickenson, and Browning)

Discog. No.	Recording/ Performance Date	RCA Victor Matrix-Take No.	RCA/BMG	Other Label	Type	Record Issue Date	Album Description and Notes
2060 [1011]	25 June 40	CS-051118-2	SR-60		78 [3]	June 40	The World's Greatest Operas. Rigoletto.
			CAL-226 (CFL-101)		LP [6]	1954 (55)	Camden. The Heart of the Opera, Vol. 6. Rigoletto.
				VAIA-1017	CD	Nov. 92	Leonard Warren: His First Recordings (1940).

Simon Boccanegra (Giuseppe Verdi)

Complete Opera. Ettore Panizza, Metropolitan Opera Orchestra and Chorus (Simon: Tibbett; Maria: Rethberg; Gabriele: Martinelli; Fiesco: Pinza; Paolo: Warren; Pietro: D'Angelo; Maidservant: Besuner; Captain: Paltrinieri)

Discog. No.	Recording/ Performance Date	RCA Victor Matrix-Take No.	RCA/BMG	Other Label	Type	Record Issue Date	Album Description and Notes
2061 [1001]	21 Jan. 39			Met 13	LP[3]	May 86	Met Historic Broadcast (Warren as Paolo).

Plebe! Patrizi! . . . Piango su voi. Wilfrid Pelletier, Metropolitan Opera Orchestra and Chorus (Warren as Paolo, with Tibbett, Bampton, Martinelli, and Nicholson)

Warren's first studio recording (Note 6).

			Format	Catalog No.	Date	Notes
2062 [1002]	3 May 39	CS-036850-1	78	15642-B	Nov. 39	Opening Nights at the Met.
			LP [3]	LM-6171	Sep. 66	50 Years of Great Opera
			LP [5]	LCT-6701-5 (Vol. 5)	May 55	Singing (Limited Edition).
			LP [3]	AGM3-4805	Sep. 83	Opening Nights at the Met.
			CD	Met 219	Sep. 93	Lawrence Tibbett: Portraits in Memory.
			CAS	CGK2-4805	Sep. 83	Opening Nights at the Met.

Dinne, perchè in quest'eremo . . . Dinne, alcun là non vedesti? . . . Figlia! a tal nome palpito. Renato Cellini, RCA Victor Orchestra (with Astrid Varnay)

			Format	Catalog No.	Date	Notes
2063 [1062]	4 Feb. 50	E0-RC-108-2	78 [3]	12-1335-A (DM-1426)	Nov. 50	Leonard Warren in Great Operatic Scenes.
		E0-RC-109-2	78 [3]	12-1336-A (DM-1426)	Nov. 50	Leonard Warren in Great Operatic Scenes.
			45 [3]	49-1390-A (WDM-1426)	Nov. 50	Leonard Warren in Great Operatic Scenes.
			45 [3]	49-1391-A (WDM-1426)	Nov. 50	Leonard Warren in Great Operatic Scenes.
			LP	LM-2453	Mar. 60	Leonard Warren: An Appreciation.
			LP	PVM1-9048 Vol. 1 [26,41372]	1976	German pressing, Leonard Warren: Arien und Szenen.
			LP	VL-42432	1978	Italian pressing, Leonard Warren: L'età d'oro del belcanto.
			CD	Met 215	Sep. 92	Leonard Warren: Portraits in Memory.

Tannhäuser (Richard Wagner)

O du mein holder Abendstern. Willard Sektberg, piano

The only Wagnerian aria that Warren recorded.

Discog. No.	Recording/ Performance Date	RCA Victor Matrix-Take No.	Catalog Number RCA/BMG	Other Label	Type	Record Issue Date	Album Description and Notes
2064 [1110]	13 May 58			MIO 49519-007	LP	1958 (?)	Public recital. Melodiya. Leonard Warren, Baritone: Arias from Operas, Songs, Romances.
				LWC-1	CD [2]	Mar. 00	Leonard Warren Commemorative. Opera Arias and Concert Songs.

Tosca (Giacomo Puccini)

Complete Opera. Dimitri Mitropoulos, Metropolitan Opera Orchestra and Chorus (Tosca: Tebaldi; Cavaradossi: Tucker; Scarpia: Warren; Sacristan: Corena; Spoletta: De Paolis; Angelotti: Harvuot; Sciarrone: Cehanovsky; Jailer: Marsh; Shepherd: Mark)

Discog. No.	Recording/ Performance Date	RCA Victor Matrix-Take No.	Catalog Number RCA/BMG	Other Label	Type	Record Issue Date	Album Description and Notes
2065 [1104]	7 Jan. 56			Met 10	LP [2]	July 58	Met Historic Broadcast.

Complete Opera. E. Leinsdorf, Rome Opera House Orchestra and Chorus (Tosca: Milanov; Cavaradossi: Björling; Scarpia: Warren; Sacristan: Corena; Spoletta: Carlin; Angelotti: Monreale; Sciarrone: Catalani; Jailer: Preziosa; Shepherd: Bianchini)

Discog. No.	Recording/ Performance Date	RCA Victor Matrix-Take No.	Catalog Number RCA/BMG	Other Label	Type	Record Issue Date	Album Description and Notes
2066 [1107]	2–18 July 57	2-H2-RB-2539-1 through 2-H2-RB-2552-1 (no 2540)	LM-6052		LP [2]	Nov. 57	
			LSC-6052		LP [3]	May 60	
			VIC/VICS-6000		LP [2]	Mar. 64	
			AGL2-4514		LP [2]	Oct. 82	
			4514-2-RG		CD [2]	Sep. 87	
			AGK2-4514		CAS [2]	Oct. 82	
			4514-4-RG		CAS [2]	Mar. 91	
2066a	Highlights 2–18 July 57		60192-2-RG		CD	June 90	
			60192-4-RG		CAS	June 90	
			V8S 1022		8T	Mar. 70	An 8-track stereo cartridge.

No.	Title / Details	Matrix	Catalog	Format	Date	Notes
2066b	Or tutto è chiaro. . . O che v'offende, dolce signora? (with Milanov and Corena) 12 July 57 2-H2-RB-2543		Met 516	CD [2]	June 92	Great Operas at the Met. *Tosca.*
2066c	Te Deum: Tre sbirri, una carrozza . . . Va Tosca, E Scarpia . . . A doppia mira 4 July 57 2-H2-RB-2544-1		VL-42432	LP	1978	Italian pressing, Leonard Warren: L'età d'oro del belcanto.
			60192-2-RG	CD	June 90	Highlights.
2066d	Te Deum: E Scarpia . . . A doppia mira 4 July 57 2-H2-RB-2544-1		VIC-1595	LP	May 71	Leonard Warren: The Great Hits of a Great Baritone.
			PVM1-9082 Vol. 2 [26.41410]	LP	1976	German pressing. Leonard Warren: Arien und Szenen.
2066e	Dov'è Angelotti? (with Björling and Milanov) 8 July 57 16 July 57 2-H2-RB-2545-1		60192-2-RG	CD	June 90	Highlights.
2066f	Floria! Amore (with Björling, Milanov, and Catalani) 14 July 57 2-H2-RB-2546-1		60192-2-RG	CD	June 90	Highlights.
2066g	Vittoria! Vittoria! (with Björling and Milanov) 14 July 57 2-H2-RB-2546-1		60192-2-RG	CD	June 90	Highlights.
2066h	Quanto? Quanto? . . . Già, mi dicon venal (with Milanov) 12 July 57 2-H2-RB-2547-1		60192-2-RG	CD	June 90	Highlights.
2066i	Ah! Piuttosto giù m'avvento! (with Milanov) 12 July 57 2-H2-RB-2547-1		60192-2-RG	CD	June 90	Highlights.
2066j	Ed ora, Tosca, finalmente mia! (with Milanov) 12 July 57 2-H2-RB-2547-1		09026-68831-2 09026-68831-4	CD CAS	July 97 July 97	Operatically Incorrect. Operatically Incorrect.

La traviata (Giuseppe Verdi)

Complete Opera. Pierre Monteux, Rome Opera House Orchestra and Chorus (Violetta: Carteri; Alfredo: Valletti; Germont: Warren; Flora: Marimpietri; Gastone: Scarlini; Douphol: La Porta; D'Obigny: Monreale; Grenvil: Caselli; Giuseppe: Di Tommaso; Messenger: Di Tommaso; Annina: Maccagnani)

Discog. No.	Recording/ Performance Date	RCA Victor Matrix-Take No.	Catalog Number RCA/BMG	Other Label	Type	Record Issue Date	Album Description and Notes
2067 [1106]	1–11 June 56	2-G2-RB-4203 through 2-G2-RB-4227 (no 4205, 4206, 4208, 4213, 4226)	LM-6040		LP [3]	Sep. 56	Special version of this album includes bound edition of *Camille* by Alexandre Dumas.
			VIC-6004		LP [2]	Sep. 70	
			EC-43		OR	Mar. 57	Act I; Act II, Scene 1.
			DC-44		OR	Mar. 57	Act II, Scene 2; Act III.
	Highlights						
2067a	1–11 June 56		549-5265 (SEP-21) through 549-5267		45 [3]	Nov. 56	
			549-5268 (ERC-2044) through 549-5270		45 [3]	Jan. 57	
			LM-2044		LP	Jan. 57	
	Ah! Dite alla giovine (with Carteri)						
2067b	9 June 56	2-G2-RB-4214	ERC-2044		45 [3]	Jan. 57	Highlights.
	11 June 56		LM-2044		LP	Jan. 57	Highlights.
	Di Provenza il mar						
2067c	2 June 56	2-G2-RB-4216	ERC-2044		45 [3]	Jan. 57	Highlights.
	9 June 56		LM-2044		LP	Jan. 57	Highlights.
			LM-2453		LP	Mar. 60	Leonard Warren: An Appreciation.
			PVM1-9048 Vol. 1 [26.41372]		LP	1976	German pressing. Leonard Warren: Arien und Szenen.

Prendi, quest' è l'immagine (with Carteri, Valletti, Maccagnani, Caselli)

2067d	11 June 56	2-G2-RB-4227	ERC-2044	45 [3]	Jan. 57	Highlights.
			LM-2044	LP	Jan. 57	Highlights.

Pura siccome un angelo . . . Così alla misera . . . Morrò! morrò! La mia memoria. Wilfrid Pelletier, symphony orchestra (with Steber)

2068 [1009]	25 June 40	CS-051113-2	SR-68	78 [3]	Sep. 40	The World's Greatest Operas. La traviata.
		CS-051114-1A	CAL-227 (CFL-101)	LP [6]	1954 (55)	Camden. The Heart of the Opera, Vol. 7. La traviata.
			VAIA-1017	CD	Nov. 92	Leonard Warren: His First Recordings (1940).

Di Provenza il mar. Renato Cellini, RCA Victor Orchestra

2069 [1063]	4 Feb. 50	E0-RC-110-1C	12-1337-A (DM-1426)	78 [3]	Nov. 50	Leonard Warren in Great Operatic Scenes.
			49-1392-A (WDM-1426)	45 [3]	Nov. 50	Leonard Warren in Great Operatic Scenes.
			447-0802	45	Sep. 57	Gold Standard Series (Note 5).
			LM-1932	LP	Dec. 55	Leonard Warren: Verdi Baritone Arias.
			LM-2071	LP	Oct. 56	The President's Favorite Music (Eisenhower).
			VIC-1595	LP	May 71	Leonard Warren: The Great Hits of a Great Baritone.
			LWC-1	CD [2]	Mar. 00	Leonard Warren Commemorative. Opera Arias and Concert Songs.

Discog. No.	Recording/ Performance Date	RCA Victor Matrix-Take No.	Catalog Number		Type	Record Issue Date	Album Description and Notes
			RCA/BMG	Other Label			
2070 [1005]	Di sprezzo degno sè stesso rende. Wilfrid Pelletier, symphony orchestra (with Steber and Tokatyan)						
	31 May 40	CS-050356-1A	SR-69		78 [3]	Sep. 40	The World's Greatest Operas. *La traviata.*
			CAL-227 (CFL-101)		LP [6]	1954 (55)	Camden. The Heart of the Opera, Vol. 7. *La traviata.*
				Met 505	CD [2]	July 89	Great Operas at the Met. *La traviata.*
				VAIA-1017	CD	Nov. 92	Leonard Warren: His First Recordings (1940).

Il trovatore (Giuseppe Verdi)

Discog. No.	Recording/ Performance Date	RCA Victor Matrix-Take No.	Catalog Number		Type	Record Issue Date	Album Description and Notes
			RCA/BMG	Other Label			
2071 [1084]	Complete Opera. Renato Cellini, RCA Victor Orchestra, Robert Shaw Chorale (Manrico: Björling; Leonora: Milanov; Di Luna: Warren; Azucena: Barbieri; Ferrando: Moscona; Inez: Roggero; Ruiz: Franke; Gypsy: Cehanovsky; Messenger: Sprinzena)						
	21 Feb. 52 through 16 Mar. 52	E2-RC-0170 through E2-RC-0191 (no 0172, 0178, 0181, 0185)	49-3874 (WDM-6008) through 49-3882		45 [9]	Oct. 52	(Note 7).
			LM-6008		LP [2]	Oct. 52	
			AVM2-0699		LP [2]	Oct. 74	
			6643-2-RG		CD [2]	Mar. 88	
			CLK2-5377P		CAS [2]	Feb. 75	
2071a	Highlights 21 Feb. 52 through 16 Mar. 52		LM-1827/LM-1827C		LP	Jan. 55	(Note 7).
			60191-2-RG		CD	June 90	
			60191-4-RG		CAS	June 90	
			DC-34		OR	Apr. 57	

2071b   Deserto sulla terra (with Björling)
21 Feb. 52   E2-RC-0173-1

Catalog	Date	Format	Description
LM-2736	Apr. 64	LP	Jussi Björling: Opera Duets and Operatic Scenes.
AGM1-4889	Jan. 84	LP	Jussi Björling: Opera Duets and Operatic Scenes.

2071c   Tutto è deserto (with Moscona)
11 Mar. 52   E2-RC-0179-1R

Catalog	Date	Format	Description
ERA-114	Nov. 53	45	Leonard Warren: Four Opera Arias.
LM-1932	Dec. 55	LP	Leonard Warren: Verdi Baritone Arias.
LM-6171	Sep. 66	LP	Opening Nights at the Met.
AGM3-4805	Sep. 83	LP	Opening Nights at the Met.
60191-2-RG	June 90	CD	Highlights.
CGK2-4805	Sep. 83	CAS	Opening Nights at the Met.

2071d   Il balen del suo sorriso
11 Mar. 52   E2-RC-0179-1R

Catalog	Date	Format	Description
ERA-114	Nov. 53	45	Leonard Warren: Four Opera Arias.
LM-1827	Jan. 55	LP	Highlights.
LM-1932	Dec. 55	LP	Leonard Warren: Verdi Baritone Arias.
LM-6171	Sep. 66	LP	Opening Nights at the Met.
AGM3-4805	Sep. 83	LP	Opening Nights at the Met.
60191-2-RG	June 90	CD	Highlights.

2071e   Qual suono! . . . Per me ora fatale . . . Ah! se l'error t'ingombra (with Moscona)
11 Mar. 52   E2-RC-0180-1R

Catalog	Date	Format	Description
ERA-114	Nov. 53	45	Leonard Warren: Four Opera Arias.
LM-1932	Dec. 55	LP	Leonard Warren: Verdi Baritone Arias.
LM-6171	Sep. 66	LP	Opening Nights at the Met.
AGM3-4805	Sep. 83	LP	Opening Nights at the Met.
60191-2-RG	June 90	CD	Highlights.

Discog. No.	Recording/Performance Date	RCA Victor Matrix-Take No.	Catalog Number RCA/BMG	Other Label	Type	Record Issue Date	Album Description and Notes
2071f	\multicolumn{7}{l}{Giorni poveri vivea (with Barbieri and Moscona)}						
	21 Feb. 52	E2-RC-0183-1R		Met 509	CD [2]	July 90	Great Operas at the Met. *Il trovatore.*
2071g	\multicolumn{7}{l}{Udiste? Come albeggi . . . Mira, di acerbe lagrime . . . Vivrà! Contende il giubilo (with Milanov)}						
	9 May 51	E1-RC-3421-1R	LM-1827		LP	Jan. 55	Highlights (Note 7).
			60191-2-RG		CD	June 90	Highlights (Note 7).
2071h	\multicolumn{7}{l}{Che! Non m'inganno! (with Milanov, Björling, and Barbieri)}						
	16 Mar. 52	E2-RC-0191-1	60191-2-RG		CD	June 90	Highlights.
				Met 509	CD [2]	July 90	Great Operas at the Met. *Il trovatore.*
2072 [1114]	\multicolumn{7}{l}{Complete Opera. Arturo Basile, Rome Opera House Orchestra and Chorus (Manrico: Tucker; Leonora: Price; Di Luna: Warren; Azucena: Elias; Ferrando: Tozzi; Inez: Londi; Ruiz: Carlin; Gypsy: Monreale; Messenger: Frascati)}						
	15–25 July 59	2-K2-RB-3338 through 2-K2-RB-3358 (no 3350)	LM/LSC-6150		LP [3]	Aug. 60	Warren's last studio recording.
			AGL3-4146		LP [3]	Oct. 81	
			60560-2-RG		CD [2]	Nov. 90	
			60560-4-RG		CAS [2]	Nov. 90	
			AGK2-4146		CAS [2]	Oct. 81	
			FTC-8000		OR	Jan. 61	
2072a	Highlights 15–25 July 59		LM/LSC-2617		LP	Sep. 62	

No.	Recording	Catalog	Format	Date	Notes
2072b	Il balen del suo sorriso 17 July 59 2-K2-RB-3347	LM-2453	LP	Mar. 60	Leonard Warren: An Appreciation.
		LM/LSC-2617	LP	Sep. 62	Highlights.
		PVM1-9048 Vol. 1 [26.41372]	LP	1976	German pressing. Leonard Warren: Arien und Szenen.
2072c	Udiste? Come albeggi (with Price) 23–24 July 59 2-K2-RB-3356	LM/LSC-2617	LP	Sep. 62	Highlights.
2073 [1025]	Il balen del suo sorriso. Wilfrid Pelletier, Victor Symphony Orchestra 11 Sep. 41 CS-066766-1, 1A	—	—	—	Unpublished (remade 2 Jan. 47).
2074 [1027]	Il balen del suo sorriso. Maximilian Pilzer, RCA Victor Orchestra 18 Dec. 44 D4-RC-682-1, 1A, 2, 2A	—	—	—	Unpublished (remade 2 Jan. 47).
2075 [1046]	Tutto è deserto . . . Il balen del suo sorriso. Jean Paul Morel, RCA Victor Orchestra 2 Jan. 47 D7-RC-7101-2	11-9956-A	78	Jan. 48	Leonard Warren in Dramatic Scenes from Verdi Operas.
		12-0463-A (MO-1245)	78 [3]	Oct. 48	Leonard Warren in Dramatic Scenes from Verdi Operas.
		49-0649-A (WDM/WMO-1245)	45 [3]	Oct. 49	Leonard Warren: Operatic Arias and Sea Shanties.
		49-0665-A	45	Dec. 49	Leonard Warren: The Great Hits of a Great Baritone.
		LM-1168	LP	Oct. 51	Leonard Warren: Portraits in Memory.
		VIC-1595	LP	May 71	
		Met 215	CD	Sep. 92	Leonard Warren Commemorative. Opera Arias and Concert Songs.
		LWC-1	CD [2]	Mar. 00	

Qual suono! . . . Per me ora fatale . . . . Ah! se l'error t'ingombra. Paul Morel, RCA Victor Orchestra (with unidentified bass)

Discog. No.	Recording/ Performance Date	RCA Victor Matrix-Take No.	Catalog Number RCA/BMG	Other Label	Type	Record Issue Date	Album Description and Notes
2076 [1047]	2 Jan. 47	D7-RC-7102-2	11-9956-B		78	Jan. 48	
		(Takes 2B and 2C electrically transferred on 26 Mar. 47)	12-0463-B (MO-1245)		78 [3]	Oct. 48	Leonard Warren in Dramatic Scenes from Verdi Operas.
		D7-RC-7102-1	49-0649-B (WMO-1245)		45 [3]	Oct. 49	Leonard Warren in Dramatic Scenes from Verdi Operas.
			49-0665-B		45	Dec. 49	Leonard Warren: Operatic Arias and Sea Shanties.
			LM-1168		LP	Oct. 51	
				Met 509	CD [2]	July 90	Great Operas at the Met. Il trovatore.

Udiste? Come albeggi. Renato Cellini, RCA Victor Orchestra (with Milanov)

Discog. No.	Recording/ Performance Date	RCA Victor Matrix-Take No.	Catalog Number RCA/BMG	Other Label	Type	Record Issue Date	Album Description and Notes
2077 [1076]	9 May 51	E1-RC-3421-1R	49-3740-B		45	Feb. 52	Gems from Il trovatore.
			ERA-112-1		45	Nov. 53	Highlights (Note 7).
			LM-1827		LP	Jan. 55	Highlights (Note 7).
			60191-2-RG		CD	June 90	

Section III. Nonopera Audio Recordings by Song

Discog. No.	Recording/ Performance Date	RCA Victor Matrix-Take No.	Catalog Number RCA/BMG	Other Label	Type	Record Issue Date	Album Description and Notes
3001 [1048]	A Rovin' (sea shanty, arr. by Tom Scott) Morris Levine, orchestra and chorus						
	8 July 47	D7-RB-1261-1		10-1386-B (MO/DM-1186)	78 [4]	Apr. 48	Leonard Warren: Sea Shanties.
				49-1149-B (WDM-1186)	45 [4]	Feb. 51	Leonard Warren: Sea Shanties.
			LM-1168		LP	Oct. 51	Leonard Warren: Operatic Arias and Sea Shanties.
				Met 215	CD	Sep. 92	Leonard Warren: Portraits in Memory.
				LWC-2	CD [2]	Mar. 00	Leonard Warren Commemorative. Opera Arias and Concert Songs.
3002 [1111]	Agnus Dei (Georges Bizet) Willard Sektberg, piano						
	May 58		LM-2266		LP	Oct. 58	Leonard Warren on Tour in Russia.
			7807-2-RG		CD	Jan. 89	Leonard Warren on Tour in Russia.
				LWC-2	CD [2]	Mar. 00	Leonard Warren Commemorative. Opera Arias and Concert Songs.
3003 [1111]	Amarilli (Giulio Caccini) Willard Sektberg, piano						
	May 58		LM-2266		LP	Oct. 58	Leonard Warren on Tour in Russia.
			7807-2-RG		CD	Jan. 89	Leonard Warren on Tour in Russia.

Discog. No.	Recording/ Performance Date	RCA Victor Matrix-Take No.	Catalog Number RCA/BMG	Other Label	Type	Record Issue Date	Album Description and Notes
3004 [1072]	America the Beautiful (Samuel A. Ward, Katherine Lee Bates) Frank Black, RCA Victor Orchestra						
	28 Sep. 50	E0-RB-5673-<u>1</u>	49-3287-A (WDM-1526)		45 [4]	July 51	Leonard Warren: Songs for Everyone.
			ERA-178		45	Mar. 54	Leonard Warren Sings.
			LM-94		LP	July 51	Leonard Warren: Songs for Everyone (10").
			LM-2206		LP	Aug. 58	Leonard Warren: Rolling Down to Rio.
				LWC-2	CD [2]	Mar. 00	Leonard Warren Commemorative. Opera Arias and Concert Song.
3005 [1073]	Battle Hymn of the Republic (William Steffe, Julia Ward Howe) Frank Black; RCA Victor Orchestra						
	28 Sep. 50	E0-RB-5674-<u>1</u>	49-3287-B (WDM-1526)		45 [4]	July 51	Leonard Warren: Songs for Everyone.
			ERA-178		45	Mar. 54	Leonard Warren Sings.
			LM-94		LP	July 51	Leonard Warren: Songs for Everyone (10").
			LM-2206		LP	Aug. 58	Leonard Warren: Rolling Down to Rio.
				LWC-2	CD [2]	Mar. 00	Leonard Warren Commemorative. Opera Arias and Concert Songs.
3006 [1056]	Because (Guy d'Hardelot, Edward Teschemacher) Willard Sektberg, piano (Guy d'Hardelot is the pseudonym of Helen Rhodes.)						
	3 Sep. 47	D7-RB-1604-<u>2A</u>	10-1406-B		78	May 48	
			49-1019-B		45	June 50	(10").

3007 [1111]

		Label/No.	Format	Date	Description
		LWC-2	CD [2]	Mar. 00	Leonard Warren Commemorative. Opera Arias and Concert Songs.

Les berçeaux (Gabriel Fauré) Willard Sektberg, piano
May 58

Label/No.	Format	Date	Description
LM-2266	LP	Oct. 58	Leonard Warren on Tour in Russia.
7807-2-RG	CD	Jan. 89	Leonard Warren on Tour in Russia.

3008 [1049]

Blow the Man Down (sea shanty, arr. by Tom Scott) Morris Levine, orchestra and chorus
8 July 47   D7-RB-1262-1A

Matrix	Label/No.	Format	Date	Description
10-1383-A (MO/DM-1186)		78 [4]	Apr. 48	Leonard Warren: Sea Shanties (10").
10-1500-A		78	Apr. 48	(10").
49-1146-A (WDM-1186)		45 [4]	Feb. 51	Leonard Warren: Sea Shanties.
LM-1168		LP	Oct. 51	Leonard Warren: Operaic Arias and Sea Shanties.

3009 [1111]

Blow the Man Down (sea shanty, arr. by Tom Scott) Willard Sektberg, piano
May 58

Label/No.	Format	Date	Description
7807-2-RG	CD	Jan. 89	Leonard Warren on Tour in Russia.

3010 [1078]

Boots (J. P. McCall, Rudyard Kipling) Frank Black; RCA Victor Orchestra (J. P. McCall is the pseudonym of Australian bass-baritone Peter Dawson.)
2 Oct. 51   E1-RB-3736-1

Matrix	Label/No.	Format	Date	Description
49-3700-A (WDM-1630)		45 [4]	Apr. 52	Leonard Warren: Songs of Rudyard Kipling.
	LM-147	LP	Apr. 52	Leonard Warren: Songs of Rudyard Kipling (10").
	LM-2206	LP	Aug. 58	Leonard Warren: Rolling Down to Rio.
	Met 215	CD	Sep. 92	Leonard Warren: Portraits in Memory.
	LWC-2	CD [2]	Mar. 00	Leonard Warren Commemorative. Opera Arias and Concert Songs.

Discog. No.	Recording/ Performance Date	RCA Victor Matrix-Take No.	Catalog Number RCA/BMG	Other Label	Type	Record Issue Date	Album Description and Notes
3011 [1092]	Canto di primavera (Pietro Cimara, Fausto Salvatori) Willard Sektberg, piano						
	9 June 54	E4-RC-0255-1	M70L0162		LP	1954 (?)	(10").
				LWC-2	CD [2]	Mar. 00	Leonard Warren Commemorative. Opera Arias and Concert Songs.
3012 [1111]	Canto di primavera (Pietro Cimara, Fausto Salvatori) Willard Sektberg, piano						
	May 58		7807-2-RG		CD	Jan. 89	Leonard Warren on Tour in Russia.
3013 [1111]	Canto popolare (Pietro Cimara) Willard Sektberg, piano						
	May 58		7807-2-RG		CD	Jan. 89	Leonard Warren on Tour in Russia.
3014 [1111]	Chanson à boire (Maurice Ravel, *Don Quichotte à Dulcinée*) Willard Sektberg, piano						
	May 58		LM-2266		LP	Oct. 58	Leonard Warren on Tour in Russia.
			7807-2-RG		CD	Jan. 89	Leonard Warren on Tour in Russia.
3015 [1110]	Chanson à boire (Maurice Ravel, *Don Quichotte à Dulcinée*) Willard Sektberg, piano						
	13 May 58			MIO 49519-007	LP	1958 (?)	Public recital. Melodiya. Leonard Warren, Baritone: Arias from Operas, Songs, Romances.
3016 [1111]	Colorado Trail (traditional, arr. by Tom Scott) Willard Sektberg, piano						
	May 58		LM-2266		LP	Oct. 58	Leonard Warren on Tour in Russia.
			7807-2-RG		CD	Jan. 89	Leonard Warren on Tour in Russia.

3017 [1058] Danny Boy (old Irish air, arr. by Fred E. Weatherly) Willard Sektberg, piano

3 Sep. 47	D7-RB-1606-1	10-1421-B	78	July 48	(10").
		49-0284-B (WDM-1460)	45 [3]	Mar. 49	A Leonard Warren Collection.
		Met 215	CD	Sep. 92	Leonard Warren: Portraits in Memory.
		LWC-2	CD [2]	Mar. 00	Leonard Warren Commemorative. Opera Arias and Concert Songs.

3018 [1083] Danny Deever (Walter Damrosch, Rudyard Kipling) Frank Black; RCA Victor Orchestra

5 Oct. 51	E1-RB-3735-1	49-3703-A (WDM-1630)	45 [4]	Apr. 52	Leonard Warren: Songs of Rudyard Kipling.
		ERA-93	45	Aug. 53	Leonard Warren: Kipling Favorites.
		LM-147	LP	Apr. 52	Leonard Warren: Songs of Rudyard Kipling (10").
		LM-2206	LP	Aug. 58	Leonard Warren: Rolling Down to Rio.
		LWC-2	CD [2]	Mar. 00	Leonard Warren Commemorative. Opera Arias and Concert Songs.

3019 [1013] Drake's Drum (Sir Charles Villiers Stanford, Sir Henry Newbolt, *Songs of the Sea*) Miguel Sandoval, piano

4 Feb. 41	BS-060703-1, 2	—		—	Unpublished.

3020 [1050] The Drummer and the Cook (sea shanty, arr. by Tom Scott) Morris Levine; orchestra and chorus

8 July 47	D7-RB-1263-1A	10-1384-A (MO/DM-1186)	78 [4]	Apr. 48	Leonard Warren: Sea Shanties (10").
		49-1147-A (WDM-1186)	45 [4]	Feb. 51	Leonard Warren: Sea Shanties.
		LM-1168	LP	Oct. 51	Leonard Warren: Operatic Arias and Sea Shanties.

Discog. No.	Recording/ Performance Date	RCA Victor Matrix-Take No.	Catalog Number RCA/BMG	Other Label	Type	Record Issue Date	Album Description and Notes
3021 [1051]	8 July 47	The Drunken Sailor (sea shanty, arr. by Tom Scott) Morris Levine; orchestra and chorus					
		D7-RB-1264-1	10-1386-A	(MO/DM-1186)	78 [4]	Apr. 48	Leonard Warren: Sea Shanties (10").
			10-1500-B		78	Apr. 48	(10").
			49-1149-A	(WDM-1186)	45 [4]	Feb. 51	Leonard Warren: Sea Shanties.
			LM-1168		LP	Oct. 51	Leonard Warren: Operatic Arias and Sea Shanties.
3022 [1110]	13 May 58	The Drunken Sailor (sea shanty, arr. by Tom Scott) Willard Sektberg, piano		MIO 49519-007	LP	1958 (?)	Public recital. Melodiya. Leonard Warren, Baritone: Arias from Operas, Songs, Romances.
3023 [1017]	10 June 41	L'esperto nocchiero (Giovanni Bononcini, *Astarto*) Miguel Sandoval, piano					
		BS-065695-1	—		—	—	Unpublished (Note 8).
3024 [1111]	May 58	Good Fellows Be Merry (J. S. Bach, Cantata No. 212, Bauer/Peasant) Willard Sektberg, piano					
			LM-2266		LP	Oct. 58	Leonard Warren on Tour in Russia.
			7807-2-RG		CD	Jan. 89	Leonard Warren on Tour in Russia.
3025 [1079]	2 Oct. 51	Gunga Din (Charles Gilbert Spross, Rudyard Kipling) Frank Black; RCA Victor Orchestra					
		E1-RB-3737-1	49-3701-A (WDM-1630)		45 [4]	Apr. 52	Leonard Warren: Songs of Rudyard Kipling.
			ERA-93		45	Aug. 53	Leonard Warren: Kipling Favorites.

| | LM-147 | LP | Apr. 52 | Leonard Warren: Songs of Rudyard Kipling (10"). |
| | LM-2206 | LP | Aug. 58 | Leonard Warren: Rolling Down to Rio. |

Haul-A-Way, Joe (sea shanty, arr. by Tom Scott) Morris Levine; orchestra and chorus

3026 [1052]	9 July 47 D7-RB-1265-2			
	10-1385-A (MO/DM-1186)	78 [4]	Apr. 48	Leonard Warren: Sea Shanties (10").
	49-1148-A (WDM-1186)	45 [4]	Feb. 51	Leonard Warren: Sea Shanties.
	LM-1168	LP	Oct. 51	Leonard Warren: Operatic Arias and Sea Shanties.
	LWC-2	CD [2]	Mar. 00	Leonard Warren Commemorative. Opera Arias and Concert Songs.

Home on the Range (David W. Guion) Frank Black; RCA Victor Orchestra

3027 [1067]	26 Sep. 50 E0-RB-5668-1			
	49-3290-B (WDM-1526)	45 [4]	July 51	Leonard Warren: Songs for Everyone.
	ERA-49 (45 EP)	45	Aug. 52	Leonard Warren Sings.
	LM-94	LP	July 51	Leonard Warren: Songs for Everyone (10").
	LM-2206	LP	Aug. 58	Leonard Warren: Rolling Down to Rio.
	LWC-2	CD [2]	Mar. 00	Leonard Warren Commemorative. Opera Arias and Concert Songs.

Ideale (Francesco Paolo Tosti, Carmelo Errico) Willard Sektberg, piano

3028 [1089]	9 June 54 E4-RC-0252-1			
	LM/LSC-2361	LP	Oct. 59	S. Hurok Presents. Leonard Warren
	LWC-2	CD [2]	Mar. 00	Leonard Warren Commemorative. Opera Arias and Concert Songs.

Discog. No.	Recording/ Performance Date	RCA Victor Matrix-Take No.	Catalog Number RCA/BMG	Other Label	Type	Record Issue Date	Album Description and Notes
3029 [1111]	In questa tomba oscura (Ludwig van Beethoven, Giuseppe Carpani) Willard Sektberg, piano						
	May 58		LM-2266		LP	Oct. 58	Leonard Warren on Tour in Russia.
			7807-2-RG		CD	Jan. 89	Leonard Warren on Tour in Russia.
3030 [1028]	A Little Bit of Heaven (Ernest R. Ball, J. Keirn Brennan) Maximilian Pilzer; RCA Victor Orchestra						
	18 Dec. 44	D4-RB-717-1, 1A			—	—	Unpublished (remade 26 Sep. 50).
3031 [1070]	A Little Bit of Heaven (Ernest R. Ball, J. Keirn Brennan) Frank Black; RCA Victor Orchestra						
	26 Sep. 50	E0-RB-5671-2	49-3290-A (WDM-1526)		45 [4]	July 51	Leonard Warren: Songs for Everyone.
			LM-94		LP	July 51	Leonard Warren: Songs for Everyone (10").
			LM-2206		LP	Aug. 58	Leonard Warren: Rolling Down to Rio.
				LWC-2	CD [2]	Mar. 00	Leonard Warren Commemorative. Opera Arias and Concert Songs.
3032 [1060]	The Lord's Prayer (Albert Hay Malotte) Willard Sektberg, piano						
	29 Nov. 47	D7-RB-2546-2C	10-1421-A		78	July 48	(10").
			49-0284-A (WDM-1460)		45 [3]	Mar. 49	A Leonard Warren Collection.
			ERA-49		45	Aug. 52	Leonard Warren Sings.
				LWC-2	CD [2]	Mar. 00	Leonard Warren Commemorative. Opera Arias and Concert .

3033 [1069] Love's Old Sweet Song (J. L. Malloy, G. C. Bingham) Frank Black, RCA Victor Orchestra
26 Sep. 50

Matrix	Catalog	Format	Date	Album
E0-RB-5670-1	49-3288-A (WDM-1526)	45 [4]	July 51	Leonard Warren: Songs for Everyone.
	LM-94	LP	July 51	Leonard Warren: Songs for Everyone (10").
	LM-2206	LP	Aug. 58	Leonard Warren: Rolling Down to Rio.
	LWC-2	CD [2]	Mar. 00	Leonard Warren Commemorative. Opera Arias and Concert Songs.

3034 [1054] Low Lands (sea shanty, arr. by Tom Scott) Morris Levine, orchestra and chorus
9 July 47

Matrix	Catalog	Format	Date	Album
D7-RB-1267-1A	10-1385-B (MO/DM-1186)	78 [4]	Apr. 48	Leonard Warren: Sea Shanties (10").
	49-1148-B (WDM-1186)	45 [4]	Feb. 51	Leonard Warren: Sea Shanties.
	LM-1168	LP	Oct. 51	Leonard Warren: Operatic Arias and Sea Shanties.
	Met 215	CD	Sep. 92	Leonard Warren: Portraits in Memory.
	LWC-2	CD [2]	Mar. 00	Leonard Warren Commemorative. Opera Arias and Concert Songs.

3035 [1111] Madrigal (Vincent d'Indy) Willard Sektberg, piano
May 58

Catalog	Format	Date	Album
LM-2266	LP	Oct. 58	Leonard Warren on Tour in Russia.
7807-2-RG	CD	Jan. 89	Leonard Warren on Tour in Russia.

3036 [1111] Mattinata (Ruggiero Leoncavallo) Willard Sektberg, piano
May 58

Catalog	Format	Date	Album
LM-2266	LP	Oct. 58	Leonard Warren on Tour in Russia.
7807-2-RG	CD	Jan. 89	Leonard Warren on Tour in Russia.

Discog. No.	Recording/ Performance Date	RCA Victor Matrix-Take No.	Catalog Number RCA/BMG	Other Label	Type	Record Issue Date	Album Description and Notes
	Mother Machree (Chauncey Olcott, Ernest R. Ball, Rida Johnson Young) Frank Black, RCA Victor Orchestra						
3037 [1068]	26 Sep. 50	E0-RB-5669-1	49-3289-A (WDM-1526)		45 [4]	July 51	Leonard Warren: Songs for Everyone.
			LM-94		LP	July 51	Leonard Warren: Songs for Everyone (10").
			LM-2206		LP	Aug. 58	Leonard Warren: Rolling Down to Rio.
				LWC-2	CD [2]	Mar. 00	Leonard Warren Commemorative. Opera Arias and Concert Songs.
	Mother o' Mine (Frank E. Tours, Rudyard Kipling) Frank Black; RCA Victor Orchestra						
3038 [1082]	5 Oct. 51	E1-RB-3734-1R	49-3702-B (WDM-1630)		45 [4]	Apr. 52	Leonard Warren: Songs of Rudyard Kipling.
			ERA-93		45	Aug. 53	Leonard Warren: Kipling Favorites.
			LM-147		LP	Apr. 52	Leonard Warren: Songs of Rudyard Kipling (10").
			LM-2206		LP	Aug. 58	Leonard Warren: Rolling Down to Rio.
	Nel giardino (Francesco Santoliquido) Willard Sektberg, piano						
3039 [1093]	9 June 54	E4-RC-0256-1	M70L0162		LP	1954 (?)	(10").
				LWC-2	CD [2]	Mar. 00	Leonard Warren Commemorative. Opera Arias and Concert Songs.
	Nel giardino (Francesco Santoliquido) Willard Sektberg, piano						
3040 [1111]	May 58		7807-2-RG		CD	Jan. 89	Leonard Warren on Tour in Russia.

None But the Lonely Heart (Peter Ilyitch Tchaikovsky, Arthur Westbrook) Willard Sektberg, piano

| 3041 [1057] | 3 Sep. 47 | D7-RB-1605-2 | 10-1406-A 49-1019-A LWC-2 | 78 45 CD [2] | May 48 June 50 Mar. 00 | Leonard Warren Commemorative. Opera Arias and Concert Songs. (10"). |

O del mio amato Ben (Stefano Donaudy) Willard Sektberg, piano

| 3042 [1111] | May 58 | 7807-2-RG | CD | Jan. 89 | Leonard Warren on Tour in Russia. |

O del mio amato Ben (Stefano Donaudy) Willard Sektberg, piano

| 3043 [1110] | 13 May 58 | MIO 49519-007 | LP | 1958 (?) | Public recital. Melodiya. Leonard Warren, Baritone: Arias from Operas, Songs, Romances. |

O Ruddier Than the Cherry (George Frideric Handel, *Acis and Galatea*) Willard Sektberg, piano

| 3044 [1111] | May 58 | 7807-2-RG | CD | Jan. 89 | Leonard Warren on Tour in Russia. |

O That It Were So (Frank Bridge) Willard Sektberg, piano

| 3045 [1111] | May 58 | LM-2266 | LP | Oct. 58 | Leonard Warren on Tour in Russia. |
| | | 7807-2-RG | CD | Jan. 89 | Leonard Warren on Tour in Russia. |

O That It Were So (Frank Bridge) Willard Sektberg, piano

| 3046 [1110] | 13 May 58 | MIO 49519-007 | LP | 1958 (?) | Melodiya. Leonard Warren, Baritone: Arias from Operas, Songs, Romances. |

Occhi di fata (Luigi Denza, Tromacoldo) Willard Sektberg, piano

| 3047 [1090] | 9 June 54 | E4-RC-0253-1 M70L0162 LWC-2 | LP CD [2] | 1954 (?) Mar. 00 | Leonard Warren Commemorative. Opera Arias and Concert Songs. (10"). |

Discog. No.	Recording/ Performance Date	RCA Victor Matrix-Take No.	Catalog Number RCA/BMG Other Label	Type	Record Issue Date	Album Description and Notes
	An Old Song Resung (Charles Tomlinson Griffes, John Masefield) Willard Sektberg, piano					
3048 [1111]	May 58		LM-2266	LP	Oct. 58	Leonard Warren on Tour in Russia.
			7807-2-RG	CD	Jan. 89	Leonard Warren on Tour in Russia.
	The Old Superb (Sir Charles Villiers Stanford, Sir Henry Newbolt, *Songs of the Sea*) Miguel Sandoval, piano					
3049 [1015]	4 Feb. 41	BS-060705-1, 2, 2A	—	—	—	Unpublished.
	Ol' Man River (Jerome Kern, Oscar Hammerstein II, *Show Boat*) Frank Black; RCA Victor Orchestra					
3050 [1071]	28 Sep. 50	E0-RB-5672-1	49-3288-B (WDM-1526)	45 [4]	July 51	Leonard Warren: Songs for Everyone.
			49-3307-A	45	Sep. 51	Leonard Warren Sings.
			ERA-49	45	Aug. 52	Leonard Warren: Songs for Everyone (10").
			LM-94	LP	July 51	Leonard Warren-Rolling Down to Rio.
			LM-2206	LP	Aug. 58	
	On the Road to Mandalay (Oley Speaks, Rudyard Kipling) Willard Sektberg, piano					
3051 [1061]	29 Nov. 47	D7-RB-2545-1	10-1447-A	78	Oct. 48	(10").
			49-0572-A (WDM-1460)	45 [3]	Oct. 49	A Leonard Warren Collection.
	On the Road to Mandalay (Oley Speaks, Rudyard Kipling) Frank Black; RCA Victor Orchestra					
3052 [1074]	28 Sep. 50	E0-RB-5675-1	49-3289-B (WDM-1526)	45 [4]	July 51	Leonard Warren: Songs for Everyone.
			49-3307-B	45	Sep. 51	

3053
[1014]

Outward Bound (Sir Charles Villiers Stanford, Sir Henry Newbolt, *Songs of the Sea*) Miguel Sandoval, piano

4 Feb. 41   BS-060704-1, 1A, 2, 2A, 3   —   —   Unpublished.

Catalog	Format	Date	Release
49-3700-B (WDM-1630)	45 [4]	Apr. 52	Leonard Warren: Songs of Rudyard Kipling.
ERA-49	45	Aug. 52	Leonard Warren Sings.
LM-94	LP	July 51	Leonard Warren: Songs for Everyone (10").
LM-147	LP	Apr. 52	Leonard Warren: Songs of Rudyard Kipling (10").
LM-2206	LP	Aug. 58	Leonard Warren: Rolling Down to Rio.
LWC-2	CD [2]	Mar. 00	Leonard Warren Commemorative. Opera Arias and Concert Songs.

3054
[1077]

Recessional (Reginald de Koven, Rudyard Kipling) Frank Black; RCA Victor Orchestra

2 Oct. 51   E1-RB-3731-1

Catalog	Format	Date	Release
49-3702-A (WDM-1630)	45 [4]	Apr. 52	Leonard Warren: Songs of Rudyard Kipling.
ERA-178	45	Mar. 54	Leonard Warren Sings.
LM-147	LP	Apr. 52	Leonard Warren: Songs of Rudyard Kipling (10").
LM-2206	LP	Aug. 58	Leonard Warren: Rolling Down to Rio.
Met 215	CD	Sep. 92	Leonard Warren: Portraits in Memory.

3055
[1053]

Rio Grande (sea shanty, arr. by Tom Scott) Morris Levine, orchestra and chorus

9 July 47   D7-RB-1266-1B

Catalog	Format	Date	Release
10-1383-B (MO/DM-1186)	78 [4]	Apr. 48	Leonard Warren: Sea Shanties (10").
49-1146-B (WDM-1186)	45 [4]	Feb. 51	Leonard Warren: Sea Shanties.
LM-1168	LP	Oct. 51	Leonard Warren: Operatic Arias and Sea Shanties.

Discog. No.	Recording/ Performance Date	RCA Victor Matrix-Take No.	Catalog Number RCA/BMG	Other Label	Type	Record Issue Date	Album Description and Notes
	Rolling Down to Rio (Edward German, Rudyard Kipling) Frank Black; RCA orchestra						
3056 [1081]	5 Oct. 51	E1-RB-3733-1	49-3703-B	(WDM-1630)	45 [4]	Apr. 52	Leonard Warren: Songs of Rudyard Kipling.
			ERA-93		45	Aug. 53	Leonard Warren: Kipling Favorites.
			LM-147		LP	Apr. 52	Leonard Warren: Songs of Rudyard Kipling (10").
			LM-2206		LP	Aug. 58	Leonard Warren: Rolling Down to Rio.
				LWC-2	CD [2]	Mar. 00	Leonard Warren Commemorative. Opera Arias and Concert Songs.
	Shenandoah (sea shanty, arr. by Tom Scott) Morris Levine; orchestra and chorus						
3057 [1055]	9 July 47	D7-RB-1268-2	10-1384-B	(MO/DM-1186)	78 [4]	Apr. 48	Leonard Warren: Sea Shanties (10").
			49-1147-B	(WDM-1186)	45 [4]	Feb. 51	Leonard Warren: Sea Shanties.
			LM-1168		LP	Oct. 51	Leonard Warren: Operatic Arias and Sea Shanties.
				Met 210	LP	Nov. 90	Songs Our Mothers Taught Us.
				Met 210	CD	Nov. 90	
				Met 210	CAS	Nov. 90	
				LWC-2	CD [2]	Mar. 00	Leonard Warren Commemorative. Opera Arias and Concert Songs.

ID	Date	Matrix	Catalog	Format	Release	Notes
3058 [1110]	**Shenandoah (sea shanty, arr. by Tom Scott) Willard Sektberg, piano**					
	13 May 58		MIO 49519-007	LP	1958 (?)	Public recital. Melodiya. Leonard Warren, Baritone: Arias from Operas, Songs, Romances.
3059 [1080]	**Smugglers' Song (Marshall Kernochan, Rudyard Kipling) Frank Black; RCA Victor Orchestra**					
	5 Oct. 51	E1-RB-3732-1	49-3701-B (WDM-1630)	45 [4]	Apr. 52	Leonard Warren: Songs of Rudyard Kipling.
			ERA-178	45	Mar. 54	Leonard Warren Sings.
			LM-147	LP	Apr. 52	Leonard Warren: Songs of Rudyard Kipling (10").
			LM-2206	LP	Aug. 58	Leonard Warren: Rolling Down to Rio.
			LWC-2	CD [2]	Mar. 00	Leonard Warren Commemorative. Opera Arias and Concert Songs.
3060 [1091]	**Stornello (Pietro Cimara, Arnaldo Frateilli) Willard Sektberg, piano**					
	9 June 54	E4-RC-0254-1	—	—	—	Unpublished.
3061 [1111]	**Tell Me, O Blue, Blue Sky (Vittorio Giannini, Karl Flaster) Willard Sektberg, piano**					
	May 58		LM-2266	LP	Oct. 58	Leonard Warren on Tour in Russia.
			7807-2-RG	CD	Jan. 89	Leonard Warren on Tour in Russia.
3062 [1016]	**Tu lo sai (Giuseppe Torelli) Miguel Sandoval, piano**					
	4 Feb. 41	BS-060706-1, 2, 2A, 3, 3A	—			Unpublished (Note 8).
	10 June 41	BS-060706-4, 4A	—			Unpublished.
3063 [1018]	**Turn Ye to Me (old Scottish song, arr. by Miguel Sandoval) Miguel Sandoval, piano**					
	10 June 41	BS-065696-1, 2, 3, 3A	—			Unpublished (Note 8).

Discog. No.	Recording/ Performance Date	RCA Victor Matrix-Take No.	Catalog Number RCA/BMG	Other Label	Type	Record Issue Date	Album Description and Notes
	L'ultima canzone (Francesco Paolo Tosti, Francesco Cimmino) Willard Sektberg, piano						
3064 [1088]	9 June 54	E4-RC-0251-1	LM-1802		LP	Sep. 54	An Adventure in High Fidelity.
	L'ultima canzone (Francesco Paolo Tosti, Francesco Cimmino) Willard Sektberg, piano						
3065 [1111]	May 58		LM-2266		LP	Oct. 58	Leonard Warren on Tour in Russia.
			7807-2-RG		CD	Jan. 89	Leonard Warren on Tour in Russia.
	L'ultima canzone (Francesco Paolo Tosti, Francesco Cimmino) Willard Sektberg, piano						
3066 [1110]	13 May 58			MIO 49519-007	LP	1958 (?)	Public recital. Melodiya. Leonard Warren, Baritone: Arias from Operas, Songs, Romances.
	Until (Wilfred Sanderson, Edward Teschemacher) Willard Sektberg, piano						
3067 [1059]	29 Nov. 47	D7-RB-2544-1	10-1447-B		78	Oct. 48	(10").
			49-0572-B	(WDM-1460)	45 [3]	Oct. 49	A Leonard Warren Collection.
	When Irish Eyes Are Smiling (Ernest R. Ball, Chauncey Olcott, George Graff Jr.) Maximilian Pilzer, RCA Victor Orchestra						
3068 [1029]	18 Dec. 44	D4-RB-718-1, 1A, 2, 2A	—		—	—	Unpublished.
	When Lights Go Rolling Round the Sky (John Ireland, James Vila Blake) Willard Sektberg, piano						
3069 [1110]	13 May 58			MIO 49519-007	LP	1958 (?)	Public recital. Melodiya. Leonard Warren, Baritone: Arias from Operas, Songs, Romances.

Section IV. Unauthorized Audio Recordings by Opera

Discog. No.	Performance Date and Source	Producer/ Label	Catalog Number	Type	Author Comments
	Aida (Giuseppe Verdi)				
	28 May 40, 17 June 40 RCA recording session	Wilfrid Pelletier (with Bampton, Summers, Carron, Cordon, Alvary)			
4001		Parade Records	EP 1003	45	Copied from RCA Victor SR 51, SR 52, SR 53, SR 54. See Discog. Nos. 2002, 2003.
			EP 1003	LP	
			EP 1014	LP	
			OP-103 (Excerpts)	LP	
	22 Mar. 41 Met Opera broadcast	Ettore Panizza (with Cordon, Castagna, Roman, Martinelli, Pinza, Oliviero, Gurney, Stellman)			
4002		GAO	EJS 101 (Complete)	LP [3]	
4003		The 40s Label	FTO 327.28 (Complete)	CD [2]	
4004		Walhall	WHL 3 (Complete)	CD [2]	
	8 Mar. 52 Met Opera broadcast	Fausto Cleva (with Milanov, Del Monaco, Rankin, Hines)			
4005		Myto Records	MCD 953.129 (Complete)	CD [2]	
4006		UORC	UORC 325 Complete	LP [2]	

Discog. No.	Performance Date and Source	Producer/ Label	Catalog Number	Type	Author Comments
Alceste (Christoph Willibald von Gluck)					
	8 Mar. 41 Met Opera broadcast				Dieu puissant! . . . Perce d'un rayon éclatant. Ettore Panizza (Warren as High Priest)
4007		GAO	EjS 212	LP	Ettore Panizza (with Maison, Bampton, Warren as High Priest, Kent, Cehanovsky, De Paolis, Farell)
4008		GAO	EjS 545 (Excerpts)	LP	
4009		Naxos Historical	8.1100067 (Complete)	CD [2]	
Andrea Chénier (Umberto Giordano)					
	4 Dec. 54 Met Opera broadcast		Fausto Cleva (with Del Monaco, Milanov, Elias)		See Discog. No. 2004.
4010		MRF	MRF 15 (Complete)	LP [3]	
4011		Nuova Era	2364/65 (Complete)	CD [2]	
	28 Dec. 57 Met Opera broadcast		Fausto Cleva (with Tucker, Milanov, Elias, Lipton)		
4012		Arkadia	CDMP 476.2 (Complete)	CD [2]	
4013		ERR	ERR 110-2 (Complete)	LP [2]	

Un ballo in maschera (Giuseppe Verdi)

15 Jan. 44 / Met Opera broadcast — Bruno Walter (with Peerce, Milanov, Thorborg, Greer, Cordon, Baker, Moscona)

No.	Label	Catalog	Format	Notes
4014	AS Disc	AS 428/9 (Complete)	CD [2]	
4015	BWS	BWS-805 (Complete)	LP [2]	
4016	The 40s Label	FTO 311.12 (Complete)	CD [2]	

22 Nov 47 / Met Opera broadcast — Giuseppe Antonicelli (with Peerce, Ilitsch, Harshaw, Alarie, Baker, Vaghi, Alvary)

No.	Label	Catalog	Format	Notes
4017	Classic Editions	CE 5001 (Complete)	LP [3]	Performers shown on album cover are incorrect.
4018	Myto Records	MCD 942.100 (Excerpts)	CD [2]	A bonus to another *Ballo* radio broadcast recording.

9 Jan. 55, 21 Jan. 55 / RCA recording session — Dimitri Mitropoulos (with Peerce, Milanov, Anderson, Peters)

No.	Label	Catalog	Format	Notes
4019	Melodiya (Russia)	D031891/2 (Highlights)	LP	Copied from RCA LM-1911 (LP). See Discog. No. 2008.
4020	Theorema	TH 121.146 (Highlights)	CD	Copied from RCA LM-1911 (LP). See Discog. No. 2008.

Boris Godunov (Modest Mussorgsky)

9 Dec. 39 / Met Opera broadcast — Ettore Panizza (with Pinza, Petina, Farell, Kaskas, De Paolis, Cehanovsky, Moscona, Cordon, Thorborg, Kullman, and Warren as Rangoni)

No.	Label	Catalog	Format	Notes
4021	ERR	ERR-138-3 (Complete)	LP [3]	Also Library of Congress: Curtis Institute discs 1770/1776 (Complete).
4022	GAO	EJS-215 (Complete)	LP [3]	
4023	The 40s Label	FTO 329.30	CD [2]	

Discog. No.	Performance Date and Source	Producer/ Label	Catalog Number	Type	Author Comments
	13 Feb. 43 Met Opera broadcast	George Szell (with Kipnis, Petina, Farell, De Paolis, Moscona, Maison, Thorborg, Cordon, and Warren as Rangoni)			
4024		GAO	EJS 550 (Excerpts)	LP	
4025		The 40s Label	FTO 1505-6 (Complete)	CD [2]	
4026		Walhall	WHL 12 (Complete)	CD [2]	
	4 Dec. 43 Met Opera broadcast	George Szell (with Pinza, De Paolis, Moscona, Thorborg, Farell, Baccaloni, and Warren as Rangoni)			
4027		GAO	EJS 561 (Excerpts)	LP	
4028		UORC	UORC 258 (Complete)	LP [3]	
	Carmen (Georges Bizet)				
	31 May 40 RCA recording session	Wilfrid Pelletier (with Peebles, Jobin, Votipka, Oelheim, Cehanovsky, Bontempi)			
4029		Parade Records	EP 1001	45	Copied from RCA Victor SR 45, SR 46, SR 47 (78 rpm). See Discog. No. 2014.
			EP 1001	LP	
			EP 1013	LP	
			OP-101	LP	
			(Excerpts)	LP	
	27 Mar. 43 Met Opera broadcast	Thomas Beecham (with Djanel, Jobin, Albanese)			
4030		UORC	UORC 289 (Excerpts)	LP	
4031		Walhall	WHL 31 (Complete)	CD [2]	

Cavalleria rusticana (Pietro Mascagni)

1 Feb. 41
Met Opera broadcast
Ferruccio Calusio (with Roman, Jagel, Kaskas, Doe)

4032	UORC	UORC 112	LP (Complete)
4033	Walhall	WHL 20	CD (Complete)

Ernani (Giuseppe Verdi)

29 Dec. 56
Met Opera broadcast
Dimitri Mitropoulos (with Del Monaco, Milanov, Siepi, Vanni, McCracken, Cehanovsky)

4034	Arkadia	CDMP 470.2	CD [2] (Complete)
	Cetra	LO-12	LP [3] (Complete)
4035	Foyer	FO 1021	LP [3] (Complete)
	Foyer	CF 2006	CD [2] (Complete)
4036	Gli Dei Della Musica	DMV 17/18/19	LP [3] (Complete)
4037	MRF	MRF 6	LP [2] (Complete)

Falstaff (Giuseppe Verdi)

26 Feb. 49
Met Opera broadcast
Fritz Reiner (with Valdengo, Di Stefano, Resnik, Albanese, Chabay, Lipton, De Paolis, Alvary)

4038	Arlecchino	ARLA 85-A86	CD [2] (Complete)
4039	GAO	EJS 250	LP [2] (Complete)

Faust (Charles Gounod)

Discog. No.	Performance Date and Source	Producer/ Label	Catalog Number	Type	Author Comments
4040	16 Mar. 40 Met Opera broadcast				Wilfrid Pelletier (with Crooks, Jepson, Pinza, Browning, Votipka, Engelman)
		UORC	UORC 275 (Complete)	LP [2]	Also Library of Congress Tape 8944-1 (Complete).
	6 Apr. 40 Met Opera broadcast, Boston				Wilfrid Pelletier (with Crooks, Jepson, Pinza, Olheim, Votipka, Engleman)
4041		GAO	EJS 188 (Complete)	LP [3]	
4042		Naxos Historical	8.110016/7 (Complete)	CD [2]	
	31 Dec. 49 Met Opera broadcast				Wilfrid Pelletier (with Di Stefano, Kirsten, Tajo)
4043		Arkadia	CDMP 478.2 (Complete)	CD [2]	
4044		Cetra	Cetra LO 1-3 (Complete)	LP [3]	
4045		Fonit Cetra	DOC 53 (Complete)	LP [3]	
4046		Giuseppe Di Stefano	GDS 2105 (Complete)	CD [2]	
4047		Historic Opera Performances	HOPE 223 (Complete)	LP [2]	
4048		UORC	UORC 144 (Excerpts)	LP	

La forza del destino (Giuseppe Verdi)

No.	Date / Event	Conductor (Cast)	Label	Catalog	Format	Notes
4049	27 Dec. 46 RCA recording session	Invano, Alvaro . . . Ah! Una suora mí lasciasti. Jean Paul Morel (with Peerce)	Legato Classics	LCD-205-1	CD	Copied from RCA Victor 11-9768A and 11 9768B (78 rpm). See Discog. No. 2032.
4050	29 Nov. 52 Met Opera broadcast	Fritz Steidry (with Milanov, Tucker, Hines)	Music & Arts	CD 693 (Complete)	CD [2]	See Discog. No. 2026.
4051	12 or 14 Mar. 53 New Orleans Opera performance	Walter Herbert (with Milanov, Del Monaco, Wildermann, Turner, Treigle)	UORC	UORC 222 (Complete)	LP [3]	Some cuts to the score.
4052			Legato Classics	LCD-118-2 (Complete)	CD [2]	Overture given after Scene 1.
4053			VOCE	VOCE-97 (Selections with Mario Del Monaco)	LP	
4054	17 Mar. 56 Met Opera broadcast	Fritz Stiedry (with Milanov, Tucker, Elias, Siepi)	Movimento Musica	03.028 (Complete)	LP [3]	
4055			Gli Dei Della Musica	DMV 20/21/22 (Complete)	LP [3]	
4056			Myto Records	MCD 943.106 (Complete)	CD [2]	

Discog. No.	Performance Date and Source	Producer/Label	Catalog Number	Type	Author Comments
4057	July/Aug. 58 Decca recording session	Fernando Previtali (with Milanov, Di Stefano, Tozzi)			
		Theorema	TH 121.157/9 (Complete)	CD [3]	Copied from either RCA LM 6406/LSC-6406 (LP) or Decca Records OSA 13122 (LP). See Discog. No. 2025.

La Gioconda (Amilcare Ponchielli)

Discog. No.	Performance Date and Source	Producer/Label	Catalog Number	Type	Author Comments
4058	3 Mar. 45 Met Opera broadcast	Emil Cooper (with Roman, Jagel, Castagna, Moscona)			
		UORC	UORC 277 (Excerpts)	LP	
4059	16 Mar. 46 Met Opera broadcast	Emil Cooper (with Milanov, Tucker, Stevens)			See Discog. No. 2035.
		Myto Records	MCD 952.127 (Complete)	CD [2]	
4060	19 Oct. 47 The Standard Hour broadcast, KFI, Hollywood	Gaetano Merola (with Baum, Roman, Thebom, Harshaw)			
		GAO	EJS 321 (Excerpts)	LP	
4061	20 Apr. 57 Met Opera broadcast	Fausto Cleva (with Milanov, Rankin, Amparan, Poggi, Siepi)			
		Arkadia	CDMP 477.2 (Complete)	CD [2]	
4062		I Gioielli Della Lirica	77 (Excerpts)	LP	

Fernando Previtali (with Milanov, Di Stefano, Elias, Clabassi)

No.	Date	Conductor / Cast	Label	Issue	Format	Notes
4063	July/Aug. 57 Decca recording session	Fernando Previtali (with Milanov, Di Stefano, Elias, Clabassi)	Theorema	TH 121.182/4 (Complete)	CD [3]	Copied from either RCA LM-6139/LSC-6139 (LP) or Decca Records OSA 13123 (LP). See Discog. No. 2036.

Lohengrin (Richard Wagner)

No.	Date	Conductor / Cast	Label	Issue	Format	Notes
4064	27 Jan. 40 Met Opera broadcast	Erich Leinsdorf (with Rethberg, Melchior, Thorborg, Huehn, List, and Warren as the Herald)	GAO	EJS 135 (Complete except for Act I Prelude)	LP [3]	
4065			Walhall	WHL 18 (Complete)	CD [3]	

Lucia di Lammermoor (Gaetano Donizetti)

No.	Date	Conductor / Cast	Label	Issue	Format	Notes
4066	8 Jan. 44 Met Opera broadcast	Cesare Sodero (with Pons, Melton, Votipka, Moscona, De Paolis, Dudley)	The 40s Label	FTO 323.24 (Complete)	CD [2]	

Macbeth (Giuseppe Verdi)

No.	Date	Conductor / Cast	Label	Issue	Format	Notes
4067	21 Feb. 59 Met Opera broadcast	Erich Leinsdorf (with Rysanek, Hines, Bergonzi, Olvis, Ordassy, Pechner)	Arkadia	CDMP 471.2 (Complete)	CD [2]	
4068			Movimento Musica	03.029 (Complete)	LP [3]	Album performance date of 21 Feb. 58 is incorrect.

Discog. No.	Performance Date and Source	Producer/ Label	Catalog Number	Type	Author Comments
4069	Feb./Mar. 59 RCA recording session	Erich Leinsdorf (with Rysanek, Hines, Bergonzi)			
		Melodiya (Russia)	D029529/34 (Complete)	LP [3]	Copied from RCA No. LM-6147/LSC-6147 (LP). See Discog. No. 2039.
	Otello (Giuseppe Verdi)				
4070	16 Nov. 46 Met Opera broadcast	George Szell (with Ralf, Roman, Lipton, De Paolis, Moscona)			
		Giuseppe Di Stefano	GDS 21013 (Complete)	CD [2]	
4071	26 Oct. 47 The Standard Hour broadcast, KFI, Hollywood	D'un uom che geme. Gaetano Merola (with Albanese, Svanholm, Turner)			
		GAO	EJS 282	LP	
4072	18 Dec. 48 Met Opera broadcast	Fritz Busch (with Vinay, Albanese, Garris, Hayward, Moscona)			
		Melodram	MEL 27501 (Complete)	CD [2]	
4073		Penzanze	PR 18 (Complete)	LP [2]	
4074	8 or 10 Jan. 54 Teatro alla Scala, Milan radio broadcast	Antonino Votto (with Del Monaco, Tebaldi, Zampieri, Della Pergola, Tozzi, Campi, Pedani, Caneli)			
		Cetra	LO 74 (Complete)	LP [3]	Album performance date of 7 Jan. 54 is incorrect.

8 Mar. 58
Met Opera broadcast

Fausto Cleva (with Del Monaco, De Los Angeles, Franke, Anthony, Moscona)
See Discog. No. 2040.
Three excerpts with Warren.

No.	Label	Number	Format	Notes
4075	ERI Edizioni	V 29 (Excerpts)	LP	
4076	RAI	3183 (Mono) (Excerpts)	LP	Album information indicates incorrectly that the performance was held in Moscow at the Bolshoi Theatre.
	Everest Records	6183 (Stereo) (Excerpts)	LP	
4077	Everest Records	GDS 4001 (Excerpts)	LP [2]	
4078	Gli Dei Della Musica	DMV 06/07/08 (Complete)	LP [3]	
4079	Melodram	MEL 675 (One selection)	LP [2]	Si, pel ciel marmoreo giuro! (with Del Monaco)
4080	Myto Records	MCD 944.107 (Complete)	CD [2]	
4081	Opera Viva	OPV-027 (Abridged)	CD	
4082	Paragon	DVS 52007 (Complete)	LP [3]	
4083	Replica	RPL 2404/06 (Complete)	LP [3]	

Note: "Giuseppe Di Stefano" appears between entries 4077 and 4078.

Pagliacci (Ruggiero Leoncavallo)

17 June 40
RCA recording session

Wilfrid Pelletier (with Carron, Steber, Bontempi, Cehanovsky)

No.	Label	Number	Format	Notes
4084	Parade Records	EP 1004	45	Copied from RCA Victor SR 70, SR 71, SR 72 (78 rpm). See Discog. No. 2047.
		EP 1004	LP	
		EP 1014	LP	
		OP-109 (Excerpts)	LP	

Discog. No.	Performance Date and Source	Producer/ Label	Catalog Number	Type	Author Comments
	20 Mar. 43 Met Opera broadcast	Cesare Sodero (with Martinelli, Farell, Cassel, Dudley)			
4085		GAO	EJS 240 (Excerpts)	LP	Si puo?; Nome di Dio! . . . to end of opera
4086		GAO	EJS 448 (Complete)	LP	
	3 Jan. 59 Met Opera broadcast	Dimitri Mitropoulos (with Del Monaco, Amara, Sereni, Anthony)			
4087		Arkadia	MP 473.2 (Complete)	CD	
4088		I Gioielli Della Lirica	11 (Excerpts)	LP	
4089		Melodram	CDM 270103 (Excerpts)	CD	
	Rigoletto (Giuseppe Verdi)				
	31 May 40, 25 June 40 RCA recording sessions	Wilfrid Pelletier (with Dickenson, Tokatyan, Browning, Alvary, Bontempi)			
4090		Parade Records	EP 1007	45	Copied from RCA Victor SR 58, SR 59, SR 60 (78 rpm). See Discog. Nos. 2052, 2055, 2060.
			EP 1007	LP	
			EP 1014	LP	
			OP-105 (Excerpts)	LP	
	25 May 44 Red Cross Benefit, Madison Square Garden	Arturo Toscanini (with Milanov, Merriman, Peerce, Moscona) (Act IV only)			
4091		Grammofono	AB 78535/36	CD [2]	Possibly copied from RCA LM-6041 (LP) or

4092	2000 (Cedar)	(Act IV)		BMG 60276-2-RG (CD). See Discog. No. 2059.
	Movimento Musica	011.008 (Act IV)	CD	Possibly copied from RCA LM-6041 (LP) or BMG 60276-2-RG (CD). See Discog. No. 2059.

29 Dec. 45
Met Opera broadcast

Cesare Sodero (with Sayão, Björling, Cordon, Lipton, Altman, Hargrave)

4093	GAO	EJS 209 (Excerpts)	LP
4094	Grammofono 2000	AB 78776/77	CD [2]
4095	Historic Opera Performances	HOPE 204 (Complete)	LP [2]
4096	Melodram	MEL 27079 (Complete)	CD [2]
4097	Music & Arts	CD 636 (Complete)	CD [2]
4098	Operatic Archives	OPA 1019/20 (Complete)	LP [2]
4099	UORC	UORC 176 (Complete)	LP [2]

3 or 5 Apr. 52
New Orleans Opera performance

Walter Herbert (with Gueden, Conley, Wildermann, Treigle, Muhs)

4100	Legendary Recordings	LR 205-2 (Complete)	LP [2]

17 Oct. 54
The Standard Hour broadcast, KNBC, San Francisco

Tutte le feste . . . Si, vendetta. Kurt Herbert Adler (with Robin)

4101	A.N.N.A. Record Co.	ANNA 1072	LP	ANNA 1072 was Edward J. Smith's last LP issue in 1982 and Warren's only appearance on the ANNA label.

Discog. No.	Performance Date and Source	Producer/Label	Catalog Number	Type	Author Comments
	25 Feb. 56 Met Opera broadcast	Fausto Cleva (with Peters, Tucker, Tozzi, Elias, Scott, Votipka, Leone)			
4102		ERI Edizioni RAI	V 24 (Excerpts)	LP	Three excerpts with Warren.
4103		Gli Dei Della Musica	DMV 04/05 (Complete)	LP [2]	
4104		Grand Tier	ENGT-CD 2 (Complete)	CD [2]	
4105		Replica	RPL 2426/27 (Complete)	LP [2]	

Simon Boccanegra (Giuseppe Verdi)

Discog. No.	Performance Date and Source	Producer/Label	Catalog Number	Type	Author Comments
	21 Jan. 39 Met Opera broadcast	Ettore Panizza (with Tibbett as Simon, Rethberg, Pinza, Martinelli, and Warren as Paolo) See Discog. No. 2061.			
4106		GAO	EJS 108 (Complete)	LP [3]	
4107		Historic Opera Performances	HOPE 203 (Complete)	LP [3]	
4108		Melodram	CDM 27507 (Complete)	CD [2]	
4109		Myto Records	MCD 954.134 (Complete)	CD [2]	
	28 Jan. 50 Met Opera broadcast	Fritz Stiedry (with Varnay, Székely, Valdengo, Alvary, Tucker)			
4110		ERR	ERR 105 (Complete)	LP [3]	Album performance date of 28 Jan. 49 is incorrect.
4111		Melodram	MEL 037 (Complete)	LP [3]	Album performance date of 28 Jan. 59 is incorrect.

4112	Myto Records	MCD 945.113	CD [2] (Complete)	
4113	Robin Hood Records	RHR 506-B	LP [2] (Complete)	

1 July 50
Ópera Nacional, Mexico City
Renato Cellini (with Garcia, Filippeschi, Silva, Morelli, Ruffino, Fuess)

4114	Legato Classics	LCD 185-1	CD (Abridged)	

Tosca (Giacomo Puccini)

7 Jan. 56
Met Opera broadcast
Dimitri Mitropoulos (with Tebaldi, Tucker, Corena, De Paolis, Cehanovsky, Mark) See Discog. No. 2065.

4115	Dino Classics	CD 9075-102	CD [2] (Complete)	
4116	ERR	MC 9057-101C ERR 143-2	CAS LP [2] (Complete)	
4117	Fonit Cetra	DOC 7	LP [2] (Complete)	Album performance date of 8 Dec. 55 is incorrect. There was no radio broadcast on that date.
4118	Frequenz	043-007	CD [2] (Complete)	
4119	I Gioielli Della Lirica	17 (Excerpts)	LP	Album performance date of 8 Dec. 55 is incorrect.
4120	Paragon	DVS 52003	LP [3] (Complete)	Album performance date of 8 Dec. 55 is incorrect.
4121	TA NEA (Cetra)	CDTA.006	CD [2] (Complete)	

La traviata (Giuseppe Verdi)

Discog. No.	Performance Date and Source	Producer/ Label	Catalog Number	Type	Author Comments
4122	31 May 40, 25 June 40 RCA recording session	Wilfrid Pelletier (with Steber, Tokatyan, Alvary)			
		Parade Records	EP 1009	45	Copied from RCA Victor SR 67, SR 68, SR 69 (78 rpm). See Discog. Nos. 2068, 2070.
			EP 1009	LP	
			EP 1014	LP	
			OP-108 (Excerpts)	LP	
4123	24 Apr. 43 Met Opera broadcast	Cesare Sodero (with Sayão, Kullman, Votipka, De Paolis, Cehanovsky)			
		Historic Opera Performances	HOPE 202 (Complete)	LP [3]	
4124		Operatic Archives	AU 4685/86/87 (Complete)	LP [3]	OPA 1001
4125		Walhall	WHL 33 (Complete)	CD [2]	
4126	6 Apr. 57 Met Opera broadcast	Fausto Cleva (with Tebaldi, Campora, Vanni, Cundari, De Paolis, McCracken)			
		Melodram	MEL 013 (Complete)	LP [2]	

Il trovatore (Giuseppe Verdi)

Discog. No.	Performance Date and Source	Producer/ Label	Catalog Number	Type	Author Comments
4127	31 Mar. 45 Met Opera broadcast	Cesare Sodero (with Milanov, Baum, Castagna, Moscona)			
		Walhall	WHL 36 (Complete)	CD [2]	

No.	Date/Venue	Conductor/Cast	Label	Number	Format	Notes
4128	25 May 48 Ópera Nacional, XEX Radio broadcast, Mexico City	Guido Picco (with Varnay, Baum, Heidt, Silva, Sagarminaga)	UORC	UORC 320 (Excerpts)	LP	
4129	20 June 50 Palacio de las Bellas Artes, Mexico City	Guido Picco (with Callas, Simionato, Baum, Moscona)	BJR	BJR-102 (Excerpts)	LP	
4130			FWR	FWR-651 (Excerpts)	LP	
4131			Historical Recording Enterprises	HRE 207-2 (Complete)	LP [2]	
4132			Melodram	CDM 26017 (Complete)	CD [2]	
4133	Feb./Mar. 52 RCA recording session	Renato Cellini (with Björling, Milanov, Barbieri, Moscona)	Melodiya (Russia)	D 033317/22 (Complete)	LP [3]	Copied from RCA No. LM-6008 (LP). See Discog. No. 2071.
4134	14 Apr. 56 Met Opera broadcast	Fausto Cleva (with Milanov, Baum, Tozzi, Rankin)	Gli Dei Della Musica	DMV 23/24/25 (Complete)	LP [3]	
4135			Melodram	MEL 009 (Complete)	LP [3]	
4136			Sonata	9064/3 (Complete)	LP [3]	

Discog. No.	Performance Date and Source	Producer/ Label	Catalog Number	Type	Author Comments
Miscellaneous Unauthorized Recordings					
Petite Messe Solennelle (Gioachino Rossini)					
4137	9 Apr. 39 WABC Radio broadcast, Carnegie Hall	Mass for Soloists, Chorus, and Orchestra: Ginster, Castagna, Kullman, Warren. (New York Philharmonic conducted by John Barbirolli; Westminster Choir directed by Dr. John Finley Williamson; Deems Taylor, Commentator).			
		UORC	UORC 162	LP	According to the *New York Times*, this was the first complete American broadcast of *Petite Messe Solennelle.*
Biographies in Music—Leonard Warren: Live Radio Broadcasts					
4138	—	Cantabile	BIM-707-1	CD	Fourteen operatic selections, dates and sources unknown. Not all from radio broadcasts.
La forza del destino: Great Tenor-Baritone Scenes with Richard Tucker and Leonard Warren					
4139	—	Historical Recording Enterprises	HRE 427-1	LP	Album indicates incorrectly that selections were taken from a 1958 live performance in New Orleans.
Great Voices: Public Performances 1945–1959: Leonard Warren					
4140	—	Memories	HR 4460 HR 4461	CD CD	Eight operatic selections on HR 4460; four operatic and four nonoperatic selections on HR 4461. Exact dates and sources not listed. Most were taken from Met Opera radio broadcasts and the Voice of Firestone broadcasts.

Leonard Warren: His First Live Recording Sessions (1940–1944)

4141	RCA recording sessions	Minerva	MN-A9	CD

Eleven operatic selections. Ten originally recorded in May/June 1940 were copied from RCA recordings and/or VAI Audio recording No. VAIA 1017 (CD). One selection is probably from a Met Opera broadcast.

J. Peerce in Scenes and Arias

La bohème selections include "In un coupé? ...O Mimì, tu più non torni" with Leonard Warren (Jean Paul Morel cond). This Jan Peerce–Leonard Warren duet was copied from either RCA 11-9767-A (78 rpm), RCA 11-9769-A (78 rpm), or RCA 49-0630-A (45 rpm). See Discog. No. 2013. It was included in the Myto CD as a bonus to another *La traviata* recording.

4142	RCA recording sessions	Myto Records	MCD 933.80	CD [2]

Recital: Leonard Warren (1941–1947)

4143	RCA recording sessions	Myto Records	MCD 955.93	CD

Fifteen operatic selections. All appear to be copies of RCA commercial recordings (78 rpm).

Parnassus Recordings Presents the Renowned Baritone Leonard Warren

4144	—	Parnassus Recordings	PAR 1011	LP

Ten operatic selections and "One Alone" from *The Desert Song*, dates and sources unknown. The *Desert Song* selection appears to be from the Voice of Firestone broadcast of 23 Jan. 50.

Leonard Warren—Robert Weede: Previously Unissued Recordings

Leonard Warren (1911–1960)

Leonard Warren Sings American and Other Songs

Discog. No.	Performance Date and Source	Producer/ Label	Catalog Number	Type	Author Comments
4145	—	VOCE	VOCE-114	LP	Includes seven operatic selections by Warren. Most were taken from The Standard Hour radio broadcasts.
4146	RCA recording sessions	Preiser-Lebendige Vergangenheit	MONO 89145	CD	Fourteen operatic selections copied from RCA recordings that Warren made from 1941 through 1947.
4147	RCA recording sessions	Myto Records	MCD 991.201	CD	Nineteen concert songs copied from RCA recordings that Warren made from 1947 through 1951.

Section V. Opera Roles Recorded by Opera

Discog. No.	Opera	Role	RCA Recording Sessions			Authorized Recordings of Public Performances			
			Complete Opera	Highlights	Selections	Met Historic Broadcasts (Complete Opera)	New Orleans Opera (Complete Opera)	Madison Square Garden (Act IV)	On Tour In Russia (Selections)
5001	Aida	Amonasro	July 55	—	May/June 40	—	—	—	—
5002	Andrea Chénier	Gérard	—	—	Mar. 55	Dec. 54	—	—	May 58 RCA and Melodiya
5003	Un ballo in maschera	Renato	—	Jan. 55	Dec. 45	—	—	—	—
5004	Il barbiere di Siviglia	Figaro	—	—	Mar. 45	—	—	—	—
5005	La bohème	Marcello	—	Mar. 51	Dec. 46	—	—	—	—
5006	Carmen	Escamillo	—	—	May 40 Mar. 45	—	—	—	May 58 (Melodiya)
5007	Les contes d'Hoffmann	Dapertutto	—	—	Sep. 41	—	—	—	—
5008	Falstaff	Falstaff	—	—	—	—	May 56	—	—
		Ford	—	—	Sep. 41 July 55	—	—	—	May 58 (RCA)
5009	Faust	Valentin	—	—	Sep. 41	—	—	—	May 58 (RCA)

| Discog. No. | Opera | Role | RCA Recording Sessions | | | Authorized Recordings of Public Performances | | | |
			Complete Opera	Highlights	Selections	Met Historic Broadcasts (Complete Opera)	New Orleans Opera (Complete Opera)	Madison Square Garden (Act IV)	On Tour In Russia (Selections)
5010	La forza del destino	Don Carlo	July/Aug. 58 (Decca)	Apr. 55	June 46 Dec. 46 Feb. 50	Nov. 52 (Excerpts)	—	—	—
5011	La Gioconda	Barnaba	July/Aug. 57 (Decca)	—	Sep. 41 Jan. 47	Mar. 46	—	—	—
5012	Macbeth	Macbeth	Feb./Mar. 59	—	—	—	—	—	—
5013	Otello	Iago	—	—	Mar. 46 Feb. 50 Mar. 55 July 55	Mar. 58	—	—	May 58 (Melodiya)
5014	Pagliacci	Tonio	Jan. 53	—	June 40 Mar. 46	—	—	—	—
5015	Rigoletto	Rigoletto	Mar./May 50	—	May/June 40 Dec. 45	—	Apr. 52	May 44 (Act IV)	—
5016	Simon Boccanegra	Paolo Simon	— —	— —	May 39 Feb. 50	Jan. 39	—	—	—
5017	Tannhäuser	Wolfram	—	—	—	—	—	—	May 58 (Melodiya)

5018	Tosca	Scarpia	July 57	—	Jan. 56	—	—	—
5019	La traviata	Germont	June 56	May/June 40 Feb. 50	—	—	—	—
5020	Il trovatore	Count di Luna	Feb./Mar. 52 July 59	Jan. 47 May 51	—	—	—	—

Section VI. Video Excerpts from the Voice of Firestone Telecasts (Conductor Howard Barlow)

Discog. No.	Telecast Date	Selection (Opera)	Music-Lyrics	VAI Video Catalog No.
6001	7 Nov. 49	A Little Bit of Heaven	Ball-Brennan	VAI-69105
6002	7 Nov. 49	None But the Lonely Heart	Tchaikovsky	VAI-69105
6003	7 Nov. 49	Toreador Song (*Carmen*)	Bizet	VAI-69105
6004	7 Nov. 49	On the Road to Mandalay	Speaks-Kipling	VAI-69110
6005	5 Dec. 49	Invictus	Henley-Huhn	VAI-69110
6006	5 Dec. 49	Largo al factotum (*Il barbiere di Siviglia*)	Rossini	VAI-69110
6007	5 Dec. 49	Will You Remember? (*Maytime*) (Duet with Eleanor Steber)	Romberg-Johnson	VAI-69110
6008	2 June 52	Until	Sanderson-Teschemacher	VAI-69105
6009	2 June 52	Eri tu? (*Un ballo in maschera*)	Verdi	VAI-69105
6010	2 June 52	Blow the Man Down	Sea Shanty (Arr. by T. Scott)	VAI-69105
6011	2 June 52	On the Road to Mandalay	Speaks-Kipling	VAI-69105
6012	24 Aug. 53	A Rovin'	Sea Shanty (Arr. by T. Scott)	VAI-69105
6013	24 Aug. 53	O sainte médaille . . . Avant de quitter ces lieux (*Faust*)	Gounod	VAI-69105
6014	24 Aug. 53	I Believe	Drake-Graham, Schirl-Stillman	VAI-69105
6015	24 Aug. 53	March of the Musketeers (*The Three Musketeers*)	Friml	VAI-69105

Section VII. Metropolitan Opera Radio Broadcast Performances by Opera

Discog. No.	Opera	Composer	Role	Broadcast Date	Comments
7001	*Aida*	Verdi	Amonasro	19 Jan. 40 2 Mar. 40 22 Mar. 41 28 Dec. 46 21 Feb. 48 8 Mar. 52 20 Feb. 54 28 Nov. 59	
7002	*Alceste*	Gluck	High Priest	8 Mar. 41	
7003	*Andrea Chénier*	Giordano	Gérard	4 Dec. 54	Met Historic Broadcast. (MET 15) [2004].
7004	*Un ballo in maschera*	Verdi	Renato	15 Jan. 44 22 Apr. 44 8 Dec. 45 22 Nov. 47	
7005	*Boris Godunov*	Mussorgsky	Rangoni	9 Dec. 39 13 Feb. 43 4 Dec. 43	
7006	*Carmen*	Bizet	Escamillo	21 Feb. 41 15 Mar. 41 24 Jan. 42 27 Mar. 43	Sung in Italian. Sung in Italian. Sung in Italian.
7007	*Cavalleria rusticana*	Mascagni	Alfio	1 Feb. 41	
7008	*Ernani*	Verdi	Don Carlo	29 Dec. 56	

Discog. No.	Opera	Composer	Role	Broadcast Date	Comments
7009	*Falstaff*	Verdi	Falstaff	11 Mar. 44 26 Feb. 49	Sung in English.
7010	*Faust*	Gounod	Valentin	16 Mar. 40 6 Apr. 40 14 Mar. 42 31 Dec. 49	
7011	*La forza del destino*	Verdi	Don Carlo	29 Nov. 52	Met Historic Broadcast. (MET 100) [2026].
7012	*La Gioconda*	Ponchielli	Barnaba	20 Mar. 54 17 Mar. 56 3 Mar. 45 16 Mar. 46	Met Historic Broadcast. (MET 17) [2035].
7013	*Lohengrin*	Wagner	Herald	3 Jan. 53 2 Apr. 55 20 Apr. 57 27 Jan. 40 17 Jan. 42	
7014	*Lucia di Lammermoor*	Donizetti	Enrico	8 Jan. 44 6 Jan. 45	
7015	*Macbeth*	Verdi	Macbeth	21 Feb. 59 2 Jan. 60	
7016	*Otello*	Verdi	Iago	23 Feb. 46 16 Nov. 46 18 Dec. 48	

No.	Opera	Composer	Role	Dates	Notes
				9 Feb. 52; 12 Mar. 55; 8 Mar. 58	Met Historic Broadcast. (MET 20) [2040].
7017	*Pagliacci*	Leoncavallo	Tonio	20 Dec. 58	
7018	*Rigoletto*	Verdi	Rigoletto	20 Mar. 43; 25 Mar. 44; 28 Feb. 48; 3 Mar. 51; 3 Jan. 59; 18 Dec. 43; 29 Dec. 45; 1 Mar. 47; Mar. 49; 4 Mar. 50; 8 Dec. 51; 7 Mar. 53; 25 Feb. 56; 28 Mar. 59	
7019	*Samson et Dalila*	Saint-Saëns	High Priest	13 Dec. 41	
7020	*Simon Boccanegra*	Verdi	Paolo	21 Jan. 39	Met Historic Broadcast. (MET 13) [2061].
7021	*Simon Boccanegra*	Verdi	Simon	28 Jan. 50	
7022	*Tosca*	Puccini	Scarpia	7 Jan. 56; 23 Mar. 57; 15 Mar. 58	Met Historic Broadcast. (MET 10) [2065].

Discog. No.	Opera	Composer	Role	Broadcast Date	Comments
7023	*La traviata*	Verdi	Germont	24 Apr. 43 23 Mar. 46 21 Dec. 46 6 Feb. 54 6 Apr. 57	
7024	*Il trovatore*	Verdi	Count di Luna	18 Mar. 44 31 Mar. 45 15 Feb. 47 27 Dec. 47 13 June 51 16 Jan. 54 14 Apr. 56	

✦

Chronology of Opera Performances

by Barrett Crawford

From 1939 through 1960, Leonard Warren appeared in 833 opera perform-ances worldwide:

	Performances
Metropolitan Opera, New York City	400
Metropolitan Opera, on tour	207
	607
San Francisco Opera	50
Teatro Municipal, Rio de Janeiro	43
Teatro Colón, Buenos Aires	41
Ópera Nacional, Mexico City	19
Chicago Opera Company	12
Teatro Municipal, São Paulo	9
Teatro alla Scala, Milan	8
Sixteen other locations	44
	833

Warren's most frequently performed operas were:

	Metropolitan Opera	Other Locations	Total
Rigoletto	89	53	142
Aida	58	22	80
La traviata	52	27	79
Il trovatore	45	21	66
Otello	45	10	55
Pagliacci	40	10	50
La forza del destino	26	19	45
Un ballo in maschera	25	15	40
La Gioconda	33	5	38
Tosca	26	2	28
Fourteen other operas	168	42	210
	607	226	833

This chronology divides Warren's performances into two sections: Metropolitan Opera Performances and Other Opera Performances. Information on Metropolitan Opera performances was abstracted from the *Annals of the Metropolitan Opera*, courtesy of the Metropolitan Opera Guild, © 1989 Metropolitan Opera Guild, Inc. With the exception of *Lucia di Lammermoor*, cast members are listed in the same order as are the roles in the *Annals*. First names or initials are given for artists not listed in the *Annals*.

I. Metropolitan Opera Performances

Leonard Warren's association with the Metropolitan Opera began at a concert on 27 November 1938 and ended with his tragic final performance in *La forza del destino* on 4 March 1960. During twenty-two seasons, Warren performed in twenty-six roles of twenty-four operas. He appeared in 607 performances, of which 207 were on tour in the United States and Canada. In addition, Warren appeared at five gala performances, forty-one concerts, and two special events.

Opera	Role	Debut	Performances
Aida	Amonasro	19 January 1940	58
Alceste	High Priest	24 January 1941	4
Andrea Chénier	Gérard	16 November 1954	17
Un ballo in maschera	Renato	17 December 1943	25
Boris Godunov	Rangoni	7 March 1939	17
Boris Godunov	Shchelkalov	7 March 1939	— (a)
Carmen	Escamillo	18 December 1940	19

Cavalleria rusticana	Alfio	9 January 1941	6
Ernani	Carlo	23 November 1956	4
Falstaff	Falstaff	11 March 1944	5
Faust	Valentin	15 December 1939	22
La forza del destino	Carlo	11 February 1943	26 (b)
La Gioconda	Barnaba	8 February 1940	33
The Island God	Ilo	20 February 1942	4
(*Ilo e Zeus)*			
Lohengrin	Herald	3 January 1940	22
Lucia di Lammermoor	Enrico	11 December 1942	21
Macbeth	Macbeth	5 February 1959	12
Otello	Iago	23 February 1946	45
Pagliacci	Tonio	20 March 1943	40
Rigoletto	Rigoletto	18 December 1943	89
Samson et Dalila	High Priest	3 December 1941	4
Simon Boccanegra	Paolo	13 January 1939	4
Simon Boccanegra	Simon	28 November 1949	7
Tosca	Scarpia	8 December 1955	26 (c)
La traviata	Germont	14 January 1942	52
Il trovatore	Di Luna	5 February 1943	45
			607

(a) Two roles in same performance count as only one performance.
(b) Includes Warren's fatal performance on 4 March 1960.
(c) Includes 28 April 1959 performance when Warren canceled after Act I.

II. Other Opera Performances

		Operas	Performances
United States	San Francisco Opera	15	50
	Chicago Opera Company	5	12
	New Orleans Opera Association	4	8
	Kansas City Philharmonic Association	2	4
	Connecticut Opera (Hartford)	2	2
	San Antonio Opera	3	3
	Cincinnati Summer Opera	1	2
	Robin Hood Dell (Philadelphia)	1	2
	Tulsa Opera	1	2
	Pittsburgh Opera	1	1
	New York City Opera (Detroit)	1	1
			87

(continued)

[II. Other Opera Performances]

		Operas	Performances
Argentina	Teatro Colón, Buenos Aires	7	41
Brazil	Teatro Municipal, Rio de Janeiro	6	43
	Teatro Municipal, São Paulo	5	9
Canada	France Film et les Festivals de Montréal	3	3
Cuba	Sociedad Pro-Art Musical, Havana	5	7
Italy	Teatro alla Scala, Milan	2	8
Mexico	Ópera Nacional, Mexico City	8	19
Puerto Rico	Opera Puerto Rico, San Juan	6	6
Soviet Union	Bolshoi Opera, Moscow	1	1
	Ukrainian Opera, Kiev	1	1
	Latvian Opera, Riga	1	1
			139

Warren debuted in seven operas before appearing in them at the Metropolitan Opera:

Opera	Role	Debut	Location
Il trovatore	Di Luna	26 September 1940	San Juan
La traviata	Germont	28 September 1940	San Juan
Pagliacci	Tonio	1 October 1940	San Juan
Simon Boccanegra	Simon	12 June 1942	Buenos Aires
Un ballo in maschera	Renato	21 July 1942	Buenos Aires
Rigoletto	Rigoletto	11 June 1943	Buenos Aires
Falstaff	Falstaff	22 June 1943	Buenos Aires

Acknowledgments

In compiling the chronology, I received invaluable help from many people to whom I am deeply grateful. Two colleagues have been particularly generous: Jack Belsom, archivist, New Orleans Opera; and George Shelby Weaver, Louisiana record collector and discographer. I am especially indebted to Agatha Warren, Leonard Warren's wife, whose handwritten compilation of his appearances made it possible to verify performance details.

I would also like to acknowledge with sincere thanks the assistance of José Carlos Benedito, Diretor do Departamento de Teatros, Prefeitura do Município de São Paulo, Secretaria Municipal de Cultura, São Paulo, Brazil; Clare Alice Conner; Constanza Corbeira, Press Department, Teatro Colón, Buenos Aires, Argentina; Edward F. Durbeck III, founder of the Durbeck Archive; Sonja Figueiredo, assistant, President's Office, Secretaria de Estado de Cultura e Esporte, Fundação Teatro Municipal do Rio de Janeiro, Brazil; James Franklin; Paul Gruber, executive director, program development, Metropolitan Opera Guild; Stuart Hinds, special collections librarian, Kansas City Public Library; Edward M. Johnson, central region chairman, Metropolitan Opera National Council; Richard Koprowski, assistant archivist, the Stanford Archive of Recorded Sound; Zoila Lapique, historian, researcher, and author of *Catalogación y clasificación de la musica Cubana*; Koraljka Lockhart, publications editor, San Francisco Opera; Elwood A. McKee, collector and researcher; James B. McPherson, opera historian; William R. Moran, author, discographer, and cofounder and honorary curator of the Stanford Archive of Recorded Sound; Mary Jane Phillips-Matz; James A. Santiago-Ramos, professor, Conservatory of Music of Puerto Rico; Octavio Sosa, author of *200 años de ópera en México*; and Victoria Turk, librarian, *Detroit Free Press*.

Bibliography

Caamaño, Roberto. *La historia del Teatro Colón: 1908–1968*, vol. 2. Buenos Aires: Editorial Cinetea, 1969.

De Brito Chaves, Jr., Edgardo. *Memórias e glórias um teatro: sessenta años de história do Teatro Municipal do Rio de Janeiro*. Rio de Janeiro: Companhia Editora Americana, 1971.

De Oliveira Castro Cerquera, Paul. *Um século de opera em São Paulo, Brasil*. São Paulo: Emprêsa Gráfica, Editôra Guia Fiscal, 1954.

Díaz Du-Pond, Carlos. *Cincuenta años de ópera en México*. Mexico City: Universidad Nacional Autónoma de México, 1978.

Gatti, Carlo. *Il Teatro alla Scala nella storia e nell'arte*. Milan: Ricordi, 1964.

Pasarell, Emilio Julio. *Orígenes y desarrollo de la afición teatral en Puerto Rico*. Santurce, Puerto Rico: Editorial del Departamento de Instrucción Pública, 1967.

Thierstein, Eldred A. *Cincinnati Opera: From the Zoo to Music Hall*. Hillsdale, Michigan: Deerstone Books, 1995.

I. Metropolitan Opera Performances

* Denotes broadcast performance

1939

13 Jan.	*Simon Boccanegra* (Paolo)	Tibbett, Caniglia, Martinelli, Pinza, Panizza cond.
21 Jan.*	*Simon Boccanegra* (Paolo)	Tibbett, Rethberg, Martinelli, Pinza, Panizza cond.
7 Mar.	*Boris Godunov* (Rangoni, Shchelkalov)	Pinza, De Paolis, Cordon, Kullman, Thorborg, Panizza cond.
10 Mar.	*Boris Godunov* (Rangoni)	Pinza, De Paolis, Cordon, Kullman, Thorborg, Panizza cond.
27 Nov.	*Simon Boccanegra* (Paolo)	Tibbett, Rethberg, Martinelli, Pinza, Panizza cond.
28 Nov. Philadelphia	*Boris Godunov* (Rangoni)	Pinza, De Paolis, Moscona, Kullman, Thorborg, Panizza cond.
1 Dec.	*Boris Godunov* (Rangoni)	Pinza, De Paolis, Moscona, Kullman, Thorborg, Panizza cond.
9 Dec.*	*Boris Godunov* (Rangoni)	Pinza, De Paolis, Moscona, Kullman, Thorborg, Panizza cond.
15 Dec.	*Faust*	Kullman, Jepson, Moscona, Browning, Pelletier cond.
18 Dec.	*Boris Godunov* (Rangoni)	Pinza, De Paolis, Moscona, Kullman, Thorborg, Panizza cond.
20 Dec.	*Simon Boccanegra* (Paolo)	Tibbett, Jessner, Jagel, Pinza, Panizza cond.

1940

3 Jan.	*Lohengrin* (Herald)	Melchior, Flagstad, Pauly, Huehn, List, Leinsdorf cond.
6 Jan.	*Faust*	Kullman, Jepson, Moscona, Olheim, Pelletier cond.
10 Jan.	*Boris Godunov* (Rangoni)	Pinza, De Paolis, Moscona, Tokatyan, Thorborg, Panizza cond.
13 Jan.	*Lohengrin*	Melchior, Rethberg, Branzell, Huehn, Cordon, Leinsdorf cond.
19 Jan.*	*Aida*	Bampton, Carron, Castagna, Moscona, Gurney, Panizza cond.
26 Jan.	*Aida*	Milanov, Carron, Bampton, Lazzari, D'Angelo, Panizza cond.
27 Jan.*	*Lohengrin*	Melchoir, Rethberg, Thorborg, Huehn, List, Leinsdorf cond.

8 Feb.	*La Gioconda*	Milanov, Jagel, Castagna, Lazzari, Kaskas, Panizza cond.
21 Feb.	*Aida*	Milanov, Martinelli, Castagna, Cordon, Gurney, Panizza cond.
23 Feb.	*Lohengrin*	Maison, Flagstad, Lawrence, Huehn, Cordon, Leinsdorf cond.
2 Mar.*	*Aida*	Bampton, Carron, Castagna, Pinza, Gurney, Panizza cond.
4 Mar.	*Lohengrin*	Melchior, Flagstad, Lawrence, Janssen, Cordon, Leinsdorf cond.
8 Mar.	*Faust*	Kullman, Jepson, Moscona, Browning, Pelletier cond.
14 Mar.	*Lohengrin*	Melchior, Flagstad, Lawrence, Janssen, List, Leinsdorf cond.
16 Mar.*	*Faust*	Crooks, Jepson, Pinza, Browning, Pelletier cond.
2 Apr. Boston	*La Gioconda*	Milanov, Martinelli, Castagna, Moscona, Kaskas, Panizza cond.
3 Apr. Boston	*Lohengrin*	Melchior, Flagstad, Branzell, Huehn, List, Leinsdorf cond.
4 Apr. Boston	*Boris Godunov* (Rangoni)	Pinza, De Paolis, Moscona, Kullman, Thorborg, Cordon, Panizza cond.
6 Apr.* Boston	*Faust*	Crooks, Jepson, Pinza, Olheim, Pelletier cond.
8 Apr. Cleveland	*Aida*	Bampton, Martinelli, Castagna, Pinza, Cordon, Panizza cond.
13 Apr. Cleveland	*La Gioconda*	Milanov, Martinelli, Castagna, Pinza, Swarthout, Panizza cond.
17 Apr. Dallas	*Faust*	Crooks, Jepson, Pinza, Olheim, Pelletier cond.
20 Apr. New Orleans	*Faust*	Crooks, Jepson, Pinza, Olheim, Pelletier cond.
18 Dec.	*Carmen*	Swarthout, Kullman, Farell, Pelletier cond.
25 Dec.	*Faust*	Björling, Jepson, Moscona, Olheim, Pelletier cond.

1941

9 Jan.	*Cavalleria rusticana*	Roman, Jagel, Kaskas, Doe, Calusio cond.
16 Jan.	*Aida*	Roman, Jagel, Thorborg, Pinza, Cordon, Panizza cond.
24 Jan.	*Alceste* (High Priest)	Lawrence, Maison, Cehanovsky, De Paolis, Panizza cond.

[1941]

30 Jan.	*Alceste*	Lawrence, Maison, Kent, De Paolis, Panizza cond.
31 Jan.	*Lohengrin*	Melchior, Flagstad, Lawrence, Huehn, List, Leinsdorf cond.
1 Feb.*	*Cavalleria rusticana*	Roman, Jagel, Kaskas, Doe, Calusio cond.
21 Feb.*	*Carmen*	Swarthout, Jobin, Albanese, Pelletier cond.
22 Feb.	*Aida*	Milanov, Carron, Thorborg, Pinza, Cordon, Panizza cond.
28 Feb.	*Lohengrin*	Maison, Rethberg, Lawrence, Janssen, Cordon, Leinsdorf cond.
5 Mar.	*Carmen*	Castagna, Jobin, Steber, Pelletier cond.
8 Mar.*	*Alceste*	Bampton, Maison, Kent, De Paolis, Panizza cond.
15 Mar.*	*Carmen*	Swarthout, Kullman, Albanese, Pelletier cond.
19 Mar.	*Alceste*	Lawrence, Jagel, Kent, De Paolis, Panizza cond.
20 Mar.	*Lohengrin*	Melchior, Jessner, Thorborg, Huehn, Cordon, Leinsdorf cond.
22 Mar.*	*Aida*	Roman, Martinelli, Castagna, Pinza, Cordon, Panizza cond.
29 Mar. Boston	*Cavalleria rusticana*	Roman, Jagel, Kaskas, Doe, Papi cond.
4 Apr. Boston	*Lohengrin*	Melchior, Flagstad, Thorborg, Huehn, Cordon, Leinsdorf cond.
18 Apr. Cleveland	*Cavalleria rusticana*	Milanov, Jagel, Kaskas, Doe, Papi cond.
23 Apr. New Orleans	*Cavalleria rusticana*	Roman, Tokatyan, Kaskas, Votipka, Papi cond.
28 Apr. Atlanta	*Cavalleria rusticana*	Roman, Jagel, Kaskas, Votipka, Papi cond.
30 Apr. Atlanta	*Lohengrin*	Melchior, Rethberg, Thorborg, Janssen, Cordon, Leinsdorf cond.
3 Dec.	*Samson et Dalila* (High Priest)	Maison, Stevens, Cordon, Moscona, Pelletier cond.
9 Dec. Philadelphia	*Samson et Dalila*	Maison, Stevens, Cordon, Moscona, Pelletier cond.
12 Dec.	*Aida*	Roman, Carron, Branzell, Cordon, Gurney, Breisach cond.
13 Dec.*	*Samson et Dalila*	Maison, Stevens, Cordon, Moscona, Pelletier cond.

30 Dec.	*Aida*	Roman, Carron, Thorborg, Pinza, Hatfield, Breisach cond.

1942

9 Jan.	*Lohengrin*	Melchior, Varnay, Thorborg, Janssen, Cordon, Leinsdorf cond.
14 Jan.	*La traviata*	Novotná, Kullman, Votipka, De Paolis, Panizza cond.
17 Jan.*	*Lohengrin*	Melchior, Varnay, Thorborg, Janssen, Cordon, Leinsdorf cond.
24 Jan.*	*Carmen*	Djanel, Kullman, Albanese, Beecham cond.
29 Jan.	*Lohengrin*	Melchior, Varnay, Branzell, Huehn, Cordon, Leinsdorf cond.
3 Feb. Philadelphia	*Lohengrin*	Maison, Varnay, Thorborg, Huehn, List, Leinsdorf cond.
4 Feb.	*Carmen*	Djanel, Kullman, Albanese, Beecham cond.
6 Feb.	*Samson et Dalila*	Maison, Thorborg, Hatfield, Moscona, Pelletier cond.
18 Feb.	*Lohengrin*	Melchior, Rethberg, Branzell, Huehn, List, Leinsdorf cond.
20 Feb.	*The Island God* (Ilo)	Cordon, Varnay, Jobin, Carter, Panizza cond. (World premiere.)
28 Feb.	*Carmen*	Djanel, Jobin, Albanese, Pelletier cond.
2 Mar.	*The Island God*	Cordon, Varnay, Jobin, Carter, Panizza cond.
3 Mar. Philadelphia	*Carmen*	Djanel, Jobin, Albanese, Beecham cond.
6 Mar.	*Aida*	Rethberg, Carron, Castagna, Moscona, Hatfield, Pelletier cond.
9 Mar.	*Carmen*	Djanel, Jobin, Albanese, Beecham cond.
10 Mar. Philadelphia	*The Island God*	Cordon, Varnay, Jobin, Carter, Panizza cond.
12 Mar.	*The Island God*	Cordon, Varnay, Jobin, Carter, Panizza cond.
14 Mar.*	*Faust*	Kullman, Albanese, Cordon, Browning, Beecham cond.
17 Mar. Baltimore	*Carmen*	Djanel, Jobin, Albanese, Beecham cond.
19 Mar. Boston	*Lohengrin*	Melchior, Varnay, Thorborg, Huehn, Cordon, Panizza cond.
21 Mar. Boston	*La traviata*	Novotná, Peerce, Votipka, De Paolis, Panizza cond.

[1942]

25 Mar. Boston	*Carmen*	Djanel, Jobin, Albanese, Beecham cond.
26 Mar. Boston	*Aida*	Roman, Martinelli, Castagna, Cordon, Gurney, Pelletier cond.
28 Mar. Boston	*Faust*	Crooks, Albanese, Cordon, Browning, Beecham cond.
7 Apr. Cleveland	*Lohengrin*	Melchior, Varnay, Thorborg, Huehn, Cordon, Leinsdorf cond.
8 Apr. Cleveland	*Carmen*	Djanel, Jobin, Albanese, Beecham cond.
13 Apr. Bloomington	*Aida*	Bampton, Carron, Castagna, Cordon, Gurney, Pelletier cond.
17 Apr. Dallas	*Carmen*	Djanel, Jobin, Albanese, Pelletier cond.
18 Apr. Dallas	*Aida*	Roman, Carron, Castagna, Moscona, Gurney, Cleva cond.
11 Dec.	*Lucia di Lammermoor*	Pons, Peerce, Moscona, De Paolis, St. Leger cond.
18 Dec.	*Faust*	Jobin, Jepson, Cordon, Browning, Pelletier cond.
21 Dec.	*Lucia di Lammermoor*	Pons, Peerce, Moscona, De Paolis, St. Leger cond.
26 Dec.	*La traviata*	Albanese, Peerce, Votipka, De Paolis, Sodero cond.
29 Dec. Philadelphia	*Lucia di Lammermoor*	Pons, Peerce, Cordon, De Paolis, St. Leger cond.
30 Dec.	*Boris Godunov* (Rangoni)	Pinza, De Paolis, Moscona, Maison, Thorborg, Szell cond.

1943

1 Jan.	*Carmen*	Petina, Gérard, Albanese, Beecham cond.
6 Jan.	*Lucia di Lammermoor*	Pons, Peerce, Cordon, Garris, St. Leger cond.
11 Jan.	*Boris Godunov* (Rangoni)	Pinza, De Paolis, Moscona, Kullman, Thorborg, Szell cond.
13 Jan.	*Lohengrin*	Melchior, Varnay, Thorborg, Sved, Cordon, Leinsdorf cond.
19 Jan. Philadelphia	*Boris Godunov* (Rangoni)	Kipnis, De Paolis, Moscona, Maison, Thorborg, Szell cond.
20 Jan.	*Faust*	Jobin, Albanese, Cordon, Browning, Beecham cond.

28 Jan.	*Lohengrin*	Melchior, Varnay, Branzell, Huehn, Cordon, Leinsdorf cond.
5 Feb.	*Il trovatore*	Martinelli, Milanov, Kaskas, Moscona, Sodero cond.
11 Feb.	*La forza del destino*	Milanov, Baum, Pinza, Petina, Pechner, Walter cond.
13 Feb.*	*Boris Godunov* (Rangoni)	Kipnis, De Paolis, Moscona, Maison, Thorborg, Szell cond.
15 Feb.	*Carmen*	Swarthout, Jobin, Albanese, Beecham cond.
19 Feb.	*Boris Godunov* (Rangoni)	Kipnis, De Paolis, Moscona, Maison, Thorborg, Szell cond.
1 Mar.	*La forza del destino*	Roman, Jagel, Pinza, Petina, Pechner, Walter cond.
5 Mar.	*Lohengrin*	Melchior, Bampton, Branzell, Sved, Cordon, Leinsdorf cond.
12 Mar.	*La forza del destino*	Milanov, Martinelli, Pinza, Petina, Baccaloni, Walter cond.
13 Mar.	*Carmen*	Petina, Jobin, Albanese, Beecham cond.
15 Mar.	*Aida*	Roman, Baum, Thorborg, Pinza, Alvary, Pelletier cond.
17 Mar.	*Faust*	Jobin, Steber, Pinza, Petina, Beecham cond.
20 Mar.*	*Pagliacci*	Farell, Martinelli, Cassel, De Paolis, Sodero cond.
25 Mar. Chicago	*La traviata*	Jepson, Melton, Stellman, De Paolis, Sodero cond.
27 Mar.* Chicago	*Carmen*	Djanel, Jobin, Albanese, Beecham cond.
2 Apr. Chicago	*Boris Godunov* (Rangoni)	Kipnis, De Paolis, Moscona, Kullman, Thorborg, Szell cond.
8 Apr. Cleveland	*Carmen*	Petina, Jobin, Albanese, Beecham cond.
10 Apr. Cleveland	*Il trovatore*	Martinelli, Bampton, Castagna, Moscona, Sodero cond.
24 Apr.*	*La traviata*	Sayão, Kullman, Votipka, De Paolis, Sodero cond.
22 Nov.	*Boris Godunov* (Rangoni)	Pinza, De Paolis, Moscona, Tokatyan, Thorborg, Szell cond.
25 Nov.	*Lucia di Lammermoor*	Pons, Peerce, Moscona, De Paolis, Sodero cond.
4 Dec.*	*Boris Godunov* (Rangoni)	Pinza, De Paolis, Moscona, Tokatyan, Thorborg, Szell cond.

[1943]

6 Dec.	*Lucia di Lammermoor*	Pons, Peerce, Moscona, Garris, Sodero cond.
17 Dec.	*Un ballo in maschera*	Milanov, Peerce, Thorborg, Greer, Cordon, Moscona, Baker, Walter cond.
18 Dec.*	*Rigoletto*	Pons, Kullman, Kaskas, Moscona. Hawkins, Sodero cond. (Warren's first Rigoletto as a last-minute replacement for the ailing Tibbett.)
22 Dec.	*Lucia di Lammermoor*	Pons, Melton, Moscona, De Paolis, Cimara cond.
25 Dec.	*Pagliacci*	Albanese, Jobin, Cassel, De Paolis, Pelletier cond.
27 Dec.	*Rigoletto*	Pons, Peerce, Kaskas, Lazzari, Hawkins, Sodero cond.

1944

1 Jan.	*Boris Godunov* (Rangoni)	Pinza, De Paolis, Moscona, Tokatyan, Thorborg, Szell cond.
4 Jan. Philadelphia	*Un ballo in maschera*	Milanov, Peerce, Thorborg, Greer, Cordon, Moscona, Cehanovsky, Walter cond.
8 Jan.*	*Lucia di Lammermoor*	Pons, Melton, Moscona, De Paolis, Sodero cond.
15 Jan.*	*Un ballo in maschera*	Milanov, Peerce, Thorborg, Greer, Cordon, Moscona, Baker, Walter cond.
19 Jan.	*La traviata*	Albanese, Melton, Votipka, De Paolis, Sodero cond.
27 Jan.	*Un ballo in maschera*	Milanov, Peerce, Thorborg, Greer, Lazzari, Moscona, Cehanovsky, Walter cond.
29 Jan.	*Pagliacci*	Albanese, Jobin, Valentino, De Paolis, Sodero cond.
21 Feb.	*Un ballo in maschera*	Milanov, Peerce, Castagna, Carroll, Lazzari, Moscona, Cehanovsky, Walter cond.
25 Feb.	*Il trovatore*	Carron, Roman, Harshaw, Moscona, Sodero cond.
29 Feb.	*Aida*	Milanov, Baum, Castagna, Moscona, Alvary, Pelletier cond.
1 Mar.	*La forza del destino*	Roman, Jagel, Moscona, Petina, Pechner, Walter cond.
7 Mar. Philadelphia	*Aida*	Milanov, Baum, Castagna, Moscona, Alvary, Pelletier cond.
11 Mar.*	*Falstaff*	Steber, Brownlee, Harshaw, Greer, Kullman, Beecham cond.

18 Mar.*	*Il trovatore*	Baum, Milanov, Harshaw, Moscona, Sodero cond.
22 Mar.	*Falstaff*	Steber, Brownlee, Harshaw, Greer, Kullman, Beecham cond.
25 Mar.*	*Pagliacci*	Albanese, Jobin, Valentino, De Paolis, Sodero cond.
3 Apr.	*Aida*	Milanov, Baum, Harshaw, Lazzari, Gurney, Pelletier cond.
5 Apr.	*Carmen*	Petina, Jobin, Albanese, Pelletier cond.
10 Apr. Boston	*Un ballo in maschera*	Milanov, Peerce, Thorborg, Greer, Lazzari, Moscona, Baker, Walter cond.
15 Apr. Boston	*La traviata*	Steber, Peerce, Stellman, De Paolis, Sodero cond.
18 Apr. Chicago	*La traviata*	Albanese, Tokatyan, Votipka, De Paolis, Cimara cond.
22 Apr.* Chicago	*Un ballo in maschera*	Milanov, Peerce, Thorborg, Greer, Lazzari, Moscona, Baker, Walter cond.
27 Apr. Chicago	*Aida*	Milanov, Baum, Harshaw, Lazzari, Alvary, Pelletier cond.
5 May Cleveland	*Lucia di Lammermoor*	Pons, Peerce, Moscona, De Paolis, Sodero cond.
2 Dec.	*La traviata*	Albanese, Kullman, Stellman, De Paolis, Sodero cond.
6 Dec.	*Il trovatore*	Baum, Resnik, Harshaw, Lazzari, Sodero cond.
9 Dec.	*Pagliacci*	Albanese, Carron, Valentino, Manning, Sodero cond.
13 Dec.	*Lucia di Lammermoor*	Munsel, Peerce, Moscona, Manning, Sodero cond.
16 Dec.	*Aida*	Kirk, Baum, Harshaw, Moscona, Whitfield, Cooper cond.
19 Dec. Philadelphia	*La traviata*	Sayão, Melton, Votipka, De Paolis, Cimara cond.
21 Dec.	*Pagliacci*	Albanese, Jobin, Cassel, Manning, Sodero cond.
28 Dec.	*La traviata*	Albanese, Peerce, Stellman, De Paolis, Sodero cond.
29 Dec.	*Faust*	Jobin, Conner, Pinza, Lipton, Pelletier cond.

1945

| 3 Jan. | *Rigoletto* | Antoine, Landi, Kaskas, Moscona, Hargrave, Sodero cond. |

[1945]

6 Jan.*	*Lucia di Lammermoor*	Munsel, Peerce, Moscona, Manning, Sodero cond.
10 Jan.	*Pagliacci*	Albanese, Jobin, Cassel, De Paolis, Sodero cond.
15 Feb.	*Faust*	Jobin, Albanese, Cordon, Lipton, Pelletier cond.
22 Feb.	*Lucia di Lammermoor*	Munsel, Melton, Lazzari, Marlowe, Sodero cond.
24 Feb.	*Rigoletto*	Benzell, Landi, Kaskas, Hargrave, Hawkins, Sodero cond.
3 Mar.*	*La Gioconda*	Roman, Jagel, Castagna, Moscona, Harshaw, Cooper cond.
6 Mar.	*Aida*	Roman, Baum, Castagna, Lazzari, Gurney, Sodero cond.
11 Mar.	*Aida*	Milanov, Baum, Castagna, Cordon, Gurney, Sodero cond.
13 Mar. Philadelphia	*La Gioconda*	Roman, Jagel, Castagna, Lazzari, Harshaw, Cooper cond.
23 Mar.	*Aida*	Roman, Carron, Harshaw, Lazzari, Hawkins, Breisach cond.
30 Mar.	*Pagliacci*	Albanese, Jobin, Thompson, De Paolis, Sodero cond.
31 Mar.*	*Il trovatore*	Baum, Milanov, Castagna, Moscona, Sodero cond.
2 Apr. Baltimore	*Aida*	Milanov, Carron, Harshaw, Cordon, Hawkins, Cooper cond.
4 Apr.	*La traviata*	Albanese, Kullman, Stellman, De Paolis, Sodero cond.
7 Apr. Boston	*Lucia di Lammermoor*	Munsel, Peerce, Moscona, Garris, Sodero cond.
11 Apr. Boston	*Aida*	Milanov, Carron, Harshaw, Cordon, Hawkins, Sodero cond.
14 Apr. Boston	*Rigoletto*	Antoine, Peerce, Castagna, Moscona, Hargrave, Sodero cond.
16 Apr. Cleveland	*Faust*	Jobin, Albanese, Pinza, Browning, Pelletier cond.
21 Apr. Cleveland	*La Gioconda*	Roman, Jagel, Thebom, Moscona, Harshaw, Cooper cond.
26 Apr. Minneapolis	*Lucia di Lammermoor*	Munsel, Melton, Moscona, Garris, Cimara cond.
30 Apr. Chicago	*Lucia di Lammermoor*	Pons, Peerce, Moscona, Garris, Sodero cond.

29 Nov.	*Rigoletto*	Sayão, Björling, Lipton, Moscona, Hargrave, Sodero cond.
8 Dec.*	*Un ballo in maschera*	Milanov, Peerce, Harshaw, Alarie, Cordon, Alvary, Baker, Walter cond.
10 Dec.	*Rigoletto*	Sayão, Björling, Lipton, Moscona, Hawkins, Sodero cond.
21 Dec.	*La Gioconda*	Milanov, Tucker, Stevens, Pinza, Harshaw, Cooper cond.
26 Dec.	*Un ballo in maschera*	Milanov, Peerce, Harshaw, Alarie, Cordon, Alvary, Baker, Walter cond.
29 Dec.*	*Rigoletto*	Sayão, Björling, Lipton, Cordon, Hargrave, Sodero cond.

1946

2 Jan.	*La Gioconda*	Milanov, Tucker, Stevens, Pinza, Harshaw, Cooper cond.
4 Feb.	*Lucia di Lammermoor*	Munsel, Peerce, Lazzari, Hayward, Cimara cond.
16 Feb.	*Un ballo in maschera*	Roman, Peerce, Harshaw, Alarie, Lazzari, Moscona, Baker, Walter cond.
23 Feb.*	*Otello*	Ralf, Roman, Lipton, De Paolis, Moscona, Szell cond.
26 Feb.	*Rigoletto*	Benzell, Peerce, Lipton, Cordon, Hargrave, Sodero cond.
28 Feb.	*La Gioconda*	Roman, Tokatyan, Thebom, Vaghi, Lipton, Cooper cond.
5 Mar. Philadelphia	*Rigoletto*	Munsel, Peerce, Lipton, Vaghi, Hawkins, Sodero cond.
11 Mar.	*Otello*	Ralf, Roman, Lipton, De Paolis, Moscona, Szell cond.
16 Mar.*	*La Gioconda*	Milanov, Tucker, Stevens, Vaghi, Harshaw, Cooper cond.
19 Mar. Philadelphia	*Otello*	Ralf, Roman, Lipton, De Paolis, Moscona, Szell cond.
23 Mar.*	*La traviata*	Albanese, Tucker, Votipka, Manning, Sodero cond.
25 Mar.	*La Gioconda*	Milanov, Tucker, Thebom, Pinza, Harshaw, Cooper cond.
29 Mar.	*Otello*	Ralf, Roman, Lipton, De Paolis, Moscona, Szell cond.
1 Apr. Baltimore	*La Gioconda*	Milanov, Tucker, Stevens, Pinza, Harshaw, Cooper cond.

[1946]

6 Apr. Boston	*La traviata*	Steber, Tucker, Votipka, De Paolis, Sodero cond.
11 Apr. Boston	*Un ballo in maschera*	Milanov, Peerce, Thorborg, Alarie, Cordon, Alvary, Baker, Walter cond.
17 Apr.	*Un ballo in maschera*	Milanov, Björling, Harshaw, Alarie, Cordon, Alvary, Baker, Walter cond.
20 Apr.	*Rigoletto*	Antoine, Björling, Lipton, Cordon, Hawkins, Sodero cond.
27 Apr. Cleveland	*Un ballo in maschera*	Milanov, Peerce, Harshaw, Alarie, Cordon, Alvary, Baker, Walter cond.
3 May Minneapolis	*La traviata*	Steber, Peerce, Votipka, De Paolis, Sodero cond.
8 May Chicago	*La Gioconda*	Milanov, Tucker, Stevens, Pinza, Harshaw, Cooper cond.
11 May Chicago	*Un ballo in maschera*	Milanov, Peerce, Harshaw, Alarie, Cordon, Alvary, Baker, Walter cond.
15 May St. Louis	*Rigoletto*	Munsel, Peerce, Lipton, Pinza, Hawkins. Sodero cond.
18 May Dallas	*Rigoletto*	Antoine, Peerce, Lipton, Cordon, Hargrave, Sodero cond.
22 May Chattanooga	*Rigoletto*	Munsel, Peerce, Browning, Pinza, Hawkins, Sodero cond.
12 Nov. Philadelphia	*Aida*	Milanov, Vinay, Thebom, Moscona, Kinsman, Sodero cond.
16 Nov.*	*Otello*	Ralf, Roman, Lipton, De Paolis, Moscona, Busch cond.
18 Nov.	*Aida*	Milanov, Vinay, Thebom, Moscona, Kinsman, Sodero cond.
22 Nov.	*Otello*	Ralf, Roman, Lipton, De Paolis, Moscona, Busch cond.
27 Nov.	*Lucia di Lammermoor*	Pons, Peerce, Moscona, Hayward, Sodero cond.
4 Dec.	*Aida*	Milanov, Svanholm, Turner, Moscona, Kinsman, Sodero cond.
7 Dec.	*Il trovatore*	Baum, Roman, Harshaw, Vaghi, Sodero cond.
9 Dec.	*Otello*	Vinay, Roman, Lipton, De Paolis, Moscona, Busch cond.
12 Dec.	*Lucia di Lammermoor*	Pons, Peerce, Moscona, Hayward, Sodero cond.
21 Dec.*	*La traviata*	Albanese, Peerce, Votipka, Chabay, Sodero cond.

28 Dec.*	*Aida*	Roman, Svanholm, Thebom, Moscona, Kinsman, Sodero cond.

1947

1 Jan.	*Il trovatore*	Baum, Resnik, Harshaw, Vaghi, Sodero cond.
7 Feb.	*Rigoletto*	Benzell, Tucker, Browning, Moscona, Hawkins, Sodero cond.
12 Feb.	*La Gioconda*	Milanov, Tucker, Stevens, Vaghi, Harshaw, Cooper cond.
15 Feb.*	*Il trovatore*	Baum, Milanov, Harshaw, Vaghi, Sodero cond.
19 Feb.	*Rigoletto*	Schymberg, Peerce, Browning, Moscona, Hargrave, Sodero cond.
22 Feb.	*Otello*	Ralf, Quartararo, Lipton, De Paolis, Moscona, Busch cond.
24 Feb.	*La Gioconda*	Milanov, Tucker, Stevens, Vaghi, Browning, Cooper cond.
1 Mar.*	*Rigoletto*	Schymberg, Peerce, Lipton, Vaghi, Hawkins, Sodero cond.
6 Mar.	*La Gioconda*	Milanov, Tucker, Lipton, Vaghi, Harshaw, Cooper cond.
12 Mar.	*Otello*	Vinay, Ilitsch, Lipton, De Paolis, Moscona, Busch cond.
15 Mar.	*Aida*	Milanov, Svanholm, Harshaw, Vaghi, Kinsman, Sodero cond.
25 Mar. Boston	*Rigoletto*	Munsel, Peerce, Lipton, Vaghi, Hawkins, Sodero cond.
28 Mar. Boston	*Otello*	Ralf, Ilitsch, Lipton, De Paolis, Moscona, Busch cond.
31 Mar.	*Rigoletto*	Antoine, Tagliavini, Browning, Vaghi, Hawkins, Cimara cond.
5 Apr.	*Il trovatore*	Björling, Ilitsch, Harshaw, Moscona, Sodero cond.
10 Apr. Cleveland	*La traviata*	Steber, Peerce, Votipka, Chabay, Cimara cond.
12 Apr. Cleveland	*Aida*	Ilitsch, Baum, Thebom, Vaghi, Kinsman, Rudolf cond.
25 Apr. Chicago	*Aida*	Ilitsch, Baum, Thebom, Lazzari, Kinsman, Sodero cond.
29 Apr. Atlanta	*Aida*	Kirk, Baum, Thebom, Moscona, Kinsman, Sodero cond.

[1947]

10 Nov.	*Un ballo in maschera*	Ilitsch, Peerce, Harshaw, Alarie, Vaghi, Alvary, Baker, Antonicelli cond.
19 Nov.	*Il trovatore*	Baum, Roman, Elmo, Vaghi, Cooper cond.
22 Nov.*	*Un ballo in maschera*	Ilitsch, Peerce, Harshaw, Alarie, Vaghi, Alvary, Baker, Antonicelli cond.
28 Nov.	*Il trovatore*	Baum, Roman, Elmo, Vaghi, Cooper cond.
5 Dec.	*Aida*	Ilitsch, Ralf, Harshaw, Vaghi, Kinsman, Cooper cond.
10 Dec.	*Un ballo in maschera*	Roman, Tucker, Elmo, Alarie, Moscona, Alvary, Baker, Antonicelli cond.
18 Dec.	*La Gioconda*	Ilitsch, Tucker, Stevens, Vaghi, Harshaw, Cooper cond.
25 Dec.	*Rigoletto*	Pons, Björling, Petina, Székely, Schon, Cimara cond.
27 Dec.*	*Il trovatore*	Björling, Roman, Harshaw, Vaghi, Cooper cond.
29 Dec.	*Lucia di Lammermoor*	Pons, Peerce, Moscona, F. Knight, Cimara cond.

1948

2 Jan.	*La Gioconda*	Ilitsch, Tucker, Thebom, Vaghi, Harshaw, Cooper cond.
8 Jan.	*Un ballo in maschera*	Roman, Björling, Harshaw, Alarie, Moscona, Alvary, Baker, Busch cond.
10 Jan.	*Rigoletto*	Benzell, Björling, Browning, Vaghi, Schon, Cimara cond.
21 Feb.*	*Aida*	Ilitsch/Kirk, Baum, Harshaw, Moscona, Kinsman, Cooper cond.
25 Feb.	*Rigoletto*	Gracia, Di Stefano, Elmo, Székely, Hawkins, Cimara cond.
28 Feb.*	*Pagliacci*	Quartararo, Vinay, Thompson, Chabay, Antonicelli cond.
4 Mar.	*Aida*	Kirk, Baum, Harshaw, Vaghi, Kinsman, Cooper cond.
9 Mar. Baltimore	*Rigoletto*	Gracia, Di Stefano, Elmo, Vaghi, Hawkins, Cimara cond.
20 Mar. Boston	*La traviata*	Albanese, Tucker, Manski, Chabay, Antonicelli cond.
31 Mar. Richmond	*La traviata*	Steber, Peerce, Manski, Chabay, Antonicelli cond.
2 Apr. Atlanta	*Lucia di Lammermoor*	Pons, Melton, Moscona, Hayward, Cimara cond.

5 Apr. Chicago	*Aida*	Ilitsch, Baum, Thebom, Moscona, Kinsman, Cooper cond.
8 Apr. Dallas	*Un ballo in maschera*	Ilitsch, Björling, Elmo, Manski, Vaghi, Alvary, Baker, Busch cond.
10 Apr. Dallas	*Pagliacci*	Kirsten, Jagel, Thompson, Chabay, Antonicelli cond.
16 Apr. Los Angeles	*Il trovatore*	Björling, Resnik, Elmo, Hines, Cooper cond.
18 Apr. Los Angeles	*Aida*	Ilitsch, Vinay, Harshaw, Moscona, Kinsman, Cooper cond.
21 Apr. Los Angeles	*Un ballo in maschera*	Roman, Björling, Elmo, I. Manski, Vaghi, Alvary, Harvuot, Busch cond.
24 Apr. Los Angeles	*La traviata*	Sayão, Peerce, Votipka, De Paolis, Antonicelli cond.
26 Apr. Denver	*Aida*	Roman, Baum, Thebom, Hines, Kinsman, Cooper cond.
8 May Minneapolis	*Il trovatore*	Björling, Resnik, Elmo, Moscona, Cooper cond.
29 Nov.	*Otello*	Vinay, Albanese, Lipton, Garris, Moscona, Busch cond. (First telecast from the Met stage.)
4 Dec.	*Rigoletto*	Munsel, Peerce, Lipton, Vichey, Harvuot, Cimara cond.
9 Dec.	*Otello*	Vinay, Albanese, Lipton, Garris, Moscona, Busch cond.
15 Dec.	*Rigoletto*	Pons, Peerce, Elmo, Vichey, Schon, Cimara cond.
18 Dec.*	*Otello*	Vinay, Albanese, Lipton, Garris, Moscona, Busch cond.
25 Dec.	*Rigoletto*	Munsel, Peerce, Elmo, Vichey, Schon, Cimara cond.
31 Dec.	*La traviata*	Albanese, Peerce, Stellman, Chabay, Antonicelli cond.

1949

5 Jan.	*Otello*	Vinay, Albanese, Lipton, Garris, Moscona, Busch cond.
26 Feb.*	*Falstaff*	Resnik, Valdengo, Elmo, Albanese, Di Stefano, Reiner cond.
3 Mar.	*Falstaff*	Resnik, Valdengo, Elmo, Albanese, Di Stefano, Reiner cond.
7 Mar.	*Falstaff*	Resnik, Valdengo, Elmo, Albanese, Di Stefano, Reiner cond.

[1949]

12 Mar.	*Otello*	Vinay, Roman, Lipton, Garris, Moscona, Busch cond.
15 Mar. Philadelphia	*La traviata*	Albanese, Peerce, Votipka, Chabay, Antonicelli cond.
19 Mar.*	*Rigoletto*	Munsel, Peerce, Lipton, Ernster, Schon, Cimara cond.
21 Mar. Baltimore	*Otello*	Vinay, Albanese, Lipton, Garris, Moscona, Cellini cond.
2 Apr. Boston	*Otello*	Vinay, Albanese, Lipton, Garris, Moscona, Cellini cond.
7 Apr. Cleveland	*Rigoletto*	Pons, Björling, Lipton, Moscona, Harvuot, Cimara cond.
9 Apr. Cleveland	*Otello*	Vinay, Albanese, Lipton, Garris, Moscona, Busch cond.
18 Apr. Atlanta	*Otello*	Vinay, Albanese, Lipton, Garris, Moscona, Busch cond.
22 Apr. Dallas	*Otello*	Vinay, Albanese, Lipton, De Paolis, Moscona, Busch cond.
26 Apr. Los Angeles	*Rigoletto*	Conner, Peerce, Lipton, Hines, Harvuot, Cimara cond.
12 May Minneapolis	*Otello*	Vinay, Albanese, Lipton, Chabay, Moscona, Busch cond.
28 Nov.	*Simon Boccanegra* (Simon)	Varnay, Tucker, Székely, Valdengo, Alvary, Stiedry cond.
4 Dec.	*Rigoletto*	Berger, Tucker, Lipton, Ernster, Harvuot, Perlea cond.
9 Dec.	*Simon Boccanegra*	Varnay, Tucker, Székely, Valdengo, Alvary, Stiedry cond.
23 Dec.	*Faust*	Di Stefano, Kirsten, Tajo, Manski, Pelletier cond.
31 Dec.*	*Faust*	Di Stefano, Kirsten, Tajo, Manski, Pelletier cond.

1950

3 Jan Philadelphia	*Simon Boccanegra*	Varnay, Tucker, Székely, Valdengo, Alvary, Stiedry cond.
6 Jan.	*Rigoletto*	Berger, Di Stefano, Petina, Vichey, Harvuot, Perlea cond.
16 Jan.	*Rigoletto*	Munsel, Peerce, Browning, Székely, Schon, Perlea cond.
24 Jan.	*La traviata*	Albanese, Tagliavini, Votipka, De Paolis, Perlea cond.

28 Jan.*	*Simon Boccanegra*	Varnay, Tucker, Székely, Valdengo, Alvary, Stiedry cond.
1 Feb.	*Rigoletto*	Berger, Tucker, Madeira, Vichey, Schon, Perlea cond.
24 Feb.	*La traviata*	Conner, Tucker, Manski, De Paolis, Perlea cond.
1 Mar.	*Simon Boccanegra*	Varnay, Tucker, Vichey, Thompson, Alvary, Stiedry cond.
4 Mar.*	*Rigoletto*	Munsel, Peerce, Lipton, Moscona, Harvuot, Perlea cond.
29 Mar. Boston	*Rigoletto*	Conner, Peerce, Lipton, Moscona, Harvuot, Perlea cond.
31 Mar. Boston	*Simon Boccanegra*	Roman, Tucker, Vichey, Thompson, Alvary, Stiedry cond.
8 Apr.	*Rigoletto*	Munsel, Di Stefano, Madeira, Ernster, Hawkins, Perlea cond.
12 Apr. Cleveland	*Faust*	Di Stefano, Albanese, Tajo, Bollinger, Pelletier cond.
22 Apr. St. Louis	*Rigoletto*	Munsel, Di Stefano, Madeira, Hines, Schon, Perlea cond.
26 Apr. Atlanta	*Rigoletto*	Munsel, Tucker, Madeira, Hines, Hawkins, Perlea cond.
29 Apr. Dallas	*Faust*	Di Stefano, Conner, Hines, Manski, Pelletier cond.
10 May Chicago	*La traviata*	Albanese, Di Stefano, Manski, Franke, Perlea cond.
12 May Chicago	*Rigoletto*	Munsel, Björling, Madeira, Hines, Schon, Perlea cond.
18 Dec.	*La traviata*	Albanese, Tagliavini, Browning, De Paolis, Erede cond.
28 Dec.	*Il trovatore*	Baum, Rigal, Barbieri, Moscona, Erede cond.

1951

1 Jan.	*Faust*	Björling, Steber, Siepi, Bollinger, Cleva cond.
3 Jan.	*Il trovatore*	Baum, Rigal, Barbieri, Moscona, Erede cond.
13 Jan.*	*Il trovatore*	Baum, Rigal, Barbieri, Moscona, Erede cond.
17 Jan.	*Pagliacci*	Rigal, Vinay, Guarrera, Hayward, Erede cond.

[1951]

19 Jan.	*Pagliacci*	Rigal, Vinay, Guarrera, Hayward, Erede cond.
27 Jan.	*Il trovatore*	Baum, Milanov, Barbieri, Moscona, Erede cond.
29 Jan.	*Pagliacci*	Rigal, Vinay, Guarrera, Hayward, Erede cond.
8 Feb.	*Il trovatore*	Baum, Milanov, Barbieri, Moscona, Erede cond.
12 Feb.	*Il trovatore*	Baum, Milanov, Barbieri, Moscona, Erede cond.
17 Feb.	*La traviata*	Conner, Tucker, Browning, De Paolis, Erede cond.
20 Feb. Philadelphia	*Pagliacci*	Rigal, Vinay, Guarrera, Hayward, Erede cond.
1 Mar.	*Faust*	Tucker, Rigal, Siepi, Bollinger, Cleva cond.
3 Mar.*	*Pagliacci*	Rigal, Baum, Guarrera, Hayward, Erede cond.
7 Mar.	*Pagliacci*	Rigal, Baum, Guarrera, Hayward, Erede cond.
22 Mar.	*Pagliacci*	Rigal, Baum, Guarrera, Hayward, Erede cond.
31 Mar.	*La traviata*	Rigal, Tucker, Browning, De Paolis, Erede cond.
17 Apr. Cleveland	*La traviata*	Kirsten, Conley, Votipka, De Paolis, Cleva cond.
2 May Oklahoma City	*La traviata*	Kirsten, Tucker, Browning, Chabay, Erede cond.
5 May Minneapolis	*Pagliacci*	Rigal, Vinay, Guarrera, Hayward, Erede cond.
15 Nov.	*Rigoletto*	Gueden, Tucker, Madeira, Pernerstorfer, Scott, Erede cond.
19 Nov.	*Rigoletto*	Gueden, Tucker, Madeira, Pernerstorfer, Scott, Erede cond.
23 Nov.	*Rigoletto*	Gueden, Tucker, Madeira, Pernerstorfer, Scott, Erede cond.
28 Nov.	*Rigoletto*	Peters, Tucker, Rankin, Moscona, Scott, Erede cond.
1 Dec.	*Pagliacci*	Rigal, Vinay, Guarrera, Hayward, Erede cond.
4 Dec. Philadelphia	*Rigoletto*	Gueden, Tucker, Madeira, Pernerstorfer, Scott, Erede cond.

8 Dec.*	*Rigoletto*	Gueden, Tucker, Madeira, Pernerstorfer, Scott, Erede cond.
14 Dec.	*Pagliacci*	Amara, Baum, Guarrera, Carelli, Erede cond.
16 Dec.	*Rigoletto*	Peters, Prandelli, Rankin, Pernerstorfer, Scott, Erede cond.
22 Dec.	*Rigoletto*	Pons, Di Stefano, Madeira, Moscona, Scott, Erede cond.
27 Dec.	*Pagliacci*	Rigal, Vinay, Capecchi, Hayward, Erede cond.
29 Dec.	*Aida*	Milanov, Del Monaco, Nikolaidi, Siepi, Vichey, Cleva cond.

1952

29 Jan.	*Aida*	Rigal, Del Monaco, Barbieri, Moscona, Scott, Cleva cond.
5 Feb.	*Rigoletto*	Peters, Peerce, Rankin, Pernerstorfer, Scott, Erede cond.
9 Feb.*	*Otello*	Vinay, Steber, Lipton, Hayward, Vichey, Stiedry cond.
15 Feb.	*Otello*	Del Monaco, Steber, Lipton, Hayward, Vichey, Stiedry cond.
20 Feb.	*Otello*	Vinay, Steber, Lipton, Hayward, Moscona, Stiedry cond.
3 Mar.	*Otello*	Vinay, Steber, Lipton, Hayward, Vichey, Stiedry cond.
8 Mar.*	*Aida*	Milanov, Del Monaco, Rankin, Hines, Vichey, Cleva cond.
26 Mar. Baltimore	*Il trovatore*	Baum, Milanov, Barbieri, Moscona, Erede cond.
14 Apr. Cleveland	*Aida*	Milanov, Del Monaco, Thebom, Hines, Vichey, Cleva cond.
16 Apr. Cleveland	*Rigoletto*	Gueden, Tucker, Madeira, Moscona, Scott, Erede cond.
21 Apr. Boston	*Aida*	Milanov, Del Monaco, Thebom, Hines, Vichey, Cleva cond.
26 Apr. Boston	*Rigoletto*	Gueden, Tucker, Madeira, Hines, Scott, Erede cond.
28 Apr. Washington, D.C.	*Aida*	Milanov, Del Monaco, Thebom, Hines, Scott, Cleva cond.
3 May Atlanta	*Aida*	Milanov, Del Monaco, Thebom, Hines, Scott, Cleva cond.

[1952]

8 May Memphis	*Rigoletto*	Gueden, Tucker, Madeira, Moscona, Scott, Erede cond.
13 May Houston	*Rigoletto*	Warner, Tucker, Madeira, Moscona, Scott, Erede cond.
16 May Minneapolis	*Rigoletto*	Peters, Di Stefano, Madeira, Hines, Scott, Erede cond.
24 May St. Louis	*La traviata*	Kirsten, Peerce, Lenchner, Franke, Cleva cond.
29 May Toronto	*Rigoletto*	Munsel, Tucker, Glaz, Moscona, Scott, Erede cond.
31 May Montréal	*La traviata*	Steber, Peerce, Lenchner, Carelli, Cleva cond.
10 Nov.	*La forza del destino*	Milanov, Tucker, Siepi, Miller, Pechner, Stiedry cond.
18 Nov. Philadelphia	*La forza del destino*	Milanov, Tucker, Hines, Miller, Pechner, Stiedry cond.
21 Nov.	*La forza del destino*	Milanov, Baum, Siepi, Miller, Pechner, Stiedry cond.
29 Nov.*	*La forza del destino*	Milanov, Tucker, Hines, Miller, Pechner, Stiedry cond.
3 Dec.	*Rigoletto*	Peters, Prandelli, Glaz, Hines, Scott, Erede cond.
10 Dec.	*La forza del destino*	Milanov, Del Monaco, Hines, Miller, Pechner, Stiedry cond.
16 Dec.	*La Gioconda*	Milanov, Del Monaco, Barbieri, Siepi, Madeira, Cleva cond.
18 Dec.	*Rigoletto*	Pons, Prandelli, Glaz, Moscona, Scott, Erede cond.
23 Dec.	*Rigoletto*	Gueden, Prandelli, Glaz, Vichey, Scott, Erede cond.
25 Dec.	*La Gioconda*	Milanov, Del Monaco, Barbieri, Siepi, Madeira, Cleva cond.
29 Dec.	*La forza del destino*	Milanov, Baum, Siepi, Miller, Pechner, Stiedry cond.

1953

3 Jan.*	*La Gioconda*	Milanov, Baum, Barbieri, Siepi, Madeira, Cleva cond.
5 Jan.	*Rigoletto*	Pons, Tagliavini, Madeira, Moscona, Scott, Erede cond.
16 Jan.	*La Gioconda*	Milanov, Del Monaco, Barbieri, Moscona, Madeira, Cleva cond.

21 Jan.	*Pagliacci*	Rigal, Del Monaco, Capecchi, Hayward, Erede cond.
28 Jan.	*La Gioconda*	Milanov, Del Monaco, Barbieri, Moscona, Madeira, Cleva cond.
31 Jan.	*Rigoletto*	Warner, Peerce, Lipton, Vichey, Scott, Erede cond.
2 Feb.	*La Gioconda*	Milanov, Tucker, Thebom, Moscona, Madeira, Cleva cond.
5 Feb.	*Aida*	Rigal, Del Monaco, Rankin, Moscona, Scott, Cleva cond.
7 Feb.	*Rigoletto*	Gueden, Björling, Lipton, Vichey, Scott, Erede cond.
7 Mar.*	*Rigoletto*	Gueden, Conley, Madeira, Moscona, Scott, Erede cond.
14 Apr. Cleveland	*La Gioconda*	Milanov, Tucker, Thebom, Siepi, Madeira, Cleva cond.
17 Apr. Cleveland	*La forza del destino*	Milanov, Tucker, Hines, Miller, Pechner, Stiedry cond.
20 Apr. Boston	*La forza del destino*	Milanov, Tucker, Siepi, Miller, Pechner, Stiedry cond.
25 Apr. Boston	*Rigoletto*	Gueden, Peerce, Madeira, Hines, Scott, Erede cond.
28 Apr. Washington, D.C.	*Rigoletto*	Peters, Conley, Madeira, Hines, Scott, Erede cond.
30 Apr. Atlanta	*Rigoletto*	Gueden, Tucker, Madeira, Hines, Scott, Erede cond.
5 May Birmingham	*Aida*	Milanov, Del Monaco, Thebom, Moscona, Scott, Cleva cond.
14 May Des Moines	*Aida*	Milanov, Baum, Thebom, Moscona, Vichey, Cleva cond.
18 May Bloomington	*Rigoletto*	Gueden, Conley, Madeira, Siepi, Scott, Erede cond.
22 May Montréal	*Rigoletto*	Peters, Tucker, Madeira, Vichey, Scott, Erede cond.
25 May Toronto	*La forza del destino*	Milanov, Tucker, Siepi, Miller, Pechner, Stiedry cond.
29 May Toronto	*Rigoletto*	Gueden, Conley, Lipton, Vichey, Scott, Erede cond.

1954

| 16 Jan.* | *Il trovatore* | Baum, Milanov, Nikolaidi, Moscona, Cleva cond. |

[1954]

20 Jan.	*Rigoletto*	Gueden, Conley, Lipton, Vichey, Scott, Erede cond.
2 Feb.	*La forza del destino*	Milanov, Baum, Siepi, Roggero, Davidson, Cimara cond.
6 Feb.*	*La traviata*	Albanese, Tucker, Roggero, Carelli, Cleva cond.
13 Feb.	*Aida*	Milanov, Baum, Thebom, Hines, Vichey, Cleva cond.
17 Feb.	*La forza del destino*	Nelli, Penno, Moscona, Roggero, Pechner, Cellini cond.
20 Feb.*	*Aida*	Milanov, Baum, Barbieri, Hines, Vichey, Cleva cond.
22 Feb.	*Il trovatore*	Penno, Milanov, Barbieri, Moscona, Cleva cond.
3 Mar.	*Il trovatore*	Penno, Milanov, Barbieri, Scott, Cleva cond.
5 Mar.	*Aida*	Nelli, Penno, Thebom, Moscona, Vichey, Cleva cond.
18 Mar.	*Pagliacci*	Amara, Vinay, Capecchi, Franke, Erede cond.
20 Mar.*	*La forza del destino*	Milanov, Penno, Hines, Madeira, Pechner, Stiedry cond.
24 Mar.	*Pagliacci*	Amara, Penno, Capecchi, Anthony, Cellini cond.
2 Apr.	*Pagliacci*	Amara, Vinay, Capecchi, Anthony, Erede cond.
19 Apr. Cleveland	*Lucia di Lammermoor*	Pons, Peerce, Scott, Hayward, McCracken, Cleva cond.
24 Apr. Cleveland	*Il trovatore*	Baum, Milanov, Nikolaidi, Scott, Cleva cond.
29 Apr. Boston	*Il trovatore*	Baum, Nelli, Madeira, Moscona, Cleva cond.
1 May Boston	*La traviata*	Albanese, Tucker, Roggero, Carelli, Cleva cond.
5 May Atlanta	*La forza del destino*	Milanov, Tucker, Siepi, Roggero, Pechner, Stiedry cond.
6 May Birmingham	*La traviata*	Albanese, Peerce, Krall, Carelli, Cleva cond.
9 May Dallas	*La traviata*	Steber, Tucker, Krall, Franke, Cleva cond.
14 May Minneapolis	*La forza del destino*	Milanov, Tucker, Moscona, Madeira, Pechner, Cimara cond.

19 May Lafayette	*Rigoletto*	Peters, Peerce, Madeira, Moscona, Scott, Erede cond.
21 May Chicago	*Aida*	Milanov, Baum, Thebom, Moscona, Vichey, Cleva cond.
23 May Chicago	*Rigoletto*	Peters, Conley, Madeira, Vichey, Scott, Erede cond.
27 May Toronto	*La traviata*	Albanese, Peerce, Roggero, Carelli, Cimara cond.
29 May Toronto	*Rigoletto*	Peters, Tucker, Madeira, Moscona, Scott, Erede cond.
16 Nov.	*Andrea Chénier*	Del Monaco, Milanov, Elias, Rankin, De Paolis, Cleva cond.
20 Nov.	*La traviata*	Albanese, Prandelli, Krall, Carelli, Erede cond.
23 Nov. Philadelphia	*Andrea Chénier*	Del Monaco, Milanov, Elias, Rankin, De Paolis, Cleva cond.
4 Dec.*	*Andrea Chénier*	Del Monaco, Milanov, Elias, Warfield, De Paolis, Cleva cond.
17 Dec.	*Pagliacci*	Amara, Vinay, Guarrera, Anthony, Erede cond.
23 Dec.	*Andrea Chénier*	Tucker, Milanov, Elias, Rankin, Anthony, Cleva cond.

1955

7 Jan.	*Un ballo in maschera*	Milanov, Tucker, M. Anderson, Peters, Moscona, Scott, Marsh, Mitropoulos cond.
11 Jan. Philadelphia	*Un ballo in maschera*	Nelli, Tucker, M. Anderson, Peters, Moscona, Scott, Marsh, Mitropoulos cond.
31 Jan.	*Otello*	Del Monaco, Tebaldi, Lipton, Franke, Vichey, Stiedry cond.
4 Feb.	*La traviata*	Kirsten, Hayward, Krall, Franke, Cimara cond.
11 Feb.	*Otello*	Del Monaco, Tebaldi, Lipton, Franke, Vichey, Stiedry cond.
1 Mar.	*Otello*	Del Monaco, Tebaldi, Lipton, Franke, Vichey, Stiedry cond.
5 Mar.	*Otello*	Del Monaco, Tebaldi, Lipton, Franke, Vichey, Stiedry cond.
9 Mar.	*La Gioconda*	Milanov, Baum, Rankin, Tozzi, Warfield, Cleva cond.
12 Mar.*	*Otello*	Del Monaco, Tebaldi, Lipton, Franke, Vichey, Stiedry cond.

[1955]

17 Mar.	*Otello*	Svanholm, Amara, Lipton, Franke, Vichey, Stiedry cond.
21 Mar.	*La Gioconda*	Milanov, Baum, Thebom, Tozzi, Warfield, Cleva cond.
28 Mar. Baltimore	*Andrea Chénier*	Del Monaco, Milanov, Elias, Warfield, De Paolis, Cleva cond.
2 Apr.*	*La Gioconda*	Milanov, Baum, Rankin, Tozzi, Warfield, Cleva cond.
13 Apr. Cleveland	*La Gioconda*	Milanov, Campora, Thebom, Moscona, Warfield, Cleva cond.
15 Apr. Cleveland	*Andrea Chénier*	Baum, Milanov, Elias, Warfield, Anthony, Cleva cond.
18 Apr. Boston	*Andrea Chénier*	Tucker, Milanov, Elias, Warfield, De Paolis, Cleva cond.
20 Apr. Boston	*Pagliacci*	Amara, Baum, Guarrera, Anthony, Kozma cond.
22 Apr. Boston	*Otello*	Svanholm, Amara, Lipton, Franke, Moscona, Stiedry cond.
25 Apr. Washington, D.C.	*La traviata*	Albanese, Tucker, Roggero, Carelli, Cleva cond.
29 Apr. Atlanta	*Andrea Chénier*	Baum, Nelli, Elias, Warfield, De Paolis, Cleva cond.
6 May Dallas	*Pagliacci*	Amara, Baum, Guarrera, Anthony, Kozma cond.
9 May Houston	*La traviata*	Kirsten, Conley, Krall, Franke, Cimara cond.
13 May Minneapolis	*Andrea Chénier*	Tucker, Milanov, Elias, Warfield, Anthony, Cleva cond.
16 May Bloomington	*Andrea Chénier*	Baum, Milanov, Roggero, Warfield, Anthony, Cleva cond.
19 May Chicago	*Andrea Chénier*	Tucker, Milanov, Elias, Warfield, De Paolis, Cleva cond.
22 May Chicago	*La traviata*	Kirsten, Peerce, Krall, Carelli, Cimara cond.
24 May Toronto	*Pagliacci*	Amara, Baum, Guarrera, Anthony, Kozma cond.
27 May Toronto	*Andrea Chénier*	Tucker, Milanov, Elias, Warfield, De Paolis, Cleva cond.
1 June Montréal	*La traviata*	Albanese, Conley, Krall, Carelli, Cleva cond.

17 Nov.	Rigoletto	Peters, Conley, Elias, Tozzi, Scott, Cleva cond.
21 Nov.	Rigoletto	Peters, Peerce, Elias, Tozzi, Scott, Cleva cond.
8 Dec.	Tosca	Tebaldi, Tucker, Baccaloni, De Paolis, Mitropoulos cond.
13 Dec.	Tosca	Tebaldi, Tucker, Baccaloni, De Paolis, Mitropoulos cond.
15 Dec.	Andrea Chénier	Tucker, Nelli, Elias, Warfield, Anthony, Cleva cond.
26 Dec.	Un ballo in maschera	Nelli, Peerce, M. Anderson, Hurley, Tozzi, Scott, Marsh, Mitropoulos cond.
30 Dec.	Tosca	Tebaldi, Campora, Baccaloni, De Paolis, Mitropoulos cond.

1956

2 Jan.	Andrea Chénier	Tucker, Tebaldi, Elias, Warfield, De Paolis, Cleva cond.
7 Jan.*	Tosca	Tebaldi, Tucker, Corena, De Paolis, Mitropoulos cond.
14 Jan.	Andrea Chénier	Ortica, Tebaldi, Elias, Lipton, De Paolis, Cleva cond.
21 Jan.	La forza del destino	Tebaldi, Tucker, Tozzi, Elias, Corena, Cimara cond.
21 Feb.	La forza del destino	Milanov, Baum, Siepi, Elias, Pechner, Stiedry cond.
25 Feb.*	Rigoletto	Peters, Tucker, Elias, Tozzi, Scott, Cleva cond.
29 Feb.	Il trovatore	Baum, Milanov, Madeira, Scott, Cleva cond.
5 Mar.	Il trovatore	Penno, Milanov, Madeira, Scott, Cleva cond.
17 Mar.*	La forza del destino	Milanov, Tucker, Siepi, Elias, Corena, Stiedry cond.
2 Apr.	La forza del destino	Milanov, Baum, Vichey, Elias, Corena, Stiedry cond.
10 Apr. Baltimore	Tosca	Milanov, Björling, Pechner, Franke, Mitropoulos cond.
14 Apr.*	Il trovatore	Baum, Milanov, Rankin, Tozzi, Cleva cond.
17 Apr. Boston	Un ballo in maschera	Nelli, Björling, M. Anderson, Wilson, Moscona, Scott, Cehanovsky, Kozma cond.
24 Apr. Cleveland	Un ballo in maschera	Milanov, Björling, M. Anderson, Wilson, Moscona, Scott, Cehanovsky, Kozma cond.

[1956]

27 Apr. Cleveland	*Rigoletto*	Peters, Björling, Elias, Tozzi, Scott, Cleva cond.
8 May Birmingham	*Rigoletto*	Peters, Conley, Elias, Tozzi, Scott, Cleva cond.
12 May Dallas	*Tosca*	Milanov, Campora, Pechner, Franke, Mitropoulos cond.
16 May Oklahoma City	*Tosca*	Milanov, Campora, Pechner, De Paolis, Mitropoulos cond.
19 May Minneapolis	*Rigoletto*	Peters, Peerce, Elias, Tozzi, Scott, Cimara cond.
26 May Chicago	*Rigoletto*	Pons, Peerce, Elias, Moscona, Scott, Cleva cond.
2 June Toronto	*Rigoletto*	Peters, Tucker, Elias, Tozzi, Scott, Cimara cond.
5 Nov.	*Il trovatore*	Baum, Milanov, Barbieri, Tozzi, Rudolf cond.
9 Nov.	*Rigoletto*	Dobbs, Peerce, Elias, Tozzi, Sgarro, Cleva cond.
23 Nov.	*Ernani*	Del Monaco, Milanov, Siepi, Vanni, McCracken, Mitropoulos cond.
28 Nov.	*Ernani*	Del Monaco, Milanov, Siepi, Vanni, McCracken, Mitropoulos cond.
30 Nov.	*Tosca*	Rigal, Barioni, Corena, Franke, Mitropoulos cond.
22 Dec.	*Ernani*	Del Monaco, Milanov, Siepi, Vanni, McCracken, Mitropoulos cond.
26 Dec.	*Rigoletto*	Gueden, Peerce, Warfield, Tozzi, Sgarro, Cleva cond.
29 Dec.*	*Ernani*	Del Monaco, Milanov, Siepi, Vanni, McCracken, Mitropoulos cond.

1957

29 Jan.	*Rigoletto*	Hurley, Peerce, Warfield, Scott, Sgarro, Cleva cond.
9 Feb.	*Rigoletto*	Hurley, Poggi, Warfield, Scott, Sgarro, Cleva cond.
13 Feb.	*Il trovatore*	Baum, Curtis-Verna, Madeira, Moscona, Rudolf cond.
21 Feb.	*La traviata*	Tebaldi, Campora, Vanni, Anthony, Cleva cond.

27 Feb.	*Tosca*	Tebaldi, Björling, Baccaloni, De Paolis, Mitropoulos cond.
2 Mar.	*La traviata*	Tebaldi, Campora, Vanni, Anthony, Cleva cond.
7 Mar.	*La Gioconda*	Milanov, Tucker, Rankin, Tozzi, Amparán, Cleva cond.
18 Mar.	*La Gioconda*	Milanov, Poggi, Resnik, Siepi, Amparán, Cleva cond.
23 Mar.*	*Tosca*	Albanese, Barioni, Pechner, De Paolis, Mitropoulos cond.
28 Mar.	*Pagliacci*	Rigal, Ortica, Guarrera, Carelli, Cleva cond.
3 Apr.	*La Gioconda*	Milanov, Poggi, Lipton, Siepi, Amparán, Cleva cond.
6 Apr.*	*La traviata*	Tebaldi, Campora, Vanni, De Paolis, Cleva cond.
10 Apr. Boston	*Rigoletto*	Hurley, Poggi, Roggero, Tozzi, Scott, Cleva cond.
16 Apr.	*Pagliacci*	Albanese, Da Costa, Marsh, Anthony, Adler cond.
20 Apr.*	*La Gioconda*	Milanov, Poggi, Rankin, Siepi, Amparán, Cleva cond.
23 Apr. Cleveland	*La traviata*	Tebaldi, Poggi, Vanni, De Paolis, Cleva cond.
27 Apr. Cleveland	*Tosca*	Tebaldi, Poggi, Davidson, Franke, Adler cond.
1 May Atlanta	*Il trovatore*	Baum, Milanov, Rankin, Tozzi, Rudolf cond.
3 May Atlanta	*La traviata*	Tebaldi, Campora, Vanni, Anthony, Cleva cond.
7 May Birmingham	*Il trovatore*	Baum, Milanov, Rankin, Scott, Rudolf cond.
10 May Dallas	*Il trovatore*	Baum, Milanov, Madeira, Scott, Rudolf cond.
18 May Minneapolis	*Il trovatore*	Baum, Milanov, Madeira, Moscona, Rudolf cond.
21 May Bloomington	*La traviata*	Tebaldi, Campora, Vanni, Carelli, Cleva cond.
24 May Chicago	*Il trovatore*	Baum, Milanov, Madeira, Tozzi, Rudolf cond.
29 May Toronto	*Il trovatore*	Baum, Milanov, Madeira, Scott, Rudolf cond.
4 June Montréal	*Il trovatore*	Da Costa, Milanov, Madeira, Moscona, Rudolf cond.

[1957]

2 Nov.	*La traviata*	De Los Angeles, Barioni, Vanni, Carelli, Cleva cond.
9 Nov.	*Tosca*	Stella, Peerce, Pechner, Franke, Mitropoulos cond.
12 Nov.	*Tosca*	Stella, Peerce, Pechner, Franke, Mitropoulos cond.
16 Nov.	*La traviata*	De Los Angeles, Campora, Vanni, Carelli, Cleva cond.
21 Nov.	*Tosca*	Stella, Campora, Pechner, Franke, Mitropoulos cond.
29 Nov.	*La forza del destino*	Milanov, Labò, Hines, Roggero, Corena, Stiedry cond.
5 Dec.	*Tosca*	Milanov, Bergonzi, Pechner, Franke, Mitropoulos cond.
7 Dec.	*La forza del destino*	Milanov, Labò, Hines, Roggero, Corena, Stiedry cond.
11 Dec.	*Andrea Chénier*	Baum, Milanov, Roggero, Amparán, Anthony, Cleva cond.
18 Dec.	*Tosca*	Milanov, Labò, Pechner, De Paolis, Mitropoulos cond.
28 Dec.*	*Andrea Chénier*	Tucker, Milanov, Elias, Amparán, Anthony, Cleva cond.

1958

2 Jan.	*La forza del destino*	Curtis-Verna, Labò, Tozzi, Amparán, Pechner, Stiedry cond.
3 Jan.	*Aida*	Curtis-Verna, Bergonzi, Dalis, Scott, Sgarro, Cleva cond.
8 Feb.	*Tosca*	Steber, Campora, Baccaloni, Franke, Adler cond.
12 Feb.	*Aida*	Davy, Baum, Dalis, Wildermann, Sgarro, Cleva cond.
27 Feb.	*Otello*	Del Monaco, De Los Angeles, Elias, Franke, Moscona, Cleva cond.
8 Mar.*	*Otello*	Del Monaco, De Los Angeles, Elias, Franke, Moscona, Cleva cond.
15 Mar.*	*Tosca*	Stella, Tucker, Baccaloni, Franke, Mitropoulos cond.
17 Mar.	*Otello*	Del Monaco, Milanov, Elias, Franke, Moscona, Cleva cond.
25 Mar. Baltimore	*Otello*	Del Monaco, De Los Angeles, Lipton, Franke, Scott, Cleva cond.

28 Mar.	*Otello*	Del Monaco, Milanov, Lipton, Franke, Scott, Cleva cond.
9 Apr.	*Otello*	Del Monaco, De Los Angeles, Elias, Franke, Moscona, Cleva cond.
18 Apr. Boston	*Otello*	Del Monaco, Milanov, Elias, Franke, Scott, Cleva cond.
26 Apr. Cleveland	*Otello*	Del Monaco, Milanov, Elias, Franke, Scott, Cleva cond.
30 Oct.	*Rigoletto*	Peters, Fernandi, Amparán, Moscona, Scott, Cleva cond.
7 Nov.	*Pagliacci*	Amara, Del Monaco, Sereni, Anthony, Mitropoulos cond.
10 Nov.	*Pagliacci*	Amara, Del Monaco, Sereni, Anthony, Mitropoulos cond.
15 Nov.	*Otello*	Del Monaco, Tebaldi, Lipton, Franke, Moscona, Cleva cond.
20 Nov.	*Pagliacci*	Amara, Del Monaco, Sereni, Anthony, Mitropoulos cond.
24 Nov.	*Otello*	Del Monaco, Tebaldi, Lipton, Franke, Moscona, Cleva cond.
20 Dec.*	*Otello*	Del Monaco, Tebaldi, Lipton, Franke, Moscona, Cleva cond.
23 Dec.	*Pagliacci*	Amara, Del Monaco, Guarrera, Anthony, Mitropoulos cond.
28 Dec.	*Otello*	Del Monaco, Tebaldi, Lipton, Franke, Moscona, Cleva cond.

1959

3 Jan.*	*Pagliacci*	Amara, Del Monaco, Sereni, Anthony, Mitropoulos cond.
13 Jan. Philadelphia	*Rigoletto*	Gueden, Fernandi, Amparán, Wildermann, Scott, Cleva cond.
16 Jan.	*Tosca*	Curtis-Verna, Fernandi, Pechner, Franke, Mitropoulos cond.
24 Jan.	*Otello*	Uzunov, Milanov, Lipton, Franke, Scott, Cleva cond.
5 Feb.	*Macbeth*	Rysanek, Hines, Bergonzi, Olvis, Leinsdorf cond.
10 Feb.	*Macbeth*	Rysanek, Hines, Bergonzi, Olvis, Leinsdorf cond.
18 Feb.	*Rigoletto*	Dobbs, Morell, Roggero, Wildermann, Scott, Schick cond.

[1959]

21 Feb.*	Macbeth	Rysanek, Hines, Bergonzi, Olvis, Leinsdorf cond.
25 Feb.	Aida	Rysanek, Bergonzi, Rankin, Siepi, Flagello, Cleva cond.
28 Feb.	Macbeth	Rysanek, Hines, Bergonzi, Olvis, Leinsdorf cond.
6 Mar.	Macbeth	Rysanek, Hines, Bergonzi, Olvis, Leinsdorf cond.
10 Mar. Philadelphia	Macbeth	Rysanek, Tozzi, Morrell, Olvis, Leinsdorf cond.
16 Mar.	Macbeth	Rysanek, Hines, Morell, Olvis, Leinsdorf cond.
28 Mar.*	Rigoletto	Peters, Fernandi, Roggero, Wildermann, Scott, Cleva cond.
15 Apr. Boston	Tosca	Milanov, Morell, Alvary, De Paolis, Cleva cond.
18 Apr. Boston	Pagliacci	Amara, Baum, Sereni, Anthony, Adler cond.
20 Apr. Cleveland	Tosca	Steber, Morell, Alvary, De Paolis, Cleva cond.
25 Apr. Cleveland	Pagliacci	Amara, Baum, Sereni, Anthony, Adler cond.
28 Apr. Washington, D.C.	Tosca	Curtis-Verna, Peerce, Alvary, De Paolis, Cleva cond. (Warren canceled after Act I and was replaced as Scarpia by Mario Zanasi.)
16 May Minneapolis	Pagliacci	Amara, Bergonzi, Sereni, Anthony, Adler cond.
22 May Detroit	Pagliacci	Amara, Bergonzi, Sereni, Anthony, Adler cond.
25 May Toronto	Tosca	Steber, Fernandi, Flagello, Franke, Cleva cond.
29 May Toronto	Rigoletto	Hurley, Tucker, Elias, Tozzi, Harvuot, Cleva cond.
26 Oct.	Il trovatore	Bergonzi, Stella, Simionato, Wildermann, Cleva cond.
29 Oct.	Tosca	Milanov, Fernandi, Davidson, Franke, Mitropoulos cond.
3 Nov.	Il trovatore	Bergonzi, Stella, Simionato, Wildermann, Cleva cond.
10 Nov. Philadelphia	Il trovatore	Bergonzi, Stella, Simionato, Wildermann, Cleva cond.

14 Nov.	*Il trovatore*	Bergonzi, Stella, Simionato, Wildermann, Cleva cond.
22 Nov.	*Aida*	Amara, Uzunov, Rankin, Wildermann, Sgarro, Cleva cond.
28 Nov.*	*Aida*	Amara, Uzunov, Rankin, Tozzi, Sgarro, Cleva cond.
30 Nov.	*La traviata*	Moffo, Morell, Vanni, Carelli, Verchi cond.
3 Dec.	*Il trovatore*	Bergonzi, Stella, Madeira, Wildermann, Cleva cond.
7 Dec.	*Il trovatore*	Bergonzi, Stella, Dunn, Wildermann, Cleva cond.
11 Dec.	*Tosca*	Milanov, Björling, Pechner, Franke, Mitropoulos cond.
16 Dec.	*Tosca*	Albanese, Björling, Davidson, Franke, Mitropoulos cond.

1960

2 Jan.*	*Macbeth*	Rysanek, Hines, Barioni, Olvis, Leinsdorf cond.
18 Jan.	*Macbeth*	Rysanek, Hines, Barioni, Olvis, Leinsdorf cond.
4 Feb.	*Macbeth*	Dalis, Tozzi, Morell, Olvis, Leinsdorf cond.
10 Feb.	*Macbeth*	Rysanek, Tozzi, Morell, Nagy, Leinsdorf cond.
20 Feb.	*Macbeth*	Rysanek, Hines, Morell, Olvis, Leinsdorf cond.
1 Mar.	*Simon Boccanegra*	Curtis-Verna, Tucker, Tozzi, Flagello, Mitropoulos cond.
4 Mar.	*La forza del destino*	Tebaldi, Tucker, Hines, Baccaloni, Sgarro, Ordassy, Reitan, Schippers cond. (Acts I, II, fragment of Act III only; Warren died onstage during Act III.)

II. Other Opera Performances

1940

Cincinnati Summer Opera at the Zoo

30 June	*Aida*	Bampton, Carron, Castagna, Moscona,
3 July		Alvary, Cleva cond.

Robin Hood Dell, Philadelphia

8 July	*Aida*	Tentoni, Carron, Szánthó, Harold Kravitt,
9 July		Abrasha Rubofsky, Alexander Smallens cond.

Opera Puerto Rico, San Juan

26 Sep.	*Il trovatore*	Carron, Delphina Samoiloff, Eleanor
		Longone, Nino Ruisi, Canarutto cond.
28 Sep.	*La traviata*	Jepson, Martini, Adele Verneri, Lázló
		Halász cond.
1 Oct.	*Pagliacci*	Burke, Carron, Engelman, Canarutto cond.

1941

France Film et les Festivals de Montréal

26 Sep.	*Aida*	Bampton, Martinelli, Kaskas, Cordon,
		Hatfield, Pelletier cond.
28 Sep.	*Faust*	Berini, Jepson, Cordon, Browning, Morel
		cond.
30 Sep.	*Carmen*	Tourel, Tokatyan, Raymondi, Pelletier cond.

1942

Teatro Colón, Buenos Aires

29 May	*Aida*	Milanov, Jagel, Castagna/Sara César, Vaghi,
31 May		Joaquín Zanín, Panizza cond.
6 June		
17 June		
12 June	*Simon Boccanegra*	Milanov/Rigal, Jagel, Vaghi, Felipe Romito,
14 June		Joaquín Alsina, Panizza cond.
20 June		
24 June		
29 June		
21 July	*Un ballo in maschera*	Kirk, Jagel, Lydia Kindermann, A. Morelli,
25 July		Joaquín Zanín, Joaquín Alsina, Calusio
29 July		cond.

Teatro Municipal, Rio de Janeiro

14 Aug.	*Simon Boccanegra*	Kirk, Jagel, Duilio Baronti, Silvio Vieira,
16 Aug.		José Perrota, Calusio cond.
26 Aug.	*Un ballo in maschera*	Kirk, Jagel, Marion Matthaus, Ghita Taghi,
30 Aug.		Nino Ruisi, José Perrota, Calusio cond.
5 Sep.		
1 Sep.	*La traviata*	Greco, Kullman, Vera Eltzova, Calusio
12 Sep.		cond.
20 Sep.		
30 Sep.		
11 Sep.	*Faust*	Tokatyan, Solange Petit-Renaux, Felipe
19 Sep.		Romito, Olga Nobre, Wolff cond.

23 Sep.	*Aida*	Greco/Heloisa de Albuquerque, Jagel, Julita
26 Sep.		Fonseca, Nino Ruisi, Lisandro Sergenti,
		Edoardo De Guarnieri cond.

Teatro Municipal, São Paulo

3 Oct.	*Il trovatore*	Elia Reis e Silva, Greco, Vera Eltzova, José
		Perrota, Armando Belardi cond.
4 Oct.	*La traviata*	Maria Sá Earp, Armando De Assis Pacheco,
		Vera Eltzova, Arturo De Angelis cond.

1943

Teatro Colón, Buenos Aires

28 May	*La traviata*	Novotná/Rigal, Landi/Alvaro Bandini,
2 June		Cecilia Oyuela/Maria de Benedictis,
5 June		Panizza/Roberto Kinsky cond.
24 June		
26 June		
6 July		
11 July		
30 July		
11 June	*Rigoletto*	Reggiani, Landi, Zaira Negroni, Cordon/
13 June		Joaquín Zanín, Renato Cesari, Panizza/
16 June		Calusio cond.
3 July		
13 July		
24 July		
22 June	*Falstaff*	Novotná, Victor Damiani, Lydia
30 June		Kindermann, Isabel Marengo, Landi,
		Panizza cond.
6 Aug.	*Pagliacci*	Isabel Marengo, Pedro Mirassou, Renato
8 Aug.		Cesari, Alvaro Bandini, Calusio cond.
10 Aug.		

Teatro Municipal, Rio de Janeiro

19 Aug.	*Simon Boccanegra*	Kirk, Jagel, Vaghi, Silvio Vieira, José
22 Aug.		Perrota, Edoardo De Guarnieri cond.
25 Aug.	*Rigoletto*	Maria Sá Earp, Kullman, Julita Fonesca/
28 Aug.		Vera Eltzova/Gilda Rosa, Vaghi, Guilherme
5 Sep.		Damiano, Edoardo De Guarnieri cond.
15 Sep.		
10 Sep.	*La traviata*	Novotná, Kullman, Vera Eltzova/Olga
12 Sep.		Nobre, Edoardo De Guarnieri cond.
18 Sep.		

Teatro Municipal, São Paulo

20 Sep.	*La traviata*	Maria Sá Earp, Kullman, Vera Eltzova,
		Arturo De Angelis cond.
22 Sep.	*Rigoletto*	Maria Sá Earp, Vera Eltzova, Kullman,
		Américo Bàsso, Leonel Cavinato, Arturo De
		Angelis cond.

San Francisco Opera

7 Oct.	*Samson et Dalila*	Jobin, Thorborg, Cehanovsky, Alvary,
		Merola cond.

[1943]

11 Oct.	La forza del destino	Milanov, Jagel, Pinza, Petina, Baccaloni, Merola cond.
17 Oct.	La forza del destino	Milanov, Baum, Pinza, Petina, Baccaloni, Merola cond.
18 Oct.	Lucia di Lammermoor	Pons, Peerce, Alvary, Randall Evans, Votipka, Cimara cond.
26 Oct.	Samson et Dalila	Jobin, Thorborg, Roberto Silva, Alvary, Merola cond.
6 Nov. Los Angeles	La forza del destino	Giannini, Jagel, Pinza, Johnson, Merola cond.

1944

Teatro Municipal, Rio de Janeiro

9 Aug. 13 Aug.	Falstaff	Alice Ribeiro, Silvio Vieira, Sarah César, Maria Sá Earp, Roberto Miranda, Edoardo De Guarnieri cond.
16 Aug. 20 Aug. 26 Aug.	La traviata	Alice Ribeiro, Kullman, Vera Eltzova, Edoardo De Guarnieri cond.
24 Aug. 3 Sep.	Rigoletto	Maria Augusta Costa, Kullman, Gretel Bruno/Julita Fonseca, Américo Bàsso, Guilherme Damiano, Edoardo De Guarnieri cond.
6 Sep.	Pagliacci	Nadir Figueiredo, Pedro Mirassou, Silvio Vieira, Bruno Magnavita, Edoardo De Guarnieri cond.

San Francisco Opera

29 Sep.	Aida	Roman, Jagel, Harshaw, Pinza, Alvary, Merola cond.
1 Oct.	La forza del destino	Roman, Jagel, Pinza, Glaz, Baccaloni, Merola cond.
7 Oct. Sacramento	La forza del destino	Roman, Jagel, Pinza, Glaz, Baccaloni, Merola cond.
15 Oct.	Aida	Roman, Jagel, Harshaw, Pinza, Alvary, Merola cond.
17 Oct.	Rigoletto	Pons, Peerce, Glaz, Roberto Silva, Robin Nelson, Cimara cond.
18 Oct.	Faust	Jobin, Della Chiesa, Pinza, Glaz, Steinberg cond.
20 Oct.	Un ballo in maschera	Roman, Peerce, Harshaw, MacWatters, Alvary, Charles Goodwin, Steinberg cond.
2 Nov.	La forza del destino	Roman, Jagel, Pinza, Glaz, Merola cond.

Chicago Opera Company

| 11 Nov. 17 Nov. | Rigoletto | Antoine, Peerce, Browning, Lazzari, Alexander Kulpak, Bamboschek cond. |

1945

Teatro Municipal, Rio de Janeiro

| 14 Aug. 18 Aug. | Rigoletto | Reggiani, Landi, Rosalind Nadell, Américo Bàsso, Guilherme Damiano, Edoardo De Guarnieri cond. |

22 Aug. 25 Aug. 9 Sep. 16 Sep.	*La forza del destino*	Roman, Baum, Roberto Silva, Rosalind Nadell, Georges Sebastian/Edoardo De Guarnieri cond.
4 Sep.	*Pagliacci*	Greco, Baum, Daniel Duno, Bruno Magnavita, Edoardo De Guarnieri cond.
11 Sep.	*La traviata*	Greco, Kullman, Gretel Bruno, Edoardo De Guarnieri cond.

Teatro Municipal, São Paulo

6 Sep.	*Rigoletto*	Reggiani, Landi, Rosalind Nadell, Roberto Silva, Ernesto de Marco, Arturo De Angelis cond.
14 Sep.	*La forza del destino*	Roman, Baum, Roberto Silva, Rosalind Nadell, Arturo De Angelis cond.
17 Sep.	*La traviata*	Greco, Roberto Miranda, Ida Dertonio, Arturo De Angelis cond.

Chicago Opera Company

12 Oct. 20 Oct.	*Il trovatore*	Baum, Selma Kaye, Margery Mayer, Lazzari, Rescigno cond.
26 Oct.	*Pagliacci*	Carole Stafford, Martinelli, Louis Sudler, Oliviero, Cleva cond.
29 Oct. 7 Nov.	*La forza del destino*	Roman, Baum, Moscona, Rosalind Nadell, Ralph Telasko, Walter cond.

1946

Teatro Colón, Buenos Aires

| 21 June
30 June
3 July
6 July
30 July | *Simon Boccanegra* | Rigal/Margherita Rinaldi, Antonio Vela, Vaghi, Angel Mattiello, Joaquín Alsina, Panizza cond. |
| 19 July
21 July
24 July
27 July
1 Aug. | *Un ballo in maschera* | Rigal, Koloman von Pataky, Sara César, Olgan Chelavine/Nilda Hofmann, Joaquín Zanín, Calusio/Panizza cond. |

Chicago Opera Company

30 Sep.	*Aida*	Milanov, Baum, Ellen Repp, Tajo, Ralph Telasko, Cleva cond.
5 Oct.	*Rigoletto*	Antoine, Björling, Winifred Heckman, Lazarri, Ralph Telasko, Rescigno cond.
11 Oct.	*Aida*	Milanov, Baum, Ellen Repp, Tajo, Ralph Telasko, Cleva cond.
12 Oct. 30 Oct.	*Rigoletto*	Antoine, Tucker, Winifred Heckman, Lazzari, Ralph Telasko, Rescigno cond. (The 30 October *Rigoletto* was substituted for the canceled performance of *Mignon*.)

1947

San Francisco Opera

16 Sep.	*La traviata*	Albanese, Peerce, Votipka, Merola cond.
25 Sep.	*Aida*	Roman, Baum, Thebom, Moscona, Alvary, Breisach cond.
30 Sep.	*La Gioconda*	Roman, Baum, Thebom, Moscona, Harshaw, Dick Marzollo cond.
4 Oct.	*La traviata*	Albanese, Kullman, Votipka, Adler cond.
16 Oct.	*La Gioconda*	Resnik, Baum, Thebom, Moscona, Harshaw, Dick Marzollo cond.
20 Oct.	*La Gioconda*	Roman, Baum, Thebom, Moscona, Harshaw, Dick Marzollo cond.

1948

San Antonio Grand Opera Festival

14 Feb.	*Rigoletto*	Conner, Conley, Lazzari, Désiré Ligeti, Max Reiter cond.

Ópera Nacional, Mexico City

25 May 29 May	*Il trovatore*	Baum, Varnay, Heidt, Roberto Silva, Guido Picco cond.
1 June 5 June	*La Gioconda*	Varnay, Baum, Heidt, Roberto Silva, Fanny Anitúa, Guido Picco cond.
8 June 12 June	*Otello*	Vinay, Varnay, Concha de Los Santos, Carlos Sagarminaga, Cellini cond.

San Francisco Opera

24 Sep.	*La forza del destino*	Sara Menkes, Baum, Pinza, Turner, Baccaloni, Merola cond.
26 Sep.	*Rigoletto*	Conner, Peerce, Glaz, Alvary, Désiré Ligeti, Adler cond.
30 Sep.	*Il trovatore*	Baum, Sara Menkes, Elmo, Moscona, Dick Marzollo cond.
9 Oct. Sacramento	*Il trovatore*	Björling, Sara Menkes, Elmo, Moscona, Dick Marzollo cond.
16 Oct.	*Otello*	Svanholm, Albanese, Turner, De Paolis, Steinberg cond.

1949

San Antonio Grand Opera Festival

12 Feb.	*Il trovatore*	Baum, Suzy Morris, Harshaw, Alvary, Max Reiter cond.

Ópera Nacional, Mexico City

24 May 28 May 9 June	*Rigoletto*	Evangelina Magaña/Verdad Luz Guajardo, Poggi, Oralia Domínguez, Ignacio Ruffino, Gilberto Cerda, Cellini cond.
31 May 4 June	*Un ballo in maschera*	Celia García, Poggi, Oralia Domínguez, Evangelina Magaña, Guido Picco cond.
7 June 11 June	*La traviata*	Onelia Fineschi, Poggi, Graciela Milera, Cellini cond.

1950

Ópera Nacional, Mexico City

20 June	Il trovatore	Baum, Callas, Simionato, Moscona, Guido
22 June		Picco cond.
29 June	Simon Boccanegra	Celia García, Mario Filippeschi, Roberto
1 July		Silva, Carlo Morelli, Ignacio Ruffino, Cellini cond.
4 July	Falstaff	Alicia Noti, Ivan Petroff, Simionato,
8 July		Eugenia Rocabruna, Rodolfo Ibáñez, Cellini cond.

Teatro Municipal, Rio de Janeiro

8 Aug.	Un ballo in maschera	Barbato, Poggi, Maria Henriques, Lia Roberti, Serafin cond.
11 Aug.	Rigoletto	(Warren was indisposed and was replaced by Enzo Mascherini after "Pari siamo" in Act I.)
18 Aug.	Il trovatore	Del Monaco, Barbato, Elena Nicolai,
20 Aug.		Américo Bàsso, Juan Emilio Martini cond.
24 Aug.	Otello	Del Monaco, Barbato, Vera Maia, Adélio Zagonara, Antonino Votto cond.
8 Sep.	Rigoletto	Maria Sá Earp, Poggi, Gilda Rosa, Américo Bàsso, Asdrubal Lima, Santiago Guerra cond.

Teatro Municipal, São Paulo

30 Aug.	Otello	Del Monaco, Barbato, Vera Maia, Adélio Zagonara, Antonino Votto cond.
2 Sep.	Rigoletto	Agnes Ayres, Poggi, Gilda Rosa, Américo Bàsso, Guilherme Damiano, Antonino Votto cond.

1951

Sociedad Pro-Art Musical, Havana, Cuba

16 May	Otello	Del Monaco, Rigal, Edith Evans, Hubert
19 May		Norville, Rosenstock cond.

1952

New Orleans Opera Association

3 Apr.	Rigoletto	Gueden, Conley, Muhs, Wildermann,
5 Apr.		Treigle, Walter Herbert cond.

Sociedad Pro-Art Musical, Havana, Cuba

7 June	Il trovatore	Del Monaco, Ribla, Madeira, Jan Rubes, Antonicelli cond.
10 June	Pagliacci	Adelaide Bishop, Del Monaco, Thompson, Luigi Velucci, Antonicelli cond.

Connecticut Opera, Hartford

1 Dec.	Rigoletto	Peters, Conley, Madeira, Wildermann, Carlo Moresco cond.

1953

San Antonio Grand Opera Festival

14 Feb.	*Rigoletto*	Rivera, Tucker, Frances Bible, Jan Gbur, Dunning, Victor Alessandro cond.

New Orleans Opera Association

12 Mar.	*La forza del destino*	Milanov, Del Monaco, Wildermann,
14 Mar.		Turner, Walter Herbert cond.

Sociedad Pro-Art Musical, Havana, Cuba

3 June	*Un ballo in maschera*	Milanov, Tucker, Madeira, Hurley, Scott,
6 June		Erede cond.
8 June	*Rigoletto*	Peters, Campora, Madeira, Scott, Celestino Ramos, Thomas Mayer cond.

New York City Opera (Detroit)

11 Nov.	*Rigoletto*	Adelaide Bishop, David Poleri, Winifred Heckman, Treigle, Richard Wentworth, Rudel cond.

Il Teatro alla Scala, Milan, Italy

16 Dec.	*Rigoletto*	Rosanna Carteri, Di Stefano, Luisa
19 Dec.		Ribacchi, Nicola Zaccaria, Antonio Zerbini,
22 Dec.		Nino Sanzogno cond.
27 Dec.		
31 Dec.		

1954

Il Teatro alla Scala, Milan, Italy

3 Jan.	*Rigoletto*	Rosanna Carteri, Di Stefano, Luisa Ribacchi, Nicola Zaccaria, Antonio Zerbini, Nino Sanzogno cond.
8 Jan.	*Otello*	Del Monaco, Tebaldi, Anna Maria Canali,
10 Jan.		Giuseppe Zampieri, Antonino Votto cond.

San Francisco Opera

17 Sep.	*Rigoletto*	Mado Robin, Tucker, Turner, Moscona, Carl Palangi, Cleva cond.
21 Sep.	*La forza del destino*	Carla Martinis, Tucker, Siepi, Turner, Baccaloni, Cleva cond.
26 Sep.	*Rigoletto*	Mado Robin, Sullivan, Rosalind Nadell, Désiré Ligeti, Carl Palangi, Kritz cond.
30 Sep.	*La forza del destino*	Carla Martinis, Roberto Turrini, Siepi, Turner, Baccaloni, Cleva cond.
9 Oct. Sacramento	*Rigoletto*	Mado Robin, Peerce, Rosalind Nadell, Moscona, Carl Palangi, Kritz cond.
14 Oct.	*Rigoletto*	Mado Robin, Prandelli, Rosalind Nadell, Alvary, Carl Palangi, Kritz cond.
16 Oct.	*Rigoletto*	Gala performance, Act III only; Mado Robin, Tucker, Carl Palangi, Assandri, Kritz cond.
22 Oct. Los Angeles	*Rigoletto*	Mado Robin, Peerce, Turner, Moscona, Carl Palangi, Kritz cond.
25 Oct. Los Angeles	*La forza del destino*	Carla Martinis, Tucker, Siepi, Turner, Cleva cond.

1955

San Francisco Opera

15 Sep.	*Aida*	Tebaldi, Roberto Turrini, Turner, Tozzi, Désiré Ligeti, Cleva cond.
22 Sep.	*Aida*	Tebaldi, Roberto Turrini, Rankin, Tozzi, Désiré Ligeti, Cleva cond.
4 Oct.	*Andrea Chénier*	Tucker, Tebaldi, Frances Bible, Alvary, Cleva cond.
8 Oct.	*Andrea Chénier*	Tucker, Tebaldi, Roggero, Alvary, Cleva cond.
11 Oct.	*Pagliacci*	Albanese, Roberto Turrini, MacNeil, Virginio Assandri, Barbini cond.
16 Oct.	*Aida*	Tebaldi, Roberto Turrini, Turner, Tozzi, Désiré Ligeti, Cleva cond.
21 Oct. Los Angeles	*Andrea Chénier*	Tucker, Tebaldi, Frances Bible, Alvary, Cleva cond.
26 Oct. Los Angeles	*Aida*	Tebaldi, Roberto Turrini, Turner, Tozzi, Désiré Ligeti, Cleva cond.
30 Oct. Los Angeles	*Pagliacci*	Albanese, Roberto Turrini, Heinz Blankenburg, Virginio Assandri, Barbini cond.

1956

Kansas City Philharmonic Association

22 Mar.	*Rigoletto*	Eva Likova, Peerce, Rosalind Nadell, Scott,
24 Mar.		Ralph Williams, Hans Schwieger cond.

New Orleans Opera Association

3 May	*Falstaff*	Della Chiesa, Richard Torigi, Lizabeth
5 May		Pritchett, Audrey Schuh, André Turp, Cellini cond.

San Francisco Opera

15 Sep.	*Tosca*	Tebaldi, Richard Martell, De Paolis, Carl Palangi, Glauco Curiel cond.
21 Sep.	*Falstaff*	Schwarzkopf, Guarrera, Oralia Domínguez,
27 Sep.		Audrey Schuh, Campora, Steinberg cond.
9 Oct.	*Simon Boccanegra*	Tebaldi, Roberto Turrini, Christoff, Heinz
13 Oct.		Blankenburg, Carl Palangi, Oliviero De Fabritiis cond.
20 Oct. Los Angeles	*Simon Boccanegra*	Tebaldi, Roberto Turrini, Christoff, Heinz Blankenburg, Carl Palangi, Oliviero De Fabritiis cond.
23 Oct. Los Angeles	*Falstaff*	Schwarzkopf, Guarrera, Oralia Domínguez, Audrey Schuh, Steinberg cond.

1957

Pittsburgh Opera

31 Jan.	*Rigoletto*	Witkowska, Randall Peters, Morell, Irene Kramarich, Valfredo Patacchi, Richard Karp cond.

[1957]

Connecticut Opera, Hartford

9 Mar.   *Il trovatore*   Crain, Stella, Irene Kramarich, Sgarro,
                                    Guadagno cond.

Kansas City Philharmonic Association

14 Mar.   *Il trovatore*   Rudolf Petrak, Nelli, Rankin, Robert Bird,
16 Mar.   Hans Schwieger cond.

Cuarto Festival de Opera, San Juan, Puerto Rico

14 June   *Tosca*   Kirsten, Campora, Franke, Hecht, Emerson
                                   Buckley cond.
16 June   *Andrea Chénier*   Roberto Turrini, Steber, Altman, Lloyd
                                   Harris, Emerson Buckley cond.
20 June   *Rigoletto*   Rivera, Campora, Elias, Wildermann,
                                   Hecht, Rudel cond.

1958

New Orleans Opera Association

1 May   *Il trovatore*   Roberto Turrini, Nelli, Irene Kramarich,
3 May   Wildermann, Cellini cond.

Bolshoi Opera, Moscow

16 May   *Rigoletto*   V. M. Firsova, A. A. Grigoriev, A. V.
                                 Scherbakova, V. A. Gavriushov, L. S.
                                 Maslov, G. G. Zhemchuzhin cond.

Ukrainian Opera, Kiev, Ukraine

21 May   *Rigoletto*   Yelizaveta Chavdar, Nikolai Sergeyevich
                                 Fokin. (Additional cast information is not
                                 available.)

Latvian Opera, Riga, Latvia

29 May   *Otello*   A. Frinberg, Germena Heine-Wagner, Anna
                                 Ludina, Artur Lepe, Richard Glazup cond.

1959

Tulsa Opera

19 Mar.   *Il trovatore*   Björling, Ross, Madeira, Moscona,
21 Mar.   Bamboschek cond.

◆

Leonard Warren Foundation

The Leonard Warren Foundation was established in 1986 by Barrett Crawford and the late Vivien Warren, Leonard Warren's sister, to perpetuate Leonard Warren's artistry and aid in the career development of aspiring singers. Although many consider Leonard Warren the greatest Verdi baritone of his era, when the foundation was established no book had been written about his life and career, and most of his recordings were out of print. The founders were concerned that Warren's exceptional gifts might be inaccessible to future generations.

To carry out its goals, the foundation entered into a publishing agreement with Amadeus Press and retained Mary Jane Phillips-Matz, author of the highly acclaimed *Verdi: A Biography* and many other publications, to write this book. The foundation also signed a licensing agreement with BMG Classics/RCA for authorization to produce two Leonard Warren Commemorative CDs, comprising sixteen arias and twenty-four concert songs. Their contents are described in the discography. In addition, the foundation plans to produce a noncommercial video and to disseminate all the results of its efforts on behalf of Leonard Warren's artistry to music schools and professional apprenticeship programs for aspiring singers.

Board of Directors

Vivien Warren, Chairman†
Barrett Crawford, President
Sherrill Milnes, Vice President
Muriel L. Crawford, Esq., Secretary

Edward Warren Haber
John T. Lawrence Jr.
Mrs. John M. Richman
Alfred C. Stepan III
William N. Topaz

Advisory Board

Carlo Bergonzi
Vladimir Chernov
Giuseppe Di Stefano
Edward Downes
Henry Fogel
Thomas Hampson
Jerome Hines

Ardis Krainik†
Lotfi Mansouri
Zinka Milanov†
Rose Bampton Pelletier
Roberta Peters
Eve Queler
Tony Randall

Ellen Shade
Robert Shaw†
Risë Stevens
Renata Tebaldi
Giorgio Tozzi
Louis Quilico
Joseph Volpe
John S. White

†deceased

Benefactors

Barrett and Muriel Crawford
SFA Management Corporation
Mrs. John Richman
Ann and Gordon Getty
    Foundation
Arthur Andersen Foundation
Thomas and Katherine Brush
Donald G. Sisler
John T. Lawrence Jr.

Joseph G. Chisholm
Dorothy R. Wurlitzer
Bruce Kubert
Rose and Robert Edelman Foundation
Marise Angelucci Pokorny
Alfred C. Stepan III
Vivien Warren
Anonymous

✦

Barrett Crawford, President
Leonard Warren Foundation
100 Sugar Creek Court
Alamo, California 94507
Tel: (925) 855-2000
Fax: (925) 855-1555

Index of Names

Leonard Warren, Vivien Warren, and Agatha Leifflen Warren do not appear in this index. Composers' names mentioned in passing also do not appear here. For complete listings of Leonard Warren's repertoire, performances, and recordings, see the chronology and discography.